LEAD, FOLLOW, OR *Move Out of the Way!*

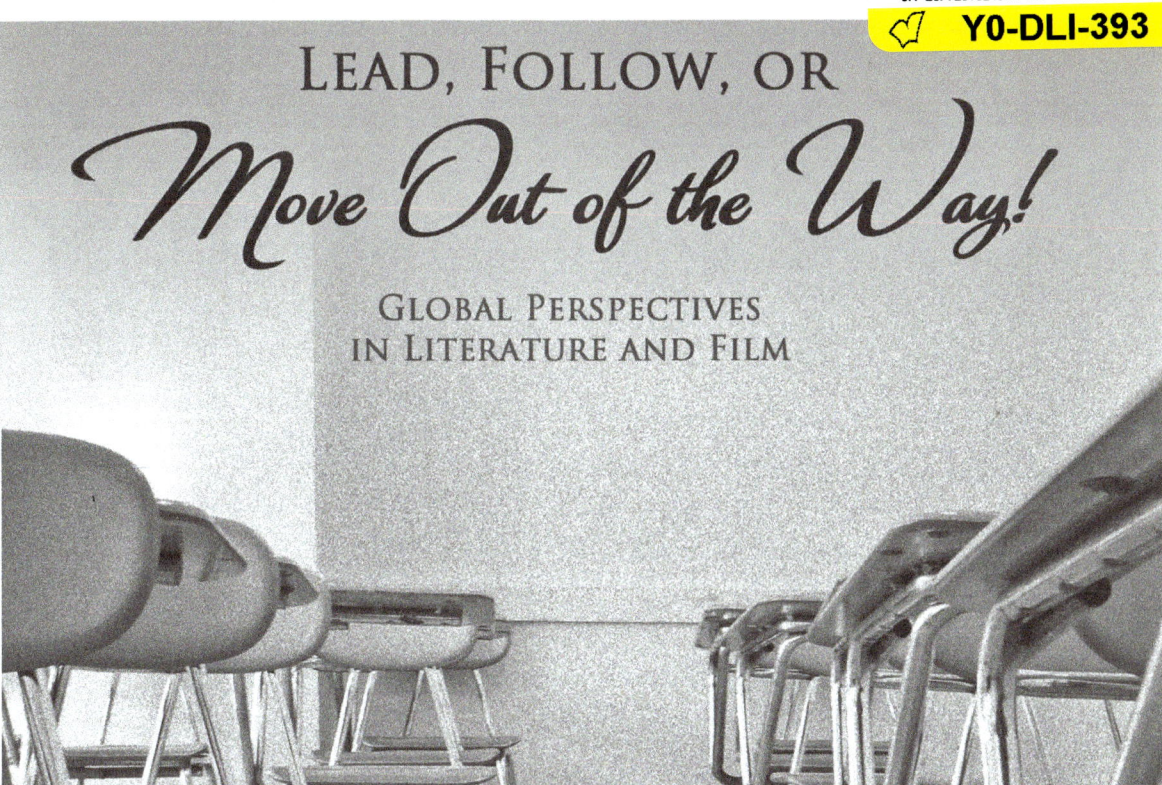

GLOBAL PERSPECTIVES IN LITERATURE AND FILM

Dr. Monique Ferrell, Associate Professor English
Dr. Julian Williams, Associate Professor of English

The City University of New York

second edition
2012 PRINTING

Kendall Hunt
publishing company

Cover images courtesy of Julian L. Williams

All interior images courtesy of Julian L. Williams

Kendall Hunt
publishing company
www.kendallhunt.com
Send all inquiries to:
4050 Westmark Drive
Dubuque, IA 52004-1840

Copyright © 2006, 2012 by Monique Ferrell and Julian Williams
Revised Printing: 2008

ISBN 978-1-4652-0398-4

Kendall Hunt Publishing Company has the exclusive rights to reproduce this work,
to prepare derivative works from this work, to publicly distribute this work,
to publicly perform this work and to publicly display this work.

All rights reserved. No part of this publication may be reproduced,
stored in a retrieval system, or transmitted, in any form or by any
means, electronic, mechanical, photocopying, recording, or otherwise,
without the prior written permission of the copyright owner.

Printed in the United States of America
10 9 8 7 6 5 4 3 2 1

Contents

FILMS xxi
FOREWORD xxi
PREFACE xxiii

CHAPTER 1 *Social Responsibility*

STANLEY CROUCH ▶ Taking Back the Music 3
Female college students challenge the stereotypical and sexist overtones in rap music by literally confronting artists and label owners.

NELLA LARSEN ▶ From the Novel *Passing* 6
Larsen's characters live within a world of racial secrecy where fair-skinned Blacks are "passing" as White. In this excerpt, a woman hoping to pass seeks to keep the evil of racism out of her house and away from her children.

RALPH WALDO EMERSON ▶ Self-Reliance 9
Emerson's essay presents the timeless call for individuals to reflect upon, study, and pursue the inner workings of their own minds, as opposed to conforming to the well-trod path of the villainous "society."

KHALED HOSSEINI ▶ From the Novel *The Kite Runner* 25
Hosseini examines how childhood friends, two Afghan boys separated by Class and religion, make devastating choices that alter their lives forever.

BIDPAI ▶ The Camel and His Friends 45
This parable asks us to consider the importance of sacrificing the self for others.

MARGARET SANGER ▶ The Turbid Ebb and Flow of Misery 47
During the 1920s, a nurse describes the frustration of visiting and treating impoverished women with large families and how she agonizes over the ethics of giving them birth control during this conservative point in American history.

NAOMI WOLF ▶ The Making of a Slut 53
The author examines the "bad girl" and positions her as a social construct for "good girls"—those females who, by separating themselves, maintain their reputations while endangering those upon whom the negative title falls.

CHAPTER 2 — *Death and Violence*

LINDA LOWEN ▶ What LaShandra Armstrong Teaches Us About
Teen Pregnancy Ten Years Out 61
Depression, neglect, and frustration drives a mother of four to murder and suicide.

TONI MORRISON ▶ From the Novel *Paradise* 64
This selection from Morrison's novel explores how acts of violence are perpetrated by men in an effort to cleanse their community of "wayward" women.

GUY DE MAUPASSANT ▶ Mother Savage 70
A mother resorts to mass murder in response to the war that has taken her child and overwhelmed her community.

IRENE ZABYTKO ▶ Home Soil 76
A father confronts his own memories about war while observing the changes in his son, a soldier, who has just returned home from combat.

MARK TWAIN ▶ From the Novel *Adventures of Huckleberry Finn* 82
This selection from Twain's most controversial work asks us to examine the "mob mentality" and its impact on the collective voice of a community.

CYNTHIA OZICK ▶ The Shawl 87
A mother, with two daughters, confronts death and survival while being held in a concentration camp.

AESOP ▶ A Lion and Other Animals Go Hunting 92
Aesop's timeless and seemingly simple tale is a poignant look at power and respect.

CHAPTER 3 — *Racial Matters*

WOODEN LEG ▶ Young Men, Go Out and Fight Them 97
Confronted with impending colonialism, a warrior challenges the men of his tribe to engage in an act of war.

ANNA LISA RAYA ▶ It's Hard Enough Being Me 102
A Hispanic woman discusses the problem of feeling as if she is always being questioned about, or asked to justify, her racial affiliation.

MAXINE HONG KINGSTON ▶ The Misery of Silence 105
The author, through her own personal reflections, examines what happens to second-language children in the classroom.

TAHIRA NAQVI ▶ Brave We Are 109
While preparing a routine dinner, a mother finds herself attempting to explain the complexities of racial mixing and how people perceive biracial children.

Contents

WILLIAM SHAKESPEARE ▶ *Othello, The Moore of Venice* 114
A former African slave rises to the highest rank in the military of his adoptive home. Suddenly he finds that the accolades and praise he receives mean little in the face of racism, Class, and true evil.

ABRAHAM LINCOLN ▶ House Divided Speech 191
Lincoln's acceptance speech for the Republican Party's nomination for U.S. Senate still remains one of the most prophetic calls for country unification—a nation divided, at the time, over the Black enslavement.

CHAPTER 4 — Class and the Culture of Power

MARK TWAIN ▶ The Lowest Animal 199
Twain's "experiments" provide cynical views of mankind that, interestingly enough, are just as distressing today as they have ever been.

KATE CHOPIN ▶ From the Novel *The Awakening* 204
A married woman discovers that marriage and motherhood are societal crosses that women must bear and sets about creating a new world for herself in the face of social norms.

NGŨGĨ WA THIONG'O ▶ Decolonising the Mind 213
The British policy of Kenyans speaking only English in classrooms after the first three years of study is seen as a major factor regarding the native speakers' self-image.

MARY SHELLY ▶ From the Novel *Frankenstein* 219
Having taken it upon himself to create life, scientist Victor Frankenstein learns firsthand from his "monster" that he has helped to contribute to the prejudice, violence, and elitism of his society.

ELIZA HAYWOOD ▶ Fantomina: Or, Love in a Maze 227
A supposed member of the weaker sex sets out to determine whether or not she can manipulate a man into thinking she is several different women.

JHUMPA LAHIRI ▶ Interpreter of Maladies 245
A poor taxi driver, who works part-time at a doctor's office, picks up a wealthy Indian-American family having an obnoxious and, as he soon learns, revealing visit.

CHARLES CHESNUT ▶ An Evening Visit   From the Novel *The House Behind The Cedars* 259
After successfully "passing" in the White world, a man returns home to visit the women he left behind.

CHAPTER 5 — Religion

AUTHOR UNKNOWN ▶ Ghost Dance Songs 271
19th century Indigenous religious songs that served as a form of political and cultural outcry.

AUDREY SMEDLY ▶ From *Race in North America* 273
The author attempts to examine the ways in which religion has been used to subjugate oppressed people as opposed to being used as an expression of faith.

BHARATI MUKHERJEE ▶ A Father 278
A father, who is a practicing Hindi, feels that the women in his family are "too" American and that their behavior will ultimately bring about disastrous consequences.

MOHAMMED NASEEHU ALI ▶ Mallam Sile 286
A Muslim man allows his faith to fight his battles and the cruelty he suffers at the hands of his community.

THE BOOK OF MATTHEW ▶ The Sermon on the Mount 295
Christ gives his followers the guidelines for leading a "good" life.

THE PROPHET MOHAMMED ▶ From *The Koran* 301
An examination of leading a "good" Muslim life.

THOMAS PAINE ▶ Age of Reason 306
The British radical and American revolutionary stresses a deistic treatise while critiquing institutionalized religion and the inerrancy of the Bible.

CHAPTER 6 *Gender, Sex, and Sexuality*

LOUIE CREW ▶ Thriving as an Outsider, Even as an Outcast,
in Smalltown America 343
A biracial, openly gay couple attempts to find a place for themselves in Middle America.

JAMES BALDWIN ▶ From the Novel *Giovanni's Room* 350
Excerpt looks at a man, conflicted with his sexuality, having sex with a woman and, throughout the entire process, feeling a great sense of sadness and regret.

DAVID MURA ▶ How America Unsexes the Asian Male 355
A look at the way the American media emasculates Asian men.

JUNOT DIAZ ▶ Fiesta 1980 359
A son recalls what it meant to discover that his father had an affair throughout his childhood.

JULIAN WILLIAMS ▶ The New Breed 369
As he experiences a sense of ethnic shame while riding the subway—notably caused by an angry teenager—a New Yorker learns that no one truly understands what it takes to rear children.

SHERMAN ALEXIE ▶ Higher Education   From the Novel *Indian Killer* 386
A frustrated Native American college student defends her cultural and political ideologies in front of her White Indian Studies Professor, who wants her removed from his class, and the Dean, who holds her future in his hands.

SAPPHIRE ▶ From the Novel *Push* 389
Victimized sexually and physically, a young teenage girl attempts to come to terms with her abuse.

CHAPTER 7 *Fork in the Road*

SIR ARTHUR CONAN DOYLE ▶ From the Novel *A Study in Scarlet*....... 397
A broken and battered Dr. Watson, weary from the pangs of war, wallows in despair until he determines to make life worthwhile by dedicating himself to working with the great Sherlock Holmes.

FRANCES A. ALTHAUS ▶ Female Circumcision: Rite of Passage
or Violation of Rights? 423
A detailed look at the culture, politics, and practice of the tradition.

JOHN CHEEVER ▶ Reunion 431
A young boy meets the father he's always wanted to know and discovers that he is not quite what he expected.

JONATHAN KOZOL ▶ The Human Cost of an Illiterate Society 435
The author exams what it means to live in a society where a large portion of the population is functionally illiterate.

MONIQUE FERRELL ▶ Go Brooklyn!.................................. 442
Dire consequences abound when a half-Black, half-Hispanic female reporter decides
to destroy Hip Hop Music and advance the cause of women by humiliating a rap artist on
live television.

CHAPTER 8 *Manmade and Natural Disasters*

THE BOOK OF GENESIS ▶ The Great Flood............................. 463
A disgruntled and angered God determines to cleanse humanity of its wickedness by sending
a great flood to Earth and, as a result, Noah is charged with collecting those deemed worthy
of saving.

CESAR ILLIANO AND TERRY WAD ▶ Chilean Miners Rescued
after 69 Days Underground 469
A detailed examination of the global, political, and cultural impact of this manmade and natural
disaster, as well as the media sensationalism that followed.

SCOTT GOLD ▶ Little to Reclaim in the Lower 9th 473
LA Times article that looks at the tragedy and devastation that remains after the most horrific
natural disaster in American history.

SIMON ROMERO ▶ Quake Accentuated Chasm That Has Defined Haiti 477
In the wake of the horrific natural disaster that all but decimated the already impoverished
nation, a reporter finds that the divide between the rich and poor has widened with devastating
effects.

STEVEN ERLANGER ▶ Amid Tears, Flickering Candles and Flowers,
a Shaken Norway Mourns.. 481
People of Norway attempt to understand how and why one of its very own citizens committed an
act of racially motivated mass murder.

FREDERICK DOUGLASS ▶ What to the Slave is the 4th of July?
From Independence Day speech at Rochester, 1852 485
On July 5, 1852, Douglass gave a speech commemorating the signing of the Declaration of
Independence. During the speech, Douglass pointed out that this celebratory holiday is a "sham"
to the enslaved American and asserted that America was guilty of the most shocking and bloody
crimes imaginable.

JEEVAN LOWEN ▶ The Nightwalkers 488
40,000 Ugandan children attempt to avoid being kidnapped and turned into murderous soldiers
by walking to safe houses each night.

IAN URBINA ▶ Mobs Are Born as Word Grows by Text Message 492
Philadelphia teens use social media to orchestrate riots and vandalize their communities.

INDEX   495

Our students, like the majority of the world's population, love movies. Whether it's drama or action/adventure or mystery or comedy or the love story or, with ever increasing audiences, the documentary, film has proven that it is arguably the main vehicle used to both express sentiment and entertain viewers. Even though this point is virtually inarguable, literary materials still remain the core for most classrooms. However, books are now, more than ever, forced to compete with our growing technological societies. Let's be honest: today's students relate more readily to wireless communication devices and the internet than they do with paper texts. With the advent of wireless portable reading devices—such as The Kindle, Nook, and iPad—there is now further proof that the text-only based classroom must adjust to this new visual world or be left behind. As such, we strongly promote a blending of what the students love with what they need. Alongside these written works, we strongly encourage that selected films—movies that round out the world's regions not addressed in the readings—be incorporated into the classroom curriculum. The infusion of these two impacting mediums allows the students to not only read and discuss texts but, also, to visualize the topics and themes that come out of classroom examinations.

We have carefully selected the following films. In an attempt to help both professor and students choose which film goes best with what written work, we have placed specific films in chapter sections and provided a brief review that gives insight into who, what, when, and where for each film.

Note to Professors/Instructors

*Please review each film before showing it to your students. Some films contain serious, adult content.

CHAPTER 1 *Social Responsibility*

The Agronomist: **A documentary on the assassination of Haitian political activist Jean Dominique.**

Aunt Diane: **Exploration of the mystery surrounding the tragic 2009 wrong-way crash that killed a mother and seven others on NY's Taconic Parkway.**

The Business of Being Born: **Documentary that explores issues surrounding child birthing, noting that the U.S. spends twice as much per birth than any other industrialized country, while, interestingly, having the second worst mortality rate for both mothers and infants.**

Dead Poet's Society: **In the spirit of Emerson, a prep-school teacher challenges his male students to be nonconformists and tap into their inner genius.**

Fight Club: **Looking at the duality that resides within men—males who prove themselves by fighting bare knuckled—the film examines a specific question: Does a man belong to himself or is maleness a societal construct to which he inevitably falls prey?**

Flowers of Evil: **A love story between Gecko, an Algerian-French hotel bellman and parkourer, and Anahita, an Iranian student forced to leave her country for her own safety after the controversial elections in 2009. Via Youtube and Twitter, the film explores the power of social networking for change.**

Gun Fight: **An eye-opening documentary that looks at the complicated issues surrounding private gun ownership in America.**

Hot Coffee: **Documentary that looks at the real story behind the infamous McDonald's coffee scalding and three other cases that impacted the tort-reform movement.**

Hotel Rwanda: **An examination of a man who stands up to be counted when the "new" norm in his African homeland is violence and warfare.**

I Am Because We Are: **Writer-producer Madonna exposes the tragic stories of the millions of Malawi children orphaned by AIDS.**

In the Year of the Pig: **Emile de Antonio's ground breaking 1968 protest documentary against the Vietnam War, where he reveals the American government's lies; moreover, the director calls into question all versions of the war released to the public.**

Jump Tomorrow: **A Nigerian pledged in an arranged marriage questions "his situation."**

Juno: **Two adolescent outcasts find themselves expecting a child in a reserved Minnesota community. Film examines abortion, adoption, and the growing pains of the protagonists and everyone around them.**

Keane: **A film dedicated to unearthing the reality of what it means to live with mental illness.**

The Kite Runner: **The subtitled film adaptation of Khalid Hosseini's best selling novel on Afghanistan, lost childhoods, betrayal, and redemption.**

The Last Supper: **Five midwestern graduate students decide to rid the world of those who hold opposing political ideas, by offering them dinners and a very special glass of wine.**

Mama Africa: **Documentary is packed with five decades of rare archival footage that examine the history and music of Miriam Makeba, whose songs exposed the world to the injustices of Apartheid in South Africa and resulted in a thirty year exile from her home country.**

Moolaaddé: **A mother who experienced female circumcision as a child attempts to prevent her daughter from being forced to take part in the ceremony.**

School Ties: **In the 1950s, an all-male school is challenged to open the prejudiced minds and hearts of its privileged students after one of their own admits he is Jewish.**

The Tillman Story: **Government turns former professional football player turned Army Ranger Pat Tillman's death into propaganda.**

Twilight Zone: **Eye of the Beholder: A woman struggles to change her face so that she can look like everyone else in order to avoid being evicted from her community.**

Young Rebels: **A documentary on young Cuban revolutionaries who use Hip-Hop music as a forum to discuss race and class issues in their native Cuba.**

Weatherman: **Local weatherman's convoluted journey to find his place in the world while dealing with the disintegration of his family.**

Without the King: **This lively documentary looks at the tiny African nation of Swaziland, one of the last existing absolute monarchies. This look at the African kingdom exposes a life expectancy that is one of the shortest in the world—the rate of HIV infection is the globe's highest—as well as thousands of citizens who subsist on some of the most revolting food imaginable.**

CHAPTER 2 *Death and Violence*

American Gun: **Vignettes on gun violence and how this epidemic is devastating American families.**

An Omar Broadway Film: **Using a contraband video camera inside the gang unit at Newark's Northern State Prison, a jailed Bloods member puts his life on the line to document guards' corruption and excessive force. Documentary exposes the often corrupt and violent world behind bars.**

Apocalypse Now: **Francis Ford Coppola's surrealistic and symbolic film details the confusion, violence, fear, and madness that encompassed the Vietnam War.**

Beautiful Boy: **A school shooting rampage is viewed from the perspective of the killer's bewildered parents.**

Better this World: **Film looks at the "Texas Two," David McKay and Bradley Crowder, two teens who, at the volatile Republican Convention, cross a line that results in high-stakes entrapment. The result is a movie that presents a story of loyalty, betrayal, and the world of civil liberties post-9/11.**

Bowling for Columbine: **Documentary filmmaker Michael Moore examines how the culture of fear, class, racism, and violence may have led to America's most horrific school shooting.**

Crying Ladies: **Comedy that follows the lives of three women who cry at funerals—professionally.**

El Sicario, Room 164: **Sitting in a motel room in Mexico, a hooded former hit man for the Ciudad Juarez drug cartel recounts his troubled adolescence, his entry into a corrupt police academy, and the many kidnappings and murders he committed.**

Freak: **Told with seamless comic flare, comedian John Leguizamo's stand-up show explores what it means to grow up in a house of domestic abuse.**

Give up Tomorrow: **Documentary that re-examines the 1997 murder of two sisters on a provincial island in the Phillipines. For the next thirteen years, Paco Larranaga's case received the highest profile in the nation's history. The film seems to be a murder mystery and a courtroom drama, but evolves into a powerful indictment of national corruption.**

How I Killed a Saint: **A woman living abroad in America returns to her native war-torn Balkans and discovers that both her family and country are in utter turmoil.**

Kassim the Dream: **Documentary that follows Kassim "The Dream" Ouma, who went from Ugandan child soldier to world champion boxer.**

Love Story: **Harvard rich kid meets Radcliffe musician. They fall in love and then discover that she is terminally ill. (Original, 1970)**

Munyurangabo: **Following the relationship between two boys traveling on a vengeance mission across Rwanda's countryside, the film, which has a completely nonprofessional cast, takes a potent look at genocide, as it depicts friendships and familial betrayals.**

Mystic River: **Boston community implodes as the death of a teenage girl puts her father at odds with his childhood friends—men bonded through a horrible childhood experience.**

Nanking: **Powerful documentary that provides first person recollections of the near-total destruction of the Chinese city and its inhabitants by imperial Japanese troops in 1937.**

Ordinary People: **The accidental death of an older son from an affluent family deeply strains the relationships between the bitter mother, the good-natured father, and the guilt-ridden son. (Original, 1980)**

Paradise Now: **After a horrific experience, two Palestinian friends decide to become suicide bombers in Tel Aviv.**

The Passion of the Christ: **An exploration of the violence Christ endured during his last days.**

Raging Bull: **The story details the main stages of temperamental, paranoid, and abusive boxer Jake Lamotta: his rise, fall, and in-between life.**

Saving Face: **Oscar-winning documentary about women disfigured by acid attacks in Pakistan.**

Series 7: The Contenders: **Movie looks at how far reality television can go, as well as presenting a sobering look at what we consider entertainment. The violent "series" has contestants actually winning and moving forward in the game by killing each other.**

Sleepers: **Supposedly based on a true crime, four teenage pranksters are sent to a juvenile detention center where they are physically and sexually abused by the guards. Ten years later, two of the boys murder the ringleader, leading to a highly publicized trial.**

State of Fear: **Documentary that offers a balanced view of the atrocities occurring during Peru's sordid twenty-year cycle of violence and corruption.**

Taxi Driver: **The quintessential average man is compelled to seek social validation through the only means available: violence.**

Terms of Endearment: **Movie traces the lives of mother and daughter, women always trying to find happiness, who march to the beat of different drummers—women reunited when one becomes stricken with cancer.**

United 93: **Reenactment of the final hours of the doomed flight that plunged out of the Pennsylvania sky on September 11, 2001.**

The War of the Roses: **A married couple turns to horrendous acts of violence after the collapse of their "ideal" marriage.**

We Were Soldiers: **Story of the first major battle of the American phase of the Vietnam War and the soldiers on both sides who fought.**

Winter Soldier: **True-life accounts from actual soldiers who returned from Vietnam—men physically and mentally left too scarred to rejoin society.**

The Whistleblower: **Based on true events, this political thriller follows Kathryn, a UN peacekeeper who arrives in post-war Bosnia. There, she is met with chaos and disorder and unearths an underworld of human trafficking.**

Wit: **Literary scholar faced with cancer discovers human kindness.**

CHAPTER 3 — *Racial Matters*

Arranged: **Movie revolves around the friendship of two young teachers in Brooklyn—one Muslim, one an Orthodox Jew—who meet at a racially and culturally diverse Brooklyn grade school. The film tackles arranged marriages, faith, secular Americanism, and the boundaries of family tolerance.**

Blind Faith: **In this powerful and historically centered film, a Black Lawyer's nephew is accused of murdering a White man.**

The Boy Who Played on the Buddhas of Bamiyan: **Family of Afghani refugees lives among the ruins of a tourist attraction that was destroyed by the Taliban.**

Cairo Exit: **A look into the collapsing world of an eighteen year-old unwed mother in Egypt who struggles with choices that become more complicated after she is robbed and fired from her job.**

Color of the Cross: **An examination of the last forty-eight hours of Jesus Christ as a Black man.**

C.S.A.: The Confederate States of America: **An alternate historical society where the South won the Revolutionary War and America has embraced racism as a part of life.**

The Defiant Ones: **Two escaped convicts—one White, the other Black—must overcome their own prejudices in an attempt to evade their pursuers, survive in a racist society, and, most of all, overcome their own social conditioning.** (Original, 1958)

Donkey in Lahore: **An unusual love story style documentary of an Australian puppeteer who falls in love with a Muslim woman he met in Pakistan. Can this unlikely couple survive the challenges they are about to face?**

Freedomland: **A portrait of a White mother who claims her child was abducted by a Black male and how this accusation fuels negative race relations in a segregated, racially charged community.**

The Help: **Film follows the lives of two maids and best friends who live in Jackson, Mississippi during the Jim Crow era. They meet and open up to a budding White writer who wants to write an explosive tell-all book about their subservient existence.**

The Interrupters: **Powerful documentary that chronicles a year spent with Chicago's antiviolence crusaders CeaseFire and their attempts to intervene in gang warfare.**

In the Heat of the Night: **Black Philadelphia police detective reluctantly becomes embroiled in a murder investigation in racially hostile 1960s Mississippi.** (Original, 1967)

Kippur: **Portrait of the 1973 Yom Kippur between Syria and Israel, told from the perspective of a skeptical soldier.**

La Vita e Bella (Life Is Beautiful): **Man uses humor and fantasy to protect his son in a Nazi death camp.**

The Loving Story: **Evocative documentary that recounts the unknown love story of Mildred and Richard Loving, the couple behind the 1967 Supreme Court ruling overturning anti-miscegenation laws in the United States.**

Michael Collins: **Leader fights to establish Irish Free State in the 1920s while becoming vilified by those hoping to create a completely independent Irish Republic.**

Mississippi Burning: **Two FBI agents are sent to Mississippi to investigate the disappearance of missing civil rights workers. The film is an exploration of one of the ugliest chapters in American history, examining White supremacy, corruption, and extreme conflicts of social conscience.**

My Life Inside: **Film follows the tragic life of Rosa Jimenez who, at seventeen, came to the U.S. to provide a better life for her family back in Mexico. This heartbreaking documentary examines how she came to stand accused of murder in a Texas courtroom.**

Occupation: Dreamland: **Documentary filmmakers record soldiers who are stationed in Iraq and gain insight about how and why they are perceived as invaders.**

The Order of Myths: **Based on Alabama's 2007 Mardi Gras, an annual event that has existed since the 1700s, this documentary examines Mobile's first ethnically blended events, where the African-American community's regents attended their White counterparts' coronation and vice-versa. The result is a microcosmic look at race relations that proves how largely divided this nation still remains.**

Planet of the Apes: **An astronaut crew crash-lands on a planet in the distant future where talking apes are the dominant species and humans are oppressed and enslaved.** (Original, 1968)

The Price of the Ticket: **Documentary on the life and literary career of one of America's most prolific writers, James Baldwin. This is an American Masters Series.**

Protocols of Zion: **Documentary about anti-Semitism in America and the rise of anti-Jewish sentiment after 9/11.**

Rosewood: **Based on the actual massacre of Black townspeople in Rosewood Florida, this film gives an account of the events that led to White town's people attacking the Black community over several days.**

Scenes of a Crime: **Troy, NY resident Adrian Thomas was interrogated for ten hours before confessing to throwing his infant son against a bed. When the child died, Thomas was convicted of second-degree murder. When the evidence exonerates him, the documentary questions legally sanctioned coercion, race, Class and the effects all have on this tragic tale.**

Some Mother's Son: **Based on the true story of IRA prisoner Bobby Sands' 1981 hunger strike in a British prison.**

Street Fight: **Documentary that chronicles the racist overtones involved in the 2002 mayoral race in Newark, New Jersey, between Sharpe James—the "average-Joe," darker skinned incumbent—and Cory Booker—the fair-skinned, Yale Law School graduate.**

Twilight Zone: Maple Street: **After the power goes out in a small middle-America neighborhood, all hell breaks loose as neighbors and friends turn against one another.**

Undefeated: **Academy award winning documentary that follows a White Memphis football coach and his 100% Black football team. Race and Class and learning to communicate become the prevailing themes of this heart wrenching film.**

What's Cooking?: **Tensions mount amidst four families of different ethnic and economic backgrounds living in contemporary Los Angeles as they prepare dinner for family and guests.**

White Man's Burden: **The film takes an alternative view on Black/White race relations by constructing a world where Blacks hold all of the power.**

Zoned In: **Filmed over the course of nine years, this documentary traces the remarkable journey of sixteen-year-old Daniel who, beginning at a Bronx high school, goes to an Ivy League university. At the same time, this film explores the role of race and class in the American educational system.**

CHAPTER 4 — *Class and the Culture of Power*

4 Months, 3 Weeks and 2 Days: **Set in 1980s Bucharest, while still behind the Iron Curtain, movie concerns two friends—one pregnant, one supportive—as they attempt to have an illegal procedure with a black-market abortionist. The film is centered mainly in the hotel room where the negotiations are discussed, revealing to the audience the hellish dynamics of economics, power games, and sex.**

A Separation: **In modern day Iran, we see a mother who hopes to take her child abroad for a better life and a bank clerk who feels trapped because he has to care for his ailing father. This powerful movie is filled with twists that reveal catastrophic consequences between seemingly unlikely people battling Class, social responsibility, and religious devotion.**

Alexandra: **Story of an elderly woman who visits a remote military outpost in implied Chechnya and observes various degrees of soldiering: banality of barrack life and machinery placement over human beings. This moving film also provides a face and voice to the enemy, as well as the difficulties of politics and the bond of the woman and her ward.**

Amores Perros: **Three interconnected stories about the different strata of life in Mexico City, revolving around a fatal car crash.**

A Walk to Beautiful: **This documentary follows five Ethiopian women from isolated rural communities who developed obstetric fistulas after prolonged obstructed deliveries. These women are ostracized and abandoned, even though a simple surgery can correct their condition. This film is an unabashed humanitarian call to action, as it examines how superstition, poverty, and hundreds of miles to medical care all stand in the way of these women's survival.**

Ballast: **A cryptic and intimate tale of three people dealing with a tragedy in the Deep South. Film brilliantly handles people living below the poverty line with poetic sensitivity.**

Beaufort: **Well crafted movie that looks at various soldiers in Lebanon guarding the highly symbolic Beaufort Castle from Hezbollah forces in the last remaining days of Israel's occupation.**

A Bronx Tale: **The protagonist struggles to come to terms with his growing affinity for a neighborhood gangster, who treats him like a son, and his father, a working-class bus driver.**

Bubble: **Set in small-town Ohio and West Virginia, the movie examines the lives of three paycheck-to-paycheck wage earners—individuals who have lived this way for so long they have forgotten how to imagine a future. Film also contains a murder mystery twist.**

Claudine: **A classic "dramadey" that examines America's welfare system and the ways in which it forces a wedge between a mother and her garbage-man boyfriend in 1970s New York.**

The Colors of the Mountain: **This film exposes us to warfare through the eyes of children as we meet nine-year old Manuel, who lives in the rural mountains of Columbia. He has friends, plays soccer, and is learning how to read thanks to a new teacher. Unfortunately, his village just happens to be the headquarters for a rebel group taking on the country's military power.**

The Constant Gardner: **In an attempt to expose the corporate and political AIDS drug racket in Kenya, a couple risks their lives.**

Duck Season: **Adolescents spend a lazy Sunday afternoon together. Melancholy film that examines loneliness, togetherness, and the end of family in a small Mexico City apartment.**

El Inmortal: **Mercedes Moncarda Rodriguez follows the plight of a woman and her four children living in Nicaragua.**

Enron: The Smartest Guys in the Room: **Based on the 2003 investigative digest, this documentary is a methodical look at the men who became known as the largest white-collar crooks ever taken to trial in American history.**

Fire in Babylon: **Using the backdrops of the national liberation movements of the 70s and 80s, this documentary pays tribute to the golden age of cricket in the West Indies. Film shows how players set out to triumph over their former colonial masters while, simultaneously, making a name for themselves on the world stage.**

The First Grader: **In 2003, when the Kenyan government offered free education to all citizens, 84year-old villager KimaniN'gan'gaMaruge showed up at the gates of the local primary school. This movie looks at how the international media attention turns the main character into a poster boy and social pariah, as well as a celebrity and pupil.**

Goodwill Hunting: **the main character, a poor street kid from Boston's low-end—who just happens to be genius—attempts to work out his issues about who he is in relation to where he lives and the expectations of those around him.**

Hustle and Flow: **Sympathetic southern pimp attempts to better his station in life—involving everyone in his limited world—through Hip-Hop.**

In America: **Irish immigrants struggle to survive and maintain their sanity in New York City's Hell's Kitchen.**

The Inheritors: **Haunting documentary that, over the course of two years, examines children working long and hard in dirt-poor rural regions of Mexico.**

The Joy Luck Club: **Chinese mothers and daughters reflect on the roles they played in the culture clash between the mothers' traditional Chinese values and their Americanized children.**

Mardi Gras: Made in China: **Conscience-stirring documentary examines the life cycle of the bead necklaces used during this New Orleans' event, alongside the millionaires who own the Tai Kuen bead factory in China and their employees—individuals who work fourteen hour days, six days a week under horrendous conditions.**

Pray the Devil Back to Hell: **After more than a decade of civil wars leading to more than 250,000 deaths and one million refugees, the documentary looks at a group of courageous Liberian women who rose up and propelled to victory the first female head of state on the African continent.**

A Raisin in the Sun: **Desperate to be seen as the breadwinner in his family, a Black man—a son, husband, and father—blames himself, his mother, and his wife for what he sees as his personal failure with regard to not being able to provide as a "man."** (Original, 1961)

Return to the Land of Wonders: **Documentary where the filmmaker—having lived thirty-five years abroad—walks the streets in Iraq, her homeland, and interviews everyday citizens about what they have been through—both under Saddam Hussein's regime and during U.S. occupation.**

Rocky: **In this classic "underdog" tale, the self-titled main character boxes his way out of Philadelphia's underbelly, training his way to a heavyweight championship fight.**

Sarafina: **A young girl struggles to break the racial and class barriers while living in apartheid South Africa.**

Sicko: **Michael Moore's compelling documentary is a scathing indictment of America's failing health care system. He travels to Canada, England, France, and Cuba—where free universal health care is the norm—and finds himself asking, "Why can't this happen in America?"**

SlumDog Millionaire: **While consistently winning India's most popular game show, an impoverished teen who has no desire for wealth comes face to face with the social pressures associated with instant wealth; at the same time, the police suspect him of cheating because they cannot figure out how he, a street kid, continues to do so well.**

The Squid and the Whale: **A failed novelist and his successful-writer wife split and the ugliness of divorce forces their sons to choose sides.**

Terri: **More than a teen misfit movie, this film introduces us to 17year-old Terri and his hell that is high school. This movie is a genuinely touching character study, one that refuses to glamorize its hopeless hero as hip or treat him with mockery.**

Twenty-Four Eyes: **Released in 1954, this award winning Japanese film traces the close relationship between a young teacher and her twelve students over the course of twenty years, spanning the period of world-wide economic collapse and World War II.**

Wal-Mart: The High Cost of Low Price: **Documentary that chronicles the corporation's ruthless policies.**

The Weeping Meadow: **A romantic Greek tragedy. Film tracks two runaway lovers from the 1919 incursion of Bolshevism to the bitter end of World War II.**

Where Soldiers Come From: **Documentary follows three small-town friends in the National Guard who are deployed to Afghanistan in 2008.**

Young and Restless in China: **Documentary follows the lives of nine youngish Chinese citizens over the course of a few years, ranging from a Western-educated entrepreneur struggling with the ethical challenges of doing business in his home country, to a young factory worker contemplating breaking off the engagement arranged by her rural family. Film illustrates the profound changes that China's double-digit economic growth has instigated in every area of life.**

CHAPTER 5 *Religion*

Agnes of God: **When a nun is discovered in her quarters with a dead newborn, a court-appointed psychiatrist investigates.**

Constantine's Sword: **Based on the 2001 book of the same name, this documentary follows James Carroll—a former Catholic priest whose faith was rocked by Christianity's militancy and anti-Semitism—as he examines the Crusades, the infamous treaty between Pope Pius XII and Adolf Hitler, and the rise of Mega Churches and evangelical fervor.**

The Dali Lama: Peace and Prosperity: **A visual record of the Dali Lama's sold out Radio City Music Hall visit and presentation.**

Destiny: **Examines the historic battle between Islamic fundamentalists and liberals through the story of the enlightened 12th-century Andalusian philosopher and Quranic scholar Averroes.**

The Dhamma Brothers: **Documentary looks at a group of inmates sentenced to Alabama's maximum-security prison who began practicing meditation following a ten-day course in the Buddhist technique of vipassana.**

Dogma: **Two renegade angels try to exploit a religious loophole that could bring an end to humanity.**

A Door to the Sky: **Father's death forces Moroccan woman to return from her expatriate life in Paris to the constrained Muslim customs of her homeland.**

The Excorcist: **Teen is possessed by the devil and priests are forced to perform a dangerous religious ceremony.** (Original, 1973)

Guyana Tragedy—The Story of Jim Jones: **This made for TV film is based on the cult-like world of charismatic leader Jim Jones and the 1978 mass suicide of the People's Temple in Jonestown, Guyana. Not only does this real life event—one that took the lives of over 900 people—serve as one of the largest mass suicides in world history, it also serves as the greatest single loss of American civilian life in a non-natural disaster until the events of September 11th, 2001.** (Original, 1980)

History of the World: **Mel Brooks's satire where we learn what "really happened" at the last supper.**

The Kid with a Bike: **Eleven-year-old foster kid, Cyril, clings to his bicycle, which is stolen repeatedly throughout the film. This warm film has a religious parable undertone, as the boy is seen as puerile Christ figure surrounded by saintly characters who all hope to find redemption.**

Koran by Heart: **The world's preeminent Koran-recitation competition that takes place each year in Cairo is captured in this documentary that follows diverse children as the undergo intense preparation before performing in front of prominent judges.**

The Last Temptation of Christ: **At his execution, Jesus is tempted by an alluring image of a blissful life with Mary Magdelene—a temptation that tries to sway him from the sacrifice he must make.**

LoveCrimesKabul: **Inside look documentary that examines Afghanistan's Badam Baugh Women's Prison, where half of the inmates are locked up for "moral crimes."**

Mooz-Lum: **Strict Muslim student goes to college and is transformed. Then 9/11 terrorist attacks occur and he experiences distrust from angry classmates.**

The Omen: **Diplomat learns that his son is the literal anti-Christ.** (Original, 1976)

Orthodox Stance: **Documentary that looks at 25-year old Orthodox Jewish prizefighter Dmitry Salita who literally won't fight after Sundown of Friday.**

Religulous: **Bill Mahr's hilarious documentary on the current state of world religion.**

Rosemary's Baby: **Woman learns that her pregnancy is actually part of a satanic ritual.** (Original, 1968)

Saint Ralph: **A young man is forced to join his Catholic school track team after it is discovered that he has committed twenty-two sins against the flesh—his own flesh.**

Saved: **This satire looks at how religious beliefs can lead to extreme intolerance when a girl finds herself pregnant at a Baptist high school.**

Take Shelter: **Ohio man plagued by visions builds a backyard storm shelter that he insists is essential to survive the impending apocalypse.**

Twist of Faith: **Documentary that looks at a man who confronts his past sexual abuse at the hands of a Catholic priest, only to discover how this shatters his relationships with his family, community, and faith.**

West Beirut: **Follows two teenagers during the beginning of the civil war between Christians and Muslims that devastated Lebanon between 1975 and 1990 and turned cosmopolitan Beirut into a bombed-out ruin.**

Witness to Jonestown: **A powerful and extremely revealing documentary that explores the social and political worlds that allowed Jim Jones to successfully seduce the city of San Francisco. The film interviews survivors and family members on the thirty year anniversary of the Jones Town massacre—tracing Jones' unstoppable rise as reverend and community activist to this tragic last days in the jungle of Guyana.**

CHAPTER 6 — Gender, Sex, and Sexuality

12 Angry Men: **This 1957 classic introduces viewers to a jury of various male personalities who, during deliberation, are prevented from sentencing a Latino male when one of the men refuses to vote guilty. The result is a tense contrast in racist, bullying, often apathetic personas that boil to a head, leading to the film's dramatic conclusion.** (Original, 1957)

American Beauty: **A depressed suburban father in the midst of a midlife crisis decides to change his life—most notably through the pursuit of his teenage daughter's friend.**

Antwone Fisher: **An abused societal outcast attempts to understand what it means to be a man by exploring the institutions and determining factors that shaped him as a boy.**

The Ballad of Genesis and Lady Jaye: **Gender identity documentary that explores the mesmerizing love story between pioneering musician and performance artist Genesis P-Orridge and soul mate Lady Jaye.**

Beneath the Veil: **Examines women rebelling against the treatment they receive under the Taliban in Afghanistan.**

Born into Brothels: **Documentary that focuses on the children existing in Calcutta's inherently abusive red-light district.**

Boys Don't Cry: **The true story of Teena Brandon, who chose to live her short life as her male alter-ego, Brandon Teena.**

Boys in the Hood: **Coming-of-age tale about three friends—young males trying to grasp manhood in various ways—living in violent South Central, Los Angeles.**

A Boy's Life: **Documentary that follows a Mississippi family's struggle—according to the obviously disturbed grandmother—with an increasingly violent and erratic child.**

Bridget Jones' Diary: **A thirty-something woman struggles with the notion of becoming a spinster.**

Brokeback Mountain: **Love story that examines the forbidden love between two modern-day cowboys.**

The Business of Fancy Dancing: **Gay Indian poet from Spokane confronts his past when he returns to his childhood home, on the reservation, to attend a friend's funeral.**

The Carrier: **Documentary that follows a pregnant Zamibian mother who is a subsistence farmer in a polygamous marriage who has just learned she is HIV positive.**

The Circle: **Tracks the hopeless situation of a half-dozen Iranian women, including three who have escaped from jail.**

The Day I Became a Woman: **A trio of tales that simply, yet evocatively, lays out the problems of being a woman in Iran.**

Disney's Beauty and the Beast: **Young maiden offers herself to the beast—a raging and abusive male—and eventually discovers the prince inside.**

Eat Drink Man Woman: **Living in Tai Pei, a senior chef lives with his three unmarried adult daughters. Film revolves around everyone's relationships and the elaborate Sunday dinners.**

How to Murder Your Wife: **When a nationally syndicated cartoonist—one so successful he lives in a luxurious penthouse with his man-servant, Charles—attends a stag party and awakens the next day married to a young woman who barely speaks English, he finds that this mistake turns his life upside down. The end result is as complex as it is hilarious when he begins to plot his wife's murder within the pages of his cartoon. When she suddenly disappears, the cartoon is used as evidence at his trial.** (Original, 1965)

A League of Their Own: **Women grow and stand up to oppression when they start their own baseball league.**

Like Water for Chocolate: **Living in Mexico, a woman, prevented from marrying the man she loves, discovers she can do amazing things through her cooking.**

Love Actually: **Follows the lives of eight very different London couples dealing with their love lives in various interrelated tales.**

Mona Lisa Smile: **Feminist-thinking art professor challenges the conditioned lives of her students at an all-female college.**

My Beautiful Laundrette: **Omar, a young gay man of Pakistani background, opens a launderette in London and hires his former classmate, Johnny. Their developing relationship is much to the chagrin of Johnny's skinhead pals and Omar's successful immigrant family.**

No Secret Anymore: **Documentary that tackles—through the attempts of the filmmakers to develop a coalition—the prevailing belief that lesbians are illegal, immoral, and sick.**

On the Outs: **Three different Latinas and their crack-laced lives face the horrors and ravages of inner-city life.**

Pariah: **Closeted Brooklyn teen spends her nights sucking up the lesbian subculture she so desperately wants to embrace, all the while trying to escape the confines of her feminine days and the scrutiny of a religious mother.**

Paris Is Burning: **Documentary on "drag nights" among New York's underclass.**

Pretty Woman: **Prostitute elevates her social standing when a wealthy businessman decides to teach her how to be a proper woman.**

The Price of Sex: **Feature-length documentary about young Eastern European women who have been drawn into a world of sex trafficking and abuse.**

Real Women Have Curves: **Young L.A. Mexican butts heads with her matriarchal mother after expressing that she wants more out of life—namely a quality education—than simply being supportive of her family.**

Same Sex in America: **Documentary looks at same-sex marriage, as seen through several couples experiencing dilemmas.**

Second Hand Lions: **Two set-in-their-ways veterans, men who have lived full and active lives, reluctantly teach their young nephew what manhood is all about.**

The Sisterhood of the Traveling Pants: **A group of teenage friends from different backgrounds separate for the summer and have life-changing experiences—but not before discovering that they all can share a very special pair of jeans.**

The Strange History of Don't Ask, Don't Tell: **Documentary examines the legacy of gays in the military.**

Thelma & Louise: **Two women take a road trip and become wanted fugitives, all while embracing life, womanhood, and friendship.**

Thirteen: **A thirteen-year-old girl's relationship with her mother is put to the test as she discovers drugs, petty crime, and sex.**

The Three Burials of Melquiades Estrada: **Ranch hand attempts to fulfill two promises: bury his friend in his home in Mexico and punish the man who killed him.**

The World According the Garp: **Young man, who sees himself as a serious writer, is overwhelmed by his famous feminist mother and the variously distressed women that come into his life.**

Y Tu Mama Tambien: **In Mexico, two teenage boys and an attractive older woman embark on a road trip and learn about life, friendship, sex, and each other.**

CHAPTER 7 — Fork in the Road

12 Angry Lebanese: **For nearly a year and a half, forty-five prison inmates in Lebanon's largest prison found themselves working together to present their version of Reginald Rose's play** *12 Angry Men,* **which they rename in this powerful documentary.**

50/50: **After being diagnosed with cancer, Adam receives distractions from his friend, Kyle, who shows him how to turn the corner regarding his illness and, as such, strengthen his personal resolve.**

Angels Crest: **In the working class town of Angels Crest, a young father tries to raise his son. This is made more difficult because the child's mother is an alcoholic. When tragedy strikes, the tight knit community splinters as it attempts to decide where the blame lies.**

The Arbor: **Documentary that looks at a poor housing project in England's Yorkshire where real life ravages of alcohol and drug abuse become the centerpiece of playwright Andrea Dunbar's life.**

Beats, Rhymes, & Life: The Travels of a Tribe Called Quest: **Documentary that explores one of the most ground breaking Hip-Hop groups of the early 90s.**

The Big One: **On his book tour, Michael Moore exposes wrongdoings by greedy big businesses and callous politicians.**

Bigger, Stronger, Faster: **Documentary that examines America's fascination—athletes and amateurs—with being the biggest, strongest, and the fastest.**

Billy the Kid: **Documentary on teenager Billy Price and his dignified coping with Asperger's syndrome.**

Boli Zhi Cheng (City of Glass): **Twenty years after a college couple's break-up and marriage to other people, their children—from respective marriages—meet and join forces to help them live out a dream.**

Changing Lanes: **Road rage spirals into a all-consuming feud between two men who both find they are at crossroads in their lives.**

City of God: **Poor Brazilian youth decides to pick up a camera and abandon his life of crime and embrace his new hobby: recording the violence and disparity of his world on film.**

Dorian Blues: **One night, a closeted high school senior—saddled with a domineering father, an athletic brother, and a loopy mother—challenges his father's conservative views and, during their argument, has an epiphany: he is gay.**

The English Sheik and the Yemeni Gentleman: **Follows a British filmmaker who returns to Yemen—the home of his father—and meets a British expatriate. Together they roam the land and discover a true sense of belonging.**

Fame: **Students at NYC's School for the Performing Arts attempt to overcome social and personal barriers and fulfill their artistic dreams.** (Original, 1980)

Flight of the Red Balloon: **Film deals with a Parisian summer filled with uncertainty, with each of the characters—mother, son, and Chinese au pair—expressing loss and pain.**

Footnote: **Dueling Talmudic scholars—the wizened father who has been overlooked in academia, and his middle aged son who reaps the rewards of success—seek their homeland's Israel Prize. When the father mistakenly thinks the prize is for him, the world of academia and its approval seeking recognition becomes the focus for this comedy's scrutiny.**

The Good Life: **Timely documentary that looks at a mother and daughter in costal Portuguese who, once rich, now live off a small pension. The film is a character study of the women's struggle to adapt to their new situation during uncertain financial times.**

Imitation of Life: **Explores the practice of passing by a young Black woman attempting to prosper in segregated America.** (Original, 1934 and 1959 remake)

The Journals of Musan: **Story of a North Korean defector forging a new life in capitalist South Korea. This film is a vision of loneliness, disconnect, and ethical ambiguity.**

Khodorkovsky: **Documentary that unpacks the biographical rise and current imprisonment of Mikhail Khodorkovsky—a Russian oligarch who, a victim of Vladimir Putin's enmity, was imprisoned after fabricated tax-evasion charges.**

Look at Me: **A Parisian choral student lives in a world of disconnectedness. Notably, there is a subplot on weight obsession after the father marries a rail-thin trophy wife, leaving his heavyset daughter feeling threatened.**

Marathon Boy: **Documentary that looks at the rags-to-riches story of an Indian boy who rose to fame as a long-distance runner before his coach was caught up in a damaging scandal.**

Mildred Pierce: **After her cheating husband leaves her, title character proves she can thrive independently.** (Original, 1945)

My Brother is an Only Child: **A coming of age story that chronicles the political awakening of a rural Italian boy in the 1960s and 70s. The film follows the contentious protagonist as he drifts from a seminary stint to Fascist party membership to Communist activism in search of a purpose.**

The Reception: **Frenchwoman, her daughter, and new son-in-law, along with a gay African American painter, drink and unleash a torrent of frank talk about sex, race, class, and hopelessly damaged family relationships.**

Thumbsucker: **Whenever the teenage protagonist feels overwhelmed, he indulges in the infantile oral fixation of sucking his thumb. Once teen discovers Ritalin, he goes from vulnerable to being overly aggressive.**

To Be Heard: **For students at the Power Writers program at East Harlem's Renaissance Charter High School for Innovation, poetry is an essential part of their survival. In this documentary** that spans four years, the kids come from various challenging backgrounds that expose personal tribulations as they try to develop a positive mode of self-expression.

Trudell: Documentary that examines Native American activist, actor, and poet John Trudell's political life, which changed drastically and tragically twelve hours after he burned an American flag on the steps of FBI's Washington, D.C., headquarters in 1979.

Tsotsi: Set in postapartheid Johannesburg, film follows the moral rehabilitation of a street thug who, after carjacking an affluent woman, decides to nurture her baby as his own.

Two for the Road: Couple drives across Europe at three different, precarious points in their relationship. Film focuses on specific questions: Are they a happy twosome facing a rough road, or a mismatch finally realizing their mutual error; or, is marriage just about the journey itself? (Original, 1967)

Where in the World is Osama bin Laden?: Morgan Spurlock, the director of the documentary *Super Size Me,* chronicles his search for Osama bin Laden and other high ranking Al Qaeda officials. Film travels through Egypt, Morocco, Israel, Jordan, Saudi Arabia, Afghanistan, and Pakistan. While comedic in many ways, the film reveals rampant poverty and people who would love to have some semblance of justice and peace.

Winter Passing: East Village young woman, eventually joined by other lost souls desperately trying to stay numb by any means necessary, attempt to heal.

CHAPTER 8 — Manmade and Natural Disaters

Children of Men: Futuristic thriller in which humankind is facing extinction because women have become infertile.

City of Life and Death: Filmed in black-and-white, this movie is a sobering depiction of Japan's 1937 three-day siege of Nanking and its bloody aftermath.

Contagion: In this epidemic thriller, an airborne virus kills millions.

Bully: Socially awkward twelve-year-old Alex is tormented daily in Sioux City, Iowa. This documentary looks closely at several stories of victimization, none more so than Alex, in an attempt to shine a light on the spiraling bullying epidemic that is impacting Middle America.

Deep Impact: Meteors are going to destroy the planet and the government starts a raffle to determine who is worthy of survival.

Extremely Loud and Incredibly Close: After 9/11, the "worst day" in American history, a son, whose father dies when the Towers collapse, attempts to discover said parent's final message while traveling through the shaken city and meeting others in need of healing.

How to Survive a Plague: Archival video tells this heroic story of AIDS during the hysteria of the Reagan administration, focusing on the activists who fought to generate compassion while battling shame and hatred.

If God is Willing and Da Creek Don't Rise: A post Hurricane Katrina documentary by Spike Lee that examines 2010 New Orleans. Included within the film is an examination of the BP oil spill.

The Island President: **Looking at the Maldives, off the coast of India, this documentary examines the island paradise alongside former President Mohamed Nasheed as he prepared to discuss the devastating impact Global Warming is having on his nation at the Copenhagen climate summit.**

Lazarus Effect: **A documentary look at the HIV/AIDS pandemic in East Africa and the impact drug treatments can have on a person's chances for survival.**

New York Says Thank You: **New Yorkers impacted by the events of 911 travel the country helping communities rebuild after disasters in this moving documentary.**

Outbreak: **Film follows scientist as they try to stop the spread of the Motaba virus that has infected a town and is wiping out the population, as well as examines the extreme military response to the threat.**

Panic in the Streets: **Shot on location in New Orleans 1950, the manhunt is on after a waterfront murder victim is discovered to carry pneumonic plague.**

Semper Fi: Always Faithful: **After Marine Master Sergeant Jerry Ensminger's daughter dies of a rare leukemia, he relentlessly searches for answers. This documentary shows how he uncovers one of the largest water contamination sites in U.S. history and struggles for justice on behalf of his family and fellow soldiers.**

Twister: **Tornado chasers follow the deadly funnels' paths of destruction across the Midwest.**

When the Levees Broke: **Spike Lee's investigative documentary explores the most devastating natural disaster in American history.**

When the Mountains Tremble: **Documentary looks at Guatemalan death squads in the early 1980s that roamed the countryside in a war against the unarmed indigenous population.**

You Don't Like the Truth: 4 Days Inside Guantanamo: **Guantanamo Bay Prison interrogation footage of Canadian citizen Omar Khadr, who is grilled about his possible terrorist ties in Afghanistan. The documentary brilliantly explores—through interviews with Khadr's lawyers, family members, and former cell mates— the debate over ends justifying the means during an era of endless war.**

Foreword

We don't write writing—we write about, because, in order to. We write to say something—something best expressed in a medium with permanency—to someone—readers who want to understand our proclamations and questions, who want to engage with us. Oftentimes, other people's texts play an essential role in inspiring, provoking, even inciting writing. Here, then, we have a collection of provocative, insightful, opinionated, and sometimes thoroughly disturbing pieces. What better way to launch authentic communication through writing?

Beyond that, *Lead, Follow or Move Out of the Way* amply demonstrates that there are public purposes for education and schooling, that learning to write well is not just a matter of accumulating skills but, rather, an occasion for examining the real and pressing issues of the social and political context in which we live. Education has moral dimensions. Thus, educators have a responsibility to build a citizenry that is not only competent but informed, not only informed but willing and able to participate in our emerging democracy. Education ought to produce participants, not bystanders.

There are several riffs on Thomas Paine here. One is, of course, the title, but the content and structure of this text instantiates another deeply held belief of Paine. In the same text from which the title comes (*The American Crisis*, 1776), Paine asserts, "Moderation in temper is always a virtue; but moderation in principle is always a vice." This anthology provides multiple opportunities to be informed and provoked, and thereby to develop strong commitments, grounded in reason and tested through deliberation.

The pieces contained in the collection are, however, not mere polemic. Their strength lies in how varied they are in genre, historical and geographical location, and authorial voice. Moreover, unlike the customary organization of anthologies—by genre, geography, or historical period—the thematic organization here creates a truly global perspective, one which is both timeless and timely, as the reader can see how the most perplexing socio-political issues know no bounds. Man-made and Natural Disasters, a theme new to this edition, enhances the global and social justice perspectives. Readers are helped to see that even the seemingly neutral acts of Mother Nature impact the poor and the voiceless disproportionately.

This text is a rich resource for teachers and students alike as its thoughtful selection and organization encourage what Short, Harste& Burke (1995) call "wondering and wandering," the central impulses of self-directed exploration and investigation. The films provide another means to access the texts and themes and are particularly useful for struggling readers. They enhance each theme and the editors' thoughtful commentary provides an orientation for both teachers and students so that they might make informed choices about where to wander and what to wonder about.

Of particular note is that *Lead, Follow, Move Out of the Way* can be used within a wide range of pedagogies, from student directed to teacher directed. Instructors can create curricula that invite students to inquire into a theme, or a particular incident, time period, author, or geographic location. Students can work alone or collaboratively. They may explore their own points of view, compare perspectives and even construct ways to put their new knowledge to use outside of the classroom. They can turn their school knowledge into action knowledge through social justice and service learning projects that emerge from their readings and viewing. Alternatively, assignments can be created that ask students to create their own mimetic texts or to construct critical reflections, analyses, and arguments.

This anthology waits for students and teachers to bring it to life. In every instance, the discussions, writing and actions that result will be purposeful, passionate, and informed. And that's what we want novice writers to learn about writing—that it serves genuine purposes and is meant for real audiences, and can make things happen in the world. Beyond that, this collection opens up a space to understand how text and film can serve social and political purposes, purposes beyond information or aesthetic delights. Readers will have a hard time maintaining moderate positions. Rather, they can develop informed and passionate principles, just as Thomas Paine would wish.

Dr. Cynthia Onore
Emeritus Professor of Education
Montclair State University

Preface

Since this book's first incarnation in 2006, our Global Community has undergone quite a bit of change. Entire countries dove headfirst into the gaping maw of a recession. Middle Eastern nations saw a record number of citizen led protests. An earthquake and subsequent tsunami devastated parts of Japan. An Icelandic volcano suspended international travel for what felt like forever. Kim Jong Il, the former leader of North Korea, died. Osama bin Laden, the orchestrator of the September 11th attacks in America, was killed. The war in Iraq ended. On top of that, environmentally, the global community saw a record number of changes to the climate. America elected its first African American President but, still grasping and hoping for a post racial society, the nation sat stunned as the details of the murder of unarmed Florida teen Trayvon Martin read like an old Jim Crow case. Additionally, the end of the world has been predicted twice by an American religious fundamentalist. And, not to be undone, if the Mayan Calendar is correct, humanity's days on planet Earth are numbered.

Of course, there were other significant and monumental happenings. But, the point that we are trying to make is that our world-at-large is at a crossroads in time.

Now, more than ever, knowledge and critical thought are so very important to who we will all become.

Perhaps the easiest part of this text was creating the title. We were hoping that the words "Lead, Follow, or Move Out of the Way" would become a new mantra that students would carry with them alongside all their other social and cultural interests. It is still our greatest desire and belief that the works within this anthology will also pique their academic interest in such a way that these varied articles, essays, short stories, novel excerpts, plays, and films will become part of their everyday discussions outside of the classroom.

Some would have us believe that today's students are apathetic or unaware of the world's ever-changing social, cultural, and political landscapes; moreover, that they are unable to create well-informed, articulately written works that address such issues. *Lead, Follow, or Move Out of the Way* takes the position that students are not only able to engage in critical discussions and writing, but that they are also looking forward to it.

We still believe that we have compiled a selection of texts that can create a dynamic atmosphere for classroom discussion and build bridges from one country to another, turning our rather large global world into a small-town community of shared learning and experience.

The authors included within this anthology differ in ethnicity, faith, gender, sexual orientation, political assertions, and overall life ideology, but the point we believe the texts make is that no matter where we fall on the battlefield that is life, we are all, at the very core, intrinsically the same. Our world is changing; our students get that. Perhaps what we take for apathy is in fact an uncertainty about how best to navigate the process of life. *Lead, Follow, or Move Out of the Way* is perhaps a tool for providing a safe space to learn, express, and develop a clearer picture of who our students wish to become.

Outside of the diverse texts, professors will find annotated film selections that will provide students with a visual companion to better digest written texts. Furthermore, each reading selection—divided into three parts—is followed by what we have termed the Critical Eye, which includes For Discussion, Reapproaching the Literature, and Writing Assignment features. These Critical Eye components are designed to facilitate classroom discussions and, in many cases, ask the student to examine the text alongside other works, different historical perspectives, and other outside texts. Because the world has changed so much since the first inception of this book in 2006, for this edition, we have added a new section entitled Manmade and Natural Disasters. In this chapter, you will find texts that examine global inhumanity and the wrath of nature.

All in all, we believe the anthology makes for a positive learning experience for the instructor and the student. This is *Lead, Follow, or Move Out of the Way*. Welcome!

—The Editors

CHAPTER 1

Social Responsibility

Never in the field of human conflict has so much been owed by so many to so few.
Winston Churchill

Today's world is one in which the threat of war and natural disasters looms over the heads of all persons everywhere. The ravages of a world involved in manmade combat have now been equaled by nature's vengeful forces affecting our ocean shores—issues that must be watched closely. With worry and fear becoming the call of the day, our need to be more socially conscious has become insistent. No longer can the citizens of the world ignore or exclude their brethren, no matter where they reside or what their ethnic, gender, class, or religious backgrounds may be. The world has awoken in peril, and we, as a world community, must demonstrate an unprecedented sense of communal responsibility. And, for those who ask, "what is my role to be?" the reality is that social responsibility in our world community might be more than just a little perplexing.

Because our human role is ever-evolving—a result of culture, technology, and policy—human beings, indeed, find themselves puzzled as to where they fit in, let alone how to accommodate or support others outside of their immediate surroundings. At the same time, citizens may find themselves questioning the ethical weight of whether or not their first allegiance is to their individual surroundings as opposed to the wide embrace of humankind. On the other hand, a large section of our population recognizes that humanity's plights and responses are the clearly defined moral obligations of everyone.

The texts in this section explore the various ways that people from all walks of life interpret the notion of social responsibility. Hopefully, the authors and their writings provide us with ways to examine and articulate these ideas to their communities, their families, their enemies, and themselves.

STANLEY CROUCH

Taking Back the Music
They're smart, they're black and they're gonna change rap's image of women

When Bill and Camille Cosby donated $20 million to the historically black Spelman College in 1988, consternation went through the black community because the size of the check was so shocking. No one, even Bill Cosby himself, could have imagined that within two decades the young black women at Spelman would spark what is easily the most important American cultural movement in this new century.

In April of last year, under the leadership of Asha Jennings, who now attends New York University as a law major, the Spelman women gave voice to the fact that they had had enough of the dehumanizing images of black women in rap. They went after the rapper Nelly, who was scheduled to appear on campus, for the images in his "Tip-Drill" video.

Nelly hid under his bed and chose to stay away from that female ire. Maybe it would blow away. It did not.

On Friday, Atlanta was set afire by the emotion and the hard thinking of black women. Spelman and Essence magazine presented a hip hop town meeting at the Cosby Academic Center Auditorium as part of their Take Back the Music campaign. The campaign is a response across generations that Essence has covered in its last two issues and will continue to address as long as necessary. One can easily see that many women find the overt hatred of females and the reductive, pornographic images of the worst hip hop quite disturbing.

The overflow audience filled three additional rooms. Michaela Angela Davis, an editor at Essence, was the moderator. The panelists were Tarshia Stanley, assistant professor of English at Spelman; Moya Bailey, Spelman senior; Kevin Powell, author and activist; Michael Lewellen, vice president of BET public relations; Brian Leach, vice president of A&R, TVT Records, and hip hop artist and actress MC Lyte.

The event lasted three hours. Said Davis: "It was most heated and most uncomfortable for those representing the companies. Lewellen and Leach received the most fire from the audience. These women are in pain and are confused. One woman asked, 'What did we do to make you all seemingly hate us so much?' There was a great silence, and a feeling of collective pain filled the air."

This mysogynistic and brutal turn in music is damaging the image of black American women to the point that they are approached outside of the U.S. like freelance prostitutes.

The Spelman women made their voices heard and have inspired thinking young men to fight the stereotypes and question the images. This is no less than an extension of the civil rights movement. But true change will only come when white females begin to identify with the dues their black sisters must pay as

© Daily News, L.P. (New York). Used with permission.

this hostility and exploitation continues to be splattered through radio and television. White women have to open up on white men, who buy four out of five rap recordings. Once they declare it uncool for white guys to support the dehumanization of black women, we will see much more than a sea of change.

I'm an optimist. I think the tide is about to turn.

CRITICAL EYE

▶ For Discussion

a. Is Hip Hop music responsible for the decline of America's youth?

b. More Hip Hop records are bought by White males than Black males. According to the article, White women should speak to "their" men about the negative images of women in Hip Hop music. Do you agree?

c. Is it true that Hip Hop music is causing nations around the globe to view all Black women as prostitutes?

d. Are the arguments against Rap any different from those made about Rock 'n' Roll during the 1950s?

▶ Re-approaching the Reading

Feminist writer Naomi Wolf asserts that our society creates "bad girls" so that women without reputations can feel safe. In what ways is this true?

▶ Writing Assignment

To imply that one form of music is creating a problematic gender structure among American youth is an astounding assertion. Do you agree?

NELLA LARSEN

From the Novel
PASSING

The main character Irene—who, unbeknownst to her spouse, occasionally passes for White— refuses to discuss a racial matter with her family. She is racked with guilt because of her racial duplicity and fears that her husband, Brian, is being unfaithful with her nemesis Clare—a Black woman who actually lives as a White woman in 1920s Harlem.

The next morning brought with it a snowstorm that lasted throughout the day.

After a breakfast which had been eaten almost in silence and which she was relieved to have done with, Irene Redfield lingered for a little while in the downstairs hall, looking out at the soft flakes fluttering down. She was watching them immediately fill some ugly irregular gaps left by the feet of hurrying pedestrians when Zulena came to her, saying: "The telephone, Mrs. Redfield. It's Mrs. Bellew."

"Take the message, Zulena, please."

Though she continued to stare out of the window, Irene saw nothing now, stabbed as she was by fear—and hope. Had anything happened between Clare and Bellew? And if so, what? And was she to be freed at last from the aching anxiety of the past weeks? Or was there to be more, and worse? She had a wrestling moment in which it seemed that she must rush after Zulena and hear for herself what it was that Clare had to say. But she waited.

Zulena, when she came back, said: "She says, ma'am, that she'll be able to go to Mrs. Freeland's tonight. She'll be here sometime between eight and nine."

"Thank you, Zulena."

The day dragged on to its end.

At dinner Brian spoke bitterly of a lynching that he had been reading about in the evening paper.

"Dad, why is it that they only lynch colored people?" Ted asked.

"Because they hate 'em, son."

"Brian!" Irene's voice was a plea and a rebuke.

Ted said: "Oh! And why do they hate 'em?"

"Because they are afraid of them."

"But what makes them afraid of 'em?"

"Because—"

"Brian!"

"It seems, son, that is a subject we can't go into at the moment without distressing the ladies of our family," he told the boy with mock seriousness, "but we'll take it up sometime when we're alone together."

Ted nodded in his engaging grave way. "I see. Maybe we can talk about it tomorrow on the way to school."

"That'll be fine."

"Brian!"

"Mother," Junior remarked, "that's the third time you've said 'Brian' like that."

"But not the last, Junior, never you fear," his father told him.

After the boys had gone up to their own floor, Irene said suavely: "I do wish, Brian, that you wouldn't talk about lynching before Ted and Junior. It was really inexcusable for you to bring up a thing like that at dinner. There'll be time enough for them to learn about such horrible things when they're older."

"You're absolutely wrong! If, as you're so determined, they've got to live in this damned country, they'd better find out what sort of thing they're up against as soon as possible. The earlier they learn it, the better prepared they'll be."

"I don't agree. I want their childhood to be happy and as free from the knowledge of such things as it possibly can be."

"Very laudable," was Brian's sarcastic answer. "Very laudable indeed, all things considered. But can it?"

"Certainly it can. If you'll only do your part."

"Stuff! You know as well as I do, Irene, that it can't. What was the use of our trying to keep them from learning the word 'nigger' and its connotation? They found out, didn't they? And how? Because somebody called Junior a dirty nigger."

"Just the same, you're not to talk to them about the race problem. I won't have it."

They glared at each other.

"I tell you, Irene, they've got to know these things, and it might as well be now as later."

"They do not!" she insisted, forcing back the tears of anger that were threatening to fall.

Brian growled: "I can't understand how anybody as intelligent as you like to think you are can show evidences of such stupidity." He looked at her in a puzzled harassed way.

"Stupid!" she cried. "Is it stupid to want my children to be happy?" Her lips were quivering.

"At the expense of proper preparation for life and their future happiness, yes. And I'd feel I hadn't done my duty by them if I didn't give them some inkling of what's before them. It's the least I can do. I wanted to get them out of this hellish place years ago. You wouldn't let me. I gave up the idea, because you objected. Don't expect me to give up everything."

Under the lash of his words she was silent. Before any answer came to her, he had turned and gone from the room.

Sitting there alone in the forsaken dining room, unconsciously pressing the hands lying in her lap tightly together, she was seized by a convulsion of shivering. For, to her, there had been something ominous in the scene that she had just had with her husband. Over and over in her mind his last words: "Don't expect me to give up everything," repeated themselves. What had they meant? What could they mean? Clare Kendry?

Surely she was going mad with fear and suspicion. She must not work herself up. She must not! Where were all the self-control, the common sense, that she was so proud of? Now, if ever, was the time for it.

CRITICAL EYE

▶ For Discussion

a. The Father says that he is preparing his children for "what's before them." Should parents expose children to the harsh realities of racism?

b. What is the danger of not discussing social intolerance with children?

▶ Re-approaching the Reading

What, exactly, is a nigger? Has the meaning of the word—historically, culturally, politically—changed over time?

▶ Writing Assignment

Consider the father in the story. Is he preparing his son for life as a "Black man" in America? What exactly does that mean these days, and how crucial is it?

Social Responsibility

RALPH WALDO EMERSON

SELF-RELIANCE
from Essays: First Series (1841)

> *"Ne te quaesiveris extra."*
> *"Man is his own star; and the soul that can*
> *Render an honest and a perfect man,*
> *Commands all light, all influence, all fate;*
> *Nothing to him falls early or too late.*
> *Our acts our angels are, or good or ill,*
> *Our fatal shadows that walk by us still."*
> Epilogue to Beaumont and
> Fletcher's *Honest Man's Fortune*

> *Cast the bantling on the rocks,*
> *Suckle him with the she-wolf's teat;*
> *Wintered with the hawk and fox,*
> *Power and speed be hands and feet.*

Essay II Self-reliance

I read the other day some verses written by an eminent painter which were original and not conventional. The soul always hears an admonition in such lines, let the subject be what it may. The sentiment they instill is of more value than any thought they may contain. To believe your own thought, to believe that what is true for you in your private heart is true for all men,—that is genius. Speak your latent conviction, and it shall be the universal sense; for the inmost in due time becomes the outmost,—and our first thought is rendered back to us by the trumpets of the Last Judgment. Familiar as the voice of the mind is to each, the highest merit we ascribe to Moses, Plato, and Milton is, that they set at naught books and traditions, and spoke not what men but what they thought. A man should learn to detect and watch that gleam of light which flashes across his mind from within, more than the lustre of the firmament of bards and sages. Yet he dismisses without notice his thought, because it is his. In every work of genius we recognize our own rejected thoughts: they come back to us with a certain alienated majesty. Great works of art have no more affecting lesson for us than this. They teach us to abide by our spontaneous impression with good-humored inflexibility then most when the whole cry of voices is on the other side. Else, to-morrow a stranger will say with masterly good sense precisely what we have thought and felt all the time, and we shall be forced to take with shame our own opinion from another.

There is a time in every man's education when he arrives at the conviction that envy is ignorance; that imitation is suicide; that he must take himself for better, for worse, as his portion; that though the wide universe is full of good, no kernel of nourishing corn can come to him but through his toil bestowed on that plot of ground which is given to him to till. The power which resides in him is new in nature, and none but he knows what that is which he can do, nor does he know until he has tried. Not for nothing one face, one character, one fact, makes much impression on him, and another none. This sculpture in the memory is not without preestablished harmony. The eye was placed where one ray should fall, that it might testify of that particular ray. We but half express ourselves, and are ashamed of that divine idea which each of us represents. It may be safely trusted as proportionate and of good issues, so it be faithfully imparted, but God will not have his work made manifest by cowards. A man is relieved and gay when he has put his heart into his work and done his best; but what he has said or done otherwise, shall give him no peace. It is a deliverance which does not deliver. In the attempt his genius deserts him; no muse befriends; no invention, no hope.

Trust thyself: every heart vibrates to that iron string. Accept the place the divine providence has found for you, the society of your contemporaries, the connection of events. Great men have always done so, and confided themselves childlike to the genius of their age, betraying their perception that the absolutely trustworthy was seated at their heart, working through their hands, predominating in all their being. And we are now men, and must accept in the highest mind the same transcendent destiny; and not minors and invalids in a protected corner, not cowards fleeing before a revolution, but guides, redeemers, and benefactors, obeying the Almighty effort, and advancing on Chaos and the Dark.

What pretty oracles nature yields us on this text, in the face and behaviour of children, babes, and even brutes! That divided and rebel mind, that distrust of a sentiment because our arithmetic has computed the strength and means opposed to our purpose, these have not. Their mind being whole, their eye is as yet unconquered, and when we look in their faces, we are disconcerted. Infancy conforms to nobody: all conform to it, so that one babe commonly makes four or five out of the adults who prattle and play to it. So God has armed youth and puberty and manhood no less with its own piquancy and charm, and made it enviable and gracious and its claims not to be put by, if it will stand by itself. Do not think the youth has no force, because he cannot speak to you and me. Hark! in the next room his voice is sufficiently clear and emphatic. It seems he knows how to speak to his contemporaries. Bashful or bold, then, he will know how to make us seniors very unnecessary.

The nonchalance of boys who are sure of a dinner, and would disdain as much as a lord to do or say aught to conciliate one, is the healthy attitude of human nature. A boy is in the parlour what the pit is in the playhouse; independent, irresponsible, looking out from his corner on such people and facts as pass by, he tries and sentences them on their merits, in the swift, summary way of boys, as good, bad, interesting, silly, eloquent, troublesome. He cumbers himself never about consequences, about interests: he gives an independent, genuine verdict. You must court him: he does not court you. But the man is, as it were, clapped into jail by his consciousness. As soon as he has once acted or spoken with eclat, he is a committed person, watched by the sympathy or the hatred of hundreds, whose affections must now enter into his account. There is no Lethe for this. Ah, that he could pass again into his neutrality! Who can thus avoid all pledges, and having observed, observe again from the same unaffected, unbiased, unbribable, unaffrighted innocence, must always be formidable. He would utter opinions on all passing affairs, which being seen to be not private, but necessary, would sink like darts into the ear of men, and put them in fear.

These are the voices which we hear in solitude, but they grow faint and inaudible as we enter into the world. Society everywhere is in conspiracy against the manhood of every one of its members. Society is a joint-stock company, in which the members agree, for the better securing of his bread to each shareholder, to surrender the liberty and culture of the eater. The virtue in most request is conformity. Self-reliance is its aversion. It loves not realities and creators, but names and customs.

Whoso would be a man must be a nonconformist. He who would gather immortal palms must not be hindered by the name of goodness, but must explore if it be goodness. Nothing is at last sacred but the integrity of your own mind. Absolve you to yourself, and you shall have the suffrage of the world. I remember an answer which when quite young I was prompted to make to a valued adviser, who was wont to importune me with the dear old doctrines of the church. On my saying, What have I to do with the sacredness of traditions, if I live wholly from within? my friend suggested,—"But these impulses may be from below, not from above." I replied, "They do not seem to me to be such; but if I am the Devil's child, I will live then from the Devil." No law can be sacred to me but that of my nature. Good and bad are but names very readily transferable to that or this; the only right is what is after my constitution, the only wrong what is against it. A man is to carry himself in the presence of all opposition, as if every thing were titular and ephemeral but he. I am ashamed to think how easily we capitulate to badges and names, to large societies and dead institutions. Every decent and well-spoken individual affects and sways me more than is right. I ought to go upright and vital, and speak the rude truth in all ways. If malice and vanity wear the coat of philanthropy, shall that pass? If an angry bigot assumes this bountiful cause of Abolition, and comes to me with his last news from Barbadoes, why should I not say to him, 'Go love thy infant; love thy wood-chopper: be good-natured and modest: have that grace; and never varnish your hard, uncharitable ambition with this incredible tenderness for black folk a thousand miles off. Thy love afar is spite at home.' Rough and graceless would be such greeting, but truth is handsomer than the affectation of love. Your goodness must have some edge to it,—else it is none. The doctrine of hatred must be preached as the counteraction of the doctrine of love when that pules and whines. I shun father and mother and wife and brother, when my genius calls me. I would write on the lintels of the door-post, Whim. I hope it is somewhat better than whim at last, but we cannot spend the day in explanation. Expect me not to show cause why I seek or why I exclude company. Then, again, do not tell me, as a good man did to-day, of my obligation to put all poor men in good situations. Are they my poor? I tell thee, thou foolish philanthropist, that I grudge the dollar, the dime, the cent, I give to such men as do not belong to me and to whom I do not belong. There is a class of persons to whom by all spiritual affinity I am bought and sold; for them I will go to prison, if need be; but your miscellaneous popular charities; the education at college of fools; the building of meeting-houses to the vain end to which many now stand; alms to sots; and the thousandfold Relief Societies;—though I confess with shame I sometimes succumb and give the dollar, it is a wicked dollar which by and by I shall have the manhood to withhold.

Virtues are, in the popular estimate, rather the exception than the rule. There is the man *and* his virtues. Men do what is called a good action, as some piece of courage or charity, much as they would pay a fine in expiation of daily non-appearance on parade. Their works are done as an apology or extenuation of their living in the world,—as invalids and the insane pay a high board. Their virtues are penances. I do not wish to expiate, but to live. My life is for itself and not for a spectacle. I much prefer that it should be of a lower strain, so it be genuine and equal, than that it should be glittering and unsteady. I wish it to be sound and sweet, and not to need diet and bleeding. I ask primary evidence that you are a man, and refuse this appeal from the man to his actions. I know that for myself it makes no difference whether I do or forbear those actions which are reckoned excellent. I cannot consent to pay for a privilege where I have intrinsic right.

Few and mean as my gifts may be, I actually am, and do not need for my own assurance or the assurance of my fellows any secondary testimony.

What I must do is all that concerns me, not what the people think. This rule, equally arduous in actual and in intellectual life, may serve for the whole distinction between greatness and meanness. It is the harder, because you will always find those who think they know what is your duty better than you know it. It is easy in the world to live after the world's opinion; it is easy in solitude to live after our own; but the great man is he who in the midst of the crowd keeps with perfect sweetness the independence of solitude.

The objection to conforming to usages that have become dead to you is, that it scatters your force. It loses your time and blurs the impression of your character. If you maintain a dead church, contribute to a dead Bible-society, vote with a great party either for the government or against it, spread your table like base housekeepers,—under all these screens I have difficulty to detect the precise man you are. And, of course, so much force is withdrawn from your proper life. But do your work, and I shall know you. Do your work, and you shall reinforce yourself. A man must consider what a blindman's-buff is this game of conformity. If I know your sect, I anticipate your argument. I hear a preacher announce for his text and topic the expediency of one of the institutions of his church. Do I not know beforehand that not possibly can he say a new and spontaneous word? Do I not know that, with all this ostentation of examining the grounds of the institution, he will do no such thing? Do I not know that he is pledged to himself not to look but at one side,—the permitted side, not as a man, but as a parish minister? He is a retained attorney, and these airs of the bench are the emptiest affectation. Well, most men have bound their eyes with one or another handkerchief, and attached themselves to some one of these communities of opinion. This conformity makes them not false in a few particulars, authors of a few lies, but false in all particulars. Their every truth is not quite true. Their two is not the real two, their four not the real four; so that every word they say chagrins us, and we know not where to begin to set them right. Meantime nature is not slow to equip us in the prison-uniform of the party to which we adhere. We come to wear one cut of face and figure, and acquire by degrees the gentlest asinine expression. There is a mortifying experience in particular, which does not fail to wreak itself also in the general history; I mean "the foolish face of praise," the forced smile which we put on in company where we do not feel at ease in answer to conversation which does not interest us. The muscles, not spontaneously moved, but moved by a low usurping wilfulness, grow tight about the outline of the face with the most disagreeable sensation.

For nonconformity the world whips you with its displeasure. And therefore a man must know how to estimate a sour face. The by-standers look askance on him in the public street or in the friend's parlour. If this aversation had its origin in contempt and resistance like his own, he might well go home with a sad countenance; but the sour faces of the multitude, like their sweet faces, have no deep cause, but are put on and off as the wind blows and a newspaper directs. Yet is the discontent of the multitude more formidable than that of the senate and the college. It is easy enough for a firm man who knows the world to brook the rage of the cultivated classes. Their rage is decorous and prudent, for they are timid as being very vulnerable themselves. But when to their feminine rage the indignation of the people is added, when the ignorant and the poor are aroused, when the unintelligent brute force that lies at the bottom of society is made to growl and mow, it needs the habit of magnanimity and religion to treat it godlike as a trifle of no concernment.

The other terror that scares us from self-trust is our consistency; a reverence for our past act or word, because the eyes of others have no other data for computing our orbit than our past acts, and we are loath to disappoint them.

But why should you keep your head over your shoulder? Why drag about this corpse of your memory, lest you contradict somewhat you have stated in this or that public place? Suppose you should contradict yourself; what then? It seems to be a rule of wisdom never to rely on your memory alone, scarcely even in acts of pure memory, but to bring the past for judgment into the thousand-eyed present, and live ever in a new day. In your metaphysics you have denied personality to the Deity: yet when the devout motions of the soul come, yield to them heart and life, though they should clothe God with shape and color. Leave your theory, as Joseph his coat in the hand of the harlot, and flee.

A foolish consistency is the hobgoblin of little minds, adored by little statesmen and philosophers and divines. With consistency a great soul has simply nothing to do. He may as well concern himself with his shadow on the wall. Speak what you think now in hard words, and to-morrow speak what to-morrow thinks in hard words again, though it contradict every thing you said to-day.—'Ah, so you shall be sure to be misunderstood.'—Is it so bad, then, to be misunderstood? Pythagoras was misunderstood, and Socrates, and Jesus, and Luther, and Copernicus, and Galileo, and Newton, and every pure and wise spirit that ever took flesh. To be great is to be misunderstood.

I suppose no man can violate his nature. All the sallies of his will are rounded in by the law of his being, as the inequalities of Andes and Himmaleh are insignificant to the curve of the sphere. Nor does it matter how you gauge and try him. A character is like an acrostic or Alexandrian stanza;—read it forward, backward, or across, it still spells the same thing. In this pleasing, contrite wood-life which God allows me, let me record day by day my honest thought without prospect or retrospect, and, I cannot doubt, it will be found symmetrical, though I mean it not, and see it not. My book should smell of pines and resound with the hum of insects. The swallow over my window should interweave that thread or straw he carries in his bill into my web also. We pass for what we are. Character teaches above our wills. Men imagine that they communicate their virtue or vice only by overt actions, and do not see that virtue or vice emit a breath every moment.

There will be an agreement in whatever variety of actions, so they be each honest and natural in their hour. For of one will, the actions will be harmonious, however unlike they seem. These varieties are lost sight of at a little distance, at a little height of thought. One tendency unites them all. The voyage of the best ship is a zigzag line of a hundred tacks. See the line from a sufficient distance, and it straightens itself to the average tendency. Your genuine action will explain itself, and will explain your other genuine actions. Your conformity explains nothing. Act singly, and what you have already done singly will justify you now. Greatness appeals to the future. If I can be firm enough to-day to do right, and scorn eyes, I must have done so much right before as to defend me now. Be it how it will, do right now. Always scorn appearances, and you always may. The force of character is cumulative. All the foregone days of virtue work their health into this. What makes the majesty of the heroes of the senate and the field, which so fills the imagination? The consciousness of a train of great days and victories behind. They shed an united light on the advancing actor. He is attended as by a visible escort of angels. That is it which throws thunder into Chatham's voice, and dignity into Washington's port, and America into Adams's eye. Honor is venerable to us because it is no ephemeris. It is always ancient virtue. We worship it to-day because it is not of to-day. We love it and pay it homage, because it is not a trap for our love and homage, but is self-dependent, self-derived, and therefore of an old immaculate pedigree, even if shown in a young person.

I hope in these days we have heard the last of conformity and consistency. Let the words be gazetted and ridiculous henceforward. Instead of the gong for dinner, let us hear a whistle from the Spartan fife. Let us never bow and apologize more. A great man is coming to eat at my house. I do not wish to please him; I wish that he should wish to please me. I will stand here for humanity, and though I would make it kind, I would make it true. Let us affront and reprimand the smooth mediocrity and squalid contentment of the times, and hurl in the face of custom, and trade, and office, the fact which is the upshot of all history, that there is a great responsible Thinker and Actor working wherever a man works; that a true man belongs to no other time or place, but is the centre of things. Where he is, there is nature. He measures you, and all men, and all events. Ordinarily, every body in society reminds us of somewhat else, or of some other person. Character, reality, reminds you of nothing else; it takes place of the whole creation. The man must be so much, that he must make all circumstances indifferent. Every true man is a cause, a country, and an age; requires infinite spaces and numbers and time fully to accomplish his design;—and posterity seem to follow his steps as a train of clients. A man Caesar is born, and for ages after we have a Roman Empire. Christ is born, and millions of minds so grow and cleave to his genius, that he is confounded with virtue and the possible of man. An institution is the lengthened shadow of one man; as, Monachism, of the Hermit Antony; the Reformation, of Luther; Quakerism, of Fox; Methodism, of Wesley; Abolition, of Clarkson. Scipio, Milton called "the height of Rome"; and all history resolves itself very easily into the biography of a few stout and earnest persons.

Let a man then know his worth, and keep things under his feet. Let him not peep or steal, or skulk up and down with the air of a charity-boy, a bastard, or an interloper, in the world which exists for him. But the man in the street, finding no worth in himself which corresponds to the force which built a tower or sculptured a marble god, feels poor when he looks on these. To him a palace, a statue, or a costly book have an alien and forbidding air, much like a gay equipage, and seem to say like that, 'Who are you, Sir?' Yet they all are his, suitors for his notice, petitioners to his faculties that they will come out and take possession. The picture waits for my verdict: it is not to command me, but I am to settle its claims to praise. That popular fable of the sot who was picked up dead drunk in the street, carried to the duke's house, washed and dressed and laid in the duke's bed, and, on his waking, treated with all obsequious ceremony like the duke, and assured that he had been insane, owes its popularity to the fact, that it symbolizes so well the state of man, who is in the world a sort of sot, but now and then wakes up, exercises his reason, and finds himself a true prince.

Our reading is mendicant and sycophantic. In history, our imagination plays us false. Kingdom and lordship, power and estate, are a gaudier vocabulary than private John and Edward in a small house and common day's work; but the things of life are the same to both; the sum total of both is the same. Why all this deference to Alfred, and Scanderbeg, and Gustavus? Suppose they were virtuous; did they wear out virtue? As great a stake depends on your private act to-day, as followed their public and renowned steps. When private men shall act with original views, the lustre will be transferred from the actions of kings to those of gentlemen.

The world has been instructed by its kings, who have so magnetized the eyes of nations. It has been taught by this colossal symbol the mutual reverence that is due from man to man. The joyful loyalty with which men have everywhere suffered the king, the noble, or the great proprietor to walk among them by a law of his own, make his own scale of men and things, and reverse theirs, pay for benefits not with money but with honor, and represent the law in his person, was the hieroglyphic by which they obscurely signified their consciousness of their own right and comeliness, the right of every man.

The magnetism which all original action exerts is explained when we inquire the reason of self-trust. Who is the Trustee? What is the aboriginal Self, on which a universal reliance may be grounded? What is the nature and power of that science-baffling star, without parallax, without calculable elements, which shoots a ray of beauty even into trivial and impure actions, if the least mark of independence appear? The inquiry leads us to that source, at once the essence of genius, of virtue, and of life, which we call Spontaneity or Instinct. We denote this primary wisdom as Intuition, whilst all later teachings are tuitions. In that deep force, the last fact behind which analysis cannot go, all things find their common origin. For, the sense of being which in calm hours rises, we know not how, in the soul, is not diverse from things, from space, from light, from time, from man, but one with them, and proceeds obviously from the same source whence their life and being also proceed. We first share the life by which things exist, and afterwards see them as appearances in nature, and forget that we have shared their cause. Here is the fountain of action and of thought. Here are the lungs of that inspiration which giveth man wisdom, and which cannot be denied without impiety and atheism. We lie in the lap of immense intelligence, which makes us receivers of its truth and organs of its activity. When we discern justice, when we discern truth, we do nothing of ourselves, but allow a passage to its beams. If we ask whence this comes, if we seek to pry into the soul that causes, all philosophy is at fault. Its presence or its absence is all we can affirm. Every man discriminates between the voluntary acts of his mind, and his involuntary perceptions, and knows that to his involuntary perceptions a perfect faith is due. He may err in the expression of them, but he knows that these things are so, like day and night, not to be disputed. My wilful actions and acquisitions are but roving;—the idlest reverie, the faintest native emotion, command my curiosity and respect. Thoughtless people contradict as readily the statement of perceptions as of opinions, or rather much more readily; for, they do not distinguish between perception and notion. They fancy that I choose to see this or that thing. But perception is not whimsical, but fatal. If I see a trait, my children will see it after me, and in course of time, all mankind,—although it may chance that no one has seen it before me. For my perception of it is as much a fact as the sun.

The relations of the soul to the divine spirit are so pure, that it is profane to seek to interpose helps. It must be that when God speaketh he should communicate, not one thing, but all things; should fill the world with his voice; should scatter forth light, nature, time, souls, from the centre of the present thought; and new date and new create the whole. Whenever a mind is simple, and receives a divine wisdom, old things pass away,—means, teachers, texts, temples fall; it lives now, and absorbs past and future into the present hour. All things are made sacred by relation to it,—one as much as another. All things are dissolved to their centre by their cause, and, in the universal miracle, petty and particular miracles disappear. If, therefore, a man claims to know and speak of God, and carries you backward to the phraseology of some old mouldered nation in another country, in another world, believe him not. Is the acorn better than the oak which is its fulness and completion? Is the parent better than the child into whom he has cast his ripened being? Whence, then, this worship of the past? The centuries are conspirators against the sanity and authority of the soul. Time and space are but physiological colors which the eye makes, but the soul is light; where it is, is day; where it was, is night; and history is an impertinence and an injury, if it be any thing more than a cheerful apologue or parable of my being and becoming.

Man is timid and apologetic; he is no longer upright; he dares not say 'I think,' 'I am,' but quotes some saint or sage. He is ashamed before the blade of grass or the blowing rose. These roses under my window make no reference to former roses or to better ones; they are for what they are; they exist with God to-day. There is no time to them. There is simply the rose; it is perfect in every moment of its existence. Before a leaf-bud has burst, its whole life acts; in the full-blown flower there is no more; in the leafless root there is no less. Its nature is satisfied, and it satisfies nature, in all moments alike. But man postpones or remembers; he does not live in the present, but with reverted eye laments the past, or, heedless of the riches that surround him, stands on tiptoe to foresee the future. He cannot be happy and strong until he too lives with nature in the present, above time.

This should be plain enough. Yet see what strong intellects dare not yet hear God himself, unless he speak the phraseology of I know not what David, or Jeremiah, or Paul. We shall not always set so great a price on a few texts, on a few lives. We are like children who repeat by rote the sentences of grandames and tutors, and, as they grow older, of the men of talents and character they chance to see,—painfully recollecting the exact words they spoke; afterwards, when they come into the point of view which those had who uttered these sayings, they understand them, and are willing to let the words go; for, at any time, they can use words as good when occasion comes. If we live truly, we shall see truly. It is as easy for the strong man to be strong, as it is for the weak to be weak. When we have new perception, we shall gladly disburden the memory of its hoarded treasures as old rubbish. When a man lives with God, his voice shall be as sweet as the murmur of the brook and the rustle of the corn.

And now at last the highest truth on this subject remains unsaid; probably cannot be said; for all that we say is the far-off remembering of the intuition. That thought, by what I can now nearest approach to say it, is this. When good is near you, when you have life in yourself, it is not by any known or accustomed way; you shall not discern the foot-prints of any other; you shall not see the face of man; you shall not hear any name;—the way, the thought, the good, shall be wholly strange and new. It shall exclude example and experience. You take the way from man, not to man. All persons that ever existed are its forgotten ministers. Fear and hope are alike beneath it. There is somewhat low even in hope. In the hour of vision, there is nothing that can be called gratitude, nor properly joy. The soul raised over passion beholds identity and eternal causation, perceives the self-existence of Truth and Right, and calms itself with knowing that all things go well. Vast spaces of nature, the Atlantic Ocean, the South Sea,—long intervals of time, years, centuries,—are of no account. This which I think and feel underlay every former state of life and circumstances, as it does underlie my present, and what is called life, and what is called death.

Life only avails, not the having lived. Power ceases in the instant of repose; it resides in the moment of transition from a past to a new state, in the shooting of the gulf, in the darting to an aim. This one fact the world hates, that the soul becomes; for that for ever degrades the past, turns all riches to poverty, all reputation to a shame, confounds the saint with the rogue, shoves Jesus and Judas equally aside. Why, then, do we prate of self-reliance? Inasmuch as the soul is present, there will be power not confident but agent. To talk of reliance is a poor external way of speaking. Speak rather of that which relies, because it works and is. Who has more obedience than I masters me, though he should not raise his finger. Round him I must revolve by the gravitation of spirits. We fancy it rhetoric, when we speak of eminent virtue. We do not yet see that virtue is Height, and that a man or a company of men, plastic and permeable to principles, by the law of nature must overpower and ride all cities, nations, kings, rich men, poets, who are not.

This is the ultimate fact which we so quickly reach on this, as on every topic, the resolution of all into the ever-blessed ONE. Self-existence is the attribute of the Supreme Cause, and it constitutes the measure of good by the degree in which it enters into all lower forms. All things real are so by so much virtue as they contain. Commerce, husbandry, hunting, whaling, war, eloquence, personal weight, are somewhat, and engage my respect as examples of its presence and impure action. I see the same law working in nature for conservation and growth. Power is in nature the essential measure of right. Nature suffers nothing to remain in her kingdoms which cannot help itself. The genesis and maturation of a planet, its poise and orbit, the bended tree recovering itself from the strong wind, the vital resources of every animal and vegetable, are demonstrations of the self-sufficing, and therefore self-relying soul.

Thus all concentrates: let us not rove; let us sit at home with the cause. Let us stun and astonish the intruding rabble of men and books and institutions, by a simple declaration of the divine fact. Bid the invaders take the shoes from off their feet, for God is here within. Let our simplicity judge them, and our docility to our own law demonstrate the poverty of nature and fortune beside our native riches.

But now we are a mob. Man does not stand in awe of man, nor is his genius admonished to stay at home, to put itself in communication with the internal ocean, but it goes abroad to beg a cup of water of the urns of other men. We must go alone. I like the silent church before the service begins, better than any preaching. How far off, how cool, how chaste the persons look, begirt each one with a precinct or sanctuary! So let us always sit. Why should we assume the faults of our friend, or wife, or father, or child, because they sit around our hearth, or are said to have the same blood? All men have my blood, and I have all men's. Not for that will I adopt their petulance or folly, even to the extent of being ashamed of it. But your isolation must not be mechanical, but spiritual, that is, must be elevation. At times the whole world seems to be in conspiracy to importune you with emphatic trifles. Friend, client, child, sickness, fear, want, charity, all knock at once at thy closet door, and say,—'Come out unto us.' But keep thy state; come not into their confusion. The power men possess to annoy me, I give them by a weak curiosity. No man can come near me but through my act. "What we love that we have, but by desire we bereave ourselves of the love."

If we cannot at once rise to the sanctities of obedience and faith, let us at least resist our temptations; let us enter into the state of war, and wake Thor and Woden, courage and constancy, in our Saxon breasts. This is to be done in our smooth times by speaking the truth. Check this lying hospitality and lying affection. Live no longer to the expectation of these deceived and deceiving people with whom we converse. Say to them, O father, O mother, O wife, O brother, O friend, I have lived with you after appearances hitherto. Henceforward I am the truth's. Be it known unto you that henceforward I obey no law less than the eternal law. I will have no covenants but proximities. I shall endeavour to nourish my parents, to support my family, to be the chaste husband of one wife,—but these relations I must fill after a new and unprecedented way. I appeal from your customs. I must be myself. I cannot break myself any longer for you, or you. If you can love me for what I am, we shall be the happier. If you cannot, I will still seek to deserve that you should. I will not hide my tastes or aversions. I will so trust that what is deep is holy, that I will do strongly before the sun and moon whatever inly rejoices me, and the heart appoints. If you are noble, I will love you; if you are not, I will not hurt you and myself by hypocritical attentions. If you are true, but not in the same truth with me, cleave to your companions; I will seek my own. I do this not selfishly, but humbly and truly. It is alike your interest, and mine, and all men's, however long we have dwelt in lies, to live in truth. Does this sound harsh today? You will soon love what is dictated by your nature as well as mine, and, if we follow the truth, it will bring us out safe at last.—But so you may give these friends pain. Yes, but I cannot sell my liberty and my power, to save their sensibility. Besides, all persons have their moments of reason, when they look out into the region of absolute truth; then will they justify me, and do the same thing.

The populace think that your rejection of popular standards is a rejection of all standard, and mere antinomianism; and the bold sensualist will use the name of philosophy to gild his crimes. But the law of consciousness abides. There are two confessionals, in one or the other of which we must be shriven. You may fulfil your round of duties by clearing yourself in the *direct*, or in the *reflex* way. Consider whether you have satisfied your relations to father, mother, cousin, neighbour, town, cat, and dog; whether any of these can upbraid you. But I may also neglect this reflex standard, and absolve me to myself. I have my own stern claims and perfect circle. It denies the name of duty to many offices that are called duties. But if I can discharge its debts, it enables me to dispense with the popular code. If any one imagines that this law is lax, let him keep its commandment one day.

And truly it demands something godlike in him who has cast off the common motives of humanity, and has ventured to trust himself for a taskmaster. High be his heart, faithful his will, clear his sight, that he may in good earnest be doctrine, society, law, to himself, that a simple purpose may be to him as strong as iron necessity is to others!

If any man consider the present aspects of what is called by distinction *society*, he will see the need of these ethics. The sinew and heart of man seem to be drawn out, and we are become timorous, desponding whimperers. We are afraid of truth, afraid of fortune, afraid of death, and afraid of each other. Our age yields no great and perfect persons. We want men and women who shall renovate life and our social state, but we see that most natures are insolvent, cannot satisfy their own wants, have an ambition out of all proportion to their practical force, and do lean and beg day and night continually. Our housekeeping is mendicant, our arts, our occupations, our marriages, our religion, we have not chosen, but society has chosen for us. We are parlour soldiers. We shun the rugged battle of fate, where strength is born.

If our young men miscarry in their first enterprises, they lose all heart. If the young merchant fails, men say he is *ruined*. If the finest genius studies at one of our colleges, and is not installed in an office within one year afterwards in the cities or suburbs of Boston or New York, it seems to his friends and to himself that he is right in being disheartened, and in complaining the rest of his life. A sturdy lad from New Hampshire or Vermont, who in turn tries all the professions, who *teams it, farms it, peddles,* keeps a school, preaches, edits a newspaper, goes to Congress, buys a township, and so forth, in successive years, and always, like a cat, falls on his feet, is worth a hundred of these city dolls. He walks abreast with his days, and feels no shame in not 'studying a profession,' for he does not postpone his life, but lives already. He has not one chance, but a hundred chances. Let a Stoic open the resources of man, and tell men they are not leaning willows, but can and must detach themselves; that with the exercise of self-trust, new powers shall appear; that a man is the word made flesh, born to shed healing to the nations, that he should be ashamed of our compassion, and that the moment he acts from himself, tossing the laws, the books, idolatries, and customs out of the window, we pity him no more, but thank and revere him,—and that teacher shall restore the life of man to splendor, and make his name dear to all history.

It is easy to see that a greater self-reliance must work a revolution in all the offices and relations of men; in their religion; in their education; in their pursuits; their modes of living; their association; in their property; in their speculative views.

    1. In what prayers do men allow themselves! That which they call a holy office is not so much as brave and manly. Prayer looks abroad and asks for some foreign addition to come through some foreign virtue, and loses itself in endless mazes of natural and supernatural, and mediatorial and miraculous. Prayer that craves a particular commodity,—any thing less than all good,—is vicious. Prayer is the contemplation of the facts of life from the highest point of view. It is the soliloquy of a beholding and jubilant soul. It is the spirit of God pronouncing his works good. But prayer as a means to effect a private end is meanness and theft. It supposes dualism and not unity in nature and consciousness. As soon as the man is at one with God, he will not beg. He will then see prayer in all action. The prayer of the farmer kneeling in his field to weed it, the prayer of the rower kneeling with the stroke of his oar, are true prayers heard throughout nature, though for cheap ends. Caratach, in Fletcher's Bonduca, when admonished to inquire the mind of the god Audate, replies,—

> "His hidden meaning lies in our
>   endeavours;
> Our valors are our best gods."

Another sort of false prayers are our regrets. Discontent is the want of self-reliance: it is infirmity of will. Regret calamities, if you can thereby help the sufferer; if not, attend your own work, and already the evil begins to be repaired. Our sympathy is just as base. We come to them who weep foolishly, and sit down and cry for company, instead of imparting to them truth and health in rough electric shocks, putting them once more in communication with their own reason. The secret of fortune is joy in our hands. Welcome evermore to gods and men is the self-helping man. For him all doors are flung wide: him all tongues greet, all honors crown, all eyes follow with desire. Our love goes out to him and embraces him, because he did not need it. We solicitously and apologetically caress and celebrate him, because he held on his way and scorned our disapprobation. The gods love him because men hated him. "To the persevering mortal," said Zoroaster, "the blessed Immortals are swift."

As men's prayers are a disease of the will, so are their creeds a disease of the intellect. They say with those foolish Israelites, 'Let not God speak to us, lest we die. Speak thou, speak any man with us, and we will obey.' Everywhere I am hindered of meeting God in my brother, because he has shut his own temple doors, and recites fables merely of his brother's, or his brother's brother's God. Every new mind is a new classification. If it prove a mind of uncommon activity and power, a Locke, a Lavoisier, a Hutton, a Bentham, a Fourier, it imposes its classification on other men, and lo! a new system. In proportion to the depth of the thought, and so to the number of the objects it touches and brings within reach of the pupil, is his complacency. But chiefly is this apparent in creeds and churches, which are also classifications of some powerful mind acting on the elemental thought of duty, and man's relation to the Highest. Such is Calvinism, Quakerism, Swedenborgism. The pupil takes the same delight in subordinating every thing to the new terminology, as a girl who has just learned botany in seeing a new earth and new seasons thereby. It will happen for a time, that the pupil will find his intellectual power has grown by the study of his master's mind. But in all unbalanced minds, the classification is idolized, passes for the end, and not for a speedily exhaustible means, so that the walls of the system blend to their eye in the remote horizon with the walls of the universe; the luminaries of heaven seem to them hung on the arch their master built. They cannot imagine how you aliens have any right to see,—how you can see; 'It must be somehow that you stole the light from us.' They do not yet perceive, that light, unsystematic, indomitable, will break into any cabin, even into theirs. Let them chirp awhile and call it their own. If they are honest and do well, presently their neat new pinfold will be too strait and low, will crack, will lean, will rot and vanish, and the immortal light, all young and joyful, million-orbed, million-colored, will beam over the universe as on the first morning.

2. It is for want of self-culture that the superstition of Travelling, whose idols are Italy, England, Egypt, retains its fascination for all educated Americans. They who made England, Italy, or Greece venerable in the imagination did so by sticking fast where they were, like an axis of the earth. In manly hours, we feel that duty is our place. The soul is no traveller; the wise man stays at home, and when his necessities, his duties, on any occasion call him from his house, or into foreign lands, he is at home still, and shall make men sensible by the expression of his countenance, that he goes the missionary of wisdom and virtue, and visits cities and men like a sovereign, and not like an interloper or a valet.

I have no churlish objection to the circumnavigation of the globe, for the purposes of art, of study, and benevolence, so that the man is first domesticated, or does not go abroad with the hope of finding somewhat greater than he knows. He who travels to be amused, or to get somewhat which he does not carry, travels away from himself, and grows old even in youth among old things. In Thebes, in Palmyra, his will and mind have become old and dilapidated as they. He carries ruins to ruins.

Travelling is a fool's paradise. Our first journeys discover to us the indifference of places. At home I dream that at Naples, at Rome, I can be intoxicated with beauty, and lose my sadness. I pack my trunk, embrace my friends, embark on the sea, and at last wake up in Naples, and there beside me is the stern fact, the sad self, unrelenting, identical, that I fled from. I seek the Vatican, and the palaces. I affect to be intoxicated with sights and suggestions, but I am not intoxicated. My giant goes with me wherever I go.

3. But the rage of travelling is a symptom of a deeper unsoundness affecting the whole intellectual action. The intellect is vagabond, and our system of education fosters restlessness. Our minds travel when our bodies are forced to stay at home. We imitate; and what is imitation but the travelling of the mind? Our houses are built with foreign taste; our shelves are garnished with foreign ornaments; our opinions, our tastes, our faculties, lean, and follow the Past and the Distant. The soul created the arts wherever they have flourished. It was in his own mind that the artist sought his model. It was an application of his own thought to the thing to

be done and the conditions to be observed. And why need we copy the Doric or the Gothic model? Beauty, convenience, grandeur of thought, and quaint expression are as near to us as to any, and if the American artist will study with hope and love the precise thing to be done by him, considering the climate, the soil, the length of the day, the wants of the people, the habit and form of the government, he will create a house in which all these will find themselves fitted, and taste and sentiment will be satisfied also.

Insist on yourself; never imitate. Your own gift you can present every moment with the cumulative force of a whole life's cultivation; but of the adopted talent of another, you have only an extemporaneous, half possession. That which each can do best, none but his Maker can teach him. No man yet knows what it is, nor can, till that person has exhibited it. Where is the master who could have taught Shakspeare? Where is the master who could have instructed Franklin, or Washington, or Bacon, or Newton? Every great man is a unique. The Scipionism of Scipio is precisely that part he could not borrow. Shakspeare will never be made by the study of Shakspeare. Do that which is assigned you, and you cannot hope too much or dare too much. There is at this moment for you an utterance brave and grand as that of the colossal chisel of Phidias, or trowel of the Egyptians, or the pen of Moses, or Dante, but different from all these. Not possibly will the soul all rich, all eloquent, with thousand-cloven tongue, deign to repeat itself; but if you can hear what these patriarchs say, surely you can reply to them in the same pitch of voice; for the ear and the tongue are two organs of one nature. Abide in the simple and noble regions of thy life, obey thy heart, and thou shalt reproduce the Foreworld again.

    4. As our Religion, our Education, our Art look abroad, so does our spirit of society. All men plume themselves on the improvement of society, and no man improves.

Society never advances. It recedes as fast on one side as it gains on the other. It undergoes continual changes; it is barbarous, it is civilized, it is christianized, it is rich, it is scientific; but this change is not amelioration. For every thing that is given, something is taken. Society acquires new arts, and loses old instincts. What a contrast between the well-clad, reading, writing, thinking American, with a watch, a pencil, and a bill of exchange in his pocket, and the naked New Zealander, whose property is a club, a spear, a mat, and an undivided twentieth of a shed to sleep under! But compare the health of the two men, and you shall see that the white man has lost his aboriginal strength. If the traveller tell us truly, strike the savage with a broad axe, and in a day or two the flesh shall unite and heal as if you struck the blow into soft pitch, and the same blow shall send the white to his grave.

The civilized man has built a coach, but has lost the use of his feet. He is supported on crutches, but lacks so much support of muscle. He has a fine Geneva watch, but he fails of the skill to tell the hour by the sun. A Greenwich nautical almanac he has, and so being sure of the information when he wants it, the man in the street does not know a star in the sky. The solstice he does not observe; the equinox he knows as little; and the whole bright calendar of the year is without a dial in his mind. His note-books impair his memory; his libraries overload his wit; the insurance-office increases the number of accidents; and it may be a question whether machinery does not encumber; whether we have not lost by refinement some energy, by a Christianity entrenched in establishments and forms, some vigor of wild virtue. For every Stoic was a Stoic; but in Christendom where is the Christian?

There is no more deviation in the moral standard than in the standard of height or bulk. No greater men are now than ever were. A singular equality may be observed between the great men of the first and of the last ages; nor can all the science, art, religion, and philosophy of the nineteenth century avail to educate greater men than Plutarch's heroes, three or four and twenty centuries ago. Not in time is the race progressive. Phocion, Socrates, Anaxagoras, Diogenes, are great men, but they leave no class. He who is really of their class will not be called by their name, but will be his own man, and, in his turn, the founder of a sect. The arts and inventions of each period are only its costume, and do not invigorate men. The harm of the improved machinery may compensate its good. Hudson and Behring accomplished so much in their fishing-boats, as to astonish Parry and Franklin, whose equipment exhausted the resources of science and art. Galileo, with an opera-glass, discovered a more splendid series of celestial phenomena than any one since. Columbus found the New World in an undecked boat. It is curious to see the periodical disuse and perishing of means and machinery, which were introduced with loud laudation a few years or centuries before. The great genius returns to essential man. We reckoned the improvements of the art of war among the triumphs of science, and yet Napoleon conquered Europe by the bivouac, which consisted of falling back on naked valor, and disencumbering it of all aids. The Emperor held it impossible to make a perfect army, says Las Casas, "without abolishing our arms, magazines, commissaries, and carriages, until, in imitation of the Roman custom, the soldier should receive his supply of corn, grind it in his hand-mill, and bake his bread himself."

Society is a wave. The wave moves onward, but the water of which it is composed does not. The same particle does not rise from the valley to the ridge. Its unity is only phenomenal. The persons who make up a nation to-day, next year die, and their experience with them.

And so the reliance on Property, including the reliance on governments which protect it, is the want of self-reliance. Men have looked away from themselves and at things so long, that they have come to esteem the religious, learned, and civil institutions as guards of property, and they deprecate assaults on these, because they feel them to be assaults on property. They measure their esteem of each other by what each has, and not by what each is. But a cultivated man becomes ashamed of his property, out of new respect for his nature. Especially he hates what he has, if he see that it is accidental,—came to him by inheritance, or gift, or crime; then he feels that it is not having; it does not belong to him, has no root in him, and merely lies there, because no revolution or no robber takes it away. But that which a man is does always by necessity acquire, and what the man acquires is living property, which does not wait the beck of rulers, or mobs, or revolutions, or fire, or storm, or bankruptcies, but perpetually renews itself wherever the man breathes. "Thy lot or portion of life," said the Caliph Ali, "is seeking after thee; therefore be at rest from seeking after it." Our dependence on these foreign goods leads us to our slavish respect for numbers. The political parties meet in numerous conventions; the greater the concourse, and with each new uproar of announcement, The delegation from Essex! The Democrats from New Hampshire! The Whigs of Maine! the young patriot feels himself stronger than before by a new thousand of eyes and arms. In like manner the reformers summon conventions, and vote and resolve in multitude. Not so, O friends! will the God deign to enter and inhabit you, but by a method precisely the reverse. It is only as a man puts off all foreign support, and stands alone, that I see him to be strong and to prevail. He is weaker by every recruit to his banner. Is not a man better than a town? Ask nothing of men, and in the endless mutation, thou only firm column must presently appear the upholder of all that surrounds thee. He who knows that power is inborn, that he is weak because he has looked for good out of him and elsewhere, and so perceiving, throws himself unhesitatingly on his thought, instantly rights himself, stands in the erect position, commands his limbs, works miracles; just as a man who stands on his feet is stronger than a man who stands on his head.

So use all that is called Fortune. Most men gamble with her, and gain all, and lose all, as her wheel rolls. But do thou leave as unlawful these winnings, and deal with Cause and Effect, the chancellors of God. In the Will work and acquire, and thou hast chained the wheel of Chance, and shalt sit hereafter out of fear from her rotations. A political victory, a rise of rents, the recovery of your sick, or the return of your absent friend, or some other favorable event, raises your spirits, and you think good days are preparing for you. Do not believe it. Nothing can bring you peace but yourself. Nothing can bring you peace but the triumph of principles.

CRITICAL EYE

▶ **For Discussion**

a. Emerson asserts that every individual has an inner genius and that it is our responsibility to honor it. Do you agree with this sentiment?

b. According to Emerson, we have all become conformists because we refuse to speak "the rude truth." In your opinion, is his assessment accurate?

▶ **Re-approaching the Reading**

Rap music has been called a kind of poetry that speaks to the youth of today. Are rap artists following their "inner genius" or are they conformists?

▶ **Writing Assignment**

Why is conformity dangerous? How does this conformity speak to Emerson's notions of "self-trust" and "foolish consistency"?

KHALED HOSSEINI

From the Novel
THE KITE RUNNER

Five

Something roared like thunder. The earth shook a little and we heard the *rat-a-tat-tat* of gunfire. "Father!" Hassan cried. We sprung to our feet and raced out of the living room. We found Ali hobbling frantically across the foyer.

"Father! What's that sound?" Hassan yelped, his hands out-stretched toward Ali. Ali wrapped his arms around us. A white light flashed, lit the sky in silver. It flashed again and was followed by a rapid staccato of gunfire.

"They're hunting ducks," Ali said in a hoarse voice. "They hunt ducks at night, you know. Don't be afraid."

A siren went off in the distance. Somewhere glass shattered and someone shouted. I heard people on the street, jolted from sleep and probably still in their pajamas, with ruffled hair and puffy eyes. Hassan was crying. Ali pulled him close, clutched him with tenderness. Later, I would tell myself I hadn't felt envious of Hassan. Not at all.

We stayed huddled that way until the early hours of the morning. The shootings and explosions had lasted less than an hour, but they had frightened us badly, because none of us had ever heard gunshots in the streets. They were foreign sounds to us then. The generation of Afghan children whose ears would know nothing but the sounds of bombs and gunfire was not yet born. Huddled together in the dining room and waiting for the sun to rise, none of us had any notion that a way of life had ended. *Our* way of life. If not quite yet, then at least it was the beginning of the end. The end, the *official* end, would come first in April 1978 with the communist coup d'état, and then in December 1979, when Russian tanks would roll into the very same streets where Hassan and I played, bringing the death of the Afghanistan I knew and marking the start of a still ongoing era of bloodletting.

Just before sunrise, Baba's car peeled into the driveway. His door slammed shut and his running footsteps pounded the stairs. Then he appeared in the doorway and I saw something on his face. Something I didn't recognize right away because I'd never seen it before: fear. "Amir! Hassan!" he exclaimed as he ran to us, opening his arms wide. "They blocked all the roads and the telephone didn't work. I was so worried!"

We let him wrap us in his arms and, for a brief insane moment, I was glad about whatever had happened that night.

They weren't shooting ducks after all. As it turned out, they hadn't shot much of anything that night of July 17, 1973. Kabul awoke the next morning to find that the monarchy was a thing of the past. The king, Zahir Shah, was away in Italy. In his absence, his cousin Daoud

"Fremont, California. 1980s," from *The Kite Runner* by Khaled Hosseini, copyright © 2003 by Khaled Hosseini. Used by permission of Riverhead Books, an imprint of Penguin Group (USA) Inc.

Khan had ended the king's forty-year reign with a bloodless coup.

I remember Hassan and I crouching that next morning outside my father's study, as Baba and Rahim Khan sipped black tea and listened to breaking news of the coup on Radio Kabul.

"Amir agha?" Hassan whispered.

"What?"

"What's a 'republic'?"

I shrugged. "I don't know." On Baba's radio, they were saying that word, "republic," over and over again.

"Amir agha?"

"What?"

"Does 'republic' mean Father and I will have to move away?"

"I don't think so," I whispered back.

Hassan considered this. "Amir agha?"

"What?"

"I don't want them to send me and Father away."

I smiled. "*Bas*, you donkey. No one's sending you away."

"Amir agha?"

"What?"

"Do you want to go climb our tree?"

My smile broadened. That was another thing about Hassan. He always knew when to say the right thing—the news on the radio was getting pretty boring. Hassan went to his shack to get ready and I ran upstairs to grab a book. Then I went to the kitchen, stuffed my pockets with handfuls of pine nuts, and ran outside to find Hassan waiting for me. We burst through the front gates and headed for the hill.

We crossed the residential street and were trekking through a barren patch of rough land that led to the hill when, suddenly, a rock struck Hassan in the back. We whirled around and my heart dropped. Assef and two of his friends, Wali and Kamal, were approaching us.

Assef was the son of one of my father's friends, Mahmood, an airline pilot. His family lived a few streets south of our home, in a posh, high-walled compound with palm trees. If you were a kid living in the Wazir Akbar Khan section of Kabul, you knew about Assef and his famous stainless-steel brass knuckles, hopefully not through personal experience. Born to a German mother and Afghan father, the blond, blue-eyed Assef towered over the other kids. His well-earned reputation for savagery preceded him on the streets. Flanked by his obeying friends, he walked the neighborhood like a Khan strolling through his land with his eager-to-please entourage. His word was law, and if you needed a little legal education, then those brass knuckles were just the right teaching tool. I saw him use those knuckles once on a kid from the Karteh-Char district. I will never forget how Assef's blue eyes glinted with a light not entirely sane and how he grinned, how he *grinned*, as he pummeled that poor kid unconscious. Some of the boys in Wazir Akbar Khan had nicknamed him Assef *Goshkhor*, or Assef "the Ear Eater." Of course, none of them dared utter it to his face unless they wished to suffer the same fate as the poor kid who had unwittingly inspired that nickname when he had fought Assef over a kite and ended up fishing his right ear from a muddy gutter. Years later, I learned an English word for the creature that Assef was, a word for which a good Farsi equivalent does not exist: "sociopath."

Of all the neighborhood boys who tortured Ali, Assef was by far the most relentless. He was, in fact, the originator of the Babalu jeer, *Hey, Babalu, who did you eat today? Huh? Come on, Babalu, give us a smile!* And on days when he felt particularly inspired, he spiced up his badgering a little, *Hey, you flat-nosed Babalu, who did you eat today? Tell us, you slant-eyed donkey!*

Social Responsibility

Now he was walking toward us, hands on his hips, his sneakers kicking up little puffs of dust.

"Good morning, *kunis!*" Assef exclaimed, waving. "Fag," that was another of his favorite insults. Hassan retreated behind me as the three older boys closed in. They stood before us, three tall boys dressed in jeans and T-shirts. Towering over us all, Assef crossed his thick arms on his chest, a savage sort of grin on his lips. Not for the first time, it occurred to me that Assef might not be entirely sane. It also occurred to me how lucky I was to have Baba as my father, the sole reason, I believe, Assef had mostly refrained from harassing me too much.

He tipped his chin to Hassan. "Hey, Flat-Nose," he said. "How is Babalu?"

Hassan said nothing and crept another step behind me.

"Have you heard the news, boys?" Assef said, his grin never faltering. "The king is gone. Good riddance. Long live the president! My father knows Daoud Khan, did you know that, Amir?"

"So does my father," I said. In reality, I had no idea if that was true or not.

"'So does my father,'" Assef mimicked me in a whining voice. Kamal and Wali cackled in unison. I wished Baba were here.

"Well, Daoud Khan dined at our house last year," Assef went on. "How do you like that, Amir?"

I wondered if anyone would hear us scream in this remote patch of land. Baba's house was a good kilometer away, I wished we'd stayed at the house.

"Do you know what I will tell Daoud Khan the next time he comes to our house for dinner?" Assef said. "I'm going to have a little chat with him, man to man, *mard* to *mard*. Tell him what I told my mother. About Hitler. Now, there was a leader. A great leader. A man with vision. I'll tell Daoud Khan to remember that if they had let Hitler finish what he had started, the world would be a better place now."

"Baba says Hitler was crazy, that he ordered a lot of innocent people killed," I heard myself say before I could clamp a hand on my mouth.

Assef snickered. "He sounds like my mother, and she's German; she should know better. But then they want you to believe that, don't they? They don't want you to know the truth."

I didn't know who "they" were, or what truth they were hiding, and I didn't want to find out. I wished I hadn't said anything. I wished again I'd look up and see Baba coming up the hill.

"But you have to read books they don't give out in school," Assef said. "I have. And my eyes have been opened. Now I have a vision, and I'm going to share it with our new president. Do you know what it is?"

I shook my head. He'd tell me anyway; Assef always answered his own questions.

His blue eyes flicked to Hassan. "Afghanistan is the land of Pashtuns. It always has been, always will be. We are the true Afghans, the pure Afghans, not this Flat-Nose here. His people pollute our homeland, our *watan*. They dirty our blood." He made a sweeping, grandiose gesture with his hands. "Afghanistan for Pashtuns, I say. That's my vision."

Assef shifted his gaze to me again. He looked like someone coming out of a good dream. "Too late for Hitler," he said. "But not for us."

He reached for something from the back pocket of his jeans. "I'll ask the president to do what the king didn't have the *quwat* to do. To rid Afghanistan of all the dirty, *kasseef* Hazaras."

"Just let us go, Assef", I said, hating the way my voice trembled. "We're not bothering you."

"Oh, you're bothering me," Assef said. And I saw with a sinking heart what he had fished out of his pocket. Of course. His stainless-steel brass knuckles sparkled in the sun. "You're bothering me very much. In fact, you bother me more than this Hazara here. How can you talk to him, play with him, let him touch you?" he said, his voice dripping with disgust. Wali and Kamal nodded and grunted in agreement. Assef narrowed his eyes. Shook his head. When he spoke again, he sounded as baffled as he looked. "How can you call him your 'friend'?"

But he's not my friend! I almost blurted. *He's my servant!* Had I really thought that? Of course I hadn't. I hadn't. I treated Hassan well, just like a friend, better even, more like a brother. But if so, then why, when Baba's friends came to visit with their kids, didn't I ever include Hassan in our games? Why did I play with Hassan only when no one else was around?

Assef slipped on the brass knuckles. Gave me an icy look. "You're part of the problem, Amir. If idiots like you and your father didn't take these people in, we'd be rid of them by now. They'd all just go rot in Hazarajat where they belong. You're a disgrace to Afghanistan."

I looked in his crazy eyes and saw that he meant it. He *really* meant to hurt me. Assef raised his fist and came for me.

There was a flurry of rapid movement behind me. Out of the corner of my eye, I saw Hassan bend down and stand up quickly. Assef's eyes flicked to something behind me and widened with surprise. I saw that same look of astonishment on Kamal and Wali's faces as they too saw what had happened behind me.

I turned and came face to face with Hassan's slingshot. Hassan had pulled the wide elastic band all the way back. In the cup was a rock the size of a walnut. Hassan held the slingshot pointed directly at Assef's face. His hand trembled with the strain of the pulled elastic band and beads of sweat had erupted on his brow.

"Please leave us alone, Agha," Hassan said in a flat tone. He'd referred to Assef as "Agha," and I wondered briefly what it must be like to live with such an ingrained sense of one's place in a hierarchy.

Assef gritted his teeth. "Put it down, you motherless Hazara."

"Please leave us be, Agha," Hassan said.

Assef smiled. "Maybe you didn't notice, but there are three of us and two of you."

Hassan shrugged. To an outsider, he didn't look scared. But Hassan's face was my earliest memory and I knew all of its subtle nuances, knew each and every twitch and flicker that ever rippled across it. And I saw that he was scared. He was scared plenty.

"You are right, Agha. But perhaps you didn't notice that I'm the one holding the slingshot. If you make a move, they'll have to change your nickname from Assef 'the Ear Eater' to 'One-Eyed Assef,' because I have this rock pointed at your left eye." He said this so flatly that even I had to strain to hear the fear that I knew hid under that calm voice.

Assef's mouth twitched. Wali and Kamal watched this exchange with something akin to fascination. Someone had challenged their god. Humiliated him. And, worst of all, that someone was a skinny Hazara. Assef looked from the rock to Hassan. He searched Hassan's face intently. What he found in it must have convinced him of the seriousness of Hassan's intentions, because he lowered his fist.

"You should know something about me, Hazara," Assef said gravely. "I'm a very patient person. This doesn't end today, believe me." He turned to me. "This isn't the end for you either, Amir. Someday, I'll make you face me one on one." Assef retreated a step. His disciples followed.

"Your Hazara made a big mistake today, Amir," he said. They then turned around, walked away. I watched them walk down the hill and disappear behind a wall.

Hassan was trying to tuck the slingshot in his waist with a pair of trembling hands. His mouth curled up into something that was supposed to be a reassuring smile. It took him five tries to tie the string of his trousers. Neither one of us said much of anything as we walked home in trepidation, certain that Assef and his friends would ambush us every time we turned a corner. They didn't and that should have comforted us a little. But it didn't. Not at all.

Six

Winter.

Here is what I do on the first day of snowfall every year: I step out of the house early in the morning, still in my pajamas, hugging my arms against the chill. I find the driveway, my father's car, the walls, the trees, the rooftops, and the hills buried under a foot of snow. I smile. The sky is seamless and blue, the snow so white my eyes burn. I shovel a handful of the fresh snow into my mouth, listen to the muffled stillness broken only by the cawing of crows. I walk down the front steps, barefoot, and call for Hassan to come out and see.

Winter was every kid's favorite season in Kabul, at least those whose fathers could afford to buy a good iron stove. The reason was simple: They shut down school for the icy season. Winter to me was the end of long division and naming the capital of Bulgaria, and the start of three months of playing cards by the stove with Hassan, free Russian movies on Tuesday mornings at Cinema Park, sweet turnip *qurma* over rice for a lunch after a morning of building snowmen.

And kites, of course. Flying kites. And running them.

For a few unfortunate kids, winter did not spell the end of the school year. There were the so-called voluntary winter courses. No kid I knew ever volunteered to go to these classes; parents, of course, did the volunteering for them. Fortunately for me, Baba was not one of them. I remember one kid, Ahmad, who lived across the street from us. His father was some kind of doctor, I think. Ahmad had epilepsy and always wore a wool vest and thick black-rimmed glasses—he was one of Assef's regular victims. Every morning, I watched from my bedroom window as their Hazara servant shoveled snow from the driveway, cleared the way for the black Opel. I made a point of watching Ahmad and his father get into the car, Ahmad in his wool vest and winter coat, his schoolbag filled with books and pencils. I waited until they pulled away, turned the corner, then I slipped back into bed in my flannel pajamas. I pulled the blanket to my chin and watched the snowcapped hills in the north through the window. Watched them until I drifted back to sleep.

I loved wintertime in Kabul. I loved it for the soft pattering of snow against my window at night, for the way fresh snow crunched under my black rubber boots, for the warmth of the cast-iron stove as the wind screeched through the yards, the streets. But mostly because, as the trees froze and ice sheathed the roads, the chill between Baba and me thawed a little. And the reason for that was the kites. Baba and I lived in the same house, but in different spheres of existence. Kites were the one paper-thin slice of intersection between those spheres.

Every winter, districts in Kabul held a kite-fighting tournament. And if you were a boy living in Kabul, the day of the tournament was undeniably the highlight of the cold season. I never slept the night before the tournament. I'd roll from side to side, make shadow animals on the wall, even sit on the balcony in the dark, a blanket wrapped around me. I felt like a soldier trying to sleep in the trenches the night before a major battle. And that wasn't so far off. In Kabul, fighting kites was a little like going to war.

As with any war, you had to ready yourself for battle. For a while, Hassan and I used to build our own kites. We saved our weekly allowances in the fall, dropped the money in a little porcelain horse Baba had brought one time from Herat. When the winds of winter began to blow and snow fell in chunks, we undid the snap under the horse's belly. We went to the bazaar and bought bamboo, glue, string, and paper. We spent hours every day shaving bamboo for the center and cross spars, cutting the thin tissue paper which made for easy dipping and recovery. And then, of course, we had to make our own string, or *tar*. If the kite was the gun, then *tar*, the glass-coated cutting line, was the bullet in the chamber. We'd go out in the yard and feed up to five hundred feet of string through a mixture of ground glass and glue. We'd then hang the line between the trees, leave it to dry. The next day, we'd wind the battle-ready line around a wooden spool. By the time the snow melted and the rains of spring swept in, every boy in Kabul bore telltale horizontal gashes on his fingers from a whole winter of fighting kites. I remember how my classmates and I used to huddle, compare our battle scars on the first day of school. The cuts stung and didn't heal for a couple of weeks, but I didn't mind. They were reminders of a beloved season that had once again passed too quickly. Then the class captain would blow his whistle and we'd march in a single file to our classrooms, longing for winter already, greeted instead by the specter of yet another long school year.

But it quickly became apparent that Hassan and I were better kite fighters than kite makers. Some flaw or other in our design always spelled its doom. So Baba started taking us to Saifo's to buy our kites. Saifo was a nearly blind old man who was a *moochi* by profession—a shoe repairman. But he was also the city's most famous kite maker, working out of a tiny hovel on Jadeh Maywand, the crowded street south of the muddy banks of the Kabul River. I remember you had to crouch to enter the prison cell–sized store, and then had to lift a trapdoor to creep down a set of wooden steps to the dank basement where Saifo stored his coveted kites. Baba would buy us each three identical kites and spools of glass string. If I changed my mind and asked for a bigger and fancier kite, Baba would buy it for me—but then he'd buy it for Hassan too. Sometimes I wished he wouldn't do that. Wished he'd let me be the favorite.

The kite-fighting tournament was an old winter tradition in Afghanistan. It started early in the morning on the day of the contest and didn't end until only the winning kite flew in the sky—I remember one year the tournament outlasted daylight. People gathered on sidewalks and roofs to cheer for their kids. The streets filled with kite fighters, jerking and tugging on their lines, squinting up to the sky, trying to gain position to cut the opponent's line. Every kite fighter had an assistant—in my case, Hassan—who held the spool and fed the line.

One time, a bratty Hindi kid whose family had recently moved into the neighborhood told us that in his hometown, kite fighting had strict rules and regulations. "You have to play in a boxed area and you have to stand at a right angle to the wind," he said proudly. "And you can't use aluminum to make your glass string."

Hassan and I looked at each other. Cracked up. The Hindi kid would soon learn what the British learned earlier in the century, and what the Russians would eventually learn by the late 1980s: the Afghans are an independent people. Afghans cherish custom but abhor rules. And so it was with kite fighting. The rules were simple: No rules. Fly your kite. Cut the opponents. Good luck.

Except that wasn't all. The real fun began when a kite was cut. That was where the kite runners came in, those kids who chased the windblown kite drifting through the neighborhoods until it came spiraling down in a field, dropping in someone's yard, on a tree, or a rooftop. The chase got pretty fierce; hordes of kite runners swarmed the streets, shoved past each other like those people from Spain I'd read about once, the ones who ran from the bulls. One year a neighborhood kid climbed a pine tree for a kite. A branch snapped under his weight and he fell thirty feet. Broke his back and never walked again. But he fell with the kite still in his hands. And when a kite runner had his hands on a kite, no one could take it from him. That wasn't a rule. That was custom.

For kite runners, the most coveted prize was the last fallen kite of a winter tournament. It was a trophy of honor, something to be displayed on a mantle for guests to admire. When the sky cleared of kites and only the final two remained, every kite runner readied himself for the chance to land this prize. He positioned himself at a spot that he thought would give him a head start. Tense muscles readied themselves to uncoil. Necks craned. Eyes crinkled. Fights broke out. And when the last kite was cut, all hell broke loose.

Over the years, I had seen a lot of guys run kites. But Hassan was by far the greatest kite runner I'd ever seen. It was downright eerie the way he always got to the spot the kite would land *before* the kite did, as if he had some sort of inner compass.

I remember one overcast winter day, Hassan and I were running a kite. I was chasing him through neighborhoods, hopping gutters, weaving through narrow streets. I was a year older than him, but Hassan ran faster than I did, and I was falling behind.

"Hassan! Wait!" I yelled, my breathing hot and ragged.

He whirled around, motioned with his hand. "This way!" he called before dashing around another corner. I looked up, saw that the direction we were running was opposite to the one the kite was drifting.

"We're losing it! We're going the wrong way!" I cried out.

"Trust me!" I heard him call up ahead. I reached the corner and saw Hassan bolting along, his head down, not even looking at the sky, sweat soaking through the back of his shirt. I tripped over a rock and fell—I wasn't just slower than Hassan but clumsier too; I'd always envied his natural athleticism. When I staggered to my feet, I caught a glimpse of Hassan disappearing around another street corner. I hobbled after him, spikes of pain battering my scraped knees.

I saw we had ended up on a rutted dirt road near Isteqlal Middle School. There was a field on one side where lettuce grew in the summer, and a row of sour cherry trees on the other. I found Hassan sitting cross-legged at the foot of one of the trees, eating from a fistful of dried mulberries.

"What are we doing here?" I panted, my stomach roiling with nausea.

He smiled. "Sit with me, Amir agha."

I dropped next to him, lay on a thin patch of snow, wheezing. "You're wasting our time. It was going the other way, didn't you see?"

Hassan popped a mulberry in his mouth. "It's coming," he said. I could hardly breathe and he didn't even sound tired.

"How do you know?" I said.

"I know."

"How can you *know*?"

He turned to me. A few sweat beads rolled from his bald scalp. "Would I ever lie to you, Amir agha?"

Suddenly I decided to toy with him a little. "I don't know. Would you?"

"I'd sooner eat dirt," he said with a look of indignation.

"Really? You'd do that?"

He threw me a puzzled look. "Do what?"

"Eat dirt if I told you to," I said. I knew I was being cruel, like when I'd taunt him if he didn't know some big word. But there was something fascinating—albeit in a sick way—about teasing Hassan. Kind of like when we used to play insect torture. Except now, he was the ant and I was holding the magnifying glass.

His eyes searched my face for a long time. We sat there, two boys under a sour cherry tree, suddenly looking, *really* looking, at each other. That's when it happened again: Hassan's face changed. Maybe not *changed*, not really, but suddenly I had the feeling I was looking at two faces, the one I knew, the one that was my first memory, and another, a second face, this one lurking just beneath the surface. I'd seen it happen before—it always shook me up a little. It just appeared, this other face, for a fraction of a moment, long enough to leave me with the unsettling feeling that maybe I'd seen it someplace before. Then Hassan blinked and it was just him again. Just Hassan.

"If you asked, I would," he finally said, looking right at me. I dropped my eyes. To this day, I find it hard to gaze directly at people like Hassan, people who mean every word they say.

"But I wonder," he added. "Would you ever ask me to do such a thing, Amir agha?" And, just like that, he had thrown at me his own little test. If I was going to toy with him and challenge his loyalty, then he'd toy with me, test my integrity.

I wished I hadn't started this conversation. I forced a smile. "Don't be stupid, Hassan. You know I wouldn't."

Hassan returned the smile. Except his didn't look forced. "I know," he said. And that's the thing about people who mean everything they say. They think everyone else does too.

"Here it comes," Hassan said, pointing to the sky. He rose to his feet and walked a few paces to his left. I looked up, saw the kite plummeting toward us. I heard footfalls, shouts, an approaching melee of kite runners. But they were wasting their time. Because Hassan stood with his arms wide open, smiling, waiting for the kite. And may God—if He exists, that is—strike me blind if the kite didn't just drop into his outstretched arms.

In the winter of 1975, I saw Hassan run a kite for the last time.

Usually, each neighborhood held its own competition. But that year, the tournament was going to be held in my neighborhood, Wazir Akbar Khan, and several other districts—Karteh-Char, Karteh-Parwan, Mekro-Rayan, and Koteh-Sangi—had been invited. You could hardly go anywhere without hearing talk of the upcoming tournament. Word had it this was going to be the biggest tournament in twenty-five years.

One night that winter, with the big contest only four days away, Baba and I sat in his study in overstuffed leather chairs by the glow of the fireplace. We were sipping tea, talking. Ali had served dinner earlier—potatoes and curried cauliflower over rice—and had retired for the night with Hassan. Baba was fattening his pipe and I was asking him to tell the story about the winter a pack of wolves had descended from the mountains in Herat and forced everyone to stay indoors for a week, when he lit a match and said, casually, "I think maybe you'll win the tournament this year. What do you think?"

I didn't know what to think. Or what to say. Was that what it would take? Had he just slipped me a key? I was a good kite fighter. Actually, a very good one. A few times, I'd even come close to winning the winter tournament—once, I'd made it to the final three. But coming close wasn't the same as winning, was it? Baba hadn't *come close*. He had won because winners won and everyone else just went home. Baba was used to winning, winning at everything he set his mind to.

Didn't he have a right to expect the same from his son? And just imagine. If I did win . . .

Baba smoked his pipe and talked. I pretended to listen. But I couldn't listen, not really, because Baba's casual little comment had planted a seed in my head: the resolution that I would win that winter's tournament. I was going to win. There was no other viable option. I was going to win, and I was going to run that last kite. Then I'd bring it home and show it to Baba. Show him once and for all that his son was worthy. Then maybe my life as a ghost in this house would finally be over. I let myself dream: I imagined conversation and laughter over dinner instead of silence broken only by the clinking of silverware and the occasional grunt. I envisioned us taking a Friday drive in Baba's car to Paghman, stopping on the way at Ghargha Lake for some fried trout and potatoes. We'd go to the zoo to see Marjan the lion, and maybe Baba wouldn't yawn and steal looks at his wristwatch all the time. Maybe Baba would read one of my stories. I'd write him a hundred if I thought he'd read one. Maybe he'd call me Amir jan like Rahim Khan did. And maybe, just maybe, I would finally be pardoned for killing my mother.

Baba was telling me about the time he'd cut fourteen kites on the same day. I smiled, nodded, laughed at all the right places, but I hardly heard a word he said. I had a mission now. And I wasn't going to fail Baba. Not this time.

It snowed heavily the night before the tournament. Hassan and I sat under the *kursi* and played panjpar as wind-rattled tree branches tapped on the window. Earlier that day, I'd asked Ali to set up the kursi for us— which was basically an electric heater under a low table covered with a thick, quilted blanket. Around the table, he arranged mattresses and cushions, so as many as twenty people could sit and slip their legs under. Hassan and I used to spend entire snowy days snug under the *kursi*, playing chess, cards—mostly panjpar.

I killed Hassan's ten of diamonds, played him two jacks and a six. Next door, in Baba's study, Baba and Rahim Khan were discussing business with a couple of other men—one of them I recognized as Assef's father. Through the wall, I could hear the scratchy sound of Radio Kabul News.

Hassan killed the six and picked up the jacks. On the radio, Daoud Khan was announcing something about foreign investments.

"He says someday we'll have television in Kabul," I said.

"Who?"

"Daoud Khan, you ass, the president."

Hassan giggled. "I heard they already have it in Iran," he said.

I sighed. "Those Iranians . . ." For a lot of Hazaras, Iran represented a sanctuary of sorts—I guess because, like Hazaras, most Iranians were Shi'a Muslims. But I remembered something my teacher had said that summer about Iranians, that they were grinning smooth talkers who patted you on the back with one hand and picked your pocket with the other. I told Baba about that and he said my teacher was one of those jealous Afghans, jealous because Iran was a rising power in Asia and most people around the world couldn't even find Afghanistan on a world map. "It hurts to say that," he said, shrugging. "But better to get hurt by the truth than comforted with a lie."

"I'll buy you one someday," I said.

Hassan's face brightened. "A television? In truth?"

"Sure. And not the black-and-white kind either. We'll probably be grown-ups by then, but I'll get us two. One for you and one for me."

"I'll put it on my table, where I keep my drawings," Hassan said.

His saying that made me kind of sad. Sad for who Hassan was, where he lived. For how he'd accepted the fact that he'd grow old in the mud shack in the yard, the way his father had. I drew the last card, played him a pair of queens and a ten.

Hassan picked up the queens. "You know, I think you're going to make Agha sahib very proud tomorrow."

"You think so?"

"*Inshallah*," he said.

"*Inshallah*," I echoed, though the "God willing" qualifier didn't sound as sincere coming from my lips. That was the thing with Hassan. He was so goddamn pure, you always felt like a phony around him.

I killed his king and played him my final card, the ace of spades. He had to pick it up, I'd won, but as I shuffled for a new game, I had the distinct suspicion that Hassan had *let* me win.

"Amir agha?"

"What?"

"You know . . . I *like* where I live." He was always doing that, reading my mind. "It's my home."

"Whatever," I said. "Get ready to lose again."

Seven

The next morning, as he brewed black tea for breakfast, Hassan told me he'd had a dream. "We were at Ghargha Lake, you, me, Father, Agha sahib, Rahim Khan, and thousands of other people," he said. "It was warm and sunny, and the lake was clear like a mirror. But no one was swimming because they said a monster had come to the lake. It was swimming at the bottom, waiting."

He poured me a cup and added sugar, blew on it a few times. Put it before me, "So everyone is scared to get in the water, and suddenly you kick off your shoes, Amir agha, and take off your shirt. 'There's no monster,' you say. 'I'll show you all.' And before anyone can stop you, you dive into the water, start swimming away. I follow you in and we're both swimming."

"But you can't swim."

Hassan laughed. "It's a dream, Amir agha, you can do anything. Anyway, everyone is screaming, 'Get out! Get out!' but we just swim in the cold water. We make it way out to the middle of the lake and we stop swimming. We turn toward the shore and wave to the people. They look small like ants, but we can hear them clapping. They see now. There is no monster, just water. They change the name of the lake after that, and call it the 'Lake of Amir and Hassan, Sultans of Kabul,' and we get to charge people money for swimming in it."

"So what does it mean?" I said.

He coated my *naan* with marmalade, placed it on a plate. "I don't know. I was hoping you could tell me."

"Well, it's a dumb dream. Nothing happens in it."

"Father says dreams always mean something."

I sipped some tea. "Why don't you ask him, then? He's so smart," I said, more curtly than I had intended. I hadn't slept all night. My neck and back were like coiled springs, and my eyes stung. Still, I had been mean to Hassan. I almost apologized, then didn't. Hassan understood I was just nervous. Hassan always understood about me.

Upstairs, I could hear the water running in Baba's bathroom.

The streets glistened with fresh snow and the sky was a blameless blue. Snow blanketed every rooftop and weighed on the branches of the stunted mulberry trees that lined our street. Overnight, snow had nudged its way into every crack and gutter. I squinted against the blinding white when Hassan and I stepped through the wrought-iron gates. Ali shut the gates behind us. I heard him mutter a prayer under his breath—he always said a prayer when his son left the house.

I had never seen so many people on our street. Kids were flinging snowballs, squabbling, chasing one another, giggling. Kite fighters were huddling with their spool holders, making last-minute preparations. From adjacent streets, I could hear laughter and chatter. Already, rooftops were jammed with spectators reclining in lawn chairs, hot tea steaming from thermoses, and the music of Ahmad Zahir blaring from cassette players. The immensely popular Ahmad Zahir had revolutionized Afghan music and outraged the purists by adding electric guitars, drums, and horns to the traditional tabla and harmonium; on stage or at parties, he shirked the austere and nearly morose stance of older singers and actually smiled when he sang—sometimes even at women. I turned my gaze to our rooftop, found Baba and Rahim Khan sitting on a bench, both dressed in wool sweaters, sipping tea. Baba waved. I couldn't tell if he was waving at me or Hassan.

"We should get started," Hassan said. He wore black rubber snow boots and a bright green *chapan* over a thick sweater and faded corduroy pants. Sunlight washed over his face, and, in it, I saw how well the pink scar above his lip had healed.

Suddenly I wanted to withdraw. Pack it all in, go back home. What was I thinking? Why was I putting myself through this, when I already knew the outcome? Baba was on the roof, watching me. I felt his glare on me like the heat of a blistering sun. This would be failure on a grand scale, even for me.

"I'm not sure I want to fly a kite today," I said.

"It's a beautiful day," Hassan said.

I shifted on my feet. Tried to peel my gaze away from our rooftop. "I don't know. Maybe we should go home."

Then he stepped toward me and, in a low voice, said something that scared me a little. "Remember, Amir agha. There's no monster, just a beautiful day." How could I be such an open book to him when, half the time, I had no idea what was milling around in his head? I was the one who went to school, the one who could read, write. I was the smart one. Hassan couldn't read a first-grade textbook but he'd read me plenty. That was a little unsettling, but also sort of comfortable to have someone who always knew what you needed.

"No monster," I said, feeling a little better, to my own surprise.

He smiled, "No monster."

"Are you sure?"

He closed his eyes. Nodded.

I looked to the kids scampering down the street, flinging snowballs. "It is a beautiful day, isn't it?"

"Let's fly," he said.

It occurred to me then that maybe Hassan had made up his dream. Was that possible? I decided it wasn't. Hassan wasn't that smart. *I* wasn't that smart. But made up or not, the silly dream had lifted some of my anxiety. Maybe I *should* take off my shirt, take a swim in the lake. Why not?

"Let's do it," I said.

Hassan's face brightened. "Good," he said. He lifted our kite, red with yellow borders, and, just beneath where the central and cross spars met, marked with Saifo's unmistakable signature. He licked his finger and held it up, tested the wind, then ran in its direction—on those rare occasions we flew kites in the summer, he'd kick up dust to see which way the wind blew it. The spool rolled in my hands until Hassan stopped, about fifty feet away. He held the kite high over his head, like an Olympic athlete showing his gold medal. I jerked the string twice, our usual signal, and Hassan tossed the kite.

Caught between Baba and the mullahs at school, I still hadn't made up my mind about God. But when a Koran *ayat* I had learned in my *diniyat* class rose to my lips, I muttered it. I took a deep breath, exhaled, and pulled on the string. Within a minute, my kite was rocketing to the sky. It made a sound like a paper bird flapping its wings. Hassan clapped his hands, whistled, and ran back to me. I handed him the spool, holding on to the string, and he spun it quickly to roll the loose string back on.

At least two dozen kites already hung in the sky, like paper sharks roaming for prey. Within an hour, the number doubled, and red, blue, and yellow kites glided and spun in the sky. A cold breeze wafted through my hair. The wind was perfect for kite flying, blowing just hard enough to give some lift, make the sweeps easier. Next to me, Hassan held the spool, his hands already bloodied by the string.

Soon, the cutting started and the first of the defeated kites whirled out of control. They fell from the sky like shooting stars with brilliant, rippling tails, showering the neighborhoods below with prizes for the kite runners. I could hear the runners now, hollering as they ran the streets. Someone shouted reports of a fight breaking out two streets down.

I kept stealing glances at Baba sitting with Rahim Khan on the roof, wondered what he was thinking. Was he cheering for me? Or did a part of him enjoy watching me fail? That was the thing about kite flying: Your mind drifted with the kite.

They were coming down all over the place now, the kites, and I was still flying. I was still flying. My eyes keep wandering over to Baba, bundled up in his wool sweater. Was he surprised I had lasted as long as I had? *You don't keep your eyes to the sky, you won't last much longer.* I snapped my gaze back to the sky. A red kite was closing in on me—I'd caught it just in time. I tangled a bit with it, ended up besting him when he became impatient and tried to cut me from below.

Up and down the streets, kite runners were returning triumphantly, their captured kites held high. They showed them off to their parents, their friends. But they all knew the best was yet to come. The biggest prize of all was still flying. I sliced a bright yellow kite with a coiled white tail. It cost me another gash on the index finger and blood trickled down into my palm. I had Hassan hold the string and sucked the blood dry, blotted my finger against my jeans.

Within another hour, the number of surviving kites dwindled from maybe fifty to a dozen. I was one of them. I'd made it to the last dozen. I knew this part of the tournament would take a while, because the guys who had lasted this long were good—they wouldn't easily fall into simple traps like the old lift-and-dive, Hassan's favorite trick.

By three o'clock that afternoon, tufts of clouds had drifted in and the sun had slipped behind them. Shadows started to lengthen. The spectators on the roofs bundled up in scarves and thick coats. We were down to a half dozen and I was still flying. My legs ached and my neck was stiff. But with each defeated kite, hope grew in my heart, like snow collecting on a wall, one flake at a time.

My eyes kept returning to a blue kite that had been wreaking havoc for the last hour.

"How many has he cut?" I asked.

"I counted eleven," Hassan said.

"Do you know whose it might be?"

Hassan clucked his tongue and tipped his chin. That was a trademark Hassan gesture, meant he had no idea. The blue kite sliced a big purple one and swept twice in big loops. Ten minutes later, he'd cut another two, sending hordes of kite runners racing after them.

Social Responsibility

After another thirty minutes, only four kites remained. And I was still flying. It seemed I could hardly make a wrong move, as if every gust of wind blew in my favor. I'd never felt so in command, so lucky. It felt intoxicating. I didn't dare look up to the roof. Didn't dare take my eyes off the sky. I had to concentrate, play it smart. Another fifteen minutes and what had seemed like a laughable dream that morning had suddenly become reality: It was just me and the other guy. The blue kite.

The tension in the air was as taut as the glass string I was tugging with my bloody hands. People were stomping their feet, clapping, whistling, chanting, "*Boboresh! Boboresh!*" *Cut him! Cut him!* I wondered if Baba's voice was one of them. Music blasted. The smell of steamed *mantu* and fried *pakora* drifted from rooftops and open doors.

But all I heard—all I willed myself to hear—was the thudding of blood in my head. All I saw was the blue kite. All I smelled was victory. Salvation. Redemption. If Baba was wrong and there *was* a God like they said in school, then He'd let me win. I didn't know what the other guy was playing for, maybe just bragging rights. But this was my one chance to become someone who was looked at, not seen, listened to, not heard. If there was a God, He guide the winds, let them blow for me so that, with a tug of my string, I'd cut loose my pain, my longing. I'd endured too much, come too far. And suddenly, just like that, hope became knowledge. I was going to win. It was just a matter of when.

It turned out to be sooner than later. A gust of wind lifted my kite and I took advantage. Fed the string, pulled up. Looped my kite on top of the blue one. I held position. The blue kite knew it was in trouble. It was trying desperately to maneuver out of the jam, but I didn't let go. I held position. The crowd sensed the end was at hand. The chorus of "Cut him! Cut him!" grew louder, like Romans chanting for the gladiators to kill, kill!

"You're almost there, Amir agha! Almost there!" Hassan was panting.

Then the moment came. I closed my eyes and loosened my grip on the string. It sliced my fingers again as the wind dragged it. And then . . . I didn't need to hear the crowd's roar to know. I didn't need to see either. Hassan was screaming and his arm was wrapped around my neck.

"Bravo! Bravo, Amir agha!"

I opened my eyes, saw the blue kite spinning wildly like a tire come loose from a speeding car. I blinked, tried to say something. Nothing came out. Suddenly I was hovering, looking down on myself from above. Black leather coat, red scarf, faded jeans. A thin boy, a little sallow, and a tad short of his twelve years. He had narrow shoulders and a hint of dark circles around his pale hazel eyes. The breeze rustled his light brown hair. He looked up to me and we smiled at each other.

Then I was screaming, and everything was color and sound, everything was alive and good. I was throwing my free arm around Hassan and we were hopping up and down, both of us laughing, both of us weeping. "You won, Amir agha! You won!"

"*We* won! *We* won!" was all I could say. This wasn't happening. In a moment, I'd blink and rouse from this beautiful dream, get out of bed, march down to the kitchen to eat breakfast with no one to talk to but Hassan. Get dressed. Wait for Baba. Give up. Back to my old life. Then I saw Baba on our roof. He was standing on the edge, pumping both of his fists. Hollering and clapping. And that right there was the single greatest moment of my twelve years of life, seeing Baba on that roof, proud of me at last.

But he was doing something now, motioning with his hands in an urgent way. Then I understood. "Hassan, we—"

"I know," he said, breaking our embrace. "*Inshallah,* we'll celebrate later. Right now, I'm going to run that blue kite for you," he said. He dropped the spool and took off running, the hem of his green *chapan* dragging in the snow behind him.

"Hassan!" I called. "Come back with it!"

He was already turning the street corner, his rubber boots kicking up snow. He stopped, turned. He cupped his hands around his mouth. "For you a thousand times over!" he said. Then he smiled his Hassan smile and disappeared around the corner. The next time I saw him smile unabashedly like that was twenty-six years later, in a faded Polaroid photograph.

I began to pull my kite back as people rushed to congratulate me. I shook hands with them, said my thanks. The younger kids looked at me with an awestruck twinkle in their eyes; I was a hero. Hands patted my back and tousled my hair. I pulled on the string and returned every smile, but my mind was on the blue kite.

Finally, I had my kite in hand. I wrapped the loose string that had collected at my feet around the spool, shook a few more hands, and trotted home. When I reached the wrought-iron gates, Ali was waiting on the other side. He stuck his hand through the bars. "Congratulations," he said.

I gave him my kite and spool, shook his hand, "*Tashakor,* Ali jan."

"I was praying for you the whole time."

"Then keep praying. We're not done yet."

I hurried back to the street. I didn't ask Ali about Baba. I didn't want to see him yet. In my head, I had it all planned: I'd make a grand entrance, a hero, prized trophy in my bloodied hands. Heads would turn and eyes would lock. Rostam and Sohrab sizing each other up. A dramatic moment of silence. Then the old warrior would walk to the young one, embrace him, acknowledge his worthiness. Vindication. Salvation. Redemption. And then? Well . . . happily ever after, of course. What else?

The streets of Wazir Akbar Khan were numbered and set at right angles to each other like a grid. It was a new neighborhood then, still developing, with empty lots of land and half-constructed homes on every street between compounds surrounded by eight-foot walls. I ran up and down every street, looking for Hassan. Everywhere, people were busy folding chairs, packing food and utensils after a long day of partying. Some, still sitting on their rooftops, shouted their congratulations to me.

Four streets south of ours, I saw Omar, the son of an engineer who was a friend of Baba's. He was dribbling a soccer ball with his brother on the front lawn of their house. Omar was a pretty good guy. We'd been classmates in fourth grade, and one time he'd given me a fountain pen, the kind you had to load with a cartridge.

"I heard you won, Amir," he said. "Congratulations."

"Thanks. Have you seen Hassan?"

"Your Hazara?"

I nodded.

Omar headed the ball to his brother. "I hear he's a great kite runner." His brother headed the ball back to him. Omar caught it, tossed it up and down. "Although I've always wondered how he manages. I mean, with those tight little eyes, how does he *see* anything?"

His brother laughed, a short burst, and asked for the ball. Omar ignored him.

"Have you seen him?"

Omar flicked a thumb over his shoulder, pointing southwest. "I saw him running toward the bazaar awhile ago."

"Thanks." I scuttled away.

Social Responsibility

By the time I reached the marketplace, the sun had almost sunk behind the hills and dusk had painted the sky pink and purple. A few blocks away, from the Haji Yaghoub Mosque, the mullah bellowed *azan,* calling for the faithful to unroll their rugs and bow their heads west in prayer. Hassan never missed any of the five daily prayers. Even when we were out playing, he'd excuse himself, draw water from the well in the yard, wash up, and disappear into the hut. He'd come out a few minutes later, smiling, find me sitting against the wall or perched on a tree. He was going to miss prayer tonight, though, because of me.

The bazaar was emptying quickly, the merchants finishing up their haggling for the day. I trotted in the mud between rows of closely packed cubicles where you could buy a freshly slaughtered pheasant in one stand and a calculator from the adjacent one. I picked my way through the dwindling crowd, the lame beggars dressed in layers of tattered rags, the vendors with rugs on their shoulders, the cloth merchants and butchers closing shop for the day. I found no sign of Hassan.

I stopped by a dried fruit stand, described Hassan to an old merchant loading his mule with crates of pine seeds and raisins. He wore a powder blue turban.

He paused to look at me for a long time before answering. "I might have seen him."

"Which way did he go?"

He eyed me up and down. "What is a boy like you doing here at this time of the day looking for a Hazara?" His glance lingered admiringly on my leather coat and my jeans—*cowboy pants,* we used to call them. In Afghanistan, owning anything American, especially if it wasn't secondhand, was a sign of wealth.

"I need to find him, Agha."

"What is he to you" he said. I didn't see the point of his question, but I reminded myself that impatience wasn't going to make him tell me any faster.

"He's our servant's son," I said.

The old man raised a pepper gray eyebrow. "He is? Lucky Hazara, having such a concerned master. His father should get on his knees, sweep the dust at your feet with his eyelashes."

"Are you going to tell me or not?"

He rested an arm on the mule's back, pointed south. "I think I saw the boy you described running that way. He had a kite in his hand. A blue one."

"He did?" I said. *For you a thousand times over,* he'd promised. Good old Hassan. Good old reliable Hassan. He'd kept his promise and run the last kite for me.

"Of course, they've probably caught him by now," the old merchant said, grunting and loading another box on the mule's back.

"Who?"

"The other boys," he said. "The ones chasing him. They were dressed like you." He glanced to the sky and sighed. "Now, run along, you're making me late for *namaz.*"

But I was already scrambling down the lane.

For the next few minutes, I scoured the bazaar in vain. Maybe the old merchant's eyes had betrayed him. Except he'd seen the blue kite. The thought of getting my hands on that kite . . . I poked my head behind every lane, every shop. No sign of Hassan.

I had begun to worry that darkness would fall before I found Hassan when I heard voices from up ahead. I'd reached a secluded, muddy road. It ran perpendicular to the end of the main thoroughfare bisecting the bazaar. I turned onto the rutted track and followed the voices. My boot squished in mud with every step and my breath puffed out in white clouds before me. The narrow path ran parallel on one side to a snow-filled ravine through which a stream may have tumbled in the spring. To my other side stood rows of snow-burdened cypress trees peppered among flat-topped clay houses—no more than mud shacks in most cases—separated by narrow alleys.

I heard the voices again, louder this time, coming from one of the alleys. I crept close to the mouth of the alley. Held my breath. Peeked around the corner.

Hassan was standing at the blind end of the alley in a defiant stance: fists curled, legs slightly apart. Behind him, sitting on piles of scrap and rubble, was the blue kite. My key to Baba's heart.

Blocking Hassan's way out of the alley were three boys, the same three from that day on the hill, the day after Daoud Khan's coup, when Hassan had saved us with his slingshot. Wali was standing on one side, Kamal on the other, and in the middle, Assef. I felt my body clench up, and something cold rippled up my spine. Assef seemed relaxed, confident. He was twirling his brass knuckles. The other two guys shifted nervously on their feet, looking from Assef to Hassan, like they'd cornered some kind of wild animal that only Assef could tame.

"Where is your slingshot, Hazara?" Assef said, turning the brass knuckles in his hand. "What was it you said? 'They'll have to call you One-Eyed Assef.' That's right. One-Eyed Assef. That was clever. Really clever. Then again, it's easy to be clever when you're holding a loaded weapon."

I realized I still hadn't breathed out. I exhaled, slowly, quietly. I felt paralyzed. I watched them close in on the boy I'd grown up with, the boy whose harelipped face had been my first memory.

"But today is your lucky day, Hazara," Assef said. He had his back to me, but I would have bet he was grinning. "I'm in a mood to forgive. What do you say to that, boys?"

"That's generous," Kamal blurted, "Especially after the rude manners he showed us last time." He was trying to sound like Assef, except there was a tremor in his voice. Then I understood: He wasn't afraid of Hassan, not really. He was afraid because he had no idea what Assef had in mind.

Assef waved a dismissive hand. "*Bakhshida*. Forgiven. It's done." His voice dropped a little. "Of course, nothing is free in this world, and my pardon comes with a small price."

"That's fair," Kamal said.

"Nothing is free," Wali added.

"You're a lucky Hazara," Assef said, taking a step toward Hassan. "Because today, it's only going to cost you that blue kite. A fair deal, boys, isn't it?"

"More than fair," Kamal said.

Even from where I was standing, I could see the fear creeping into Hassan's eyes, but he shook his head. "Amir agha won the tournament and I ran this kite for him. I ran it fairly. This is his kite."

"A loyal Hazara. Loyal as a dog," Assef said.

Kamal's laugh was a shrill, nervous sound.

"But before you sacrifice yourself for him, think about this: Would he do the same for you? Have you ever wondered why he never includes you in games when he has guests? Why he only plays with you when no one else is around? I'll tell you why, Hazara. Because to him, you're nothing but an ugly pet. Something he can play with when he's bored, something he can kick when he's angry. Don't ever fool yourself and think you're something more."

"Amir agha and I are friends," Hassan said. He looked flushed.

"Friends?" Assef said, laughing. "You pathetic fool! Someday you'll wake up from your little fantasy and learn just how good of a friend he is. Now, bas! Enough of this. Give us that kite."

Hassan stooped and picked up a rock.

Assef flinched. He began to take a step back, stopped. "Last chance, Hazara."

Hassan's answer was to cock the arm that held the rock.

"Whatever you wish." Assef unbuttoned his winter coat, took it off, folded it slowly and deliberately. He placed it against the wall.

I opened my mouth, almost said something. Almost. The rest of my life might have turned out differently if I had. But I didn't. I just watched. Paralyzed.

Assef motioned with his hand, and the other two boys separated, forming a half circle, trapping Hassan in the alley.

"I've changed my mind," Assef said. "I'm letting you keep the kite, Hazara. I'll let you keep it so it will always remind you of what I'm about to do."

Then he charged. Hassan hurled the rock. It struck Assef in the forehead. Assef yelped as he flung himself at Hassan, knocking him to the ground. Wali and Kamal followed.

I bit on my fist. Shut my eyes.

A memory:

Did you know Hassan and you fed from the same breast? Did you know that, Amir agha? Sakina, her name was. She was a fair, blue-eyed Hazara woman from Bamiyan and she sang you old wedding songs. They say there is a brotherhood between people who've fed from the same breast. Did you know that?

A memory:

"*A* rupia *each, children. Just one* rupia *each and I will part the curtain of truth.*" *The old man sits against a mud wall. His sightless eyes are like molten silver embedded in deep, twin craters. Hunched over his cane, the fortune-teller runs a gnarled hand across the surface of his deflated cheeks. Cups it before us.* "*Not much to ask for the truth, is it, a* rupia *each?*" *Hassan drops a coin in the leathery palm. I drop mine too.* "*In the name of Allah most beneficent, most merciful,*" *the old fortune-teller whispers. He takes Hassan's hand first, strokes the palm with one hornlike fingernail, round and round, round and round. The finger then floats to Hassan's face and makes a dry, scratchy sound as it slowly traces the curve of his cheeks, the outline of his ears. The calloused pads of his fingers brush against Hassan's eyes. The hand stops there. Lingers. A shadow passes across the old man's face. Hassan and I exchange a glance. The old man takes Hassan's hand and puts the rupia back in Hassan's palm. He turns to me.* "*How about you, young friend?*" *he says. On the other side of the wall, a rooster crows. The old man reaches for my hand and I withdraw it.*

A dream:

I am lost in a snowstorm. The wind shrieks, blows stinging sheets of snow into my eyes. I stagger through layers of shifting white. I call for help but the wind drowns my cries. I fall and lie panting on the snow, lost in the white, the wind wailing in my ears. I watch the snow erase my fresh footprints. I'm a ghost now, I think, a ghost with no footprints. I cry out again, hope fading like my footprints. But this time, a muffled reply. I shield my eyes and manage to sit up. Out of the swaying curtains of snow, I catch a glimpse of movement, a flurry of color. A familiar shape materializes. A hand reaches out for me. I see deep, parallel gashes across the palm, blood dripping, staining the snow. I take the hand and suddenly the snow is gone. We're standing in a field of apple green grass with soft wisps of clouds drifting above. I look up and see the clear sky is filled with kites, green, yellow, red, orange. They shimmer in the afternoon light.

A havoc of scrap and rubble littered the alley. Worn bicycle tires, bottles with peeled labels, ripped up magazines, yellowed newspapers, all scattered amid a pile of bricks and slabs of cement. A rusted cast-iron stove with a gaping hole on its side tilted against a wall. But there were two things amid the garbage that I couldn't stop looking at: One was the blue kite resting against the wall, close to the cast-iron stove; the other was Hassan's brown corduroy pants thrown on a heap of eroded bricks.

"I don't know," Wali was saying. "My father says it's sinful." He sounded unsure, excited, scared, all at the same time. Hassan lay with his chest pinned to the ground. Kamal and Wali each gripped an arm, twisted and bent at the elbow so that Hassan's hands were pressed to his back. Assef was standing over them, the heel of his snow boots crushing the back of Hassan's neck.

"Your father won't find out," Assef said. "And there's nothing sinful about teaching a lesson to a disrespectful donkey."

"I don't know," Wali muttered.

"Suit yourself," Assef said. He turned to Kamal. "What about you?"

"I . . . well . . ."

"It's just a Hazara," Assef said. But Kamal kept looking away.

"Fine," Assef snapped. "All I want you weaklings to do is hold him down. Can you manage that?"

Wali and Kamal nodded. They looked relieved.

Assef knelt behind Hassan, put his hands on Hassan's hips and lifted his bare buttocks. He kept one hand on Hassan's back and undid his own belt buckle with his free hand. He unzipped his jeans. Dropped his underwear. He positioned himself behind Hassan. Hassan didn't struggle. Didn't even whimper. He moved his head slightly and I caught a glimpse of his face. Saw the resignation in it. It was a look I had seen before. It was the look of the lamb.

Tomorrow is the tenth day of Dhul-Hijjah, *the last month of the Muslim calendar, and the first of three days of Eid Al-Adha, or* Eid-e-Qorban, *as Afghans call it—a day to celebrate how the prophet Ibrahim almost sacrificed his own son for God. Baba has handpicked the sheep again this year, a powder white one with crooked black ears.*

We all stand in the backyard, Hassan, Ali, Baba, and I. The mullah recites the prayer, rubs his beard. Baba mutters, Get on with it, *under his breath. He sounds annoyed with the endless praying, the ritual of making the meat halal. Baba mocks the story behind this* Eid, *like he mocks everything religious. But he respects the tradition of* Eid-e-Qorban. *The custom is to divide the meat in thirds, one for the family, one for friends, and one for the poor. Every year, Baba gives it all to the poor.* The rich are fat enough already, *he says.*

The mullah finishes the prayer. Ameen. *He picks up the kitchen knife with the long blade. The custom is to not let the sheep see the knife. Ali feeds the animal a cube of sugar—another custom, to make death sweeter. The sheep kicks, but not much. The mullah grabs it under its jaw and places the blade on its neck. Just a second before he slices the throat in one expert motion, I see the sheep's eyes. It is a look that will haunt my dreams for weeks. I don't know why I watch this yearly ritual in our backyard; my nightmares persist long after the bloodstains on the grass have faded. But I always watch. I watch because of that look of acceptance in the animal's eyes. Absurdly, I imagine the animal understands. I imagine the animal sees that its imminent demise is for a higher purpose. This is the look. . .*

I STOPPED WATCHING, turned away from the alley. Something warm was running down my wrist. I blinked, saw I was still biting down on my fist, hard enough to draw blood from the knuckles. I realized something else. I was weeping. From just around the corner, I could hear Assef's quick, rhythmic grunts.

I had one last chance to make a decision. One final opportunity to decide who I was going to be. I could step into that alley, stand up for Hassan—the way he'd stood up for me all those times in the past—and accept whatever would happen to me. Or I could run.

In the end, I ran.

I ran because I was a coward. I was afraid of Assef and what he would do to me. I was afraid of getting hurt. That's what I told myself as I turned my back to the alley, to Hassan. That's what I made myself believe. I actually *aspired* to cowardice, because the alternative, the real reason I was running, was that Assef was right: Nothing was free in this world. Maybe Hassan was the price I had to pay, the lamb I had to slay, to win Baba. Was it a fair price? The answer floated to my conscious mind before I could thwart it: He was just a Hazara, wasn't he?

I ran back the way I'd come. Ran back to the all but deserted bazaar. I lurched to a cubicle and leaned against the padlocked swinging doors. I stood there panting, sweating, wishing things had turned out some other way.

About fifteen minutes later, I heard voices and running footfalls. I crouched behind the cubicle and watched Assef and the other two sprinting by, laughing as they hurried down the deserted lane. I forced myself to wait ten more minutes. Then I walked back to the rutted track that ran along the snow-filled ravine. I squinted in the dimming light and spotted Hassan walking slowly toward me. I met him by a leafless birch tree on the edge of the ravine.

He had the blue kite in his hands; that was the first thing I saw. And I can't lie now and say my eyes didn't scan it for any rips. His *chapan* had mud smudges down the front and his shirt was ripped just below the collar. He stopped. Swayed on his feet like he was going to collapse. Then he steadied himself. Handed me the kite.

"Where were you? I looked for you," I said. Speaking those words was like chewing on a rock.

Hassan dragged a sleeve across his face, wiped snot and tears. I waited for him to say something, but we just stood there in silence, in the fading light. I was grateful for the early-evening shadows that fell on Hassan's face and concealed mine. I was glad I didn't have to return his gaze. Did he know I knew? And if he knew, then what would I see if I *did* look in his eyes? Blame? Indignation? Or, God forbid, what I feared most: guileless devotion? That, most of all, I couldn't bear to see.

He began to say something and his voice cracked. He closed his mouth, opened it, and closed it again. Took a step back. Wiped his face. And that was as close as Hassan and I ever came to discussing what had happened in the alley. I thought he might burst into tears, but, to my relief, he didn't, and I pretended I hadn't heard the crack in his voice. Just like I pretended I hadn't seen the dark stain in the seat of his pants. Or those tiny drops that fell from between his legs and stained the snow black.

"Agha sahib will worry," was all he said. He turned from me and limped away.

It happened just the way I'd imagined. I opened the door to the smoky study and stepped in. Baba and Rahim Khan were drinking tea and listening to the news crackling on the radio. Their heads turned. Then a smile played on my father's lips. He opened his arms. I put the kite down and walked into his thick hairy arms. I buried my face in the warmth of his chest and wept. Baba held me close to him, rocking me back and forth. In his arms, I forgot what I'd done. And that was good.

CRITICAL EYE

▶ **For Discussion**

a. Are all friendships equal, or is there usually one personality that controls the relationship?

b. Why is Amir unable to help Hassan?

c. Can a friendship survive if the parties are members of different classes?

d. Is Hassan stronger than Amir? Why?

▶ **Re-approaching the Reading**

Would the story change if Hassan's character were a girl? Would this make the assault even more tragic? If so, why? If not, why?

▶ **Writing Assignment**

Historically, are there successful accounts of the strong coming to the aid of the weak?

BIDPAI

The Camel and His Friends
c. 4th century

Once a merchant was leading a caravan of heavily-laden camels through a jungle when one of them, overcome by fatigue, collapsed. The merchant decided to leave the camel in the jungle and go on his way. Later, when the camel recovered his strength, he realized that he was alone in a strange jungle. Fortunately there was plenty of grass, and he survived.

One day the king of the jungle, a lion, arrived along with his three friends—a leopard, a fox, and a crow. The king lion wondered what the camel was doing in the jungle! He came near the camel and asked how he, a creature of the desert, had ended up in the hostile jungle. The camel tearfully explained what happened. The lion took pity on him and said, "You have nothing to fear now. Henceforth, you are under my protection and can stay with us." The camel began to live happily in the jungle.

Then one day the lion was wounded in a fight with an elephant. He retired to his cave and stayed there for several days. His friends came to offer their sympathy. They tried to catch prey for the hungry lion but failed. The camel had no problem as he lived on grass while the others were starving.

The fox came up with a plan. He secretly went to the lion and suggested that the camel be sacrificed for the good of the others. The lion got furious, "I can never kill an animal who is under my protection."

The fox humbly said, "But Lord, you have provided us food all the time. If any one of us voluntarily offered himself to save your life, I hope you won't mind!" The hungry lion did not object to that and agreed to take the offer.

The fox went back to his companions and said, "Friends, our king is dying of starvation. Let us go and beg him to eat one of us. It is the least we can do for such a noble soul."

So they went to the king and the crow offered his life. The fox interrupted, and said, "You are a small creature, the master's hunger will hardly be appeased by eating you. May I humbly offer my life to satisfy my master's hunger."

The leopard stepped forward and said, "You are no bigger than the crow, it is me whom our master should eat."

The foolish camel thought, "Everyone has offered to lay down their lives for the king, but he has not hurt any one. It is now my turn to offer myself." So he stepped forward and said, "Stand aside friend leopard, the king and you have close family ties. It is me whom the master must eat."

An ominous silence greeted the camel's offer. Then the king gladly said, "I accept your offer, O noble camel." And in no time he was killed by the three rogues, the false friends.

Moral: Be careful in choosing your friends.

"The Camel and His Friends" (originally titled "The Unreliable Friends") by Bidpai, from *Panchatantra* edited by Arundhati Khanwalkar. Reprinted by permission of Arundhati Khanwalkar.

CRITICAL EYE

▶ For Discussion

a. Do we live in a society where people are willing to sacrifice themselves for a greater good or in defense of the weak?

b. Why are the animals "false friends"?

c. Should the leaders of nations expect/demand their citizens to make sacrifices?

d. Does the story suggest that the masses cannot trust those who are in charge?

▶ Re-approaching the Reading

Imagine the animals of the story are people of different races, faiths, and genders. With these new factors in mind, what would the story be saying about human nature?

▶ Writing Assignment

Why should we feel compelled to sacrifice ourselves for strangers when they need our help? What is gained by doing so?

MARGARET SANGER

THE TURBID EBB AND FLOW OF MISERY

> *Every night and every morn*
> *Some to misery are born.*
> *Every morn and every night*
> *Some are born to sweet delight.*
> *Some are born to sweet delight,*
> *Some are born to endless night.*
> — William Blake

During these years [about 1912] in New York trained nurses were in great demand. Few people wanted to enter hospitals; they were afraid they might be "practiced" upon, and consented to go only in desperate emergencies. Sentiment was especially vehement in the matter of having babies. A woman's own bedroom, no matter how inconveniently arranged, was the usual place for her lying-in. I was not sufficiently free from domestic duties to be a general nurse, but I could ordinarily manage obstetrical cases because I was notified far enough ahead to plan my schedule. And after serving my two weeks I could get home again.

Sometimes I was summoned to small apartments occupied by young clerks, insurance salesmen, or lawyers, just starting out, most of them under thirty and whose wives were having their first or second baby. They were always eager to know the best and latest method in infant care and feeding. In particular, Jewish patients, whose lives centered around the family, welcomed advice and followed it implicitly.

But more and more my calls began to come from the Lower East Side, as though I were being magnetically drawn there by some force outside my control. I hated the wretchedness and hopelessness of the poor, and never experienced that satisfaction in working among them that so many noble women have found. My concern for my patients was now quite different from my earlier hospital attitude. I could see that much was wrong with them which did not appear in the physiological or medical diagnosis. A woman in childbirth was not merely a woman in childbirth. My expanded outlook included a view of her background, her potentialities as a human being, the kind of children she was bearing, and what was going to happen to them.

The wives of small shopkeepers were my most frequent cases, but I had carpenters, truck drivers, dishwashers, and pushcart vendors. I admired intensely the consideration most of these people had for their own. Money to pay doctor and nurse had been carefully saved months in advance—parents-in-law, grandfathers, grandmothers, all contributing.

As soon as the neighbors learned that a nurse was in the building they came in a friendly way to visit, often carrying fruit, jellies, or

---

Chapter 7 of *An Autobiography* (1938). Sanger has taken her chapter title from a line in Matthew Arnold's poem "Dover Beach" [Editor's note].

gefüllter fish made after a cherished recipe. It was infinitely pathetic to me that they, so poor themselves, should bring me food. Later they drifted in again with the excuse of getting the plate, and sat down for a nice talk; there was no hurry. Always back of the little gift was the question, "I am pregnant (or my daughter, or my sister is). Tell me something to keep from having another baby. We cannot afford another yet."

I tried to explain the only two methods I had ever heard of among the middle classes, both of which were invariably brushed aside as unacceptable. They were of no certain avail to the wife because they placed the burden of responsibility solely upon the husband—a burden which he seldom assumed. What she was seeking was self-protection she could herself use, and there was none.

Below this stratum of society was one in truly desperate circumstances. The men were sullen and unskilled, picking up odd jobs now and then, but more often unemployed, lounging in and out of the house at all hours of the day and night. The women seemed to slink on their way to market and were without neighborliness.

These submerged, untouched classes were beyond the scope of organized charity or religion. No labor union, no church, not even the Salvation Army reached them. They were apprehensive of everyone and rejected help of any kind, ordering all intruders to keep out: both birth and death they considered their own business. Social agents, who were just beginning to appear, were profoundly mistrusted because they pried into homes and lives, asking questions about wages, how many were in the family, had any of them ever been in jail. Often two or three had been there or were now under suspicion of prostitution, shoplifting, purse snatching, petty thievery, and, in consequence, passed furtively by the big blue uniforms on the corner.

The utmost depression came over me as I approached this surreptitious region. Below Fourteenth Street I seemed to be breathing a different air, to be in another world and country where the people had habits and customs alien to anything I had ever heard about.

There were then approximately ten thousand apartments in New York into which no sun ray penetrated directly; such windows as they had opened only on a narrow court from which rose fetid odors. It was seldom cleaned, though garbage and refuse often went down into it. All these dwellings were pervaded by the foul breath of poverty, that moldy, indefinable, indescribable smell which cannot be fumigated out, sickening to me but apparently unnoticed by those who lived there. When I set to work with antiseptics, their pungent sting, at least temporarily, obscured the stench.

I remember one confinement case to which I was called by the doctor of an insurance company. I climbed up the five flights and entered the airless rooms, but the baby had come with too great speed. A boy of ten had been the only assistant. Five flights was a long way; he had wrapped the placenta in a piece of newspaper and dropped it out the window into the court.

Many families took in "boarders," as they were termed, whose small contributions paid the rent. These derelicts, wanderers, alternately working and drinking, were crowded in with the children; a single room sometimes held as many as six sleepers. Little girls were accustomed to dressing and undressing in front of the men, and were often violated, occasionally by their own fathers or brothers, before they reached the age of puberty.

Pregnancy was a chronic condition among the women of this class. Suggestions as to what to do for a girl who was "in trouble" or a married woman who was "caught" passed from mouth to mouth—herb teas, turpentine, steaming, rolling downstairs, inserting slippery

Social Responsibility

elm, knitting needles, shoe-hooks. When they had word of a new remedy they hurried to the drugstore, and if the clerk were inclined to be friendly he might say, "Oh, that won't help you, but here's something that may." The younger druggists usually refused to give advice because, if it were to be known, they would come under the law; midwives were even more fearful. The doomed women implored me to reveal the "secret" rich people had, offering to pay me extra to tell them; many really believed I was holding back information for money. They asked everybody and tried anything, but nothing did them any good. On Saturday nights I have seen groups of from fifty to one hundred with their shawls over their heads waiting outside the office of a five-dollar abortionist.

Each time I returned to this district, which was becoming a recurrent nightmare, I used to hear that Mrs. Cohen "had been carried to a hospital, but had never come back," or that Mrs. Kelly "had sent the children to a neighbor and had put her head into the gas oven." Day after day such tales were poured into my ears—a baby born dead, great relief—the death of an older child, sorrow but again relief of a sort—the story told a thousand times of death from abortion and children going into institutions. I shuddered with horror as I listened to the details and studied the reasons back of them—destitution linked with excessive childbearing. The waste of life seemed utterly senseless. One by one worried, sad, pensive, and aging faces marshaled themselves before me in my dreams, sometimes appealingly, sometimes accusingly.

These were not merely "unfortunate conditions among the poor" such as we read about. I knew the women personally. They were living, breathing, human beings, with hopes, fears, and aspirations like my own, yet the weary, misshapen bodies, "always ailing, never failing," were destined to be thrown on the scrap heap before they were thirty-five. I could not escape from the facts of their wretchedness; neither was I able to see any way out. My own cozy and comfortable family existence was becoming a reproach to me.

Then one stifling mid-July day of 1912 I was summoned to a Grand Street tenement. My patient was a small, slight Russian Jewess, about twenty-eight years old, of the special cast of feature to which suffering lends a madonna-like expression. The cramped three-room apartment was in a sorry state of turmoil. Jake Sachs, a truck driver scarcely older than his wife, had come home to find the three children crying and her unconscious from the effects of a self-induced abortion. He had called the nearest doctor, who in turn had sent for me. Jake's earnings were trifling, and most of them had gone to keep the none-too-strong children clean and properly fed. But his wife's ingenuity had helped them to save a little, and this he was glad to spend on a nurse rather than have her go to a hospital.

The doctor and I settled ourselves to the task of fighting the septicemia. Never had I worked so fast, never so concentratedly. The sultry days and nights were melted into a torpid inferno. It did not seem possible there could be such heat, and every bit of food, ice, and drugs had to be carried up three flights of stairs.

Jake was more kind and thoughtful than many of the husbands I have encountered. He loved his children, and had always helped his wife wash and dress them. He had brought water up and carried garbage down before he left in the morning, and did as much as he could for me while he anxiously watched her progress.

After a fortnight Mrs. Sachs' recovery was in sight. Neighbors, ordinarily fatalistic as to the results of abortion, were genuinely pleased that she had survived. She smiled wanly at all who came to see her and thanked them gently, but she could not respond to their hearty congratulations. She appeared to be more despondent and anxious than she should have been, and spent too much time in meditation.

At the end of three weeks, as I was preparing to leave the fragile patient to take up her difficult life once more, she finally voiced her fears. "Another baby will finish me, I suppose?"

"It's too early to talk about that," I temporized.

But when the doctor came to make his last call, I drew him aside. "Mrs. Sachs is terribly worried about having another baby."

"She well may be," replied the doctor, and then he stood before her and said, "Any more such capers, young woman, and there'll be no need to send for me."

"I know, doctor," she replied timidly, "but," and she hesitated as though it took all her courage to say it, "what can I do to prevent it?"

The doctor was a kindly man, and he had worked hard to save her, but such incidents had become so familiar to him that he had long since lost whatever delicacy he might once have had. He laughed good-naturedly. "You want to have your cake and eat it too, do you? Well, it can't be done."

Then picking up his hat and bag to depart he said, "Tell Jake to sleep on the roof."

I glanced quickly at Mrs. Sachs. Even through my sudden tears I could see stamped on her face an expression of absolute despair. We simply looked at each other, saying no word until the door had closed behind the doctor. Then she lifted her thin, blue-veined hands and clasped them beseechingly. "He can't understand. He's only a man. But you do, don't you? Please tell me the secret, and I'll never breathe it to a soul. *Please!*"

What was I to do? I could not speak the conventionally comforting phrases which would be of no comfort. Instead, I made her as physically easy as I could and promised to come back in a few days to talk with her again. A little later, when she slept, I tiptoed away.

Night after night the wistful image of Mrs. Sachs appeared before me. I made all sorts of excuses to myself for not going back. I was busy on other cases; I really did not know what to say to her or how to convince her of my own ignorance; I was helpless to avert such monstrous atrocities. Time rolled by and I did nothing.

The telephone rang one evening three months later, and Jake Sachs' agitated voice begged me to come at once; his wife was sick again and from the same cause. For a wild moment I thought of sending someone else, but actually, of course, I hurried into my uniform, caught up my bag, and started out. All the way I longed for a subway wreck, an explosion, anything to keep me from having to enter that home again. But nothing happened, even to delay me. I turned into the dingy doorway and climbed the familiar stairs once more. The children were there, young little things.

Mrs. Sachs was in a coma and died within ten minutes. I folded her still hands across her breast, remembering how they had pleaded with me, begging so humbly for the knowledge which was her right. I drew a sheet over her pallid face. Jake was sobbing, running his hands through his hair and pulling it out like an insane person. Over and over again he wailed, "My God! My God! My God!"

I left him pacing desperately back and forth, and for hours I myself walked and walked and walked through the hushed streets. When I finally arrived home and let myself quietly in, all the household was sleeping. I looked out my window and down upon the dimly lighted city. Its pains and griefs crowded in upon me, a moving picture rolled before my eyes with photographic clearness: women writhing in travail to bring forth little babies; the babies themselves naked and hungry, wrapped in newspapers to keep them from the cold; six-year-old children with pinched, pale, wrinkled faces, old in concentrated wretchedness, pushed into gray and fetid cellars, crouching on stone floors, their small scrawny hands scuttling through rags, making lamp shades, artificial flowers; white coffins, black coffins, coffins, coffins interminably passing in never-ending succession. The scenes piled one upon another on another. I could bear it no longer.

As I stood there the darkness faded. The sun came up and threw its reflection over the house tops. It was the dawn of a new day in my life also. The doubt and questioning, the experimenting and trying, were now to be put behind me. I knew I could not go back merely to keeping people alive.

I went to bed, knowing that no matter what it might cost, I was finished with palliatives and superficial cures; I was resolved to seek out the root of evil, to do something to change the destiny of mothers whose reveries were vast as the sky.

CRITICAL EYE

▶ **For Discussion**

a. What is Sanger arguing regarding the notion of poverty and the lack of opportunities it affords women?

b. Was the distribution of birth control the best answer?

c. Does anyone have the right to determine that a segment of the population is overbreeding?

d. Are marriage and childbearing the best options for women?

▶ **Re-approaching the Reading**

If Sanger were a man, would her story change? How?

▶ **Writing Assignment**

What would happen in America if *Roe vs. Wade* were overturned?

NAOMI WOLF

The Making of a Slut

So much of the debate over issues relating to women and sexuality today is stereotypical, grinding together false dualisms of good and evil, saints and villains. All too often we discuss important issues such as teen pregnancy and date rape with a lot of name-calling but with too little real-life experience providing a background against which to measure myths and distortions.

Because sexual awakening for girls and sexuality for women are almost always complex, contextual and nuanced, I felt a need to "unpack" the statistics and the polemics. As a writer, I have faith in the power of stories to get at truths that numbers and political screeds can't reach. So this is my effort to tell some of the stories that statistics can't and that polemics won't.

Many women of my mother's generation told their stories of sexual coming-of-age in the shadow of the repressive hypocrisy of the fifties, and of "finding themselves" by casting off that era's inhibitions. For a quarter century, their conclusions have shaped our discussions of sex, women, and freedom. Those conclusions no longer fit the experiences of the two generations that have grown into womanhood during and after the sexual and feminist revolutions—generations whose experiences are sometimes so very different from those of their mothers that in some ways their stories are harder to tell, and, consequently, harder to learn from.

It is still more difficult to lay claim to the personal experiences of the slut than to those of the virgin. Women's sexual past is still materially used against them. This can happen in a court of law, a place of business, a congressional hearing, or an intimate negotiation. When someone's past "catches up with her," that woman is scapegoated and separated from the "good girls." But the punishment aimed at her inhibits all of us, and can keep us from actions ranging from charging a supervisor with sexual harassment to running for school board office to fighting for custody of children. And, in the wake of the sexual revolution, the line between "good" and "bad" girls is always shifting, keeping us unsteady, as it is meant to do.

It will not be safe for us to live comfortably in our skins until we say: "You can no longer separate us out one from another. We are all 'bad' girls."

In any group of girls, someone has to be the slut.

In our group, Dinah became the slut. She found that role—or rather, it found her—and she did not deign to fight it. She put it on with dignity.

We were fourteen and a half; it was our eighth-grade year at our junior high. After school, before she became an outcast, I used to go over to Dinah's house in the Fillmore District almost every day.

"The Making of a Slut" by Naomi Wolf. Reprinted by permission of the author.

She had the gift not only of inventing a more alluring world, but of extending it to others so they could see it too. When the two of us were alone, a glamour would descend on us. Dinah had a chewed-up collection of records of musicals, and for her these created an alternative world. Singing along with them, her pointed chin would lift upward as she sang, and her red-rimmed eyes would light up, and she would lose her tough scrapper quality. The headache-tight Lee jeans, the hair darkened with henna streaks, the pookah shell necklaces, the run-down hiking boots, would all disappear. She became Mary Martin in the South Seas or Auntie Mame loose on Manhattan.

But Dinah was the slut. She became the slut because of conditions so tangential that they could almost never have been, or could as easily have slipped the designation to someone else. She was poor; that is, poorer than the other white kids. And her body changed faster than many of the other girls'. Her breasts were large and high by seventh grade—but that visitation had come to other girls, too. It was how she decided to carry it that did her in.

She refused the good-girl slump, the binder held crosswise across her chest. She would not back down and rest her weight on her pelvis and ruin her line. Instead she flagrantly kept walking with her spine extended to her full height, her back slightly swayed. I understood what she was doing with her tailbone tucked under and her torso supple and erect like a figure on the prow of a ship, and her feet turned carefully out: she was being a star. She was thinking of the technique of stage movement that she was reading about in the books on drama, and trying always to imagine a fine filament connecting the top of her talented head to the heavens. She was walking always out to her public, graciously, for an encore. But there was no visual language in our world for a poor girl with big breasts walking tall except "slut."

By watching what happened to Dinah, we discovered that sex—for girls at least—was a game of musical chairs. It was very important to stay in the game, if always nervously moving; but finding yourself suddenly singled out was nothing short of fatal. And—just like that game—the rules that isolated one or another of us were arbitrary and capricious. One thing was certain: if you were targeted, no matter how randomly, whether you had moved not fast enough or too fast for the music, in some sure way your exclusion was your own fault.

Dinah was a spectacular dancer. On late afternoons, she could usually be found practicing steps alone in our school's shabby music room, head up, facing solemnly into the wall-length mirror. Dinah's kicks were higher and her splits deeper than those of any of the other girls over whom she towered in our class. She was more than disciplined with herself—she was almost brutal in the service of what she thought of, very levelly, as her art. There was a genre of teenage-girl novel in which a hardworking and usually orphaned ballet student pits her all to attain the great performance and accolades, and then a life of grace and ease. Dinah devoured these books.

It was no surprise that, when the call for cheerleader auditions went out, it provoked her competitive spirit. We were not the kind of girls to approach the cheerleader squad with straight faces. But the idea of a test—even more compellingly, a test of skill and charm—seduced us. Cheerleading was sexy, but for once it was a sexuality that was also absolutely safe for us.

The junior high school cheerleading squad would be chosen not by P.E. or drama teachers on the basis of physical skill, but rather, by a panel of regular subject teachers. These teachers thought of themselves as the conscience of the school. ("And," as one was overheard to say, "the cheerleaders represent the school.") They saw a heavily made-up girl,

Social Responsibility

in her short red-leather jacket and midriff cropped T-shirt, leaning against a graffiti-stained wall every afternoon with the guys in the band, smoking; and they thought they knew all about Dinah.

For weeks, Dinah prepared. She believed in merit. In the try-out red plush outfit that she had sewn herself, she played the role of "wholesome cheerleader"—the only jarring note being the crease of metallic blue eye shadow that, against the dictates of Seventeen magazine, she insisted on applying daily. On the afternoon of the tryout, Dinah was tense. But her performance of the two cheers was, insofar as such a crude and bouncy set piece could be, a star turn. She held out her arms to the dark and silent auditorium seats, pom-poms lifted in an exuberant V, and then swooped them low.

The panel of teachers sat in the center of the pit, in the otherwise empty auditorium, their faces impassive.

Then the other girls and I tried out, sheepishly, in jeans. None of us were any better than pedestrian in contrast to Dinah. We went back outside to wait for the panel's decision.

A secretary posted a typewritten list outside the gym door. She avoided our eyes. All the new members of the team consisted of commonly acknowledged "popular" older girls. And me. In a mostly poor and working-class school, almost all of the chosen were daughters of the middle class. And—in a student population that was mostly Chinese, Japanese, Filipino, or African American—almost all were white. Dinah was not even an alternate.

I felt sick.

Dinah looked at the list on the door. She made her "Judy Garland chin-out struggling" face, then laughed at herself. "You," she said, "don't know what to say."

She shrugged her shoulders under her leather jacket. "It's that I hang out with the wrong group, that's all," she said. She looked past me to the hills above the playground, and assumed the ironic detachment she was so good at. "Well," she said crisply, lighting a Marlboro and then making one perfect French curl of smoke, "it can't be because they think I don't know how to dance."

We filed to the bus stop together in silence. We had been classified differently and we knew it. Our companionship was never exactly the same again.

The girl named head cheerleader, called "the cutest girl in ninth grade" and paragon of her church group, was no angel. But her parents were "nice" and her clothes were good. The popular girls whom the teachers approved of often conducted their sexual experiences after sneaking away from their parents' cabanas on the white-sand beaches of family vacations. Dinah went out with nineteen-year-old store clerk motorcycle rockers and lay around on foam mattresses in garages.

Dinah got called a slut because she was too poor and she was too proud of her body, and, by implication, she was too proud of her sexuality.

By the time we reached high school, Dinah had found a new gang. They were mostly guys, the rough kind of guys. Class considerations, which were like invisible, undeniable hands moving us over a school-sized chessboard, directed Dinah to a whole new group of girls. The whole school spread rumors that girls in that gang had mastered every technique in *The Sensuous Woman*.

Years later, another woman who as a girl was familiar with what was becoming Dinah's world, said that fellatio was the first genuine adult skill she ever mastered except driving, and that it made her feel just as powerful, just as valuable and free of her childhood helplessness. She spoke about the feeling among the girls in that subculture that sex was a performance for the benefit of boys.

Dinah's reputation worsened as we got older. But I also guess from having known her that during the same time in her life that her name became a fixture on the boys' bathroom walls, she was probably studying and trying to keep her family life together. According to the junior high and high school grapevine, when she heard about the graffiti in the bathrooms that talked about her blow jobs, she thought it was funny. At least, I heard she laughed. I believed it. She liked to shock the world that had repudiated her.

By our junior year in high school, her clothes tighter and her makeup heavier than ever, Dinah still seemed proud, and she still carried herself with that head-held-high, fuck-you regalness. I don't know for sure what she was thinking because I stopped knowing her—the result of that adolescent social dynamic, when class or race or gender pulls friends apart, that is so irrevocable. Class had declared her a slut by fourteen, while she was still technically a virgin, and kept her there, and kept me and my other wild little middle-class friends safe. As she passed us in the halls, her face grew more and more impassive with every year. That still haunts me.

From her story, and the stories of so many others, I knew that "keeping control of my desire was the only key to keeping myself and my emerging identity safe." So much depended on my taking the careful, balanced paces of a tightrope walker. Go—but DON'T JUMP!!! Go, but go slow, and keep watching. Yet part of me wanted above all else the experience of shutting my eyes and falling through the air.

I knew I was dangerous to myself the day that I let a boy walk me home from school and drew me into the overgrown alley that ran alongside the stone staircase up the hill to my house. He pushed the hair away from my forehead and then kissed my forehead, as if to make everything all right. He kissed down the side of my face to the corner of my mouth, too shy to look me in the eyes, but moving always closer to my lips. All I had to do was turn my face up toward him, and hold perfectly still. It was the easiest important thing I had ever done.

I knew that arching my neck just a little meant, "That's all right; go on." His hand lay against my clavicle and then against my chest above my collar. Finally, he slid just the tips of his fingers not even to my breast but to the skin between that lay just inside the line of my clothing. Through my closed eyes, the light went red. He withdrew his hand and watched my face. Even as the cold air rippled my shirt, his fingerprints were still burning.

He was watching to see if it was all right. It wasn't all right. I was capable of anything. I was capable of being Dinah.

Almost every society punishes its sluts in its own ways. It's just that right now, our own sometimes pretends it does not. The summer that I went back home to ask my friends about our girlhoods, there was a rash of sex industry films coming out of Hollywood. *Striptease* and *Showgirls* were following their predecessor, *Pretty Woman*. Teenage girls were reading about how Demi Moore worked out for hours each day to play a stripper; how she would go to the strip joints and hang with the dancers to "get it right."

As we drove through the hills above Marin, I asked a friend who had grown up with us what she thought about those films. Her opinion was better informed than most of ours was, for she had spent time as a stripper, and later as a professional mistress. She embodied the contradiction we live under: a college-educated, happily married, community-minded woman with curly black hair, a hip way of wearing her tailored clothes, a timid grin—indistinguishable from any of the rest of our tribe. But by the standards of the culture she had been a real whore, a true, dyed-in-the-wool, no-argument, verifiable slut. She had gone all the way. The bad girl, the good girl—

the dimorphism was a fantasy. They were both here in the car; in her, in myself, in us all.

As she drove, the carefree mood of two women in their early thirties thinking about girlhood in an open car, feet on the dashboard and reggae on the radio, evaporated. "Here is all I have to say about how they are glamorizing those images for girls, who are just sucking it in," she said. Her words became slow and deliberate. "When men think a woman is a whore, it's open . . . season . . . on her. They can say anything to her they want, they can do anything they want, they can be absolutely as crass and vile and violent and cruel and uncaring as the darkest part of their personality wants to be. And it's okay. They don't have to afford the woman one ounce of respect for being a human being. She's not a human being. She's a thing.

"Since the sexual revolution, there's a license, and there's terror, and we're living under . . . both."

Then the words came out in a torrent. "I was shocked. I was shocked. I thought that because of the progress that women have made in our society men would have a clue that prostitutes are human beings and that they don't deserve to be treated so poorly, but they don't. It's almost as if now they see sex workers as the only women that they can be so aggressive and cruel to. They can't get away with it in their jobs anymore, they can't get away with it in their marriages, but with sex workers, it's okay. That's what they're paid for! They're paid to be sexually harassed, they're paid to be assaulted. Women outside the sex industry won't put up with it anymore."

I was quiet. I was thinking: if all women, even nice women, can do what only whores used to do, but you can no longer treat all women who do such things like whores—that is, if feminism is succeeding at breaking down some of the penalties that used to be directed at nonprofessional, sexually licentious women—then society will all the more rigidly professionalize and demarcate the bad girl for sale, to whom anything can be done. My friend was explaining that "real" prostitutes used to bear the burden of the fact that nice girls had a limited repertoire; now they bear the burden of the fact that nice girls have gotten wild.

The feeling of foreboding that had hung over the word "slut" in my sexually libertine girlhood became clearer. The culture had said: Take it off. Take it all off. The culture had also said, of the raped girl, of the hitchhiker, of the dead girl: She was in the wrong place at the wrong time, doing the wrong thing.

Suddenly, as the soft round hills sped by, I saw flash before my eyes a photograph from one of the social histories I had been reading. It was of the nearly intact, mummified remains, dating from the first century a.d., of a fourteen-year-old German girl. Her long, shapely legs and slender feet were intact, and her right arm still clutched the garrote that had been used to twist the rope around her neck. Her lips were still in an O of surprise or pain, and a twisted rag was still securely bound against her eyes. At fourteen, the girl had been blindfolded, strangled, and drowned, most likely as retribution for "adultery"—for what we would call a teenage love affair.

Given these origins, it is no wonder that even today fourteen-year-old girls who notice, let alone act upon, desire have the heart-racing sense that they are doing something obscurely, but surely, dangerous. It is also in part because of this inheritance that a contemporary woman wakes up after a night of being erotically "out of control" feeling sure, on some primal level, that something punitive is bound to happen to her—and that if it doesn't, it should.

CRITICAL EYE

▶ For Discussion

a. Why are women held to a different sexual standard than men?

b. Are mothers now, in our modern-day society, more capable of speaking to their daughters about their own sexual experiences and desires?

c. Wolf argues that we make life very dangerous for the "bad girl." How is this true?

▶ Re-approaching the Reading

Imagine a world where all women embrace the title of "slut." How would such a feat affect gender relations in America?

▶ Writing Assignment

Can you argue that so-called "bad girls" are actually living Emerson's idea of being nonconformists?

CHAPTER 2

Death and Violence

A punishment to some, to some a gift, and to many a favor.
Lucius Annaeus Seneca

To answer brutality with brutality is to admit one's moral and intellectual bankruptcy, and it can only start a vicious cycle.
Mahatma Gandhi

Everything that lives dies. There is no escaping this reality. Birds, plants, fish, mammals—large and small—all, at some point, perish. Even though many variations of trees and reptiles may exist for what seems like forever, death is the only truly inevitable cycle for anything that breathes and grows. When it comes to people, Stewart Alsop's explanation seems right on: "A dying man needs to die, as a sleepy man needs to sleep, and there comes a time when it is wrong, as well as useless, to resist." If fortunate, death is about the end of days. If lucky, the race has been run and it is time to embrace the eternal rest. Whimsically speaking, the "internal clock will no longer reset," and "the end of the road is in sight." More succinctly put, we all hope and pray that when life is suspended and there is no more, it was "time."

Yet, as the world evolves and mankind pushes forward into this new millennium, there is an understood axiom that seems to be inescapable: earth's species will continue to reproduce, and human beings will, both indiscriminately and discriminately, try to kill them all. It does not matter if it grows out of the ground or swims in the ocean or soars through the sky or, even more tragically, looks just like themselves—humans have proven that nothing that breathes is sacred from their wrath. Since the dawn of time, man's reasons for violent behavior have ranged from accidental to self-defense to calculated murder. Unfortunately, as time progresses, women have proven that they too are capable of committing aggressively heinous acts, sometimes at the expense of their children.

Understandably, violence as a mode of preservation is not uncommon. Many would argue that these types of acts are necessary for the very survival of our species. As a matter of fact, few would deny that the defense of one's family—one's way of life, for that matter—is a right of the living. Killing for food actually speaks to the essence of perpetuating the species. Yet, we live in a world where cruelties—not those deeds that speak to survival—have become the norm. Everyday, we are bombarded by brutal and often sadistic images: children's games are now based on mayhem; the news, our lens into everyday living, relays the horrendous acts that plague our world; and murder sells books and music more than the idea of love and harmony ever has. This embracement suggests that our social media have become so steeped in the world of violence that we have learned to expect that a destructive hand will one day knock upon our door.

As a result, too often the end comes too soon: the loss of a child; a tragic mishap that ends someone's life before being fully lived; the ominous hand of murder and unexplainable loss. No matter what the causes—be they accident, crime, war, or mental illness—what seems fascinating about death and violence is not only how we die, or who else is involved, but how family and friends—often passersby—are forced to adjust and bereave in the aftermath.

The chosen selections in this chapter can in no way answer the question, "why must we die?" Instead, they ponder how death and violence—so often joined at the hip—are received and accepted, even measured out, across gender, class, and ethnic boundaries.

LINDA LOWEN

WHAT LASHANDA ARMSTRONG TEACHES US ABOUT TEEN PREGNANCY TEN YEARS OUT

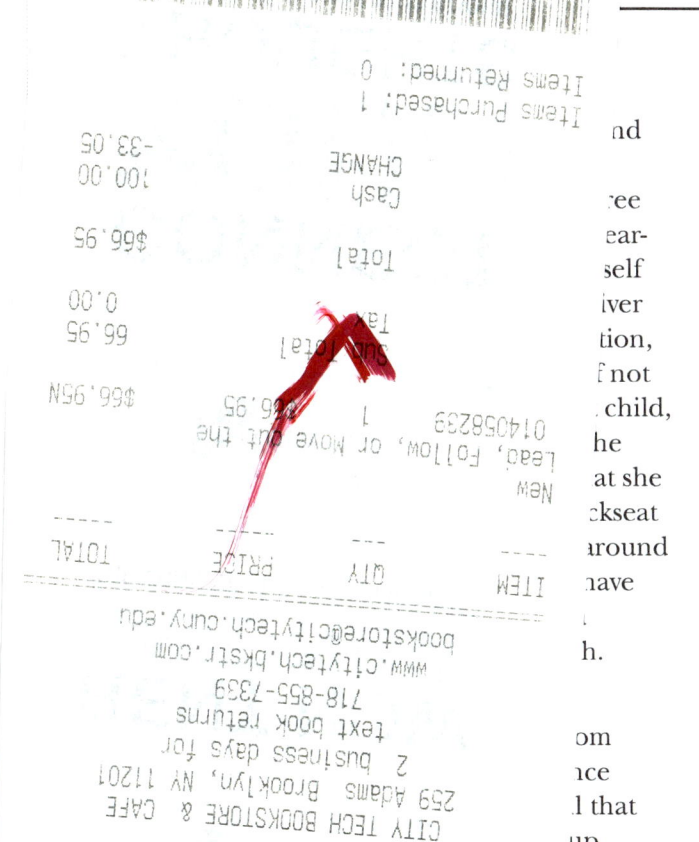

noted that the children were happy, polite, neatly dressed and well-cared for.

Here's the truth of the matter. Armstrong was the single mom of four children, 10, 5, 2 and 11 months. Newburgh was not her home town; she'd moved there from New Jersey to be with the father of her three youngest children, and they'd recently fought, so she had no support structure in place. She was not only a working mom but a student at the local community college, and often her day did not end until 10 PM. According to the *Los Angeles Times*, she was overwhelmed by trying to raise a family of 4 children alone and provide a decent life for them all.

Her story is heartbreaking but all too commonplace. The deck was stacked against her, beginning with the challenges she faced as a teen mother at age 15.

What LaShanda Armstrong represents is the face of teen mothers a decade down the road. It's one aspect of reality that shows like MTV's Teen Mom should be covering. The teen mothers MTV features may have struggles, but they're caring for just one child and most have their own parents to rely on—a critical safety net for teen moms trying to work and complete their education. Plus, they're receiving $60,000 in compensation, a point MTV never seems to mention.

Where will the cameras be 5 or 10 years down the road? Long gone and far away from the reality faced by women who give birth early and are stymied by a workplace that makes no allowances for single mothers and is especially

© 2012 Linda Lowen (http://womensissues.about.com/). Used with permission of About, Inc., which can be found line at www.about.com. All rights reserved.

challenging for under-educated single mothers. Imagine trying to balance schooling, working, and raising a family all by yourself. No wonder these women live in a state of constant pressure. This alone, notwithstanding the economic aspect, hampers their efforts to be good mothers.

This reality is echoed in a study of teenage mothers' children co-authored by Stefanie Molborn, Assistant Professor of Sociology at the University of Colorado at Boulder. Molborn finds that "compared to children of adult mothers, teenage mothers' children are disadvantaged across many domains. Their home environments have some greater risks, and their mothers' parenting behaviors are not rated as favorably. Many health and developmental measures at age 2 are compromised for teenage mothers' children."

Armstrong, by all accounts, did the best she could. When the father of her three youngest children allegedly showed abusive behavior, she attempted to get a restraining order against him.

Statistically speaking, none of this is a surprise. Teens who've had sex by age 14 are nearly four times more likely to be physically abused by their partners than teens who wait to have sex until 17 or 18.

Armstrong's partner also dodged child support payments, dumping the cost of raising four children solely on her. The fear of not being able to keep a roof over the family's head must have plagued Armstrong as she'd already had a car reposessed last year and clearly struggled financially. As Sophie Vorsburg, President of the National Child Support Foundation notes, non-payment of child support is a major cause of childhood poverty.

As I said earlier, this is not a post that blames LaShanda Armstrong. Instead, it's a wake-up call as to why becoming a teen mom is never a good idea, especially when compared to becoming a mother at age 20 or later.

According to the National Campaign to Prevent Teen Pregnancy, only 40% of teen mothers 17 and younger complete high school; less than 2% complete college by age 30. Women age 18–35 who have their first child at age 18–19 earn almost $70,000 less during that time period than women who wait until age 20–21 to have their first child; even in their early to mid 30s, these teen mothers earned on average $11,000 less per year than women who became mothers at age 20–21.

As a teen mom, LaShanda Armstrong started out at a disadvantage and her circumstances only worsened over time. For reasons we'll never fully know, something inside her snapped—something that made her believe death was the answer. This is not an excuse, but it is one possible answer to the question, "What would lead a mother to kill herself and her children?" A child giving birth to a child, too many children too young, too little money and too few prospects for a better life, the father of her children cheating on her, no child support and the threat of poverty always looming, a feeling of loneliness and of being overwhelmed—all of these contributed to the state of mind that convinced her there was nothing she could do to get out from under it.

As ample research shows, the odds would have been in her favor had she given birth at age 20 instead of 15. Being a teen mother didn't make her kill herself and her children, but it did create a climate in which she felt trapped, alone, desperate; and those feelings are likely shared by thousands of now-grown-up teen moms who understand Armstrong's tragic impulse. In both her unplanned pregnancy and her moment of madness she must have thought "What have I gotten myself into?" The former she endured alone, but the latter has become a national story that has moved us all.

It's heartbreaking to learn—from her son's account—that she came to her senses in the final seconds of life. But by then it was just too late.

CRITICAL EYE

▶ For Discussion

a. Is the journalist correct? Is there a danger attached to teen pregnancy when it comes to stereotyping, poverty, and depression?

b. Who failed LaShaundra the most: her parents, the school system, social services, or the law?

c. How much personal responsibility does LaShaundra bear for her circumstances and her death?

▶ Re-approaching the Reading

How can we take the plight of teen moms seriously when shows like *16 and Pregnant* and *Teen Mom* appear to glorify what happens to young mothers?

▶ Writing Assignment

In previous generations, there used to be a stigma attached to becoming a young mother out of wedlock. Can you argue that this new acceptance of young mothers is part of the problem?

TONI MORRISON

From the Novel
PARADISE

Set in the all Black town of Ruby, Oklahoma during the post-slavery decades of segregation and civil disobedience, **Paradise** *focuses on the a puritanical town of patriarchs and their desire to destroy five women beyond their reach. The following excerpt depicts the showdown between these self-proclaimed defenders of decency and the women they've come to massacre.*

This selection opens the novel and begins after the men have invaded this "female" space—a renovated convent previously used as a missionary school designed to "Americanize" young Native American girls. The reader is privy to the internal monologues of each of the men after they have gunned down the five female inhabitants.

They shoot the white girl first. With the rest they can take their time. No need to hurry out here. They are seventeen miles from a town which has ninety miles between it and any other. Hiding places will be plentiful in the Convent, but there is time and the day has just begun.

They are nine, over twice the number of the women they are obliged to stampede or kill and they have the paraphernalia for either requirement: rope, a palm leaf cross, handcuffs, Mace and sunglasses, along with clean, handsome guns.

They have never been this deep in the Convent. Some of them have parked Chevrolets near its porch to pick up a string of peppers or have gone into the kitchen for a gallon of barbecue sauce; but only a few have seen the halls, the chapel, the schoolroom, the bedrooms. Now they all will. And at last they will see the cellar and expose its filth to the light that is soon to scour the Oklahoma sky. Meantime they are startled by the clothes they are wearing—suddenly aware of being ill-dressed. For at the dawn of a July day how could they have guessed the cold that is inside this place? Their T-shirts, work shirts and dashikis soak up cold like fever. Those who have worn work shoes are unnerved by the thunder of their steps on marble floors; those in Pro-Keds by the silence. Then there is the grandeur. Only the two who are wearing ties seem to belong here and one by one each is reminded that before it was a Convent, this house was an embezzler's folly. A mansion where bisque and rose-tone marble floors segue into teak ones. Isinglass holds yesterday's light and patterns walls that were stripped and whitewashed fifty years ago. The ornate bathroom fixtures, which sickened the nuns, were replaced with good plain spigots, but the princely tubs and sinks, which could not be inexpensively removed, remain coolly corrupt. The embezzler's joy that could be demolished was, particularly in the dining room, which the nuns converted to a schoolroom, where stilled Arapaho girls once sat and learned to forget.

From *Paradise* by Toni Morrison, copyright © 1997 by Toni Morrison. Used by permission of Alfred A. Knopf, a division of Random House, Inc.

Now armed men search rooms where macramé baskets float next to Flemish candelabra; where Christ and His mother glow in niches trimmed in grapevines. The Sisters of the Sacred Cross chipped away all the nymphs, but curves of their marble hair still strangle grape leaves and tease the fruit. The chill intensifies as the men spread deeper into the mansion, taking their time, looking, listening, alert to the female malice that hides here and the yeast-and-butter smell of rising dough.

One of them, the youngest, looks back, forcing himself to see how the dream he is in might go. The shot woman, lying uncomfortably on marble, waves her fingers at him—or seems to. So his dream is doing okay, except for its color. He has never before dreamed in colors such as these: imperial black sporting a wild swipe of red, then thick, feverish yellow. Like the clothes of an easily had woman. The leading man pauses, raising his left hand to halt the silhouettes behind him. They stop, editing their breath, making friendly adjustments in the grip of rifles and handguns. The leading man turns and gestures the separations: you two over there to the kitchen; two more upstairs; two others into the chapel. He saves himself, his brother and the one who thinks he is dreaming for the cellar.

They part gracefully without words or haste. Earlier, when they blew open the Convent door, the nature of their mission made them giddy. But the target, after all, is detritus: throwaway people that sometimes blow back into the room after being swept out the door. So the venom is manageable now. Shooting the first woman (the white one) has clarified it like butter: the pure oil of hatred on top, its hardness stabilized below.

Outside, the mist is waist high. It will turn silver soon and make grass rainbows low enough for children's play before the sun burns it off, exposing acres of bluestem and maybe witch tracks as well.

The kitchen is bigger than the house in which either man was born. The ceiling barn-rafter high. More shelving than Ace's Grocery Store. The table is fourteen feet long if an inch, and it's easy to tell that the women they are hunting have been taken by surprise. At one end a full pitcher of milk stands near four bowls of shredded wheat. At the other end vegetable chopping has been interrupted: scallions piled like a handful of green confetti nestles brilliant disks of carrot, and the potatoes, peeled and whole, are bone white, wet and crisp. Stock simmers on the stove. It is restaurant size with eight burners and on a shelf beneath the great steel hood a dozen loaves of bread swell. A stool is overturned. There are no windows.

One man signals the other to open the pantry while he goes to the back door. It is closed but unlocked. Peering out he sees an old hen, her puffed and bloody hind parts cherished, he supposes, for delivering freaks—double, triple yolks in outsize and misshapen shells. Soft stuttering comes from the coop beyond; fryers padding confidently into the yard's mist disappear, reappear and disappear again, each flat eye indifferent to anything but breakfast. No footprints disturb the mud around the stone steps. This man closes the door and joins his partner at the pantry. Together they scan dusty mason jars and what is left of last year's canning: tomatoes, green beans, peaches. Slack, they think. August just around the corner and these women have not even sorted, let alone washed, the jars.

He turns the fire off under the stockpot. His mother bathed him in a pot no bigger than that. A luxury in the sod house where she was born. The house he lives in is big, comfortable, and this town is resplendent compared to his birthplace, which had gone from feet to belly in fifty years. From Haven, a dreamtown in Oklahoma Territory, to Haven, a ghosttown in Oklahoma State. Freedmen who stood tall in 1889 dropped to their knees in 1934 and were stomach-crawling by 1948. That is why they are here in this Convent. To make sure it never happens again. That nothing inside or out rots the one all-black town worth the pain. All the others he knew about or heard tell of knuckled to or merged with white towns; otherwise, like Haven, they had shriveled into tracery: foundation outlines marked by the way grass grew there, wallpaper turned negative behind missing windowpanes, schoolhouse floors moved aside by elder trees growing toward the bell housing. One thousand citizens in 1905 becoming five hundred by 1934. Then two hundred, then eighty as cotton collapsed or railroad companies laid their tracks elsewhere. Subsistence farming, once the only bounty a large family needed, became just scrap farming as each married son got his bit, which had to be broken up into more pieces for his children, until finally the owners of the bits and pieces who had not walked off in disgust welcomed any offer from a white speculator, so eager were they to get away and try someplace else. A big city this time, or a small town that was already built.

But he and the others, veterans all, had a different idea. Loving what Haven had been—the idea of it and its reach—they carried that devotion, gentling and nursing it from Bataan to Guam, from Iwo Jima to Stuttgart, and they made up their minds to do it again. He touched the stove hood admiring its construction and power. It was the same length as the brick oven that once sat in the middle of his hometown. When they got back to the States, they took it apart, carrying the bricks, the hearthstone and its iron plate two hundred and forty miles west—far far from the old Creek Nation which once upon a time a witty government called "unassigned land." He remembers the ceremony they'd had when the Oven's iron lip was recemented into place and its worn letters polished for all to see. He himself had helped clean off sixty-two years of carbon and animal fat so the words shone as brightly as they did in 1890 when they were new. And if it hurt—pulling asunder what their grandfathers had put together—it was nothing compared to what they had endured and what they might become if they did not begin anew. As new fathers, who had fought the world, they could not (would not) be less than the Old Fathers who had outfoxed it; who had not let danger or natural evil keep them from cutting Haven out of mud and who knew enough to seal their triumph with that priority. An Oven. Round as a head, deep as desire. Living in or near their wagons, boiling meal in the open, cutting sod and mesquite for shelter, the Old Fathers did that first: put most of their strength into constructing the huge, flawlessly designed Oven that both nourished them and monumentalized what they had done. When it was finished—each pale brick perfectly pitched; the chimney wide, lofty; the pegs and grill secure; the draft pulling steadily from the tail hole; the fire door plumb—then the ironmonger did his work. From barrel staves and busted axles, from kettles and bent nails, he fashioned an iron plate five feet by two and set it at the base of the Oven's mouth. It is still not clear where the words came from. Something he heard, invented, or something whispered to him while he slept curled over his tools in a wagon bed. His name was Morgan and who knew if he invented or stole the half-dozen or so words he forged. Words that seemed at first to bless them; later to confound them; finally to announce that they had lost.

The man eyes the kitchen sink. He moves to the long table and lifts the pitcher of milk. He sniffs it first and then, the pistol in his right hand, he uses his left to raise the pitcher to his mouth, taking such long, measured swallows the milk is half gone by the time he smells the wintergreen.

On the floor above two men walk the hall and examine the four bedrooms, each with a name card taped on its door. The first name, written in lipstick, is Seneca. The next, Divine, is inked in capital letters. They exchange knowing looks when they learn that each woman sleeps not in a bed, like normal people, but in a hammock. Other than that, and except for a narrow desk or an end table, there is no additional furniture. No clothes in the closets, of course, since the women wore no-fit dirty dresses and nothing you could honestly call shoes. But there are strange things nailed or taped to the walls or propped in a corner. A 1968 calendar, large X's marking various dates (April 4, July 19): a letter written in blood so smeary its satanic message cannot be deciphered; an astrology chart; a fedora tilted on the plastic neck of a female torso, and, in a place that once housed Christians—well. Catholics anyway—not a cross of Jesus anywhere. But what alarms the two men most is the series of infant booties and shoes ribboned to a cord hanging from a crib in the last bedroom they enter. A teething ring, cracked and stiff, dangles among the tiny shoes. Signaling with his eyes, one man directs his partner to four more bedrooms on the opposite side of the hall. He himself moves closer to the bouquet of baby shoes. Looking for what? More evidence? He isn't sure. Blood? A little toe, maybe, left in a white calfskin shoe? He slides the safety on his gun and joins the search across the hall.

These rooms are normal. Messy—the floor in one of them is covered with food-encrusted dishes, dirty cups, its bed invisible under a hill of clothes; another room sports two rocking chairs full of dolls; a third the debris and smell of a heavy drinker—but normal at least.

His saliva is bitter and although he knows this place is diseased, he is startled by the whip of pity flicking in his chest. What, he wonders, could do this to women? How can their plain brains think up such things: revolting sex, deceit and the sly torture of children? Out here in wide-open space tucked away in a mansion—no one to bother or insult them— they managed to call into question the value of almost every woman he knew. The winter coat money for which his father saved in secret for two harvests; the light in his mother's eyes when she stroked its seal collar. The surprise party he and his brothers threw for a sister's sixteenth birthday. Yet here, not twenty miles away from a quiet, orderly community, there were women like none he knew or ever heard tell of. In this place of all places. Unique and isolated, his was a town justifiably pleased with itself. It neither had nor needed a jail. No criminals had ever come from his town. And the one or two people who acted up, humiliated their families or threatened the town's view of itself were taken good care of. Certainly there wasn't a slack or sloven woman anywhere in town and the reasons, he thought, were clear. From the beginning its people were free and protected. A sleepless woman could always rise from her bed, wrap a shawl around her shoulders and sit on the steps in the moonlight. And if she felt like it she could walk out the yard and on down the road. No lamp and no fear. A hiss-crackle from the side of the road would never scare her because whatever it was that made the sound, it wasn't something creeping up on her. Nothing for ninety miles around thought she was prey. She could stroll as slowly as she liked, think of food preparations, war, of family things, or lift her eyes to stars and think of nothing at all. Lampless and without fear she could make her way. And if a light shone from a house up a ways and the cry of a colicky baby caught her attention, she might step over to the house and call out softly to the woman inside trying to soothe the baby. The two of them might take turns massaging the infant stomach, rocking, or trying to get a little soda water down. When the baby quieted they could sit together for a spell, gossiping, chuckling low so as not to wake anybody else.

The woman could decide to go back to her own house then, refreshed and ready to sleep, or she might keep her direction and walk further down the road, past other houses, past the three churches, past the feedlot. On out, beyond the limits of town, because nothing at the edge thought she was prey.

At each end of the hall is a bathroom. As each man enters one, neither is working his jaws because both believe they are prepared for anything. In one bathroom, the biggest, the taps are too small and dowdy for the wide sink. The bathtub rests on the backs of four mermaids— their tails split wide for the tub's security, their breasts arched for stability. The tile underfoot is bottle green. A Modess box is on the toilet tank and a bucket of soiled things stands nearby. There is no toilet paper. Only one mirror has not been covered with chalky paint and that one the man ignores. He does not want to see himself stalking females or their liquid. With relief he backs out and closes the door. With relief he lets his handgun point down.

CRITICAL EYE

▶ For Discussion

a. What distinctions does the narrator make between what makes a woman good or bad?

b. It is clear that the men who enter the convent are in conflict with these women and mean to do them harm. For these men, why does violence seem to be the "best" way to handle conflict rather than discussion?

▶ Re-approaching the Reading

The women in the text are seen as "bad" women/girls. Feminist critic Naomi Wolf suggests that there is, in fact, no such thing as a "bad girl" and, moreover, we have created the bad girl persona in order to have someone to mistreat. Taking this idea into consideration, determine whether or not these women are indeed "bad" or are simply living outside of the stereotypical female archetype.

▶ Writing Topic

As human beings, we often deal harshly with those we feel are encroaching upon our territory or are not following our social/cultural mores. Why is this?

GUY DE MAUPASSANT

MOTHER SAVAGE

I

It had been fifteen years since I had visited Virelogne. One autumn I returned to do some hunting and stayed with my friend Serval, who had finally rebuilt the château that the Prussians had destroyed.

I was madly in love with the area. It is one of those delightful corners of the world that possess a sensual appeal for the eyes. This is almost a physical kind of love. Those of us who are easily seduced by landscapes retain fond memories of certain springs, certain woods, certain streams, and certain hills which have become familiar to us and which can move our hearts like happy events. Sometimes our daydreams return to a wooded spot, or a riverbank, or an orchard bursting into blossom, seen only once on a lovely day but held in our hearts like images of women strolling the streets on a spring morning with fresh, clean faces, stirring body and soul with unrequited desire, with the unforgettable sensation of fleeting joy.

At Virelogne, I loved the whole countryside, dotted with little woods and traversed by streams that course though the soil like veins carrying blood to the earth. We fished for crawfish, for trout and eels. Such blessed happiness! There were spots to swim, and we could flush snipe from the tall weeds that grew along the banks of these narrow ribbons of water.

I walked along, lightly as a goat, watching my two dogs range in front of me. Serval, a hundred meters to my right, beat through a field of high grass. As I came around the bushes that mark the border of the Saudres Forest, I saw a thatched cottage in ruins.

Suddenly I recalled that I had seen it before, the last time in 1869, well kept up, covered with vines, and with a few chickens around the front door. What can be sadder than a dead house with its skeleton still standing, ruined and sinister?

I also recalled that the good woman who lived there had asked me in, one day when I was bone-tired, for a glass of wine, and that Serval had later told me the family history. The father, an old poacher, had been shot by the police. The son, whom I had seen before, was a tall, wiry fellow who also had a reputation as a fierce killer of game. They were called the Savages.

Was this their name or nickname?

I called out to Serval. He walked over to me with his long, ambling stride.

I asked him:

"What's become of the people who lived here?"

And he told me this story.

Gwynn, R.S., *Fiction: A Pocket Anthology*, (Penguin Academics Series), 4th Edition, © 2005. Reprinted by permission of Pearson Education Inc., Upper Saddle River, NJ. Printed and reproduced by permission of Pearson Education, Inc., Upper Saddle River, New Jersey.

II

When the war broke out, Mother Savage's son, who was then thirty-three years old, volunteered, leaving his mother all alone. However, no one felt sorry for the old woman because everybody knew that she had money.

So she lived by herself in her isolated cottage, far from the village at the edge of the forest. But she was not a bit afraid, being made of the same stuff as the men of the countryside—a hardy old woman, tall and gaunt, who seldom laughed and whom nobody dared to cross. The women of the countryside do not laugh much. That's the men's business! The souls of these women are melancholy and narrow, for their lives are dismal and rarely brightened by an hour of joy. The peasant husbands or sons enjoy a little noisy gaiety in taverns, but their wives or mothers remain serious, with perpetually severe expressions. The muscles of their faces have never learned the movements of laughter.

Mother Savage continued to live as she always had in her cottage, which was soon covered with snow. Once a week she used to come to the village to buy bread and meat, after which she would return home. As there was quite a bit of talk about wolves, she never went out without a gun slung on her shoulder, her son's rifle, a rusty weapon whose stock was quite worn from the hands that had rubbed against it; she made a strange sight, that tall old woman, a little stooped by age, walking with slow steps through the snow with the barrel of the gun sticking up behind the black scarf which covered her head and concealed the white hair that no one had ever seen.

One day the Prussians came. They were billeted with the people of the area, according to the wealth and resources of each family. The old woman had to take four of them because she was known to have money.

These were four big fellows with fair skin, blond beards, and blue eyes who had not grown thin in spite of all the wear and tear they had endured; they seemed to be good boys, even though they were in a conquered country. Finding themselves alone with the old woman, they took pains to show her all possible consideration and did everything they could to save her trouble or expense. You could see them every morning, all four of them, washing up at the well in their shirt sleeves, pouring great quantities of cold water over that fair, rosy Northern skin of theirs even on the days when it was snowing most heavily—while Mother Savage came and went, getting their soup ready. Later they could be seen cleaning up the kitchen, washing windows, chopping wood, peeling potatoes, washing linen—in short, doing all the chores like four good boys working for their own mother.

But the old woman was always thinking of her own son—her tall, gaunt boy with his hooked nose and brown eyes and thick mustache that seemed to cover his upper lip like a pelt of black fur. And every day she used to ask the four soldiers quartered in her home, "Do you know where that French regiment is, the 23rd of the line? My son is in it."

They would reply, "No, not know, not nothing." And sensing her pain and fear, they, who had mothers far away themselves, showed her a thousand little courtesies. She liked them well enough, too, those four enemies of hers; for country people do not as a rule feel patriotic hatred—those feelings are reserved for the upper classes. The humble folk—those who pay the most because they are poor and are always being weighed down with new burdens, those who are slaughtered wholesale, those who make up the real cannon fodder because there are so many of them, those who, to tell the truth, suffer most hideously from the miserable atrocities of war because they are the most vulnerable and the least powerful—such people do not understand war fever or the fine points of military honor or, even less, those so-called political necessities which exhaust two nations in six months, both victor and vanquished alike.

Speaking of Mother Savage's Germans, folks in the area would say, "Well, those four landed in a safe enough spot."

One morning while Mother Savage was at home alone, she caught sight of a man far off across the fields, hurrying towards her gate. He soon came near enough for her to recognize him: it was the rural postman. He handed her a sheet of folded paper, and she took her glasses, which she always wore when sewing, out of their case, and read:

> *Madam Savage,*
> *This letter has a sad story to tell you. Your boy Victor was killed yesterday by a cannonball, which cut him practically in two. I was right there when it happened, for we stood next to each other in line and he was always talking to me about you so that I could let you know at once if he had any bad luck.*
> *I took his watch out of his pocket to bring to you when the war is over.*
> *Cordially,*
> *Césaire Rivot, Private Second Class in the Twenty-third Regiment of the Line*

The letter was dated three weeks earlier.

She did not cry. She remained motionless, so overwhelmed, so stupefied by the blow that she did not immediately feel anything. She thought, "There's Victor, and now he's been killed." Then, little by little, tears slowly rose in her eyes, and sorrow invaded her heart. Thoughts came to her, one after the other—frightful, torturing ones. She would never kiss him again, her only child, her big, tall boy—never! The police had killed his father, and now the Prussians had killed the son . . . he had been cut in two by a cannonball. And it seemed to her she could see it all, the whole horrible thing: his head falling with his eyes wide open, his teeth still gnawing the corners of his thick mustache the way he used to do when he was angry.

What had they done afterward with his body? Couldn't they have brought her son back the same way they brought her husband back to her, with a bullet hole in the middle of his forehead?

But then she heard the sound of loud voices. It was the Prussians returning from the village. Quickly she hid the letter in her pocket and met them very calmly with her usual expression, for she had managed to wipe her eyes.

All four of them were laughing, quite delighted that they had been able to bring home a fine rabbit—doubtless stolen—and they made signs to the old woman that they were all going to have something really good to eat.

She set to work at once to prepare their dinner, but when the time came to kill the rabbit she did not have the heart to do it. Yet surely this wasn't the first rabbit she had ever been given to kill! One of the soldiers knocked it out by striking it behind the ears with his hand. Once it was dead she pulled the red body out of its skin, but the sight of the blood she was handling, which covered her fingers—the warm blood that she could feel cooling and coagulating—made her tremble from head to toe; all the while she kept seeing her tall son, cut in two and all red just like the body of the still quivering animal.

She sat down at the table with her Prussians, but she could not eat, not so much as a mouthful. They devoured the rabbit without paying any attention to her. Meanwhile she watched them from the corners of her eyes, not speaking—turning an idea over and over in her head, but with such an impassive face that none of them noticed anything unusual.

All of a sudden she said, "I don't even know your names, and we've been together for a whole month." They understood, with some difficulty, what she wanted and told her their names. But that was not enough; she made them write them down on a piece of paper along with the addresses of their families, and, placing her reading glasses on her big nose, she looked over the foreign writing; then she folded up the paper and put it into her pocket, next to the letter which had told her about the death of her son.

When the meal was over she said to them:

"Now I'm going to do something for you."

And she started carrying straw up into the loft where they slept.

They thought this was rather strange, but when she explained to them that it would keep them warmer they helped her. They stacked the bales all the way up to the thatched ceiling and made themselves a sort of large room with four walls of forage, warm and fragrant, where they could sleep peacefully.

At supper one of them became worried that Mother Savage still had not eaten anything. She told him that she had stomach cramps. Then she lit a good fire to warm herself, and the four Germans climbed up into their loft on the ladder they used every evening.

As soon as they had closed the trapdoor, the old woman took away the ladder, and, going outside without a sound, she began to collect straw and filled her kitchen with it. She walked barefoot through the snow—so softly that no one could hear her. From time to time she heard the loud and fitful snoring of the four sleeping soldiers.

When she decided that her preparations were complete, she thrust one of the bundles of straw into the fire, then flung the burning handful on top of the others and went outside to watch.

In several seconds a fierce glare lit the inside of the cottage; then the whole thing became a terrible furnace, a gigantic oven whose violent light blazed through the single narrow window and sent a bright ray reflecting over the snow.

Loud cries rang out from the upper part of the house. Then they were followed by a clamor of human screams full of agony and terror. Then, the trapdoor having been lifted, a storm of flame roared up into the loft, burnt through the roof of straw, rose up to the heavens like a vast bonfire, and the whole cottage went up in flames.

Nothing could now be heard but the crackling of the fire, the crumbling of the walls, the falling of the beams. The last fragments of the roof fell in, and the red-hot shell of the dwelling flung a huge shower of sparks skyward through clouds of thick smoke.

The snow-covered fields, lit up by the fire, shone like a sheet of silver tinged with crimson.

Far away, a bell began to ring.

Old Mother Savage stood at attention in front of the ruins of her home, armed with a gun, her dead son's rifle, to make sure that none of them could escape.

When she saw that it was all over, she threw the weapon into the fire. A single shot rang out.

People came running to the scene—the neighbors, the Prussian soldiers.

They found the old woman sitting on a tree stump, calm and satisfied.

A German officer, who spoke French like a son of France, asked her:

"Where are your soldiers?"

She stretched out her skinny arm towards the smoldering mass of ruins where the fire was dying down at last and answered in a strong voice:

"There! Inside!"

Everyone gathered around her. The Prussian asked:

"How did the fire start?"

She answered:

"I started it."

They could not believe her, and they thought that the disaster had driven her mad. Then, when everyone had moved closer to listen to her, she told the whole story from beginning to end—from the arrival of the letter down to the final screams of the burning men inside her house. She did not leave out a single detail of what she had felt and what she had done.

When she finished, she took two pieces of paper out of her pocket and, so she could tell one from the other by the last light of the fire, adjusted her glasses and announced, holding up one piece of paper, "This one is Victor's death." Holding up the other, she added, nodding her head towards the still-red ruins, "This one has their names on it so you can write home about them." She calmly handed the white sheet to the officer, who was now holding her by the shoulders, and she continued:

"You can write them how this all happened, and you can tell their parents that I was the one who did it—I, Victoire Simon, The Savage! Never forget it."

The officer screamed some orders in German. They seized her and pushed her up against the still-warm walls of her house. Then a dozen men lined up in front of her, twenty meters away. She never blinked an eye. She knew what was coming, and she waited.

An order rang out, followed by a loud volley. One shot echoed all by itself after the others.

The old woman did not fall. She sank straight down as though her legs had been cut away from under her.

The Prussian officer approached to look. She had been cut almost in two, and her stiffened fingers still clutched the letter, bathed in blood.

III

My friend Serval added, "In reprisal, the Germans destroyed the local château, which I owned."

For my own part, I thought about the mothers of those four poor boys who had burned inside, and of the terrible heroism of that other mother, shot dead against that wall.

And I picked up a little stone, which still bore the scorch marks of the fire.

—1884

CRITICAL EYE

▶ For Discussion

a. Does a parent have the right to seek revenge after their child has been harmed?

b. Does an act of revenge actually remedy a problem?

c. Consider the case of Trayvon Martin. What is unique or important about the way his parents have chosen to speak for their son since his death?

▶ Re-approaching the Reading

Locate a copy of Luigi Pirandello's short-story "War." Why is the mother in "Mother Savage" unable to reconcile her grief the way the parents in "War" are?

▶ Writing Assignment

Our entire legal system exists not only to determine guilt or innocence, but also to punish those it deems guilty of a crime. How is it any different than the mother who acts as judge, jury, and executioner?

IRENE ZABYTKO

HOME SOIL

I watch my son crack his knuckles, oblivious to the somber sounds of the Old Slavonic hymns the choir behind us is singing.

We are in the church where Bohdan, my son, was baptized nineteen years ago. It is Sunday. The pungent smell of frankincense permeates the darkened atmosphere of this cathedral. Soft sun rays illuminate the stained-glass windows. I sit near the one that shows Jesus on the cross looking down on some unidentifiable Apostles who are kneeling beneath His nailed feet. In the background, a tiny desperate Judas swings from a rope, the thirty pieces of silver thrown on the ground.

There is plenty of room in my pew, but my son chooses not to sit with me. I see him staring at the round carapace of a ceiling, stoic icons staring directly back at him. For the remainder of the Mass, he lightly drums his nervous fingers on top of the cover of *My Divine Friend*, the Americanized prayer book of the Ukrainian service. He took bongo lessons before he graduated high school, and learned the basic rolls from off a record, "Let's Swing with Bongos." I think it was supposed to make him popular with the girls at parties. I also think he joined the army because he wanted the virile image men in uniforms have that the bongos never delivered. When he returned from Nam, he mentioned after one of our many conversational silences that he lost the bongos, and the record is cracked, with the pieces buried somewhere deep inside the duffel bag he still hasn't unpacked.

Bohdan, my son, who calls himself Bob, has been back for three weeks. He looks so "American" in his green tailored uniform: his spit-shined vinyl dress shoes tap against the red-cushioned kneelers. It was his idea to go to church with me. He has not been anywhere since he came home. He won't even visit my garden.

Luba, my daughter, warned me he would be moody. She works for the Voice of America and saw him when he landed from Nam in San Francisco, "Just don't worry tato,"° she said to me on the telephone. "He's acting weird. Culture shock."

"Explain what you mean."

"Just, you know, strange." For a disc jockey, and a bilingual one at that, she is so inarticulate. She plays American jazz and tapes concerts for broadcasts for her anonymous compatriots in Ukraine. That's what she was doing when she was in San Francisco, taping some jazz concert. Pure American music for the huddled gold-toothed youth who risk their *komsomol* privileges and maybe their lives listening to these clandestine broadcasts and to my daughter's sweet voice. She will never be able to visit our relatives back there because American security won't allow it, and she would lose her job. But that doesn't matter.

"Home Soil" by Irene Zabytko from *The Perimeter of Light* edited by Vivian Vie Balfour. Copyright © 1992 New Rivers Press. Reprinted by permission. All rights reserved.

tato: "Father" or "Dad."

Death and Violence

After my wife died, I have not bothered to keep up with anyone there, and I don't care if they have forgotten all about me. It's just as well.

I noticed how much my son resembled my wife when I first saw him again at the airport. He was alone, near the baggage claim ramp. He was taller than ever, and his golden hair was bleached white from the jungle sun. He inherited his mother's high cheekbones, but he lost his baby fat, causing his cheeks to jut out from his lean face as sharp as the arrowheads he used to scavenge for when he was a kid.

We hugged briefly. I felt his medals pinch through my thin shirt "You look good, son," I lied. I avoided his eyes and concentrated on a pin shaped like an open parachute that he wore over his heart.

"Hi, *tato*," he murmured. We spoke briefly about his flight home from San Francisco, how he'd seen Luba. We stood apart, unlike the other soldiers with their families who were hugging and crying on each other's shoulders in a euphoric delirium.

He grabbed his duffle bag from the revolving ramp and I walked behind him to see if he limped or showed any signs of pain. He showed nothing.

"Want to drive?" I asked, handing him the keys to my new Plymouth.

"Nah," he said. He looked around at the cars crowding the parking lot, and I thought he seemed afraid. "I don't remember how the streets go anymore."

An usher in his best borscht-red polyester suit waits for me to drop some money into the basket. It is old Pan° Medved, toothless except for the prominent gold ones he flashes at me as he pokes me with his basket.

"*Nu*, give," he whispers hoarsely, but loud enough for a well-dressed woman with lacquered hair who sits in front of me to turn around and stare in mute accusation.

I take out the gray and white snakeskin wallet Bohdan brought back for me, and transfer out a ten dollar bill. I want the woman to see it before it disappears into the basket. She smiles at me and nods.

Women always smile at me like that. Especially after they see my money and find out that I own a restaurant in the neighborhood. None of the Ukies° go there; they don't eat fries and burgers much. But the "jackees"—the Americans—do when they're sick of eating in the cafeteria at the plastics factory. My English is pretty good for a D.P., and no one has threatened to bomb my business because they accuse me of being a no-good bohunk commie. Not yet anyway.

But the women are always impressed. I usually end up with the emigrés—some of them Ukrainians. The Polish women are the greediest for gawdy trinkets and for a man to give them money so that they can return to their husbands and children in Warsaw. I like them the best anyway because they laugh more than the other women I see, and they know how to have a good time.

Bohdan knows nothing about my lecherous life. I told the women to stay clear after my son arrived. He is so lost with women. I think he was a virgin when he joined the army, but I'm sure he isn't now. I can't ask him.

After mass ends, I lose Bohdan in the tight clusters of people leaving their pews and genuflecting toward the iconostasis. He waits for me by the holy water font. It looks like a regular porcelain water fountain but without a spout. There is a sponge in the basin that is moistened with the holy water blessed by

---

Pan: a term of respect for adult males, the equivalent of Mr.
Ukies: Ukrainian Americans.

the priests here. Bohdan stands towering over the font, dabs his fingers into the sponge, but doesn't cross himself the way he was taught to do as a boy.

"What's the matter?" I ask in English. I hope he will talk to me if I speak to him in his language.

But Bohdan ignores me and watches an elderly woman gingerly entering the door of the confessional. "What she got to say? Why is she going in there?"

"Everyone has sins."

"Yeah, but who forgives?"

"God forgives," I say. I regret it because it makes me feel like a hypocrite whenever I parrot words I still find difficult to believe.

We walk together in the neighborhood; graffiti visible in the alley-ways despite the well-trimmed lawns with flowers and "bathtub" statues of the Blessed Mary smiling benevolently at us as we pass by the small bungalows. I could afford to move out of here, out of Chicago and into some nearby cushy suburb, Skokie or something. But what for? Some smart Jewish lawyer or doctor would be my next door neighbor and find out that I'm a Ukie and complain to me about how his grandmother was raped by Petliura.° I heard it before. Anyway, I like where I am. I bought a three-flat apartment building after my wife died and I live in one of the apartments rent-free. I can walk to my business, and see the past—old women in babushkas sweeping the sidewalks in front of their cherished gardens; men in Italian-made venetian-slat sandals and woolen socks rushing to a chess match at the Soyuiez, a local meeting place where the D.P.s sit for hours rehashing the war over beers and chess.

Bohdan walks like a soldier. Not exactly a march, but stiff gait that a good posture in a rigid uniform demands. He looks masculine, but tired and worn. Two pimples are sprouting above his lip where a faint moustache is starting.

"Want a cigarette?" I ask. Soldiers like to smoke. During the forties, I smoked that horrible cheap tobacco, *mahorka*. I watch my son puff heavily on the cigarette I've given him, with his eyes partially closed, delicately cupping his hands to protect it from the wind. In my life, I have seen so many soldiers in that exact pose; they all look the same. When their faces are contorted from sucking the cigarette, there is an unmistakable shadow of vulnerability and fear of living. That gesture and stance are more eloquent than the blood and guts war stories men spew over their beers.

Pan Medved, the battered gold-toothed relic in the church, has that look. Pan Holewski, one of my tenants, has it too. I would have known it even if he never openly displayed his old underground soldier's cap that sits on a bookshelf in the living room between small Ukrainian and American flags. I see it every time I collect the rent.

I wish Bohdan could tell me what happened to him in Vietnam. What did he do? What was done to him? Maybe now isn't the time to tell me. He may never tell me. I never told anyone either.

I was exactly his age when I became a soldier. At nineteen, I was a student at the university in L'vov, which the Poles occupied. I was going to be a poet, to study poetry and write it, but the war broke out, and my family could not live on the romantic epics I tried to publish, so I was paid very well by the Nazis to write propaganda pamphlets "Freedom for Ukrainians" I wrote "Freedom for our people. Fight the Poles and Russians alongside our German brothers"

Petliura: Simeon Petliura (1879–1926), an anti-Bolshevik Ukrainian leader who was accused of responsibility for Jewish pogroms during World War I. When his forces were defeated by the Russians he went into exile in Paris where he was ultimately assassinated by a Jewish nationalist.

and other such dreck. I even wrote light verse that glorified Hitler as the protector of the free Ukrainian nation that the Germans promised us. My writing was as naïve as my political ideas.

My new career began in a butcher shop, commandeered after the Polish owner was arrested and shot. I set my battered Underwood typewriter atop an oily wooden table where crescents of chicken feathers still clung between the cracks. Meat hooks that once held huge sides of pork hung naked in a back room, and creaked ominously like a deserted gallows whenever anyone slammed the frontdoor. Every shred of meat had been stolen by looters after the Germans came into the city. Even the little bell that shopkeepers kept at the entrance was taken. But I was very comfortable in my surroundings. I thought only about how I was to play a part in a historical destiny that my valiant words would help bring about. That delusion lasted only about a week or so until three burly Nazis came in. "*Schnell!*" they said to me, pushing me out of my chair and pointing to the windows where I saw crowds chaotically swarming about. Before I could question the soldiers, one of them shoved a gun into my hands and pushed me out into the streets. I felt so bewildered until the moment I pointed my rifle at a man who was about—I thought—to hit me with a club of some sort. Suddenly, I felt such an intense charge of power, more so than I had ever felt writing some of my best poems. I was no longer dealing with abstract words and ideas for a mythological cause; I was responsible for life and death.

I enjoyed that power, until it seeped into my veins and poisoned my soul. It was only an instant, a brief interlude, a matter of hours until that transformation occurred. I still replay that scene in my mind almost forty years after it happened, no matter what I am doing, or who I am with.

I think she was a village girl. Probably a Jew, because on that particular day, the Jews were the ones chosen to be rounded up and sent away in cattle cars. Her hair was golden red, short and wavy as was the style, and her neck was awash in freckles. It was a crowded station in the center of the town, not far from the butcher shop. There were Germans shouting and women crying and church bells ringing. I stood with that German regulation rifle I hardly knew how to handle, frozen because I was too lightheaded and excited. I too began to yell at people and held the rifle against my chest, and I was very much aware of how everyone responded to my authority.

Then, this girl appeared in my direct line of vision. Her back was straight, her shoulders tensed; she stopped in the middle of all the chaos. Simply stopped. I ran up and pushed her. I pushed her hard, she almost fell. I kept pushing her, feeling the thin material of her cheap wool jacket against my chapped eager hand; her thin muscles forced forward by my shoves. Once, twice, until she toppled into the open door of a train and fell toward a heap of other people moving deeper into the tiny confines of the stinking cattle car. She never turned around.

I should have shot her. I should have spared her from whatever she had to go through. I doubt she survived. I should have tried to find out what her name was, so I could track down her relatives and confess to them. At least in that way, they could have spat at me in justice and I would have finally received the absolution I will probably never find in this life.

• • •

I don't die. Instead, I go to the garden. It is Sunday evening. I am weeding the crop of beets and cabbages I planted in the watch in my backyard. The sun is lower, a breeze kicks up around me, but my forehead sweats. I breathe in the thick deep earth smells as the dirt crumbles and rotates against the blade of my hoe. I should destroy the honeysuckle vine that is slowly choking my plants, but the scent is so sweet, and its intoxicating perfume reminds me of a woman's gentleness.

I hoe for a while, but not for long, because out of the corner of my eye, I see Bohdan sitting on the grass tearing the firm green blades with his clenched hands. He is still wearing his uniform, all except the jacket, tie, and cap. He sits with his legs apart, his head down, ignoring the black flies that nip at his ears.

I wipe my face with a bright red bandana, which I brought with me to tie up the stalks of my drooping sunflowers. "Bohdan," I say to my son. "Why don't we go into the house and have a beer. I can finish this another time." I look at the orange sun. "It's humid and there's too many flies—means rain will be coming."

My son is quietly crying to himself.

"*Tato*, I didn't know anything," he cries out. "You know, I just wanted to jump out from planes with my parachute. I just wanted to fly . . ."

"I should have stopped you," I say more to myself than to him. Bohdan lets me stroke the thin spikes of his army regulation crew-cut which is soft and warm and I am afraid of how easily my hand can crush his skull.

I rock him in my arms the way I saw his mother embrace him when he was afraid to sleep alone.

There is not much more I can do right now except to hold him. I will hold him until he pulls away.

CRITICAL EYE

▶ For Discussion

a. It is one thing to survive a life-or-death situation; it is quite another to hold the life and death of another human being in your hands. According to this story, which is worse? Is there really any difference at all?

b. How is it that experiencing something as overwhelming as war can cause someone to question his or her faith?

▶ Re-approaching the Reading

During the events of 9/11, strangers opened their hearts to their fellow country men and women. During natural disasters, people across economic, racial, and cultural divides open their wallets to aid those in need. We wish to believe that we present our best selves in times of trauma. As you see it, is this true?

▶ Writing Assignment

Once an adult child experiences a traumatic event that irrevocably changes his or her life, is there anything that a parent can do to make the child feel safe again?

MARK TWAIN

From the Novel
ADVENTURES OF HUCKLEBERRY FINN
Chapters 21–22 excerpted

Chapter XXI.

The nearer it got to noon that day the thicker and thicker was the wagons and horses in the streets, and more coming all the time. Families fetched their dinners with them from the country, and eat them in the wagons. There was considerable whisky drinking going on, and I seen three fights. By and by somebody sings out:

"Here comes old Boggs!—in from the country for his little old monthly drunk; here he comes, boys!"

All the loafers looked glad; I reckoned they was used to having fun out of Boggs. One of them says:

"Wonder who he's a-gwyne to chaw up this time. If he'd a-chawed up all the men he's ben a-gwyne to chaw up in the last twenty year he'd have considerable ruputation now."

Another one says, "I wisht old Boggs 'd threaten me, 'cuz then I'd know I warn't gwyne to die for a thousan' year."

Boggs comes a-tearing along on his horse, whooping and yelling like an Injun, and singing out:

"Cler the track, thar. I'm on the waw-path, and the price uv coffins is a-gwyne to raise."

He was drunk, and weaving about in his saddle; he was over fifty year old, and had a very red face. Everybody yelled at him and laughed at him and sassed him, and he sassed back, and said he'd attend to them and lay them out in their regular turns, but he couldn't wait now because he'd come to town to kill old Colonel Sherburn, and his motto was, "Meat first, and spoon vittles to top off on."

He see me, and rode up and says:

"Whar'd you come f'm, boy? You prepared to die?"

Then he rode on. I was scared, but a man says:

"He don't mean nothing; he's always a-carryin' on like that when he's drunk. He's the best naturedest old fool in Arkansaw—never hurt nobody, drunk nor sober."

Boggs rode up before the biggest store in town, and bent his head down so he could see under the curtain of the awning and yells:

"Come out here, Sherburn! Come out and meet the man you've swindled.

You're the houn' I'm after, and I'm a-gwyne to have you, too!"

And so he went on, calling Sherburn everything he could lay his tongue to, and the whole street packed with people listening and laughing and going on. By and by a proud-looking man about fifty-five–and he was a heap the best dressed man in that town, too—steps out of the store, and the crowd drops back on each side to let him come. He says to Boggs, mighty ca'm and slow—he says:

"I'm tired of this, but I'll endure it till one o'clock. Till one o'clock, mind—no longer. If you open your mouth against me only once after that time you can't travel so far but I will find you."

Then he turns and goes in. The crowd looked mighty sober; nobody stirred, and there warn't no more laughing. Boggs rode off blackguarding Sherburn as loud as he could yell, all down the street; and pretty soon back he comes and stops before the store, still keeping it up. Some men crowded around him and tried to get him to shut up, but he wouldn't; they told him it would be one o'clock in about fifteen minutes, and so he MUST go home–he must go right away. But it didn't do no good. He cussed away with all his might, and threwed his hat down in the mud and rode over it, and pretty soon away he went a-raging down the street again, with his gray hair a-flying. Everybody that could get a chance at him tried their best to coax him off of his horse so they could lock him up and get him sober; but it warn't no use–up the street he would tear again, and give Sherburn another cussing. By and by somebody says:

"Go for his daughter!—quick, go for his daughter; sometimes he'll listen to her. If anybody can persuade him, she can."

So somebody started on a run. I walked down street a ways and stopped. In about five or ten minutes here comes Boggs again, but not on his horse. He was a-reeling across the street towards me, bare-headed, with a friend on both sides of him a-holt of his arms and hurrying him along. He was quiet, and looked uneasy; and he warn't hanging back any, but was doing some of the hurrying himself. Somebody sings out:

"Boggs!"

I looked over there to see who said it, and it was that Colonel Sherburn. He was standing perfectly still in the street, and had a pistol raised in his right hand–not aiming it, but holding it out with the barrel tilted up towards the sky. The same second I see a young girl coming on the run, and two men with her. Boggs and the men turned round to see who called him, and when they see the pistol the men jumped to one side, and the pistol-barrel come down slow and steady to a level–both barrels cocked. Boggs throws up both of his hands and says, "O Lord, don't shoot!" Bang! goes the first shot, and he staggers back, clawing at the air–bang! goes the second one, and he tumbles backwards on to the ground, heavy and solid, with his arms spread out. That young girl screamed out and comes rushing, and down she throws herself on her father, crying, and saying, "Oh, he's killed him, he's killed him!" The crowd closed up around them, and shouldered and jammed one another, with their necks stretched, trying to see, and people on the inside trying to shove them back and shouting, "Back, back! give him air, give him air!"

Colonel Sherburn he tossed his pistol on to the ground, and turned around on his heels and walked off.

They took Boggs to a little drug store, the crowd pressing around just the same, and the whole town following, and I rushed and got a good place at the window, where I was close to him and could see in. They laid him on the floor and put one large Bible under his head, and opened another one and spread it on his breast; but they tore open his shirt first, and I seen where one of the bullets went in. He made about a dozen long gasps, his breast lifting the Bible up when he drawed in his breath, and letting it down again when he breathed it out—and after that he laid still; he was dead. Then they pulled his daughter away from him, screaming and crying, and took her off. She was about sixteen, and very sweet and gentle looking, but awful pale and scared.

Well, pretty soon the whole town was there, squirming and scrouging and pushing and shoving to get at the window and have a look, but people that had the places wouldn't give them up, and folks behind them was saying all the time, "Say, now, you've looked enough, you fellows; 'tain't right and 'tain't fair for you to stay thar all the time, and never give nobody a chance; other folks has their rights as well as you."

There was considerable jawing back, so I slid out, thinking maybe there was going to be trouble. The streets was full, and everybody was excited. Everybody that seen the shooting was telling how it happened, and there was a big crowd packed around each one of these fellows, stretching their necks and listening. One long, lanky man, with long hair and a big white fur stovepipe hat on the back of his head, and a crooked-handled cane, marked out the places on the ground where Boggs stood and where Sherburn stood, and the people following him around from one place to t'other and watching everything he done, and bobbing their heads to show they understood, and stooping a little and resting their hands on their thighs to watch him mark the places on the ground with his cane; and then he stood up straight and stiff where Sherburn had stood, frowning and having his hat-brim down over his eyes, and sung out, "Boggs!" and then fetched his cane down slow to a level, and says "Bang!" staggered backwards, says "Bang!" again, and fell down flat on his back. The people that had seen the thing said he done it perfect; said it was just exactly the way it all happened. Then as much as a dozen people got out their bottles and treated him.

Well, by and by somebody said Sherburn ought to be lynched. In about a minute everybody was saying it; so away they went, mad and yelling, and snatching down every clothes-line they come to to do the hanging with.

Chapter XXII.

They swarmed up towards Sherburn's house, a-whooping and raging like Injuns, and everything had to clear the way or get run over and tromped to mush, and it was awful to see. Children was heeling it ahead of the mob, screaming and trying to get out of the way; and every window along the road was full of women's heads, and there was nigger boys in every tree, and bucks and wenches looking over every fence; and as soon as the mob would get nearly to them they would break and skaddle back out of reach. Lots of the women and girls was crying and taking on, scared most to death.

They swarmed up in front of Sherburn's palings as thick as they could jam together, and you couldn't hear yourself think for the noise. It was a little twenty-foot yard. Some sung out "Tear down the fence! tear down the fence!" Then there was a racket of ripping and tearing and smashing, and down she goes, and the front wall of the crowd begins to roll in like a wave.

Just then Sherburn steps out on to the roof of his little front porch, with a double-barrel gun in his hand, and takes his stand, perfectly ca'm and deliberate, not saying a word. The racket stopped, and the wave sucked back.

Sherburn never said a word—just stood there, looking down. The stillness was awful creepy and uncomfortable. Sherburn run his eye slow along the crowd; and wherever it struck the people tried a little to out-gaze him, but they couldn't; they dropped their eyes and looked sneaky. Then pretty soon Sherburn sort of laughed; not the pleasant kind, but the kind that makes you feel like when you are eating bread that's got sand in it.

Then he says, slow and scornful:

"The idea of YOU lynching anybody! It's amusing. The idea of you thinking you had pluck enough to lynch a MAN! Because you're brave enough to tar and feather poor friendless cast-out women that come along here, did that make you think you had grit enough to lay your hands on a MAN? Why, a MAN'S safe in the hands of ten thousand of your kind—as long as it's daytime and you're not behind him.

"Do I know you? I know you clear through was born and raised in the South, and I've lived in the North; so I know the average all around. The average man's a coward. In the North he lets anybody walk over him that wants to, and goes home and prays for a humble spirit to bear it. In the South one man all by himself, has stopped a stage full of men in the daytime, and robbed the lot. Your newspapers call you a brave people so much that you think you are braver than any other people—whereas you're just AS brave, and no braver. Why don't your juries hang murderers? Because they're afraid the man's friends will shoot them in the back, in the dark—and it's just what they WOULD do.

"So they always acquit; and then a MAN goes in the night, with a hundred masked cowards at his back and lynches the rascal. Your mistake is, that you didn't bring a man with you; that's one mistake, and the other is that you didn't come in the dark and fetch your masks. You brought PART of a man—Buck Harkness, there—and if you hadn't had him to start you, you'd a taken it out in blowing.

"You didn't want to come. The average man don't like trouble and danger. YOU don't like trouble and danger. But if only HALF a man—like Buck Harkness, there—shouts 'Lynch him! lynch him!' you're afraid to back down—afraid you'll be found out to be what you are—COWARDS—and so you raise a yell, and hang yourselves on to that half-a-man's coat-tail, and come raging up here, swearing what big things you're going to do. The pitifulest thing out is a mob; that's what an army is—a mob; they don't fight with courage that's born in them, but with courage that's borrowed from their mass, and from their officers. But a mob without any

MAN at the head of it is BENEATH pitifulness. Now the thing for YOU to do is to droop your tails and go home and crawl in a hole. If any real lynching's going to be done it will be done in the dark, Southern fashion; and when they come they'll bring their masks, and fetch a MAN along. Now LEAVE—and take your half-a-man with you"—tossing his gun up across his left arm and cocking it when he says this.

The crowd washed back sudden, and then broke all apart, and went tearing off every which way, and Buck Harkness he heeled it after them, looking tolerable cheap. I could a stayed if I wanted to, but I didn't want to.

CRITICAL EYE

▶ **For Discussion**

a. Why does the mob retreat in the presence of a "real man"?

b. Looking at Twain's "The Lowest Animal," how does this iconic novel figure into the points raised by Twain in this essay?

▶ **Re-approaching the Reading**

Col. Sherburn has maliciously killed Boggs, yet he is presented to the reader as being wise and heroic—a man of character. What commentary is Twain making on responsibility and keeping one's word?

▶ **Writing Assignment**

Examine this excerpt alongside of Shakespeare's *Othello*. In what way(s) is the "mob mentality" at work within the play? Why does the mob succeed in one text and fail in the other?

CYNTHIA OZICK

The Shawl

Stella, cold, cold the coldness of hell. How they walked on the roads together, Rosa with Magda curled up between sore breasts, Magda wound up in the shawl. Sometimes Stella carried Magda. But she was jealous of Magda. A thin girl of fourteen, too small, with thin breasts of her own, Stella wanted to be wrapped in a shawl, hidden away, asleep, rocked by the march, a baby, a round infant in arms. Magda took Rosa's nipple, and Rosa never stopped walking, a walking cradle. There was not enough milk; sometimes Magda sucked air; then she screamed. Stella was ravenous. Her knees were tumors on sticks, her elbows chicken bones.

Rosa did not feel hunger; she felt light, not like someone walking but like someone in a faint, in trance, arrested in a fit, someone who is already a floating angel, alert and seeing everything, but in the air, not there, not touching the road. As if teetering on the tips of her fingernails. She looked into Magda's face through a gap in the shawl: a squirrel in a nest, safe, no one could reach her inside the little house of the shawl's windings. The face, very round, a pocket mirror of a face: but it was not Rosa's bleak complexion, dark like cholera, it was another kind of face altogether, eyes blue as air, smooth feathers of hair nearly as yellow as the Star sewn into Rosa's coat. You could think she was one of *their* babies.

Rosa, floating, dreamed of giving Magda away in one of the villages. She could leave the line for a minute and push Magda into the hands of any woman on the side of the road. But if she moved out of line they might shoot. And even if she fled the line for half a second and pushed the shawl-bundle at a stranger, would the woman take it? She might be surprised, or afraid; she might drop the shawl, and Magda would fall out and strike her head and die. The little round head. Such a good child, she gave up screaming, and sucked now only for the taste of the drying nipple itself. The neat grip of the tiny gums. One mite of a tooth tip sticking up in the bottom gum, how shining, an elfin tombstone of white marble gleaming there. Without complaining, Magda relinquished Rosa's teats, first the left, then the right; both were cracked, not a sniff of milk. The duct crevice extinct, a dead volcano, blind eye, chill hole, so Magda took the corner of the shawl and milked it instead. She sucked and sucked, flooding the threads with wetness. The shawl's good flavor, milk of linen.

It was a magic shawl, it could nourish an infant for three days and three nights. Magda did not die, she stayed alive, although very quiet. A peculiar smell, of cinnamon and almonds, lifted out of her mouth. She held her eyes open every moment, forgetting how to blink or nap, and Rosa and sometimes Stella studied their blueness. On the road they raised one burden of a leg after another and studied Magda's face. "Aryan," Stella said, in a voice grown as thin as a string; and Rosa thought

"The Shawl" from *The Shawl* by Cynthia Ozick, copyright © 1980, 1983 by Cynthia Ozick. Used by permission of Alfred A. Knopf, a division of Random House, Inc.

how Stella gazed at Magda like a young cannibal. And the time that Stella said "Aryan," it sounded to Rosa as if Stella had really said "Let us devour her."

But Magda lived to walk. She lived that long, but she did not walk very well, partly because she was only fifteen months old, and partly because the spindles of her legs could not hold up her fat belly. It was fat with air, full and round. Rosa gave almost all her food to Magda, Stella gave nothing; Stella was ravenous, a growing child herself, but not growing much. Stella did not menstruate. Rosa did not menstruate. Rosa was ravenous, but also not; she learned from Magda how to drink the taste of a finger in one's mouth. They were in a place without pity, all pity was annihilated in Rosa, she looked at Stella's bones without pity. She was sure that Stella was waiting for Magda to die so she could put her teeth into the little thighs.

Rosa knew Magda was going to die very soon; she should have been dead already, but she had been buried away deep inside the magic shawl, mistaken there for the shivering mound of Rosa's breasts; Rosa clung to the shawl as if it covered only herself. No one took it away from her. Magda was mute. She never cried. Rosa hid her in the barracks, under the shawl, but she knew that one day someone would inform; or one day someone, not even Stella, would steal Magda to eat her. When Magda began to walk Rosa knew that Magda was going to die very soon, something would happen. She was afraid to fall asleep; she slept with the weight of her thigh on Magda's body; she was afraid she would smother Magda under her thigh. The weight of Rosa was becoming less and less; Rosa and Stella were slowly turning into air.

Magda was quiet, but her eyes were horribly alive, like blue tigers. She watched. Sometimes she laughed—it seemed a laugh, but how could it be? Magda had never seen anyone laugh. Still, Magda laughed at her shawl when the wind blew its corners, the bad wind with pieces of black in it, that made Stella's and Rosa's eyes tear. Magda's eyes were always clear and tearless. She watched like a tiger. She guarded her shawl. No one could touch it; only Rosa could touch it. Stella was not allowed. The shawl was Magda's own baby, her pet, her little sister. She tangled herself up in it and sucked on one of the corners when she wanted to be very still.

Then Stella took the shawl away and made Magda die.

Afterward Stella said: "I was cold."

And afterward she was always cold, always. The cold went into her heart: Rosa saw that Stella's heart was cold. Magda flopped onward with her little pencil legs scribbling this way and that, in search of the shawl; the pencils faltered at the barracks opening, where the light began. Rosa saw and pursued. But already Magda was in the square outside the barracks, in the jolly light. It was the roll-call arena. Every morning Rosa had to conceal Magda under the shawl against a wall of the barracks and go out and stand in the arena with Stella and hundreds of others, sometimes for hours, and Magda, deserted, was quiet under the shawl, sucking on her corner. Every day Magda was silent, and so she did not die. Rosa saw that today Magda was going to die, and at the same time a fearful joy ran into Rosa's two palms, her fingers were on fire, she was astonished, febrile: Magda, in the sunlight, swaying on her pencil legs, was howling. Ever since the drying up of Rosa's nipples, ever since Magda's last scream on the road, Magda had been devoid of any syllable; Magda was a mute. Rosa believed that something had gone wrong with her vocal cords, with her windpipe, with the cave of her larynx; Magda was defective, without a voice; perhaps she was deaf; there might be something amiss with her intelligence; Magda was dumb. Even the laugh that came when the ash-stippled wind made a clown out of Magda's shawl was only the air-blown showing of her teeth. Even when the lice, head lice and body lice, crazed her so that she became as wild as one of the big rats that plundered the barracks at daybreak looking for carrion, she rubbed and scratched and kicked and bit and rolled without a whimper. But now Magda's mouth was spilling a long viscous rope of clamor.

"Maaaa—"

It was the first noise Magda had ever sent out from her throat since the drying up of Rosa's nipples.

"Maaaa . . . aaa!"

Again! Magda was wavering in the perilous sunlight of the arena, scrabbling on such pitiful little bent shins. Rosa saw. She saw that Magda was grieving for the loss of her shawl, she saw that Magda was going to die. A tide of commands hammered in Rosa's nipples: Fetch, get, bring! But she did not know which to go after first, Magda or the shawl. If she jumped out into the arena to snatch Magda up, the howling would not stop, because Magda would still not have the shawl; but if she ran back into the barracks to find the shawl, and if she found it, and if she came after Magda holding it and shaking it, then she would get Magda back, Magda would put the shawl in her mouth and turn dumb again.

Rosa entered the dark. It was easy to discover the shawl. Stella was heaped under it, asleep in her thin bones. Rosa tore the shawl free and flew—she could fly, she was only air—into the arena. The sunheat murmured of another life, of butterflies in summer. The light was placid, mellow. On the other side of the steel fence, far away, there were green meadows speckled with dandelions and deep-colored violets; beyond them, even farther, innocent tiger lilies, tall, lifting their orange bonnets. In the barracks they spoke of "flowers," of "rain": excrement, thick turd-braids, and the slow stinking maroon waterfall that slunk down from the upper bunks, the stink mixed with a bitter fatty floating smoke that greased Rosa's skin. She stood for an instant at the margin of the arena. Sometimes the electricity inside the fence would seem to hum; even Stella said it was only an imagining, but Rosa heard real sounds in the wire: grainy sad voices. The farther she was from the fence, the more clearly the voices crowded at her. The lamenting voices strummed so convincingly, so passionately, it was impossible to suspect them of being phantoms. The voices told her to hold up the shawl, high; the voices told her to shake it, to whip with it, to unfurl it like a flag. Rosa lifted, shook, whipped, unfurled. Far off, very far, Magda leaned across her air-fed belly, reaching out with the rods of her arms. She was high up, elevated, riding someone's shoulder. But the shoulder that carried Magda was not coming toward Rosa and the shawl, it was drifting away, the speck of Magda was moving more and more into the smoky distance. Above the shoulder a helmet glinted. The light tapped the helmet and sparkled it into a goblet. Below the helmet a black body like a domino and a pair of black boots hurled themselves in the direction of the electrified fence. The electric voices began to chatter wildly. "Maa-maa, maaamaaa," they all hummed together. How far Magda was from Rosa now, across the whole square, past a dozen barracks, all the way on the other side! She was no bigger than a moth.

All at once Magda was swimming through the air. The whole of Magda traveled through loftiness. She looked like a butterfly touching a silver vine. And the moment Magda's feathered round head and her pencil legs and balloonish belly and zigzag arms splashed against the fence, the steel voices went mad in their growling, urging Rosa to run and run to the spot where Magda had fallen from her flight against the electrified fence; but of course Rosa did not obey them. She only stood, because if she ran they would shoot, and if she tried to pick up the sticks of Magda's body they would shoot, and if she let the wolf's screech ascending now through the ladder of her skeleton break out, they would shoot; so she took Magda's shawl and filled her own mouth with it, stuffed it in and stuffed it in, until she was swallowing up the wolf's screech and tasting the cinnamon and almond depth of Magda's saliva; and Rosa drank Magda's shawl until it dried.

CRITICAL EYE

▶ For Discussion

a. In what ways does Ozick's story discuss how the horrors of trauma affect the mind?

b. Many Jews survived the atrocity of the Holocaust, and they remember with vivid clarity the horrors that occurred around them. What are we learning from their remembrances?

▶ Re-approaching the Reading

Examine the mother in this story alongside the article about Lashaundra Armstrong. Why was one mother able to see past the madness around her while the other was not?

▶ Writing Assignment

The mother considers two costly choices as a means of saving/ending Magda's life. Can her choices be excused because of the circumstances?

AESOP

A Lion and Other Animals Go Hunting

A lion, an ass, a jackal, and a wolf went hunting one day, and every one was to share and share alike in what they took. They plucked down a stag, and cut him up into four parts, but as they were beginning to divide shares, the lion said, "Hands off. *This* quarter is mine, by privilege of my rank, as King of Beasts. *This* quarter is mine because I frightened the stag with my roar. *This* quarter is mine because I delivered the first blow. As for *this* quarter, well, take it who dares." So the mouths of the allies were shut, and they went away, quiet as fishes.

Moral: There is no partnership with those who have the power.

CRITICAL EYE

▶ For Discussion

a. Does the lion's final statement speak to the historical posturing of the bully?

b. Provide current or historical evidence that presents a nation or governing body as a bully.

c. Thinking in terms of gender, race, and politics, who is generally seen as the bully?

d. Does historical evidence exist in which the "other," or those presumed to be powerless, assumed power and, subsequently, took on the persona of the bully?

▶ Re-approaching the Reading

Look at the relationships between the animals in terms of political domination. How will the lion's behavior affect those deemed lesser? Be sure to juxtapose the story with issues of domination from our larger global society.

▶ Writing Assignment

Using Aseop's tale as a platform, argue that the notion of the bully is a myth and that those in power are entitled to lead and set the gender, social, political, and cultural standards for those deemed weaker.

CHAPTER 3

Racial Matters

George Bush does not care about Black people!
Kanye West

If I can send the flower of the German nation into the hell of war without the smallest pity for the shedding of precious German blood, then surely I have the right to remove millions of an inferior race that breeds like vermin.
Adolf Hitler

Humans are essentially comprised of ethnic, cultural, and regional groupings that we generally oversimplify by lumping into what we call "races" of people. Actually, Homosapiens are all of one race—the human race. Yet, we still continue—based on skin color and language, cultural and religious affiliations, social mandates and values—to separate ourselves to the extent of judgment and, too often, violent segregation. These problems with those who are "other" in our worlds frequently result in blaming and, more tragically, self-incrimination. As a result, these so-called racial conflicts continue to flare up and burn out of control. But, when examined from a position of personal intuitiveness, these moments of narrow-mindedness seem to be, moreso, issues of how we see ourselves—those flawed reflections we cast in the mirror.

Perceived differences have represented the largest gap among humankind. Historically, the world has demonstrated little tolerance for difference, making so-called matters of race the most debated issue since the evolution of our species. That said, how do we move forward in a world that, currently, seems as ethnically intolerant as at any point in history? Moreover, how do we learn to embrace ourselves and our neighbors when the diverse images of our reflective lives continue to be attacked and subjugated to the point of self-hatred and confusion?

What seems most perplexing about the issue of race is that, in fact, there is an issue of "race." Somehow, we do not look at our fellow humans and see our own humanity. Perhaps what we must do is not examine the areas where racism is a threat or problem, but, instead, excise the very roots of difference, in order to define, combat, and eliminate one of, if not the, largest quandary to ever impact our world. The following selections allow readers to consider who they are in relation to the skin color that defines them and further question how and why these notions of race and racial matters color their views of the world.

WOODEN LEG

Young Men, Go Out and Fight Them

The gold rush of 1874, which lured thousands of white prospectors into the Black Hills of South Dakota, was a crucial factor in provoking a major confrontation between the United States and the Plains Indians. To the powerful Sioux nation these mountains were sacred terrain, and also properly protected by the Fort Laramie Treaty of 1868, signed by the Sioux and the United States government. It was Lieutenant Colonel George Armstrong Custer who originally violated that treaty. In July 1874, ostensibly to locate a site for a new fort, but covertly to hunt for mineral resources, Custer led the expedition into the Black Hills and reported that there was gold "from the grassroots down."

So it was poetic justice that in late June 1876 Custer's small command should blunder into the largest gathering of Plains Indian fighters ever assembled—an estimated twelve to fifteen thousand Indians, with at least four thousand fighting men, drawn from the Teton, Santee and Yankton Sioux, Assiniboine, Cheyenne, Arapaho, and Gros Ventre, camped together along three miles of the bank of the Little Big Horn River in central Montana. Under the leadership of the Sioux war chiefs Sitting Bull and Crazy Horse and the Cheyenne headman Two Moons, the natives comprised die-hard hostiles and recent reservation runaways come together momentarily as a united front.

Here is one warrior's memory of the tumultuous day of "many soldiers falling into camp," the battle of the Little Big Horn. Wooden Leg, the narrator, was about eighteen years old when Custer disastrously divided his Seventh Cavalry forces, ignored warnings from his Crow scouts, and was cut down along with all 225 of his officers and men. The battle was a freakish victory for the Indians, stunning the victors along with the vanquished. The tribes did not have sufficient unity or ammunition to follow it up with a broader offensive. Their forces quickly scattered, with Sitting Bull and his followers hiding out in Canada until 1881.

In my sleep I dreamed that a great crowd of people were making lots of noise. Something in the noise startled me. I found myself wide awake, sitting up and listening. My brother too awakened, and we both jumped to our feet. A great commotion was going on among the camps. We heard shooting. We hurried out from the trees so we might see as well as hear.

The shooting was somewhere at the upper part of the camp circles. It looked as if all of the Indians there were running away toward the hills to the westward or down toward the village. Women were screaming and men were letting out war cries. Through it all we could hear old men calling: "Soldiers are here! Young men, go out and fight them."

"Young Men, Go Out and Fight Them" from *Wooden Leg: A Warrior Who Fought Custer.* Interpreted by Thomas B. Marquis. Published by the University of Nebraska Press.

We ran to our camp and to our home lodge. Everybody there was excited. Women were hurriedly making up little packs for flight. Some were going off northward or across the river without any packs. Children were hunting for their mothers. Mothers were anxiously trying to find their children. I got my lariat and my six-shooter. I hastened on down toward where had been our horse herd. . . .

My father had caught my favorite horse from the herd brought in by the boys and Bald Eagle. I quickly emptied out my war bag and set myself at getting ready to go into battle. I jerked off my ordinary clothing. I jerked on a pair of new breeches that had been given to me by an Uncpapa Sioux. I had a good cloth shirt, and I put it on. My old moccasins were kicked off and a pair of beaded moccasins substituted for them.

My father strapped a blanket upon my horse and arranged the rawhide lariat into a bridle. He stood holding my mount. "Hurry," he urged me.

The air was so full of dust I could not see where to go. But it was not, needful that I see that far. I kept my horse headed in the direction of movement by the crowd of Indians on horseback. I was led out around and far beyond the Uncpapa camp circle. Many hundreds of Indians on horseback were dashing to and fro in front of a body of soldiers. The soldiers were on the level valley ground and were shooting with rifles. Not many bullets were being sent back at them, but thousands of arrows were falling among them. I went on with a throng of Sioux until we got beyond and behind the white men. By this time, though, they had mounted their horses and were hiding themselves in the timber. . . .

Suddenly the hidden soldiers came tearing out on horseback, from the woods. I was around on that side where they came out. I whirled my horse and lashed it into a dash to escape from them. All others of my companions did the same. But soon we discovered they were not following us. They were running away from us. They were going as fast as their tired horses could carry them across an open valley space and toward the river. We stopped, looked a moment, and then we whipped our ponies into swift pursuit. A great throng of Sioux also were coming after them. A distant position put them among the leaders in the chase. The soldier horses moved slowly, as if they were very tired. Ours were lively. We gained rapidly on them.

I fired four shots with my six-shooter. I do not know whether or not any of my bullets did harm. I saw a Sioux put an arrow into the back of a soldier's head. Another arrow went into his shoulder. He tumbled from his horse to the ground. Others fell dead either from arrows or from stabbings or jabbings or from blows by the stone war clubs of the Sioux. Horses limped or staggered or sprawled out dead or dying.

Our war cries and war songs were mingled with many jeering calls, such as: "You are only boys. You ought not to be fighting. We whipped you on the Rosebud. You should have brought more Crows or Shoshones with you to do your fighting."

Little Bird and I were after one certain soldier. Little Bird was wearing a trailing warbonnet. He was at the right and I was at the left of the fleeing man. We were lashing him and his horse with our pony whips. It seemed not brave to shoot him. Besides, I did not want to waste my bullets. He pointed back his revolver, though, and sent a bullet into Little Bird's thigh. Immediately I whacked the white man fighter on his head with the heavy elk-horn handle of my pony whip. The blow dazed him. I seized the rifle strapped on his back. I wrenched it and dragged the looping strap over his head. As I was getting possession of this weapon, he fell to the ground. I did not harm him further. I do not know what became of him. The jam of oncoming Indians swept me on. . . .

I returned to the west side of the river. Lots of Indians were hunting around there for dead soldiers or for wounded ones to kill. I joined in this search. I got some tobacco from the pockets of one dead man. I got also a belt having in it a few cartridges. All of the weapons and clothing and all other possessions were being taken from the bodies. The warriors were doing this. No old people nor women were there. They all had run away to the hill benches to the westward.

I went to a dead horse, to see what might be found there. Leather bags were on them, behind the saddles. I rummaged into one of these bags. I found there two pasteboard boxes. I broke open one of them. "Oh, cartridges!"

There were twenty of them in each box, forty in all. Thirty of them were used to fill up the vacant places in my belt. The remaining ten I wrapped into a piece of cloth and dropped them down into my own little kit bag. Now I need not be so careful in expending ammunition. Now I felt very brave. . . .

The shots quit coming from the soldiers. Warriors who had crept close to them began to call out that all of the white men were dead. All of the Indians then jumped up and rushed forward. All of the boys and old men on their horses came tearing into the crowd. The air was full of dust and smoke. Everybody was greatly excited. It looked like thousands of dogs might look if all of them were mixed together in a fight. All of the Indians were saying these soldiers also went crazy and killed themselves. I do not know. I could not see them. But I believe they did so. . . .

I took one scalp. As I went walking and leading my horse among the dead, I observed one face that interested me. The dead man had a long beard growing from both sides of his face and extending several inches below the chin. He had also a full mustache. All of the beard hair was of a light, yellow color, as I now recall it. Most of the soldiers had beards growing, in different lengths, but this was the longest one I saw among them. I think the dead man may have been thirty or more years old. "Here is a new kind of scalp," I said to a companion. I skinned one side of the face and half of the chin, so as to keep the long beard yet on the part removed. I got an arrow shaft and tied the strange scalp to the end of it. . . .

I waved my scalp as I rode among our people. The first person I met who took special interest in me was my mother's mother. She was living in a little willow dome lodge of her own. "What is that?" she asked me when I flourished the scalp stick toward her. I told her. "I give it to you," I said, and I held it out to her. She screamed and shrank away. "Take it," I urged. "It will be good medicine for you." Then I went on to tell her about my having killed the Crow or Shoshone at the first right up the river, about my getting the two guns, about my knocking in the head two soldiers in the river, about what I had done in the next fight on the hill where all of the soldiers had been killed. We talked about my soldier clothing. She said I looked good dressed that way. I had thought so too, but neither the coat nor the breeches fit me well. The arms and legs were too short for me. Finally she decided she would take the scalp. She went then into her own little lodge. . . .

There was no dancing nor celebrating of any kind in any of the camps that night. Too many people were in mourning, among all of the Sioux as well as among the Cheyennes. Too many Cheyenne and Sioux women had gashed their arms and legs, in token of their grief. The people generally were praying, not cheering. There was much noise and confusion, but this was from other causes. Young men were going out to fight the first soldiers now hiding themselves on the hill across the river from where had been the first fighting during the morning. . . .

I did not go back that afternoon nor that night to help in fighting the first soldiers. Late in the night, though, I went as a scout. Five young men of the Cheyennes were appointed to guard our camp while other people slept. These were Big Nose, Yellow Horse, Little Shield, Horse Road and Wooden Leg. One or other of us was out somewhere looking over the country all the time. Two of us went once over to the place where the soldiers were hidden. We got upon hill points higher than they were. We could look down among them. We could have shot among them, but we did not do this. We just saw that they yet were there.

Five other young men took our duties in the last part of the night. I was glad to be relieved. I did not go to my family group for rest. I let loose my horse and dropped myself down upon a thick pad of grassy sod.

WOODEN LEG, *Northern Cheyenne*

CRITICAL EYE

▶ For Discussion

a. Why does war seem to be such a necessary component of every society?

b. Why was the resistance to the colonists of such grave importance to the tribal peoples, even though their battles, in many cases, were futile?

▶ Re-approaching the Reading

Some people say that the conquering of "weaker" peoples is a part of human nature. Keeping this in mind, discuss the rights of the settlers to the native lands.

▶ Writing Assignment

Many ethnic groups in the United States, such as the Irish and Blacks, have undergone some form of harsh treatment at the hands of those perceived to be stronger or more superior. Have we resolved our differences or, racially speaking, are we worse off than at any time in American history?

ANNA LISA RAYA

It's Hard Enough Being Me

When I entered college, I *discovered* I was Latina. Until then, I had never questioned who I was or where I was from: My father is a second-generation Mexican-American, born and raised in Los Angeles, and my mother was born in Puerto Rico and raised in Compton, Calif. My home is El Sereno, a predominantly Mexican neighborhood in L.A. Every close friend I have back home is Mexican. So I was always just Mexican. Though sometimes I was just Puerto Rican—like when we would visit Mamo (my grandma) or hang out with my Aunt Titi.

Upon arriving in New York as a first-year student, 3000 miles from home, I not only experienced extreme culture shock, but for the first time I had to define myself according to the broad term "Latina." Although culture shock and identity crisis are common for the newly minted collegian who goes away to school, my experience as a newly minted Latina was, and still is, even more complicating. In El Sereno, I felt like I was part of a majority, whereas at the College I am a minority.

I've discovered that many Latinos like myself have undergone similar experiences. We face discrimination for being a minority in this country while also facing criticism for being "whitewashed" or "sellouts" in the countries of our heritage. But as an ethnic group in college, we are forced to define ourselves according to some vague, generalized Latino experience. This requires us to know our history, our language, our music, and our religion. I can't even be a content "Puerto Mexican" because I have to be a politically-and-socially-aware-Latina-with-a-chip-on-my-shoulder-because-of-how-repressed-I-am-in-this-country.

I am none of the above. I am the quintessential imperfect Latina. I can't dance salsa to save my life, I learned about Montezuma and the Aztecs in sixth grade, and I haven't prayed to the *Virgen de Guadalupe* in years.

Apparently I don't even look Latina. I can't count how many times people have just assumed that I'm white or asked me if I'm Asian. True, my friends back home call me *güera* ("whitey") because I have green eyes and pale skin, but that was as bad as it got. I never thought I would wish my skin were a darker shade or my hair a curlier texture, but since I've been in college, I have—many times.

Another thing: my Spanish is terrible. Every time I call home, I berate my mama for not teaching me Spanish when I was a child. In fact, not knowing how to speak the language of my home countries is the biggest problem that I have encountered, as have many Latinos. In Mexico there is a term, *pocha*, which is used by native Mexicans to ridicule Mexican-Americans. It expresses a deep-rooted antagonism and dislike for those of us who were raised on the other side of the border. Our failed attempts to speak pure, Mexican Spanish are largely responsible for the dislike. Other Latin American natives have this same

---

"It's Hard Enough Being Me" by Anna Lisa Raya from *Columbia College Today,* Winter/Spring 1994. Reprinted with permission from Columbia College Today, © 1994.

attitude. No matter how well a Latino speaks Spanish, it can never be good enough.

Yet Latinos can't even speak Spanish in the U.S. without running the risk of being called "spic" or "wetback." That is precisely why my mother refused to teach me Spanish when I was a child. The fact that she spoke Spanish was constantly used against her: It prevented her from getting good jobs, and it would have placed me in bilingual education—a construct of the Los Angeles public school system that has proved to be more of a hindrance to intellectual development than a help.

To be fully Latina in college, however, I *must* know Spanish. I must satisfy the equation: Latina [equals] Spanish-speaking.

So I'm stuck in this black hole of an identity crisis, and college isn't making my life any easier, as I thought it would. In high school, I was being prepared for an adulthood in which I would be an individual, in which I wouldn't have to wear a Catholic school uniform anymore. But though I led an anonymous adolescence, I knew who I was. I knew I was different from white, black, or Asian people. I knew there was a language other than English that I could call my own if I only knew how to speak it better. I knew there were historical reasons why I was in this country, distinct reasons that make my existence here easier or more difficult than other people's existence. Ultimately, I was content.

Now I feel pushed into a corner, always defining, defending, and proving myself to classmates, professors, or employers. Trying to understand who and why I am, while understanding Plato or Homer, is a lot to ask of myself.

A month ago, I heard three Nuyorican (Puerto Ricans born and raised in New York) writers discuss how New Your City has influenced their writing. One problem I have faced as a young writer is finding a voice that is true to my community. I was surprised and reassured to discover that as Latinos, these writers had faced similar pressures and conflicts as myself; some weren't even taught Spanish in childhood. I will never forget the advice that one of them gave me that evening: She said that I need to be true to myself. "Because people will always complain about what you are doing—you're a 'gringa' or a 'spic' no matter what," she explained. "So you might as well do things for yourself and not for them."

I don't know why it has taken 20 years to hear this advice, but I'm going to give it a try. *Soy yo* and no one else. *Punto.*[1]

(1994)

---

[1] *Soy yo . . . Punto* I'm me . . . Period. (Editors' note.)

CRITICAL EYE

▶ **For Discussion**

a. Do you believe that most children of immigrants who live in America suffer from the same issues as the author?

b. How plausible do you think it would be to have all immigrants rid themselves of monikers such as Chinese American and Hispanic American and to simply be Americans in the interest of racial harmony?

▶ **Re-approaching the Reading**

What could the college experience have done to make the author's transition better or alleviate her racial tensions?

▶ **Writing Assignment**

Why are we all so obsessed with racial identity in America?

MAXINE HONG KINGSTON

THE MISERY OF SILENCE[1]

When I went to kindergarten and had to speak English for the first time, I became silent. A dumbness—a shame—still cracks my voice in two, even when I want to say "hello" casually, or ask an easy question in front of the checkout counter, or ask directions of a bus driver. I stand frozen, or I hold up the line with the complete, grammatical sentence that comes squeaking out at impossible length. "What did you say?" says the cab driver, or "Speak up," so I have to perform again, only weaker the second time. A telephone call makes my throat bleed and takes up that day's courage. It spoils my day with self-disgust when I hear my broken voice come skittering out into the open. It makes people wince to hear it. I'm getting better, though. Recently I asked the postman for special-issue stamps; I've waited since childhood for postmen to give me some of their own accord. I am making progress, a little every day.

My silence was thickest—total—during the three years that I covered my school paintings with black paint. I painted layers of black over houses and flowers and suns, and when I drew on the blackboard, I put a layer of chalk on top. I was making a stage curtain, and it was the moment before the curtain parted or rose. The teachers called my parents to school, and I saw they had been saving my pictures, curling and cracking, all alike and black. The teachers pointed to the pictures and looked serious, talked seriously too, but my parents did not understand English. ("The parents and teachers of criminals were executed," said my father.) My parents took the pictures home. I spread them out (so black and full of possibilities) and pretended the curtains were swinging open, flying up, one after another, sunlight underneath, mighty operas.

During the first silent year I spoke to no one at school, did not ask before going to the lavatory, and flunked kindergarten. My sister also said nothing for three years, silent in the playground and silent at lunch. There were other quiet Chinese girls not of our family, but most of them got over it sooner than we did. I enjoyed the silence. At first it did not occur to me I was supposed to talk or to pass kindergarten. I talked at home and to one or two of the Chinese kids in class. I made motions and even made some jokes. I drank out of a toy saucer when the water spilled out of the cup, and everybody laughed, pointing at me, so I did it some more. I didn't know that Americans don't drink out of saucers.

I liked the Negro students (Black Ghosts) best because they laughed the loudest and talked to me as if I were a daring talker too. One of the Negro girls had her mother coil braids over her ears Shanghai-style like mine; we were Shanghai twins except that she was covered with black like my paintings. Two Negro kids enrolled in Chinese school, and the teachers

---

[1]Editor's title.

From *The Woman Warrior* by Maxine Hong Kingston, copyright © 1975, 1976 by Maxine Hong Kingston. Used by permission of Alfred A. Knopf, a division of Random House, Inc.

gave them Chinese names. Some Negro kids walked me to school and home, protecting me from the Japanese kids, who hit me and chased me and stuck gum in my ears. The Japanese kids were noisy and tough. They appeared one day in kindergarten, released from concentration camp, which was a tic-tac-toe mark, like barbed wire, on the map.

It was when I found out I had to talk that school become a misery, that the silence became a misery. I did not speak and felt bad each time that I did not speak. I read aloud in first grade, though, and heard the barest whisper with little squeaks come out of my throat. "Louder," said the teacher, who scared the voice away again. The other Chinese girls did not talk either, so I knew the silence had to do with being a Chinese girl.

Reading out loud was easier than speaking because we did not have to make up what to say, but I stopped often, and the teacher would think I'd gone quiet again. I could not understand "I." The Chinese "I" has seven strokes, intricacies. How could the American "I," assuredly wearing a hat like the Chinese, have only three strokes, the middle so straight? Was it out of politeness that this writer left off the strokes the way a Chinese has to write her own name small and crooked? No, it was not politeness; "I" is a capital and "you" is lower-case. I stared at that middle line and waited so long for its black center to resolve into tight strokes and dots that I forgot to pronounce it. The other troublesome word was "here," no strong consonant to hang on to, and so flat, when "here" is two mountainous ideographs. The teacher, who had already told me every day how to read "I" and "here," put me in the low corner under the stairs again, where the noisy boys usually sat.

When my second grade class did a play, the whole class went to the auditorium except the Chinese girls. The teacher, lovely and Hawaiian, should have understood about us, but instead left us behind in the classroom. Our voices were too soft or nonexistent, and our parents never signed the permission slips anyway. They never signed anything unnecessary. We opened the door a crack and peeked out, but closed it again quickly. One of us (not me) won every spelling bee, though.

I remember telling the Hawaiian teacher, "We Chinese can't sing 'land where our fathers died.'" She argued with me about politics, while I meant because of curses. But how can I have that memory when I couldn't talk? My mother says that we, like the ghosts, have no memories.

After American school, we picked up our cigar boxes, in which we had arranged books, brushes, and an inkbox neatly, and went to Chinese school, from 5:00 to 7:30 P.M. There we chanted together, voices rising and falling, loud and soft, some boys shouting, everybody reading together, reciting together and not alone with one voice. When we had a memorization test, the teacher let each of us come to his desk and say the lesson to him privately, while the rest of the class practiced copying or tracing. Most of the teachers were men. The boys who were so well behaved in the American school played tricks on them and talked back to them. The girls were not mute. They screamed and yelled during recess, when there were no rules; they had fistfights. Nobody was afraid of children hurting themselves or of children hurting school property. The glass doors to the red and green balconies with the gold joy symbols were left wide open so that we could run out and climb the fire escapes. We played capture-the-flag in the auditorium, where Sun Yat-sen and Chiang Kai-shek's pictures hung at the back of the stage, the Chinese flag on their left and the American flag on their right. We climbed the teak ceremonial chairs and made flying leaps off the stage. One flag headquarters was behind the glass door and the other on stage right. Our feet drummed on the hollow stage. During recess the teachers locked themselves up in their office with the shelves of books, copybooks, inks from China. They drank tea and warmed their hands at a stove. There was no play supervision. At recess we had the school to ourselves, and also we could roam as far as we could go—downtown, Chinatown stores, home—as long as we returned before the bell rang.

At exactly 7:30 the teacher again picked up the brass bell that sat on his desk and swung it over our heads, while we charged down the stairs, our cheering magnified in the stairwell. Nobody had to line up.

Not all of the children who were silent at American school found voice at Chinese school. One new teacher said each of us had to get up and recite in front of the class, who was to listen. My sister and I had memorized the lesson perfectly. We said it to each other at home, one chanting, one listening. The teacher called on my sister to recite first. It was the first time a teacher had called on the second-born to go first. My sister was scared. She glanced at me and looked away; I looked down at my desk. I hoped that she could do it because if she could, then I would have to. She opened her mouth and a voice came out that wasn't a whisper, but it wasn't a proper voice either. I hoped that she would not cry, fear breaking up her voice like twigs underfoot. She sounded as if she were trying to sing through weeping and strangling. She did not pause or stop to end the embarrassment. She kept going until she said the last word, and then she sat down. When it was my turn, the same voice came out, a crippled animal running on broken legs. You could hear splinters in my voice, bones rubbing jagged against one another. I was loud, though. I was glad I didn't whisper.

How strange that the emigrant villagers are shouters, hollering face to face. My father asks, "Why is it I can hear Chinese from blocks away? Is it that I understand the language? Or is it they talk loud?" They turn the radio up full blast to hear the operas, which do not seem to hurt their ears. And they yell over the singers that wail over the drums, everybody talking at once, big arm gestures, spit flying. You can see the disgust on American faces looking at women like that. It isn't just the loudness. It is the way Chinese sounds, ching-chong ugly, to American ears, not beautiful like Japanese sayonara words with the consonants and vowels as regular as Italian. We make guttural peasant noise and have Ton Duc Thang names you can't remember. And the Chinese can't hear Americans at all; the language is too soft and western music unhearable. I've watched a Chinese audience laugh, visit, talk-story, and holler during a piano recital, as if the musician could not hear them. A Chinese-American, somebodyson, was playing Chopin, which has no punctuation, no cymbals, no gongs. Chinese piano music is five black keys. Normal Chinese women's voices are strong and bossy. We American-Chinese girls had to whisper to make ourselves American-feminine. Apparently we whispered even more softly than the Americans. Once a year the teachers referred my sister and me to speech therapy, but our voices would straighten out, unpredictably normal, for the therapists. Some of us gave up, shook our heads, and said nothing, not one word. Some of us could not even shake our heads. At times shaking my head no is more self-assertion than I can manage. Most of us eventually found some voice, however faltering. We invented an American-feminine speaking personality.

CRITICAL EYE

▶ **For Discussion**

a. Do you believe the issues presented in the text are experienced by most non-native speakers?

b. How is it that, for the most part, Asian Americans are viewed as the "model minority" in terms of professions and academics while Hong Kingston's experience seems so horrific?

▶ **Re-approaching the Reading**

How does this story and the essay "The Human Cost of an Illiterate Society" speak to each other?

▶ **Writing Assignment**

Is what happened to Hong Kingston an example of racism?

TAHIRA NAQVI

BRAVE WE ARE

"Mom, Ammi," he asks, the little boy Kasim who is my son, who has near-black eyes and whose buck teeth give him a Bugs Bunny look when his mouth is open, as it is now, in query. "What does hybrid mean?"

"Hybrid?" I'm watching the water in the pot very closely; the tiny bubbles quivering restlessly on its surface indicate it's about to come to boil. Poised over the pot, clutching a batch of straw-colored Prince spaghetti, is my hand, suspended, warm from the steam and waiting for the moment when the bubbles will suddenly and turbulently come to life.

I'm not fussy about brands, especially where spaghetti is concerned (it's all pasta, after all), but I wish there was one which would fit snugly at the outset into my largest pot. As things stand now, the strands bend uncomfortably, contort, embroiling themselves in something of a struggle within the confines of the pot once they've been dropped into the boiling water. Someday of course, I will have a pot large enough to accommodate all possible lengths and varieties.

"Yeah, hybrid. Do you know what it means?"

The note of restive insistence in his voice compels me to tear my gaze away from the water. Kasim's face looks darker now than when he left for school this morning. Perhaps running up the steep driveway with the March wind lashing against his lean nine-year-old frame has forced the blood to rush to his face. Flushed, his face reminds me he's still only a child, 'only ten, just a baby,' as my mother often says when I sometimes take him to task in her presence, arguing with him as if he were a man behaving like a child.

A new spelling word? Such a difficult word for a fourth-grader. "Are you studying plants?"

"No, but can you tell me what it means?" Impatient, so impatient, so like the water that's hissing and tumbling in the pot, demanding immediate attention. He slides against the kitchen counter and hums, his fingers beating an indecipherable rhythm on the Formica, his eyes raised above mine, below mine, behind me, to the window outside which white, lavender and gray have mingled to become a muddied brown. Just as he reaches for the cookie jar I quickly throw in the spaghetti.

"Well, that's a hard word. Let me see." Helplessly I watch as he breaks off a Stella Doro biscuit in his mouth and crumbs disperse in a steady fall-out, over the counter, on the kitchen tile, some getting caught in his blue-and-green striped sweater, like flies in a spider's web. "It's a sort of mixture, a combination of different sorts of things," I say wisely, with the absolute knowledge that 'things' is susceptible to misinterpretation. I rack my brain for a good example. If I don't hurry up with one he's going to move away with the notion that his mother doesn't know what hybrid means.

"You mean if you mix orange juice with lemonade it's going to become hybrid juice?"

"Brave We Are" from *Dying in a Strange Country* (Tsar, 2001), reprinted by permission of Tsar Publications.

The idea has proved ticklish, he smiles, crumbs from the Stella Doro dangling on the sides of his face; they obviously don't bother him as much as they bother me. I lean forward and rub a hand around his mouth just as he lunges toward the cookie jar again. He squirms and recoils at the touch of my ministering hand. Another biscuit is retrieved. I turn down the heat under the spaghetti to medium and start chopping onions.

Today I'm making spaghetti the way my mother makes it in Lahore, like pulao, the way I used to make it after I got married and was just learning to cook for a husband who had selective tastes in food. That was about the only thing I could make then so I worked hard to embellish and innovate. There, we call it noodles, although it's unmistakably spaghetti, with no tomato sauce or meatballs in or anywhere near it, no cheese either, and no one has heard of mozzarella or romano. The idea of cheese with our recipe would surprise the people in Lahore; even the ones with the most adventurous palates will cringe.

"Well, that too." And why not? My eyes smart from the sharpness of the onions, tears fill my eyes and spill over my cheeks. I turn away from the chopping board. "The word is used when you breed two different kinds of plants or animals, it's called cross-breeding." I snaffle. This gets harder. I know his knowledge of breeding is limited and 'cross' isn't going to help at all.

"*What's cross-what you may call it?*"

An example. One that will put the seal on hybrid forever. So he can boast his mother knows everything.

I wipe my watering eyes with a paper napkin and turn to the onions again. These, chopped thinly, are for the ground beef which will be cooked with small green peas, cubed potatoes and cut-leaf spinach and will be spiced with coriander, garlic, cumin, a touch of turmeric and half-inch long bristly strands of fresh ginger root. I'll throw the beef into the spaghetti when it's done and my husband and I alone will eat what I make. My children like spaghetti the way it should be, the way it is in America.

Moisture runs down my cheeks and my eyes smart. I place the knife down on the chopping board, tear out another sheet from the roll of Bounty towels on my right and rub my eyes and nose with it, my attention driven to the stark, brown limbs of trees outside as I wipe my face. The kitchen window that I now face as I do innumerable times during the day, faithfully reflects the movements of time and seasons of the small town in Connecticut where we live, compelling the spirit to buoyancy or, when the tones on its canvas are achromatous and dark, to melancholy, to sadness. Today, the sun is visible again and the white of the snow is distinguishable from the lavender of the bare, thin, stalky birches, unhealthy because we haven't tended them well. Sharply the sun cuts shadows on the clean, uncluttered snow.

Why does snow in February always remind me of February in Lahore? Incongruent, disparate, the seasons have so little in common. March is spring, grass so thick your foot settles into it, roses that bloom firm, their curves fleshy, the colors like undisturbed paint on an artist's palette, the air timberous, weaving in and out of swishing tree branches with the *sar, sar, sar* of a string instrument. Why do I turn to Eileen, my cleaning lady, and say, "Eileen, do you know it's spring in Lahore?" She looks up from the pot she's scrubbing in the kitchen sink with a good-humored smile. "No kidding? Really?" she asks, as if she didn't already know, as if she hadn't already heard it from me before.

An example, yes. "Now take an apple. A farmer can cross-breed a Macintosh apple with a Golden Yellow and get something which is a little bit like both. That will be a hybrid apple." I look closely at the boy's face for some signs of comprehension.

"You mean the apple's going to have a new name, like Macintosh Yellow?" he asks, his forehead creased thoughtfully.

"Yes." Relieved, I return to the onions, making a mental note to check the spaghetti soon, which, languorously swelled now, will have to be taken off from the stove and drained.

"But what about animals? You said there's *cross what you may call it* in animals too." He sprawls against the counter, up and down, right and left, like a gymnast.

"Yes there is. A cow from one family may be bred with a steer from another family and they'll end up with a calf that's a bit like the two of them." I wash my hands and he skips on the floor, dance-like steps, his arms raised.

"But man's an animal too, teacher says. Do people also cross . . . umm . . . breed?"

He's humming again. I know the tune now; "*Suzie Q/ Suzie Q/ I love you/O Suzie Q!*" It's from a song on his older brother Haider's tape, a catchy tune, sort of stays with you and you can't stop humming it. Both Haider and my younger son, Asghar, were amused when I showed an interest in the song. What do I know about music, their kind of music? Once, nearly two years ago, I tried to bribe Haider to memorize a ghazal by the poet Ghalib. The greatest Urdu poet of the subcontinent, I said passionately, the most complex. Egged on by the fifty dollars I was offering, he mastered the first verse by listening to a tape of ghazals sung by Mehdi Hasan.

> *Yeh naa thi hamari qismet ke visal-e-yaar ho*
> *Agar aurjeete rehte yehi intizar hota*

> It was not fated that I should meet my beloved,
> Life will merely prolong the waiting

Then, unable to sustain his interest, despite the now thirty-dollar a verse rate, Haider abandoned the project.

"The words are too hard," he complained when I protested, somewhat angrily. "The music's easy, but I can't keep up with the lyrics."

And I would have given him the money too. Actually I had decided to give him all of it after he had moved on to the second verse.

"Does that mean Mary is also hybrid?" Kasim's voice crashes into my thoughts of Suzie Q with a loud boom.

I lower the heat under the spaghetti—so what if it's a bit overdone. The yellow-white strands jump at each other in frantic embraces, hurried, as if there's no time to be lost.

"Mary? What are you talking about?" I know exactly what he's talking about. His vagueness passes through the sieve in my head and comes out as clarity. I fill in any blanks, uncannily, never ceasing to be surprised at the way this peculiar magic works.

"You know, Mary Khan, Dr. Khan's daughter? She's in my class Mom, you know her."

Yes, I know Mary well. Her full name is Marium. Her father, Amjad Khan and my husband, Ali, were together in the same medical school in Lahore, they graduated the same year, they completed residencies together at the same hospital in New York, where Amjad met and married Helen, a nurse. Helen is English. She's a few years older than I, very tall, almost a half-inch taller than Amjad, and has sleek, golden hair. We're good friends, Helen and I, and at least once a week we meet for lunch at a restaurant, an activity we decided to call 'sampling restaurants for later.' Over salmon lasagna or papadi chat and dosa or tandoori chicken she'll tell me how difficult Amjad is when it comes to their children, how upset he is that their son has taken it upon himself to date without his father's consent or approval. I'll shake my head and try to explain that Amjad might have dated *her*, but like a good Muslim father, he can't accept that his son can have girlfriends. "Wait till Mary is older," I say with my hand on Helen's arm, "the Muslim father in him will drop all his masks." Together we do what most women do quite unabashedly: spend a great deal of time talking about husbands.

When Mary was born Amjad said, "We're going to call her Marium, it's a name everyone knows." Familiar and convenient is what he meant, since it's tri-religious. That doesn't sound right, but if we can say bisexual, surely we can say tri-religious too. Why not? After all Islam, Christianity and Judaism all profess a claim to this name. However, before the child was quite one 'Marium' was shortened permanently to Mary.

Kasim is at the breakfast table now, some of his earlier energy dissipated. A small piece of biscuit lies forlornly before him on the table and he fusses with it slowly, obviously unwilling to pop the last bit in his mouth, content just to play with it.

"You know, her mother's English and her father's Pakistani like Dad, and she's got blue eyes and black hair."

"Yes, she does have lovely blue eyes and they look so pretty with her dark hair." I grapple with something to blunt the sharpness of his next question which I anticipate and I know I cannot repel.

"Well, then she's hybrid too, isn't she?" He's looking straight at me. His eyes are bright with the defiance of someone who knows he's scored a point.

Brave we are, we who answer questions that spill forth artlessly from the mouths of nine-year-old purists, questions that can neither be waved nor dismissed with flippant ambiguity. Vigilant and alert, we must be ready with our answers.

"Technically speaking she is, I mean, wait, you can say she is." I lift a hand and stop him before he says more. "But we don't use the word for people." The firmness in my voice sounds forced. "Don't say anything to her, okay?"

"Why? Is it a swear?"

"No!" I hasten with denial. "Of course not. It's just a word we don't use for people, that's all. Understand?"

"But what do you call them then?" He persists. "Mary's like the apple, isn't she? Isn't she? Her name's Mary Khan, isn't it?"

"Yes, Kas, it is. But there's nothing wrong with that name, a name's a name." Kasim looks contemplative. I know he's saying to himself, *Mom doesn't really know, but Mary's a hybrid, she's got blue eyes and black hair.*

"She's a person Kasim, not an apple. Anyway, you didn't tell me where you heard that word. Is it on your spelling list for this week?"

"No, Mrs. Davis was reading us something about plants in the *Weekly Reader*. It's not homework." He shrugs, abandons the Stella Doro and humming, leaves the kitchen.

"Get to homework now," I call after him, wondering if there's an equivalent of 'hybrid' in Urdu, a whole word, not one or two strung together in a phrase to mean the same thing. Offhand I can't think of one.

Without meaning to I throw some oregano into the boiling spaghetti. I shouldn't have done that. How's oregano going to taste in the company of coriander and cumin? Well, no matter, it's too late anyway.

After I've drained the spaghetti I will take some out for the meat mixture, saving the rest for my children. Then I'll add to our portion, my husband's and mine, the beef and vegetable mixture and turn everything over ever so gently, making sure that the spaghetti isn't squelched. The strands must remain smooth, elusive, separate.

Critical Eye

▶ For Discussion

a. Can you make the argument that issues of race are very difficult for parents to discuss with their children?

b. Is it necessary for a child from a mixed background to choose a race?

c. In your opinion, why is the mother uncomfortable?

d. What do you think about the mother's responses to her child's questions about the notion of a "hybrid"?

e. Compare the mother in "Brave We Are" to the mother in Nella Larsen's *Passing*. In what ways are their views on race similar?

▶ Re-approaching the Reading

Consider how the story would change if the mother were to simply tell her child that race should never be an issue when determining one's worth.

▶ Writing Assignment

Imagine a world where everyone has a mixed background. Would we then finally be rid of racial intolerance?

WILLIAM SHAKESPEARE

Othello, the Moore of Venice

ACT I

SCENE I. Venice. A street.

Enter RODERIGO and IAGO

RODERIGO

Tush! never tell me; I take it much unkindly
That thou, Iago, who hast had my purse
As if the strings were thine, shouldst know
of this.

IAGO

'Sblood, but you will not hear me:
If ever I did dream of such a matter, Abhor
me.

RODERIGO

Thou told'st me thou didst hold him in thy
hate.

IAGO

Despise me, if I do not. Three great ones of
the city,
In personal suit to make me his lieutenant,
Off-capp'd to him: and, by the faith of man,
I know my price, I am worth no worse a
place:
But he; as loving his own pride and
purposes,
Evades them, with a bombast circumstance
Horribly stuff'd with epithets of war;
And, in conclusion,
Nonsuits my mediators; for, 'Certes,' says he,
'I have already chose my officer.'
And what was he?
Forsooth, a great arithmetician,
One Michael Cassio, a Florentine,
A fellow almost damn'd in a fair wife;
That never set a squadron in the field,
Nor the division of a battle knows
More than a spinster; unless the bookish
theoric,
Wherein the toged consuls can propose
As masterly as he: mere prattle, without
practise,
Is all his soldiership. But he, sir, had the
election:
And I, of whom his eyes had seen the proof
At Rhodes, at Cyprus and on other grounds
Christian and heathen, must be be-lee'd and
calm'd
By debitor and creditor: this counter-caster,
He, in good time, must his lieutenant be,
And I–God bless the mark!–his Moorship's
ancient.

RODERIGO

By heaven, I rather would have been his
hangman.

IAGO

Why, there's no remedy; 'tis the curse of
service,
Preferment goes by letter and affection,
And not by old gradation, where each
second
Stood heir to the first. Now, sir, be judge
yourself,

Whether I in any just term am affined
To love the Moor.

RODERIGO

I would not follow him then.

IAGO

O, sir, content you;
I follow him to serve my turn upon him:
We cannot all be masters, nor all masters
Cannot be truly follow'd. You shall mark
Many a duteous and knee-crooking knave,
That, doting on his own obsequious bondage,
Wears out his time, much like his master's ass,
For nought but provender, and when he's old, cashier'd:
Whip me such honest knaves. Others there are
Who, trimm'd in forms and visages of duty,
Keep yet their hearts attending on themselves,
And, throwing but shows of service on their lords,
Do well thrive by them and when they have lined their coats
Do themselves homage: these fellows have some soul;
And such a one do I profess myself. For, sir,
It is as sure as you are Roderigo,
Were I the Moor, I would not be Iago:
In following him, I follow but myself;
Heaven is my judge, not I for love and duty,
But seeming so, for my peculiar end:
For when my outward action doth demonstrate
The native act and figure of my heart
In compliment extern, 'tis not long after
But I will wear my heart upon my sleeve
For daws to peck at: I am not what I am.

RODERIGO

What a full fortune does the thicklips owe
If he can carry't thus!

IAGO

Call up her father,
Rouse him: make after him, poison his delight,
Proclaim him in the streets; incense her kinsmen,
And, though he in a fertile climate dwell,
Plague him with flies: though that his joy be joy,
Yet throw such changes of vexation on't,
As it may lose some colour.

RODERIGO

Here is her father's house; I'll call aloud.

IAGO

Do, with like timorous accent and dire yell
As when, by night and negligence, the fire
Is spied in populous cities.

RODERIGO

What, ho, **BRABANTIO**! Signior **BRABANTIO**, ho!

IAGO

Awake! what, ho, **BRABANTIO**! thieves! thieves! thieves!
Look to your house, your daughter and your bags!
Thieves! thieves!

BRABANTIO appears above, at a window

BRABANTIO

What is the reason of this terrible summons?
What is the matter there?

RODERIGO

Signior, is all your family within?

IAGO

Are your doors lock'd?

BRABANTIO

Why, wherefore ask you this?

IAGO

'Zounds, sir, you're robb'd; for shame, put on your gown;
Your heart is burst, you have lost half your soul;
Even now, now, very now, an old black ram
Is topping your white ewe. Arise, arise;
Awake the snorting citizens with the bell,
Or else the devil will make a grandsire of you:
Arise, I say.

BRABANTIO

What, have you lost your wits?

RODERIGO

Most reverend signior, do you know my voice?

BRABANTIO

Not I what are you?

RODERIGO

My name is Roderigo.

BRABANTIO

The worser welcome:
I have charged thee not to haunt about my doors:
In honest plainness thou hast heard me say
My daughter is not for thee; and now, in madness,
Being full of supper and distempering draughts,
Upon malicious bravery, dost thou come
To start my quiet.

RODERIGO

Sir, sir, sir,—

BRABANTIO

But thou must needs be sure
My spirit and my place have in them power
To make this bitter to thee.

RODERIGO

Patience, good sir.

BRABANTIO

What tell'st thou me of robbing? this is Venice;
My house is not a grange.

RODERIGO

Most grave Brabantio,
In simple and pure soul I come to you.

IAGO

'Zounds, sir, you are one of those that will not serve God, if the devil bid you. Because we come to do you service and you think we are ruffians, you'll have your daughter covered with a Barbary horse; you'll have your nephews neigh to you; you'll have coursers for cousins and gennets for germans.

BRABANTIO

What profane wretch art thou?

IAGO

I am one, sir, that comes to tell you your daughter and the Moor are now making the beast with two backs.

BRABANTIO

Thou art a villain.

IAGO

You are—a senator.

BRABANTIO

This thou shalt answer; I know thee, Roderigo.

RODERIGO

Sir, I will answer any thing. But, I beseech you,
If 't be your pleasure and most wise consent,
As partly I find it is, that your fair daughter,
At this odd-even and dull watch o' the night,
Transported, with no worse nor better guard
But with a knave of common hire, a gondolier,

To the gross clasps of a lascivious Moor–
If this be known to you and your allowance,
We then have done you bold and saucy wrongs;
But if you know not this, my manners tell me
We have your wrong rebuke. Do not believe
That, from the sense of all civility,
I thus would play and trifle with your reverence:
Your daughter, if you have not given her leave,
I say again, hath made a gross revolt;
Tying her duty, beauty, wit and fortunes
In an extravagant and wheeling stranger
Of here and every where. Straight satisfy yourself:
If she be in her chamber or your house,
Let loose on me the justice of the state
For thus deluding you.

BRABANTIO

Strike on the tinder, ho!
Give me a taper! call up all my people!
This accident is not unlike my dream:
Belief of it oppresses me already.
Light, I say! light!

Exit above

IAGO

Farewell; for I must leave you:
It seems not meet, nor wholesome to my place,
To be produced—as, if I stay, I shall—
Against the Moor: for, I do know, the state,
However this may gall him with some cheque,
Cannot with safety cast him, for he's embark'd
With such loud reason to the Cyprus wars,
Which even now stand in act, that, for their souls,
Another of his fathom they have none,
To lead their business: in which regard,
Though I do hate him as I do hell-pains.
Yet, for necessity of present life,
I must show out a flag and sign of love,
Which is indeed but sign. That you shall surely find him,
Lead to the Sagittary the raised search;
And there will I be with him. So, farewell.

Exit

Enter, below, Brabantio, and Servants with torches

BRABANTIO

It is too true an evil: gone she is;
And what's to come of my despised time
Is nought but bitterness. Now, Roderigo,
Where didst thou see her? O unhappy girl!
With the Moor, say'st thou? Who would be a father!
How didst thou know 'twas she? O she deceives me
Past thought! What said she to you? Get more tapers:
Raise all my kindred. Are they married, think you?

RODERIGO

Truly, I think they are.

BRABANTIO

O heaven! How got she out? O treason of the blood!
Fathers, from hence trust not your daughters' minds
By what you see them act. Is there not charms
By which the property of youth and maidhood
May be abused? Have you not read, Roderigo,
Of some such thing?

RODERIGO

Yes, sir, I have indeed.

BRABANTIO

Call up my brother. O, would you had had her!
Some one way, some another. Do you know
Where we may apprehend her and the Moor?

RODERIGO

I think I can discover him, if you please,
To get good guard and go along with me.

BRABANTIO

Pray you, lead on. At every house I'll call;
I may command at most. Get weapons, ho!
And raise some special officers of night.
On, good Roderigo: I'll deserve your pains.

Exeunt

SCENE II. Another street.

Enter OTHELLO, IAGO, and Attendants with torches

IAGO

Though in the trade of war I have slain men,
Yet do I hold it very stuff o' the conscience
To do no contrived murder: I lack iniquity
Sometimes to do me service: nine or ten times
I had thought to have yerk'd him here under the ribs.

OTHELLO

'Tis better as it is.

IAGO

Nay, but he prated,
And spoke such scurvy and provoking terms
Against your honour
That, with the little godliness I have,
I did full hard forbear him. But, I pray you, sir,
Are you fast married? Be assured of this,
That the magnifico is much beloved,
And hath in his effect a voice potential
As double as the duke's: he will divorce you;
Or put upon you what restraint and grievance
The law, with all his might to enforce it on,
Will give him cable.

OTHELLO

Let him do his spite:
My services which I have done the signiory
Shall out-tongue his complaints. 'Tis yet to know,—
Which, when I know that boasting is an honour,
I shall promulgate–I fetch my life and being
From men of royal siege, and my demerits
May speak unbonneted to as proud a fortune
As this that I have reach'd: for know, Iago,
But that I love the gentle Desdemona,
I would not my unhoused free condition
Put into circumscription and confine
For the sea's worth. But, look! what lights come yond?

IAGO

Those are the raised father and his friends:
You were best go in.

OTHELLO

Not I I must be found:
My parts, my title and my perfect soul
Shall manifest me rightly. Is it they?

IAGO

By Janus, I think no.

Enter CASSIO, and certain Officers with torches

OTHELLO

The servants of the duke, and my lieutenant.
The goodness of the night upon you, friends!
What is the news?

CASSIO

The duke does greet you, general,
And he requires your haste-post-haste appearance,
Even on the instant.

OTHELLO

What is the matter, think you?

Racial Matters

CASSIO

Something from Cyprus as I may divine:
It is a business of some heat: the galleys
Have sent a dozen sequent messengers
This very night at one another's heels,
And many of the consuls, raised and met,
Are at the duke's already: you have been hotly call'd for;
When, being not at your lodging to be found,
The senate hath sent about three several guests
To search you out.

OTHELLO

'Tis well I am found by you.
I will but spend a word here in the house,
And go with you.

Exit

CASSIO

Ancient, what makes he here?

IAGO

'Faith, he to-night hath boarded a land carack:
If it prove lawful prize, he's made for ever.

CASSIO

I do not understand.

IAGO

He's married.

CASSIO

To who?

Re-enter OTHELLO

IAGO

Marry, to—Come, captain, will you go?

OTHELLO

Have with you.

CASSIO

Here comes another troop to seek for you.

IAGO

It is Brabantio. General, be advised;
He comes to bad intent.

Enter BRABANTIO, RODERIGO, and Officers with torches and weapons

OTHELLO

Holla! stand there!

RODERIGO

Signior, it is the Moor.

BRABANTIO

Down with him, thief!

They draw on both sides

IAGO

You, Roderigo! come, sir, I am for you.

OTHELLO

Keep up your bright swords, for the dew will rust them.
Good signior, you shall more command with years
Than with your weapons.

BRABANTIO

O thou foul thief, where hast thou stow'd my daughter?
Damn'd as thou art, thou hast enchanted her;
For I'll refer me to all things of sense,
If she in chains of magic were not bound,
Whether a maid so tender, fair and happy,
So opposite to marriage that she shunned
The wealthy curled darlings of our nation,
Would ever have, to incur a general mock,
Run from her guardage to the sooty bosom
Of such a thing as thou, to fear, not to delight.
Judge me the world, if 'tis not gross in sense
That thou hast practised on her with foul charms,
Abused her delicate youth with drugs or minerals
That weaken motion: I'll have't disputed on;

'Tis probable and palpable to thinking.
I therefore apprehend and do attach thee
For an abuser of the world, a practiser
Of arts inhibited and out of warrant.
Lay hold upon him: if he do resist,
Subdue him at his peril.

OTHELLO

Hold your hands,
Both you of my inclining, and the rest:
Were it my cue to fight, I should have known it
Without a prompter. Where will you that I go
To answer this your charge?

BRABANTIO

To prison, till fit time
Of law and course of direct session
Call thee to answer.

OTHELLO

What if I do obey?
How may the duke be therewith satisfied,
Whose messengers are here about my side,
Upon some present business of the state
To bring me to him?

FIRST OFFICER

'Tis true, most worthy signior;
The duke's in council and your noble self,
I am sure, is sent for.

BRABANTIO

How! the duke in council!
In this time of the night! Bring him away:
Mine's not an idle cause: the duke himself,
Or any of my brothers of the state,
Cannot but feel this wrong as 'twere their own;
For if such actions may have passage free,
Bond-slaves and pagans shall our statesmen be.

Exeunt

SCENE III. A council-chamber.

The DUKE and Senators sitting at a table; Officers attending

DUKE OF VENICE

There is no composition in these news
That gives them credit.

FIRST SENATOR

Indeed, they are disproportion'd;
My letters say a hundred and seven galleys.

DUKE OF VENICE

And mine, a hundred and forty.

SECOND SENATOR

And mine, two hundred:
But though they jump not on a just account,—
As in these cases, where the aim reports,
'Tis oft with difference—yet do they all confirm
A Turkish fleet, and bearing up to Cyprus.

DUKE OF VENICE

Nay, it is possible enough to judgment:
I do not so secure me in the error,
But the main article I do approve
In fearful sense.

SAILOR

[Within] What, ho! what, ho! what, ho!

FIRST OFFICER

A messenger from the galleys.

Enter a Sailor

DUKE OF VENICE

Now, what's the business?

SAILOR

The Turkish preparation makes for Rhodes;
So was I bid report here to the state
By Signior Angelo.

DUKE OF VENICE

How say you by this change?

FIRST SENATOR

This cannot be,
By no assay of reason: 'tis a pageant,
To keep us in false gaze. When we consider
The importancy of Cyprus to the Turk,
And let ourselves again but understand,
That as it more concerns the Turk than Rhodes,
So may he with more facile question bear it,
For that it stands not in such warlike brace,
But altogether lacks the abilities
That Rhodes is dress'd in: if we make thought of this,
We must not think the Turk is so unskilful
To leave that latest which concerns him first,
Neglecting an attempt of ease and gain,
To wake and wage a danger profitless.

DUKE OF VENICE

Nay, in all confidence, he's not for Rhodes.

FIRST OFFICER

Here is more news.

Enter a Messenger

MESSENGER

The Ottomites, reverend and gracious,
Steering with due course towards the isle of Rhodes,
Have there injointed them with an after fleet.

FIRST SENATOR

Ay, so I thought. How many, as you guess?

MESSENGER

Of thirty sail: and now they do restem
Their backward course, bearing with frank appearance
Their purposes toward Cyprus. Signior Montano,
Your trusty and most valiant servitor,
With his free duty recommends you thus,
And prays you to believe him.

DUKE OF VENICE

'Tis certain, then, for Cyprus.
Marcus Luccicos, is not he in town?

FIRST SENATOR

He's now in Florence.

DUKE OF VENICE

Write from us to him; post-post-haste dispatch.

FIRST SENATOR

Here comes Brabantio and the valiant Moor.

Enter BRABANTIO, OTHELLO, IAGO, RODERIGO, and Officers

DUKE OF VENICE

Valiant Othello, we must straight employ you
Against the general enemy Ottoman.

To BRABANTIO

I did not see you; welcome, gentle signior;
We lack'd your counsel and your help tonight.

BRABANTIO

So did I yours. Good your grace, pardon me;
Neither my place nor aught I heard of business
Hath raised me from my bed, nor doth the general care
Take hold on me, for my particular grief
Is of so flood-gate and o'erbearing nature
That it engluts and swallows other sorrows
And it is still itself.

DUKE OF VENICE

Why, what's the matter?

BRABANTIO

My daughter! O, my daughter!

DUKE OF VENICE Senator

Dead?

BRABANTIO

Ay, to me;
She is abused, stol'n from me, and corrupted
By spells and medicines bought of mountebanks;
For nature so preposterously to err,
Being not deficient, blind, or lame of sense,
Sans witchcraft could not.

DUKE OF VENICE

Whoe'er he be that in this foul proceeding
Hath thus beguiled your daughter of herself
And you of her, the bloody book of law
You shall yourself read in the bitter letter
After your own sense, yea, though our proper son
Stood in your action.

BRABANTIO

Humbly I thank your grace.
Here is the man, this Moor, whom now, it seems,
Your special mandate for the state-affairs
Hath hither brought.

DUKE OF VENICE Senator

We are very sorry for't.

DUKE OF VENICE

[To OTHELLO] What, in your own part, can you say to this?

BRABANTIO

Nothing, but this is so.

OTHELLO

Most potent, grave, and reverend signiors,
My very noble and approved good masters,
That I have ta'en away this old man's daughter,
It is most true; true, I have married her:
The very head and front of my offending
Hath this extent, no more. Rude am I in my speech,
And little bless'd with the soft phrase of peace:
For since these arms of mine had seven years' pith,
Till now some nine moons wasted, they have used
Their dearest action in the tented field,
And little of this great world can I speak,
More than pertains to feats of broil and battle,
And therefore little shall I grace my cause
In speaking for myself. Yet, by your gracious patience,
I will a round unvarnish'd tale deliver
Of my whole course of love; what drugs, what charms,
What conjuration and what mighty magic,
For such proceeding I am charged withal,
I won his daughter.

BRABANTIO

A maiden never bold;
Of spirit so still and quiet, that her motion
Blush'd at herself; and she, in spite of nature,
Of years, of country, credit, every thing,
To fall in love with what she fear'd to look on!
It is a judgment maim'd and most imperfect
That will confess perfection so could err
Against all rules of nature, and must be driven
To find out practises of cunning hell,
Why this should be. I therefore vouch again
That with some mixtures powerful o'er the blood,
Or with some dram conjured to this effect,
He wrought upon her.

DUKE OF VENICE

To vouch this, is no proof,
Without more wider and more overt test
Than these thin habits and poor likelihoods
Of modern seeming do prefer against him.

FIRST SENATOR

But, Othello, speak:
Did you by indirect and forced courses
Subdue and poison this young maid's affections?
Or came it by request and such fair question
As soul to soul affordeth?

OTHELLO

I do beseech you,
Send for the lady to the Sagittary,
And let her speak of me before her father:
If you do find me foul in her report,
The trust, the office I do hold of you,
Not only take away, but let your sentence
Even fall upon my life.

DUKE OF VENICE

Fetch Desdemona hither.

OTHELLO

Ancient, conduct them: you best know the place.

Exeunt IAGO and Attendants

And, till she come, as truly as to heaven
I do confess the vices of my blood,
So justly to your grave ears I'll present
How I did thrive in this fair lady's love,
And she in mine.

DUKE OF VENICE

Say it, Othello.

OTHELLO

Her father loved me; oft invited me;
Still question'd me the story of my life,
From year to year, the battles, sieges, fortunes,
That I have passed.
I ran it through, even from my boyish days,
To the very moment that he bade me tell it;
Wherein I spake of most disastrous chances,
Of moving accidents by flood and field
Of hair-breadth scapes i' the imminent deadly breach,
Of being taken by the insolent foe
And sold to slavery, of my redemption thence
And portance in my travels' history:
Wherein of antres vast and deserts idle,
Rough quarries, rocks and hills whose heads touch heaven
It was my hint to speak,—such was the process;
And of the Cannibals that each other eat,
The Anthropophagi and men whose heads
Do grow beneath their shoulders. This to hear
Would Desdemona seriously incline:
But still the house-affairs would draw her thence:
Which ever as she could with haste dispatch,
She'd come again, and with a greedy ear
Devour up my discourse: which I observing,
Took once a pliant hour, and found good means
To draw from her a prayer of earnest heart
That I would all my pilgrimage dilate,
Whereof by parcels she had something heard,
But not intentively: I did consent,
And often did beguile her of her tears,
When I did speak of some distressful stroke
That my youth suffer'd. My story being done,
She gave me for my pains a world of sighs:
She swore, in faith, twas strange, 'twas passing strange,
'Twas pitiful, 'twas wondrous pitiful:
She wish'd she had not heard it, yet she wish'd
That heaven had made her such a man: she thank'd me,
And bade me, if I had a friend that loved her,
I should but teach him how to tell my story.
And that would woo her. Upon this hint I spake:
She loved me for the dangers I had pass'd,
And I loved her that she did pity them.
This only is the witchcraft I have used:
Here comes the lady; let her witness it.

Enter DESDEMONA, IAGO, and Attendants

DUKE OF VENICE

I think this tale would win my daughter too.
Good Brabantio,
Take up this mangled matter at the best:
Men do their broken weapons rather use
Than their bare hands.

BRABANTIO

I pray you, hear her speak:
If she confess that she was half the wooer,
Destruction on my head, if my bad blame
Light on the man! Come hither, gentle mistress:
Do you perceive in all this noble company
Where most you owe obedience?

DESDEMONA

My noble father,
I do perceive here a divided duty:
To you I am bound for life and education;
My life and education both do learn me
How to respect you; you are the lord of duty;
I am hitherto your daughter: but here's my husband,
And so much duty as my mother show'd
To you, preferring you before her father,
So much I challenge that I may profess
Due to the Moor my lord.

BRABANTIO

God be wi' you! I have done.
Please it your grace, on to the state-affairs:
I had rather to adopt a child than get it.
Come hither, Moor:
I here do give thee that with all my heart
Which, but thou hast already, with all my heart
I would keep from thee. For your sake, jewel,
I am glad at soul I have no other child:
For thy escape would teach me tyranny,
To hang clogs on them. I have done, my lord.

DUKE OF VENICE

Let me speak like yourself, and lay a sentence,
Which, as a grise or step, may help these lovers
Into your favour.
When remedies are past, the griefs are ended
By seeing the worst, which late on hopes depended.
To mourn a mischief that is past and gone
Is the next way to draw new mischief on.
What cannot be preserved when fortune takes
Patience her injury a mockery makes.
The robb'd that smiles steals something from the thief;
He robs himself that spends a bootless grief.

BRABANTIO

So let the Turk of Cyprus us beguile;
We lose it not, so long as we can smile.
He bears the sentence well that nothing bears
But the free comfort which from thence he hears,
But he bears both the sentence and the sorrow
That, to pay grief, must of poor patience borrow.
These sentences, to sugar, or to gall,
Being strong on both sides, are equivocal:
But words are words; I never yet did hear
That the bruised heart was pierced through the ear.
I humbly beseech you, proceed to the affairs of state.

DUKE OF VENICE

The Turk with a most mighty preparation makes for Cyprus. Othello, the fortitude of the place is best known to you; and though we have there a substitute of most allowed sufficiency, yet opinion, a sovereign mistress of effects, throws a more safer voice on you: you must therefore be content to slubber the gloss of your new fortunes with this more stubborn and boisterous expedition.

OTHELLO

The tyrant custom, most grave senators,
Hath made the flinty and steel couch of war
My thrice-driven bed of down: I do agnise
A natural and prompt alacrity
I find in hardness, and do undertake
These present wars against the Ottomites.
Most humbly therefore bending to your state,
I crave fit disposition for my wife.
Due reference of place and exhibition,
With such accommodation and besort
As levels with her breeding.

DUKE OF VENICE

If you please,
Be't at her father's.

BRABANTIO

I'll not have it so.

OTHELLO

Nor I.

DESDEMONA

Nor I; I would not there reside,
To put my father in impatient thoughts
By being in his eye. Most gracious duke,
To my unfolding lend your prosperous ear;
And let me find a charter in your voice,
To assist my simpleness.

DUKE OF VENICE

What would You, Desdemona?

DESDEMONA

That I did love the Moor to live with him,
My downright violence and storm of fortunes
May trumpet to the world: my heart's subdued
Even to the very quality of my lord:
I saw Othello's visage in his mind,
And to his honour and his valiant parts
Did I my soul and fortunes consecrate.
So that, dear lords, if I be left behind,
A moth of peace, and he go to the war,
The rites for which I love him are bereft me,
And I a heavy interim shall support
By his dear absence. Let me go with him.

OTHELLO

Let her have your voices.
Vouch with me, heaven, I therefore beg it not,
To please the palate of my appetite,
Nor to comply with heat—the young affects
In me defunct—and proper satisfaction.
But to be free and bounteous to her mind:
And heaven defend your good souls, that you think
I will your serious and great business scant
For she is with me: no, when light-wing'd toys
Of feather'd Cupid seal with wanton dullness
My speculative and officed instruments,
That my disports corrupt and taint my business,
Let housewives make a skillet of my helm,
And all indign and base adversities
Make head against my estimation!

DUKE OF VENICE

Be it as you shall privately determine,
Either for her stay or going: the affair cries haste,
And speed must answer it.

FIRST SENATOR

You must away to-night.

OTHELLO

With all my heart.

DUKE OF VENICE

At nine i' the morning here we'll meet again.
Othello, leave some officer behind,
And he shall our commission bring to you;
With such things else of quality and respect
As doth import you.

OTHELLO

So please your grace, my ancient;
A man he is of honest and trust:

To his conveyance I assign my wife,
With what else needful your good grace shall think
To be sent after me.

DUKE OF VENICE

Let it be so.
Good night to every one.

To **BRABANTIO**

And, noble signior,
If virtue no delighted beauty lack,
Your son-in-law is far more fair than black.

FIRST SENATOR

Adieu, brave Moor, use Desdemona well.

BRABANTIO

Look to her, Moor, if thou hast eyes to see:
She has deceived her father, and may thee.

Exeunt DUKE OF VENICE, Senators, Officers, &c

OTHELLO

My life upon her faith! Honest Iago,
My Desdemona must I leave to thee:
I prithee, let thy wife attend on her:
And bring them after in the best advantage.
Come, Desdemona: I have but an hour
Of love, of worldly matters and direction,
To spend with thee: we must obey the time.

Exeunt OTHELLO and DESDEMONA

RODERIGO

Iago,—

IAGO

What say'st thou, noble heart?

RODERIGO

What will I do, thinkest thou?

IAGO

Why, go to bed, and sleep.

RODERIGO

I will incontinently drown myself.

IAGO

If thou dost, I shall never love thee after. Why, thou silly gentleman!

RODERIGO

It is silliness to live when to live is torment; and then have we a prescription to die when death is our physician.

IAGO

O villainous! I have looked upon the world for four times seven years; and since I could distinguish betwixt a benefit and an injury, I never found man that knew how to love himself. Ere I would say, I would drown myself for the love of a guinea-hen, I would change my humanity with a baboon.

RODERIGO

What should I do? I confess it is my shame to be so fond; but it is not in my virtue to amend it.

IAGO

Virtue! a fig! 'tis in ourselves that we are thus or thus. Our bodies are our gardens, to the which our wills are gardeners: so that if we will plant nettles, or sow lettuce, set hyssop and weed up thyme, supply it with one gender of herbs, or distract it with many, either to have it sterile with idleness, or manured with industry, why, the power and corrigible authority of this lies in our wills. If the balance of our lives had not one scale of reason to poise another of sensuality, the blood and baseness of our natures would conduct us to most preposterous conclusions: but we have reason to cool our raging motions, our carnal stings, our unbitted lusts, whereof I take this that you call love to be a sect or scion.

RODERIGO

It cannot be.

IAGO

It is merely a lust of the blood and a permission of the will. Come, be a man. Drown thyself! drown cats and blind puppies. I have professed me thy friend and I confess me knit to thy deserving with cables of perdurable toughness; I could never better stead thee than now. Put money in thy purse; follow thou the wars; defeat thy favour with an usurped beard; I say, put money in thy purse. It cannot be that Desdemona should long continue her love to the Moor,—put money in thy purse,—nor he his to her: it was a violent commencement, and thou shalt see an answerable sequestration:—put but money in thy purse. These Moors are changeable in their wills: fill thy purse with money:—the food that to him now is as luscious as locusts, shall be to him shortly as bitter as coloquintida. She must change for youth: when she is sated with his body, she will find the error of her choice: she must have change, she must: therefore put money in thy purse. If thou wilt needs damn thyself, do it a more delicate way than drowning. Make all the money thou canst: if sanctimony and a frail vow betwixt an erring barbarian and a supersubtle Venetian not too hard for my wits and all the tribe of hell, thou shalt enjoy her; therefore make money. A pox of drowning thyself! it is clean out of the way: seek thou rather to be hanged in compassing thy joy than to be drowned and go without her.

RODERIGO

Wilt thou be fast to my hopes, if I depend on the issue?

IAGO

Thou art sure of me:–go, make money:—I have told thee often, and I re-tell thee again and again, I hate the Moor: my cause is hearted; thine hath no less reason. Let us be conjunctive in our revenge against him: if thou canst cuckold him, thou dost thyself a pleasure, me a sport. There are many events in the womb of time which will be delivered. Traverse! go, provide thy money. We will have more of this to-morrow. Adieu.

RODERIGO

Where shall we meet i' the morning?

IAGO

At my lodging.

RODERIGO

I'll be with thee betimes.

IAGO

Go to; farewell. Do you hear, Roderigo?

RODERIGO

What say you?

IAGO

No more of drowning, do you hear?

RODERIGO

I am changed: I'll go sell all my land.

Exit

IAGO

Thus do I ever make my fool my purse:
For I mine own gain'd knowledge should profane,
If I would time expend with such a snipe.
But for my sport and profit. I hate the Moor:
And it is thought abroad, that 'twixt my sheets
He has done my office: I know not if't be true;
But I, for mere suspicion in that kind,
Will do as if for surety. He holds me well;
The better shall my purpose work on him.
Cassio's a proper man: let me see now:
To get his place and to plume up my will

In double knavery—How, how? Let's see:—
After some time, to abuse Othello's ear
That he is too familiar with his wife.
He hath a person and a smooth dispose
To be suspected, framed to make women false.
The Moor is of a free and open nature,
That thinks men honest that but seem to be so,
And will as tenderly be led by the nose
As asses are.
I have't. It is engender'd. Hell and night
Must bring this monstrous birth to the world's light.

Exit

ACT II

SCENE I. A Sea-port in Cyprus. An open place near the quay.

Enter MONTANO and two Gentlemen

MONTANO

What from the cape can you discern at sea?

FIRST GENTLEMAN

Nothing at all: it is a highwrought flood;
I cannot, 'twixt the heaven and the main,
Descry a sail.

MONTANO

Methinks the wind hath spoke aloud at land;
A fuller blast ne'er shook our battlements:
If it hath ruffian'd so upon the sea,
What ribs of oak, when mountains melt on them,
Can hold the mortise? What shall we hear of this?

SECOND GENTLEMAN

A segregation of the Turkish fleet:
For do but stand upon the foaming shore,
The chidden billow seems to pelt the clouds;
The wind-shaked surge, with high and monstrous mane,
seems to cast water on the burning bear,
And quench the guards of the ever-fixed pole:
I never did like molestation view
On the enchafed flood.

MONTANO

If that the Turkish fleet
Be not enshelter'd and embay'd, they are drown'd:
It is impossible they bear it out.

Enter a third Gentleman

THIRD GENTLEMAN

News, lads! our wars are done.
The desperate tempest hath so bang'd the Turks,
That their designment halts: a noble ship of Venice
Hath seen a grievous wreck and sufferance
On most part of their fleet.

MONTANO

How! is this true?

THIRD GENTLEMAN

The ship is here put in,
A Veronesa; Michael Cassio,
Lieutenant to the warlike Moor Othello,
Is come on shore: the Moor himself at sea,
And is in full commission here for Cyprus.

MONTANO

I am glad on't; 'tis a worthy governor.

THIRD GENTLEMAN

But this same Cassio, though he speak of comfort
Touching the Turkish loss, yet he looks sadly,
And prays the Moor be safe; for they were parted
With foul and violent tempest.

MONTANO

Pray heavens he be;
For I have served him, and the man commands

Like a full soldier. Let's to the seaside, ho!
As well to see the vessel that's come in
As to throw out our eyes for brave Othello,
Even till we make the main and the aerial blue
An indistinct regard.

THIRD GENTLEMAN

Come, let's do so:
For every minute is expectancy
Of more arrivance.

Enter CASSIO

CASSIO

Thanks, you the valiant of this warlike isle,
That so approve the Moor! O, let the heavens
Give him defence against the elements,
For I have lost us him on a dangerous sea.

MONTANO

Is he well shipp'd?

CASSIO

His bark is stoutly timber'd, his pilot
Of very expert and approved allowance;
Therefore my hopes, not surfeited to death,
Stand in bold cure.

A cry within 'A sail, a sail, a sail!'

Enter a fourth Gentleman

CASSIO

What noise?

FOURTH GENTLEMAN

The town is empty; on the brow o' the sea
Stand ranks of people, and they cry 'A sail!'

CASSIO

My hopes do shape him for the governor.

Guns heard

SECOND GENTLEMEN

They do discharge their shot of courtesy:
Our friends at least.

CASSIO

I pray you, sir, go forth,
And give us truth who 'tis that is arrived.

SECOND GENTLEMAN

I shall.

Exit

MONTANO

But, good lieutenant, is your general wived?

CASSIO

Most fortunately: he hath achieved a maid
That paragons description and wild fame;
One that excels the quirks of blazoning pens,
And in the essential vesture of creation
Does tire the ingener.

Re-enter second Gentleman

How now! who has put in?

SECOND GENTLEMAN

'Tis one Iago, ancient to the general.

CASSIO

Has had most favourable and happy speed:
Tempests themselves, high seas, and howling winds,
The gutter'd rocks and congregated sands—
Traitors ensteep'd to clog the guiltless keel,—
As having sense of beauty, do omit
Their mortal natures, letting go safely by
The divine Desdemona.

MONTANO

What is she?

CASSIO

She that I spake of, our great captain's captain,
Left in the conduct of the bold Iago,
Whose footing here anticipates our thoughts
A se'nnight's speed. Great Jove, Othello guard,

And swell his sail with thine own powerful breath,
That he may bless this bay with his tall ship,
Make love's quick pants in Desdemona's arms,
Give renew'd fire to our extincted spirits
And bring all Cyprus comfort!

Enter DESDEMONA, EMILIA, IAGO, RODERIGO, and Attendants

O, behold,
The riches of the ship is come on shore!
Ye men of Cyprus, let her have your knees.
Hail to thee, lady! and the grace of heaven,
Before, behind thee, and on every hand,
Enwheel thee round!

DESDEMONA

I thank you, valiant Cassio.
What tidings can you tell me of my lord?

CASSIO

He is not yet arrived: nor know I aught
But that he's well and will be shortly here.

DESDEMONA

O, but I fear–How lost you company?

CASSIO

The great contention of the sea and skies
Parted our fellowship—But, hark! a sail.

Within 'A sail, a sail!' Guns heard

SECOND GENTLEMAN

They give their greeting to the citadel;
This likewise is a friend.

CASSIO

See for the news.

Exit Gentleman

Good ancient, you are welcome.

To EMILIA

Welcome, mistress.
Let it not gall your patience, good Iago,
That I extend my manners; 'tis my breeding
That gives me this bold show of courtesy.

Kissing her

IAGO

Sir, would she give you so much of her lips
As of her tongue she oft bestows on me,
You'll have enough.

DESDEMONA

Alas, she has no speech.

IAGO

In faith, too much;
I find it still, when I have list to sleep:
Marry, before your ladyship, I grant,
She puts her tongue a little in her heart,
And chides with thinking.

EMILIA

You have little cause to say so.

IAGO

Come on, come on; you are pictures out of doors,
Bells in your parlors, wild-cats in your kitchens,
Saints m your injuries, devils being offended,
Players in your housewifery, and housewives' in your beds.

DESDEMONA

O, fie upon thee, slanderer!

IAGO

Nay, it is true, or else I am a Turk:
You rise to play and go to bed to work.

EMILIA

You shall not write my praise.

IAGO

No, let me not.

DESDEMONA

What wouldst thou write of me, if thou shouldst praise me?

IAGO

O gentle lady, do not put me to't;
For I am nothing, if not critical.

DESDEMONA

Come on assay. There's one gone to the harbour?

IAGO

Ay, madam.

DESDEMONA

I am not merry; but I do beguile
The thing I am, by seeming otherwise.
Come, how wouldst thou praise me?

IAGO

I am about it; but indeed my invention
Comes from my pate as birdlime does from frize;
It plucks out brains and all: but my Muse labours,
And thus she is deliver'd.
If she be fair and wise, fairness and wit,
The one's for use, the other useth it.

DESDEMONA

Well praised! How if she be black and witty?

IAGO

If she be black, and thereto have a wit,
She'll find a white that shall her blackness fit.

DESDEMONA

Worse and worse.

EMILIA

How if fair and foolish?

IAGO

She never yet was foolish that was fair;
For even her folly help'd her to an heir.

DESDEMONA

These are old fond paradoxes to make fools laugh i' the alehouse. What miserable praise hast thou for her that's foul and foolish?

IAGO

There's none so foul and foolish thereunto,
But does foul pranks which fair and wise ones do.

DESDEMONA

O heavy ignorance! thou praisest the worst best.
But what praise couldst thou bestow on a deserving woman indeed, one that, in the authority of her merit, did justly put on the vouch of very malice itself?

IAGO

She that was ever fair and never proud,
Had tongue at will and yet was never loud,
Never lack'd gold and yet went never gay,
Fled from her wish and yet said 'Now I may,'
She that being anger'd, her revenge being nigh,
Bade her wrong stay and her displeasure fly,
She that in wisdom never was so frail
To change the cod's head for the salmon's tail;
She that could think and ne'er disclose her mind,
See suitors following and not look behind,
She was a wight, if ever such wight were,—

DESDEMONA

To do what?

IAGO

To suckle fools and chronicle small beer.

DESDEMONA

O most lame and impotent conclusion! Do not learn of him, Emilia, though he be thy husband. How say you, Cassio? is he not a most profane and liberal counsellor?

CASSIO

He speaks home, madam: You may relish him more in the soldier than in the scholar.

IAGO

[Aside] He takes her by the palm: ay, well said, whisper: with as little a web as this will I ensnare as great a fly as Cassio. Ay, smile upon her, do; I will gyve thee in thine own courtship. You say true; 'tis so, indeed: if such tricks as these strip you out of your lieutenantry, it had been better you had not kissed your three fingers so oft, which now again you are most apt to play the sir in. Very good; well kissed! an excellent courtesy! 'tis so, indeed. Yet again your fingers to your lips? would they were clyster-pipes for your sake!

Trumpet within

The Moor! I know his trumpet.

CASSIO

'Tis truly so.

DESDEMONA

Let's meet him and receive him.

CASSIO

Lo, where he comes!

Enter OTHELLO and Attendants

OTHELLO

O my fair warrior!

DESDEMONA

My dear Othello!

OTHELLO

It gives me wonder great as my content
To see you here before me. O my soul's joy!
If after every tempest come such calms,
May the winds blow till they have waken'd death!
And let the labouring bark climb hills of seas
Olympus-high and duck again as low
As hell's from heaven! If it were now to die,
'Twere now to be most happy; for, I fear,
My soul hath her content so absolute
That not another comfort like to this
Succeeds in unknown fate.

DESDEMONA

The heavens forbid
But that our loves and comforts should increase,
Even as our days do grow!

OTHELLO

Amen to that, sweet powers!
I cannot speak enough of this content;
It stops me here; it is too much of joy:
And this, and this, the greatest discords be

Kissing her

That e'er our hearts shall make!

IAGO

[Aside] O, you are well tuned now!
But I'll set down the pegs that make this music,
As honest as I am.

OTHELLO

Come, let us to the castle.
News, friends; our wars are done, the Turks are drown'd.
How does my old acquaintance of this isle?
Honey, you shall be well desired in Cyprus;
I have found great love amongst them.
O my sweet,
I prattle out of fashion, and I dote
In mine own comforts. I prithee, good Iago,
Go to the bay and disembark my coffers:
Bring thou the master to the citadel;
He is a good one, and his worthiness
Does challenge much respect. Come, Desdemona,
Once more, well met at Cyprus.

Exeunt OTHELLO, DESDEMONA, and Attendants

IAGO

Do thou meet me presently at the harbour.
Come hither. If thou be'st valiant,—as, they

say, base men being in love have then a nobility in their natures more than is native to them—list me. The lieutenant tonight watches on the court of guard:—first, I must tell thee this—Desdemona is directly in love with him.

RODERIGO

With him! why, 'tis not possible.

IAGO

Lay thy finger thus, and let thy soul be instructed. Mark me with what violence she first loved the Moor, but for bragging and telling her fantastical lies: and will she love him still for prating? let not thy discreet heart think it. Her eye must be fed; and what delight shall she have to look on the devil? When the blood is made dull with the act of sport, there should be, again to inflame it and to give satiety a fresh appetite, loveliness in favour, sympathy in years, manners and beauties; all which the Moor is defective in: now, for want of these required conveniences, her delicate tenderness will find itself abused, begin to heave the gorge, disrelish and abhor the Moor; very nature will instruct her in it and compel her to some second choice. Now, sir, this granted,—as it is a most pregnant and unforced position–who stands so eminent in the degree of this fortune as Cassio does? a knave very voluble; no further conscionable than in putting on the mere form of civil and humane seeming, for the better compassing of his salt and most hidden loose affection? why, none; why, none: a slipper and subtle knave, a finder of occasions, that has an eye can stamp and counterfeit advantages, though true advantage never present itself; a devilish knave. Besides, the knave is handsome, young, and hath all those requisites in him that folly and green minds look after: a pestilent complete knave; and the woman hath found him already.

RODERIGO

I cannot believe that in her; she's full of most blessed condition.

IAGO

Blessed fig's-end! the wine she drinks is made of grapes: if she had been blessed, she would never have loved the Moor. Blessed pudding! Didst thou not see her paddle with the palm of his hand? didst not mark that?

RODERIGO

Yes, that I did; but that was but courtesy.

IAGO

Lechery, by this hand; an index and obscure prologue to the history of lust and foul thoughts. They met so near with their lips that their breaths embraced together. Villanous thoughts, Roderigo! when these mutualities so marshal the way, hard at hand comes the master and main exercise, the incorporate conclusion, Pish! But, sir, be you ruled by me: I have brought you from Venice. Watch you to-night; for the command, I'll lay't upon you. Cassio knows you not. I'll not be far from you: do you find some occasion to anger Cassio, either by speaking too loud, or tainting his discipline; or from what other course you please, which the time shall more favourably minister.

RODERIGO

Well.

IAGO

Sir, he is rash and very sudden in choler, and haply may strike at you: provoke him, that he may; for even out of that will I cause these of Cyprus to mutiny; whose qualification shall come into no true taste again but by the displanting of Cassio. So shall you have a shorter journey to your desires by the means I shall then have to prefer them; and the impediment most profitably removed, without the which there were no expectation of our prosperity.

RODERIGO

I will do this, if I can bring it to any opportunity.

IAGO

I warrant thee. Meet me by and by at the citadel:
I must fetch his necessaries ashore. Farewell.

RODERIGO

Adieu.

Exit

IAGO

That Cassio loves her, I do well believe it;
That she loves him, 'tis apt and of great credit:
The Moor, howbeit that I endure him not,
Is of a constant, loving, noble nature,
And I dare think he'll prove to Desdemona
A most dear husband. Now, I do love her too;
Not out of absolute lust, though peradventure
I stand accountant for as great a sin,
But partly led to diet my revenge,
For that I do suspect the lusty Moor
Hath leap'd into my seat; the thought whereof
Doth, like a poisonous mineral, gnaw my inwards;
And nothing can or shall content my soul
Till I am even'd with him, wife for wife,
Or failing so, yet that I put the Moor
At least into a jealousy so strong
That judgment cannot cure. Which thing to do,
If this poor trash of Venice, whom I trash
For his quick hunting, stand the putting on,
I'll have our Michael Cassio on the hip,
Abuse him to the Moor in the rank garb–
For I fear Cassio with my night-cap too–
Make the Moor thank me, love me and reward me.
For making him egregiously an ass
And practising upon his peace and quiet
Even to madness. 'Tis here, but yet confused:
Knavery's plain face is never seen tin used.

Exit

SCENE II. A street.

Enter a Herald with a proclamation; People following

HERALD

It is Othello's pleasure, our noble and valiant general, that, upon certain tidings now arrived, importing the mere perdition of the Turkish fleet, every man put himself into triumph; some to dance, some to make bonfires, each man to what sport and revels his addiction leads him: for, besides these beneficial news, it is the celebration of his nuptial. So much was his pleasure should be proclaimed. All offices are open, and there is full liberty of feasting from this present hour of five till the bell have told eleven. Heaven bless the isle of Cyprus and our noble general Othello!

Exeunt

SCENE III. A hall in the castle.

Enter OTHELLO, DESDEMONA, CASSIO, and Attendants

OTHELLO

Good Michael, look you to the guard to-night:
Let's teach ourselves that honourable stop,
Not to outsport discretion.

CASSIO

Iago hath direction what to do;
But, notwithstanding, with my personal eye
Will I look to't.

OTHELLO

Iago is most honest.
Michael, good night: to-morrow with your earliest
Let me have speech with you.

To DESDEMONA

Come, my dear love,
The purchase made, the fruits are to ensue;
That profit's yet to come 'tween me and you.
Good night.

Exeunt OTHELLO, DESDEMONA, and Attendants

Enter IAGO

CASSIO

Welcome, Iago; we must to the watch.

IAGO

Not this hour, lieutenant; 'tis not yet ten o' the clock. Our general cast us thus early for the love of his Desdemona; who let us not therefore blame: he hath not yet made wanton the night with her; and she is sport for Jove.

CASSIO

She's a most exquisite lady.

IAGO

And, I'll warrant her, fun of game.

CASSIO

Indeed, she's a most fresh and delicate creature.

IAGO

What an eye she has! methinks it sounds a parley of provocation.

CASSIO

An inviting eye; and yet methinks right modest.

IAGO

And when she speaks, is it not an alarum to love?

CASSIO

She is indeed perfection.

IAGO

Well, happiness to their sheets! Come, lieutenant, I have a stoup of wine; and here without are a brace of Cyprus gallants that would fain have a measure to the health of black Othello.

CASSIO

Not to-night, good Iago: I have very poor and unhappy brains for drinking: I could well wish courtesy would invent some other custom of entertainment.

IAGO

O, they are our friends; but one cup: I'll drink for you.

CASSIO

I have drunk but one cup to-night, and that was craftily qualified too, and, behold, what innovation it makes here: I am unfortunate in the infirmity, and dare not task my weakness with any more.

IAGO

What, man! 'tis a night of revels: the gallants desire it.

CASSIO

Where are they?

IAGO

Here at the door; I pray you, call them in.

CASSIO

I'll do't; but it dislikes me.

Exit

IAGO

If I can fasten but one cup upon him,
With that which he hath drunk to-night already,
He'll be as full of quarrel and offence
As my young mistress' dog. Now, my sick fool Roderigo,
Whom love hath turn'd almost the wrong side out,
To Desdemona hath to-night caroused
Potations pottle-deep; and he's to watch:
Three lads of Cyprus, noble swelling spirits,
That hold their honours in a wary distance,
The very elements of this warlike isle,
Have I to-night fluster'd with flowing cups,
And they watch too. Now, 'mongst this flock of drunkards,
Am I to put our Cassio in some action
That may offend the isle.—But here they come:
If consequence do but approve my dream,
My boat sails freely, both with wind and stream.

Re-enter CASSIO; with him MONTANO and Gentlemen; servants following with wine

CASSIO

'Fore God, they have given me a rouse already.

MONTANO

Good faith, a little one; not past a pint, as I am a soldier.

IAGO

Some wine, ho!

Sings

And let me the canakin clink, clink;
And let me the canakin clink
A soldier's a man;
A life's but a span;
Why, then, let a soldier drink.
Some wine, boys!

CASSIO

'Fore God, an excellent song.

IAGO

I learned it in England, where, indeed, they are most potent in potting: your Dane, your German, and your swag-bellied Hollander—Drink, ho!—are nothing to your English.

CASSIO

Is your Englishman so expert in his drinking?

IAGO

Why, he drinks you, with facility, your Dane dead drunk; he sweats not to overthrow your Almain; he gives your Hollander a vomit, ere the next pottle can be filled.

CASSIO

To the health of our general!

MONTANO

I am for it, lieutenant; and I'll do you justice.

IAGO

O sweet England!
King Stephen was a worthy peer,
His breeches cost him but a crown;
He held them sixpence all too dear,
With that he call'd the tailor lown.
He was a wight of high renown,
And thou art but of low degree:
'Tis pride that pulls the country down;
Then take thine auld cloak about thee.
Some wine, ho!

CASSIO

Why, this is a more exquisite song than the other.

IAGO

Will you hear't again?

CASSIO

No; for I hold him to be unworthy of his place that does those things. Well, God's above all; and there be souls must be saved, and there be souls must not be saved.

IAGO

It's true, good lieutenant.

CASSIO

For mine own part,—no offence to the general, nor any man of quality,—I hope to be saved.

IAGO

And so do I too, lieutenant.

CASSIO

Ay, but, by your leave, not before me; the lieutenant is to be saved before the ancient. Let's have no more of this; let's to our affairs.—Forgive us our sins!—Gentlemen, let's look to our business. Do not think, gentlemen. I am drunk: this is my ancient; this is my right hand, and this is my left: I am not drunk now; I can stand well enough, and speak well enough.

ALL

Excellent well.

CASSIO

Why, very well then; you must not think then that I am drunk.

Exit

MONTANO

To the platform, masters; come, let's set the watch.

IAGO

You see this fellow that is gone before;
He is a soldier fit to stand by Caesar
And give direction: and do but see his vice;
'Tis to his virtue a just equinox,
The one as long as the other: 'tis pity of him.
I fear the trust Othello puts him in.
On some odd time of his infirmity,
Will shake this island.

MONTANO

But is he often thus?

IAGO

'Tis evermore the prologue to his sleep:
He'll watch the horologe a double set,
If drink rock not his cradle.

MONTANO

It were well
The general were put in mind of it.
Perhaps he sees it not; or his good nature
Prizes the virtue that appears in Cassio,
And looks not on his evils: is not this true?

Enter RODERIGO

IAGO

[Aside to him] How now, Roderigo!
I pray you, after the lieutenant; go.

Exit RODERIGO

MONTANO

And 'tis great pity that the noble Moor
Should hazard such a place as his own second
With one of an ingraft infirmity:
It were an honest action to say
So to the Moor.

IAGO

Not I, for this fair island:
I do love Cassio well; and would do much
To cure him of this evil—But, hark! what noise?

Cry within: 'Help! help!'

Re-enter CASSIO, driving in RODERIGO

CASSIO

You rogue! you rascal!

MONTANO

What's the matter, lieutenant?

CASSIO

A knave teach me my duty!
I'll beat the knave into a twiggen bottle.

RODERIGO

Beat me!

CASSIO

Dost thou prate, rogue?

Striking RODERIGO

MONTANO

Nay, good lieutenant;

Staying him

I pray you, sir, hold your hand.

CASSIO

Let me go, sir,
Or I'll knock you o'er the mazzard.

MONTANO

Come, come,
you're drunk.

CASSIO

Drunk!

They fight

IAGO

[Aside to RODERIGO] Away, I say; go out, and cry a mutiny.

Exit RODERIGO

Nay, good lieutenant,—alas, gentlemen;—
Help, ho!—Lieutenant,—sir,—Montano,—sir;
Help, masters!—Here's a goodly watch indeed!

Bell rings

Who's that which rings the bell?—Diablo, ho!
The town will rise: God's will, lieutenant, hold!
You will be shamed for ever.

Re-enter OTHELLO and Attendants

OTHELLO

What is the matter here?

MONTANO

'Zounds, I bleed still; I am hurt to the death.

Faints

OTHELLO

Hold, for your lives!

IAGO

Hold, ho! Lieutenant,—sir-Montano,—gentlemen,—
Have you forgot all sense of place and duty?
Hold! the general speaks to you; hold, hold, for shame!

OTHELLO

Why, how now, ho! from whence ariseth this?
Are we turn'd Turks, and to ourselves do that
Which heaven hath forbid the Ottomites?
For Christian shame, put by this barbarous brawl:
He that stirs next to carve for his own rage
Holds his soul light; he dies upon his motion.
Silence that dreadful bell: it frights the isle
From her propriety. What is the matter, masters?
Honest Iago, that look'st dead with grieving,
Speak, who began this? on thy love, I charge thee.

IAGO

I do not know: friends all but now, even now,
In quarter, and in terms like bride and groom
Devesting them for bed; and then, but now–
As if some planet had unwitted men–
Swords out, and tilting one at other's breast,

Racial Matters

In opposition bloody. I cannot speak
Any beginning to this peevish odds;
And would in action glorious I had lost
Those legs that brought me to a part of it!

OTHELLO

How comes it, Michael, you are thus forgot?

CASSIO

I pray you, pardon me; I cannot speak.

OTHELLO

Worthy Montano, you were wont be civil;
The gravity and stillness of your youth
The world hath noted, and your name is great
In mouths of wisest censure: what's the matter,
That you unlace your reputation thus
And spend your rich opinion for the name
Of a night-brawler? give me answer to it.

MONTANO

Worthy Othello, I am hurt to danger:
Your officer, Iago, can inform you,—
While I spare speech, which something now offends me,—
Of all that I do know: nor know I aught
By me that's said or done amiss this night;
Unless self-charity be sometimes a vice,
And to defend ourselves it be a sin
When violence assails us.

OTHELLO

Now, by heaven,
My blood begins my safer guides to rule;
And passion, having my best judgment collied,
Assays to lead the way: if I once stir,
Or do but lift this arm, the best of you
Shall sink in my rebuke. Give me to know
How this foul rout began, who set it on;
And he that is approved in this offence,
Though he had twinn'd with me, both at a birth,
Shall lose me. What! in a town of war,
Yet wild, the people's hearts brimful of fear,
To manage private and domestic quarrel,
In night, and on the court and guard of safety!
'Tis monstrous. Iago, who began't?

MONTANO

If partially affined, or leagued in office,
Thou dost deliver more or less than truth,
Thou art no soldier.

IAGO

Touch me not so near:
I had rather have this tongue cut from my mouth
Than it should do offence to Michael Cassio;
Yet, I persuade myself, to speak the truth
Shall nothing wrong him. Thus it is, general.
Montano and myself being in speech,
There comes a fellow crying out for help:
And Cassio following him with determined sword,
To execute upon him. Sir, this gentleman
Steps in to Cassio, and entreats his pause:
Myself the crying fellow did pursue,
Lest by his clamour—as it so fell out—
The town might fall in fright: he, swift of foot,
Outran my purpose; and I return'd the rather
For that I heard the clink and fall of swords,
And Cassio high in oath; which till to-night
I ne'er might say before. When I came back—For this was brief—I found them close together,
At blow and thrust; even as again they were
When you yourself did part them.
More of this matter cannot I report:
But men are men; the best sometimes forget:
Though Cassio did some little wrong to him,
As men in rage strike those that wish them best,
Yet surely Cassio, I believe, received
From him that fled some strange indignity,
Which patience could not pass.

OTHELLO

I know, Iago,
Thy honesty and love doth mince this matter,
Making it light to Cassio. Cassio, I love thee
But never more be officer of mine.

Re-enter DESDEMONA, attended

Look, if my gentle love be not raised up!
I'll make thee an example.

DESDEMONA

What's the matter?

OTHELLO

All's well now, sweeting; come away to bed.
Sir, for your hurts, myself will be your surgeon:
Lead him off.

To MONTANO, who is led off

Iago, look with care about the town,
And silence those whom this vile brawl distracted.
Come, Desdemona: 'tis the soldiers' life
To have their balmy slumbers waked with strife.

Exeunt all but IAGO and CASSIO

IAGO

What, are you hurt, lieutenant?

CASSIO

Ay, past all surgery.

IAGO

Marry, heaven forbid!

CASSIO

Reputation, reputation, reputation! O, I have lost my reputation! I have lost the immortal part of myself, and what remains is bestial. My reputation, Iago, my reputation!

IAGO

As I am an honest man, I thought you had received some bodily wound; there is more sense in that than in reputation. Reputation is an idle and most false imposition: oft got without merit, and lost without deserving: you have lost no reputation at all, unless you repute yourself such a loser. What, man! there are ways to recover the general again: you are but now cast in his mood, a punishment more in policy than in malice, even so as one would beat his offenceless dog to affright an imperious lion: sue to him again, and he's yours.

CASSIO

I will rather sue to be despised than to deceive so good a commander with so slight, so drunken, and so indiscreet an officer. Drunk? and speak parrot? and squabble? swagger? swear? and discourse fustian with one's own shadow? O thou invisible spirit of wine, if thou hast no name to be known by, let us call thee devil!

IAGO

What was he that you followed with your sword? What had he done to you?

CASSIO

I know not.

IAGO

Is't possible?

CASSIO

I remember a mass of things, but nothing distinctly; a quarrel, but nothing wherefore. O God, that men should put an enemy in their mouths to steal away their brains! that we should, with joy, pleasance revel and applause, transform ourselves into beasts!

IAGO

Why, but you are now well enough: how came you thus recovered?

CASSIO

It hath pleased the devil drunkenness to give place to the devil wrath; one unperfectness shows me another, to make me frankly despise myself.

IAGO

Come, you are too severe a moraler: as the time, the place, and the condition of this country stands, I could heartily wish this had not befallen; but, since it is as it is, mend it for your own good.

CASSIO

I will ask him for my place again; he shall tell me I am a drunkard! Had I as many mouths as Hydra, such an answer would stop them all. To be now a sensible man, by and by a fool, and presently a beast! O strange! Every inordinate cup is unblessed and the ingredient is a devil.

IAGO

Come, come, good wine is a good familiar creature, if it be well used: exclaim no more against it. And, good lieutenant, I think you think I love you.

CASSIO

I have well approved it, sir. I drunk!

IAGO

You or any man living may be drunk! at a time, man. I'll tell you what you shall do. Our general's wife is now the general: may say so in this respect, for that he hath devoted and given up himself to the contemplation, mark, and denotement of her parts and graces: confess yourself freely to her; importune her help to put you in your place again: she is of so free, so kind, so apt, so blessed a disposition, she holds it a vice in her goodness not to do more than she is requested: this broken joint between you and her husband entreat her to splinter; and, my fortunes against any lay worth naming, this crack of your love shall grow stronger than it was before.

CASSIO

You advise me well.

IAGO

I protest, in the sincerity of love and honest kindness.

CASSIO

I think it freely; and betimes in the morning I will beseech the virtuous Desdemona to undertake for me: I am desperate of my fortunes if they cheque me here.

IAGO

You are in the right. Good night, lieutenant; I must to the watch.
CASSIO: Good night, honest Iago.

Exit

IAGO

And what's he then that says I play the villain?
When this advice is free I give and honest,
Probal to thinking and indeed the course
To win the Moor again? For 'tis most easy
The inclining Desdemona to subdue
In any honest suit: she's framed as fruitful
As the free elements. And then for her
To win the Moor—were't to renounce his baptism,
All seals and symbols of redeemed sin,
His soul is so enfetter'd to her love,
That she may make, unmake, do what she list,
Even as her appetite shall play the god
With his weak function. How am I then a villain
To counsel Cassio to this parallel course,
Directly to his good? Divinity of hell!

When devils will the blackest sins put on,
They do suggest at first with heavenly shows,
As I do now: for whiles this honest fool
Plies Desdemona to repair his fortunes
And she for him pleads strongly to the Moor,
I'll pour this pestilence into his ear,
That she repeals him for her body's lust;
And by how much she strives to do him good,
She shall undo her credit with the Moor.
So will I turn her virtue into pitch,
And out of her own goodness make the net
That shall enmesh them all.

Re-enter RODERIGO

How now, Roderigo!

RODERIGO

I do follow here in the chase, not like a hound that hunts, but one that fills up the cry. My money is almost spent; I have been to-night exceedingly well cudgelled; and I think the issue will be, I shall have so much experience for my pains, and so, with no money at all and a little more wit, return again to Venice.

IAGO

How poor are they that have not patience!
What wound did ever heal but by degrees?
Thou know'st we work by wit, and not by witchcraft;
And wit depends on dilatory time.
Does't not go well? Cassio hath beaten thee.
And thou, by that small hurt, hast cashier'd Cassio:
Though other things grow fair against the sun,
Yet fruits that blossom first will first be ripe:
Content thyself awhile. By the mass, 'tis morning;
Pleasure and action make the hours seem short.
Retire thee; go where thou art billeted:
Away, I say; thou shalt know more hereafter:
Nay, get thee gone.

Exit RODERIGO

Two things are to be done:
My wife must move for Cassio to her mistress;
I'll set her on;
Myself the while to draw the Moor apart,
And bring him jump when he may Cassio find
Soliciting his wife: ay, that's the way
Dull not device by coldness and delay.

Exit

ACT III

SCENE I. Before the castle.

Enter CASSIO and some Musicians

CASSIO

Masters, play here; I will content your pains;
Something that's brief; and bid 'Good morrow, general.'

Music

Enter Clown

CLOWN

Why masters, have your instruments been in Naples, that they speak i' the nose thus?

FIRST MUSICIAN

How, sir, how!

CLOWN

Are these, I pray you, wind-instruments?

FIRST MUSICIAN

Ay, marry, are they, sir.

CLOWN

O, thereby hangs a tail.

FIRST MUSICIAN

Whereby hangs a tale, sir?

CLOWN

Marry. sir, by many a wind-instrument that I know. But, masters, here's money for you:

and the general so likes your music, that he desires you, for love's sake, to make no more noise with it.

FIRST MUSICIAN

Well, sir, we will not.

CLOWN

If you have any music that may not be heard, to't again: but, as they say to hear music the general does not greatly care.

FIRST MUSICIAN

We have none such, sir.

CLOWN

Then put up your pipes in your bag, for I'll away: go; vanish into air; away!

Exeunt Musicians

CASSIO

Dost thou hear, my honest friend?

CLOWN

No, I hear not your honest friend; I hear you.

CASSIO

Prithee, keep up thy quillets. There's a poor piece of gold for thee: if the gentlewoman that attends the general's wife be stirring, tell her there's one Cassio entreats her a little favour of speech: wilt thou do this?

CLOWN

She is stirring, sir: if she will stir hither, I shall seem to notify unto her.

CASSIO

Do, good my friend.

Exit Clown

Enter IAGO

In happy time, Iago.

IAGO

You have not been a-bed, then?

CASSIO

Why, no; the day had broke
Before we parted. I have made bold, Iago,
To send in to your wife: my suit to her
Is, that she will to virtuous Desdemona
Procure me some access.

IAGO

I'll send her to you presently;
And I'll devise a mean to draw the Moor
Out of the way, that your converse and business
May be more free.

CASSIO

I humbly thank you for't.

Exit IAGO

I never knew
A Florentine more kind and honest.

Enter EMILIA

EMILIA

Good morrow, good Lieutenant: I am sorry
For your displeasure; but all will sure be well.
The general and his wife are talking of it;
And she speaks for you stoutly: the Moor replies,
That he you hurt is of great fame in Cyprus,
And great affinity, and that in wholesome wisdom
He might not but refuse you; but he protests he loves you
And needs no other suitor but his likings
To take the safest occasion by the front
To bring you in again.

CASSIO

Yet, I beseech you,
If you think fit, or that it may be done,
Give me advantage of some brief discourse
With Desdemona alone.

EMILIA

Pray you, come in;
I will bestow you where you shall have time
To speak your bosom freely.

CASSIO

I am much bound to you.

Exeunt

SCENE II. A room in the castle.

Enter OTHELLO, IAGO, and Gentlemen

OTHELLO

These letters give, Iago, to the pilot;
And by him do my duties to the senate:
That done, I will be walking on the works;
Repair there to me.

IAGO

Well, my good lord, I'll do't.

OTHELLO

This fortification, gentlemen, shall we see't?

GENTLEMAN

We'll wait upon your lordship.

Exeunt

SCENE III. The garden of the castle.

Enter DESDEMONA, CASSIO, and EMILIA

DESDEMONA

Be thou assured, good Cassio, I will do
All my abilities in thy behalf.

EMILIA

Good madam, do: I warrant it grieves my husband,
As if the case were his.

DESDEMONA

O, that's an honest fellow. Do not doubt, Cassio,
But I will have my lord and you again
As friendly as you were.

CASSIO

Bounteous madam,
Whatever shall become of Michael Cassio,
He's never any thing but your true servant.

DESDEMONA

I know't; I thank you. You do love my lord:
You have known him long; and be you well assured
He shall in strangeness stand no further off
Than in a polite distance.

CASSIO

Ay, but, lady,
That policy may either last so long,
Or feed upon such nice and waterish diet,
Or breed itself so out of circumstance,
That, I being absent and my place supplied,
My general will forget my love and service.

DESDEMONA

Do not doubt that; before Emilia here
I give thee warrant of thy place: assure thee,
If I do vow a friendship, I'll perform it
To the last article: my lord shall never rest;
I'll watch him tame and talk him out of patience;
His bed shall seem a school, his board a shrift;
I'll intermingle every thing he does
With Cassio's suit: therefore be merry, Cassio;
For thy solicitor shall rather die
Than give thy cause away.

EMILIA

Madam, here comes my lord.

CASSIO

Madam, I'll take my leave.

DESDEMONA

Why, stay, and hear me speak.

CASSIO

Madam, not now: I am very ill at ease,
Unfit for mine own purposes.

DESDEMONA

Well, do your discretion.

Exit CASSIO

Enter OTHELLO and IAGO

IAGO

Ha! I like not that.

OTHELLO

What dost thou say?

IAGO

Nothing, my lord: or if—I know not what.

OTHELLO

Was not that Cassio parted from my wife?

IAGO

Cassio, my lord! No, sure, I cannot think it,
That he would steal away so guilty-like,
Seeing you coming.

OTHELLO

I do believe 'twas he.

DESDEMONA

How now, my lord!
I have been talking with a suitor here,
A man that languishes in your displeasure.

OTHELLO

Who is't you mean?

DESDEMONA

Why, your lieutenant, Cassio. Good my lord,
If I have any grace or power to move you,
His present reconciliation take;
For if he be not one that truly loves you,
That errs in ignorance and not in cunning,
I have no judgment in an honest face:
I prithee, call him back.

OTHELLO

Went he hence now?

DESDEMONA

Ay, sooth; so humbled
That he hath left part of his grief with me,
To suffer with him. Good love, call him back.

OTHELLO

Not now, sweet Desdemona; some other time.

DESDEMONA

But shall't be shortly?

OTHELLO

The sooner, sweet, for you.

DESDEMONA

Shall't be to-night at supper?

OTHELLO

No, not to-night.

DESDEMONA

To-morrow dinner, then?

OTHELLO

I shall not dine at home;
I meet the captains at the citadel.

DESDEMONA

Why, then, to-morrow night; or Tuesday morn;
On Tuesday noon, or night; on Wednesday morn:
I prithee, name the time, but let it not
Exceed three days: in faith, he's penitent;
And yet his trespass, in our common reason—
Save that, they say, the wars must make examples
Out of their best—is not almost a fault
To incur a private cheque. When shall he come?
Tell me, Othello: I wonder in my soul,
What you would ask me, that I should deny,

OTHELLO

Or stand so mammering on. What! Michael Cassio,
That came a-wooing with you, and so many a time,
When I have spoke of you dispraisingly,
Hath ta'en your part; to have so much to do
To bring him in! Trust me, I could do much,—

OTHELLO

Prithee, no more: let him come when he will;
I will deny thee nothing.

DESDEMONA

Why, this is not a boon;
'Tis as I should entreat you wear your gloves,
Or feed on nourishing dishes, or keep you warm,
Or sue to you to do a peculiar profit
To your own person: nay, when I have a suit
Wherein I mean to touch your love indeed,
It shall be full of poise and difficult weight
And fearful to be granted.

OTHELLO

I will deny thee nothing:
Whereon, I do beseech thee, grant me this,
To leave me but a little to myself.

DESDEMONA

Shall I deny you? no: farewell, my lord.

OTHELLO

Farewell, my Desdemona: I'll come to thee straight.

DESDEMONA

Emilia, come. Be as your fancies teach you;
Whate'er you be, I am obedient.

Exeunt DESDEMONA and EMILIA

OTHELLO

Excellent wretch! Perdition catch my soul,
But I do love thee! and when I love thee not,
Chaos is come again.

IAGO

My noble lord—

OTHELLO

What dost thou say, Iago?

IAGO

Did Michael Cassio, when you woo'd my lady,
Know of your love?

OTHELLO

He did, from first to last: why dost thou ask?

IAGO

But for a satisfaction of my thought;
No further harm.

OTHELLO

Why of thy thought, Iago?

IAGO

I did not think he had been acquainted with her.

OTHELLO

O, yes; and went between us very oft.

IAGO

Indeed!

OTHELLO

Indeed! ay, indeed: discern'st thou aught in that?
Is he not honest?

IAGO

Honest, my lord!

OTHELLO

Honest! ay, honest.

IAGO

My lord, for aught I know.

OTHELLO

What dost thou think?

IAGO

Think, my lord!

OTHELLO

Think, my lord!
By heaven, he echoes me,
As if there were some monster in his thought
Too hideous to be shown. Thou dost mean something:
I heard thee say even now, thou likedst not that,
When Cassio left my wife: what didst not like?
And when I told thee he was of my counsel
In my whole course of wooing, thou criedst 'Indeed!'
And didst contract and purse thy brow together,
As if thou then hadst shut up in thy brain
Some horrible conceit: if thou dost love me,
Show me thy thought.

IAGO

My lord, you know I love you.

OTHELLO

I think thou dost;
And, for I know thou'rt full of love and honesty,
And weigh'st thy words before thou givest them breath,
Therefore these stops of thine fright me the more:
For such things in a false disloyal knave
Are tricks of custom, but in a man that's just
They are close delations, working from the heart
That passion cannot rule.

IAGO

For Michael Cassio,
I dare be sworn I think that he is honest.

OTHELLO

I think so too.

IAGO

Men should be what they seem;
Or those that be not, would they might seem none!

OTHELLO

Certain, men should be what they seem.

IAGO

Why, then, I think Cassio's an honest man.

OTHELLO

Nay, yet there's more in this:
I prithee, speak to me as to thy thinkings,
As thou dost ruminate, and give thy worst of thoughts
The worst of words.

IAGO

Good my lord, pardon me:
Though I am bound to every act of duty,
I am not bound to that all slaves are free to.
Utter my thoughts? Why, say they are vile and false;
As where's that palace whereinto foul things
Sometimes intrude not? who has a breast so pure,
But some uncleanly apprehensions
Keep leets and law-days and in session sit
With meditations lawful?

OTHELLO

Thou dost conspire against thy friend, Iago,
If thou but think'st him wrong'd and makest his ear
A stranger to thy thoughts.

IAGO

I do beseech you–
Though I perchance am vicious in my guess,
As, I confess, it is my nature's plague
To spy into abuses, and oft my jealousy
Shapes faults that are not–that your wisdom yet,
From one that so imperfectly conceits,

Would take no notice, nor build yourself a trouble
Out of his scattering and unsure observance.
It were not for your quiet nor your good,
Nor for my manhood, honesty, or wisdom,
To let you know my thoughts.

OTHELLO

What dost thou mean?

IAGO

Good name in man and woman, dear my lord,
Is the immediate jewel of their souls:
Who steals my purse steals trash; 'tis something, nothing;
'Twas mine, 'tis his, and has been slave to thousands:
But he that filches from me my good name
Robs me of that which not enriches him
And makes me poor indeed.

OTHELLO

By heaven, I'll know thy thoughts.

IAGO

You cannot, if my heart were in your hand;
Nor shall not, whilst 'tis in my custody.

OTHELLO

Ha!

IAGO

O, beware, my lord, of jealousy;
It is the green-eyed monster which doth mock
The meat it feeds on; that cuckold lives in bliss
Who, certain of his fate, loves not his wronger;
But, O, what damned minutes tells he o'er
Who dotes, yet doubts, suspects, yet strongly loves!

OTHELLO

O misery!

IAGO

Poor and content is rich and rich enough,
But riches fineless is as poor as winter
To him that ever fears he shall be poor.
Good heaven, the souls of all my tribe defend
From jealousy!

OTHELLO

Why, why is this?
Think'st thou I'ld make a life of jealousy,
To follow still the changes of the moon
With fresh suspicions? No; to be once in doubt
Is once to be resolved: exchange me for a goat,
When I shall turn the business of my soul
To such exsufflicate and blown surmises,
Matching thy inference. 'Tis not to make me jealous
To say my wife is fair, feeds well, loves company,
Is free of speech, sings, plays and dances well;
Where virtue is, these are more virtuous:
Nor from mine own weak merits will I draw
The smallest fear or doubt of her revolt;
For she had eyes, and chose me. No, Iago;
I'll see before I doubt; when I doubt, prove;
And on the proof, there is no more but this,—
Away at once with love or jealousy!

IAGO

I am glad of it; for now I shall have reason
To show the love and duty that I bear you
With franker spirit: therefore, as I am bound,
Receive it from me. I speak not yet of proof.
Look to your wife; observe her well with Cassio;
Wear your eye thus, not jealous nor secure:
I would not have your free and noble nature,
Out of self-bounty, be abused; look to't:
I know our country disposition well;
In Venice they do let heaven see the pranks
They dare not show their husbands; their best conscience

Is not to leave't undone, but keep't unknown.

OTHELLO

Dost thou say so?

IAGO

She did deceive her father, marrying you;
And when she seem'd to shake and fear your looks,
She loved them most.

OTHELLO

And so she did.

IAGO

Why, go to then;
She that, so young, could give out such a seeming,
To seal her father's eyes up close as oak-
He thought 'twas witchcraft—but I am much to blame;
I humbly do beseech you of your pardon
For too much loving you.

OTHELLO

I am bound to thee for ever.

IAGO

I see this hath a little dash'd your spirits.

OTHELLO

Not a jot, not a jot.

IAGO

I' faith, I fear it has.
I hope you will consider what is spoke
Comes from my love. But I do see you're moved:
I am to pray you not to strain my speech
To grosser issues nor to larger reach
Than to suspicion.

OTHELLO

I will not.

IAGO

Should you do so, my lord,
My speech should fall into such vile success
As my thoughts aim not at. Cassio's my worthy friend—
My lord, I see you're moved.

OTHELLO

No, not much moved:
I do not think but Desdemona's honest.

IAGO

Long live she so! and long live you to think so!

OTHELLO

And yet, how nature erring from itself,—

IAGO

Ay, there's the point: as—to be bold with you—
Not to affect many proposed matches
Of her own clime, complexion, and degree,
Whereto we see in all things nature tends—
Foh! one may smell in such a will most rank,
Foul disproportion thoughts unnatural.
But pardon me; I do not in position
Distinctly speak of her; though I may fear
Her will, recoiling to her better judgment,
May fall to match you with her country forms
And happily repent.

OTHELLO

Farewell, farewell:
If more thou dost perceive, let me know more;
Set on thy wife to observe: leave me, Iago:

IAGO

[Going] My lord, I take my leave.

OTHELLO

Why did I marry? This honest creature doubtless
Sees and knows more, much more, than he unfolds.

IAGO

[Returning] My lord, I would I might entreat your honour
To scan this thing no further; leave it to time:
Though it be fit that Cassio have his place,
For sure, he fills it up with great ability,
Yet, if you please to hold him off awhile,
You shall by that perceive him and his means:
Note, if your lady strain his entertainment
With any strong or vehement importunity;
Much will be seen in that. In the mean time,
Let me be thought too busy in my fears–
As worthy cause I have to fear I am–
And hold her free, I do beseech your honour.

OTHELLO

Fear not my government.

IAGO

I once more take my leave.

Exit

OTHELLO

This fellow's of exceeding honesty,
And knows all qualities, with a learned spirit,
Of human dealings. If I do prove her haggard,
Though that her jesses were my dear heartstrings,
I'd whistle her off and let her down the wind,
To pray at fortune. Haply, for I am black
And have not those soft parts of conversation
That chamberers have, or for I am declined
Into the vale of years,—yet that's not much—
She's gone. I am abused; and my relief
Must be to loathe her. O curse of marriage,
That we can call these delicate creatures ours,
And not their appetites! I had rather be a toad,
And live upon the vapour of a dungeon,
Than keep a corner in the thing I love
For others' uses. Yet, 'tis the plague of great ones;
Prerogatived are they less than the base;
'Tis destiny unshunnable, like death:
Even then this forked plague is fated to us
When we do quicken. Desdemona comes:

Re-enter DESDEMONA and EMILIA

If she be false, O, then heaven mocks itself!
I'll not believe't.

DESDEMONA

How now, my dear Othello!
Your dinner, and the generous islanders
By you invited, do attend your presence.

OTHELLO

I am to blame.

DESDEMONA

Why do you speak so faintly?
Are you not well?

OTHELLO

I have a pain upon my forehead here.

DESDEMONA

'Faith, that's with watching; 'twill away again:
Let me but bind it hard, within this hour
It will be well.

OTHELLO

Your napkin is too little:

He puts the handkerchief from him; and it drops

Let it alone. Come, I'll go in with you.

DESDEMONA

I am very sorry that you are not well.

Exeunt OTHELLO and DESDEMONA

EMILIA

I am glad I have found this napkin:
This was her first remembrance from the Moor:
My wayward husband hath a hundred times

Woo'd me to steal it; but she so loves the token,
For he conjured her she should ever keep it,
That she reserves it evermore about her
To kiss and talk to. I'll have the work ta'en out,
And give't Iago: what he will do with it
Heaven knows, not I;
I nothing but to please his fantasy.

Re-enter Iago

IAGO

How now! what do you here alone?

EMILIA

Do not you chide; I have a thing for you.

IAGO

A thing for me? it is a common thing—

EMILIA

Ha!

IAGO

To have a foolish wife.

EMILIA

O, is that all? What will you give me now
For the same handkerchief?

IAGO

What handkerchief?

EMILIA

What handkerchief?
Why, that the Moor first gave to Desdemona;
That which so often you did bid me steal.

IAGO

Hast stol'n it from her?

EMILIA

No, 'faith; she let it drop by negligence.
And, to the advantage, I, being here,
took't up.
Look, here it is.

IAGO

A good wench; give it me.

EMILIA

What will you do with 't, that you have been so earnest
To have me filch it?

IAGO

[Snatching it] Why, what's that to you?

EMILIA

If it be not for some purpose of import,
Give't me again: poor lady, she'll run mad
When she shall lack it.

IAGO

Be not acknown on 't; I have use for it.
Go, leave me.

Exit EMILIA

I will in Cassio's lodging lose this napkin,
And let him find it. Trifles light as air
Are to the jealous confirmations strong
As proofs of holy writ: this may do something.
The Moor already changes with my poison:
Dangerous conceits are, in their natures, poisons.
Which at the first are scarce found to distaste,
But with a little act upon the blood.
Burn like the mines of Sulphur. I did say so:
Look, where he comes!

Re-enter OTHELLO

Not poppy, nor mandragora,
Nor all the drowsy syrups of the world,
Shall ever medicine thee to that sweet sleep
Which thou owedst yesterday.

OTHELLO

Ha! ha! false to me?

IAGO

Why, how now, general! no more of that.

OTHELLO

Avaunt! be gone! thou hast set me on the rack:
I swear 'tis better to be much abused
Than but to know't a little.

IAGO

How now, my lord!

OTHELLO

What sense had I of her stol'n hours of lust?
I saw't not, thought it not, it harm'd not me:
I slept the next night well, was free and merry;
I found not Cassio's kisses on her lips:
He that is robb'd, not wanting what is stol'n,
Let him not know't, and he's not robb'd at all.

IAGO

I am sorry to hear this.

OTHELLO

I had been happy, if the general camp,
Pioners and all, had tasted her sweet body,
So I had nothing known. O, now, for ever
Farewell the tranquil mind! farewell content!
Farewell the plumed troop, and the big wars,
That make ambition virtue! O, farewell!
Farewell the neighing steed, and the shrill trump,
The spirit-stirring drum, the ear-piercing fife,
The royal banner, and all quality,
Pride, pomp and circumstance of glorious war!
And, O you mortal engines, whose rude throats
The immortal Jove's dead clamours counterfeit,
Farewell! Othello's occupation's gone!

IAGO

Is't possible, my lord?

OTHELLO

Villain, be sure thou prove my love a whore,
Be sure of it; give me the ocular proof:
Or by the worth of man's eternal soul,
Thou hadst been better have been born a dog
Than answer my waked wrath!

IAGO

Is't come to this?

OTHELLO

Make me to see't; or, at the least, so prove it,
That the probation bear no hinge nor loop
To hang a doubt on; or woe upon thy life!

IAGO

My noble lord,—

OTHELLO

If thou dost slander her and torture me,
Never pray more; abandon all remorse;
On horror's head horrors accumulate;
Do deeds to make heaven weep, all earth amazed;
For nothing canst thou to damnation add
Greater than that.

IAGO

O grace! O heaven forgive me!
Are you a man? have you a soul or sense?
God be wi' you; take mine office.
O wretched fool.
That livest to make thine honesty a vice!
O monstrous world! Take note, take note, O world,
To be direct and honest is not safe.
I thank you for this profit; and from hence
I'll love no friend, sith love breeds such offence.

OTHELLO

Nay, stay: thou shouldst be honest.

IAGO

I should be wise, for honesty's a fool
And loses that it works for.

OTHELLO

By the world,
I think my wife be honest and think she is not;

I think that thou art just and think thou art not.
I'll have some proof. Her name, that was as fresh
As Dian's visage, is now begrimed and black
As mine own face. If there be cords, or knives,
Poison, or fire, or suffocating streams,
I'll not endure it. Would I were satisfied!

IAGO

I see, sir, you are eaten up with passion:
I do repent me that I put it to you.
You would be satisfied?

OTHELLO

Would! nay, I will.

IAGO

And may: but, how? how satisfied, my lord?
Would you, the supervisor, grossly gape on—
Behold her topp'd?

OTHELLO

Death and damnation! O!

IAGO

It were a tedious difficulty, I think,
To bring them to that prospect: damn them then,
If ever mortal eyes do see them bolster
More than their own! What then? how then?
What shall I say? Where's satisfaction?
It is impossible you should see this,
Were they as prime as goats, as hot as monkeys,
As salt as wolves in pride, and fools as gross
As ignorance made drunk. But yet, I say,
If imputation and strong circumstances,
Which lead directly to the door of truth,
Will give you satisfaction, you may have't.

OTHELLO

Give me a living reason she's disloyal.

IAGO

I do not like the office:
But, sith I am enter'd in this cause so far,
Prick'd to't by foolish honesty and love,
I will go on. I lay with Cassio lately;
And, being troubled with a raging tooth,
I could not sleep.
There are a kind of men so loose of soul,
That in their sleeps will mutter their affairs:
One of this kind is Cassio:
In sleep I heard him say 'Sweet Desdemona,
Let us be wary, let us hide our loves;'
And then, sir, would he gripe and wring my hand,
Cry 'O sweet creature!' and then kiss me hard,
As if he pluck'd up kisses by the roots
That grew upon my lips: then laid his leg
Over my thigh, and sigh'd, and kiss'd; and then
Cried 'Cursed fate that gave thee to the Moor!'

OTHELLO

O monstrous! monstrous!

IAGO

Nay, this was but his dream.

OTHELLO

But this denoted a foregone conclusion:
'Tis a shrewd doubt, though it be but a dream.

IAGO

And this may help to thicken other proofs
That do demonstrate thinly.

OTHELLO

I'll tear her all to pieces.

IAGO

Nay, but be wise: yet we see nothing done;
She may be honest yet. Tell me but this,
Have you not sometimes seen a handkerchief
Spotted with strawberries in your wife's hand?

OTHELLO

I gave her such a one; 'twas my first gift.

IAGO

I know not that; but such a handkerchief—
I am sure it was your wife's—did I to-day
See Cassio wipe his beard with.

OTHELLO

If it be that—

IAGO

If it be that, or any that was hers,
It speaks against her with the other proofs.

OTHELLO

O, that the slave had forty thousand lives!
One is too poor, too weak for my revenge.
Now do I see 'tis true. Look here, Iago;
All my fond love thus do I blow to heaven.
'Tis gone.
Arise, black vengeance, from thy hollow cell!
Yield up, O love, thy crown and hearted throne
To tyrannous hate! Swell, bosom, with thy fraught,
For 'tis of aspics' tongues!

IAGO

Yet be content.

OTHELLO

O, blood, blood, blood!

IAGO

Patience, I say; your mind perhaps may change.

OTHELLO

Never, Iago: Like to the Pontic sea,
Whose icy current and compulsive course
Ne'er feels retiring ebb, but keeps due on
To the Propontic and the Hellespont,
Even so my bloody thoughts, with violent pace,
Shall ne'er look back, ne'er ebb to humble love,
Till that a capable and wide revenge
Swallow them up. Now, by yond marble heaven,

Kneels

In the due reverence of a sacred vow
I here engage my words.

IAGO

Do not rise yet.

Kneels

Witness, you ever-burning lights above,
You elements that clip us round about,
Witness that here Iago doth give up
The execution of his wit, hands, heart,
To wrong'd Othello's service! Let him command,
And to obey shall be in me remorse,
What bloody business ever.

They rise

OTHELLO

I greet thy love,
Not with vain thanks, but with acceptance bounteous,
And will upon the instant put thee to't:
Within these three days let me hear thee say
That Cassio's not alive.

IAGO

My friend is dead; 'tis done at your request:
But let her live.

OTHELLO

Damn her, lewd minx! O, damn her!
Come, go with me apart; I will withdraw,
To furnish me with some swift means of death
For the fair devil. Now art thou my lieutenant.

IAGO

I am your own for ever.

Exeunt

Racial Matters

SCENE IV. Before the castle.

Enter DESDEMONA, EMILIA, and Clown

DESDEMONA

Do you know, sirrah, where Lieutenant Cassio lies?

CLOWN

I dare not say he lies any where.

DESDEMONA

Why, man?

CLOWN

He's a soldier, and for one to say a soldier lies, is stabbing.

DESDEMONA

Go to: where lodges he?

CLOWN

To tell you where he lodges, is to tell you where I lie.

DESDEMONA

Can any thing be made of this?

CLOWN

I know not where he lodges, and for me to devise a lodging and say he lies here or he lies there, were to lie in mine own throat.

DESDEMONA

Can you inquire him out, and be edified by report?

CLOWN

I will catechise the world for him; that is, make questions, and by them answer.

DESDEMONA

Seek him, bid him come hither: tell him I have moved my lord on his behalf, and hope all will be well.

CLOWN

To do this is within the compass of man's wit: and therefore I will attempt the doing it.

Exit

DESDEMONA

Where should I lose that handkerchief, Emilia?

EMILIA

I know not, madam.

DESDEMONA

Believe me, I had rather have lost my purse
Full of crusadoes: and, but my noble Moor
Is true of mind and made of no such baseness
As jealous creatures are, it were enough
To put him to ill thinking.

EMILIA

Is he not jealous?

DESDEMONA

Who, he? I think the sun where he was born
Drew all such humours from him.

EMILIA

Look, where he comes.

DESDEMONA

I will not leave him now till Cassio
Be call'd to him.

Enter OTHELLO

How is't with you, my lord

OTHELLO

Well, my good lady.

Aside

O, hardness to dissemble!–
How do you, Desdemona?

DESDEMONA

Well, my good lord.

OTHELLO

Give me your hand: this hand is moist, my lady.

DESDEMONA

It yet hath felt no age nor known no sorrow.

OTHELLO

This argues fruitfulness and liberal heart:
Hot, hot, and moist: this hand of yours requires
A sequester from liberty, fasting and prayer,
Much castigation, exercise devout;
For here's a young and sweating devil here,
That commonly rebels. 'Tis a good hand,
A frank one.

DESDEMONA

You may, indeed, say so;
For 'twas that hand that gave away my heart.

OTHELLO

A liberal hand: the hearts of old gave hands;
But our new heraldry is hands, not hearts.

DESDEMONA

I cannot speak of this. Come now, your promise.

OTHELLO

What promise, chuck?

DESDEMONA

I have sent to bid Cassio come speak with you.

OTHELLO

I have a salt and sorry rheum offends me;
Lend me thy handkerchief.

DESDEMONA

Here, my lord.

OTHELLO

That which I gave you.

DESDEMONA

I have it not about me.

OTHELLO

Not?

DESDEMONA

No, indeed, my lord.

OTHELLO

That is a fault.
That handkerchief
Did an Egyptian to my mother give;
She was a charmer, and could almost read
The thoughts of people: she told her, while she kept it,
'Twould make her amiable and subdue my father
Entirely to her love, but if she lost it
Or made gift of it, my father's eye
Should hold her loathed and his spirits should hunt
After new fancies: she, dying, gave it me;
And bid me, when my fate would have me wive,
To give it her. I did so: and take heed on't;
Make it a darling like your precious eye;
To lose't or give't away were such perdition
As nothing else could match.

DESDEMONA

Is't possible?

OTHELLO

'Tis true: there's magic in the web of it:
A sibyl, that had number'd in the world
The sun to course two hundred compasses,
In her prophetic fury sew'd the work;
The worms were hallow'd that did breed the silk;
And it was dyed in mummy which the skilful
Conserved of maidens' hearts.

DESDEMONA

Indeed! is't true?

OTHELLO

Most veritable; therefore look to't well.

DESDEMONA

Then would to God that I had never seen't!

OTHELLO

Ha! wherefore?

DESDEMONA

Why do you speak so startingly and rash?

OTHELLO

Is't lost? is't gone? speak, is it out o' the way?

DESDEMONA

Heaven bless us!

OTHELLO

Say you?

DESDEMONA

It is not lost; but what an if it were?

OTHELLO

How!

DESDEMONA

I say, it is not lost.

OTHELLO

Fetch't, let me see't.

DESDEMONA

Why, so I can, sir, but I will not now.
This is a trick to put me from my suit:
Pray you, let Cassio be received again.

OTHELLO

Fetch me the handkerchief: my mind misgives.

DESDEMONA

Come, come;
You'll never meet a more sufficient man.

OTHELLO

The handkerchief!

DESDEMONA

I pray, talk me of Cassio.

OTHELLO

The handkerchief!

DESDEMONA

A man that all his time
Hath founded his good fortunes on your love,
Shared dangers with you,–

OTHELLO

The handkerchief!

DESDEMONA

In sooth, you are to blame.

OTHELLO

Away!

Exit

EMILIA

Is not this man jealous?

DESDEMONA

I ne'er saw this before.
Sure, there's some wonder in this handkerchief:
I am most unhappy in the loss of it.

EMILIA

'Tis not a year or two shows us a man:
They are all but stomachs, and we all but food;
To eat us hungerly, and when they are full,
They belch us. Look you, Cassio and my husband!

Enter CASSIO and IAGO

IAGO

There is no other way; 'tis she must do't:
And, lo, the happiness! go, and importune her.

DESDEMONA

How now, good Cassio! what's the news with you?

CASSIO

Madam, my former suit: I do beseech you
That by your virtuous means I may again
Exist, and be a member of his love
Whom I with all the office of my heart
Entirely honour: I would not be delay'd.
If my offence be of such mortal kind
That nor my service past, nor present sorrows,
Nor purposed merit in futurity,
Can ransom me into his love again,
But to know so must be my benefit;
So shall I clothe me in a forced content,
And shut myself up in some other course,
To fortune's alms.

DESDEMONA

Alas, thrice-gentle Cassio!
My advocation is not now in tune;
My lord is not my lord; nor should I know him,
Were he in favour as in humour alter'd.
So help me every spirit sanctified,
As I have spoken for you all my best
And stood within the blank of his displeasure
For my free speech! you must awhile be patient:
What I can do I will; and more I will
Than for myself I dare: let that suffice you.

IAGO

Is my lord angry?

EMILIA

He went hence but now,
And certainly in strange unquietness.

IAGO

Can he be angry? I have seen the cannon,
When it hath blown his ranks into the air,
And, like the devil, from his very arm
Puff'd his own brother:—and can he be angry?
Something of moment then: I will go meet him:
There's matter in't indeed, if he be angry.

DESDEMONA

I prithee, do so.

Exit IAGO

Something, sure, of state,
Either from Venice, or some unhatch'd practise
Made demonstrable here in Cyprus to him,
Hath puddled his clear spirit: and in such cases
Men's natures wrangle with inferior things,
Though great ones are their object. 'Tis even so;
For let our finger ache, and it indues
Our other healthful members even to that sense
Of pain: nay, we must think men are not gods,
Nor of them look for such observances
As fit the bridal. Beshrew me much, Emilia,
I was, unhandsome warrior as I am,
Arraigning his unkindness with my soul;
But now I find I had suborn'd the witness,
And he's indicted falsely.

EMILIA

Pray heaven it be state-matters, as you think,
And no conception nor no jealous toy
Concerning you.

DESDEMONA

Alas the day! I never gave him cause.

EMILIA

But jealous souls will not be answer'd so;
They are not ever jealous for the cause,
But jealous for they are jealous: 'tis a monster
Begot upon itself, born on itself.

DESDEMONA

Heaven keep that monster from Othello's mind!

EMILIA

Lady, amen.

DESDEMONA

I will go seek him. Cassio, walk hereabout:
If I do find him fit, I'll move your suit
And seek to effect it to my uttermost.

CASSIO

I humbly thank your ladyship.

Exeunt DESDEMONA and EMILIA

Enter BIANCA

BIANCA

Save you, friend Cassio!

CASSIO

What make you from home?
How is it with you, my most fair Bianca?
I' faith, sweet love, I was coming to your house.

BIANCA

And I was going to your lodging, Cassio.
What, keep a week away? seven days and nights?
Eight score eight hours? and lovers' absent hours,
More tedious than the dial eight score times?
O weary reckoning!

CASSIO

Pardon me, Bianca:
I have this while with leaden thoughts been press'd:
But I shall, in a more continuate time,
Strike off this score of absence. Sweet Bianca,

Giving her DESDEMONA's handkerchief

Take me this work out.

BIANCA

O Cassio, whence came this?
This is some token from a newer friend:
To the felt absence now I feel a cause:
Is't come to this? Well, well.

CASSIO

Go to, woman!
Throw your vile guesses in the devil's teeth,
From whence you have them. You are jealous now
That this is from some mistress, some remembrance:
No, in good troth, Bianca.

BIANCA

Why, whose is it?

CASSIO

I know not, sweet: I found it in my chamber.
I like the work well: ere it be demanded–
As like enough it will–I'd have it copied:
Take it, and do't; and leave me for this time.

BIANCA

Leave you! wherefore?

CASSIO

I do attend here on the general;
And think it no addition, nor my wish,
To have him see me woman'd.

BIANCA

Why, I pray you?

CASSIO

Not that I love you not.

BIANCA

But that you do not love me.
I pray you, bring me on the way a little,
And say if I shall see you soon at night.

CASSIO

'Tis but a little way that I can bring you;
For I attend here: but I'll see you soon.

BIANCA

'Tis very good; I must be circumstanced.

Exeunt

ACT IV

SCENE I. Cyprus. Before the castle.

Enter OTHELLO and IAGO

IAGO

Will you think so?

OTHELLO

Think so, Iago!

IAGO

What,
To kiss in private?

OTHELLO

An unauthorized kiss.

IAGO

Or to be naked with her friend in bed
An hour or more, not meaning any harm?

OTHELLO

Naked in bed, Iago, and not mean harm!
It is hypocrisy against the devil:
They that mean virtuously, and yet do so,
The devil their virtue tempts, and they tempt heaven.

IAGO

So they do nothing, 'tis a venial slip:
But if I give my wife a handkerchief,—

OTHELLO

What then?

IAGO

Why, then, 'tis hers, my lord; and, being hers,
She may, I think, bestow't on any man.

OTHELLO

She is protectress of her honour too:
May she give that?

IAGO

Her honour is an essence that's not seen;
They have it very oft that have it not:
But, for the handkerchief,—

OTHELLO

By heaven, I would most gladly have forgot it.
Thou said'st, it comes o'er my memory,
As doth the raven o'er the infected house,
Boding to all—he had my handkerchief.

IAGO

Ay, what of that?

OTHELLO

That's not so good now.

IAGO

What,
If I had said I had seen him do you wrong?
Or heard him say,—as knaves be such abroad,
Who having, by their own importunate suit,
Or voluntary dotage of some mistress,
Convinced or supplied them, cannot choose
But they must blab—

OTHELLO

Hath he said any thing?

IAGO

He hath, my lord; but be you well assured,
No more than he'll unswear.

OTHELLO

What hath he said?

IAGO

'Faith, that he did—I know not what he did.

OTHELLO

What? what?

IAGO

Lie—

OTHELLO

With her?

IAGO

With her, on her; what you will.

OTHELLO

Lie with her! lie on her! We say lie on her, when they belie her. Lie with her! that's fulsome.—Handkerchief—confessions—handkerchief!—To confess, and be hanged for his labour;—first, to be hanged, and then to confess.—I tremble at it. Nature would not invest herself in such shadowing passion without some instruction. It is not words that shake me thus. Pish! Noses, ears, and lips.—Is't possible?—Confess—handkerchief!—O devil!—

Falls in a trance

IAGO

Work on,
My medicine, work! Thus credulous fools are caught;
And many worthy and chaste dames even thus,
All guiltless, meet reproach. What, ho! my lord!
My lord, I say! Othello!

Enter CASSIO

How now, Cassio!

CASSIO

What's the matter?

IAGO

My lord is fall'n into an epilepsy:
This is his second fit; he had one yesterday.

CASSIO

Rub him about the temples.

IAGO

No, forbear;
The lethargy must have his quiet course:
If not, he foams at mouth and by and by
Breaks out to savage madness. Look he stirs:
Do you withdraw yourself a little while,
He will recover straight: when he is gone,
I would on great occasion speak with you.

Exit CASSIO

How is it, general? have you not hurt your head?

OTHELLO

Dost thou mock me?

IAGO

I mock you! no, by heaven.
Would you would bear your fortune like a man!

OTHELLO

A horned man's a monster and a beast.

IAGO

There's many a beast then in a populous city,
And many a civil monster.

OTHELLO

Did he confess it?

IAGO

Good sir, be a man;
Think every bearded fellow that's but yoked
May draw with you: there's millions now alive
That nightly lie in those unproper beds
Which they dare swear peculiar: your case is better.
O, 'tis the spite of hell, the fiend's arch-mock,
To lip a wanton in a secure couch,
And to suppose her chaste! No, let me know;
And knowing what I am, I know what she shall be.

OTHELLO

O, thou art wise; 'tis certain.

IAGO

Stand you awhile apart;
Confine yourself but in a patient list.
Whilst you were here o'erwhelmed with your grief–
A passion most unsuiting such a man–
Cassio came hither: I shifted him away,
And laid good 'scuse upon your ecstasy,
Bade him anon return and here speak with me;
The which he promised. Do but encave yourself,
And mark the fleers, the gibes, and notable scorns,
That dwell in every region of his face;
For I will make him tell the tale anew,
Where, how, how oft, how long ago, and when
He hath, and is again to cope your wife:
I say, but mark his gesture. Marry, patience;
Or I shall say you are all in all in spleen,
And nothing of a man.

OTHELLO

Dost thou hear, Iago?
I will be found most cunning in my patience;
But—dost thou hear?—most bloody.

IAGO

That's not amiss;
But yet keep time in all. Will you withdraw?

OTHELLO retires

Now will I question Cassio of Bianca,
A housewife that by selling her desires
Buys herself bread and clothes: it is a creature
That dotes on Cassio; as 'tis the strumpet's plague
To beguile many and be beguiled by one:
He, when he hears of her, cannot refrain
From the excess of laughter. Here he comes:

Re-enter CASSIO

As he shall smile, Othello shall go mad;
And his unbookish jealousy must construe
Poor Cassio's smiles, gestures and light behavior,
Quite in the wrong. How do you now, lieutenant?

CASSIO

The worser that you give me the addition
Whose want even kills me.

IAGO

Ply Desdemona well, and you are sure on't.

Speaking lower

Now, if this suit lay in Bianco's power,
How quickly should you speed!

CASSIO

Alas, poor caitiff!

OTHELLO

Look, how he laughs already!

IAGO

I never knew woman love man so.

CASSIO

Alas, poor rogue! I think, i' faith, she loves me.

OTHELLO

Now he denies it faintly, and laughs it out.

IAGO

Do you hear, Cassio?

OTHELLO

Now he importunes him
To tell it o'er: go to; well said, well said.

IAGO

She gives it out that you shall marry hey:
Do you intend it?

CASSIO

Ha, ha, ha!

OTHELLO

Do you triumph, Roman? do you triumph?

CASSIO

I marry her! what? a customer! Prithee, bear some charity to my wit: do not think it so unwholesome. Ha, ha, ha!

OTHELLO

So, so, so, so: they laugh that win.

IAGO

'Faith, the cry goes that you shall marry her.

CASSIO

Prithee, say true.

IAGO

I am a very villain else.

OTHELLO

Have you scored me? Well.

CASSIO

This is the monkey's own giving out: she is persuaded I will marry her, out of her own love and flattery, not out of my promise.

OTHELLO

Iago beckons me; now he begins the story.

CASSIO

She was here even now; she haunts me in every place. I was the other day talking on the sea-bank with certain Venetians; and thither comes the bauble, and, by this hand, she falls me thus about my neck—

OTHELLO

Crying 'O dear Cassio!' as it were: his gesture imports it.

CASSIO

So hangs, and lolls, and weeps upon me; so hales, and pulls me: ha, ha, ha!

OTHELLO

Now he tells how she plucked him to my chamber. O, I see that nose of yours, but not that dog I shall throw it to.

CASSIO

Well, I must leave her company.

IAGO

Before me! look, where she comes.

CASSIO

'Tis such another fitchew! marry a perfumed one.

Enter **BIANCA**

What do you mean by this haunting of me?

BIANCA

Let the devil and his dam haunt you! What did you mean by that same handkerchief you gave me even now? I was a fine fool to take it. I must take out the work?–A likely piece of work, that you should find it in your chamber, and not know who left it there! This is some minx's token, and I must take out the work? There; give it your hobby-horse: wheresoever you had it, I'll take out no work on't.

CASSIO

How now, my sweet Bianca! how now! how now!

OTHELLO

By heaven, that should be my handkerchief!

BIANCA

An you'll come to supper to-night, you may; an you will not, come when you are next prepared for.

Exit

IAGO

After her, after her.

CASSIO

'Faith, I must; she'll rail in the street else.

IAGO

Will you sup there?

CASSIO

'Faith, I intend so.

IAGO

Well, I may chance to see you; for I would very fain speak with you.

CASSIO

Prithee, come; will you?

IAGO

Go to; say no more.

Exit CASSIO

OTHELLO

[Advancing] How shall I murder him, Iago?

IAGO

Did you perceive how he laughed at his vice?

OTHELLO

O Iago!

IAGO

And did you see the handkerchief?

OTHELLO

Was that mine?

IAGO

Yours by this hand: and to see how he prizes the foolish woman your wife! she gave it him, and he hath given it his whore.

OTHELLO

I would have him nine years a-killing. A fine woman! a fair woman! a sweet woman!

IAGO

Nay, you must forget that.

OTHELLO

Ay, let her rot, and perish, and be damned to-night; for she shall not live: no, my heart is turned to stone; I strike it, and it hurts my hand. O, the world hath not a sweeter creature: she might lie by an emperor's side and command him tasks.

IAGO

Nay, that's not your way.

OTHELLO

Hang her! I do but say what she is: so delicate with her needle: an admirable musician: O! she will sing the savageness out of a bear: of so high and plenteous wit and invention:—

IAGO

She's the worse for all this.

OTHELLO

O, a thousand thousand times: and then, of so gentle a condition!

IAGO

Ay, too gentle.

OTHELLO

Nay, that's certain: but yet the pity of it, Iago! O Iago, the pity of it, Iago!

IAGO

If you are so fond over her iniquity, give her patent to offend; for, if it touch not you, it comes near nobody.

OTHELLO

I will chop her into messes: cuckold me!

IAGO

O, 'tis foul in her.

OTHELLO

With mine officer!

IAGO

That's fouler.

OTHELLO

Get me some poison, Iago; this night: I'll not expostulate with her, lest her body and beauty unprovide my mind again: this night, Iago.

IAGO

Do it not with poison, strangle her in her bed, even the bed she hath contaminated.

OTHELLO

Good, good: the justice of it pleases: very good.

IAGO

And for Cassio, let me be his undertaker: you shall hear more by midnight.

OTHELLO

Excellent good.

A trumpet within

What trumpet is that same?

IAGO

Something from Venice, sure. 'Tis Lodovico Come from the duke: and, see, your wife is with him.

Enter LODOVICO, DESDEMONA, and Attendants

LODOVICO

Save you, worthy general!

OTHELLO

With all my heart, sir.

LODOVICO

The duke and senators of Venice greet you.

Gives him a letter

OTHELLO

I kiss the instrument of their pleasures.

Opens the letter, and reads

DESDEMONA

And what's the news, good cousin Lodovico?

IAGO

I am very glad to see you, signior Welcome to Cyprus.

LODOVICO

I thank you. How does Lieutenant Cassio?

IAGO

Lives, sir.

DESDEMONA

Cousin, there's fall'n between him and my lord
An unkind breach: but you shall make all well.

OTHELLO

Are you sure of that?

DESDEMONA

My lord?

OTHELLO

[Reads] 'This fail you not to do, as you will—'

LODOVICO

He did not call; he's busy in the paper.
Is there division 'twixt my lord and Cassio?

DESDEMONA

A most unhappy one: I would do much
To atone them, for the love I bear to Cassio.

OTHELLO

Fire and brimstone!

DESDEMONA

My lord?

OTHELLO

Are you wise?

DESDEMONA

What, is he angry?

LODOVICO

May be the letter moved him;
For, as I think, they do command him home,
Deputing Cassio in his government.

DESDEMONA

Trust me, I am glad on't.

OTHELLO

Indeed!

DESDEMONA

My lord?

OTHELLO

I am glad to see you mad.

DESDEMONA

Why, sweet Othello,–

OTHELLO

[Striking her] Devil!

DESDEMONA

I have not deserved this.

LODOVICO

My lord, this would not be believed in Venice,
Though I should swear I saw't: 'tis very much:
Make her amends; she weeps.

OTHELLO

O devil, devil!
If that the earth could teem with woman's tears,
Each drop she falls would prove a crocodile.
Out of my sight!

DESDEMONA

I will not stay to offend you.

Going

LODOVICO

Truly, an obedient lady:
I do beseech your lordship, call her back.

OTHELLO

Mistress!

DESDEMONA

My lord?

OTHELLO

What would you with her, sir?

LODOVICO

Who, I, my lord?

OTHELLO

Ay; you did wish that I would make her turn:
Sir, she can turn, and turn, and yet go on,
And turn again; and she can weep, sir, weep;
And she's obedient, as you say, obedient,
Very obedient. Proceed you in your tears.
Concerning this, sir,–O well-painted passion!–
I am commanded home. Get you away;
I'll send for you anon. Sir, I obey the mandate,
And will return to Venice. Hence, avaunt!

Exit DESDEMONA

Cassio shall have my place. And, sir, tonight,
I do entreat that we may sup together:
You are welcome, sir, to Cyprus.—Goats and monkeys!

Exit

LODOVICO

Is this the noble Moor whom our full senate
Call all in all sufficient? Is this the nature
Whom passion could not shake? whose solid virtue
The shot of accident, nor dart of chance,
Could neither graze nor pierce?

IAGO

He is much changed.

LODOVICO

Are his wits safe? is he not light of brain?

IAGO

He's that he is: I may not breathe my censure
What he might be: if what he might he is not,
I would to heaven he were!

LODOVICO

What, strike his wife!

IAGO

'Faith, that was not so well; yet would I knew
That stroke would prove the worst!

LODOVICO

Is it his use?
Or did the letters work upon his blood,
And new-create this fault?

IAGO

Alas, alas!
It is not honesty in me to speak
What I have seen and known. You shall observe him,
And his own courses will denote him so
That I may save my speech: do but go after,
And mark how he continues.

LODOVICO

I am sorry that I am deceived in him.

Exeunt

SCENE II. A room in the castle.

Enter OTHELLO and EMILIA

OTHELLO

You have seen nothing then?

EMILIA

Nor ever heard, nor ever did suspect.

OTHELLO

Yes, you have seen Cassio and she together.

EMILIA

But then I saw no harm, and then I heard
Each syllable that breath made up between them.

OTHELLO

What, did they never whisper?

EMILIA

Never, my lord.

OTHELLO

Nor send you out o' the way?

EMILIA

Never.

OTHELLO

To fetch her fan, her gloves, her mask, nor nothing?

EMILIA

Never, my lord.

OTHELLO

That's strange.

EMILIA

I durst, my lord, to wager she is honest,
Lay down my soul at stake: if you think other,
Remove your thought; it doth abuse your bosom.
If any wretch have put this in your head,
Let heaven requite it with the serpent's curse!
For, if she be not honest, chaste, and true,
There's no man happy; the purest of their wives
Is foul as slander.

OTHELLO

Bid her come hither: go.

Exit EMILIA

She says enough; yet she's a simple bawd
That cannot say as much. This is a subtle whore,
A closet lock and key of villanous secrets
And yet she'll kneel and pray; I have seen her do't.

Enter DESDEMONA with EMILIA

DESDEMONA

My lord, what is your will?

OTHELLO

Pray, chuck, come hither.

DESDEMONA

What is your pleasure?

OTHELLO

Let me see your eyes;
Look in my face.

DESDEMONA

What horrible fancy's this?

OTHELLO

[To EMILIA] Some of your function, mistress;
Leave procreants alone and shut the door;
Cough, or cry 'hem,' if any body come:
Your mystery, your mystery: nay, dispatch.

Exit EMILIA

DESDEMONA

Upon my knees, what doth your speech import?
I understand a fury in your words.
But not the words.

OTHELLO

Why, what art thou?

DESDEMONA

Your wife, my lord; your true
And loyal wife.

OTHELLO

Come, swear it, damn thyself
Lest, being like one of heaven, the devils themselves
Should fear to seize thee: therefore be double damn'd:
Swear thou art honest.

DESDEMONA

Heaven doth truly know it.

OTHELLO

Heaven truly knows that thou art false as hell.

DESDEMONA

To whom, my lord? with whom? how am I false?

OTHELLO

O Desdemona! away! away! away!

DESDEMONA

Alas the heavy day! Why do you weep?
Am I the motive of these tears, my lord?
If haply you my father do suspect
An instrument of this your calling back,
Lay not your blame on me: If you have lost him,
Why, I have lost him too.

OTHELLO

Had it pleased heaven
To try me with affliction; had they rain'd
All kinds of sores and shames on my bare head.
Steep'd me in poverty to the very lips,
Given to captivity me and my utmost hopes,
I should have found in some place of my soul
A drop of patience: but, alas, to make me
A fixed figure for the time of scorn
To point his slow unmoving finger at!
Yet could I bear that too; well, very well:
But there, where I have garner'd up my heart,

DESDEMONA

Where either I must live, or bear no life;
The fountain from the which my current runs,
Or else dries up; to be discarded thence!
Or keep it as a cistern for foul toads
To knot and gender in! Turn thy complexion there,
Patience, thou young and rose-lipp'd cherubin,–
Ay, there, look grim as hell!

DESDEMONA

I hope my noble lord esteems me honest.

OTHELLO

O, ay; as summer flies are in the shambles,
That quicken even with blowing. O thou weed,
Who art so lovely fair and smell'st so sweet
That the sense aches at thee, would thou hadst ne'er been born!

DESDEMONA

Alas, what ignorant sin have I committed?

OTHELLO

Was this fair paper, this most goodly book,
Made to write 'whore' upon? What committed!
Committed! O thou public commoner!
I should make very forges of my cheeks,
That would to cinders burn up modesty,
Did I but speak thy deeds. What committed!
Heaven stops the nose at it and the moon winks,
The bawdy wind that kisses all it meets
Is hush'd within the hollow mine of earth,
And will not hear it. What committed!
Impudent strumpet!

DESDEMONA

By heaven, you do me wrong.

OTHELLO

Are you not a strumpet?

DESDEMONA

No, as I am a Christian:
If to preserve this vessel for my lord
From any other foul unlawful touch
Be not to be a strumpet, I am none.

OTHELLO

What, not a whore?

DESDEMONA

No, as I shall be saved.

OTHELLO

Is't possible?

DESDEMONA

O, heaven forgive us!

OTHELLO

I cry you mercy, then:
I took you for that cunning whore of Venice
That married with Othello.

Raising his voice

You, mistress,
That have the office opposite to Saint Peter,
And keep the gate of hell!

Re-enter EMILIA

You, you, ay, you!
We have done our course; there's money for your pains:
I pray you, turn the key and keep our counsel.

Exit

EMILIA

Alas, what does this gentleman conceive?
How do you, madam? how do you, my good lady?

DESDEMONA

'Faith, half asleep.

EMILIA

Good madam, what's the matter with my lord?

DESDEMONA

With who?

EMILIA

Why, with my lord, madam.

DESDEMONA

Who is thy lord?

EMILIA

He that is yours, sweet lady.

DESDEMONA

I have none: do not talk to me, Emilia;
I cannot weep; nor answer have I none,
But what should go by water. Prithee, tonight
Lay on my bed my wedding sheets: remember;
And call thy husband hither.

EMILIA

Here's a change indeed!

Exit

DESDEMONA

'Tis meet I should be used so, very meet.
How have I been behaved, that he might stick
The small'st opinion on my least misuse?

Re-enter EMILIA with IAGO

IAGO

What is your pleasure, madam?
How is't with you?

DESDEMONA

I cannot tell. Those that do teach young babes
Do it with gentle means and easy tasks:
He might have chid me so; for, in good faith,
I am a child to chiding.

IAGO

What's the matter, lady?

EMILIA

Alas, Iago, my lord hath so bewhored her.
Thrown such despite and heavy terms upon her,
As true hearts cannot bear.

DESDEMONA

Am I that name, Iago?

IAGO

What name, fair lady?

DESDEMONA

Such as she says my lord did say I was.

EMILIA

He call'd her whore: a beggar in his drink
Could not have laid such terms upon his callat.

IAGO

Why did he so?

DESDEMONA

I do not know; I am sure I am none such.

IAGO

Do not weep, do not weep. Alas the day!

EMILIA

Hath she forsook so many noble matches,
Her father and her country and her friends,
To be call'd whore? would it not make one weep?

DESDEMONA

It is my wretched fortune.

IAGO

Beshrew him for't!
How comes this trick upon him?

DESDEMONA

Nay, heaven doth know.

EMILIA

I will be hang'd, if some eternal villain,
Some busy and insinuating rogue,
Some cogging, cozening slave, to get some office,
Have not devised this slander; I'll be hang'd else.

IAGO

Fie, there is no such man; it is impossible.

DESDEMONA

If any such there be, heaven pardon him!

EMILIA

A halter pardon him! and hell gnaw his bones!
Why should he call her whore? who keeps her company?
What place? what time? what form? what likelihood?
The Moor's abused by some most villanous knave,
Some base notorious knave, some scurvy fellow.
O heaven, that such companions thou'ldst unfold,
And put in every honest hand a whip
To lash the rascals naked through the world
Even from the east to the west!

IAGO

Speak within door.

EMILIA

O, fie upon them! Some such squire he was
That turn'd your wit the seamy side without,
And made you to suspect me with the Moor.

IAGO

You are a fool; go to.

DESDEMONA

O good Iago,
What shall I do to win my lord again?
Good friend, go to him; for, by this light of heaven,
I know not how I lost him. Here I kneel:
If e'er my will did trespass 'gainst his love,
Either in discourse of thought or actual deed,
Or that mine eyes, mine ears, or any sense,
Delighted them in any other form;
Or that I do not yet, and ever did.
And ever will–though he do shake me off
To beggarly divorcement–love him dearly,
Comfort forswear me! Unkindness may do much;
And his unkindness may defeat my life,
But never taint my love. I cannot say 'whore:'
It does abhor me now I speak the word;
To do the act that might the addition earn
Not the world's mass of vanity could make me.

IAGO

I pray you, be content; 'tis but his humour:
The business of the state does him offence,
And he does chide with you.

DESDEMONA

If 'twere no other–

IAGO

'Tis but so, I warrant.

Trumpets within

Hark, how these instruments summon to supper!
The messengers of Venice stay the meat;
Go in, and weep not; all things shall be well.

Exeunt DESDEMONA and EMILIA

Enter RODERIGO

How now, Roderigo!

RODERIGO

I do not find that thou dealest justly with me.

IAGO

What in the contrary?

RODERIGO

Every day thou daffest me with some device, Iago; and rather, as it seems to me now, keepest from me all conveniency than suppliest me with the least advantage of hope. I will indeed no longer endure it, nor am I yet persuaded to put up in peace what already I have foolishly suffered.

IAGO

Will you hear me, Roderigo?

RODERIGO

'Faith, I have heard too much, for your words and performances are no kin together.

IAGO

You charge me most unjustly.

RODERIGO

With nought but truth. I have wasted myself out of my means. The jewels you have had from me to deliver to Desdemona would half have corrupted a votarist: you have told me she hath received them and returned me expectations and comforts of sudden respect and acquaintance, but I find none.

IAGO

Well; go to; very well.

RODERIGO

Very well! go to! I cannot go to, man; nor 'tis not very well: nay, I think it is scurvy, and begin to find myself fobbed in it.

IAGO

Very well.

RODERIGO

I tell you 'tis not very well. I will make myself known to Desdemona: if she will return me my jewels, I will give over my suit and repent my unlawful solicitation; if not, assure yourself I will seek satisfaction of you.

IAGO

You have said now.

RODERIGO

Ay, and said nothing but what I protest intendment of doing.

IAGO

Why, now I see there's mettle in thee, and even from this instant to build on thee a better opinion than ever before. Give me thy hand, Roderigo: thou hast taken against me a most just exception; but yet, I protest, I have dealt most directly in thy affair.

RODERIGO

It hath not appeared.

IAGO

I grant indeed it hath not appeared, and your suspicion is not without wit and judgment. But, Roderigo, if thou hast that in thee indeed, which I have greater reason to believe now than ever, I mean purpose, courage and valour, this night show it: if thou the next night following enjoy not Desdemona, take me from this world with treachery and devise engines for my life.

RODERIGO

Well, what is it? is it within reason and compass?

IAGO

Sir, there is especial commission come from Venice to depute Cassio in Othello's place.

RODERIGO

Is that true? why, then Othello and Desdemona return again to Venice.

IAGO

O, no; he goes into Mauritania and takes away with him the fair Desdemona, unless his abode be lingered here by some accident: wherein none can be so determinate as the removing of Cassio.

RODERIGO

How do you mean, removing of him?

IAGO

Why, by making him uncapable of Othello's place; knocking out his brains.

RODERIGO

And that you would have me to do?

IAGO

Ay, if you dare do yourself a profit and a right. He sups to-night with a harlotry, and thither will I go to him: he knows not yet of his horrorable fortune. If you will watch his going thence, which I will fashion to fall out between twelve and one, you may take him at your pleasure: I will be near to second your attempt, and he shall fall between us. Come, stand not amazed at it, but go along with me; I will show you such a necessity in his death that you shall think yourself bound to put it on him. It is now high suppertime, and the night grows to waste: about it.

RODERIGO

I will hear further reason for this.

IAGO

And you shall be satisfied.

Exeunt

SCENE III. Another room In the castle.

Enter OTHELLO, LODOVICO, DESDEMONA, EMILIA and Attendants

LODOVICO

I do beseech you, sir, trouble yourself no further.

OTHELLO

O, pardon me: 'twill do me good to walk.

LODOVICO

Madam, good night; I humbly thank your ladyship.

DESDEMONA

Your honour is most welcome.

OTHELLO

Will you walk, sir?
O,—Desdemona,-

DESDEMONA

My lord?

OTHELLO

Get you to bed on the instant; I will be returned forthwith: dismiss your attendant there: look it be done.

DESDEMONA

I will, my lord.

Exeunt OTHELLO, LODOVICO, and Attendants

EMILIA

How goes it now? he looks gentler than he did.

DESDEMONA

He says he will return incontinent:
He hath commanded me to go to bed,
And bade me to dismiss you.

EMILIA

Dismiss me!

DESDEMONA

It was his bidding: therefore, good Emilia,.
Give me my nightly wearing, and adieu:
We must not now displease him.

EMILIA

I would you had never seen him!

DESDEMONA

So would not I my love doth so approve him,
That even his stubbornness, his cheques, his frowns–

Prithee, unpin me,–have grace and favour in them.

EMILIA

I have laid those sheets you bade me on the bed.

DESDEMONA

All's one. Good faith, how foolish are our minds!
If I do die before thee prithee, shroud me
In one of those same sheets.

EMILIA

Come, come you talk.

DESDEMONA

My mother had a maid call'd Barbara:
She was in love, and he she loved proved mad
And did forsake her: she had a song of 'willow;'
An old thing 'twas, but it express'd her fortune,
And she died singing it: that song to-night
Will not go from my mind; I have much to do,
But to go hang my head all at one side,
And sing it like poor Barbara. Prithee, dispatch.

EMILIA

Shall I go fetch your night-gown?

DESDEMONA

No, unpin me here.
This Lodovico is a proper man.

EMILIA

A very handsome man.

DESDEMONA

He speaks well.

EMILIA

I know a lady in Venice would have walked barefoot to Palestine for a touch of his nether lip.

DESDEMONA

[Singing] The poor soul sat sighing by a sycamore tree,
Sing all a green willow:
Her hand on her bosom, her head on her knee,
Sing willow, willow, willow:
The fresh streams ran by her, and murmur'd her moans;
Sing willow, willow, willow;
Her salt tears fell from her, and soften'd the stones;
Lay by these:—

Singing

Sing willow, willow, willow;
Prithee, hie thee; he'll come anon:–

Singing

Sing all a green willow must be my garland.
Let nobody blame him; his scorn I approve,-
Nay, that's not next.—Hark! who is't that knocks?

EMILIA

It's the wind.

DESDEMONA

[Singing] I call'd my love false love; but what said he then?
Sing willow, willow, willow:
If I court moe women, you'll couch with moe men!
So, get thee gone; good night Ate eyes do itch;
Doth that bode weeping?

EMILIA

'Tis neither here nor there.

DESDEMONA

I have heard it said so. O, these men, these men!
Dost thou in conscience think,—tell me, Emilia,—
That there be women do abuse their husbands In such gross kind?

EMILIA

There be some such, no question.

DESDEMONA

Wouldst thou do such a deed for all the world?

EMILIA

Why, would not you?

DESDEMONA

No, by this heavenly light!

EMILIA

Nor I neither by this heavenly light;
I might do't as well i' the dark.

DESDEMONA

Wouldst thou do such a deed for all the world?

EMILIA

The world's a huge thing: it is a great price. For a small vice.

DESDEMONA

In troth, I think thou wouldst not.

EMILIA

In troth, I think I should; and undo't when I had done. Marry, I would not do such a thing for a joint-ring, nor for measures of lawn, nor for gowns, petticoats, nor caps, nor any petty exhibition; but for the whole world,—why, who would not make her husband a cuckold to make him a monarch? I should venture purgatory for't.

DESDEMONA

Beshrew me, if I would do such a wrong
For the whole world.

EMILIA

Why the wrong is but a wrong i' the world: and having the world for your labour, tis a wrong in your own world, and you might quickly make it right.

DESDEMONA

I do not think there is any such woman.

EMILIA

Yes, a dozen; and as many to the vantage as would store the world they played for.
But I do think it is their husbands' faults
If wives do fall: say that they slack their duties,
And pour our treasures into foreign laps,
Or else break out in peevish jealousies,
Throwing restraint upon us; or say they strike us,
Or scant our former having in despite;
Why, we have galls, and though we have some grace,
Yet have we some revenge. Let husbands know
Their wives have sense like them: they see and smell
And have their palates both for sweet and sour,
As husbands have. What is it that they do
When they change us for others? Is it sport?
I think it is: and doth affection breed it?
I think it doth: is't frailty that thus errs?
It is so too: and have not we affections,
Desires for sport, and frailty, as men have?
Then let them use us well: else let them know,
The ills we do, their ills instruct us so.

DESDEMONA

Good night, good night: heaven me such uses send,
Not to pick bad from bad, but by bad mend!

Exeunt

ACT V
SCENE I. Cyprus. A street.

Enter IAGO and RODERIGO

IAGO

Here, stand behind this bulk; straight will he come:

Wear thy good rapier bare, and put it home:
Quick, quick; fear nothing; I'll be at thy elbow:
It makes us, or it mars us; think on that,
And fix most firm thy resolution.

RODERIGO

Be near at hand; I may miscarry in't.

IAGO

Here, at thy hand: be bold, and take thy stand.

Retires

RODERIGO

I have no great devotion to the deed;
And yet he hath given me satisfying reasons:
'Tis but a man gone. Forth, my sword: he dies.

IAGO

I have rubb'd this young quat almost to the sense,
And he grows angry. Now, whether he kill Cassio,
Or Cassio him, or each do kill the other,
Every way makes my gain: live Roderigo,
He calls me to a restitution large
Of gold and jewels that I bobb'd from him,
As gifts to Desdemona;
It must not be: if Cassio do remain,
He hath a daily beauty in his life
That makes me ugly; and, besides, the Moor
May unfold me to him; there stand I in much peril:
No, he must die. But so: I hear him coming.

Enter CASSIO

RODERIGO

I know his gait, 'tis he.–Villain, thou diest!

Makes a pass at CASSIO

CASSIO

That thrust had been mine enemy indeed,
But that my coat is better than thou know'st
I will make proof of thine.

Draws, and wounds RODERIGO

RODERIGO

O, I am slain!

IAGO from behind wounds CASSIO in the leg, and exit

CASSIO

I am maim'd for ever. Help, ho! murder! murder!

Falls

Enter OTHELLO

OTHELLO

The voice of Cassio: Iago keeps his word.

RODERIGO

O, villain that I am!

OTHELLO

It is even so.

CASSIO

O, help, ho! light! a surgeon!

OTHELLO

'Tis he:—O brave Iago, honest and just,
That hast such noble sense of thy friend's wrong!
Thou teachest me. Minion, your dear lies dead,
And your unblest fate hies: strumpet, I come.
Forth of my heart those charms, thine eyes, are blotted;
Thy bed, lust-stain'd, shall with lust's blood be spotted.

Exit

Enter LODOVICO and GRATIANO

CASSIO

What, ho! no watch? no passage? murder! murder!

GRATIANO

'Tis some mischance; the cry is very direful.

CASSIO

O, help!

LODOVICO

Hark!

RODERIGO

O wretched villain!

LODOVICO

Two or three groan: it is a heavy night:
These may be counterfeits: let's think't unsafe
To come in to the cry without more help.

RODERIGO

Nobody come? then shall I bleed to death.

LODOVICO

Hark!

Re-enter IAGO, with a light

GRATIANO

Here's one comes in his shirt, with light and weapons.

IAGO

Who's there? whose noise is this that ones on murder?

LODOVICO

We do not know.

IAGO

Did not you hear a cry?

CASSIO

Here, here! for heaven's sake, help me!

IAGO

What's the matter?

GRATIANO

This is Othello's ancient, as I take it.

LODOVICO

The same indeed; a very valiant fellow.

IAGO

What are you here that cry so grievously?

CASSIO

Iago? O, I am spoil'd, undone by villains!
Give me some help.

IAGO

O me, lieutenant! what villains have done this?

CASSIO

I think that one of them is hereabout,
And cannot make away.

IAGO

O treacherous villains!
What are you there? come in, and give some help.

To LODOVICO and GRATIANO

RODERIGO

O, help me here!

CASSIO

That's one of them.

IAGO

O murderous slave! O villain!

Stabs RODERIGO

RODERIGO

O damn'd Iago! O inhuman dog!

IAGO

Kill men i' the dark!–Where be these bloody thieves?–
How silent is this town!–Ho! murder! murder!–
What may you be? are you of good or evil?

LODOVICO

As you shall prove us, praise us.

IAGO

Signior Lodovico?

LODOVICO

He, sir.

IAGO

I cry you mercy. Here's Cassio hurt by villains.

GRATIANO

Cassio!

IAGO

How is't, brother!

CASSIO

My leg is cut in two.

IAGO

Marry, heaven forbid!
Light, gentlemen; I'll bind it with my shirt.

Enter BIANCA

BIANCA

What is the matter, ho? who is't that cried?

IAGO

Who is't that cried!

BIANCA

O my dear Cassio! my sweet Cassio! O Cassio, Cassio, Cassio!

IAGO

O notable strumpet! Cassio, may you suspect Who they should be that have thus many led you?

CASSIO

No.

GRATIANO

I am to find you thus: I have been to seek you.

IAGO

Lend me a garter. So. O, for a chair,
To bear him easily hence!

BIANCA

Alas, he faints! O Cassio, Cassio, Cassio!

IAGO

Gentlemen all, I do suspect this trash
To be a party in this injury.
Patience awhile, good Cassio. Come, come;
Lend me a light. Know we this face or no?
Alas my friend and my dear countryman
Roderigo! no:–yes, sure: O heaven!
Roderigo.

GRATIANO

What, of Venice?

IAGO

Even he, sir; did you know him?

GRATIANO

Know him! ay.

IAGO

Signior Gratiano? I cry you gentle pardon;
These bloody accidents must excuse my manners,
That so neglected you.

GRATIANO

I am glad to see you.

IAGO

How do you, Cassio? O, a chair, a chair!

GRATIANO

Roderigo!

IAGO

He, he 'tis he.

A chair brought in

O, that's well said; the chair!

GRATIANO

Some good man bear him carefully from hence;
I'll fetch the general's surgeon.

To BIANCA

For you, mistress,
Save you your labour. He that lies slain here, Cassio,
Was my dear friend: what malice was between you?

CASSIO

None in the world; nor do I know the man.

IAGO

[To **BIANCA**] What, look you pale? O, bear him out o' the air.

CASSIO and RODERIGO are borne off

Stay you, good gentlemen. Look you pale, mistress?
Do you perceive the gastness of her eye?
Nay, if you stare, we shall hear more anon.
Behold her well; I pray you, look upon her:
Do you see, gentlemen? nay, guiltiness will speak,
Though tongues were out of use.

Enter EMILIA

EMILIA

'Las, what's the matter? what's the matter, husband?

IAGO

Cassio hath here been set on in the dark
By Roderigo and fellows that are scaped:
He's almost slain, and Roderigo dead.

EMILIA

Alas, good gentleman! alas, good Cassio!

IAGO

This is the fruit of whoring. Prithee, Emilia,
Go know of Cassio where he supp'd to-night.

To BIANCA

What, do you shake at that?

BIANCA

He supp'd at my house; but I therefore shake not.

IAGO

O, did he so? I charge you, go with me.

EMILIA

Fie, fie upon thee, strumpet!

BIANCA

I am no strumpet; but of life as honest
As you that thus abuse me.

EMILIA

As I! foh! fie upon thee!

IAGO

Kind gentlemen, let's go see poor Cassio dress'd.
Come, mistress, you must tell's another tale.
Emilia run you to the citadel,
And tell my lord and lady what hath happ'd.
Will you go on? I pray.

Aside

This is the night
That either makes me or fordoes me quite.

Exeunt

SCENE II. A bedchamber in the castle: DESDEMONA in bed asleep;

a light burning.

Enter OTHELLO

OTHELLO

It is the cause, it is the cause, my soul,–
Let me not name it to you, you chaste stars!–
It is the cause. Yet I'll not shed her blood;
Nor scar that whiter skin of hers than snow,
And smooth as monumental alabaster.
Yet she must die, else she'll betray more men.
Put out the light, and then put out the light:
If I quench thee, thou flaming minister,
I can again thy former light restore,
Should I repent me: but once put out thy light,
Thou cunning'st pattern of excelling nature,
I know not where is that Promethean heat

That can thy light relume. When I have pluck'd the rose,
I cannot give it vital growth again.
It must needs wither: I'll smell it on the tree.

Kissing her

Ah balmy breath, that dost almost persuade
Justice to break her sword! One more, one more.
Be thus when thou art dead, and I will kill thee,
And love thee after. One more, and this the last:
So sweet was ne'er so fatal. I must weep,
But they are cruel tears: this sorrow's heavenly;
It strikes where it doth love. She wakes.

DESDEMONA

Who's there? Othello?

OTHELLO

Ay. Desdemona.

DESDEMONA

Will you come to bed, my lord?

OTHELLO

Have you pray'd to-night, Desdemona?

DESDEMONA

Ay, my lord.

OTHELLO

If you bethink yourself of any crime
Unreconciled as yet to heaven and grace,
Solicit for it straight.

DESDEMONA

Alas, my lord, what do you mean by that?

OTHELLO

Well, do it, and be brief; I will walk by:
I would not kill thy unprepared spirit;
No; heaven forfend! I would not kill thy soul.

DESDEMONA

Talk you of killing?

OTHELLO

Ay, I do.

DESDEMONA

Then heaven
Have mercy on me!

OTHELLO

Amen, with all my heart!

DESDEMONA

If you say so, I hope you will not kill me.

OTHELLO

Hum!

DESDEMONA

And yet I fear you; for you are fatal then
When your eyes roll so: why I should fear I know not,
Since guiltiness I know not; but yet I feel I fear.

OTHELLO

Think on thy sins.

DESDEMONA

They are loves I bear to you.

OTHELLO

Ay, and for that thou diest.

DESDEMONA

That death's unnatural that kills for loving.
Alas, why gnaw you so your nether lip?
Some bloody passion shakes your very frame:
These are portents; but yet I hope, I hope,
They do not point on me.

OTHELLO

Peace, and be still!

DESDEMONA

I will so. What's the matter?

OTHELLO

That handkerchief which I so loved and gave thee
Thou gavest to Cassio.

DESDEMONA

No, by my life and soul!
Send for the man, and ask him.

OTHELLO

Sweet soul, take heed,
Take heed of perjury; thou art on thy deathbed.

DESDEMONA

Ay, but not yet to die.

OTHELLO

Yes, presently:
Therefore confess thee freely of thy sin;
For to deny each article with oath
Cannot remove nor choke the strong conception
That I do groan withal. Thou art to die.

DESDEMONA

Then Lord have mercy on me!

OTHELLO

I say, amen.

DESDEMONA

And have you mercy too! I never did
Offend you in my life; never loved Cassio
But with such general warranty of heaven
As I might love: I never gave him token.

OTHELLO

By heaven, I saw my handkerchief in's hand.
O perjured woman! thou dost stone my heart,
And makest me call what I intend to do
A murder, which I thought a sacrifice:
I saw the handkerchief.

DESDEMONA

He found it then;
I never gave it him: send for him hither;
Let him confess a truth.

OTHELLO

He hath confess'd.

DESDEMONA

What, my lord?

OTHELLO

That he hath used thee.

DESDEMONA

How? unlawfully?

OTHELLO

Ay.

DESDEMONA

He will not say so.

OTHELLO

No, his mouth is stopp'd;
Honest Iago hath ta'en order for't.

DESDEMONA

O! my fear interprets: what, is he dead?

OTHELLO

Had all his hairs been lives, my great revenge
Had stomach for them all.

DESDEMONA

Alas! he is betray'd and I undone.

OTHELLO

Out, strumpet! weep'st thou for him to my face?

DESDEMONA

O, banish me, my lord, but kill me not!

OTHELLO

Down, strumpet!

DESDEMONA

Kill me to-morrow: let me live to-night!

OTHELLO

Nay, if you strive—

DESDEMONA

But half an hour!

OTHELLO

Being done, there is no pause.

DESDEMONA

But while I say one prayer!

OTHELLO

It is too late.

He stifles her

EMILIA

[Within] My lord, my lord! what, ho! my lord, my lord!

OTHELLO

What noise is this? Not dead? not yet quite dead?
I that am cruel am yet merciful;
I would not have thee linger in thy pain:
So, so.

EMILIA

[Within] What, ho! my lord, my lord!

OTHELLO

Who's there?

EMILIA

[Within] O, good my lord, I would speak a word with you!

OTHELLO

Yes: 'tis Emilia. By and by. She's dead.
'Tis like she comes to speak of Cassio's death.—
The noise was here. Ha! no more moving?
Still as the grave. Shall she come in? were't good?—
I think she stirs again:–no. What's best to do?
If she come in, she'll sure speak to my wife:
My wife! my wife! what wife? I have no wife.
O insupportable! O heavy hour!
Methinks it should be now a huge eclipse
Of sun and moon, and that the affrighted globe
Should yawn at alteration.

EMILIA

[Within] I do beseech you
That I may speak with you, O, good my lord!

OTHELLO

I had forgot thee: O, come in, Emilia;
Soft; by and by. Let me the curtains draw.
Where art thou?

Unlocks the door

Enter EMILIA

What's the matter with thee now?

EMILIA

O, my good lord, yonder's foul murders done!

OTHELLO

What, now?

EMILIA

But now, my lord.

OTHELLO

It is the very error of the moon;
She comes more nearer earth than she was wont,
And makes men mad.

EMILIA

Cassio, my lord, hath kill'd a young Venetian
Call'd Roderigo.

OTHELLO

Roderigo kill'd!
And Cassio kill'd!

EMILIA

No, Cassio is not kill'd.

OTHELLO

Not Cassio kill'd! then murder's out of tune,
And sweet revenge grows harsh.

DESDEMONA

O, falsely, falsely murder'd!

EMILIA

Alas, what cry is that?

OTHELLO

That! what?

EMILIA

Out, and alas! that was my lady's voice.
Help! help, ho! help! O lady, speak again!
Sweet Desdemona! O sweet mistress, speak!

DESDEMONA

A guiltless death I die.

EMILIA

O, who hath done this deed?

DESDEMONA

Nobody; I myself. Farewell
Commend me to my kind lord: O, farewell!

Dies

OTHELLO

Why, how should she be murder'd?

EMILIA

Alas, who knows?

OTHELLO

You heard her say herself, it was not I.

EMILIA

She said so: I must needs report the truth.

OTHELLO

She's, like a liar, gone to burning hell:
'Twas I that kill'd her.

EMILIA

O, the more angel she,
And you the blacker devil!

OTHELLO

She turn'd to folly, and she was a whore.

EMILIA

Thou dost belie her, and thou art a devil.

OTHELLO

She was false as water.

EMILIA

Thou art rash as fire, to say
That she was false: O, she was heavenly true!

OTHELLO

Cassio did top her; ask thy husband else.
O, I were damn'd beneath all depth in hell,
But that I did proceed upon just grounds
To this extremity. Thy husband knew it all.

EMILIA

My husband!

OTHELLO

Thy husband.

EMILIA

That she was false to wedlock?

OTHELLO

Ay, with Cassio. Nay, had she been true,
If heaven would make me such another world
Of one entire and Perfect chrysolite,
I'd not have sold her for it.

EMILIA

My husband!

OTHELLO

Ay, 'twas he that told me first:
An honest man he is, and hates the slime
That sticks on filthy deeds.

EMILIA

My husband!

OTHELLO

What needs this iteration, woman? I say
thy husband.

EMILIA

O mistress, villany hath made mocks with
love,
My husband say that she was false!

OTHELLO

He, woman;
I say thy husband: dost understand the word?
My friend, thy husband, honest, honest Iago.

EMILIA

If he say so, may his pernicious soul
Rot half a grain a day! he lies to the heart:
She was too fond of her most filthy bargain.

OTHELLO

Ha!

EMILIA

Do thy worst:
This deed of thine is no more worthy heaven
Than thou wast worthy her.

OTHELLO

Peace, you were best.

EMILIA

Thou hast not half that power to do me harm
As I have to be hurt. O gull! O dolt!
As ignorant as dirt! thou hast done a deed–
I care not for thy sword; I'll make thee
known,
Though I lost twenty lives.–Help! help,
ho! help!
The Moor hath kill'd my mistress! Murder!
murder!

*Enter MONTANO, GRATIANO, IAGO,
and others*

MONTANO

What is the matter? How now, general!

EMILIA

O, are you come, Iago? you have done well,
That men must lay their murders on your
neck.

GRATIANO

What is the matter?

EMILIA

Disprove this villain, if thou be'st a man:
He says thou told'st him that his wife was
false:
I know thou didst not, thou'rt not such
a villain:
Speak, for my heart is full.

IAGO

I told him what I thought, and told no more
Than what he found himself was apt and
true.

EMILIA

But did you ever tell him she was false?

IAGO

I did.

EMILIA

You told a lie, an odious, damned lie;
Upon my soul, a lie, a wicked lie.
She false with Cassio!–did you say with
Cassio?

IAGO

With Cassio, mistress. Go to, charm your
tongue.

EMILIA

I will not charm my tongue; I am bound
to speak:
My mistress here lies murder'd in her bed,—

All

O heavens forfend!

EMILIA

And your reports have set the murder on.

OTHELLO

Nay, stare not, masters: it is true, indeed.

GRATIANO

'Tis a strange truth.

MONTANO

O monstrous act!

EMILIA

Villany, villany, villany!
I think upon't, I think: I smell't: O villany!—
I thought so then:—I'll kill myself for grief:—
O villany, villany!

IAGO

What, are you mad? I charge you, get you home.

EMILIA

Good gentlemen, let me have leave to speak:
'Tis proper I obey him, but not now.
Perchance, Iago, I will ne'er go home.

OTHELLO

O! O! O!

He falls on the bed

EMILIA

Nay, lay thee down and roar;
For thou hast kill'd the sweetest innocent
That e'er did lift up eye.

OTHELLO

[Rising] O, she was foul!
I scarce did know you, uncle: there lies your niece,
Whose breath, indeed, these hands have newly stopp'd:
I know this act shows horrible and grim.

GRATIANO

Poor Desdemona! I am glad thy father's dead:
Thy match was mortal to him, and pure grief
Shore his old thread in twain: did he live now,
This sight would make him do a desperate turn,
Yea, curse his better angel from his side,
And fall to reprobation.

OTHELLO

'Tis pitiful; but yet Iago knows
That she with Cassio hath the act of shame
A thousand times committed; Cassio confess'd it:
And she did gratify his amorous works
With that recognizance and pledge of love
Which I first gave her; I saw it in his hand:
It was a handkerchief, an antique token
My father gave my mother.

EMILIA

O heaven! O heavenly powers!

IAGO

Come, hold your peace.

EMILIA

'Twill out, 'twill out: I peace!
No, I will speak as liberal as the north:
Let heaven and men and devils, let them all,
All, all, cry shame against me, yet I'll speak.

IAGO

Be wise, and get you home.

EMILIA

I will not.

IAGO offers to stab **EMILIA**

GRATIANO

Fie!
Your sword upon a woman?

EMILIA

O thou dull Moor! that handkerchief thou speak'st of
I found by fortune and did give my husband;
For often, with a solemn earnestness,
More than indeed belong'd to such a trifle,
He begg'd of me to steal it.

IAGO

Villanous whore!

EMILIA

She give it Cassio! no, alas! I found it,
And I did give't my husband.

IAGO

Filth, thou liest!

EMILIA

By heaven, I do not, I do not, gentlemen.
O murderous coxcomb! what should such a fool
Do with so good a woman?

OTHELLO

Are there no stones in heaven
But what serve for the thunder?—Precious villain!

He runs at IAGO IAGO, from behind, stabs EMILIA, and exit

GRATIANO

The woman falls; sure, he hath kill'd his wife.

EMILIA

Ay, ay: O, lay me by my mistress' side.

GRATIANO

He's gone, but his wife's kill'd.

MONTANO

'Tis a notorious villain. Take you this weapon,
Which I have here recover'd from the Moor:
Come, guard the door without; let him not pass,
But kill him rather. I'll after that same villain,
For 'tis a damned slave.

Exeunt MONTANO and GRATIANO

OTHELLO

I am not valiant neither,
But ever puny whipster gets my sword:
But why should honour outlive honesty?
Let it go all.

EMILIA

What did thy song bode, lady?
Hark, canst thou hear me? I will play the swan.
And die in music.

Singing

Willow, willow, willow,–
Moor, she was chaste; she loved thee, cruel Moor;
So come my soul to bliss, as I speak true;
So speaking as I think, I die, I die.

Dies

OTHELLO

I have another weapon in this chamber;
It is a sword of Spain, the ice-brook's temper:–
O, here it is. Uncle, I must come forth.

GRATIANO

[Within] If thou attempt it, it will cost thee dear:
Thou hast no weapon, and perforce must suffer.

OTHELLO

Look in upon me then and speak with me,
Or, naked as I am, I will assault thee.

Re-enter GRATIANO

GRATIANO

What is the matter?

OTHELLO

Behold, I have a weapon;
A better never did itself sustain
Upon a soldier's thigh: I have seen the day,
That, with this little arm and this good sword,
I have made my way through more impediments
Than twenty times your stop: but, O vain boast!
Who can control his fate? 'tis not so now.
Be not afraid, though you do see me weapon'd;
Here is my journey's end, here is my butt,
And very sea-mark of my utmost sail.
Do you go back dismay'd? 'tis a lost fear;
Man but a rush against Othello's breast,
And he retires. Where should Othello go?
Now, how dost thou look now? O ill-starr'd wench!
Pale as thy smock! when we shall meet at compt,
This look of thine will hurl my soul from heaven,
And fiends will snatch at it. Cold, cold, my girl!
Even like thy chastity. O cursed slave!
Whip me, ye devils,
From the possession of this heavenly sight!
Blow me about in winds! roast me in sulphur!
Wash me in steep-down gulfs of liquid fire!
O Desdemona! Desdemona! dead!
Oh! Oh! Oh!

Enter LODOVICO. MONTANO, CASSIO carried in a chair, and Officers with IAGO, prisoner

LODOVICO

Where is this rash and most unfortunate man?

OTHELLO

That's he that was Othello: here I am.

LODOVICO

Where is that viper? bring the villain forth.

OTHELLO

I look down towards his feet; but that's a fable.
If that thou best a devil, I cannot kill thee.

Wounds IAGO

LODOVICO

Wrench his sword from him.

IAGO

I bleed, sir; but not kill'd.

OTHELLO

I am not sorry neither: I'ld have thee live;
For, in my sense, 'tis happiness to die.

LODOVICO

O thou Othello, thou wert once so good,
Fall'n in the practise of a damned slave,
What shall be said to thee?

OTHELLO

Why, any thing:
An honourable murderer, if you will;
For nought I did in hate, but all in honour.

LODOVICO

This wretch hath part confess'd his villany:
Did you and he consent in Cassio's death?

OTHELLO

Ay.

CASSIO

Dear general, I never gave you cause.

OTHELLO

I do believe it, and I ask your pardon.
Will you, I pray, demand that demi-devil
Why he hath thus ensnared my soul and body?

IAGO

Demand me nothing: what you know, you know:
From this time forth I never will speak word.

LODOVICO

What, not to pray?

GRATIANO

Torments will ope your lips.

OTHELLO

Well, thou dost best.

LODOVICO

Sir, you shall understand what hath befall'n,
Which, as I think, you know not. Here is a letter
Found in the pocket of the slain Roderigo;
And here another: the one of them imports
The death of Cassio to be undertook
By Roderigo.

OTHELLO

O villain!

CASSIO

Most heathenish and most gross!

LODOVICO

Now here's another discontented paper,
Found in his pocket too; and this, it seems,
Roderigo meant to have sent this damned villain;
But that belike Iago in the interim
Came in and satisfied him.

OTHELLO

O the pernicious caitiff!
How came you, Cassio, by that handkerchief
That was my wife's?

CASSIO

I found it in my chamber:
And he himself confess'd but even now
That there he dropp'd it for a special purpose
Which wrought to his desire.

OTHELLO

O fool! fool! fool!

CASSIO

There is besides in Roderigo's letter,
How he upbraids Iago, that he made him
Brave me upon the watch; whereon it came
That I was cast: and even but now he spake,
After long seeming dead, Iago hurt him,
Iago set him on.

LODOVICO

You must forsake this room, and go with us:
Your power and your command is taken off,
And Cassio rules in Cyprus. For this slave,
If there be any cunning cruelty
That can torment him much and hold him long,
It shall be his. You shall close prisoner rest,
Till that the nature of your fault be known
To the Venetian state. Come, bring him away.

OTHELLO

Soft you; a word or two before you go.
I have done the state some service, and they know't.
No more of that. I pray you, in your letters,
When you shall these unlucky deeds relate,
Speak of me as I am; nothing extenuate,
Nor set down aught in malice: then must you speak
Of one that loved not wisely but too well;
Of one not easily jealous, but being wrought
Perplex'd in the extreme; of one whose hand,
Like the base Indian, threw a pearl away
Richer than all his tribe; of one whose subdued eyes,
Albeit unused to the melting mood,
Drop tears as fast as the Arabian trees
Their medicinal gum. Set you down this;
And say besides, that in Aleppo once,
Where a malignant and a turban'd Turk
Beat a Venetian and traduced the state,
I took by the throat the circumcised dog,
And smote him, thus.

Stabs himself

LODOVICO

O bloody period!

GRATIANO

All that's spoke is marr'd.

OTHELLO

I kiss'd thee ere I kill'd thee: no way but this;
Killing myself, to die upon a kiss.

Falls on the bed, and dies

CASSIO

This did I fear, but thought he had no weapon;
For he was great of heart.

LODOVICO

[To **IAGO**] O Spartan dog,
More fell than anguish, hunger, or the sea!
Look on the tragic loading of this bed;
This is thy work: the object poisons sight;
Let it be hid. Gratiano, keep the house,
And seize upon the fortunes of the Moor,
For they succeed on you. To you, lord governor,
Remains the censure of this hellish villain;
The time, the place, the torture: O, enforce it!
Myself will straight aboard: and to the state
This heavy act with heavy heart relate.

Exeunt

CRITICAL EYE

▶ **For Discussion**

a. Why is Othello unable to forge a new life for himself despite his ability to climb the social and political ranks of his society?

b. Does Iago's plan actually work because Othello still sees himself as a victim and a slave?

c. Obtain a copy of James Alan Mcpherson's story "Umbilicus," and examine *Othello* alongside of it. How are their arguments about racial tension the same?

▶ **Re-approaching the Reading**

Much of this text focuses on Othello, but what about Desdemona? In so many ways, she is a hapless victim because of her gender. How is this true?

▶ **Writing Assignment**

Examine this story from Iago's perspective. How/why is his resentment of Othello understood? In essence, why does Iago see himself as a member of the underclass?

ABRAHAM LINCOLN

HOUSE DIVIDED SPEECH
Springfield, Illinois
June 16, 1858

Mr. President and Gentlemen of the Convention.

If we could first know where we are, and *whither* we are tending, we could then better judge *what* to do, and *how* to do it. We are now far into the *fifth* year, since a policy was initiated, with the *avowed* object, and *confident* promise, of putting an end to slavery agitation. Under the operation of that policy, that agitation has not only, *not ceased,* but has *constantly augmented.* In my opinion, it *will* not cease, until a *crisis* shall have been reached, and passed. "A house divided against itself cannot stand." I believe this government cannot endure, permanently *half* slave and half *free.* I do not expect the Union to be *dissolved*—I do not expect the house to *fall*—but I *do* expect it will cease to be divided. It will become *all* one thing or *all* the other. Either the *opponents* of slavery, will arrest the further spread of it, and place it where the public mind shall rest in the belief that it is in the course of ultimate extinction; or its *advocates* will push it forward, till it shall become alike lawful in *all* the States, *old* as well as *new*—*North* as well as *South.*

Have we no *tendency* to the latter condition?

Let any one who doubts, carefully contemplate that now almost complete legal combination—piece of *machinery* so to speak—compounded of the Nebraska doctrine, and the Dred Scott decision. Let him consider not only *what* work the machinery is adapted to do, and *how well* adapted; but also, let him study the *history* of its construction, and trace, if he can, or rather *fail,* if he can, to trace the evidence of design and concert of action, among its chief architects, from the beginning.

The new year of 1854 found slavery excluded from more than half the States by State Constitutions, and from most of the national territory by congressional prohibition. Four days later, commenced the struggle, which ended in repealing that congressional prohibition. This opened all the national territory to slavery, and was the first point gained.

This necessity had not been overlooked; but had been provided for, as well as might be, in the notable argument of *"squatter sovereignty,"* otherwise called *"sacred right of self government,"* which latter phrase, though expressive of the only rightful basis of any government, was so perverted in this attempted use of it as to amount to just this: That if any *one* man, choose to enslave *another,* no *third* man shall be allowed to object. That argument was incorporated into the Nebraska bill itself, in the language which follows:

> *It being the true intent and meaning of this act not to legislate slavery into any Territory or state, not to exclude it therefrom; but to leave the people thereof perfectly free to form and regulate their domestic institutions in their own way, subject only to the Constitution of the United States."*

Then opened the roar of loose declamation in favor of "Squatter Sovereignty," and "Sacred right of self-government." "But," said opposition members, "let us be more *specific*—let us *amend* the bill so as to expressly declare that the people of the territory may exclude slavery." "Not we," said the friends of the measure; and down they voted the amendment.

While the Nebraska Bill was passing through congress, a *law case* involving the question of a negroe's freedom, by reason of his owner having voluntarily taken him first into a free state and then a territory covered by the congressional prohibition, and held him as a slave, for a long time in each, was passing through the U.S. Circuit Court for the District of Missouri; and both Nebraska bill and law suit were brought to a decision in the same month of May, 1854. The negroe's name was "Dred Scott," which name now designates the decision finally made in the case. *Before* the *then* next Presidential election, the law case came *to*, and was argued *in*, the Supreme Court of the United States; but the *decision* of it was deferred until *after* the election. Still, *before* the election, Senator Trumbull, on the floor of the Senate, requests the leading advocate of the Nebraska bill to state *his opinion* whether the people of a territory can constitutionally exclude slavery from their limits; and the latter answers: "That is a question for the Supreme Court."

The election came. Mr. Buchanan was elected, and the *indorsement,* such as it was, secured. That was the *second* point gained. The indorsement, however, fell short of a clear popular majority by nearly four hundred thousand votes, and so, perhaps, was not overwhelmingly reliable and satisfactory. The *outgoing* President, in his last annual message, as impressively as possible, *echoed back* upon the people the weight and *authority* of the indorsement. The Supreme Court met again; *did not* announce their decision, but ordered a re-argument.

The Presidential inauguration came, and still no decision of the court; but the *incoming* President, in his inaugural address, fervently exhorted the people to abide by the forthcoming decision, *whatever might be*. Then, in a few days, came the decision.

The reputed author of the Nebraska Bill finds an early occasion to make a speech at this capital indorsing the Dred Scott Decision, and vehemently denouncing all opposition to it. The new President, too, seizes the early occasion of the Silliman letter to *indorse* and strongly *construe* that decision, and to express his *astonishment* that any different view had ever been entertained!

At length a squabble springs up between the President and the author of the Nebraska Bill, on the *mere* question of *fact*, whether the Lecompton constitution was or was not, in any just sense, made by the people of Kansas; and in that squabble the latter declares that all he wants is a fair vote for the people, and that he *cares* not whether slavery be voted *down* or voted *up*. I do not understand his declaration that he cares not whether slavery be voted down or voted up, to be intended by him other than as an *apt definition* of the *policy* he would impress upon the public mind—the *principle* for which he declares he has suffered much, and is ready to suffer to the end. And well may he cling to that principle. If he has any parental feeling, well may he cling to it. That principle, is the only *shred* left of his original Nebraska doctrine.

Under the Dred Scott decision, "squatter sovereignty" squatted out of existence, tumbled down like temporary scaffolding—like the mould at the foundry served through one blast and fell back into loose sand—helped to carry an election, and then was kicked to the winds. His late *joint* struggle with the Republicans, against the Lecompton Constitution, involves nothing of the original Nebraska doctrine. That struggle was made on a point, the right of a people to make their own constitution, upon which he and the Republicans have never differed.

The several points of the Dred Scott decision, in connection with Senator Douglas's "care-not" policy, constitute the piece of machinery, in its present state of advancement. This was the third point gained. The working points of that machinery are:

First, that no negro slave, imported as such from Africa, and no descendant of such slave, can ever be a citizen of any State, in the sense of that term as used in the Constitution of the United States. This point is made in order to deprive the negro, in every possible event, of the benefit of that provision of the United States Constitution, which declares that: "The citizens of each State shall be entitled to all privileges and immunities of citizens in the several States."

Second, that "subject to the Constitution of the United States," neither Congress nor a Territorial legislature can exclude slavery from any United States Territory. This point is made in order that individual men may fill up the Territories with slaves, without danger of losing them as property, and thus to enhance the chances of permanency to the institution through all the future. Third, that whether holding a negro in actual slavery in a free State makes him free, as against the holder, the United States courts will not decide, but will leave to be decided by the courts of any slave State the negro may be forced into by the master. This point is made, not to be pressed immediately; but, if acquiesced in for a while, and apparently indorsed by the people at an election, then to sustain the logical conclusion that what Dred Scott's master might lawfully do with Dred Scott, in the free State of Illinois, every other master may lawfully do with any other one, or one thousand slaves, in Illinois, or in any other free State.

Auxiliary to all this, and working hand in hand with it, the Nebraska doctrine, or what is left of it, is to educate and mold public opinion, at least Northern public opinion, not to care whether slavery is voted down or voted up. This shows exactly where we now are; and partially, also, whither we are tending.

It will throw additional light on the latter, to go back, and run the mind over the string of historical facts already stated. Several things will now appear less dark and mysterious than they did when they were transpiring. The people were to be left "perfectly free," subject only to the Constitution. What the Constitution had to do with it, outsiders could not then see. Plainly enough now, it was an exactly fitted niche, for the Dred Scott decision to afterward come in, and declare the perfect free freedom of the people to be just no freedom at all. Why was the amendment, expressly declaring the right of the people, voted down? Plainly enough now: the adoption of it would have spoiled the niche for the Dred Scott decision. Why was the court decision held up? Why even a Senator's individual opinion withheld, till after the presidential election? Plainly enough now—the speaking out then would have damaged the perfectly free argument upon which the election was to be carried. Why the outgoing President's felicitation on the indorsement? Why the delay of a re-argument? Why the incoming President's advance exhortation in favor of the decision? These things look like the cautious patting and petting of a spirited horse, preparatory to mounting him, when it is dreaded that he may give the rider a fall. And why the hasty after-indorsement of the decision by the President and others?

We cannot absolutely know that all these exact adaptations are the result of preconcert. But when we see a lot of framed timbers, different portions of which we know have been gotten out at different times and places, and by different workmen—Stephen, Franklin, Roger, and James, for instance—and when we see these timbers joined together, and see they exactly matte the frame of a house or a mill, all the tenons and mortices exactly fitting, and all the lengths and proportions of the different l pieces exactly adapted to their respective places, and not a piece. Too many or too few, not omitting even scaffolding—or, if a single piece be lacking, we see the place in the frame exactly fitted and prepared yet to bring such piece in—in such a case we find it impossible not to believe that Stephen and Franklin and Roger and James all understood one another from the beginning and all worked upon a common plan or draft drawn up before the first blow was struck.

CRITICAL EYE

▶ For Discussion

a. Putting the racial component aside, why was it important as a leader for Mr. Lincoln to take up such a position on slavery and its place in American society?

b. Would you argue that his stance weakened or strengthened his position as President? Keep in mind that a huge section of the country stood in direct opposition to his ideas.

▶ Re-approaching the Reading

Why is it important for a leader of a nation to support and defend the oppressed and impoverished segments of their country? What is gained in doing so? What then is the signal to the rest of the society, and do they in turn become disenfranchised in favor of the oppressed and poor? In short, can there be a balance?

▶ Writing Assignment

Why, in your opinion, have racial matters always centered around Blacks and Whites? As you see it, are we still dealing with the ideas that Mr. Lincoln addresses in his speech? Are we still hurting as a nation because of the evil of African slavery?

CHAPTER 4

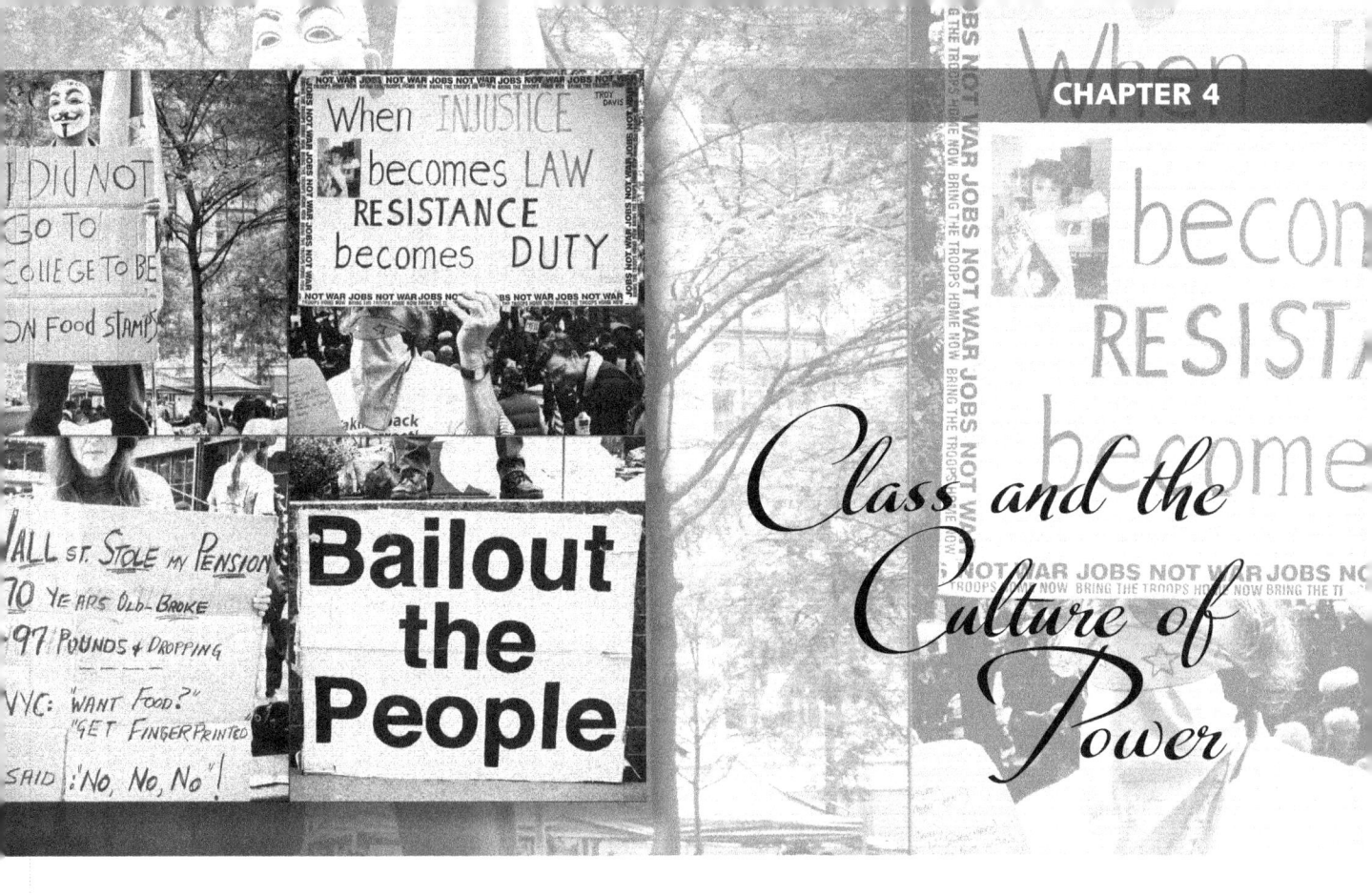

Class and the Culture of Power

> *It is a very grave matter to be forced to imitate a people for whom you know—which is the price of your performance and survival—you do not exist. It is hard to imitate a people whose existence appears, mainly, to be made tolerable by their bottomless gratitude that they are not, thank heaven, you.*
> — James Baldwin

To socially classify a group of people is an idea as old as the development of civilization itself. Since the dawn of human beings, mankind has always compared itself to those forms of nature it could most readily relate with—ultimately deeming itself the dominant species. The obvious luxury of this positioning—of recognizing the species of humankind as being number one—is that those who are beneath humans on the measuring stick are often susceptible to the whims of humans as king of the world.

With this understanding, the differentiating of humanity was inevitable. Undeniably, differentiating the "haves" and the "have-nots" has been the main platform for establishing social difference—of distinguishing a society's vision of what we have come to call "Class." When it comes to Class, individuals function in society based upon the stratification that accords their grouping status.

Scientists would argue that this separation is no different than the established hierarchy that other species employ. Yet, around the globe, sociologists, philosophers, and politicians alike have attempted to discern what exactly makes and who actually fits into particular groupings. Some suggest that it is mainly a matter of race. Others claim that gender is the dominant factor. And, many claim that Class is most notably an economic consideration. Yet, confusion and disharmony arise because the reality is that language, neighborhood, occupation, and education—even looks—often become determining factors of how we are judged by society and how we, in turn, will judge others.

Unlike the strong and domineering creatures that rule the jungle or the sea, humankind's grouping and separating is far more perplexing. The interesting thing about who fits and who does not—what determines Class and what should not be a consideration—is that even though finding a set definition of social Class is, at best, as obscure as it is convoluted, all agree that social differentiation is undeniable and inescapable. The following selections seek to explore these complexities and considerations surrounding Class.

MARK TWAIN

The Lowest Animal

I have been studying the traits and dispositions of the "lower animals" (so-called), and contrasting them with the traits and dispositions of man. I find the result humiliating to me. For it obliges me to renounce my allegiance to the Darwinian theory of the Ascent of Man from the Lower Animals; since it now seems plain to me that that theory ought to be vacated in favor of a new and truer one, this new and truer one to be named the Descent of Man from the Higher Animals.

In proceeding toward this unpleasant conclusion I have not guessed or speculated or conjectured, but have used what is commonly called the scientific method. That is to say, I have subjected every postulate that presented itself to the crucial test of actual experiment, and have adopted it or rejected it according to the result. Thus I verified and established each step of my course in its turn before advancing to the next. These experiments were made in the London Zoological Gardens, and covered many months of painstaking and fatiguing work.

Before particularizing any of the experiments, I wish to state one or two things which seem to more properly belong in this place than further along. This in the interest of clearness. The massed experiments established to my satisfaction certain generalizations, to wit:

1. That the human race is of one distinct species. It exhibits slight variations—in color, stature, mental caliber, and so on—due to climate, environment, and so forth; but it is a species by itself, and not to be confounded with any other.

2. That the quadrupeds are a distinct family, also. This family exhibits variations—in color, size, food preferences and so on; but it is a family by itself.

3. That the other families—the birds, the fishes, the insects, the reptiles, etc.—are more or less distinct, also. They are in the procession. They are links in the chain which stretches down from the higher animals to man at the bottom.

Some of my experiments were quite curious. In the course of my reading I had come across a case where, many years ago, some hunters on our Great Plains organized a buffalo hunt for the entertainment of an English earl—that, and to provide some fresh meat for his larder. They had charming sport. They killed seventy-two of those great animals; and ate part of one of them and left the seventy-one to rot. In order to determine the difference between an anaconda and an earl—if any—I caused seven young calves to be turned into the anaconda's cage. The grateful reptile immediately crushed one of them and swallowed it. Then lay back satisfied. It showed no further interest in the calves, and no disposition to harm them. I tried this experiment with other anacondas: always with the same result. The fact stood proven that the difference between an earl and an anaconda is that the earl is cruel and the anaconda isn't; and that the earl wantonly destroys what he has no use for, but the anaconda doesn't. This seemed to suggest that the anaconda was not descended from the earl. It also seemed to suggest that the earl was descended from the anaconda, and had lost a good deal in the transition.

I was aware that many men who have accumulated more millions of money than they can ever use have shown a rabid hunger for more, and have not scrupled to cheat the ignorant and the helpless out of their poor servings in order to partially appease that appetite. I furnished a hundred different kinds of wild and tame animals the opportunity to accumulate vast stores of food, but none of them would do it. The squirrels and bees and certain birds made accumulations, but stopped when they had gathered a winter's supply, and could not be persuaded to add to it either honestly or by chicane. In order to bolster up a tottering reputation the ant pretended to store up supplies, but I was not deceived. I know the ant. These experiments convinced me that there is this difference between man and the higher animals: he is avaricious and miserly, they are not.

In the course of my experiments I convinced myself that among the animals man is the only one that harbors insults and injuries, broods over them, waits till a chance offers, then takes revenge. The passion of revenge is unknown to the higher animals.

Roosters keep harems, but it is by consent of their concubines: therefore no wrong is done. Men keep harems, but it is by brute force, privileged by atrocious laws which the other sex is allowed no hand in making. In this matter man occupies a far lower place than the rooster.

Cats are loose in their morals, but not consciously so. Man, in his descent from the cat, has brought the cat's looseness with him but has left the unconsciousness behind—the saving grace which excuses the cat. The cat is innocent, man is not.

Indecency, vulgarity, obscenity—these are strictly confined to man: he invented them. Among the higher animals there is no trace of them. They hide nothing; they are not ashamed. Man, with his soiled mind, covers himself. He will not even enter a drawing room with his breast and back naked, so alive are he and his mates to indecent suggestion. Man is "The Animal that Laughs." But so does the monkey, as Mr. Darwin pointed out; and so does the Australian bird that is called the laughing jackass. No—Man is the Animal that Blushes. He is the only one that does it—or has occasion to.

At the head of this article we see how "three monks were burnt to death" a few days ago, and a prior "put to death with atrocious cruelty." Do we inquire into the details? No; or we should find out that the prior was subjected to unprintable multilations. Man—when he is a North American Indian—gouges out his prisoner's eyes; when he is King John, with a nephew to render untroublesome, he uses a red-hot iron; when he is a religious zealot dealing with heretics in the Middle Ages, he skins his captive alive and scatters salt on his back; in the first Richard's time he shuts up a multitude of Jew families in a tower and sets fire to it; in Columbus's time he captures a family of Spanish Jews and—but *that* is not printable; in our day in England a man is fined ten shillings for beating his mother nearly to death with a chair, and another man is fined forty shillings for having four pheasant eggs in his possession without being able to satisfactorily explain how he got them. Of all the animals, man is the only one that is cruel. He is the only one that inflicts pain for the pleasure of doing it. It is a trait that is not known to the higher animals. The cat plays with the frightened mouse; but she has this excuse, that she does not know that the mouse is suffering. The cat is moderate—unhumanly moderate: she only scares the mouse, she does not hurl it; she doesn't dig out its eyes, or tear off its skin, or drive splinters under its nails—man-fashion; when she is done playing with it she makes a sudden meal of it and puts it out of its trouble. Man is the Cruel Animal. He is alone in that distinction.

The higher animals engage in individual fights, but never in organized masses. Man is the only animal that deals in that atrocity of atrocities.

War. He is the only one that gathers his brethren about him and goes forth in cold blood and with calm pulse to exterminate his kind. He is the only animal that for sordid wages will march out, as the Hessians[1] did in our Revolution, and as the boyish Prince Napoleon did in the Zulu war, and help to slaughter strangers of his own species who have done him no harm and with whom he has no quarrel.

Man is the only animal that robs his helpless fellow of his country—takes possession of it and drives him out of it or destroys him. Man has done this in all the ages. There is not an acre of ground on the globe that is in possession of its rightful owner, or that has not been taken away from owner after owner, cycle after cycle, by force and bloodshed.

Man is the only Slave. And he is the only animal who enslaves. He has always been a slave in one form or another, and has always held other slaves in bondage under him in one way or another. In our day he is always some man's slave for wages, and does that man's work; and this slave has other slaves under him for minor wages, and they do *his* work. The higher animals are the only ones who exclusively do their own work and provide their own living.

Man is the only Patriot. He sets himself apart in his own country, under his own flag, and sneers at the other nations, and keeps multitudinous uniformed assassins on hand at heavy expense to grab slices of other people's countries, and keep *them* from grabbing slices of *his*. And in the intervals between campaigns he washes the blood off his hands and works for "the universal brotherhood of man"—with his mouth.

Man is the Religious Animal. He is the only Religious Animal. He is the only animal that has the True Religion—several of them. He is the only animal that loves his neighbor as himself, and cuts his throat if his theology isn't straight. He has made a graveyard of the globe in trying his honest best to smooth his brother's path to happiness and heaven. He was at it in the time of the Caesars, he was at it in Mahomet's time, he was at it in the time of the Inquisition, he was at it in France a couple of centuries, he was at it in England in Mary's day, he has been at it ever since he first saw the light, he is at it today in Crete—as per the telegrams quoted above—he will be at it somewhere else tomorrow. The higher animals have no religion. And we are told that they are going to be left out, in the Hereafter. I wonder why? It seems questionable taste.

Man is the Reasoning Animal. Such is the claim. I think it is open to dispute. Indeed, my experiments have proven to me that he is the Unreasoning Animal. Note his history, as sketched above. It seems plain to me that whatever he is he is *not* a reasoning animal. His record is the fantastic record of a maniac. I consider that the strongest count against his intelligence is the fact that with that record back of him he blandly sets himself up as the head animal of the lot: whereas by his own standards he is the bottom one.

In truth, man is incurably foolish. Simple things which the other animals easily learn, he is incapable of learning. Among my experiments was this. In an hour I taught a cat and a dog to be friends. I put them in a cage. In another hour I taught them to be friends with a rabbit. In the course of two days I was able to add a fox, a goose, a squirrel and some doves. Finally a monkey. They lived together in peace; even affectionately.

Next, in another cage I confined an Irish Catholic from Tipperary, and as soon as he seemed tame I added a Scotch Presbyterian from Aberdeen. Next a Turk from Constantinople; a Greek Christian from Crete; an Armenian; a Methodist from the wilds of Arkansas; a Buddhist from China; a Brahman from Benares. Finally, a Salvation Army Colonel from Wapping. Then I

---

[1] Hessians: the German auxillary soldiers brought over by the British to fight the Americans during the Revolutionary War.

stayed away two whole days. When I came back to note result, the cage of Higher Animals was all right, but in the other there was but a chaos of gory odds and ends of turbans and fezzes and plaids and bones and flesh—not a specimen left alive. These Reasoning Animals had disagreed on a theological detail and carried the matter to a Higher Court.

One is obliged to concede that in true loftiness of character, Man cannot claim to approach even the meanest of the Higher Animals. It is plain that he is constitutionally incapable of approaching that altitude; that he is constitutionally afflicted with a Defect which must make such approach forever impossible, for it is manifest that this defect is permanent in him, indestructible, ineradicable.

I find this Defect to be *the Moral Sense*. He is the only animal that has it. It is the secret of his degradation. It is the quality *which enables him to do wrong*. It has no other office. It is incapable of performing any other function. It could never have been intended to perform any other. Without it, man could do no wrong. He would rise at once to the level of the Higher Animals.

Since the Moral Sense has but the one office, the one capacity—to enable man to do wrong—it is plainly without value to him. It is as valueless to him as is disease. In fact, it manifestly is a disease. *Rabies* is bad, but it is not so bad as this disease. Rabies enables a man to do a thing which he could not do when in a healthy state: kill his neighbor with a poisonous bite. No one is the better man for having rabies. The Moral Sense enables a man to do wrong. It enables him to do wrong in a thousand ways. Rabies is an innocent disease, compared to the Moral Sense. No one, then, can be the better man for having the Moral Sense. What, now, do we find the Primal Curse to have been? Plainly what it was in the beginning: the infliction upon man of the Moral Sense; the ability to distinguish good from evil; and with it, necessarily, the ability to *do* evil; for there can be no evil act without the presence of consciousness of it in the doer of it.

And so I find that we have descended and degenerated, from some far ancestor—some microscopic atom wandering at its pleasure between the mighty horizons of a drop of water perchance—insect by insect, animal by animal, reptile by reptile, down the long highway of smirchless innocence, till we have reached the bottom stage of development—namable as the Human Being. Below us—nothing.

CRITICAL EYE

▶ For Discussion

   a. What commentary is Twain making about mankind?

   b. Is he making a distinction between men and women?

   c. Throughout history, what has man done to prove the validity of Twain's essay?

   d. Read Emerson's *Nature* (download) and examine how it addresses Twain's positions.

▶ Re-approaching the Reading

Apply Twain's perspective to how man continues to treat endangered species.

▶ Writing Assignment

Early American colonists believed in the notion of Manifest Destiny, which stressed the notion of the settlers being ordained by God to cultivate America and tame its inhabitants. The book of Genesis in the Old Testament stresses the right of Adam to have dominion over the Earth and the animals therein. In what way(s) do these biblical assessments subvert Twain's argument?

KATIE CHOPIN

From the Novel
THE AWAKENING

This chapter allows the reader to see the further evolution of Edna Pontellier—a young wife and mother who has recently discovered her true self and, much to the chagrin of her husband and contemporaries, abandons her societal responsibilities as a "woman." Refusing to abide by her husband's wishes, Mrs. Pontellier has also fallen in love with another man and, on a whim, has decided she would like to become an artist.

XIX

Edna could not help but think that it was very foolish, very childish, to have stamped upon her wedding ring and smashed the crystal vase upon the tiles. She was visited by no more outbursts, moving her to such futile expedients. She began to do as she liked and to feel as she liked. She completely abandoned her Tuesdays at home, and did not return the visits of those who had called upon her. She made no ineffectual efforts to conduct her household *en bonne menagere*, going and coming as it suited her fancy, and, so far as she was able, lending herself to any passing caprice.

Mr. Pontellier had been a rather courteous husband so long as he met a certain tacit submissiveness in his wife. But her new and unexpected line of conduct completely bewildered him. It shocked him. Then her absolute disregard for her duties as a wife angered him. When Mr. Pontellier became rude, Edna grew insolent. She had resolved never to take another step backward.

"It seems to me the utmost folly for a woman at the head of a household, and the mother of children, to spend in an atelier days which would be better employed contriving for the comfort of her family."

"I feel like painting," answered Edna. "Perhaps I shan't always feel like it."

"Then in God's name paint! but don't let the family go to the devil. There's Madame Ratignolle; because she keeps up her music, she doesn't let everything else go to chaos. And she's more of a musician than you are a painter."

"She isn't a musician, and I'm not a painter. It isn't on account of painting that I let things go."

"On account of what, then?"

"Oh! I don't know. Let me alone; you bother me."

It sometimes entered Mr. Pontellier's mind to wonder if his wife were not growing a little unbalanced mentally. He could see plainly that she was not herself. That is, he could not see that she was becoming herself and daily casting aside that fictitious self which we assume like a garment with which to appear before the world.

Her husband let her alone as she requested, and went away to his office. Edna went up to her atelier—a bright room in the top of the house. She was working with great energy and interest, without accomplishing anything, however, which satisfied her even in the smallest degree. For a time she had the whole household enrolled in the service of art. The boys posed for her. They thought it amusing at first, but the occupation soon lost its attractiveness when they discovered that it was not a game arranged especially for their entertainment. The quadroon sat for hours before Edna's palette, patient as a savage, while the house-maid took charge of the children, and the drawing-room went undusted. But the house-maid, too, served her term as model when Edna perceived that the young woman's back and shoulders were molded on classic lines, and that her hair, loosened from its confining cap, became an inspiration.

While Edna worked she sometimes sang low the little air, *"Ah! si tu savais!"*

It moved her with recollections. She could hear again the ripple of the water, the flapping sail. She could see the glint of the moon upon the bay, and could feel the soft, gusty beating of the hot south wind. A subtle current of desire passed through her body, weakening her hold upon the brushes and making her eyes burn.

There were days when she was very happy without knowing why. She was happy to be alive and breathing, when her whole being seemed to be one with the sunlight, the color, the odors, the luxuriant warmth of some perfect Southern day. She liked then to wander alone into strange and unfamiliar places. She discovered many a sunny, sleepy corner, fashioned to dream in. And she found it good to dream and to be alone and unmolested.

There were days when she was unhappy, she did not know why, – when it did not seem worth while to be glad or sorry, to be alive or dead; when life appeared to her like a grotesque pandemonium and humanity like worms struggling blindly toward inevitable annihilation. She could not work on such a day, nor weave fancies to stir her pulses and warm her blood.

XX

It was during such a mood that Edna hunted up Mademoiselle Reisz. She had not forgotten the rather disagreeable impression left upon her by their last interview; but she nevertheless felt a desire to see her—above all, to listen while she played upon the piano. Quite early in the afternoon she started upon her quest for the pianist. Unfortunately she had mislaid or lost Mademoiselle Reisz's card, and looking up her address in the city directory, she found that the woman lived on Bienville Street, some distance away. The directory which fell into her hands was a year or more old, however, and upon reaching the number indicated, Edna discovered that the house was occupied by a respectable family of mulattoes who had *chambres garnies* to let. They had been living there for six months, and knew absolutely nothing of a Mademoiselle Reisz. In fact, they knew nothing of any of their neighbors; their lodgers were all people of the highest distinction, they assured Edna. She did not linger to discuss class distinctions with Madame Pouponne, but hastened to a neighboring grocery store, feeling sure that Mademoiselle would have left her address with the proprietor.

He knew Mademoiselle Reisz a good deal better than he wanted to know her, he informed his questioner. In truth, he did not want to know her at all, or anything concerning her—the most disagreeable and unpopular woman who ever lived in Bienville Street. He thanked heaven she had left the neighborhood, and was equally thankful that he did not know where she had gone.

Edna's desire to see Mademoiselle Reisz had increased tenfold since these unlooked-for obstacles had arisen to thwart it. She was wondering who could give her the information she sought, when it suddenly occurred to her that Madame Lebrun would be the one most likely to do so. She knew it was useless to ask Madame Ratignolle, who was on the most distant terms with the musician, and preferred to know nothing concerning her. She had once been almost as emphatic in expressing herself upon the subject as the corner grocer.

Edna knew that Madame Lebrun had returned to the city, for it was the middle of November. And she also knew where the Lebruns lived, on Chartres Street.

Their home from the outside looked like a prison, with iron bars before the door and lower windows. The iron bars were a relic of the old *regime*, and no one had ever thought of dislodging them. At the side was a high fence enclosing the garden. A gate or door opening upon the street was locked. Edna rang the bell at this side garden gate, and stood upon the banquette, waiting to be admitted.

It was Victor who opened the gate for her. A black woman, wiping her hands upon her apron, was close at his heels. Before she saw them Edna could hear them in altercation, the woman—plainly an anomaly—claiming the right to be allowed to perform her duties, one of which was to answer the bell.

Victor was surprised and delighted to see Mrs. Pontellier, and he made no attempt to conceal either his astonishment or his delight. He was a dark-browed, good-looking youngster of nineteen, greatly resembling his mother, but with ten times her impetuosity. He instructed the black woman to go at once and inform Madame Lebrun that Mrs. Pontellier desired to see her. The woman grumbled a refusal to do part of her duty when she had not been permitted to do it all, and started back to her interrupted task of weeding the garden.

Whereupon Victor administered a rebuke in the form of a volley of abuse, which, owing to its rapidity and incoherence, was all but incomprehensible to Edna. Whatever it was, the rebuke was convincing, for the woman dropped her hoe and went mumbling into the house.

Edna did not wish to enter. It was very pleasant there on the side porch, where there were chairs, a wicker lounge, and a small table. She seated herself, for she was tired from her long tramp; and she began to rock gently and smooth out the folds of her silk parasol. Victor drew up his chair beside her. He at once explained that the black woman's offensive conduct was all due to imperfect training, as he was not there to take her in hand. He had only come up from the island the morning before, and expected to return next day. He stayed all winter at the island; he lived there, and kept the place in order and got things ready for the summer visitors.

But a man needed occasional relaxation, he informed Mrs. Pontellier, and every now and again he drummed up a pretext to bring him to the city. My! but he had had a time of it the evening before! He wouldn't want his mother to know, and he began to talk in a whisper. He was scintillant with recollections. Of course, he couldn't think of telling Mrs. Pontellier all about it, she being a woman and not comprehending such things. But it all began with a girl peeping and smiling at him through the shutters as he passed by. Oh! but she was a beauty! Certainly he smiled back, and went up and talked to her. Mrs. Pontellier did not know him if she supposed he was one to let an opportunity like that escape him. Despite herself, the youngster amused her. She must have betrayed in her look some degree of interest or entertainment. The boy grew more daring, and Mrs. Pontellier might have found herself, in a little while, listening to a highly colored story but for the timely appearance of Madame Lebrun.

That lady was still clad in white, according to her custom of the summer. Her eyes beamed an effusive welcome. Would not Mrs. Pontellier go inside? Would she partake of some refreshment? Why had she not been there before? How was that dear Mr. Pontellier and how were those sweet children? Had Mrs. Pontellier ever known such a warm November?

Victor went and reclined on the wicker lounge behind his mother's chair, where he commanded a view of Edna's face. He had taken her parasol from her hands while he spoke to her, and he now lifted it and twirled it above him as he lay on his back. When Madame Lebrun complained that it was so dull coming back to the city; that she saw so few people now; that even Victor, when he came up from the island for a day or two, had so much to occupy him and engage his time; then it was that the youth went into contortions on the lounge and winked mischievously at Edna. She somehow felt like a confederate in crime, and tried to look severe and disapproving.

There had been but two letters from Robert, with little in them, they told her. Victor said it was really not worth while to go inside for the letters, when his mother entreated him to go in search of them. He remembered the contents, which in truth he rattled off very glibly when put to the test.

One letter was written from Vera Cruz and the other from the City of Mexico. He had met Montel, who was doing everything toward his advancement. So far, the financial situation was no improvement over the one he had left in New Orleans, but of course the prospects were vastly better. He wrote of the City of Mexico, the buildings, the people and their habits, the conditions of life which he found there. He sent his love to the family. He inclosed a check to his mother, and hoped she would affectionately remember him to all his friends. That was about the substance of the two letters. Edna felt that if there had been a message for her, she would have received it. The despondent frame of mind in which she had left home began again to overtake her, and she remembered that she wished to find Mademoiselle Reisz.

Madame Lebrun knew where Mademoiselle Reisz lived. She gave Edna the address, regretting that she would not consent to stay and spend the remainder of the afternoon, and pay a visit to Mademoiselle Reisz some other day. The afternoon was already well advanced.

Victor escorted her out upon the banquette, lifted her parasol, and held it over her while he walked to the car with her. He entreated her to bear in mind that the disclosures of the afternoon were strictly confidential. She laughed and bantered him a little, remembering too late that she should have been dignified and reserved.

"How handsome Mrs. Pontellier looked!" said Madame Lebrun to her son.

"Ravishing!" he admitted. "The city atmosphere has improved her. Some way she doesn't seem like the same woman."

XXI

Some people contended that the reason Mademoiselle Reisz always chose apartments up under the roof was to discourage the approach of beggars, peddlars and callers. There were plenty of windows in her little front room. They were for the most part dingy, but as they were nearly always open it did not make so much difference. They often admitted into the room a good deal of smoke and soot; but at the same time all the light and air that there was came through them. From her windows could be seen the crescent of the river, the masts of ships and the big chimneys of the Mississippi steamers. A magnificent piano crowded the apartment. In the next room she slept, and in the third and last she harbored a gasoline stove on which she cooked her meals when disinclined to descend to the neighboring restaurant. It was there also that she ate, keeping her belongings in a rare old buffet, dingy and battered from a hundred years of use.

When Edna knocked at Mademoiselle Reisz's front room door and entered, she discovered that person standing beside the window, engaged in mending or patching an old prunella gaiter. The little musician laughed all over when she saw Edna. Her laugh consisted of a contortion of the face and all the muscles of the body. She seemed strikingly homely, standing there in the afternoon light. She still wore the shabby lace and the artificial bunch of violets on the side of her head.

"So you remembered me at last," said Mademoiselle. "I had said to myself, 'Ah, bah! she will never come.'"

"Did you want me to come?" asked Edna with a smile.

"I had not thought much about it," answered Mademoiselle. The two had seated themselves on a little bumpy sofa which stood against the wall. "I am glad, however, that you came. I have the water boiling back there, and was just about to make some coffee. You will drink a cup with me. And how is *la belle dame*? Always handsome! always healthy! always contented!" She took Edna's hand between her strong wiry fingers, holding it loosely without warmth, and executing a sort of double theme upon the back and palm.

"Yes," she went on; "I sometimes thought: 'She will never come. She promised as those women in society always do, without meaning it. She will not come.' For I really don't believe you like me, Mrs. Pontellier."

"I don't know whether I like you or not," replied Edna, gazing down at the little woman with a quizzical look.

The candor of Mrs. Pontellier's admission greatly pleased Mademoiselle Reisz. She expressed her gratification by repairing forthwith to the region of the gasoline stove and rewarding her guest with the promised cup of coffee. The coffee and the biscuit accompanying it proved very acceptable to Edna, who had declined refreshment at Madame Lebrun's and was now beginning to feel hungry. Mademoiselle set the tray which she brought in upon a small table near at hand, and seated herself once again on the lumpy sofa.

"I have had a letter from your friend," she remarked, as she poured a little cream into Edna's cup and handed it to her.

"My friend?"

"Yes, your friend Robert. He wrote to me from the City of Mexico."

"Wrote to *you?*" repeated Edna in amazement, stirring her coffee absently.

"Yes, to me. Why not? Don't stir all the warmth out of your coffee; drink it. Though the letter might as well have been sent to you; it was nothing but Mrs. Pontellier from beginning to end."

"Let me see it," requested the young woman, entreatingly.

"No; a letter concerns no one but the person who writes it and the one to whom it is written."

"Haven't you just said it concerned me from beginning to end?"

"It was written about you, not to you. 'Have you seen Mrs. Pontellier? How is she looking?' he asks. 'As Mrs. Pontellier says,' or 'as Mrs. Pontellier once said.' 'If Mrs. Pontellier should call upon you, play for her that Impromptu of Chopin's, my favorite. I heard it here a day or two ago, but not as you play it. I should like to know how it affects her,' and so on, as if he supposed we were constantly in each other's society."

"Let me see the letter."

"Oh, no."

"Have you answered it?"

"No."

"Let me see the letter."

"No, and again, no."

"Then play the Impromptu for me."

"It is growing late; what time do you have to be home?"

"Time doesn't concern me. Your question seems a little rude. Play the Impromptu."

"But you have told me nothing of yourself. What are you doing?"

"Painting!" laughed Edna. "I am becoming an artist. Think of it!"

"Ah! an artist! You have pretensions, Madame."

"Why pretensions? Do you think I could not become an artist?"

"I do not know you well enough to say. I do not know your talent or your temperament. To be an artist includes much; one must possess many gifts—absolute gifts—which have not been acquired by one's own effort. And, moreover, to succeed, the artist must possess the courageous soul."

"What do you mean by the courageous soul?"

"Courageous, *ma foi!* The brave soul. The soul that dares and defies."

"Show me the letter and play for me the Impromptu. You see that I have persistence. Does that quality count for anything in art?"

"It counts with a foolish old woman whom you have captivated," replied Mademoiselle, with her wriggling laugh.

The letter was right there at hand in the drawer of the little table upon which Edna had just placed her coffee cup. Mademoiselle opened the drawer and drew forth the letter, the topmost one. She placed it in Edna's hands, and without further comment arose and went to the piano.

Mademoiselle played a soft interlude. It was an improvisation. She sat low at the instrument, and the lines of her body settled into ungraceful curves and angles that gave it an appearance of deformity. Gradually and imperceptibly the interlude melted into the soft opening minor chords of the Chopin Impromptu.

Edna did not know when the Impromptu began or ended. She sat in the sofa corner reading Robert's letter by the fading light. Mademoiselle had glided from the Chopin into the quivering love-notes of Isolde's song, and back again to the Impromptu with its soulful and poignant longing.

The shadows deepened in the little room. The music grew strange and fantastic—turbulent, insistent, plaintive and soft with entreaty. The shadows grew deeper. The music filled the room. It floated out upon the night, over the housetops, the crescent of the river, losing itself in the silence of the upper air.

Edna was sobbing, just as she had wept one midnight at Grand Isle when strange, new voices awoke in her. She arose in some agitation to take her departure. "May I come again, Mademoiselle?" she asked at the threshold.

"Come whenever you feel like it. Be careful; the stairs and landings are dark; don't stumble."

Mademoiselle reentered and lit a candle. Robert's letter was on the floor. She stooped and picked it up. It was crumpled and damp with tears. Mademoiselle smoothed the letter out, restored it to the envelope, and replaced it in the table drawer.

XXII

One morning on his way into town Mr. Pontellier stopped at the house of his old friend and family physician, Doctor Mandelet. The Doctor was a semi-retired physician, resting, as the saying is, upon his laurels. He bore a reputation for wisdom rather than skill—leaving the active practice of medicine to his assistants and younger contemporaries—and was much sought for in matters of consultation. A few families, united to him by bonds of friendship, he still attended when they required the services of a physician. The Pontelliers were among these.

Mr. Pontellier found the Doctor reading at the open window of his study. His house stood rather far back from the street, in the center of a delightful garden, so that it was quiet and peaceful at the old gentleman's study window. He was a great reader. He stared up disapprovingly over his eye-glasses as Mr. Pontellier entered, wondering who had the temerity to disturb him at that hour of the morning.

"Ah, Pontellier! Not sick, I hope. Come and have a seat. What news do you bring this morning?" He was quite portly, with a profusion of gray hair, and small blue eyes which age had robbed of much of their brightness but none of their penetration.

"Oh! I'm never sick, Doctor. You know that I come of tough fiber—of that old Creole race of Pontelliers that dry up and finally blow away. I came to consult—no, not precisely to consult—to talk to you about Edna. I don't know what ails her."

"Madame Pontellier not well," marveled the Doctor. "Why, I saw her—I think it was a week ago—walking along Canal Street, the picture of health, it seemed to me."

"Yes, yes; she seems quite well," said Mr. Pontellier, leaning forward and whirling his stick between his two hands; "but she doesn't act well. She's odd, she's not like herself. I can't make her out, and I thought perhaps you'd help me."

"How does she act?" inquired the Doctor.

"Well, it isn't easy to explain," said Mr. Pontellier, throwing himself back in his chair. "She lets the housekeeping go to the dickens."

"Well, well; women are not all alike, my dear Pontellier. We've got to consider—"

"I know that; I told you I couldn't explain. Her whole attitude—toward me and everybody and everything—has changed. You know I have a quick temper, but I don't want to quarrel or be rude to a woman, especially my wife; yet I'm driven to it, and feel like ten thousand devils after I've made a fool of myself. She's making it devilishly uncomfortable for me," he went on nervously. "She's got some sort of notion in her head concerning the eternal rights of women; and—you understand—we meet in the morning at the breakfast table."

The old gentleman lifted his shaggy eyebrows, protruded his thick nether lip, and tapped the arms of his chair with his cushioned fingertips.

"What have you been doing to her, Pontellier?"

"Doing! *Parbleu!*"

"Has she," asked the Doctor, with a smile, "has she been associating of late with a circle of pseudo-intellectual women—super-spiritual superior beings? My wife has been telling me about them."

"That's the trouble," broke in Mr. Pontellier, "she hasn't been associating with any one. She has abandoned her Tuesdays at home, has thrown over all her acquaintances, and goes tramping about by herself, moping in the street-cars, getting in after dark. I tell you she's peculiar. I don't like it; I feel a little worried over it."

This was a new aspect for the Doctor. "Nothing hereditary?" he asked, seriously.

"Nothing peculiar about her family antecedents, is there?"

"Oh, no, indeed! She comes of sound old Presbyterian Kentucky stock. The old gentleman, her father, I have heard, used to atone for his weekday sins with his Sunday devotions. I know for a fact, that his race horses literally ran away with the prettiest bit of Kentucky farming land I ever laid eyes upon. Margaret—you know Margaret—she has all the Presbyterianism undiluted. And the youngest is something of a vixen. By the way, she gets married in a couple of weeks from now."

"Send your wife up to the wedding," exclaimed the Doctor, foreseeing a happy solution. "Let her stay among her own people for a while; it will do her good."

"That's what I want her to do. She won't go to the marriage. She says a wedding is one of the most lamentable spectacles on earth. Nice thing for a woman to say to her husband!" exclaimed Mr. Pontellier, fuming anew at the recollection.

"Pontellier," said the Doctor, after a moment's reflection, "let your wife alone for a while. Don't bother her, and don't let her bother you. Woman, my dear friend, is a very peculiar and delicate organism—a sensitive and highly organized woman, such as I know Mrs. Pontellier to be, is especially peculiar. It would require an inspired psychologist to deal successfully with them. And when ordinary fellows like you and me attempt to cope with their idiosyncrasies the result is bungling. Most women are moody and whimsical. This is some passing whim of your wife, due to some cause or causes which you and I needn't try to fathom. But it will pass happily over, especially if you let her alone. Send her around to see me."

"Oh! I couldn't do that; there'd be no reason for it," objected Mr. Pontellier.

"Then I'll go around and see her," said the Doctor. "I'll drop in to dinner some evening *en bon ami*.

"Do! by all means," urged Mr. Pontellier. "What evening will you come? Say Thursday. Will you come Thursday?" he asked, rising to take his leave.

"Very well; Thursday. My wife may possibly have some engagement for me Thursday. In case she has, I shall let you know. Otherwise, you may expect me."

Mr. Pontellier turned before leaving to say:

"I am going to New York on business very soon. I have a big scheme on hand, and want to be on the field proper to pull the ropes and handle the ribbons. We'll let you in on the inside if you say so, Doctor," he laughed.

"No, I thank you, my dear sir," returned the Doctor. "I leave such ventures to you younger men with the fever of life still in your blood."

"What I wanted to say," continued Mr. Pontellier, with his hand on the knob; "I may have to be absent a good while. Would you advise me to take Edna along?"

"By all means, if she wishes to go. If not, leave her here. Don't contradict her. The mood will pass, I assure you. It may take a month, two, three months—possibly longer, but it will pass; have patience."

"Well, good-by, *a jeudi*," said Mr. Pontellier, as he let himself out.

The Doctor would have liked during the course of conversation to ask, "Is there any man in the case?" but he knew his Creole too well to make such a blunder as that.

He did not resume his book immediately, but sat for a while meditatively looking out into the garden.

CRITICAL EYE

▶ **For Discussion**

a. Even though Kate Chopin always argued that she was not a feminist, when the text was rediscovered in 1969, it became and remains the quintessential feminist text. That said, why is this novel so important to the feminist movement?

b. What does Edna's character reveal about a woman's need to have her own money and private space?

▶ **Re-approaching the Reading**

The social norms of our society have always told us that *all* women desire to be married with children. In fact, societal strictures dictate that these are the jobs for which women are best suited. How do women like Edna upset the balance of our society when they step outside of what is expected of them?

▶ **Writing Topic**

Examine this excerpt alongside of Naomi Wolf's "The Making of a Slut." Is Edna a "bad girl"?

NGŪGĪ WA THIONG'O
DECOLONISING THE MIND

I was born into a large peasant family: father, four wives and about twenty-eight children. I also belonged, as we all did in those days, to a wider extended family and to the community as a whole.

We spoke Gĩkũyũ as we worked in the fields. We spoke Gĩkũyũ in and outside the home. I can vividly recall those evenings of story-telling around the fireside. It was mostly the grown-ups telling the children but everybody was interested and involved. We children would re-tell the stories the following day to other children who worked in the fields picking the pyrethrum flowers, tea-leaves or coffee beans of our European and African landlords.

The stories, with mostly animals as the main characters, were all told in Gĩkũyũ. Hare, being small, weak but full of innovative wit and cunning, was our hero. We identified with him as he struggled against the brutes of prey like lion, leopard, hyena. His victories were our victories and we learnt that the apparently weak can outwit the strong. We followed the animals in their struggle against hostile nature—drought, rain, sun, wind—a confrontation often forcing them to search for forms of co-operation. But we were also interested in their struggles amongst themselves, and particularly between the beasts and the victims of prey. These twin struggles, against nature and other animals, reflected real-life struggles in the human world.

Not that we neglected stories with human beings as the main characters. There were two types of characters in such human-centered narratives: the species of truly human beings with qualities of courage, kindness, mercy, hatred of evil, concern for others; and a man-eat-man two-mouthed species with qualities of greed, selfishness, individualism and hatred of what was good for the larger co-operative community. Co-operation as the ultimate good in a community was a constant theme. It could unite human beings with animals against ogres and beasts of prey, as in the story of how dove, after being fed with castor-oil seeds, was sent to fetch a smith working far away from home and whose pregnant wife was being threatened by these man-eating two-mouthed ogres.

There were good and bad story-tellers. A good one could tell the same story over and over again, and it would always be fresh to us, the listeners. He or she could tell a story told by someone else and make it more alive and dramatic. The differences really were in the use of words and images and the inflexion of voices to effect different tones.

We therefore learnt to value words for their meaning and nuances. Language was not a mere string of words. It had a suggestive power well beyond the immediate and lexical meaning. Our appreciation of the suggestive magical power of language was reinforced by the games we played with words through riddles, proverbs, transpositions of syllables, or through nonsensical but musically arranged words.[1] So we learnt the music of our language

Reprinted with permission from *Decolonising the Mind: The Politics of Language in African Literature* by Ngugi wa Thiong'o. Copyright © 1986 by Ngugi wa Thiong'o. Published by Heinemann, Portsmouth, NH. All rights reserved.

on top of the content. The language, through images and symbols, gave us a view of the world, but it had a beauty of its own. The home and the field were then our pre-primary school but what is important, for this discussion, is that the language of our evening teach-ins, and the language of our immediate and wider community, and the language of our work in the fields were one.

And then I went to school, a colonial school, and this harmony was broken. The language of my education was no longer the language of my culture. I first went to Kamaandura, missionary run, and then to another called Maanguuũ run by nationalists grouped around the Gĩkũyũ Independent and Karinga Schools Association. Our language of education was still Gĩkũyũ. The very first time I was ever given an ovation for my writing was over a composition in Gĩkũyũ. So for my first four years there was still harmony between the language of my formal education and that of the Limuru peasant community.

It was after the declaration of a state of emergency over Kenya in 1952 that all the schools run by patriotic nationalists were taken over by the colonial regime and were placed under District Education Boards chaired by Englishmen. English became the language of my formal education. In Kenya, English became more than a language: It was *the* language, and all the others had to bow before it in deference.

Thus one of the most humiliating experiences was to be caught speaking Gĩkũyũ in the vicinity of the school. The culprit was given corporal punishment—three to five strokes of the cane on bare buttocks—or was made to carry a metal plate around the neck with inscriptions such as I AM STUPID or I AM A DONKEY. Sometimes the culprits were fined money they could hardly afford. And how did the teachers catch the culprits? A button was initially given to one pupil who was supposed to hand it over to whoever was caught speaking his mother tongue. Whoever had the button at the end of the day would sing who had given it to him and the ensuing process would bring out all the culprits of the day. Thus children were turned into witch-hunters and in the process were being taught the lucrative value of being a traitor to one's immediate community.

The attitude to English was the exact opposite: any achievement in spoken or written English was highly rewarded: prizes, prestige, applause: the ticket to higher realms. English became the measure of intelligence and ability in the arts, the sciences, and all the other branches of learning. English became *the* main determinant of a child's progress up the ladder of formal education.

As you may know, the colonial system of education in addition to its apartheid racial demarcation had the structure of a pyramid: a broad primary base, a narrowing secondary middle, and an even narrower university apex. Selections from primary into secondary were through an examination, in my time called Kenya African Preliminary Examination, in which one had to pass six subjects ranging from Math to Nature Study and Kiswahili. All the papers were written in English. Nobody could pass the exam who failed the English language paper no matter how brilliantly he had done in the other subjects. I remember one boy in my class of 1954 who had distinctions in all subjects except English, which he had failed. He was made to fail the entire exam. He went on to become a turn boy in a bus company. I who had only passed but a credit in English got a place at the Alliance High School, one of the most elitist institutions for Africans in colonial

---

[1] Example from a tongue twister: 'Kaana ka Nikoora koona koora koora: na ko koora koona kaana ka Nikoora koora koora.' I'm indebted to Wangul wa Gora for this example. "Nichola's child saw a baby frog and ran away: and when the baby frog saw Nichola's child it also ran away." A Gĩkũyũ speaking child has to get the correct tone and length of vowel and pauses to get it right. Otherwise it becomes a jumble of k's and r's and na's [author's note].

Kenya. The requirements for a place at the University, Makerere University College, were broadly the same: nobody could go on to wear the undergraduate red gown, no matter how brilliantly they had performed in all the other subjects unless they had a credit—not even a simple pass!—in English. Thus the most coveted place in the pyramid and in the system was only available to the holder of an English language credit card. English was the official vehicle and the magic formula to colonial elitedom.

Literary education was now determined by the dominant language while also reinforcing that dominance. Orature (oral literature) in Kenyan languages stopped. In primary school I now read simplified Dickens and Stevenson alongside Rider Haggard. Jim Hawkins, Oliver Twist, Tom Brown—not Hare, Leopard and Lion—were now my daily companions in the world of imagination. In secondary school, Scott and G.B. Shaw vied with more Rider Haggard, John Buchan, Alan Paton, Captain W.K. Johns. At Makerere I read English: from Chaucer to T.S. Eliot with a touch of Graham Greene.

Thus language and literature were taking us further and further from ourselves to other selves, from our world to other worlds.

What was the colonial system doing to us Kenyan children? What were the consequences of, on the one hand, this systematic suppression of our languages and the literature they carried, and on the other the elevation of English and the literature it carried? To answer those questions, let me first examine the relationship of language to human experience, human culture, and the human perception of reality.

Language, any language, has a dual character: it is both a means of communication and a carrier of culture. Take English. It is spoken in Britain and in Sweden and Denmark. But for Swedish and Danish people English is only a means of communication with non-Scandinavians. It is not a carrier of their culture. For the British, and particularly the English, it is additionally, and inseparably from its use as a tool of communication, a carrier of their culture and history. Or take Swahili in East and Central Africa. It is widely used as a means of communication across many nationalities. But it is not the carrier of a culture and history of many of those nationalities. However in parts of Kenya and Tanzania, and particularly in Zanzibar, Swahili is inseparably both a means of communication and a carrier of the culture of those people to whom it is a mother-tongue.

Culture transmits or imparts those images of the world and reality through the spoken and the written language, that is through a specific language. In other words, the capacity to speak, the capacity to order sounds in a manner that makes for mutual comprehension between human beings is universal. This is the universality of language, a quality specific to human beings. It corresponds to the universality of the struggle against nature and that between human beings. But the particularity of the sounds, the words, the word order into phrases and sentences, and the specific manner, or laws, of their ordering is what distinguishes one language from another. Thus a specific culture is not transmitted through language in its universality but in its particularity as the language of a specific community with a specific history. Written literature and orature are the main means by which a particular language transmits the images of the world contained in the culture it carries.

Language as communication and as culture are then products of each other. Communication creates culture: culture is a means of communication. Language carries culture, and culture carries, particularly through orature and literature, the entire body of values by which we come to perceive ourselves and our place in the world. How people perceive themselves affects how they look at their culture, at their politics and at the social production of wealth, at their entire relationship to nature and to other beings. Language is thus inseparable from ourselves as a community of human beings with a specific form and character, a specific history, a specific relationship to the world.

So what was the colonialist imposition of a foreign language doing to us children?

The real aim of colonialism was to control the people's wealth: what they produced, how they produced it, and how it was distributed; to control, in other words, the entire realm of the language of real life. Colonialism imposed its control of the social production of wealth through military conquest and subsequent political dictatorship. But its most important area of domination was the mental universe of the colonised, the control, through culture, of how people perceived themselves and their relationship to the world. Economic and political control can never be complete or effective without mental control. To control a people's culture is to control their tools of self-definition in relationship to others.

For colonialism this involved two aspects of the same process: the destruction or the deliberate undervaluing of a people's culture, their art, dances, religions, history, geography, education, orature and literature, and the conscious elevation of the language of the coloniser. The domination of a people's language by the languages of the colonising nations was crucial to the domination of the mental universe of the colonised.

Take language as communication. Imposing a foreign language, and suppressing the native languages as spoken and written, were already breaking the harmony previously existing between the African child and the three aspects of language. Since the new language as a means of communication was a product of and was reflecting the 'real language of life' elsewhere, it could never as spoken or written properly reflect or imitate the real life of that community. This may in part explain why technology always appears to us as slightly external, their product and not ours. The word 'missile' used to hold an alien far-away sound until I recently learnt its equivalent in Gĩkũyũ, ngurukuhĩ, and it made me apprehend it differently. Learning, for a colonial child, became a cerebral activity and not an emotionally felt experience.

But since the new, imposed languages could never completely break the native languages as spoken, their most effective area of domination was the third aspect of language as communication, the written. The language of an African child's formal education was foreign. The language of the books he read was foreign. The language of his conceptualisation was foreign. Thought, in him, took the visible form of a foreign language. So the written language of a child's upbringing in the school (even his spoken language within the school compound) became divorced from his spoken language at home. There was often not the slightest relationship between the child's written world, which was also the language of his schooling, and the world of his immediate environment in the family and the community. For a colonial child, the harmony existing between the three aspects of language as communication was irrevocably broken. This resulted in the disassociation of the sensibility of that child from his natural and social environment, what we might call colonial alienation. The alienation became reinforced in the teaching of history, geography, music, where bourgeois Europe was always the centre of the universe.

This disassociation, divorce, or alienation from the immediate environment becomes clearer when you look at colonial language as a carrier of culture.

Since culture is a product of the history of a people which it in turn reflects, the child was now being exposed exclusively to a culture that was a product of a world external to himself. He was being made to stand outside himself to look at himself. *Catching Them Young* is the title of a book on racism, class, sex, and politics in children's literature by Bob Dixon. 'Catching them young' as an aim was even more true of a colonial child. The images of this world and his place in it implanted in a child take years to eradicate, if they ever can be.

Since culture does not just reflect the world in images but actually, through those very images, conditions a child to see that world in a certain way, the colonial child was made to see the world and where he stands in it as seen and defined by or reflected in the culture of the language of imposition.

And since those images are mostly passed on through orature and literature it meant the child would now only see the world as seen in the literature of his language of adoption. From the point of view of alienation, that is of seeing oneself from outside oneself as if one was another self, it does not matter that the imported literature carried the great humanist tradition of the best in Shakespeare, Goethe, Balzac, Tolstoy, Gorky, Brecht, Sholokhov, Dickens. The location of this great mirror of imagination was necessarily Europe and its history and culture and the rest of the universe was seen from that centre.

But obviously it was worse when the colonial child was exposed to images of his world as mirrored in the written languages of his coloniser. Where his own native languages were associated in his impressionable mind with low status, humiliation, corporal punishment, slow-footed intelligence and ability or downright stupidity, non-intelligibility and barbarism, this was reinforced by the world he met in the works of such geniuses of racism as a Rider Haggard or a Nicholas Monsarrat; not to mention the pronouncement of some of the giants of western intellectual and political establishment, such as Hume ('. . . the negro is naturally inferior to the whites . . .'),[2] Thomas Jefferson ('. . . the blacks . . . are inferior to the whites on the endowments of both body and mind . . .'),[3] or Hegel with his Africa comparable to a land of childhood still enveloped in the dark mantle of the night as far as the development of self-conscious history was concerned. Hegel's statement that there was nothing harmonious with humanity to be found in the African character is representative of the racist images of Africans and Africa such a colonial child was bound to encounter in the literature of the colonial languages.[4] The results could be disastrous.

In her paper read to the conference on the teaching of African literature in schools held in Nairobi in 1973, entitled 'Written Literature and Black Images'[5] the Kenyan writer and scholar Professor Mĩcere Mũgo related how a reading of the description of Gagool as an old African woman in Rider Haggard's *King Solomon's Mines* had for a long time made her feel mortal terror whenever she encountered old African women. In his autobiography *This Life* Sydney Poitier describes how, as a result of the literature he had read, he had come to associate Africa with snakes. So on arrival in Africa and being put up in a modern hotel in a modern city, he could not sleep because he kept on looking for snakes everywhere, even under the bed. These two have been able to pinpoint the origins of their fears. But for most others the negative image becomes internalised and it affects their cultural and even political choices in ordinary living.

---

[2] Quoted in Eric Williams, *A History of the People of Trinidad and Tobago*, London 1964, p. 32 [Author's note].

[3] Eric Williams, ibid. p. 31 [Author's note].

[4] In references to Africa in the introduction to his lectures in *The Philosophy of History,* Hegel gives historical, philosophical, rational expression and legitimacy to every conceivable European racist myth about Africa. Africa is even denied her own geography where it does not correspond to the myth. Thus Egypt is not part of Africa; and North Africa is part of Europe. Africa proper is the especial home of ravenous beasts, snakes of all kinds. The African is not part of humanity. Only slavery to Europe can raise him, possibly, to the lower ranks of humanity. Slavery is good for the African. 'Slavery is in and for itself *injustice,* for the essence of humanity is *freedom;* but for this man must be matured. The gradual abolition of slavery is therefore wiser and more equitable than its sudden removal.' (Hegel, *The Philosophy of History,* Dover edition. New York: 1956, pp. 91–9.) Hegel clearly reveals himself as the nineteenth-century Hitler of the intellect [Author's note].

[5] The paper is now in Akivaga and Gachukiah's *The Teaching of African Literature in Schools,* published by Kenya Literature Bureau [Author's note].

CRITICAL EYE

▶ For Discussion

a. Looking at the British rule of Kenya, how important are language and education to the domination of a people?

b. Looking at the oppression of Kenyans, does Thiong'o's essay suggest that the British are attempting to civilize the ignorant or dismantle their culture?

▶ Re-approaching the Reading

Given that Puerto Rico is a principality of the United States, can you find any similarities between the way the United States handles Puerto Rico and its own citizens?

▶ Writing Assignment

As Kenya is a principality, would you suggest that the colonizer has the right to rule the land and citizens of its owned property as it sees fit, or must the citizens make efforts to govern themselves?

MARY SHELLEY

From the Novel
FRANKENSTEIN

Chapter 16

"Cursed, cursed creator! Why did I live? Why, in that instant, did I not extinguish the spark of existence which you had so wantonly bestowed? I know not; despair had not yet taken possession of me; my feelings were those of rage and revenge. I could with pleasure have destroyed the cottage and its inhabitants and have glutted myself with their shrieks and misery.

"When night came I quitted my retreat and wandered in the wood; and now, no longer restrained by the fear of discovery, I gave vent to my anguish in fearful howlings. I was like a wild beast that had broken the toils, destroying the objects that obstructed me and ranging through the wood with a stag-like swiftness. Oh! What a miserable night I passed! The cold stars shone in mockery, and the bare trees waved their branches above me; now and then the sweet voice of a bird burst forth amidst the universal stillness. All, save I, were at rest or in enjoyment; I, like the arch-fiend, bore a hell within me, and finding myself unsympathized with, wished to tear up the trees, spread havoc and destruction around me, and then to have sat down and enjoyed the ruin.

"But this was a luxury of sensation that could not endure; I became fatigued with excess of bodily exertion and sank on the damp grass in the sick impotence of despair. There was none among the myriads of men that existed who would pity or assist me; and should I feel kindness towards my enemies? No; from that moment I declared everlasting war against the species, and more than all, against him who had formed me and sent me forth to this insupportable misery.

"The sun rose; I heard the voices of men and knew that it was impossible to return to my retreat during that day. Accordingly I hid myself in some thick underwood, determining to devote the ensuing hours to reflection on my situation.

"The pleasant sunshine and the pure air of day restored me to some degree of tranquillity; and when I considered what had passed at the cottage, I could not help believing that I had been too hasty in my conclusions. I had certainly acted imprudently. It was apparent that my conversation had interested the father in my behalf, and I was a fool in having exposed my person to the horror of his children. I ought to have familiarized the old De Lacey to me, and by degrees to have discovered myself to the rest of his family, when they should have been prepared for my approach. But I did not believe my errors to be irretrievable, and after much consideration I resolved to return to the cottage, seek the old man, and by my representations win him to my party.

"These thoughts calmed me, and in the afternoon I sank into a profound sleep; but the fever of my blood did not allow me to be visited by peaceful dreams. The horrible scene of the preceding day was forever acting before my eyes; the females were flying and the enraged Felix tearing me from his father's feet. I awoke exhausted, and finding that it was already night, I crept forth from my hiding-place, and went in search of food.

"When my hunger was appeased, I directed my steps towards the well-known path that conducted to the cottage. All there was at peace. I crept into my hovel and remained in silent expectation of the accustomed hour when the family arose. That hour passed, the sun mounted high in the heavens, but the cottagers did not appear. I trembled violently, apprehending some dreadful misfortune. The inside of the cottage was dark, and I heard no motion; I cannot describe the agony of this suspense.

"Presently two countrymen passed by, but pausing near the cottage, they entered into conversation, using violent gesticulations; but I did not understand what they said, as they spoke the language of the country, which differed from that of my protectors. Soon after, however, Felix approached with another man; I was surprised, as I knew that he had not quitted the cottage that morning, and waited anxiously to discover from his discourse the meaning of these unusual appearances.

"'Do you consider,' said his companion to him, 'that you will be obliged to pay three months' rent and to lose the produce of your garden? I do not wish to take any unfair advantage, and I beg therefore that you will take some days to consider of your determination.'

"'It is utterly useless,' replied Felix; 'we can never again inhabit your cottage. The life of my father is in the greatest danger, owing to the dreadful circumstance that I have related. My wife and my sister will never recover from their horror. I entreat you not to reason with me any more. Take possession of your tenement and let me fly from this place.'

"Felix trembled violently as he said this. He and his companion entered the cottage, in which they remained for a few minutes, and then departed. I never saw any of the family of De Lacey more.

"I continued for the remainder of the day in my hovel in a state of utter and stupid despair. My protectors had departed and had broken the only link that held me to the world. For the first time the feelings of revenge and hatred filled my bosom, and I did not strive to control them, but allowing myself to be borne away by the stream, I bent my mind towards injury and death. When I thought of my friends, of the mild voice of De Lacey, the gentle eyes of Agatha, and the exquisite beauty of the Arabian, these thoughts vanished and a gush of tears somewhat soothed me. But again when I reflected that they had spurned and deserted me, anger returned, a rage of anger, and unable to injure anything human, I turned my fury towards inanimate objects. As night advanced I placed a variety of combustibles around the cottage, and after having destroyed every vestige of cultivation in the garden, I waited with forced impatience until the moon had sunk to commence my operations.

"As the night advanced, a fierce wind arose from the woods and quickly dispersed the clouds that had loitered in the heavens; the blast tore along like a mighty avalanche and produced a kind of insanity in my spirits that burst all bounds of reason and reflection. I lighted the dry branch of a tree and danced with fury around the devoted cottage, my eyes still fixed on the western horizon, the edge of which the moon nearly touched. A part of its orb was at length hid, and I waved my brand; it sank, and with a loud scream I fired the straw, and heath, and bushes, which I had collected. The wind fanned the fire, and the cottage was quickly enveloped by the flames, which clung to it and licked it with their forked and destroying tongues.

"As soon as I was convinced that no assistance could save any part of the habitation, I quitted the scene and sought for refuge in the woods.

"And now, with the world before me, whither should I bend my steps? I resolved to fly far from the scene of my misfortunes; but to me, hated and despised, every country must be equally horrible. At length the thought of you crossed my mind. I learned from your papers that you were my father, my creator; and to whom could I apply with more fitness than to him who had given me life? Among the lessons that Felix had bestowed upon Safie, geography had not been omitted; I had learned from these the relative situations of the different countries of the earth. You had mentioned Geneva as the name of your native town, and towards this place I resolved to proceed.

"But how was I to direct myself? I knew that I must travel in a southwesterly direction to reach my destination, but the sun was my only guide. I did not know the names of the towns that I was to pass through, nor could I ask information from a single human being; but I did not despair. From you only could I hope for succour, although towards you I felt no sentiment but that of hatred. Unfeeling, heartless creator! You had endowed me with perceptions and passions and then cast me abroad an object for the scorn and horror of mankind. But on you only had I any claim for pity and redress, and from you I determined to seek that justice which I vainly attempted to gain from any other being that wore the human form.

"My travels were long and the sufferings I endured intense. It was late in autumn when I quitted the district where I had so long resided. I travelled only at night, fearful of encountering the visage of a human being. Nature decayed around me, and the sun became heatless; rain and snow poured around me; mighty rivers were frozen; the surface of the earth was hard and chill, and bare, and I found no shelter. Oh, earth! How often did I imprecate curses on the cause of my being! The mildness of my nature had fled, and all within me was turned to gall and bitterness. The nearer I approached to your habitation, the more deeply did I feel the spirit of revenge enkindled in my heart. Snow fell, and the waters were hardened, but I rested not. A few incidents now and then directed me, and I possessed a map of the country; but I often wandered wide from my path. The agony of my feelings allowed me no respite; no incident occurred from which my rage and misery could not extract its food; but a circumstance that happened when I arrived on the confines of Switzerland, when the sun had recovered its warmth and the earth again began to look green, confirmed in an especial manner the bitterness and horror of my feelings.

"I generally rested during the day and travelled only when I was secured by night from the view of man. One morning, however, finding that my path lay through a deep wood, I ventured to continue my journey after the sun had risen; the day, which was one of the first of spring, cheered even me by the loveliness of its sunshine and the balminess of the air. I felt emotions of gentleness and pleasure, that had long appeared dead, revive within me. Half surprised by the novelty of these sensations, I allowed myself to be borne away by them, and forgetting my solitude and deformity, dared to be happy. Soft tears again bedewed my cheeks, and I even raised my humid eyes with thankfulness towards the blessed sun, which bestowed such joy upon me.

"I continued to wind among the paths of the wood, until I came to its boundary, which was skirted by a deep and rapid river, into which many of the trees bent their branches, now budding with the fresh spring. Here I paused, not exactly knowing what path to pursue, when I heard the sound of voices, that induced me to conceal myself under the shade of a cypress. I was scarcely hid when a young girl came running towards the spot where I was concealed, laughing, as if she ran from someone in sport. She continued her course along the precipitous sides of the river, when suddenly her foot slipped, and she fell into the rapid stream. I rushed from my hiding-place and with extreme labour, from the force of the current, saved her and dragged her to shore. She was senseless, and I endeavoured by every means in my power to restore animation, when I was suddenly interrupted by the approach of a rustic, who was probably the person from whom she had playfully fled. On seeing me, he darted towards me, and tearing the girl from my arms, hastened towards the deeper parts of the wood. I followed speedily, I hardly knew why; but when the man saw me draw near, he aimed a gun, which he carried, at my body and fired. I sank to the ground, and my injurer, with increased swiftness, escaped into the wood.

"This was then the reward of my benevolence! I had saved a human being from destruction, and as a recompense I now writhed under the miserable pain of a wound which shattered the flesh and bone. The feelings of kindness and gentleness which I had entertained but a few moments before gave place to hellish rage and gnashing of teeth. Inflamed by pain, I vowed eternal hatred and vengeance to all mankind. But the agony of my wound overcame me; my pulses paused, and I fainted.

"For some weeks I led a miserable life in the woods, endeavouring to cure the wound which I had received. The ball had entered my shoulder, and I knew not whether it had remained there or passed through; at any rate I had no means of extracting it. My sufferings were augmented also by the oppressive sense of the injustice and ingratitude of their infliction. My daily vows rose for revenge—a deep and deadly revenge, such as would alone compensate for the outrages and anguish I had endured.

"After some weeks my wound healed, and I continued my journey. The labours I endured were no longer to be alleviated by the bright sun or gentle breezes of spring; all joy was but a mockery which insulted my desolate state and made me feel more painfully that I was not made for the enjoyment of pleasure.

"But my toils now drew near a close, and in two months from this time I reached the environs of Geneva.

"It was evening when I arrived, and I retired to a hiding-place among the fields that surround it to meditate in what manner I should apply to you. I was oppressed by fatigue and hunger and far too unhappy to enjoy the gentle breezes of evening or the prospect of the sun setting behind the stupendous mountains of Jura.

"At this time a slight sleep relieved me from the pain of reflection, which was disturbed by the approach of a beautiful child, who came running into the recess I had chosen, with all the sportiveness of infancy. Suddenly, as I gazed on him, an idea seized me that this little creature was unprejudiced and had lived too short a time to have imbibed a horror of deformity. If, therefore, I could seize him and educate him as my companion and friend, I should not be so desolate in this peopled earth.

"Urged by this impulse, I seized on the boy as he passed and drew him towards me. As soon as he beheld my form, he placed his hands before his eyes and uttered a shrill scream; I drew his hand forcibly from his face and said, 'Child, what is the meaning of this? I do not intend to hurt you; listen to me.'

"He struggled violently. 'Let me go,' he cried; 'monster! Ugly wretch! You wish to eat me and tear me to pieces. You are an ogre. Let me go, or I will tell my papa.'

"'Boy, you will never see your father again; you must come with me.'

"'Hideous monster! Let me go. My papa is a syndic—he is M. Frankenstein—he will punish you. You dare not keep me.'

"'Frankenstein! you belong then to my enemy—to him towards whom I have sworn eternal revenge; you shall be my first victim.'

"The child still struggled and loaded me with epithets which carried despair to my heart; I grasped his throat to silence him, and in a moment he lay dead at my feet.

"I gazed on my victim, and my heart swelled with exultation and hellish triumph; clapping my hands, I exclaimed, 'I too can create desolation; my enemy is not invulnerable; this death will carry despair to him, and a thousand other miseries shall torment and destroy him.'

"As I fixed my eyes on the child, I saw something glittering on his breast. I took it; it was a portrait of a most lovely woman. In spite of my malignity, it softened and attracted me. For a few moments I gazed with delight on her dark eyes, fringed by deep lashes, and her lovely lips; but presently my rage returned; I remembered that I was forever deprived of the delights that such beautiful creatures could bestow and that she whose resemblance I contemplated would, in regarding me, have changed that air of divine benignity to one expressive of disgust and affright.

"Can you wonder that such thoughts transported me with rage? I only wonder that at that moment, instead of venting my sensations in exclamations and agony, I did not rush among mankind and perish in the attempt to destroy them.

"While I was overcome by these feelings, I left the spot where I had committed the murder, and seeking a more secluded hiding-place, I entered a barn which had appeared to me to be empty. A woman was sleeping on some straw; she was young, not indeed so beautiful as her whose portrait I held, but of an agreeable aspect and blooming in the loveliness of youth and health. Here, I thought, is one of those whose joy-imparting smiles are bestowed on all but me. And then I bent over her and whispered, 'Awake, fairest, thy lover is near—he who would give his life but to obtain one look of affection from thine eyes; my beloved, awake!'

"The sleeper stirred; a thrill of terror ran through me. Should she indeed awake, and see me, and curse me, and denounce the murderer? Thus would she assuredly act if her darkened eyes opened and she beheld me. The thought was madness; it stirred the fiend within me—not I, but she, shall suffer; the murder I have committed because I am forever robbed of all that she could give me, she shall atone. The crime had its source in her; be hers the punishment! Thanks to the lessons of Felix and the sanguinary laws of man, I had learned now to work mischief. I bent over her and placed the portrait securely in one of the folds of her dress. She moved again, and I fled.

"For some days I haunted the spot where these scenes had taken place, sometimes wishing to see you, sometimes resolved to quit the world and its miseries forever. At length I wandered towards these mountains, and have ranged through their immense recesses, consumed by a burning passion which you alone can gratify. We may not part until you have promised to comply with my requisition. I am alone and miserable; man will not associate with me; but one as deformed and horrible as myself would not deny herself to me. My companion must be of the same species and have the same defects. This being you must create."

Chapter 17

The being finished speaking and fixed his looks upon me in the expectation of a reply. But I was bewildered, perplexed, and unable to arrange my ideas sufficiently to understand the full extent of his proposition. He continued,

"You must create a female for me with whom I can live in the interchange of those sympathies necessary for my being. This you alone can do, and I demand it of you as a right which you must not refuse to concede."

The latter part of his tale had kindled anew in me the anger that had died away while he narrated his peaceful life among the cottagers, and as he said this I could no longer suppress the rage that burned within me.

"I do refuse it," I replied; "and no torture shall ever extort a consent from me. You may render me the most miserable of men, but you shall never make me base in my own eyes. Shall I create another like yourself, whose joint wickedness might desolate the world. Begone! I have answered you; you may torture me, but I will never consent."

"You are in the wrong," replied the fiend; "and instead of threatening, I am content to reason with you. I am malicious because I am miserable. Am I not shunned and hated by all mankind? You, my creator, would tear me to pieces and triumph; remember that, and tell me why I should pity man more than he pities me? You would not call it murder if you could precipitate me into one of those ice-rifts and destroy my frame, the work of your own hands. Shall I respect man when he condemns me? Let him live with me in the interchange of kindness, and instead of injury I would bestow every benefit upon him with tears of gratitude at his acceptance. But that cannot be; the human senses are insurmountable barriers to our union. Yet mine shall not be the submission of abject slavery. I will revenge my injuries; if I cannot inspire love, I will cause fear, and chiefly towards you my arch-enemy, because my creator, do I swear inextinguishable hatred. Have a care; I will work at your destruction, nor finish until I desolate your heart, so that you shall curse the hour of your birth."

A fiendish rage animated him as he said this; his face was wrinkled into contortions too horrible for human eyes to behold; but presently he calmed himself and proceeded—

"I intended to reason. This passion is detrimental to me, for you do not reflect that YOU are the cause of its excess. If any being felt emotions of benevolence towards me, I should return them a hundred and a hundredfold; for that one creature's sake I would make peace with the whole kind! But I now indulge in dreams of bliss that cannot be realized. What I ask of you is reasonable and moderate; I demand a creature of another sex, but as hideous as myself; the gratification is small, but it is all that I can receive, and it shall content me. It is true, we shall be monsters, cut off from all the world; but on that account we shall be more attached to one another. Our lives will not be happy, but they will be harmless and free from the misery I now feel. Oh! My creator, make me happy; let me feel gratitude towards you for one benefit! Let me see that I excite the sympathy of some existing thing; do not deny me my request!"

I was moved. I shuddered when I thought of the possible consequences of my consent, but I felt that there was some justice in his argument. His tale and the feelings he now expressed proved him to be a creature of fine sensations, and did I not as his maker owe him all the portion of happiness that it was in my power to bestow? He saw my change of feeling and continued,

"If you consent, neither you nor any other human being shall ever see us again; I will go to the vast wilds of South America. My food is not that of man; I do not destroy the lamb and the kid to glut my appetite; acorns and berries afford me sufficient nourishment. My companion will be of the same nature as myself and will be content with the same fare. We shall make our bed of dried leaves; the sun will shine on us as on man and will ripen our food. The picture I present to you is peaceful and human, and you must feel that you could deny it only in the wantonness of power and cruelty. Pitiless as you have been towards me, I now see compassion in your eyes; let me seize the favourable moment and persuade you to promise what I so ardently desire."

"You propose," replied I, "to fly from the habitations of man, to dwell in those wilds where the beasts of the field will be your only companions. How can you, who long for the love and sympathy of man, persevere in this exile? You will return and again seek their kindness, and you will meet with their detestation; your evil passions will be renewed, and you will then have a companion to aid you in the task of destruction. This may not be; cease to argue the point, for I cannot consent."

"How inconstant are your feelings! But a moment ago you were moved by my representations, and why do you again harden yourself to my complaints? I swear to you, by the earth which I inhabit, and by you that made me, that with the companion you bestow I will quit the neighbourhood of man and dwell, as it may chance, in the most savage of places. My evil passions will have fled, for I shall meet with sympathy! My life will flow quietly away, and in my dying moments I shall not curse my maker."

His words had a strange effect upon me. I compassionated him and sometimes felt a wish to console him, but when I looked upon him, when I saw the filthy mass that moved and talked, my heart sickened and my feelings were altered to those of horror and hatred. I tried to stifle these sensations; I thought that as I could not sympathize with him, I had no right to withhold from him the small portion of happiness which was yet in my power to bestow.

"You swear," I said, "to be harmless; but have you not already shown a degree of malice that should reasonably make me distrust you? May not even this be a feint that will increase your triumph by affording a wider scope for your revenge?"

"How is this? I must not be trifled with, and I demand an answer. If I have no ties and no affections, hatred and vice must be my portion; the love of another will destroy the cause of my crimes, and I shall become a thing of whose existence everyone will be ignorant. My vices are the children of a forced solitude that I abhor, and my virtues will necessarily arise when I live in communion with an equal. I shall feel the affections of a sensitive being and become linked to the chain of existence and events from which I am now excluded."

I paused some time to reflect on all he had related and the various arguments which he had employed. I thought of the promise of virtues which he had displayed on the opening of his existence and the subsequent blight of all kindly feeling by the loathing and scorn which his protectors had manifested towards him. His power and threats were not omitted in my calculations; a creature who could exist in the ice caves of the glaciers and hide himself from pursuit among the ridges of inaccessible precipices was a being possessing faculties it would be vain to cope with. After a long pause of reflection I concluded that the justice due both to him and my fellow creatures demanded of me that I should comply with his request. Turning to him, therefore, I said,

"I consent to your demand, on your solemn oath to quit Europe forever, and every other place in the neighbourhood of man, as soon as I shall deliver into your hands a female who will accompany you in your exile."

"I swear," he cried, "by the sun, and by the blue sky of heaven, and by the fire of love that burns my heart, that if you grant my prayer, while they exist you shall never behold me again. Depart to your home and commence your labours; I shall watch their progress with unutterable anxiety; and fear not but that when you are ready I shall appear."

Saying this, he suddenly quitted me, fearful, perhaps, of any change in my sentiments. I saw him descend the mountain with greater speed than the flight of an eagle, and quickly lost among the undulations of the sea of ice.

CRITICAL EYE

▶ For Discussion

a. Why does Victor Frankenstein create "the monster"? What is he looking for? Why does he refuse to make his creation a mate?

b. In many ways, Frankenstein is very much like a parent who is deeply disappointed in the way his/her child turned out. How is this true?

▶ Re-approaching the Reading

How is "the monster" like Shakespeare's Othello? Why are their surrounding communities refusing to see each character's intellect and humanity and only willing to focus solely on a perceived savagery?

▶ Writing Topic

In what way is Shelly's text stating that we are responsible for what we create: our children, wars, illness, poverty, each other, hatred—essentially everything?

ELIZA HAYWOOD

Fantomina: Or, Love in a Maze
Being a Secret History of an Amour Between Two Persons of Condition

> *In love the victors from vanquished fly.*
> *They fly that wound, and they pursue that die.*
> Waller

A young Lady of distinguished Birth, Beauty, Wit, and Spirit, happened to be in a Box one Night at the Playhouse; where, though there were a great Number of celebrated Toasts, she perceived several Gentlemen extremely pleased themselves with entertaining a Woman who sat in a Corner of the Pit, and, by her Air and Manner of receiving them, might easily be known to be one of those who come there for no other Purpose, than to create Acquaintance with as many as seem desirous of it. She could not help testifying her Contempt of Men, who, regardless either of the Play, or Circle, threw away their Time in such a Manner, to some Ladies that sat by her: But they, either less surprised by being more accustomed to such Sights, than she who had been bred for the most Part in the Country, or not of a Disposition to consider any Thing very deeply, took but little Notice of it. She still thought of it, however; and the longer she reflected on it, the greater was her Wonder, that Men, some of whom she knew were accounted to have Wit, should have Tastes so very Depraved.—This excited a Curiosity in her to know in what Manner these Creatures were address'd:— She was young, a Stranger to the World, and consequently to the Dangers of it; and having no Body in Town, at that Time, to whom she was oblig'd to be accountable for her Actions, did in every Thing as her Inclinations or Humours render'd most agreeable to her: Therefore thought it not in the least a Fault to put in practice a little Whim which came immediately into her Head, to dress herself as near as she could in the Fashion of those Women who make sale of their Favours, and set herself in the Way of being accosted as such a one, having at that Time no other Aim, than the Gratification of an innocent Curiosity.— She had no sooner design'd this Frolick, than she put it in Execution; and muffling her Hoods over her Face, went the next Night into the Gallery-Box, and practising as much as she had observ'd, at that Distance, the Behaviour of that Woman, was not long before she found her Disguise had answer'd the Ends she wore it for:—A Crowd of Purchasers of all Degrees and Capacities were in a Moment gather'd about her, each endeavouring to out-bid the other, in offering her a Price for her Embraces.—She listen'd to 'em all, and was not a little diverted in her Mind at the Disappointment she shou'd give to so many, each of which thought himself secure of gaining her.—She was told by 'em all, that she was the most lovely Woman in the World; and some cry'd, *Gad, she is mighty like my fine Lady Such-a-one*,—naming her own Name. She was naturally vain, and receiv'd no small Pleasure in hearing herself prais'd, tho' in the

Person of another, and a suppos'd Prostitute; but she dispatch'd as soon as she cou'd all that had hitherto attack'd her, when she saw the accomplish'd *Beauplaisir* was making his Way thro' the Crowd as fast as he was able, to reach the Bench she sat on. She had often seen him in the Drawing-Room, had talk'd with him; but then her Quality and reputed Virtue kept him from using her with that Freedom she now expected he wou'd do, and had discover'd something in him, which had made her often think she shou'd not be displeas'd, if he wou'd abate some Part of his Reserve.—Now was the Time to have her Wishes answer'd:—He look'd in her Face, and fancy'd, as many others had done, that she very much resembled that Lady whom she really was; but the vast Disparity there appear'd between their Characters, prevented him from entertaining even the most distant Thought that they cou'd be the same.—He address'd her at first with the usual Salutations of her pretended Profession, as, *Are you engag'd, Madam?—Will you permit me to wait on you home after the Play?—By Heaven, you are a fine Girl!—How long have you us'd this House?—* And such like Questions; but perceiving she had a Turn of Wit, and a genteel Manner in her Raillery, beyond what is frequently to be found among those Wretches, who are for the most part Gentlewomen but by Necessity, few of 'em having had an Education suitable to what they affect to appear, he chang'd the Form of his Conversation, and shew'd her it was not because he understood no better, that he had made use of Expressions so little polite.—In fine, they were infinitely charm'd with each other: He was transported to find so much Beauty and Wit in a Woman, who he doubted not but on very easy Terms he might enjoy; and she found a vast deal of Pleasure in conversing with him in this free and unrestrain'd Manner. They pass'd their Time all the Play with an equal Satisfaction; but when it was over, she found herself involv'd in a Difficulty, which before never enter'd into her Head, but which she knew not well how to get over.—The Passion he profess'd for her, was not of that humble Nature which can be content with distant Adorations:—He resolv'd not to part from her without the Gratifications of those Desires she had inspir'd; and presuming on the Liberties which her suppos'd Function allow'd off, told her she must either go with him to some convenient House of his procuring, or permit him to wait on her to her own Lodgings.—Never had she been in such a *Dilemma:* Three or four Times did she open her Mouth to confess her real Quality; but the influence of her ill Stars prevented it, by putting an Excuse into her Head, which did the Business as well, and at the same Time did not take from her the Power of seeing and entertaining him a second Time with the same Freedom she had done this.—She told him, she was under Obligations to a Man who maintain'd her, and whom she durst not disappoint, having promis'd to meet him that Night at a House hard by.—This Story so like what those Ladies sometimes tell, was not at all suspected by *Beauplaisir;* and assuring her he wou'd be far from doing her a Prejudice, desir'd that in return for the Pain he shou'd suffer in being depriv'd of her Company that Night, that she wou'd order her Affairs, so as not to render him unhappy the next. She gave a solemn Promise to be in the same Box on the Morrow Evening; and they took Leave of each other; he to the Tavern to drown the Remembrance of his Disappointment; she in a Hackney-Chair hurry'd home to indulge Contemplation on the Frolick she had taken, designing nothing less on her first Reflections, than to keep the Promise she had made him, and hugging herself with Joy, that she had the good Luck to come off undiscover'd.

But these Cogitations were but of a short Continuance, they vanish'd with the Hurry of her Spirits, and were succeeded by others vastly different and ruinous:—All the Charms of *Beauplaisir* came fresh into her Mind; she languish'd, she almost dy'd for another

Opportunity of conversing with him; and not all the Admonitions of her Discretion were effectual to oblige her to deny laying hold of that which offer'd itself the next Night.—She depended on the Strength of her Virtue, to bear her fate thro' Tryals more dangerous than she apprehended this to be, and never having been address'd by him as Lady, — was resolv'd to receive his Devoirs as a Town-Mistress, imagining a world of Satisfaction to herself in engaging him in the Character of such a one, and in observing the Surprise he would be in to find himself refused by a Woman, who he supposed granted her Favours without Exception.—Strange and unaccountable were the Whimsies she was possess'd of,—wild and incoherent her Desires,—unfix'd and undetermin'd her Resolutions, but in that of seeing *Beauplaisir* in the Manner she had lately done. As for her Proceedings with him, or how a second Time to escape him, without discovering who she was, she cou'd neither assure herself, nor whither or not in the last Extremity she wou'd do so.—Bent, however, on meeting him, whatever shou'd be the Consequence, she went out some Hours before the Time of going to the Playhouse, and took lodgings in a House not very far from it, intending, that if he shou'd insist on passing some Part of the Night with her, to carry him there, thinking she might with more Security to her Honour entertain him at a Place where she was Mistress, than at any of his own chusing.

The appointed Hour being arriv'd, she had the Satisfaction to find his Love in his Assiduity: He was there before her; and nothing cou'd be more tender than the Manner in which he accosted her: But from the first Moment she came in, to that of the Play being done, he continued to assure her no Consideration shou'd prevail with him to part from her again, as she had done the Night before; and she rejoic'd to think she had taken that Precaution of providing herself with a Lodging, to which she thought she might invite him, without running any Risque, either of her Virtue or Reputation.—Having told him she wou'd admit of his accompanying her home, he seem'd perfectly satisfy'd; and leading her to the Place, which was not above twenty Houses distant, wou'd have order'd a Collation to be brought after them. But she wou'd not permit it, telling him she was not one of those who suffer'd themselves to be treated at their own Lodgings; and as soon as she was come in, sent a Servant, belonging to the House, to provide a very handsome Supper, and Wine, and every Thing was serv'd to Table in a Manner which shew'd the Director neither wanted Money, nor was ignorant how it shou'd be laid out.

This Proceeding, though it did not take from him the Opinion that she was what she appeared to be, yet it gave him Thoughts of her, which he had not before.—He believ'd her a *Mistress*, but believ'd her to be one of a superior Rank, and began to imagine the Possession of her would be much more Expensive than at first he had expected: But not being of a Humour to grudge any Thing for his Pleasures, he gave himself no further Trouble, than what were occasioned by Fears of not having Money enough to reach her Price, about him.

Supper being over, which was intermixed with a vast deal of amorous Conversation, he began to explain himself more than he had done; and both by his Words and Behaviour let her know, he would not be denied that Happiness the Freedoms she allow'd had made him hope.—It was in vain; she would have retracted the Encouragement she had given:—In vain she endeavoured to delay, till the next Meeting, the fulfilling of his Wishes:—She had now gone too far to retreat:—*He* was bold;—he was resolute: *She* fearful,—confus'd, altogether unprepar'd to resist in such Encounters, and rendered more so, by the extreme Liking she had to him.—Shock'd, however, at the Apprehension of really losing her Honour, she struggled all she could, and was just going to reveal the whole Secret of her Name and Quality, when the Thoughts of the Liberty he had taken with her, and those he still continued to prosecute, prevented her, with representing the Danger of being expos'd, and the whole Affair made a Theme for publick Ridicule.—Thus much, indeed, she told him, that she was a Virgin, and had assumed this Manner of Behaviour only to engage him. But that he little regarded, or if he had, would have been far from obliging him to desist;—nay, in the present burning Eagerness of Desire, 'tis probable, that had he been acquainted both with who and what she really was, the Knowledge of her Birth would not have influenc'd him with Respect sufficient to have curb'd the wild Exuberance of his luxurious Wishes, or made him in that longing,—that impatient Moment, change the Form of his Addresses. In fine, she was undone; and he gain'd a Victory, so highly rapturous, that had he known over whom, scarce could he have triumphed more. Her Tears, however, and the Destraction she appeared in, after the ruinous Extasy was past, as it heighten'd his Wonder, so it abated his Satisfaction:—He could not imagine for what Reason a Woman, who, if she intended not to be a *Mistress*, had counterfeited the Part of one, and taken so much Pains to engage him, should lament a Consequence which she could not but expect, and till the last Test, seem'd inclinable to grant; and was both surpris'd and troubled at the Mystery.—He omitted nothing that he thought might make her easy; and still retaining an Opinion that the Hope of Interest had been the chief Motive which had led her to act in the Manner she had done, and believing that she might know so little of him, as to suppose, now she had nothing left to give, he might not make that Recompense she expected for her Favours: To put her out of that Pain, he pulled out of his Pocket a Purse of Gold, entreating her to accept of that as an Earnest of what he intended to do for her;

assuring her, with ten thousand Protestations, that he would spare nothing, which his whole Estate could purchase, to procure her Content and Happiness. This Treatment made her quite forget the Part she had assum'd, and throwing it from her with an Air of Disdain, Is this a Reward *(said she)* for Condescensions, such as I have yeilded to?—Can all the Wealth you are possessed of, make a Reparation for my Loss of Honour?—Oh! no, I am undone beyond the Power of Heaven itself to help me!—She uttered many more such Exclamations; which the amaz'd *Beauplaisir* heard without being able to reply to, till by Degrees sinking from that Rage of Temper, her Eyes resumed their softning Glances, and guessing at the Consternation he was in, No, my dear *Beauplaisir, (added she,)* your Love alone can compensate for the Shame you have involved me in; be you sincere and constant, and I hereafter shall, perhaps, be satisfy'd with my Fate, and forgive myself the Folly that betray'd me to you.

Beauplaisir thought he could not have a better Opportunity than these Words gave him of enquiring who she was, and wherefore she had feigned herself to be of a Profession which he was now convinc'd she was not; and after he had made her thousand Vows of an Affection, as inviolable and ardent as she could wish to find in him, entreated she would inform him by what Means his Happiness has been brought about, and also to whom he was indebted for the Bliss he had enjoy'd.—Some remains of yet unextinguished Modesty, and Sense of Shame, made her Blush exceedingly at this Demand; but recollecting herself in a little Time, she told him so much of the Truth, as to what related to the Frolick she had taken of satisfying her Curiosity in what Manner *Mistresses,* of the Sort she appeared to be, were treated by those who addressed them; but forbore discovering her true Name and Quality, for the Reasons she had done before, resolving, if he boasted of this Affair, he should not have it in his Power to touch her Character: She therefore said she was the Daughter of a Country Gentleman, who was come to town to buy Cloaths, and that she was call'd *Fantomina*. He had no Reason to distrust the Truth of this Story, and was therefore satisfy'd with it; but did not doubt by the Beginning of her Conduct, but that in the End she would be in Reality, the Thing she so artfully had counterfeited; and had good Nature enough to pity the Misfortunes he imagin'd would be her Lot: But to tell her so, or offer his Advice in that Point, was not his Business, as least, as yet.

They parted not till towards Morning; and she oblig'd him to a willing Vow of visiting her the next Day at Three in the Afternoon. It was too late for her to go home that Night, therefore contented herself with lying there. In the Morning she sent for the Woman of the House to come up to her; and easily perceiving, by her Manner, that she was a Woman who might be influenced by Gifts, made her a Present of a Couple of Broad Pieces, and desir'd her, that if the Gentleman, who had been there the night before, should ask any Questions concerning her, that he should be told, she was lately come out of the Country, had lodg'd there about a Fortnight, and that her Name was *Fantomina*. I shall *(also added she)* lie but seldom here; nor, indeed, ever come but in those Times when I expect to meet him: I would, therefore, have you order it so, that he may think I am but just gone out, if he should happen by any Accident to call when I am not here; for I would not, for the World, have him imagine I do not constantly lodge here. The Landlady assur'd her she would do every Thing as she desired, and gave her to understand she wanted not the Gift of Secrecy.

Every Thing being ordered at this Home for the Security of her Reputation, she repaired to the other, where she easily excused to an unsuspecting Aunt, with whom she boarded, her having been abroad all Night, saying, she went with a Gentleman and his Lady in a Barge, to a little Country Seat of theirs up the River, all of them designing to return the same Evening; but that one of the Bargemen happ'ning to be taken ill on the sudden, and no other Waterman to be got that Night, they were oblig'd to tarry till Morning. Thus did this Lady's Wit and Vivacity assist her in all, but where it was most needful.—She had Discernment to forsee, and avoid all those Ills which might attend the Loss of her *Reputation*, but was wholly blind to those of the Ruin of her *Virtue;* and having managed her Affairs so as to secure the one, grew perfectly easy with the Remembrance, she had forfeited the *other.*—The more she reflected on the Merits of *Beauplaisir*, the more she excused herself for what she had done; and the Prospect of that continued Bliss she expected to share with him, took from her all Remorse for having engaged in an Affair which promised her so much Satisfaction, and in which she found not the least Danger of Misfortune.— If he is really *(said she, to herself)* the faithful, the constant Lover he has sworn to be, how charming will be our Amour?—And if he should be false, grow satiated, like other Men, I shall but, at the worst, have the private Vexation of knowing I have lost him;—the Intreague being a Secret, my Disgrace will be so too:—I shall hear no Whispers as I pass,—She is Forsaken:—The odious Word *Forsaken* will never wound my Ears; nor will my Wrongs excite either the Mirth or Pity of the talking World:—It will not be even in the Power of my Undoer himself to triumph over me; and while he laughs at, and perhaps despises the fond, the yielding *Fantomina*, he will revere and esteem the virtuous, the reserv'd Lady.—In this Manner did she applaud her own Conduct, and exult with the Imagination that she had more Prudence than all her Sex beside. And it must be confessed, indeed, that she preserved an OEconomy in the management of this Intreague, beyond what almost any Woman but herself ever did: In the first Place, by making no Person in the World a Confident in it; and in the next, in concealing from *Beauplaisir* himself the Knowledge who she was; for though she met him three or four Days in a Week, at the Lodging she had taken for that Purpose, yet as much as he employ'd her Time and Thoughts, she was never miss'd from any Assembly she had been accustomed to frequent.—The Business of her Love has engross'd her till Six in the Evening, and before Seven she has been dress'd in a different Habit, and in another Place.—Slippers, and a Nightgown loosely flowing, has been the Garb in which he has left the languishing *Fantomina;*—Lac'd, and adorn'd with all the Blaze of Jewels, has he, in less than an Hour after, beheld at the Royal Chapel, the Palace Gardens, Drawing-Room, Opera, or Play, the Haughty Awe-Inspiring Lady—A thousand Times has he stood amaz'd at the prodigious Likeness between his little Mistress, and this Court Beauty; but was still as far from imagining they were the same, as he was the first Hour he had accosted her in the Playhouse, though it is not impossible, but that her Resemblance to this celebrated Lady, might keep his Inclination alive something longer than otherwise they would have been; and that it was to the Thoughts of this (as he supposed) unenjoy'd Charmer, she ow'd in great measure the Vigour of his latter Caresses.

But he varied not so much from his Sex as to be able to prolong Desire, to any great Length after Possession: The rifled Charms of *Fantomina* soon lost their Poinancy, and grew tastless and insipid; and when the Season of the Year inviting the Company to the *Bath*, she offer'd to accompany him, he made an Excuse to go without her. She easily perceiv'd his Coldness, and the Reason why he pretended her going would be inconvenient, and endur'd as much from the Discovery as any of her Sex could do: She dissembled it, however, before him, and took her Leave of him with the Shew of no other Concern than his Absence occasion'd: But this she did to take from him all Suspicion of her following him, as she intended, and had already laid a Scheme for.—From her first finding out that he design'd to leave her behind, she plainly saw it was for no other Reason, than being tir'd of her Conversation, he was willing to be at liberty to pursue new Conquests; and wisely considering that Complaints, Tears, Swooning, and all the Extravagancies which Women make use of in such Cases, have little Prevailence over a Heart inclin'd to rove, and only serve to render those who practice them more contemptible, by robbing them of that Beauty which alone can bring back the fugitive Lover, she resolved to take another Course; and remembring the Height of Transport she enjoyed when the agreeable *Beauplaisir* kneel'd at her Feet, imploring her first Favours, she long'd to prove the same again. Not but a Woman of her Beauty and Accomplishments might have beheld a Thousand in that Condition *Beauplaisir* had been; but with her Sex's Modesty, she had not also thrown off another Virtue equally valuable, tho' generally unfortunate, *Constancy:* She loved *Beauplaisir;* it was only he whose Solicitations could give her Pleasure; and had she seen the whole Species despairing, dying for her sake, it might, perhaps, have been a Satisfaction to her Pride, but none to her more tender Inclination.—Her Design was once more to engage him, to hear him sigh, to see him languish, to feel the strenuous Pressures of his eager Arms, to be compelled, to be sweetly forc'd to what she wished with equal Ardour, was what she wanted, and what she had form'd a Stratagem to obtain, in which she promis'd herself Success.

She no sooner heard he had left the Town, than making a Pretence to her Aunt, that she was going to visit a Relation in the Country, went towards *Bath*, attended but by two Servants, who she found Reasons to quarrel with on the Road and discharg'd: Clothing herself in a Habit she had brought with her, she forsook the Coach, and went into a Wagon, in which Equipage she arriv'd at *Bath*. The Dress she was in, was a round-ear'd Cap, a short Red Petticoat, and a little Jacket of Grey Stuff; all the rest of her Accoutrements were answerable to these, and join'd with a broad Country Dialect, a rude unpolish'd Air, which she, having been bred in these Parts, knew very well how to imitate, with her Hair and Eye-brows black'd, made it impossible for her to be known, or taken for any other than what she seem'd. Thus disguis'd did she offer herself to Service in the House where *Beauplaisir* lodg'd, having made it her Business to find out immediately where he was. Notwithstanding this Metamorphosis she was still extremely pretty; and the Mistress of the House happening at that Time to want a Maid, was very glad of the Opportunity of taking her. She was presently receiv'd into the Family; and had a Post in it (such as she would have chose, had she been left at her Liberty,) that of making the Gentlemen's Beds, getting them their Breakfasts, and waiting on them in their Chambers. Fortune in this Exploit was extremely on her side; there were no others of the Male-Sex in the House, than an old Gentleman, who had lost the Use of his Limbs with the Rheumatism, and had come thither for the Benefit of the Waters, and her belov'd *Beauplaisir;* so that she was in no Apprehensions of any Amorous Violence, but where she wish'd to find it. Nor were her Designs disappointed: He was fir'd with the first Sight of her; and tho' he did not presently take any farther Notice of her, than giving her two or three hearty Kisses, yet she, who now understood that Language but too well, easily saw they were the Prelude to more substantial Joys.—Coming the next Morning to bring his Chocolate, as he had order'd, he catch'd her by the pretty Leg, which the Shortness of her Petticoat did not in the least oppose; then pulling her gently to him, ask'd her, how long she had been at Service?—How many Sweethearts she had? If she had ever been in Love? and many other such Questions, befitting one of the Degree she appear'd to be: All which she answer'd with such seeming Innocence, as more enflam'd the amorous Heart of him who talk'd to her. He compelled her to sit in his Lap; and gazing on her blushing Beauties, which, if possible, receiv'd Addition from her plain and rural Dress, he soon lost the Power of containing himself.— His wild Desires burst out in all his Words and Actions: he call'd her little Angel, Cherubim, swore he must enjoy her, though Death were to be the Consequence, devour'd her Lips, her Breasts with greedy Kisses, held to his burning Bosom her half-yielding, half-reluctant Body, nor suffered her to get loose, till he had ravaged all, and glutted each rapacious Sense with the sweet Beauties of the pretty *Celia,* for that was the Name she bore in this second Expedition.—Generous as Liberality itself to all who gave him Joy this way, he gave her a handsome Sum of Gold, which she durst not now refuse, for fear of creating some Mistrust, and losing the Heart she so lately had regain'd; therefore taking it with an humble Curtesy, and a well counterfeited Shew of Surprise and Joy, cry'd, O Law, Sir! what must I do for all this? He laughed at her Simplicity, and kissing her again, tho' less fervently than he had done before, bad her not be out of the Way when he came home at Night. She promis'd she would not, and very obediently kept her Word.

His Stay at *Bath* exceeded not a Month; but in that Time his suppos'd Country Lass had persecuted him so much with her Fondness, that in spite of the Eagerness with which he first enjoy'd her, he was at last grown more weary of her, than he had been of *Fantomina;* which she perceiving, would not be troublesome, but quitting her Service, remained privately in the Town till she heard he was on his Return; and in that Time provided herself of another Disguise to carry on a third Plot, which her inventing Brain had furnished her with, once more to renew his twice-decay'd Ardours. The Dress she had order'd to be made, was such as Widows wear in their first Mourning, which, together with the most afflicted and penitential Countenance that ever was seen, was no small Alteration to her who us'd to seem all Gaiety.—To add to this, her Hair, which she was accustom'd to wear very loose, both when *Fantomina* and *Celia*, was now ty'd back so straight, and her Pinners coming so very forward, that there was none of it to be seen. In fine, her Habit and her Air were so much chang'd, that she was not more difficult to be known in the rude Country *Girl*, than she was now in the sorrowful *Widow*.

She knew that *Beauplaisir* came alone in his Chariot to the *Bath*, and in the Time of her being Servant in the House where he lodg'd, heard nothing of any Body that was to accompany him to *London*, and hop'd he wou'd return in the same Manner he had gone: She therefore hir'd Horses and a Man to attend her to an Inn about ten Miles on this side *Bath*, where having discharg'd them, she waited till the Chariot should come by; which when it did, and she saw that he was alone in it, she call'd to him that drove it to stop a Moment, and going to the Door saluted the Master with these Words:

The Distress'd and Wretched, Sir, *(said she,)* never fail to excite Compassion in a generous Mind; and I hope I am not deceiv'd in my Opinion that yours is such:—You have the Appearance of a Gentleman, and cannot, when you hear my Story, refuse that Assistance which is in your Power to give to an unhappy Woman, who without it, may be rendered the most miserable of all created Beings.

It would not be very easy to represent the Surprise, so odd an Address created in the Mind of him to whom it was made.—She had not the Appearance of one who wanted Charity; and what other Favour she requir'd

he cou'd not conceive: But telling her, she might command any Thing in his Power, gave her Encouragement to declare herself in this Manner: You may judge, *(resumed she,)* by the melancholy Garb I am in, that I have lately lost all that ought to be valuable to Womankind; but it is impossible for you to guess the Greatness of my Misfortune, unless you had known my Husband, who was Master of every Perfection to endear him to a Wife's Affections.—But, notwithstanding, I look on myself as the most unhappy of my Sex in out-living him, I must so far obey the Dictates of my Discretion, as to take care of the little Fortune he left behind him, which being in the hands of a Brother of his in *London*, will be all carried off to *Holland*, where he is going to settle; if I reach not the Town before he leaves it, I am undone for ever.—To which End I left Bristol, the Place where we liv'd, hoping to get a Place in the Stage at *Bath*, but they were all taken up before I came; and being, by a Hurt I got in a Fall, render'd incapable of travelling any long Journey on Horseback, I have no Way to go to *London*, and must be inevitably ruin'd in the Loss of all I have on Earth, without you have good Nature enough to admit me to take Part of your Chariot.

Here the feigned Widow ended her sorrowful Tale, which had been several Times interrupted by a Parenthesis of Sighs and Groans; and *Beauplaisir*, with a complaisant and tender Air, assur'd her of his Readiness to serve her in Things of much greater Consequence than what she desir'd of him; and told her, it would be an Impossibility of denying a Place in his Chariot to a Lady, who he could not behold without yielding one in his Heart. She answered the Compliments he made her but with Tears, which seem'd to stream in such abundance from her Eyes, that she could not keep her Handkerchief from her Face one Moment. Being come into the Chariot, *Beauplaisir* said a thousand handsome Things to perswade her from giving way to so violent a Grief, which, he told her, would not only be distructive to her Beauty, but likewise her Health. But all his Endeavours for Consolement appear'd ineffectual, and he began to think he should have but a dull Journey, in the Company of one who seem'd so obstinately devoted to the Memory of her dead Husband, that there was no getting a Word from her on any other Theme:—But bethinking himself of the celebrated Story of the *Ephesian* Matron, it came into his Head to make Tryal, she who seem'd equally susceptible of *Sorrow*, might not also be so too of *Love;* and having begun a Discourse on almost every other Topick, and finding her still incapable of answering, resolv'd to put it to the Proof, if this would have no more Effect to rouze her sleeping Spirits:—With a gay Air, therefore, though accompany'd with the greatest Modesty and Respect, he turned the Conversation, as though without Design, on that Joy-giving Passion, and soon discover'd that was indeed the Subject she was best pleas'd to be entertained with; for on his giving her a Hint to begin upon, never any Tongue run more voluble than hers, on the prodigious Power it had to influence the Souls of those posses'd of it, to Actions even the most distant from their Intentions, Principles, or Humours.—From that she pass'd to a Description of the Happiness of mutual Affection;—the unspeakable Extasy of those who meet with equal Ardency; and represented it in Colours so lively, and disclos'd by the Gestures with which her Words were accompany'd, and the Accent of her Voice so true a Feeling of what she said, that *Beauplaisir*, without being as stupid, as he was really the contrary, could not avoid perceiving there were Seeds of Fire, not yet extinguish'd, in this fair Widow's Soul, which wanted but the kindling Breath of tender Sighs to light into a Blaze.—He now thought himself as fortunate, as some Moments before he had the Reverse; and doubted not, but, that before they parted, he should find a Way to dry the Tears of this lovely Mourner, to the Satisfaction of them both. He did not, however, offer, as he had done to *Fantomina* and *Celia,* to urge his Passion directly to her, but by a thousand little softning Artifices, which he well knew how to use, gave her leave to guess he was enamour'd. When they came to the Inn where they were to lie, he declar'd himself somewhat more freely, and perceiving she did not resent it past Forgiveness, grew more encroaching still:—He now took the Liberty of kissing away her Tears, and catching the Sighs as they issued from her Lips; telling her if Grief was infectious, he was resolv'd to have his Share; protesting he would gladly exchange Passions with her, and be content to bear her Load of *Sorrow,* if she would as willingly ease the Burden of his *Love*.—She said little in answer to the strenuous Pressures with which at last he ventur'd to enfold her, but not thinking it Decent, for the Character she had assum'd, to yield so suddenly, and unable to deny both his and her own Inclinations, she counterfeited a fainting, and fell motionless upon his Breast.— He had no great Notion that she was in a real Fit, and the Room they supp'd in happening to have a Bed in it, he took her in his Arms and laid her on it, believing, that whatever her Distemper was, that was the most proper Place to convey her to.—He laid himself down by her, and endeavour'd to bring her to herself; and she was too grateful to her kind Physician at her returning Sense, to remove from the Posture he had put her in, without his Leave.

It may, perhaps, seem strange that *Beauplaisir* should in such near Intimacies continue still deceiv'd: I know there are Men who will swear it is an Impossibility, and that no Disguise could hinder them from knowing a Woman they had once enjoy'd. In answer to these Scruples, I can only say, that besides the Alteration which the Change of Dress made in her, she was so admirably skill'd in the Art of feigning, that she had the Power of putting on almost what Face she pleas'd, and knew so exactly how to form her Behaviour to the Character she represented, that all the Comedians at both Playhouses are infinitely short of her Performances: She could vary her very Glances, tune her Voice to Accents the most different imaginable from those in which she spoke when she appear'd herself.—These Aids from Nature, join'd to the Wiles of Art, and the Distance between the Places where the imagin'd *Fantomina* and *Celia* were, might very well prevent his having any Thought that they were the same, or that the fair *Widow* was either of them: It never so much as enter'd his Head, and though he did fancy he observed in the Face of the latter, Features which were not altogether unknown to him, yet he could not recollect when or where he had known them;—and being told by her, that from her Birth, she had never remov'd from *Bristol*, a Place where he never was, he rejected the Belief of having seen her, and suppos'd his Mind had been deluded by an Idea of some other, whom she might have a Resemblance of.

They pass'd the Time of their Journey in as much Happiness as the most luxurious Gratification of wild Desires could make them; and when they came to the End of it, parted not without a mutual Promise of seeing each other often.—He told her to what Place she should direct a Letter to him; and she assur'd him she would send to let him know where to come to her, as soon as she was fixed in Lodgings.

She kept her Promise; and charm'd with the Continuance of his eager Fondness, went not home, but into private Lodgings, whence she wrote to him to visit her the first Opportunity, and enquire for the Widow *Bloomer.*—She had no sooner dispatched this Billet, than she repair'd to the House where she had lodg'd as *Fantomina,* charging the People if *Beauplaisir* should come there, not to let him know she had been out of Town. From thence she wrote to him, in a different Hand, a long Letter of Complaint, that he had been so cruel in not sending one Letter to her all the Time he had been absent, entreated to see

him, and concluded with subscribing herself his unalterably Affectionate *Fantomina.* She received in one Day Answers to both these. The first contain'd these Lines:

To the Charming Mrs. Bloomer,
It would be impossible, my Angel! for me to express the thousandth Part of that Infinity of Transport, the Sight of your dear Letter gave me.—Never was Woman form'd to charm like you: Never did any look like you,—write like you,—bless like you;—nor did ever Man adore as I do.—Since Yesterday we parted, I have seem'd a Body without a Soul; and had you not by this inspiring Billet, gave me new Life, I know not what by To-morrow I should have been.—I will be with you this Evening about Five:—O, 'tis an Age till then!—But the cursed Formalities of Duty oblige me to Dine with my Lord—who never rises from Table till that Hour;—therefore Adieu till then sweet lovely Mistress of the Soul and all the Faculties of

Your most faithful,
Beauplaisir.

The other was in this Manner:

To the Lovely Fantomina.
If you were half so sensible as you ought of your own Power of charming, you would be assur'd, that to be unfaithful or unkind to you, would be among the Things that are in their very Natures Impossibilities.—It was my Misfortune, not my Fault, that you were not persecuted every Post with a Declaration of my unchanging Passion; but I had unluckily forgot the Name of the Woman at whose House you are, and knew not how to form a Direction that it might come safe to your Hands.—And, indeed, the Reflection how you might misconstrue my Silence, brought me to Town some Weeks sooner than I intended—If you knew how I have languish'd to renew those Blessings I am permitted to enjoy in your Society, you would rather pity than condemn

Your ever faithful,
Beauplaisir.

P.S. *I fear I cannot see you till To-morrow; some Business has unluckily fallen out that will engross my Hours till then.—Once more, my Dear,* Adieu.

Traytor! *(cry'd she,)* as soon as she had read them, 'tis thus our silly, fond, believing Sex are serv'd when they put Faith in Man: So had I been deceiv'd and cheated, had I like the rest believ'd, and sat down mourning in Absence, and vainly waiting recover'd Tendernesses.— How do some Women, *(continued she)* make their Life a Hell, burning in fruitless Expectations, and dreaming out their Days in Hopes and Fears, then wake at last to all the Horror of Dispair?—But I have outwitted even the most Subtle of the deceiving Kind, and while he thinks to fool me, is himself the only beguiled Person.

She made herself, most certainly, extremely happy in the Reflection on the Success of her Stratagems; and while the Knowledge of his Inconstancy and Levity of Nature kept her from having that real Tenderness for him she would else have had, she found the Means of gratifying the Inclination she had for his agreeable Person, in as full a Manner as she could wish. She had all the Sweets of Love, but as yet had tasted none of the Gall, and was in a State of Contentment, which might be envy'd by the more Delicate.

When the expected Hour arriv'd, she found that her Lover had lost no part of the Fervency with which he had parted from her; but when the next Day she receiv'd him as *Fantomina,* she perceiv'd a prodigious Difference; which led her again into Reflections on the Unaccountableness of Men's Fancies, who still prefer the last Conquest, only because it is the last.—Here was an evident Proof of it; for there could not be a Difference in Merit, because they were the same Person; but the Widow *Bloomer* was a more new Acquaintance than *Fantomina,* and therefore esteem'd more valuable. This, indeed, must be said of Beauplaisir, that he had a greater Share of good Nature than most of his Sex, who, for the most part, when they are weary of an Intreague, break it entirely off, without any Regard to the Despair of the abandon'd Nymph. Though he retain'd no more than a bare Pity and Complaisance for *Fantomina,* yet believing she lov'd him to an Excess, would not entirely forsake her, though the Continuance of his Visits was now become rather a Penance than a Pleasure.

The Widow *Bloomer* triumph'd some Time longer over the Heart of this Inconstant, but at length her Sway was at an End, and she sunk in this Character, to the same Degree of Tastelessness, as she had done before in that of *Fantomina* and *Celia.*—She presently perceiv'd it, but bore it as she had always done; it being but what she expected, she had prepar'd herself for it, and had another Project in *embrio,* which she soon ripen'd into Action. She did not, indeed, compleat it altogether so suddenly as she had done the others, by reason there must be Persons employ'd in it; and the Aversion she had to any *Confidents* in her Affairs, and the Caution with which she had hitherto acted, and which she was still determin'd to continue, made it very difficult for her to find a Way without breaking thro' that Resolution to compass what she wish'd.—She got over the Difficulty at last, however, by proceeding in a Manner, if possible, more extraordinary than all her former Behaviour:—Muffling herself up in her Hood one Day, she went into the Park about the Hour when there are a great many necessitous Gentlemen, who think themselves above doing what they call little Things for a Maintenance, walking in the *Mall,* to take a *Camelion* Treat, and fill their Stomachs with Air instead of Meat. Two of those, who by their Physiognomy she thought most proper for her Purpose, she beckon'd to come to her; and taking them into a Walk more remote from Company, began to communicate the Business she had with them in these Words: I am sensible, Gentlemen, *(said she,)* that, through the blindness of Fortune, and Partiality of the World, Merit frequently goes unrewarded, and that those of the best Pretentions meet with the least Encouragement:—I ask your Pardon, *(continued she,)* perceiving they seem'd surpris'd, if I am mistaken in the Notion, that you two may, perhaps, be of the Number of those who have Reason to complain of the Injustice of Fate; but if you are such as I take you for, have a Proposal to make you, which may be of some little Advantage to you. Neither of them made any immediate Answer, but appear'd bury'd in Consideration for some Moments. At length, We should, doubtless, Madam, *(said one of them,)* willingly come into any Measures to oblige you, provided they are such as may bring us into no Danger, either as to our Persons or Reputations. That which I require of you, *(resumed she,)* has nothing in it criminal: All that I desire is *Secrecy* in what you are intrusted, and to disguise yourselves in such a Manner as you cannot be known, if hereafter seen by the Person on whom you are to impose.—In fine, the Business is only an innocent Frolick, but if blaz'd abroad, might be taken for too great a Freedom in me:—Therefore, if you resolve to assist me, here are five Pieces to Drink my Health, and assure you, that I have not discours'd you on an Affair, I design not to proceed in; and when it is accomplish'd fifty more lie ready for your Acceptance. These Words, and, above all, the Money, which was a Sum which, 'tis probable, they had not seen of a long Time, made them immediately assent to all she desir'd, and press for the Beginning of their Employment: But things were not yet ripe for Execution; and she told them, that the next Day they should be let into the Secret, charging them to meet her in the same Place at an hour she appointed. 'Tis hard to say, which of these Parties went away best pleas'd; *they,* that Fortune had sent them so unexpected a Windfall; or *she,* that she had found Persons, who appeared so well qualified to serve her.

Indefatigable in the Pursuit of whatsoever her Humour was bent upon, she had no sooner left her new-engag'd Emissaries, than she went in search of a House for the compleating her Project.—She pitch'd on one very large, and magnificently furnished, which she hir'd by the Week, giving them the Money beforehand, to prevent any Inquiries. The next Day she repaired to the Park, where she met the punctual 'Squires of low Degree; and ordering them to follow her to the House she had taken, told them they must condescend to appear like Servants, and gave each of them a very rich Livery. Then writing a Letter to *Beauplaisir,* in a Character vastly different from either of those she had made use of, as *Fantomina,* or the fair Widow *Bloomer,* order'd one of them to deliver it into his own Hands, to bring back an Answer, and to be careful that he sifted out nothing of the Truth.—I do not fear, *(said she,)* that you should discover to him who I am, because that is a Secret, of which you yourselves are ignorant; but I would have you be so careful in your Replies, that he may not think the Concealment springs from any other Reasons than your great Integrity to your Trust.—Seem therefore to know my whole Affairs; and let your refusing to make him Partaker in the Secret, appear to be only the Effect of your Zeal for my Interest and Reputation. Promises of entire Fidelity on the one side, and Reward on the other, being past, the Messenger made what haste he could to the House of *Beauplaisir;* and being there told where he might find him, perform'd exactly the Injunction that had been given him. But never Astonishment exceeding that which *Beauplaisir* felt at the reading this Billet, in which he found these Lines:

To the All-conquering BEAUPLAISIR.

I imagine not that 'tis a new Thing to you, to be told, you are the greatest Charm in Nature to our Sex: I shall therefore, not to fill up my Letter with any impertinent Praises on your Wit or Person, only tell you, that I am infinite in Love with both, and if you have a Heart not too deeply engag'd, should think myself the happiest of my Sex in being capable of inspiring it with some Tenderness.—There is but one Thing in my Power to refuse you, which is the Knowledge of my Name, which believing the Sight of my Face will render no Secret, you must not take it ill that I conceal from you.—The Bearer of this is a Person I can trust; send by him your Answer; but endeavour not to dive into the Meaning of this Mystery, which will be impossible for you to unravel, and at the same Time very much disoblige me:— But that you may be in no Apprehensions of being impos'd on by a Woman unworthy of your Regard, I will venture to assure you, the first and greatest Men in the Kingdom, would think themselves blest to have that Influence over me you have, though unknown to yourself acquir'd.—But I need not go about to raise your Curiosity, by giving you any Idea of what my Person is; if you think fit to be satisfied, resolve to visit me To-morrow about Three in the Afternoon; and though my Face is hid, you shall not want sufficient Demonstration, that she who takes these unusual Measures to commence a Friendship with you, is neither Old, nor Deform'd. Till then I am,

Yours,

INCOGNITA.

He had scarce come to the Conclusion, before he ask'd the Person who brought it, from what Place he came;—the Name of the Lady he serv'd;—if she were a Wife, or Widow, and several other Questions directly opposite to the Directions of the Letter; but Silence would have avail'd him as much as did all those Testimonies of Curiosity: *No Italian Bravo,* employ'd in a Business of the like Nature, perform'd his Office with more Artifice; and the impatient Enquirer was convinc'd that nothing but doing as he was desir'd, could give him any Light into the Character of the Woman who declar'd so violent a Passion for him; and little fearing any Consequence which could ensue from such an Encounter, resolv'd to rest satisfy'd till he was inform'd of every Thing from herself, not imagining this *Incognita* varied so much from the Generality of her Sex, as to be able to refuse the Knowledge of any Thing to the Man she lov'd with that Transcendency of Passion she profess'd, and which his many Successes with the Ladies gave him Encouragement enough to believe. He therefore took Pen and Paper, and answer'd her Letter in terms tender enough for a Man who had never seen the Person to whom he wrote. The Words were as follows:

To the Obliging and Witty
INCOGNITA.

Though to tell me I am happy enough to be lik'd by a Woman, such, as by your Manner of Writing, I imagine you to be, is an Honour which I can never sufficiently acknowledge, yet I know not how I am able to content myself with admiring the Wonders of your Wit alone: I am certain, a Soul like yours must shine in your Eyes with a Vivacity, which must bless all they look on.—I shall, however, endeavour to restrain myself in these Bounds you are pleas'd to set me, till by the Knowledge of my inviolable Fedility, I may be thought worthy of gazing on that Heaven I am now but to enjoy in Contemplation.—You need not doubt my glad Compliance with your obliging Summons: There is a Charm in your Lines, which gives too sweet an Idea of their lovely Author to be resisted.—I am all impatient for the blissful Moment, which is to throw me at your Feet, and give me an Opportunity of convincing you that I am,

Your everlasting Slave,

BEAUPLAISIR.

Nothing could be more pleas'd than she, to whom it was directed, at the Receipt of this Letter; but when she was told how inquisitive he had been concerning her Character and Circumstances, she could not forbear laughing heartily to think of the Tricks she had play'd him, and applauding her own Strength of Genius, and Force of Resolution, which by such unthought-of Ways could triumph over her Lover's Inconstancy, and render that very Temper, which to other Women is the greatest Curse, a Means to make herself more bless'd.—Had he been faithful to me, *(said she, to herself,)* either as *Fantomina,* or *Celia,* or the Widow *Bloomer*, the most violent Passion, if it does not change its Object, in Time will wither: Possession naturally abates the Vigour of Desire, and I should have had, at best, but a cold, insipid, husband-like Lover in my Arms; but by these Arts of passing on him as a new Mistress whenever the Ardour, which alone makes Love a Blessing, begins to diminish, for the former one, I have him always raving, wild, impatient, longing, dying.—O that all neglected Wives, and fond abandon'd Nymphs would take this Method!—Men would be caught in their own Snare, and have no Cause to scorn our easy, weeping, wailing Sex! Thus did she pride herself as if secure she never should have any Reason to repent the present Gaiety of her Humour. The Hour drawing near in which he was to come, she dress'd herself in as magnificent a Manner, as if she were to be that Night at a Ball at Court, endeavouring to repair the want of those Beauties which the Vizard should conceal, by setting forth the others with the greatest Care and Exactness. Her fine Shape, and Air, and Neck, appear'd to great Advantage; and by that which was to be seen of her, one might believe the rest to be perfectly agreeable. *Beauplaisir* was prodigiously charm'd, as well with her Appearance, as with the Manner she entertain'd him: But though he was wild with Impatience for the Sight of a Face which belong'd to so exquisite a Body, yet he would not immediately press for it, believing before he left her he should easily obtain that Satisfaction.—A noble Collation being over, he began to sue for the Performance of her Promise of granting every Thing he could ask, excepting the Sight of her Face, and Knowledge of her Name. It would have been a ridiculous Piece of Affection in her to have seem'd coy in complying with what she herself had been the first in desiring: She yielded without even a Shew of Reluctance: And if there be any true Felicity in an Armour such as theirs, both here enjoy'd it to the full. But not in the Height of all their mutual Raptures, could he prevail on her to satisfy his Curiosity with the Sight of her Face: She told him that she hop'd he knew so much of her, as might serve to convince him, she was not unworthy of his tenderest Regard; and if he cou'd not content himself with that which she was willing to reveal, and which was the Conditions of their meeting, dear as he was to her, she would rather part with him for ever, than consent to gratify an Inquisitiveness, which, in her Opinion, had no Business with his Love. It was in vain that he endeavour'd to make her sensible of her Mistake; and that this Restraint was the greatest Enemy imaginable to the Happiness of them both: She was not to be perswaded, and he was oblig'd to desist his Solicitations, though determin'd in his Mind to compass what he so ardently desir'd, before he left the House. He then turned the Discourse wholly on the Violence of the Passion he had for her; and express'd the greatest Discontent in the World at the Apprehensions of being separated;—swore he could dwell for ever in her Arms, and with such an undeniable Earnestness pressed to be permitted to tarry with her the whole Night, that had she been less charm'd with his renew'd Eagerness of Desire, she scarce would have had the Power of refusing him; but in granting this Request, she was not without a Thought that he had another Reason for making it besides the Extremity of his Passion, and had it immediately in her Head how to disappoint him.

The Hours of Repose being arriv'd, he begg'd she would retire to her Chamber; to which she consented, but oblig'd him to go to Bed first; which he did not much oppose, because he suppos'd she would not lie in her Mask, and doubted not but the Morning's Dawn would bring the wish'd Discovery.—The two imagin'd Servants usher'd him to his new Lodging; where he lay some Moments in all the Perplexity imaginable at the Oddness of this Adventure. But she suffer'd not these Cogitations to be of any long Continuance: She came, but came in the Dark; which being no more than he expected by the former Part of her Proceedings, he said nothing of; but as much Satisfaction as he found in her Embraces, nothing ever long'd for the Approach of Day with more Impatience than he did. At last it came; but how great was his Disappointment, when by the Noises he heard in the Street, the hurry of the Coaches, and the Cries of Penny-Merchants, he was convinc'd it was Night no where but with him? He was still in the same Darkness as before; for she had taken care to blind the Windows in such a manner, that not the least Chink was left to let in the Day.—He complain'd of her Behaviour in Terms that she would not have been able to resist yielding to, if she had not been certain it would have been the Ruin of her Passion:— She, therefore, answered him only as she had done before; and getting out of the Bed from him, flew out of the Room with too much Swiftness for him to have overtaken her, if he had attempted it. The Moment she left him, the two Attendants enter'd the Chamber, and plucking down the Implements which had skreen'd him from the Knowledge of that which he so much desir'd to find out, restored his Eyes once more to Day:—They attended to assist him in Dressing, brought him Tea, and by their Obsequiousness, let him see there was but one Thing which the Mistress of them would not gladly oblige him in.—He was so much out of Humour, however, at the Disappointment of his Curiosity, that he resolv'd never to make a second Visit.—Finding her in an outer Room, he made no Scruples of expressing the Sense he had of the little Trust she reposed in him, and at last plainly told her, he could not submit to receive Obligations from a Lady, who thought him uncapable of keeping a Secret, which she made no Difficulty of letting her Servants into.—He resented,—he once more entreated,—he said all that Man could do, to prevail on her to unfold the Mystery; but all his Adjurations were fruitless; and he went out of the House determin'd never to re-enter it, till she should pay the Price of his Company with the Discovery of her Face and Circumstances.—She suffer'd him to go with this Resolution, and doubted not but he would recede from it, when he reflected on the happy Moments they had pass'd together; but if he did not, she comforted herself with the Design of forming some other Stratagem, with which to impose on him a fourth Time.

She kept the House, and her Gentlemen-Equipage for about a Fortnight, in which Time she continu'd to write to him as *Fantomina* and the Widow *Bloomer,* and received the Visits he sometimes made to each; but his Behaviour to both was grown so cold, that she began to grow as weary of receiving his now insipid Caresses as he was of offering them: She was beginning to think in what Manner she should drop these two Characters, when the sudden Arrival of her Mother, who had been some Time in a foreign Country, oblig'd her to put an immediate Stop to the Course of her whimsical Adventures.— That Lady, who was severely virtuous, did not approve of many Things she had been told of the Conduct of her Daughter; and though it was not in the Power of any Person in the World to inform her of the Truth of what she had been guilty of, yet she heard enough to make her keep her afterwards in a Restraint, little agreeable to her Humour, and the Liberties to which she had been accustomed.

But this Confinement was not the greatest Part of the Trouble of this now afflicted Lady: She found the Consequences of her amorous Follies would be, without almost a Miracle, impossible to be concealed:—She was with Child; and though she would easily have found Means to have skreen'd even this from the Knowledge of the World, had she been at liberty to have acted with the same unquestionable Authority over herself, as she did before the coming of her Mother, yet now all her Invention was at a Loss for a Stratagem to impose on a Woman of her Penetration:— By eating little, lacing prodigious strait, and the Advantage of a great Hoop-Petticoat, however, her Bigness was not taken notice of, and, perhaps, she would not have been suspected till the Time of her going into the Country, where her Mother design'd to send her, and from whence she intended to make her escape to some Place where she might be delivered with Secrecy, if the Time of it had not happen'd much Sooner than she expected.—A Ball being at Court, the good Old Lady was willing she should partake of the Diversion of it as a Farewel to the Town.—It was there she was seiz'd with those Pangs, which none in her Condition are exempt from:—She could not conceal the sudden Rack which all at once invaded her; or had her Tongue been mute, her wildly rolling Eyes, the Distortion of her Features, and the Convulsions which shook her whole Frame, in spite of her, would have reveal'd she labour'd under some terrible Shock of Nature.—Every Body was surpris'd, every Body was concern'd, but few guessed at the Occasion.—Her Mother griev'd beyond Expression, doubted not but she was struct with the Hand of Death; and order'd her to be carried Home in a Chair, while herself follow'd in another.—A Physician was immediately sent for: But he was presently perceiving what was her Distemper, call'd the old Lady aside, and told her, it was not a Doctor of his Sex, but one of her own, her Daughter stood in need of.—Never was Astonishment and Horror greater than that which seiz'd the Soul of this afflicted Parent at these Words: She could not for a Time believe the Truth of what she heard; but he insisting on it, and conjuring her to send for a Midwife, she was at length convinc'd if it.—All the Pity and Tenderness she had been for some Moment before possess'd of, now vanish'd, and were succeeded by an adequate Shame and Indignation:—She flew to the Bed where her Daughter was lying, and telling her what she had been inform'd of, and which she was now far from doubting, commanded her to reveal the Name of the Person whose Insinuations had drawn her to this Dishonour.—It was a great while before she could be brought to confess any Thing, and much longer before she could be prevailed on to name the Man whom she so fatally had lov'd; but the Rack of Nature growing more fierce, and the enraged old Lady protesting no Help should be afforded her while she persisted in her Obstinacy, she, with great Difficulty and Hesitation in her Speech, at last pronounc'd the Name of *Beauplaisir*. She had no sooner satisfy'd her weeping Mother, than that sorrowful Lady sent Messengers at the same Time, for a Midwife, and for that Gentleman who had occasion'd the other's being wanted.—He happen'd by Accident to be at home, and immediately obey'd the Summons, though prodigiously surpris'd what Business a Lady so much a Stranger to him could have to impart.—But how much greater was his Amazement, when taking him into her Closet, she there acquainted him with her Daughter's Misfortune, of the Discovery she had made, and how far he was concern'd in it?—All the Idea one can form of wild Astonishment, was mean to what he felt:—He assur'd her, that the young Lady her Daughter was a Person who he had never, more than at a Distance, admir'd:—That he had indeed, spoke to her in publick Company, but that he never had a Thought which tended to her Dishonour.—His Denials, if possible, added to the Indignation she was before enflam'd with:—She had no longer Patience; and carrying him into the Chamber, where she was just deliver'd of a fine Girl, cry'd out, I will not be impos'd on: The Truth by one of you shall be reveal'd.—*Beauplaisir* being brought to the Bed side, was beginning to address himself to the Lady in it, to beg she would clear the Mistake her Mother was involv'd in; when she, covering herself with the Cloaths, and ready to die a second Time with the inward Agitations of her Soul, shriek'd out, Oh, I am undone!—I cannot live, and bear this Shame!—But the old Lady believing that now or never was the Time to dive into the Bottom of this Mystery, forcing her to rear her Head, told her, she should not hope to Escape the Scrutiny of a Parent she had dishonour'd in such a Manner, and pointing to *Beauplaisir*, Is this the Gentleman, *(said she,)* to whom you owe your Ruin? or have you deceiv'd me by a fictitious Tale? Oh! no, *(resum'd the trembling Creature,)* he is, indeed, the innocent Cause of my Undoing:—Promise me your Pardon, *(continued she,)* and I will relate the Means. Here she ceas'd, expecting what she would reply, which, on hearing *Beauplaisir* cry out, What mean you Madam? I your Undoing, who never harbour'd the least Design on you in my Life, she did in these Words, Though the Injury you have done your Family, *(said she,)* is of a Nature which cannot justly hope Forgiveness, yet be assur'd, I shall much sooner excuse you when satisfied of the Truth, than while I am kept in a Suspence, if possible, as vexatious as the Crime itself is to me. Encouraged by this she related the whole Truth. And 'tis difficult to determine, if *Beauplaisir*, or the Lady, were most surpris'd at what they heard; he, that he should have been blinded so often by her Artifices; or she, that so young a Creature should have the Skill to make use of them. Both sat for some Time in a profound Revery; till at length she broke it first in these Words: Pardon, Sir, *(said she,)* the Trouble I have given you: I must confess it was with a Design to oblige you to repair the supposed Injury you had done this unfortunate Girl, by marrying her, but now I know not what to say;—The Blame is wholly her's, and I have nothing to request further of you, than that you will not divulge the distracted Folly she has been guilty of.—He answered her in Terms perfectly polite; but made no Offer of that which, perhaps, she expected, though could not, now inform'd of her Daughter's Proceedings, demand. He assured her, however, that if she would commit the new-born Lady to his Care, he would discharge it faithfully. But neither of them would consent to that; and he took his Leave, full of Cogitations, more confus'd than ever he had known in his whole Life. He continued to visit there, to enquire after her Health every Day; but the old Lady perceiving there was nothing likely to ensue from these Civilities, but, perhaps, a Renewing of the Crime, she entreated him to refrain; and as soon as her Daughter was in a Condition, sent her to a Monastery in *France*, the Abbess of which had been her particular Friend. And thus ended an Intreague, which, considering the Time it lasted, was as full of Variety as any, perhaps, that many Ages has produced.

FINIS.

Critical Eye

▶ **For Discussion**

a. How practical is the experiment the main character engages in?

b. One of the implications of what the main character does is that she feels men are simplistic and can be fooled easily. How offensive or realistic are these claims?

c. Consider this piece alongside Wolf's "The Making of a Slut." Is Fantomina a "bad girl," or is she ahead of her time?

▶ **Re-approaching the Reading**

From a male standpoint, could this text be viewed as sexist toward men?

▶ **Writing Assignment**

How much of the main character's dilemma stems from the "dream" that women are sold about love and finding a "Prince Charming"?

JHUMPA LAHIRI

INTERPRETER OF MALADIES

At the tea stall Mr. and Mrs. Das bickered about who should take Tina to the toilet. Eventually Mrs. Das relented when Mr. Das pointed out that he had given the girl her bath the night before. In the rearview mirror Mr. Kapasi watched as Mrs. Das emerged slowly from his bulky white Ambassador, dragging her shaved, largely bare legs across the back seat. She did not hold the little girl's hand as they walked to the rest room.

They were on their way to see the Sun Temple at Konarak. It was a dry, bright Saturday, the mid-July heat tempered by a steady ocean breeze, ideal weather for sightseeing. Ordinarily Mr. Kapasi would not have stopped so soon along the way, but less than five minutes after he'd picked up the family that morning in front of Hotel Sandy Villa, the little girl had complained. The first thing Mr. Kapasi had noticed when he saw Mr. and Mrs. Das, standing with their children under the portico of the hotel, was that they were very young, perhaps not even thirty. In addition to Tina they had two boys, Ronny and Bobby, who appeared very close in age and had teeth covered in a network of flashing silver wires. The family looked Indian but dressed as foreigners did, the children in stiff, brightly colored clothing and caps with translucent visors. Mr. Kapasi was accustomed to foreign tourists; he was assigned to them regularly because he could speak English. Yesterday he had driven an elderly couple from Scotland, both with spotted faces and fluffy white hair so thin it exposed their sunburnt scalps. In comparison, the tanned, youthful faces of Mr. and Mrs. Das were all the more striking. When he'd introduced himself, Mr. Kapasi had pressed his palms together in greeting, but Mr. Das squeezed hands like an American so that Mr. Kapasi felt it in his elbow. Mrs. Das, for her part, had flexed one side of her mouth, smiling dutifully at Mr. Kapasi, without displaying any interest in him.

As they waited at the tea stall, Ronny, who looked like the older of the two boys, clambered suddenly out of the back seat, intrigued by a goat tied to a stake in the ground.

"Don't touch it," Mr. Das said. He glanced up from his paperback tour book, which said "INDIA" in yellow letters and looked as if it had been published abroad. His voice, somehow tentative and a little shrill, sounded as though it had not yet settled into maturity.

"I want to give it a piece of gum," the boy called back as he trotted ahead.

Mr. Das stepped out of the car and stretched his legs by squatting briefly to the ground. A clean-shaven man, he looked exactly like a magnified version of Ronny. He had a sapphire blue visor, and was dressed in shorts, sneakers, and a T-shirt. The camera slung around his neck, with an impressive telephoto lens and numerous buttons and markings, was the

"Interpreter of Maladies", from *Interpreter of Maladies* by Jhumpa Lahiri. Copyright © 1999 by Jhumpa Lahiri. Reprinted by permission of Houghton Mifflin Harcourt Publishing Company. All rights reserved.

only complicated thing he wore. He frowned, watching as Ronny rushed toward the goat, but appeared to have no intention of intervening. "Bobby, make sure that your brother doesn't do anything stupid."

"I don't feel like it," Bobby said, not moving. He was sitting in the front seat beside Mr. Kapasi, studying a picture of the elephant god taped to the glove compartment.

"No need to worry," Mr. Kapasi said. "They are quite tame." Mr. Kapasi was forty-six years old, with receding hair that had gone completely silver, but his butterscotch complexion and his unlined brow, which he treated in spare moments to dabs of lotus-oil balm, made it easy to imagine what he must have looked like at an earlier age. He wore gray trousers and a matching jacket-style shirt, tapered at the waist, with short sleeves and a large pointed collar, made of a thin but durable synthetic material. He had specified both the cut and the fabric to his tailor—it was his preferred uniform for giving tours because it did not get crushed during his long hours behind the wheel. Through the windshield he watched as Ronny circled around the goat, touched it quickly on its side, then trotted back to the car.

"You left India as a child?" Mr. Kapasi asked when Mr. Das had settled once again into the passenger seat.

"Oh, Mina and I were both born in America," Mr. Das announced with an air of sudden confidence. "Born and raised. Our parents live here now, in Assansol.° They retired. We visit them every couple years." He turned to watch as the little girl ran toward the car, the wide purple bows of her sundress flopping on her narrow brown shoulders. She was holding to her chest a doll with yellow hair that looked as it it had been chopped, as a punitive measure, with pair of dull scissors. "This is Tina's first trip to India, isn't it, Tina?"

"I don't have to go to the bathroom anymore," Tina announced.

"Where's Mina?" Mr. Das asked.

Mr. Kapasi found it strange that Mr. Das should refer to his wife by her first name when speaking to the little girl. Tina pointed to where Mrs. Das was purchasing something from one of the shirtless men who worked at the tea stall. Mr. Kapasi heard one of the shirtless men sing a phrase from a popular Hindi love song as Mrs. Das walked back to the car, but she did not appear to understand the words of the song, for she did not express irritation, or embarrassment, or react in any other way to the man's declarations.

He observed her. She wore a red-and-white-checkered skirt that stopped above her knees, slip-on shoes with a square wooden heel, and a close-fitting blouse styled like a man's undershirt. The blouse was decorated at chest-level with a calico appliqué in the shape of a strawberry. She was a short woman, with small hands like paws, her frosty pink fingernails painted to match her lips, and was slightly plump in her figure. Her hair, shorn only a little longer than her husband's, was parted far to one side. She was wearing large dark brown sunglasses with a pinkish tint to them, and carried a big straw bag, almost as big as her torso, shaped like a bowl, with a water bottle poking out of it. She walked slowly, carrying some puffed rice tossed with peanuts and chili peppers in a large packet made from newspapers. Mr. Kapasi turned to Mr. Das.

"Where in America do you live?"

"New Brunswick, New Jersey."

"Next to New York?"

"Exactly. I teach middle school there."

"What subject?"

"Science. In fact, every year I take my students on a trip to the Museum of Natural History in New York City. In a way we have a lot in common, you could say, you and I. How long have you been a tour guide, Mr. Kapasi?"

"Five years."

Mrs. Das reached the car. "How long's the trip?" she asked, shutting the door,

"About two and a half hours," Mr. Kapasi replied.

At this Mrs. Das gave an impatient sigh, as if she had been traveling her whole life without pause. She fanned herself with a folded Bombay film magazine written in English.

"I thought that the Sun Temple is only eighteen miles north of Puri," Mr. Das said, tapping on the tour book.

"The roads to Konarak are poor. Actually it is a distance of fifty-two miles," Mr. Kapasi explained.

Mr. Das nodded, readjusting the camera strap where it had begun to chafe the back of his neck.

Before starting the ignition. Mr. Kapasi reached back to make sure the cranklike locks on the inside of each of the back doors were secured. As soon as the car began to move the little girl began to play with the lock on her side, clicking it with some effort forward and backward, but Mrs. Das said nothing to stop her. She sat a bit slouched at one end of the back seat, not offering her puffed rice to anyone. Ronny and Tina sat on either side of her, both snapping bright green gum.

"Look," Bobby said as the car began to gather speed. He pointed with his finger to the tall trees that lined the road. "Look."

"Monkeys!" Ronny shrieked. "Wow!"

They were seated in groups along the branches, with shining black faces, silver bodies, horizontal eyebrows, and crested heads. Their long gray tails dangled like a series of ropes among the leaves. A few scratched themselves with black leathery hands, or swung their feet, staring as the car passed.

"We call them the hanuman," Mr. Kapasi said. "They are quite common in the area."

As soon as he spoke, one of the monkeys leaped into the middle of the road, causing Mr. Kapasi to brake suddenly. Another bounced onto the hood of the car, then sprang away. Mr. Kapasi beeped his horn. The children began to get excited, sucking in their breath and covering their faces partly with their hands. They had never seen monkeys outside of a zoo, Mr. Das explained. He asked Mr. Kapasi to stop the car so that he could take a picture.

While Mr. Das adjusted his telephoto lens, Mrs. Das reached into her straw bag and pulled out a bottle of colorless nail polish, which she proceeded to stroke on the tip of her index finger.

The little girl stuck out a hand. "Mine too. Mommy, do mine too."

"Leave me alone," Mrs. Das said, blowing on her nail and turning her body slightly. "You're making me mess up."

The little girl occupied herself by buttoning and unbuttoning a pinafore on the doll's plastic body.

"All set," Mr. Das said, replacing the lens cap.

The car rattled considerably as it raced along the dusty road, causing them all to pop up from their seats every now and then, but Mrs. Das continued to polish her nails. Mr. Kapasi eased up on the accelerator, hoping to produce a smoother ride. When he reached for the gearshift the boy in front accommodated him by swinging his hairless knees out of the way. Mr. Kapasi noted that this boy was slightly paler than than other children. "Daddy, why is the driver sitting on the wrong side in this car, too?" the boy asked.

"They all do that here, dummy," Ronny said.

"Don't call your brother a dummy," Mr. Das said. He turned to Mr. Kapasi. "In America, you know . . . it confuses them."

"Oh yes, I am well aware," Mr. Kapasi said. As delicately as he could, he shifted gears again, accelerating as they approached a hill in the road. "I see it on *Dallas,*° the steering wheels are on the left-hand side."

"What's *Dallas?*" Tina asked, hanging her now naked doll on the seat behind Mr. Kapasi.

"It went off the air," Mr. Das explained. "It's a television show."

They were all like siblings, Mr. Kapasi thought as they passed a row of date trees. Mr. and Mrs. Das behaved like an older brother and sister, not parents. It seemed that they were in charge of the children only for the day; it was hard to believe they were regularly responsible for anything other than themselves. Mr. Das tapped on his lens cap, and his tour book, dragging his thumbnail occasionally across the pages so that they made a scraping sound. Mrs. Das continued to polish her nails. She had still not removed her sunglasses. Every now and then Tina renewed her plea that she wanted her nails done, too, and so at one point Mrs. Das flicked a drop of polish on the little girl's finger before depositing the bottle back inside her straw bag.

"Isn't this an air-conditioned car?" she asked, still blowing on her hand. The window on Tina's side was broken and could not be rolled down.

"Quit complaining," Mr. Das said. "It isn't so hot."

"I told you to get a car with air-conditioning," Mrs. Das continued. "Why do you do this, Raj, just to save a few stupid rupees. What are you saving us, fifty cents?"

Their accents sounded just like the ones Mr. Kapasi heard on American television programs, though not like the ones on *Dallas.*

"Doesn't it get tiresome, Mr. Kapasi, showing people the same thing every day?" Mr. Das asked, rolling down his own window all the way. "Hey, do you mind stopping the car? I just want to get a shot of this guy."

Mr. Kapasi pulled over to the side of the road as Mr. Das took a picture of a barefoot man, his head wrapped in a dirty turban, seated on top of a cart of grain sacks pulled by a pair of bullocks. Both the man and the bullocks were emaciated. In the back seat Mrs. Das gazed out another window, at the sky, where nearly transparent clouds passed quickly in front of one another.

"I look forward to it, actually," Mr. Kapasi said as they continued on their way. "The Sun Temple is one of my favorite places. In that way it is a reward for me. I give tours on Fridays and Saturdays only. I have another job during the week."

"Oh? Where?" Mr. Das asked.

"I work in a doctor's office."

"You're a doctor?"

"I am not a doctor. I work with one. As an interpreter."

"What does a doctor need an interpreter for?"

"He has a number of Gujarati patients. My father was Gujarati, but many people do not speak Gujarati in this area, including the doctor. And so the doctor asked me to work in his office, interpreting what the patients say."

"Interesting. I've never heard of anything like that," Mr. Das said.

Mr. Kapasi shrugged. "It is a job like any other."

"But so romantic," Mrs. Das said dreamily, breaking her extended silence. She lifted her pinkish brown sunglasses and arranged them on top of her head like a tiara. For the first time, her eyes met Mr. Kapasi's in the rearview mirror: pale, a bit small, their gaze fixed but drowsy.

Mr. Das craned to look at her. "What's so romantic about it?"

"I don't know. Something." She shrugged, knitting her brows together for an instant. "Would you like a piece of gum, Mr. Kapasi?" she asked brightly. She reached into her straw bag and handed him a small square wrapped in green-and-striped paper. As soon as Mr. Kapasi put the gum in his mouth a thick sweet liquid burst onto his tongue.

"Tell us more about your job, Mr. Kapasi," Mrs. Das said.

"What would you like to know, madame?"

"I don't know," she shrugged, munching on some puffed rice and licking the mustard oil from the corners of her mouth. "Tell us a typical situation." She settled back in her seat, her head tilted in a patch of sun, and closed her eyes. "I want to picture what happens."

"Very well. The other day a man came in with a pain in his throat."

"Did he smoke cigarettes?"

"No. It was very curious. He complained that he felt as if there were long pieces of straw stuck in his throat. When I told the doctor he was able to prescribe the proper medication."

"That's so neat."

"Yes," Mr. Kapasi agreed after some hesitation.

"So these patients are totally dependent on you," Mrs. Das said. She spoke slowly, as if she were thinking aloud. "In a way, more dependent on you than the doctor."

"How do you mean? How could it be?"

"Well, for example, you could tell the doctor that the pain felt like a burning, not straw. The patient would never know what you had told the doctor, and the doctor wouldn't know that you had told the wrong thing. It's a big responsibility."

"Yes, a big responsibility you have there, Mr. Kapasi," Mr. Das agreed.

Mr. Kapasi had never thought of his job in such complimentary terms. To him it was a thankless occupation. He found nothing noble in interpreting people's maladies, assiduously translating the symptoms of so many swollen bones, countless cramps of bellies and bowels, spots on people's palms that changed color, shape, or size. The doctor, nearly half his age, had an affinity for bell-bottom trousers and made humorless jokes about the Congress party. Together they worked in a stale little infirmary where Mr. Kapasi's smartly tailored clothes clung to him in the heat, in spite of the blackened blades of a ceiling fan churning over their heads.

The job was a sign of his failings. In his youth he'd been a devoted scholar of foreign languages, the owner of an impressive collection of dictionaries. He had dreamed of being an interpreter for diplomats and dignitaries, resolving conflicts between people and nations, settling disputes of which he alone could understand both sides. He was a self-educated man. In a series of notebooks, in the evenings before his parents settled his marriage, he has listed the common etymologies of words, and at one point in his life he was confident that he could converse, if given the opportunity, in English, French, Russian, Portuguese, and Italian, not to mention Hindi, Bengali, Orissi, and Gujarati. Now only a handful of European phrases remained in his memory, scattered words for things like saucers and chairs. English was the only non-Indian language he spoke fluently anymore. Mr. Kapasi knew it was not a remarkable talent. Sometimes he feared that his children knew better English than he did, just from watching television. Still, it came in handy for the tours.

He had taken the job as an interpreter after his first son, at the age of seven, contracted typhoid—that was how he had first made the acquaintance of the doctor. At the time

Mr. Kapasi had been teaching English in a grammar school, and he bartered his skills as an interpreter to pay the increasingly exorbitant medical bills. In the end the boy had died one evening in his mother's arms, his limbs burning with fever, but then there was the funeral to pay for, and the other children who were born soon enough, and the newer, bigger house, and the good schools and tutors, and the fine shoes and the television, and the countless other ways he tried to console his wife and to keep her from crying in her sleep, and so when the doctor offered to pay him twice as much as he earned at the grammar school, he accepted. Mr. Kapasi knew that his wife had little regard for his career as an interpreter. He knew it reminded her of the son she'd lost, and that she resented the other lives he helped, in his own small way, to save. If ever she referred to his position, she used the phrase "doctor's assistant," as if the process of interpretation were equal to taking someone's temperature, or changing a bedpan. She never asked him about the patients who came to the doctor's office, or said that his job was a big responsibility.

For this reason it flattered Mr. Kapasi that Mrs. Das was so intrigued by his job. Unlike his wife, she had reminded him of its intellectual challenges. She had also used the word "romantic." She did not behave in a romantic way toward her husband, and yet she had used the word to describe him. He wondered if Mr. and Mrs. Das were a bad match, just as he and his wife were. Perhaps they, too, had little in common apart from three children and a decade of their lives. The signs he recognized from his own marriage were there—the bickering, the indifference, the protracted silences. Her sudden interest in him, an interest she did not express in either her husband or her children, was mildly intoxicating. When Mr. Kapasi thought once again about how she had said "romantic," the feeling of intoxication grew.

He began to check his reflection in the rearview mirror as he drove, feeling grateful that he had chosen the gray suit that morning and not the brown one, which tended to sag a little in the knees. From time to time he glanced through the mirror at Mrs. Das. In addition to glancing at her face he glanced at the strawberry between her breasts, and the golden brown hollow in her throat. He decided to tell Mrs. Das about another patient, and another: the young woman who had complained of a sensation of raindrops in her spine, the gentleman whose birthmark had begun to sprout hairs. Mrs. Das listened attentively, stroking her hair with a small plastic brush that resembled an oval bed of nails, asking more questions, for yet another example. The children were quiet, intent on spotting more monkeys in the trees, and Mr. Das was absorbed by his tour book, so it seemed like a private conversation between Mr. Kapasi and Mrs. Das. In this manner the next half hour passed, and when they stopped for lunch at a roadside restaurant that sold fritters and omelette sandwiches, usually something Mr. Kapasi looked forward to on his tours so that he could sit in peace and enjoy some hot tea, he was disappointed. As the Das family settled together under a magenta umbrella fringed with white and orange tassels, and placed their orders with one of the waiters who marched about in tricornered caps, Mr. Kapasi reluctantly headed toward a neighboring table.

"Mr. Kapasi, wait. There's room here," Mrs. Das called out. She gathered Tina onto her lap, insisting that he accompany them. And so, together, they had bottled mango juice and sandwiches and plates of onions and potatoes deep-fried in graham-flour batter. After finishing two omelette sandwiches Mr. Das took more pictures of the group as they ate.

"How much longer?" he asked Mr. Kapasi as he paused to load a new roll of film in the camera.

"About half an hour more."

By now the children had gotten up from the table to look at more monkeys perched in a nearby tree, so there was a considerable space between Mrs. Das and Mr. Kapasi. Mr. Das placed the camera to his face and squeezed one eye shut, his tongue exposed at one corner of his mouth. "This looks funny. Mina, you need to lean in closer to Mr. Kapasi."

She did. He could smell a scent on her skin, like a mixture of whiskey and rosewater. He worried suddenly that she could smell his perspiration, which he knew had collected beneath the synthetic material of his shirt. He polished off his mango juice in one gulp and smoothed his silver hair with his hands. A bit of the juice dripped onto his chin. He wondered if Mrs. Das had noticed.

She had not. "What's your address, Mr. Kapasi?" she inquired, fishing for something inside her straw bag.

"You would like my address?"

"So we can send you copies," she said. "Of the pictures." She handed him a scrap of paper which she had hastily ripped from a page of her film magazine. The blank portion was limited, for the narrow strip was crowded by lines of text and a tiny picture of a hero and heroine embracing under a eucalyptus tree.

The paper curled as Mr. Kapasi wrote his address in clear, careful letters. She would write to him, asking about his days interpreting at the doctor's office, and he would respond eloquently, choosing only the most entertaining anecdotes, ones that would make her laugh out loud as she read them in her house in New Jersey. In time she would reveal the disappointment of her marriage, and he his. In this way their friendship would grow, and flourish. He would possess a picture of the two of them, eating fried onions under a magenta umbrella, which he would keep, he decided, safely tucked between the pages of his Russian grammar. As his mind raced, Mr. Kapasi experienced a mild and pleasant shock. It was similar to a feeling he used to experience long ago when, after months of translating with the aid of a dictionary, he would finally read a passage from a French novel, or an Italian sonnet, and understand the words, one after another, unencumbered by his own efforts. In those moments Mr. Kapasi used to believe that all was right with the world, that all struggles were rewarded, that all of life's mistakes made sense in the end. The promise that he would hear from Mrs. Das now filled him with the same belief.

When he finished writing his address Mr. Kapasi handed her the paper, but as soon as he did so he worried that he had either misspelled his name, or accidentally reversed the numbers of his postal code. He dreaded the possibility of a lost letter, the photograph never reaching him, hovering somewhere in Orissa, close but ultimately unattainable. He thought of asking for the slip of paper again, just to make sure he had written his address accurately, but Mrs. Das had already dropped it into the jumble of her bag.

They reached Konarak at two-thirty. The temple, made of sandstone, was a massive pyramid-like structure in the shape of a chariot. It was dedicated to the great master of life, the sun, which struck three sides of the edifice as it made its journey each day across the sky. Twenty-four giant wheels were carved on the north and south sides of the plinth. The whole thing was drawn by a team of seven horses, speeding as if through the heavens. As they approached, Mr. Kapasi explained that the temple had been built between A.D. 1243 and 1255, with the efforts of twelve hundred artisans, by the great ruler of the Ganga dynasty, King Narasimhadeva the First, to commemorate his victory against the Muslin army.

"It says the temple occupies about a hundred and seventy acres of land," Mr. Das said, reading from his book.

"It's like a desert," Ronny said, his eyes wandering across the sand that stretched on all sides beyond the temple.

"The Chandrabhaga River once flowed one mile north of here. It is dry now," Mr. Kapasi said, turning off the engine.

They got out and walked toward the temple, posing first for pictures by the pair of lions that flanked the steps. Mr. Kapasi led them next to one of the wheels of the chariot, higher than any human being, nine feet in diameter.

"'The wheels are supposed to symbolize the wheel of life,'" Mr. Das read. "'They depict the cycle of creation, preservation, and achievement of realization.' Cool." He turned the page of his book. "'Each wheel is divided into eight thick and thin spokes, dividing the day into eight equal parts. The rims are carved with designs of birds and animals, whereas the medallions in the spokes are carved with women in luxurious poses, largely erotic in nature.'"

What he referred to were the countless friezes of entwined naked bodies, making love in various positions, women clinging to the necks of men, their knees wrapped eternally around their lovers' thighs. In addition to these were assorted scenes from daily life, of hunting and trading, of deer being killed with bows and arrows and marching warriors holding swords in their hands.

It was no longer possible to enter the temple, for it had filled with rubble years ago, but they admired the exterior, as did all the tourists Mr. Kapasi brought there, slowly strolling along each of its sides. Mr. Das trailed behind, taking pictures. The children ran ahead, pointing to figures of naked people, intrigued in particular by the Nagamithunas, the half-human, half-serpentine couples who were said, Mr. Kapasi told them, to live in the deepest waters of the sea. Mr. Kapasi was pleased that they liked the temple, pleased especially that it appealed to Mrs. Das. She stopped every three or four paces, staring silently at the carved lovers, and the processions of elephants, and the topless female musicians beating on two-sided drums.

Though Mr. Kapasi had been to the temple countless times, it occurred to him, as he, too, gazed at the topless women, that he had never seen his own wife fully naked. Even when they had made love she kept the panels of her blouse hooked together, the string of her petticoat knotted around her waist. He had never admired the backs of his wife's legs the way he now admired those of Mrs. Das, walking as if for his benefit alone. He had, of course, seen plenty of bare limbs before, belonging to the American and European ladies who took his tours. But Mrs. Das was different, Unlike the other women, who had an interest only in the temple, and kept their noses buried in a guidebook, or their eyes behind the lens of a camera, Mrs. Das had taken an interest in him.

Mr. Kapasi was anxious to be alone with her, to continue their private conversation, yet he felt nervous to walk at her side. She was lost behind her sunglasses, ignoring her husband's requests that she pose for another picture, walking past her children as if they were strangers. Worried that he might disturb her, Mr. Kapasi walked ahead, to admire, as he always did, the three life-sized bronze avatars of Surya, the sun god, each emerging from its own niche on the temple facade to greet the sun at dawn, noon, and evening. They wore elaborate headdresses, their languid, elongated eyes closed, their bare chests draped with carved chains and amulets. Hibiscus petals, offerings from previous visitors, were strewn at their gray-green feet. The last statue, on the northern wall of the temple, was Mr. Kapasi's favorite. This Surya had a tired expression, weary after a hard day of work, sitting astride a horse with folded legs. Even his horse's eyes were drowsy. Around his body were smaller sculptures of women in pairs, their hips thrust to one side.

"Who's that?" Mrs. Das asked. He was startled to see that she was standing beside him.

Class and the Culture of Power

"He is the Astachala-Surya," Mr. Kapasi said. "The setting sun."

"So in a couple of hours the sun will set right here?" She slipped a foot out of one of her square-heeled shoes, rubbed her toes on the back of her other leg.

"That is correct."

She raised her sunglasses for a moment, then put them back on again. "Neat."

Mr. Kapasi was not certain exactly what the word suggested, but he had a feeling it was a favorable response. He hoped that Mrs. Das had understood Surya's beauty, his power. Perhaps they would discuss it further in their letters. He would explain things to her, things about India, and she would explain things to him about America. In its own way this correspondence would fulfill his dream, of serving as an interpreter between nations. He looked at her straw bag, delighted that his address lay nestled among its contents. When he pictured her so many thousands of miles away he plummeted, so much so that he had an overwhelming urge to wrap his arms around her, to freeze with her, even for an instant, in an embrace witnessed by his favorite Surya. But Mrs. Das had already started walking.

"When do you return to America?" he asked, trying to sound placid.

"In ten days."

He calculated: A week to settle in, a week to develop the pictures, a few days to compose her letter, two weeks to get to India by air. According to his schedule, allowing room for delays, he would hear from Mrs. Das in approximately six weeks' time.

The family was silent as Mr. Kapasi drove them back, a little past four-thirty, to Hotel Sandy Villa. The children had bought miniature granite versions of the chariot's wheels at a souvenir stand, and they turned them round in their hands. Mr. Das continued to read his book. Mrs. Das untangled Tina's hair with her brush and divided it into two little ponytails.

Mr. Kapasi was beginning to dread the thought of dropping them off. He was not prepared to begin his six-week wait to her from Mrs. Das. As he stole glances at her in the rearview mirror, wrapping elastic bands around Tina's hair, he wondered how he might make the tour last a little longer. Ordinarily he sped back to Puri using a shortcut, eager to return home, scrub his feet and hands with sandalwood soap, and enjoy the evening newspaper and a cup of tea that his wife would serve him in silence. The though of that silence, something to which he'd long been resigned, now oppressed him. It was then that he suggested visiting the hills and Udayagiri and Khandagiri, where a number of monastic dwellings were hewn out of the ground, facing one another across a defile. It was some miles away, but well worth seeing, Mr. Kapasi told them.

"Oh yeah, there's something mentioned about it in this book," Mr. Das said. "Built by a Jain king or something."

"Shall we go then?" Mr. Kapasi asked. He paused at a turn in the road. "It's to the left."

Mr. Das turned to look at Mrs. Das. Both of them shrugged.

"Left, left," the children chanted.

Mr. Kapasi turned the wheel, almost delirious with relief. He did not know what he would do or say to Mrs. Das once they arrived at the hills. Perhaps he would tell her what a pleasing smile she had. Perhaps he would compliment her strawberry shirt, which he found irresistibly becoming. Perhaps, when Mr. Das was busy taking a picture, he would take her hand.

He did not have to worry. When they got to the hills, divided by a steep path thick with trees, Mrs. Das refused to get out of the car. All along the path, dozens of monkeys were seated on stones, as well as on the branches of the trees. Their hind legs were stretched out in front and raised to shoulder level, their arms resting on their knees.

"My legs are tired," she said, sinking low in her seat. "I'll stay here."

"Why did you have to wear those stupid shoes?" Mr. Das said. "You won't be in the pictures."

"Pretend I'm there."

"But we could use one of these pictures for our Christmas card this year. We didn't get one of all five of us at the Sun Temple. Mr. Kapasi could take it."

"I'm not coming. Anyway, those monkeys give me the creeps."

"But they're harmless," Mr. Das said. He turned to Mr. Kapasi. "Aren't they?"

"They are more hungry than dangerous," Mr. Kapasi said. "Do not provoke them with food, and they will not bother you."

Mr. Das headed up the defile with the children, the boys at his side, the little girl on his shoulders. Mr. Kapasi watched as they crossed paths with a Japanese man and woman, the only other tourists there, who paused for a final photograph, then stepped into a nearby car and drove away. As the car disappeared out of view some of the monkeys called out, emitting soft whooping sounds, and then walked on their flat black hands and feet up the path. At one point a group of them formed a little ring around Mr. Das and the children. Tina screamed in delight. Ronny ran in circles around his father. Bobby bent down and picked up a fat stick on the ground. When he extended it, one of the monkeys approached him and snatched it, then briefly beat the ground.

"I'll join them," Mr. Kapasi said, unlocking the door on his side. "There is much to explain about the caves."

"No. Stay a minute," Mrs. Das said. She got out of the back seat and slipped in beside Mr. Kapasi. "Raj has his dumb book anyway." Together, through the windshield, Mrs. Das and Mr. Kapasi watched as Bobby and the monkey passed the stick back and forth between them.

"A brave little boy," Mr. Kapasi commented.

"It's not so surprising," Mrs. Das said.

"No?"

"He's not his."

"I beg your pardon?"

"Raj's. He's not Raj's son."

Mr. Kapasi felt a prickle on his skin. He reached into his shirt pocket for the small tin of lotus-oil balm he carried with him at all times, and applied it to three spots on his forehead. He knew that Mrs. Das was watching him, but he did not turn to face her. Instead he watched as the figures of Mr. Das and the children grew smaller, climbing up the steep path, pausing every now and then for a picture, surrounded by a growing number of monkeys.

"Are you surprised?" The way she put it made him choose his words with care.

"It's not the type of thing one assumes," Mr. Kapasi replied slowly. He put the tin of lotus-oil balm back in his pocket.

"No, of course not. And no one knows, of course. No one at all. I've kept it a secret for eight whole years." She looked at Mr. Kapasi, tilting her chin as if to gain a fresh perspective. "But now I've told you."

Mr. Kapasi nodded. He felt suddenly parched, and his forehead was warm and slightly numb from the balm. He considered asking Mrs. Das for a sip of water, then decided against it.

"We met when we were very young," she said. She reached into her straw bag in search of something, then pulled out a packet of puffed rice. "Want some?"

"No, thank you."

She put a fistful in her mouth, sank into the seat a little, and looked away from Mr. Kapasi, out the window on her side of the car. "We married when we were still in college. We were in high school when he proposed. We went to the same college, of course. Back then we couldn't stand the thought of being separated, not for a day, not for a minute. Our parents were best friends who lived in the same town. My entire life I saw him every weekend, either at our house or theirs. We were sent upstairs to play together while our parents joked about our marriage. Imagine! They never caught us at anything, though in a way I think it was all more or less a setup. The things we did those Friday and Saturday nights, while our parents sat downstairs drinking tea . . . I could tell you stories, Mr. Kapasi."

As a result of spending all her time in college with Raj, she continued, she did not make many close friends. There was no one to confide in about him at the end of a difficult day, or to share a passing thought or a worry. Her parents now lived on the other side of the world, but she had never been very close to them, anyway. After marrying so young she was overwhelmed by it all, having a child so quickly, and nursing, and warming up bottles of milk and testing their temperature against her wrist while Raj was at work, dressed in sweaters and corduroy pants, teaching his students about rocks and dinosaurs. Raj never looked cross or harried, or plump as she had become after the first baby.

Always tired, she declined invitations from her one or two college girlfriends, to have lunch or shop in Manhattan. Eventually the friends stopped calling her, so that she was left at home all day with the baby, surrounded by toys that made her trip when she walked or wince when she sat, always cross and tired. Only occasionally did they go out after Ronny was born, and even more rarely did they entertain. Raj didn't mind; he looked forward to coming home from teaching and watching television and bouncing Ronny on his knee. She had been outraged when Raj told her that a Punjabi friend, someone whom she had once met but did not remember, would be staying with them for a week for some job interviews in the New Brunswick area.

Bobby was conceived in the afternoon, on a sofa littered with rubber teething toys, after the friend learned that a London pharmaceutical company had hired him, while Ronny cried to be freed from his playpen. She made no protest when the friend touched the small of her back as she was about to make a pot of coffee, then pulled her against his crisp navy suit. He made love to her swiftly, in silence, with an expertise she had never known, without the meaningful expressions and smiles Raj always insisted on afterward. The next day Raj drove the friend to JFK. He was married now, to a Punjabi girl, and they lived in London still, and every year they exchanged Christmas cards with Raj and Mina, each couple tucking photos of their families into the envelopes. He did not know that he was Bobby's father. He never would.

"I beg your pardon, Mrs. Das, but why have you told me this information?" Mr. Kapasi asked when she had finally finished speaking, and had turned to face him once again.

"For God's sake, stop calling me Mrs. Das. I'm twenty-eight. You probably have children my age."

"Not quite." It disturbed Mr. Kapasi to learn that she thought of him as a parent. The feeling he had had toward her, that had made him check his reflection in the rearview mirror as they drove, evaporated a little.

"I told you because of your talents." She put the packet of puffed rice back into her bag without folding over the top.

"I don't understand," Mr. Kapasi said.

"Don't you see? For eight years I haven't been able to express this to anybody, not friends, certainly not to Raj. He doesn't even suspect it. He thinks I'm still in love with him. Well, don't you have anything to say?"

"About what?"

"About what I've just told you. About my secret, and about how terrible it makes me feel. I feel terrible looking at my children, and at Raj, always terrible. I have terrible urges, Mr. Kapasi, to throw things away. One day I had the urge to throw everything I own out the window, the television, the children, everything. Don't you think it's unhealthy?"

He was silent.

"Mr. Kapasi, don't you have anything to say? I thought that was your job."

"My job is to give tours, Mrs. Das."

"Not that. Your other job. As an interpreter."

"But we do not face a language barrier. What need is there for an interpreter?"

"That's not what I mean. I would never have told you otherwise. Don't you realize what it means for me to tell you?"

"What does it mean?"

"It means that I'm tired of feeling so terrible all the time. Eight years, Mr. Kapasi, I've been in pain eight years. I was hoping you could help me feel better, say the right thing. Suggest some kind of remedy."

He looked at her, in her red plaid skirt and strawberry T-shirt, a woman not yet thirty, who loved neither her husband nor her children, who had already fallen out of love with life. Her confession depressed him, depressed him all the more when he thought of Mr. Das at the top of the path, Tina clinging to his shoulders, taking pictures of ancient monastic cells cut into the hills to show his students in America, unsuspecting and unaware that one of his sons was not his own. Mr. Kapasi felt insulted that Mrs. Das should ask him to interpret her common, trivial little secret. She did not resemble the patients in the doctor's office, those who came glassy-eyed and desperate, unable to sleep or breathe or urinate with ease, unable, above all, to give words to their pains. Still, Mr. Kapasi believed it was his duty to assist Mrs. Das. Perhaps he ought to tell her to confess the truth to Mr. Das. He would explain that honesty was the best policy. Honesty, surely, would help her feel better, as she'd put it. Perhaps he would offer to preside over the discussion, as a mediator. He decided to begin with the most obvious question, to get to the heart of the matter, and so he asked, "Is it really pain you feel, Mrs. Das, or is it guilt?"

She turned to him and glared, mustard oil thick on her frosty pink lips. She opened her mouth to say something, but as she glared at Mr. Kapasi some certain knowledge seemed to pass before her eyes, and she stopped. It crushed him; he knew at that moment that he was not even important enough to be properly insulted. She opened the car door and began walking up the path, wobbling a little on her square wooden heels, reaching into her straw bag to eat handfuls of puffed rice. It fell through her fingers, leaving a zigzagging trail, causing a monkey to leap down from a tree and devour the little white grains. In search of more, the monkey began to follow Mrs. Das. Others joined him, so that she was soon being followed by about half a dozen of them, their velvety tails dragging behind.

Mr. Kapasi stepped out of the car. He wanted to holler, to alert her in some way, but he worried that if she knew they were behind her, she would grow nervous. Perhaps she would lose her balance. Perhaps they would pull at her bag or her hair. He began to jog up the path, taking a fallen branch in his hand to scare away the monkeys. Mrs. Das continued walking, oblivious, trailing grains of puffed rice. Near the top of the incline, before a group of cells fronted by a row of squat stone pillars, Mr. Das was kneeling on the ground focusing the lens of his camera. The children stood under the arcade, now hiding, now emerging from view.

"Wait for me," Mrs. Das called out. "I'm coming."

Tina jumped up and down. "Here comes Mommy!"

"Great," Mr. Das said without looking up. "Just in time. We'll get Mr. Kapasi to take a picture of the five of us."

Mr. Kapasi quickened his pace, waving his branch so that the monkeys scampered away, distracted, in another direction.

"Where's Bobby?" Mrs. Das asked when she stopped.

Mr. Das looked up from the camera. "I don't know. Ronny, where's Bobby?"

Ronny shrugged, "I thought he was right here."

"Where is he?" Mrs. Das repeated sharply. "What's wrong with all of you?"

They began calling his name, wandering up and down the path a bit. Because they were calling, they did not initially hear the boy's screams. When they found him, a little farther down the path under a tree, he was surrounded by a group of monkeys, over a dozen of them, pulling at his T-shirt with their long black fingers. The puffed rice Mrs. Das had spilled was scattered at his feet, raked over by the monkeys' hands. The boy was silent, his body frozen, swift tears running down his startled face. His bare legs were dusty and red with welts from where one of the monkeys struck him repeatedly with the stick he had given to it earlier.

"Daddy, the monkey's hurting Bobby," Tina said.

Mr. Das wiped his palms on the front of his shorts. In his nervousness he accidentally pressed the shutter on his camera; the whirring noise of the advancing film excited the monkeys, and the one with the stick began to beat Bobby more intently. "What are we supposed to do? What if they start attacking?"

"Mr. Kapasi," Mrs. Das shrieked, noticing him standing to one side. "Do something, for God's sake, do something!"

Mr. Kapasi took his branch and shooed them away, hissing at the ones that remained, stomping his feet to scare them. The animals retreated slowly, with a measured gait, obedient but unintimidated. Mr. Kapasi gathered Bobby in his arms and brought him back to where his parents and siblings were standing. As he carried him he was tempted to whisper a secret into the boy's ear. But Bobby was stunned, and shivering with fright, his legs bleeding slightly where the stick had broken the skin. When Mr. Kapasi delivered him to his parents, Mrs. Das brushed some dirt off the boy's T-shirt and put the visor on him the right way. Mrs. Das reached into her straw bag to find a bandage which she taped over the cut on his knee. Ronny offered his brother a fresh piece of gum. "He's fine. Just a little scared, right, Bobby?" Mr. Das said, patting the top of his head.

"God, let's get out of here," Mrs. Das said. She folded her arms across the strawberry on her chest. "This place gives me the creeps."

"Yeah. Back to the hotel, definitely," Mr. Das agreed.

"Poor Bobby," Mrs. Das said. "Come here a second. Let Mommy fix your hair." Again she reached into her straw bag, this time for her hairbrush, and began to run it around the edges of the translucent visor. When she whipped out the hairbrush, the slip of paper with Mr. Kapasi's address on it fluttered away in the wind. No one but Mr. Kapasi noticed. He watched as it rose, carried higher and higher by the breeze, into the trees where the monkeys now sat, solemnly observing the scene below. Mr. Kapasi observed it too, knowing that this was the picture of the Das family he would preserve forever in his mind.

CRITICAL EYE

▶ For Discussion

a. How is it that all of the individuals in the story share the same ethnic identity but are so drastically different? What has informed their adult lives?

b. Discuss the metaphorical meaning of the phrase "interpreter of the maladies."

c. How is this story about the life of an unfulfilled woman?

▶ Re-approaching the Reading

Examine the main character in the film *Fight Club* and the woman from Lahiri's text. What do these two have in common, and how do both explore the notion of the need for confession?

▶ Writing Assignment

Is this story an allusion to how adults often feel that their lives have been wasted?

CHARLES CHESTNUT

AN EVENING VISIT

*From the Novel
The House Behind the Cedars*

TOWARD evening of the same day, Warwick took his way down Front Street in the gathering dusk. By the time night had spread its mantle over the earth, he had reached the gate by which he had seen the girl of his morning walk enter the cedar-bordered garden. He stopped at the gate and glanced toward the house, which seemed dark and silent and deserted.

"It's more than likely," he thought, "that they are in the kitchen. I reckon I'd better try the back door."

But as he drew cautiously near the corner, he saw a man's figure outlined in the yellow light streaming from the open door of a small house between Front Street and the cooper shop. Wishing, for reasons of his own, to avoid observation, Warwick did not turn the corner, but walked on down Front Street until he reached a point from which he could see, at a long angle, a ray of light proceeding from the kitchen window of the house behind the cedars.

"They are there," he muttered with a sigh of relief, for he had feared they might be away. "I suspect I'll have to go to the front door, after all. No one can see me through the trees."

He retraced his steps to the front gate, which he essayed to open. There was apparently some defect in the latch, for it refused to work. Warwick remembered the trick, and with a slight sense of amusement, pushed his foot under the gate and gave it a hitch to the left, after which it opened readily enough. He walked softly up the sanded path, tiptoed up the steps and across the piazza, and rapped at the front door, not too loudly, lest this too might attract the attention of the man across the street. There was no response to his rap. He put his ear to the door and heard voices within, and the muffled sound of footsteps. After a moment he rapped again, a little louder than before.

There was an instant cessation of the sounds within. He rapped a third time, to satisfy any lingering doubt in the minds of those who he felt sure were listening in some trepidation. A moment later a ray of light streamed through the keyhole.

"Who's there?" a woman's voice inquired somewhat sharply.

"A gentleman," answered Warwick, not holding it yet time to reveal himself. "Does Mis' Molly Walden live here?"

"Yes," was the guarded answer. "I'm Mis' Walden. What's yo'r business?"

"I have a message to you from your son John."

A key clicked in the lock. The door opened, and the elder of the two women Warwick had seen upon the piazza stood in the doorway, peering curiously and with signs of great excitement into the face of the stranger.

From *The House Behind the Cedars* by Charles Chestnut, Houghton Mifflin 1990.

"You've got a message from my son, you say?" she asked with tremulous agitation. "Is he sick, or in trouble?"

"No. He's well and doing well, and sends his love to you, and hopes you've not forgotten him."

"Fergot him? No, God knows I ain't fergot him! But come in, sir, an' tell me somethin' mo' about him."

Warwick went in, and as the woman closed the door after him, he threw a glance round the room. On the wall, over the mantelpiece, hung a steel engraving of General Jackson at the battle of New Orleans, and, on the opposite wall, a framed fashion-plate from "Godey's Lady's Book." In the middle of the room an octagonal centre-table with a single leg, terminating in three sprawling feet, held a collection of curiously shaped sea-shells. There was a great haircloth sofa, somewhat the worse for wear, and a well-filled bookcase. The screen standing before the fireplace was covered with Confederate bank-notes of various denominations and designs, in which the heads of Jefferson Davis and other Confederate leaders were conspicuous.

"Imperious Cæsar, dead, and turned to clay,
Might stop a hole to keep the wind away,"

murmured the young man, as his eye fell upon this specimen of decorative art.

The woman showed her visitor to a seat. She then sat down facing him and looked at him closely. "When did you last see my son?" she asked.

"I've never met your son," he replied.

Her face fell. "Then the message comes through you from somebody else?"

"No, directly from your son."

She scanned his face with a puzzled look. This bearded young gentleman, who spoke so politely and was dressed so well, surely—no, it could not be! and yet—

Warwick was smiling at her through a mist of tears. An electric spark of sympathy flashed between them. They rose as if moved by one impulse, and were clasped in each other's arms.

"John, my John! It *is* John!"

"Mother—my dear old mother!"

"I didn't think," she sobbed, "that I'd ever see you again."

He smoothed her hair and kissed her. "And are you glad to see me, mother?"

"Am I glad to see you? It's like the dead comin' to life. I thought I'd lost you forever, John, my son, my darlin' boy!" she answered, hugging him strenuously.

"I couldn't live without seeing you, mother," he said. He meant it, too, or thought he did, although he had not seen her for ten years.

"You've grown so tall, John, and are such a fine gentleman! And you *are* a gentleman now, John, ain't you—sure enough? Nobody knows the old story?"

"Well, mother, I've taken a man's chance in life, and have tried to make the most of it; and I haven't felt under any obligation to spoil it by raking up old stories that are best forgotten. There are the dear old books: have they been read since I went away?"

"No, honey, there's be'n nobody to read 'em, excep' Rena, an' she don't take to books quite like you did. But I've kep' 'em dusted clean, an' kep' the moths an' the bugs out; for I hoped you'd come back some day, an' knowed you'd like to find 'em all in their places, jus' like you left 'em."

"That's mighty nice of you, mother. You could have done no more if you had loved them for themselves. But where is Rena? I saw her on the street to-day, but she didn't know me from Adam; nor did I guess it was she until she opened the gate and came into the yard."

"I've be'n so glad to see you that I'd fergot about her," answered the mother. "Rena, oh, Rena!"

The girl was not far away; she had been standing in the next room, listening intently to every word of the conversation, and only kept from coming in by a certain constraint that made a brother whom she had not met for so many years seem almost as much a stranger as if he had not been connected with her by any tie.

"Yes, mamma," she answered, coming forward.

"Rena, child, here's yo'r brother John, who's come back to see us. Tell 'im howdy."

As she came forward, Warwick rose, put his arm around her waist, drew her toward him, and kissed her affectionately, to her evident embarrassment. She was a tall girl, but he towered above her in quite a protecting fashion; and she thought with a thrill how fine it would be to have such a brother as this in the town all the time. How proud she would be, if she could but walk up the street with such a brother by her side! She could then hold up her head before all the world, oblivious to the glance of pity or contempt. She felt a very pronounced respect for this tall gentleman who held her blushing face between his hands and looked steadily into her eyes.

"You're the little sister I used to read stories to, and whom I promised to come and see some day. Do you remember how you cried when I went away?"

"It seems but yesterday," she answered. "I've still got the dime you gave me."

He kissed her again, and then drew her down beside him on the sofa, where he sat enthroned between the two loving and excited women. No king could have received more sincere or delighted homage. He was a man, come into a household of women,—a man of whom they were proud, and to whom they looked up with fond reverence. For he was not only a son,—a brother—but he represented to them the world from which circumstances had shut them out, and to which distance lent even more than its usual enchantment; and they felt nearer to this far-off world because of the glory which Warwick reflected from it.

"You're a very pretty girl," said Warwick, regarding his sister thoughtfully. "I followed you down Front Street this morning, and scarcely took my eyes off you all the way; and yet I didn't know you, and scarcely saw your face. You improve on acquaintance; to-night, I find you handsomer still."

"Now, John," said his mother, expostulating mildly, "you'll spile her, if you don't min'."

The girl was beaming with gratified vanity. What woman would not find such praise sweet from almost any source, and how much more so from this great man, who, from his exalted station in the world, must surely know the things whereof he spoke! She believed every word of it; she knew it very well indeed, but wished to hear it repeated and itemized and emphasized.

"No, he won't, mamma," she asserted, "for he's flattering me. He talks as if I was some rich young lady, who lives on the Hill,"—the Hill was the aristocratic portion of the town,—"instead of a poor"—

"Instead of a poor young girl, who has the hill to climb," replied her brother, smoothing her hair with his hand. Her hair was long and smooth and glossy, with a wave like the ripple of a summer breeze upon the surface of still water. It was the girl's great pride, and had been sedulously cared for. "What lovely hair! It has just the wave that yours lacks, mother."

"Yes," was the regretful reply, "I've never be'n able to git that wave out. But her hair's be'n took good care of, an' there ain't nary gal in town that's got any finer."

"Don't worry about the wave, mother. It's just the fashionable ripple, and becomes her immensely. I think my little Albert favors his Aunt Rena somewhat."

"Your little Albert!" they cried. "You've got a child?"

"Oh, yes," he replied calmly, "a very fine baby boy."

They began to purr in proud contentment at this information, and made minute inquiries about the age and weight and eyes and nose and other important details of this precious infant. They inquired more coldly about the child's mother, of whom they spoke with greater warmth when they learned that she was dead. They hung breathless on Warwick's words as he related briefly the story of his life since he had left, years before, the house behind the cedars—how with a stout heart and an abounding hope he had gone out into a seemingly hostile world, and made fortune stand and deliver. His story had for the women the charm of an escape from captivity, with all the thrill of a pirate's tale. With the whole world before him, he had remained in the South, the land of his fathers, where, he conceived, he had an inalienable birthright. By some good chance he had escaped military service in the Confederate army, and, in default of older and more experienced men, had undertaken, during the rebellion, the management of a large estate, which had been left in the hands of women and slaves. He had filled the place so acceptably, and employed his leisure to such advantage, that at the close of the war he found himself—he was modest enough to think, too, in default of a better man—the husband of the orphan daughter of the gentleman who had owned the plantation, and who had lost his life upon the battlefield. Warwick's wife was of good family, and in a more settled condition of society it would not have been easy for a young man of no visible antecedents to win her hand. A year or two later, he had taken the oath of allegiance, and had been admitted to the South Carolina bar. Rich in his wife's right, he had been able to practice his profession upon a high plane, without the worry of sordid cares, and with marked success for one of his age.

"I suppose," he concluded, "that I have got along at the bar, as elsewhere, owing to the lack of better men. Many of the good lawyers were killed in the war, and most of the remainder were disqualified; while I had the advantage of being alive, and of never having been in arms against the government. People had to have lawyers, and they gave me their business in preference to the carpet-baggers. Fortune, you know, favors the available man."

His mother drank in with parted lips and glistening eyes the story of his adventures and the record of his successes. As Rena listened, the narrow walls that hemmed her in seemed to draw closer and closer, as though they must crush her. Her brother watched her keenly. He had been talking not only to inform the women, but with a deeper purpose, conceived since his morning walk, and deepened as he had followed, during his narrative, the changing expression of Rena's face and noted her intense interest in his story, her pride in his successes, and the occasional wistful look that indexed her self-pity so completely.

"An' I s'pose you're happy, John?" asked his mother.

"Well, mother, happiness is a relative term, and depends, I imagine, upon how nearly we think we get what we think we want. I have had my chance and haven't thrown it away, and I suppose I ought to be happy. But then, I have lost my wife, whom I loved very dearly, and who loved me just as much, and I'm troubled about my child."

"Why?" they demanded. "Is there anything the matter with him?"

"No, not exactly. He's well enough, as babies go, and has a good enough nurse, as nurses go. But the nurse is ignorant, and not always careful. A child needs some woman of its own blood to love it and look after it intelligently."

Mis' Molly's eyes were filled with tearful yearning. She would have given all the world to warm her son's child upon her bosom; but she knew this could not be.

"Did your wife leave any kin?" she asked with an effort.

"No near kin; she was an only child."

"You'll be gettin' married again," suggested his mother.

"No," he replied; "I think not."

Warwick was still reading his sister's face, and saw the spark of hope that gleamed in her expressive eye.

"If I had some relation of my own that I could take into the house with me," he said reflectively, "the child might be healthier and happier, and I should be much more at ease about him."

The mother looked from son to daughter with a dawning apprehension and a sudden pallor. When she saw the yearning in Rena's eyes, she threw herself at her son's feet.

"Oh, John," she cried despairingly, "don't take her away from me! Don't take her, John, darlin', for it'd break my heart to lose her!"

Rena's arms were round her mother's neck, and Rena's voice was sounding in her ears. "There, there, mamma! Never mind! I won't leave you, mamma—dear old mamma! Your Rena'll stay with you always, and never, never leave you."

John smoothed his mother's hair with a comforting touch, patted her withered cheek soothingly, lifted her tenderly to her place by his side, and put his arm about her.

"You love your children, mother?"

"They're all I've got," she sobbed, "an' they cos' me all I had. When the las' one's gone,

I'll want to go too, for I'll be all alone in the world. Don't take Rena, John; for if you do, I'll never see her again, an' I can't bear to think of it. How would you like to lose yo'r one child?"

"Well, well, mother, we'll say no more about it. And now tell me all about yourself, and about the neighbors, and how you got through the war, and who's dead and who's married—and everything."

The change of subject restored in some degree Mis' Molly's equanimity, and with returning calmness came a sense of other responsibilities.

"Good gracious, Rena!" she exclaimed. "John's be'n in the house an hour, and ain't had nothin' to eat yet! Go in the kitchen an' spread a clean tablecloth, an' git out that 'tater pone, an' a pitcher o' that las' kag o' persimmon beer, an' let John take a bite an' a sip."

Warwick smiled at the mention of these homely dainties. "I thought of your sweet-potato pone at the hotel to-day, when I was at dinner, and wondered if you'd have some in the house. There was never any like yours; and I've forgotten the taste of persimmon beer entirely."

Rena left the room to carry out her hospitable commission. Warwick, taking advantage of her absence, returned after a while to the former subject.

"Of course, mother," he said calmly, "I wouldn't think of taking Rena away against your wishes. A mother's claim upon her child is a high and holy one. Of course she will have no chance here, where our story is known. The war has wrought great changes, has put the bottom rail on top, and all that—but it hasn't wiped *that* out. Nothing but death can remove that stain, if it does not follow us even beyond the grave. Here she must forever be—nobody! With me she might have got out into the world; with her beauty she might have made a good marriage; and, if I mistake not, she has sense as well as beauty."

"Yes," sighed the mother, "she's got good sense. She ain't as quick as you was, an' don't read as many books, but she's keerful an' painstakin', an' always tries to do what's right. She's be'n thinkin' about goin' away somewhere an' tryin' to git a school to teach, er somethin', sence the Yankees have started 'em everywhere for po' white folks an' niggers too. But I don't like fer her to go too fur."

"With such beauty and brains," continued Warwick, "she could leave this town and make a place for herself. The place is already made. She has only to step into my carriage—after perhaps a little preparation— and ride up the hill which I have had to climb so painfully. It would be a great pleasure to me to see her at the top.

But of course it is impossible—a mere idle dream. *Your* claim comes first; her duty chains her here."

"It would be so lonely without her," murmured the mother weakly, "an' I love her so—my las' one!"

"No doubt—no doubt," returned Warwick, with a sympathetic sigh; "of course you love her. It's not to be thought of for a moment. It's a pity that she couldn't have a chance here—but how could she! I had thought she might marry a gentleman, but I dare say she'll do as well as the rest of her friends—as well as Mary B., for instance, who married— Homer Pettifoot, did you say? Or maybe Billy Oxendine might do for her. As long as she has never known any better, she'll probably be as well satisfied as though she married a rich man, and lived in a fine house, and kept a carriage and servants, and moved with the best in the land."

The tortured mother could endure no more. The one thing she desired above all others was her daughter's happiness. Her own life had not been governed by the highest standards, but about her love for her beautiful daughter there was no taint of selfishness. The life her son had described had been to her always the ideal but unattainable life. Circumstances, some beyond her control, and others for which she was herself in a measure responsible, had put it forever and inconceivably beyond her reach. It had been conquered by her son. It beckoned to her daughter. The comparison of this free and noble life with the sordid existence of those around her broke down the last barrier of opposition.

"O Lord!" she moaned, "what shall I do without her? It'll be lonely, John—so lonely!"

"You'll have your home, mother," said Warwick tenderly, accepting the implied surrender. "You'll have your friends and relatives, and the knowledge that your children are happy. I'll let you hear from us often, and no doubt you can see Rena now and then. But you must let her go, mother,— it would be a sin against her to refuse."

"She may go," replied the mother brokenly. "I'll not stand in her way—I've got sins enough to answer for already."

Warwick watched her pityingly. He had stirred her feelings to unwonted depths, and his sympathy went out to her. If she had sinned, she had been more sinned against than sinning, and it was not his part to judge her. He had yielded to a sentimental weakness in deciding upon this trip to Patesville. A matter of business had brought him within a day's journey of the town, and an over-mastering impulse had compelled him to seek the mother who had given him birth and the old town where he had spent the earlier years of his life. No one would have acknowledged sooner than he the folly of this visit. Men who have elected to govern their lives by principles of abstract right and reason, which happen, perhaps, to be at variance with what society considers equally right and reasonable, should, for fear of complications, be careful about descending from the lofty heights of logic to the common level of impulse and affection. Many years before, Warwick, when a lad of eighteen, had shaken the dust of the town from his feet, and with it, he fondly thought, the blight of his inheritance, and had achieved elsewhere a worthy career. But during all these years of absence he had cherished a tender feeling for his mother, and now again found himself in her house, amid the familiar surroundings of his childhood. His visit had brought joy to his mother's heart, and was now to bring its shrouded companion, sorrow. His mother had lived her life, for good or ill. A wider door was open to his sister—her mother must not bar the entrance.

"She may go," the mother repeated sadly, drying her tears. "I'll give her up for her good."

"The table's ready, mamma," said Rena, coming to the door.

The lunch was spread in the kitchen, a large unplastered room at the rear, with a wide fireplace at one end. Only yesterday, it seemed to Warwick, he had sprawled upon the hearth, turning sweet potatoes before the fire, or roasting groundpeas in the ashes; or, more often, reading, by the light of a blazing pine-knot or lump of resin, some volume from the bookcase in the hall. From Bulwer's novel, he had read the story of Warwick the Kingmaker, and upon leaving home had chosen it for his own. He was a new man, but he had the blood of an old race, and he would select for his own one of its worthy names. Overhead loomed the same smoky beams, decorated with what might have been, from all appearances, the same bunches of dried herbs, the same strings of onions and red peppers. Over in the same corner stood the same spinning-wheel, and through the open door of an adjoining room he saw the old loom, where in childhood he had more than once thrown the shuttle. The kitchen was different from the stately dining-room of the old colonial mansion where he now lived; but it was homelike, and it was familiar. The sight of it moved his heart, and he felt for the moment a sort of a blind anger against the fate which made it necessary that he should visit the home of his childhood, if at all, like a thief in the night. But he realized, after a moment, that the thought was pure sentiment, and that one who had gained so much ought not to complain if he must give up a little. He who would climb the heights of life must leave even the pleasantest valleys behind.

"Rena," asked her mother, "how'd you like to go an' pay yo'r brother John a visit? I guess I might spare you for a little while."

The girl's eyes lighted up. She would not have gone if her mother had wished her to stay, but she would always have regarded this as the lost opportunity of her life.

"Are you sure you don't care, mamma?" she asked, hoping and yet doubting.

"Oh, I'll manage to git along somehow or other. You can go an' stay till you git homesick, an' then John'll let you come back home."

But Mis' Molly believed that she would never come back, except, like her brother, under cover of the night. She must lose her daughter as well as her son, and this should be the penance for her sin. That her children must expiate as well the sins of their fathers, who had sinned so lightly, after the manner of men, neither she nor they could foresee, since they could not read the future.

The next boat by which Warwick could take his sister away left early in the morning of the next day but one. He went back to his hotel with the understanding that the morrow should be devoted to getting Rena ready for her departure, and that Warwick would visit the household again the following evening; for, as has been intimated, there were several reasons why there should be no open relations between the fine gentleman at the hotel and the women in the house behind the cedars, who, while superior in blood and breeding to the people of the neighborhood in which they lived, were yet under the shadow of some cloud which clearly shut them out from the better society of the town. Almost any resident could have given one or more of these reasons, of which any one would have been sufficient to most of them; and to some of them Warwick's mere presence in the town would have seemed a bold and daring thing.

CRITCAL EYE

▶ For Discussion

a. How significant is it that Warwick has taken "a man's chance in life" to his success? Could his sister, Rena, have taken the same chance alone?

b. Why can't Warwick risk taking his mother into his White world, too? What does his leaving her behind signify?

c. The fact that Warwick has decided to pass as a White person has led him to great success, as he is now respected and revered by all persons. Has he made the right choice? Said differently, is being a part of the majority—the ruling class by birth—worth denouncing one's true heritage?

▶ Re-approaching the Reading

Examine this story alongside of Nella Larsen's *Passing*. What are the similarities? Why are these characters struggling with the issue of race? Why is being something other than what they are so appealing and necessary?

▶ Writing Assignment

Imagine a circumstance where you would denounce your ethnicity and leave behind your family and, for that matter, all that you know. For a chance at the best education and social status, would you walk away from everything and everyone? Or, can you imagine a circumstance where you would give up the advantages afforded one based on skin color, religion, or social grouping—realities that provide ethnic privilege at birth—and willingly become part of another group?

CHAPTER 5

Religion

When I was a kid I used to pray every night for a new bicycle. Then I realized that the Lord doesn't work that way so I stole one and asked him to forgive me.
Emo Phillips

Now, now my good man, this is no time for making enemies.
Voltaire, on his deathbed, to a priest asking that he renounce Satan.

Religion is generally perceived as a belief in and, arguably—maybe more importantly—a reverence for a supernatural power or powers regarded as both the creator and governing body of the universe. A subtler notion of religion is defined as a cause, activity, or principle that is undertaken with conscientious devotion. Almost every person walking the planet has either embraced or been touched by the broad hand of a higher being and the tradition that governs it. While all humans may not believe or follow, none are unaffected by the influence and power of religion. Oddly enough, religion is, like taxes, inescapable.

Historically, religion has appeared in the embracing words and arms of the church; at the same time, at least in some cases, our faiths have harmed as many as they have helped. For some, religion, faith, and spiritual matters provide support for the people. Yet, too often have our faith-based beliefs become blurred with our worldly views on power and dominance. This blending of religion with politics, power, and—as we see as clearly in the 21st century as ever before—"intolerance" demands a converting with the snap of a merciless whip that appears as fanatical as it is blind. Which is accurate? What is the real face of our world's churches, synagogues, mosques, temples, and meeting places where people gather to worship? What happens when the "word" of deities is played out and manipulated by flawed humans who manipulate religious doctrines to fit their own vision of the world? And, moreover, what happens when religious mandates become vexing to the point of oppression? Undoubtedly, the fact that we have various religions is a blessing. But, the judgment that seems to follow—the worldwide bickering that one interpretation of a higher power is better than others—seems as absurd as it is contradictory. Surely the purpose of faith is to bring a sense of reconciliation that humankind cannot explain. As such, if spirituality is an elevation from our secular lives to a higher sense of being, then shouldn't those who so wholeheartedly claim to "believe" denounce the shallow views of politics, financial compensation, rivalry—as well as mores and rules that seem painfully outdated—in an attempt to heal our damaged world?

The selections in this chapter touch different parts of the world and brazenly cross gender lines. For some, faith not only guarantees salvation but also provides the individual with patience and fortitude in a trying world. For others, faith is neither black nor white, but, as we recognize now more than ever before, varied shades of gray that are so very difficult to muddle through.

Religion

GHOST DANCE SONGS

In an effort to defeat the colonizers, indigenous peoples reverted to the power of prayer, ceremony, song, and dance to defeat the White settlers. Indians who practiced the Ghost Dance believed that the ceremony would bring back their dead and make the Whites disappear.

I

My children, when at first I liked the whites,
My children, when at first I liked the whites,
I gave them fruits,
I gave them fruits.

II

Father, have pity on me,
Father, have pity on me;
I am crying for thirst,
I am crying for thirst;
All is gone—I have nothing to eat.
All is gone—I have nothing to eat.

III

My son, let me grasp your hand,
My son, let me grasp your hand,
Says the father,
Says the father.
You shall live,
You shall live,
Says the father,
Says the father.
I bring you a pipe,
I bring you a pipe,
Says the father,
Says the father.
By means of it you shall live,
By means of It you shall live,
Says the father,
Says the father.

IV

My children, my children,
I take pity on those who have been taught,
I take pity on those who have been taught,
Because they push on hard,
Because they push on hard,
Says our father,
Says our father.

V

The whole world is coming,
A nation is coming, a nation is coming,
The Eagle has brought the message to the tribe.
The father says so, the father says so.
Over the whole earth they are coming.
The buffalo are coming, the buffalo are coming.
The Crow has brought the message to the tribe,
The father says so, the father says so.

VI

The spirit host is advancing, they say,
The spirit host is advancing, they say,
They are coming with the buffalo, they say,
They are coming with the buffalo, they say.
They are coming with the new earth, they say,
They are coming with the new earth, they say.

VII

He' yoho' ho! He' yoho' ho!
The yellow-hide, the white skin
I have now put him aside—
I have now put him aside—
I have no more sympathy with him,
I have no more sympathy with him,
He' yoho' ho! He' yoho' ho!

CRITICAL EYE

▶ For Discussion

a. While seemingly passive, colonists viewed all Ghost Dance ceremonies as dangerous, powerful, and a grave threat to "negotiations" between Whites and the Indigenous populations. Why?

b. How are the sentiments expressed by Wooden Leg in "Young Men, Go Out and Fight Them," and those expressed in the Ghost Dance Song similar?

c. How are both texts about what is expected of men in the face of a perceived threat?

▶ Re-approaching the Reading

Examine "The Ghost Dance Song" alongside of the ideas expressed by Marie Poltakin in *Indian Killer*. How are her words true? In what way(s) does America still owe a tremendous debt to all Indigenous peoples?

▶ Writing Assignment

Marie Polatkin from *Indian Killer*, The Ghost Dance ceremonial songs, and Frederick Douglass each make the same crucial point—the forced enslavement and brutality experienced by Africans and Indians has not been forgotten by their ancestors. We are now well into the 21st century; how can we move past these historical hurts?

AUDREY SMEDLY

From RACE IN NORTH AMERICA
The Backing of God and Other Justifications for Conquest

From the very beginnings of English excursions into overseas exploration and trade, the rationale most frequently expressed was that the venture was sanctioned by God. John Hawkins, the earliest and most successful of the English slave traders, once led an expedition of slave ships with names such as *Jesus of Lubeck* and *John the Baptist* (Wright 1965, 9). Not only were ships commonly given names with biblical references, but virtually all also had clerics aboard to bless the expedition. Leaders of expeditions invariably referred to the Lord's blessings and special care for them, his children, in their ships' logs.

Without question, military dominance of the English and their success in ultimately destroying the Indians and their cultures were seen as God's will, no matter how brutal and insensitive the actions and no matter the innocence of the Indian victims. A high degree of self-righteousness and arrogance characterized the religious beliefs, particularly of the Puritans. Offshoots of the Protestant Reformation, they had evolved a sharply focused sense of the nature of salvation and what was needed to achieve it. Their theology relinquished the vast majority of souls on earth to be damned forever. Only the select few would ultimately enter the glorious kingdom of God. These were individuals who adhered strictly to Puritan ideals of proper behavior and laid claims to personal salvation through faith. Knowledge of Christ, including a personal relationship to him, were prerequisites. In their strict division of the world into the saved and the damned, there was no explicit, or intrinsic, requirement for tolerance and understanding of others. Nor was there any commitment to humanistic values that might have inhibited or curtailed the excessive cruelty dispensed to the damned. Instead, the Puritans developed the very convenient belief that all sinners, witches, and savages who opposed the word of God deserved the atrocities inflicted upon them. They were a fitting retribution for their opposition to the civilizing efforts of Christianity.

In the New England area, many settlers rejoiced at the extraordinary reduction of the Indian population from epidemic diseases. John Winthrop, who led the colony in the 1630s, wrote that the smallpox epidemic of 1617 was God's way of "thinning out" the Indian population "to make room for the Puritans." Later, he recorded that the Indians "are neere all dead of the small Poxe, so the Lord hathe cleared our title to what we possess" (quoted in Nash 1972, 136).

According to Louis B. Wright (1965), it was the preachers of England who "induced in public consciousness a sense of mission, a feeling often not put into words but nonetheless strong, that Englishmen had a destiny overseas" (151). These preachers, both Anglican and Puritan, had a powerful influence on the colonization process. From

From *Race in North America: Origin and Evolution of a Worldview* by Smedley, Audrey. Reproduced with permission of Westview Press in the format republish in a book / e-book via Copyright Clearance Center.

their pulpits and in their publications, they exhorted the public to become involved in the colonization of the New World, a region seen as a new Canaan. And the commercial companies and promoters of colonization encouraged the clergy to advertise their schemes.

The English clergy themselves were motivated by a number of considerations, all of which were highly publicized at the time. Chief among these was their desire to thwart the further spread of Catholicism. The success of Spanish proselytizing in the New World was well known; and nothing irked the Protestants so much as the idea of Spain winning the battle for new souls. Economic and political competition with the Spanish intensified these feelings of religious antagonism. The defeat of the Spanish Armada had made the planting of English colonies all the more pressing.

Another important reason for ministerial preachments had to do with the increasingly large numbers of the poor and unemployed who roamed the streets and byways of English cities. Several lines of reasoning led clergymen to advocate the exportation of these "vagabonds" to the new colonies. As educated men, they concluded that England was facing a problem of overpopulation, and there was a need to do something about this demographic situation. Moreover, unemployment was acute in many areas, and existing charitable institutions were hard pressed to provide sufficient services to an expanding impoverished class. The clergy saw colonization as a way of siphoning off an excess of able-bodied workers and putting them to useful labor in the plantations overseas.

Exhortations to send the poor and unemployed off to the colonies should be understood within a wider framework of English, and specifically, Puritan beliefs. Seventeenth-century preachers, we are told, "looked upon idleness and consequent poverty as moral iniquities" (Wright 1965, 152). Those virtues most valued in the Puritan life-style were work, sobriety, thrift, diligence, and honesty. An idle or lazy person would be lacking in all of these traits. Thus, poverty, immorality, and sloth were bound together in the Puritan mind as evils that had to be overcome, if necessary by forced labor. Hoover claims that the Puritans created a new class of evil people, the poor who were seen as "being wicked and outside the bonds of society" (1976, 31). So colonization would not only relieve the poverty at home, but, by putting sinful, idle men and women to work, it would also restore them to the true and proper values of religion and improve their characters.

Finally, Wright (1965) argues that many English clergymen, who "were almost unanimous in supporting colonization in America," (86) were motivated by a sincere desire to save the souls of the heathens of America. They were convinced, and convinced others, that God had commanded them to go forth and preach the gospel. There was no better setting in which to do this than among the indigenes of newly discovered lands. However, this missionary zeal peaked in the early stages of settlement, as we have seen. The Puritans and their church leaders soon concluded that if the savages could not be saved from themselves, their extermination would be a worthy enterprise in the sight of the Lord. This notion of a God-given right to mistreat others, especially for private gain, runs through much of Western culture, and after the emergence of capitalism it became especially acute in North America.

When they were not invoking God's blessings or permission for their mistreatment of the Indians, the colonizers had other rational and pragmatic arguments of particular use for co-opting native lands. One was that the Indians did not make proper use of the land "and thus could be justly deprived of it by the more enterprising English" (Canny 1973, 596).

Such an argument, we have seen, was invoked to force the Irish off their lands. A more pervasive argument was the ancient one of the right of conquest. This was often linked to the religious position and rationalized that since God had chosen the English to find these new shores, he must have wanted them to possess such bountiful land. Conquest was thus God's ordained plan; it was he who had led them thence. The Puritans as God's "chosen people" were responsible merely for carrying out his will.

Though God's supposed will should have been enough, an even more secular and philosophical argument was also proposed, one that derived from some knowledge of the codes of laws of the ancients. John Winthrop expressed this in his reasoning on the Englishman's rights to land. There are, he declared, two types of rights that God has given mankind: natural rights and civil rights. Natural rights were held by all men including those who lived in a state of nature, holding land and resources in common. But when some men began to enclose parcels of land and hold them separate from others, to have a settled habitation on it, and to use domesticated cattle to improve the land, then they acquired civil rights to the land. Since the Indians had not done these things, they gained no civil rights but retained only natural ones. And, since clearly the English had developed superior modes of utilizing land, they enjoyed lawful civil rights that inevitably took precedence over natural rights. Under this argument, superior "civilized" people had legitimate cause to seize land, as long as they left sufficient areas for the "uncivilized" to exercise their natural rights (Thomas 1975).

Partly because of the myths of origin that Americans created for themselves, too few of us have sufficiently noted the cruel and barbaric treatment that the English imposed on the Indians, although the evidence, largely from the pens of the colonists themselves, is overwhelming. The incidents described above—in no way exceptional—attest to extreme and callous brutality and to a policy of treachery and deceit that seems hardly consonant with the English history of concern for the rights of mankind, and even less with England's image of itself as the most "civilized" of the European nations.

Some historians have labored hard to explain this seeming paradox. Although we might accept Nash's psychologically oriented argument that the dehumanization of the Indian was "one means of justifying one's own inhumanity" (1972, 137), this is a somewhat circular or teleological explication that does not reveal much as to underlying causes. Nicholas P. Canny's (1973) explanation follows in a similar vein and is very close to that of Winthrop Jordan (1968). Both refer to the insecurities and uncertainties of the English, and of their need to know who they were in a rapidly changing society and in a setting in which they constantly felt threatened. More evident than such psychological needs, however, were the drives to achieve power and control, to establish and maintain political, economic, and social dominance, all of which arose from an English sense of moral and cultural superiority. The Indians, said Morgan, "presented a challenge . . . to their image of themselves, to their self-esteem, to their conviction of their own superiority over foreigners, and especially over barbarous foreigners like the Irish and the Indians" (1975, 89).

Christian values regarding humane behavior (the Sermon on the Mount, the Golden Rule, the Ten Commandments) had little impact on the minds, the morals, and the consciences of the settlers. Jordan gives a brief analysis of the kind of Christianity that developed among the English after the Protestant Reformation. He shows that it was "altered in the direction of Biblicism, personal piety, individual judgment, and more intense self-scrutiny and internalized control" (1968, 40). The English came to evaluate and judge themselves according to their own individual interpretations of the scriptures. The older institutional and external constraints of Catholicism were replaced with a less certain and more nebulous sense of personal responsibility and control.

Such inner controls, however, were virtually antithetical to the spirits of adventurism and greed for wealth that characterized the English in the seventeenth century and later. English colonists were caught up in a dilemma that might have evoked massive ambivalence, leading to a catatonic inability to take action. Instead, or perhaps because of this, too many of them in the New World opted for the path of moral and ethical duplicity, hypocrisy, and the priority of aggrandizing wealth at no matter what cost. A self-serving moral order had replaced the constraints once exercised by the institutions of family, kinship, class, community, and church. It was not merely self-control that the new settlers sought, it was control over others and over potentially advantageous situations and resources. Jordan's (1968) discussion of an age driven by the twin spirits of adventure and of control euphemistically glosses over this reality. But Morgan's (1975) description of the ruthless, cold-hearted, and avaricious men who led or participated in the Virginia colony leaves us little room for doubt.

CRITICAL EYE

▶ For Discussion

a. When one group conquers or dominates another, is it wrong for the conquering peoples to impose their spiritual practices upon the conquered?

b. Can religion be used as a form of subjugation? How so?

▶ Re-approaching the Reading

Read the excerpt from Alexie's *Indian Killer*. Are the ideas and anger expressed by Marie Polatkin the same sentiments expressed in the Ghost Dance Song?

▶ Writing Assignment

Outside of religion, what other ideologies/practices have been used as tools of "non-violent" domination?

BHARATI MUKHERJEE

A Father

One Wednesday morning in mid-May Mr. Bhowmick woke up as he usually did at 5:43 A.M., checked his Rolex against the alarm clock's digital readout, punched down the alarm (set for 5:45), then nudged his wife awake. She worked as a claims investigator for an insurance company that had an office in a nearby shopping mall. She didn't really have to leave the house until 8:30, but she liked to get up early and cook him a big breakfast. Mr. Bhowmick had to drive a long way to work. He was a naturally dutiful, cautious man, and he set the alarm clock early enough to accommodate a margin for accidents.

While his wife, in a pink nylon negligee she had paid for with her own Master-Card card, made him a new version of French toast from a clipping ("Eggs-cellent Recipes!") Scotchtaped to the inside of a kitchen cupboard, Mr. Bhowmick brushed his teeth. He brushed, he gurgled with the loud, hawking noises that he and his brother had been taught as children to make in order to flush clean not merely teeth but also tongue and palate.

After that he showered, then, back in the bedroom again, he recited prayers in Sanskrit to Kali, the patron goddess of his family, the goddess of wrath and vengeance. In the pokey flat of his childhood in Ranchi, Bihar, his mother had given over a whole bedroom to her collection of gods and goddesses. Mr. Bhowmick couldn't be that extravagant in Detroit. His daughter, twenty-six and an electrical engineer, slept in the other of the two bedrooms in his apartment. But he had done his best. He had taken Woodworking I and II at a nearby recreation center and built a grotto for the goddess. Kali-Mata was eight inches tall, made of metal and painted a glistening black so that the metal glowed like the oiled, black skin of a peasant woman. And though Kali-Mata was totally nude except for a tiny gilt crown and a garland strung together from sinners' chopped off heads, she looked warm, cozy, *pleased,* in her makeshift wooden shrine in Detroit. Mr. Bhowmick had gathered quite a crowd of admiring, fellow woodworkers in those final weeks of decoration.

"Hurry it up with the prayers," his wife shouted from the kitchen. She was an agnostic, a believer in ambition, not grace. She frequently complained that his prayers had gotten so long that soon he wouldn't have time to go to work, play duplicate bridge with the Ghosals, or play the tabla in the Bengali Association's one-Sunday-per-month musical soirees. Lately she'd begun to drain him in a wholly new way. He wasn't praying, she nagged; he was shutting her out of his life. There'd be no peace in the house until she hid Kali-Mata in a suitcase.

She nagged, and he threatened to beat her with his shoe as his father had threatened his mother: it was the thrust and volley of marriage. There was no question of actually taking off a shoe and applying it to his wife's

---

"A Father" by Bharati Mukherjee. Copyright © 1985 by Bharati Mukherjee. Originally published in *Darkness*. Reprinted with permission of the author.

body. She was bigger than he was. And, secretly, he admired her for having the nerve, the agnosticism, which as a college boy in backward Bihar he too had claimed.

"I have time," he shot at her. He was still wrapped in a damp terry towel.

"You have time for everything but domestic life."

It was the fault of the shopping mall that his wife had started to buy pop psychology paperbacks. These paperbacks preached that for couples who could sit down and talk about their "relationship," life would be sweet again. His engineer daughter was on his wife's side. She accused him of holding things in.

"Face it, Dad," she said. "You have an affect deficit."

But surely everyone had feelings they didn't want to talk about or talk over. He definitely did not want to blurt out anything about the sick-in-the-guts sensations that came over him most mornings and that he couldn't bubble down with Alka-Seltzer or smother with Gas-X. The women in his family were smarter than him. They were cheerful, outgoing, more American somehow.

How could he tell these bright, mocking women that in the 5:43 A.M. darkness, he sensed invisible presences: gods and snakes frolicked in the master bedroom, little white sparks of cosmic static crackled up the legs of his pajamas. Something was out there in the dark, something that could invent accidents and coincidences to remind mortals that even in Detroit they were no more than mortal. His wife would label this paranoia and dismiss it. Paranoia, premonition: whatever it was, it had begun to undermine his composure.

Take this morning. Mr. Bhowmick had woken up from a pleasant dream about a man taking a Club Med vacation, and the postdream satisfaction had lasted through the shower, but when he'd come back to the shrine in the bedroom, he'd noticed all at once how scarlet and saucy was the tongue that Kali-Mata stuck out at the world. Surely he had not lavished such alarming detail, such admonitory colors on that flap of flesh.

Watch out, ambulatory sinners. Be careful out there, the goddess warned him, and not with the affection of Sergeant Esterhaus, either.

"French toast must be eaten hot-hot," his wife nagged. "Otherwise they'll taste like rubber."

Mr. Bhowmick laid the trousers of a two-trouser suit he had bought on sale that winter against his favorite tweed jacket. The navy stripes in the trousers and the small, navy tweed flecks in the jacket looked quite good together. So what if the Chief Engineer had already started wearing summer cottons?

"I am coming, I am coming," he shouted back. "You want me to eat hot-hot, you start the frying only when I am sitting down. You didn't learn anything from Mother in Ranchi?"

"Mother cooked French toast from fancy recipes? I mean French Sandwich Toast with complicated filling?"

He came into the room to give her his testiest look. "You don't know the meaning of complicated cookery. And mother had to get the coal fire of the *chula* going first."

His daughter was already at the table. "Why don't you break down and buy her a microwave oven? That's what I mean about sitting down and talking things out." She had finished her orange juice. She took a plastic measure of Slim-Fast out of its can and poured the powder into a glass of skim milk. "It's ridiculous."

Babli was not the child he would have chosen as his only heir. She was brighter certainly than the sons and daughters of the other Bengalis he knew in Detroit, and she had been the only female student in most of her classes at Georgia Tech, but as she sat there in her beige linen business suit, her thick chin dropping into a polka-dotted cravat, he regretted again that she was not the child of his dreams. Babli would be able to help him out moneywise if something happened to him, something so bad that even his pension plans and his insurance policies and his money market schemes wouldn't be enough. But Babli could never comfort him. She wasn't womanly or tender the way that unmarried girls had been in the wistful days of his adolescence. She could sing Hindi film songs, mimicking exactly the high, artificial voice of Lata Mungeshkar, and she had taken two years of dance lessons at Sona Devi's Dance Academy in Southfield, but these accomplishments didn't add up to real femininity. Not the kind that had given him palpitations in Ranchi.

Mr. Bhowmick did his best with his wife's French toast. In spite of its filling of marshmallows, apricot jam and maple syrup, it tasted rubbery. He drank two cups of Darjeeling tea, said, "Well, I'm off," and took off.

All might have gone well if Mr. Bhowmick hadn't fussed longer than usual about putting his briefcase and his trenchcoat in the backseat. He got in behind the wheel of his Oldsmobile, fixed his seatbelt and was just about to turn the key in the ignition when his neighbor, Al Stazniak, who was starting up his Buick Skylark, sneezed. A sneeze at the start of a journey brings bad luck. Al Stazniak's sneeze was fierce, made up of five short bursts, too loud to be ignored.

Be careful out there! Mr. Bhowmick could see the goddess's scarlet little tongue tip wagging at him.

He was a modern man, an intelligent man. Otherwise he couldn't have had the options in life that he did have. He couldn't have given up a good job with perks in Bombay and found a better job with General Motors in Detroit. But Mr. Bhowmick was also a prudent enough man to know that some abiding truth lies bunkered within each wanton Hindu superstition. A sneeze was more than a sneeze. The heedless are carried off in ambulances. He had choices to make. He could ignore the sneeze, and so challenge the world unseen by men. Perhaps Al Stazniak had hay fever. For a sneeze to be a potent omen, surely it had to be unprovoked and terrifying, a thunderclap cleaving the summer skies. Or he could admit the smallness of mortals, undo the fate of the universe by starting over, and go back inside the apartment, sit for a second on the sofa, then restart his trip.

Al Stazniak rolled down his window. "Everything okay?"

Mr. Bhowmick nodded shyly. They weren't really friends in the way neighbors can sometimes be. They talked as they parked or pulled out of their adjacent parking stalls. For all Mr. Bhowmick knew, Al Stazniak had no legs. He had never seen the man out of his Skylark.

He let the Buick back out first. Everything was okay, yes, please. All the same he undid his seatbelt. Compromise, adaptability, call it what you will. A dozen times a day he made these small trade-offs between new-world reasonableness and old-world beliefs.

While he was sitting in his parked car, his wife's ride came by. For fifty dollars a month, she was picked up and dropped off by a hard up, newly divorced woman who worked at a florist's shop in the same mall. His wife came out the front door in brown K-Mart pants and a burgundy windbreaker. She waved to him, then slipped into the passenger seat of the florist's rusty Japanese car.

He was a metallurgist. He knew about rust and ways of preventing it, secret ways, thus far unknown to the Japanese.

Babli's fiery red Mitsubishi was still in the lot. She wouldn't leave for work for another eight minutes. He didn't want her to know he'd been undone by a sneeze. Babli wasn't tolerant of superstitions. She played New Wave music in her tapedeck. If asked about Hinduism, all she'd ever said to her American friends was that "it's neat." Mr. Bhowmick had heard her on the phone years before. The cosmos balanced on the head of a snake was like a beachball balanced on the snout of a circus seal. "This Hindu myth stuff," he'd heard her say, "is like a series of super graphics."

He'd forgiven her. He could probably forgive her anything. It was her way of surviving high school in a city that was both native to her, and alien.

There was no question of going back where he'd come from. He hated Ranchi. Ranchi was no place for dreamers. All through his teenage years, Mr. Bhowmick had dreamed of success abroad. What form that success would take he had left vague. Success had meant to him escape from the constant plotting and bitterness that wore out India's middle class.

Babli should have come out of the apartment and driven off to work by now. Mr. Bhowmick decided to take a risk, to dash inside and pretend he'd left his briefcase on the coffee table.

When he entered the living room, he noticed Babli's spring coat and large vinyl pocketbook on the sofa. She was probably sorting through the junk jewelry on her dresser to give her business suit a lift. She read hints about dressing in women's magazines and applied them to her person with seriousness. If his luck held, he could sit on the sofa, say a quick prayer and get back to the car without her catching on.

It surprised him that she didn't shout out from her bedroom, "Who's there?" What if he had been a rapist?

Then he heard Babli in the bathroom. He heard unladylike squawking noises. She was throwing up, A squawk, a spitting, then the horrible gurgle of a waterfall.

A revelation came to Mr. Bhowmick. A woman vomiting in the privacy of the bathroom could mean many things. She was coming down with the flu. She was nervous about a meeting. But Mr. Bhowmick knew at once that his daughter, his untender, unloving daughter whom he couldn't love and hadn't tried to love, was not, in the larger world of Detroit, unloved. Sinners are everywhere, even in the bosom of an upright, unambitious family like the Bhowmicks. It was the goddess sticking out her tongue at him.

The father sat heavily on the sofa, shrinking from contact with her coat and pocketbook. His brisk, bright engineer daughter was pregnant. Someone had taken time to make love to her. Someone had thought her tender, feminine. Someone even now was perhaps mooning over her. The idea excited him. It was so grotesque and wondrous. At twenty-six Babli had found the man of her dreams; whereas at twenty-six Mr. Bhowmick had given up on truth, beauty . . .

Mr. Bhowmick's tweed-jacketed body sagged against the sofa cushions. Babli would abort, of course. He knew his Babli. It was the only possible option if she didn't want to bring shame to the Bhowmick family. All the same, he could see a chubby baby boy on the rug, crawling to his granddaddy. Shame like that was easier to hide in Ranchi. There was always a barren womb sanctified by marriage that could claim sudden fructifying by the goddess Parvati. Babli would do what she wanted. She was headstrong and independent and he was afraid of her.

Babli staggered out of the bathroom. Damp stains ruined her linen suit, was the first time he had seen his daughter look ridiculous, quite unprofessional. She didn't come into the living room to investigate the noises he'd made. He glimpsed her shoeless stockinged feet flip-flop on collapsed arches down the hall to her bedroom.

"Are you all right?" Mr. Bhowmick asked, standing in the hall. "Do you need Sinutab?"

She wheeled around. "What're you doing here?"

He was the one who should be angry. "I'm feeling poorly too," he said. "I'm taking the day off."

"I feel fine, "Babli said.

Within fifteen minutes Babli had changed her clothes and left. Mr. Bhowmick had the apartment to himself all day. All day for praising or cursing the life that had brought him along with its other surprises an illegitimate grandchild.

It was his wife that he blamed. Coming to America to live had been his wife's idea. After the wedding, the young Bhowmicks had spent two years in Pittsburgh on his student visa, then gone back home to Ranchi for nine years. Nine crushing years. Then the job in Bombay had come through. All during those nine years his wife had screamed and wept. She was a woman of wild, progressive ideas—she'd called them her "American" ideas—and she'd been martyred by her neighbors for them. American *memsahib. Markin mem, Markin mem.* In bazaars the beggar boys had trailed her and hooted. She'd done provocative things. She'd hired a *chamar* woman who by caste rules was forbidden to cook for higher caste families, especially for widowed mothers of decent men. This had caused a blowup in the neighborhood. She'd made other, lesser errors. While other wives shopped and cooked every day, his wife had cooked the whole week's menu on weekends.

"What's the point of having a refrigerator, then?" She'd been scornful of the Ranchi women.

His mother, an old-fashioned widow, had accused her of trying to kill her by poisoning. "You are in such a hurry? You want to get rid of me quick-quick so you can go back to the States?"

Family life had been turbulent.

He had kept aloof, inwardly siding with his mother. He did not love his wife now, and he had not loved her then. In any case, he had not defended her. He felt some affection, and he felt guilty for having shunned her during those unhappy years. But he had thought of it then as revenge. He had wanted to marry a beautiful woman. Not being a young man of means, only a young man with prospects, he had had no right to yearn for pure beauty. He cursed his fate and after a while, settled for a barrister's daughter, a plain girl with a wide, flat plank of a body and myopic eyes. The barrister had sweetened the deal by throwing in an all-expenses-paid two years' study at Carnegie Tech to which Mr. Bhowmick had been admitted. Those two years had changed his wife from pliant girl to an ambitious woman.

It was his wife who had forced him to apply for permanent resident status in the U.S. even though he had a good job in Ranchi as a government engineer. The putting together of documents for the immigrant visa had been a long and humbling process. He had had to explain to a chilly clerk in the Embassy that, like most Indians of his generation, he had no birth certificate. He had to swear out affidavits, suffer through police checks, bribe orderlies whose job it was to move his dossier from desk to desk. The decision, the clerk had advised him, would take months, maybe years. He hadn't dared hope that merit might be rewarded. Merit could collapse under bad luck. It was for grace that he prayed.

While the immigration papers were being processed, he had found the job in Bombay. So he'd moved his mother in with his younger brother's family, and left his hometown for good. Life in Bombay had been lighthearted, almost fulfilling. His wife had thrown herself into charity work with the same energy that

The crazy look that had been in his wife's eyes when she'd shooed away beggar kids was in her eyes again.

"Stop it!" His own boldness overwhelmed him. "Shut up! Babli's pregnant so what? It's your fault, you made us come to the States."

Girls like Babli were caught between rules, that's the point he wished to make. They were too smart, too impulsive for a backward place like Ranchi, but not tough nor smart enough for sex-crazy places like Detroit.

"My fault?" his wife cried. "I told her to do hanky-panky with boys? I told her to shame us like this?"

She got in one blow with the rolling pin. The second glanced off Babli's shoulder and fell on his arm which he had stuck out for his grandson's sake.

"I'm calling the police," Babli shouted. She was out of the rolling pin's range "This is brutality. You can't do this to me."

"Shut up! Shut your mouth, foolish woman." He wrenched the weapon from his wife's fist. He made a show of taking off his shoe to beat his wife on the face.

"What do you know? You don't know anything." She let herself down slowly on a dining chair. Her hair, curled overnight, stood in wild whorls around her head. "Nothing."

"And you do!" He laughed. He remembered her tormentors, and laughed again. He had begun to enjoy himself. Now *he* was the one with the crazy, progressive ideas.

"Your daughter is pregnant, yes," she said, "any fool knows that. But ask her the name of the father. Go, ask."

He stared at his daughter who gazed straight ahead, eyes burning with hate, jaw clenched with fury.

"Babli?"

"Who needs a man?" she hissed. "The father of my baby is a bottle and a syringe. Men louse up your lives. I just want a baby. Oh, don't worry—he's a certified fit donor. No diseases, college graduate, above average, and he made the easiest twenty-five dollars of his life—"

"Like animals," his wife said. For the first time he heard horror in her voice. His daughter grinned at him. He saw her tongue, thick and red, squirming behind her row of perfect teeth.

"Yes, yes, yes," she screamed, "like livestock. Just like animals. You should be happy—that's what marriage is all about, isn't it? Matching bloodlines, matching horoscopes, matching castes, matching, matching, matching . . ." and it was difficult to know if she was laughing or singing, or mocking and like a madwoman.

Mr. Bhowmick lifted the rolling pin high above his head and brought it down hard on the dome of Babli's stomach. In the end, it was his wife who called the police.

had offended the Ranchi women. He was happy to be in a big city at last. Bombay was the Rio de Janeiro of the East; he'd read that in a travel brochure. He drove out to Nariman Point at least once a week to admire the necklace of municipal lights, toss coconut shells into the dark ocean, drink beer at the Oberoi-Sheraton where overseas Indian girls in designer jeans beckoned him in sly ways. His nights were full. He played duplicate bridge, went to the movies, took his wife to Bingo nights at his club. In Detroit he was a lonelier man.

Then the green card had come through. For him, for his wife, and for the daughter who had been born to them in Bombay. He sold what he could sell, and put in his brother's informal trust what he couldn't to save on taxes. Then he had left for America, and one more start.

All through the week, Mr. Bhowmick watched his daughter. He kept furtive notes on how many times she rushed to the bathroom and made hawking, wrenching noises, how many times she stayed late at the office, calling her mother to say she'd be taking in a movie and pizza afterwards with friends.

He had to tell her that he knew. And he probably didn't have much time. She shouldn't be on Slim-Fast in her condition. He had to talk things over with her. But what would he say to her? What position could he take? He had to choose between public shame for the family, and murder.

For three more weeks he watched her and kept his silence. Babli wore shifts to the office instead of business suits, and he liked her better in those garments. Perhaps she was dressing for her young man, not from necessity. Her skin was pale and blotchy by turn. At breakfast her fingers looked stiff, and she had trouble with silverware.

Two Saturdays running, he lost badly at duplicate bridge. His wife scolded him. He had made silly mistakes. When was Babli meeting this man? Where? He must be American; Mr. Bhowmick prayed only that he was white. He pictured his grandson crawling to him, and the grandson was always fat and brown and buttery-skinned, like the infant Krishna. An American son-in-law was a terrifying notion. Why was she not mentioning men, at least, preparing the way for the major announcement? He listened sharply for men's names, rehearsed little lines like, "Hello, Bob, I'm Babli's old man," with a cracked little laugh. Bob, Jack, Jimmy, Tom. But no names surfaced. When she went out for pizza and a movie it was with the familiar set of Indian girls and their strange, unpopular, American friends, all without men. Mr. Bhowmick tried to be reasonable. Maybe she had already gotten married and was keeping it secret. "Well, Bob, you and Babli sure had Mrs. Bhowmick and me going there, heh-heh," he mumbled one night with the Sahas and Ghosals, over cards. "Pardon?" asked Pronob Saha. Mr. Bhowmick dropped two tricks, and his wife glared. "Such stupid blunders," she fumed on the drive back. A new truth was dawning; there would be no marriage for Babli. Her young man probably was not so young and not so available. He must be already married. She must have yielded to passion or been raped in the office. His wife seemed to have noticed nothing. Was he a murderer, or a conspirator? He kept his secret from his wife; his daughter kept her decision to herself.

Nights, Mr. Bhowmick pretended to sleep, but as soon as his wife began her snoring—not real snores so much as loud, gaspy gulpings for breath—he turned on his side and prayed to Kali-Mata.

In July, when Babli's belly had begun to push up against the waistless dress she'd bought herself, Mr. Bhowmick came out of the shower one weekend morning and found the two women screaming at each other. His wife had a rolling pin in one hand. His daughter held up a *National Geographic* as a shield for her head.

CRITICAL EYE

▶ For Discussion

a. In what way(s) is the father's traditional role in his home being undermined? Is this a bad thing? Shouldn't the women in his family be allowed to take advantage of the freedoms granted by their new homeland?

b. The father believes that his wife and daughter have become more American. Why is this a problem for him? What does he believe has been lost culturally? Is there really something wrong, or is this merely a culture clash?

c. Why is the father moved to violence at the end of the story? What is he *really* angry about?

▶ Re-approaching the Reading

How is this story about the difficulties immigrants experience once they arrive in America? How are their traditions challenged? What are they expected to surrender?

▶ Writing Assignment

As much as this is a story about the father's moment of truth, in what ways is this story about the daughter taking her life into her own hands? Is this defining moment traumatic for most parents? If so, why? Also, once independent, do children owe parents their entire future? In short, because they gave us life, do we owe our parents our futures?

MOHAMMED NASEEHU ALI

MALLAM SILE

He was popularly known as *mai tea*, or the tea seller. His shop was situated right in the navel of Zongo Street—a stone's throw from the chief's assembly shed and adjacent to the kiosk where Mansa BBC, the town gossip, sold her provisions. Along with fried eggs and white butter bread, Mallam Sile carried all kinds of beverages: regular black tea, Japanese green tea, Milo, Bournvita, cocoa drink, instant coffee. But on Zongo Street all hot beverages were referred to just as tea, and it was common, therefore, to hear people say, "Mallam Sile, may I have a mug of cocoa tea?" or "Sile, may I have a cup of coffee tea?"

The tea shop had no windows. It was built of *wawa*, a cheap wood easily infested by termites. The floor was uncemented, and heaps of dust rose in the air whenever a customer walked in. Sile protected his merchandise from the dust by keeping everything in plastic bags. An enormous wooden "chop box," the top of which he used as a serving table, covered most of the space in the shop. There was a tall chair behind the chop box for Sile, but he never used it, preferring instead to stand on his feet even when the shop was empty. There were also three benches that were meant to be used only by those who bought tea, though the idle gossips who crowded the shop and never spent any money occupied the seats most of the time.

Old Sile had an irrational fear of being electrocuted and so he'd never tapped electricity into his shack, as was usually done on Zongo Street. Instead, he used kerosene lanterns, three of which hung from the low wooden ceiling. Sile kept a small radio in the shop, and whenever he had no customers he listened, in meditative silence, to the English programs on GBC 2, as though he understood what was being said. Mallam Sile was fluent only in his northern Sisaala tongue, though he understood Hausa—the language of the street's inhabitants—and spoke just enough pidgin to be able to conduct his business.

The mornings were usually slow for the tea seller, as a majority of the street folks preferred the traditional breakfast of *kókó da mása*, or corn porridge with rice cake. But, come evening, the shop was crowded with the street's young men and women, who gossiped and talked about the "latest news" in town. Some came to the shop just to meet their loved ones. During the shop's peak hours—from eight in the evening until around midnight—one could hardly hear oneself talk because of the boisterous chattering that went on. But anytime Mallam Sile opened his mouth to add to a conversation people would say, "Shut up, Sile, what do you know about this?" or "Close your beak, Sile, who told you that?" The tea seller learned to swallow his words, and eventually spoke only when he was engaged in a transaction with a customer. But nothing said or even whispered in the shop escaped his sharp ears.

Mallam Sile was a loner, without kin on the street or anywhere else in the city. He was born in Nanpugu, a small border town in the

---

"Madam Sile" (pp. 149–68) from *The Prophet of Zongo Street* by Mohammed Naseehu Ali. Copyright © 2005 by Mohammed Naseehu Ali. Reprinted by permission of HarperCollins Publishers.

north. He left home at age sixteen, and, all by himself, journeyed more than nine hundred miles in a cow truck to find work down south in Kumasi—the capital city of Ghana's gold-rich Ashanti region.

Within a week of his arrival in the city, Sile landed a job as a house servant. Although his monthly wages were meagre, he sent a portion of them home to his ailing parents, who lived like paupers in their drought-stricken village. Even so, Sile's efforts were not enough to save his parents from the claws of Death, who took them away in their sleep one night. They were found clinging tightly to each other, as if one of them had seen what was coming and had grabbed onto the other so that they could go together.

The young Sile received the news of his parents' death with mixed emotions. He was sad to lose them, of course, but he saw it as a well-deserved rest for them, as they both had been ill and bedridden for many months. Though Sile didn't travel up north to attend their funeral, he sent money for a decent burial. With his parents deceased, Sile suddenly found himself with more money in his hands. He quit his house-servant job and found another, selling iced *kenkey* in Kumasi's central market. Sile kept every pesewa he earned, and two years later he was able to use his savings to open a tea business. It was the first of such establishments on Zongo Street, and would remain the only one for many years to come.

Mallam Sile was short—so short, in fact, that many claimed he was a Pygmy. He stood exactly five feet one inch tall. Although he didn't have the broad, flat nose, poorly developed chin, and round head of the Pygmies, he was stout and hairy all over, as they were. A childhood illness that had caused Sile's vision to deteriorate had continued to plague him throughout his adult life. Yet he refused to go to the hospital and condemned any form of medication, traditional or Western. "God is the one who brings illness, and he is the only true healer"—this was Sile's simple, if rather mystical, explanation.

Sile's small face was covered with a thick, long beard. The wrinkles on his dark forehead and the moistness of his soft, squinted eyes gave him the appearance of a sage, one who had lived through and conquered many adversities in his life. His smile, which stretched from one wrinkled cheek to the other, baring his kola-stained teeth, radiated strength, wisdom, and self-confidence.

Sile wore the same outfit every day: a white polyester djellabah and its matching *wando*, a loose pair of slacks that tied with strings at the waist. He had eight of these suits, and wore a different one each day of the week. Also, his head was perpetually shaved, and he was never without his white embroidered Mecca hat—worn by highly devout Muslims as a reflection of their submission to Allah. Like most of the street's dwellers, Sile owned just one pair of slippers at a time, and replaced them only when they were worn out beyond repair. An unusual birth defect that caused the tea seller to grow an additional toe on each foot had made it impossible for him to find footwear that fit him properly; special slippers were made for him by Anaba the cobbler, who used discarded car tires for the soles of the shoes he made. The rascals of Zongo Street, led by Samadu, the street's most notorious bully, poked at Sile's feet and his slippers, which they called *kalabilwala*, a nonsensical term that no one could understand, let alone translate.

At forty-six, Mallam Sile was still a virgin. He routinely made passes at the divorcées and widows who came to his shop, but none showed any interest in him whatsoever. "What would I do with a dwarf?" the women would ask, feeling ashamed of having had passes made at them by Sile. A couple of them seemed receptive to tea seller Sile's advances, but everyone knew that they were flirting with him only in order to get free tea.

Eventually, Sile resigned himself to his lack of success with women. He was convinced that he would die a virgin. Yet late at night, after all the customers, idlers, and rumormongers had left the shop to seek refuge in their shanties and on their bug-ridden grass mattresses, Sile could be heard singing love songs, hoping that a woman somewhere would respond to his passionate cries:

> A beautiful woman, they say,
> Is like an elephant's meat.
> And only the man with the sharpest knife
> Can cut through.
> That's what they say.
> Young girl, I have no knife,
> I am not a hunter of meat.
> And I am not savage.
> I am only looking for love.
> This is what I say.
> Up north where I am from,
> Young girls are not what they are here.
> Up north where I am from,
> People don't judge you by your knife.
> They look at the size of your heart.
> Young girl, I don't know what you look like.
> I don't know where to look for you.
> I don't even know who you are, young girl.
> All I know is: my heart is aching.
> Oh, oh, oh! My heart is aching for you.

Sile's voice rang with melancholy when he sang his songs. But still the rascals derided him. "When are you going to give up, Sile?" they would say. "Can't you see that no woman would marry you?"

"I have given up on them long, long ago," he would reply. "But I am never going to give up on myself!" "You keep fooling yourself," they told him, laughing.

The rascals' mocking didn't end there. Knowing that Mallam Sile couldn't see properly, they often used fake or banned cedi notes to purchase tea from him at night. The tea seller pinned the useless bills to the walls of his shop as if they were good-luck charms. He believed that it was hunger—and not mischief—that had led the rascals to cheat him. And, since he considered it inhuman to refuse a hungry person food, Mallam Sile allowed them to get away with their frauds.

To cool off the hot tea for his customers, Sile poured the contents of one mug into another, raising one over the other. The rascals would push Sile in the middle of this process, causing the hot liquid to spill all over his arms. The tea seller was never angered by such pranks. He merely grinned and, without saying a word, wiped off the spilled tea and continued to serve his customers. And when the rascals blew out the lanterns in the shop, so as to steal bread and Milo while he was trying to rekindle the light, Sile accepted that, too. He managed to rid his heart of any ill feelings. He would wave his short arms to anyone who walked past his shop, and shout, by way of greeting, "How are the heavens with you, boy?" Sile called everyone "boy," including women and older people, and he hardly ever uttered a sentence without referring to the heavens.

He prided himself on his hard work, and smiled whenever he looked in the mirror and saw his dwarfish body and ailing eyes, two abnormalities that he had learned to love. A few months before the death of his parents, he had come to the conclusion that if Allah had made him any differently he would not have been Mallam Sile—and Mallam Sile was an individual whom Sile's heart, mind, and spirit had come to accept and respect. This created within him a peace that made it possible for him not only to tolerate the rascals' ill treatment but also to forgive them. Though in their eyes Sile was only a buffoon.

One sunny afternoon during the dry season, Mallam Sile was seen atop the roof of his shack with hammers, saws, pliers, and all kinds of building tools. He lingered there all day long like a stray monkey, and by dusk he had dismantled all the aluminum roofing sheets that had once sheltered him and his business. He resumed work early the following morning, and by about one-thirty, before *azafar*, the first of the two afternoon prayers, Sile had no place to call either home or tea shop—he had demolished the shack down to its dusty floor.

At three-thirty, after *la-asar*, the second afternoon worship, Mallam Sile moved his personal belongings and all his tea paraphernalia to a room in the servants' quarters of the chiefs' palace. The room had been arranged for him by the chief's wazir, or right-hand man, who was sympathetic to the tea seller.

During the next two days, Mallam Sile ordered plywood and planks of *odum*, a wood superior to the *wawa* used for the old shop. He also ordered a few bags of cement and truckloads of sand and stones, and immediately began building a new shack, much bigger than the first.

The street folks were shocked by Sile's new building—they wondered where he had got the money to embark on such an enterprise. Sile was rumored to be constructing a mini-market store to compete with Alhaji Saifa, the owner of the street's provision store. (And though the tea seller denied the rumor, it rapidly spread up and down the street, eventually creating bad blood between Sile and Alhaji Saifa.)

It took three days for Mallam Sile to complete work on the new shop's foundation, and an additional three weeks for him to erect the wooden walls and the aluminum roofing sheets. While Sile was busy at work, passersby would call out, "How is the provision store coming?" or "*Mai tea*, how is the mansion coming?" Sile would reply simply, "It is coming well, boy. It will be completed soon, *Inshallah*." He would grin his usual wide grin and wave his short hairy arms, and then return to his work.

Meanwhile, as the days and weeks passed, the street folks grew impatient and somewhat angry at the closing of Sile's shop. The nearest tea shack was three hundred metres away, on Zerikyi Road—and not only that but the owner of the shack, Abongo, was generally abhorred. And for good reason. Abongo, also a northerner, was quite unfriendly even to his loyal customers. He maintained a rigid no-credit policy, and made customers pay him even before they were served. No one was an exception to this policy—even if he or she was dying of hunger. And, unlike Sile, Abongo didn't tolerate idlers or loud conversation in his shop. If a customer persisted in chatting, Abongo reached for the customer's mug, poured the contents in a plastic basin, and refunded his money. He then chased the customer out of the shop, brandishing his bullwhip and cursing after him, "If your mama and papa never teach you manners, I'll teach you some! I'll sew those careless lips of yours together, you bastard son of a bastard woman!"

As soon as work on the shop was completed, Sile left for his home town. Soon afterward, yet another rumor surfaced: it was said that the tea seller had travelled up north in search of "black medicine" for his bad eyesight.

Sile finally returned one Friday evening, some six weeks after he'd begun work on the shop, flanked by a stern woman who looked to be in her late thirties and was three times larger than the tea seller. The woman, whose name was Abeeba, turned out to be Mallam Sile's wife. She was tall and massive, with a face as gloomy as that of someone mourning a dead relative. Like her husband, Abeeba said very little to people in or out of the shop. She, too, grinned and waved her huge arms whenever she greeted people, though, unlike the tea seller, she seemed to have something harder lurking behind her cheerful smile. Abeeba carried herself with the grace and confidence of a lioness, and covered her head and part of her face with an Islamic veil, a practice that had been dropped by most of the married women on Zongo Street.

The rascals asked Sile, when they ran into him at the market, "From where did you get this elephant? Better not get on her bad side; she'll sit on you till you sink into the ground." To this, the tea seller did not say a word.

Exactly one week after Sile's return from his village, he and his wife opened the doors of the new shop to their customers. Among the most talked-about features were the smooth concrete floor and the bright gas lantern that illuminated every corner. In a small wooden box behind the counter, Sile and his wife burned *tularen mayu,* or witches' lavender, a strong yet sweet-smelling incense that doubled as a jinx repellent—to drive bad spirits away from the establishment.

On the first night, the tea shop was so crowded that some customers couldn't find a seat, even with the twelve new metal folding chairs that Sile had bought. The patrons sang songs of praise to the variety of food on the new menu, which included meat pies, brown bread, custard, and Tom Brown, an imported grain porridge. Some of the patrons even went so far as to thank Sile and his wife for relieving them of "Abongo's nastiness." But wise old Sile, who was as familiar with the street folks' cynicism as he was with the palms of his hands, merely nodded and grinned his sheepish grin. He knew that, despite their praise, and despite the smiles they flashed his way, some customers were at that very moment thinking of ways to cheat him.

While Sile prepared the tea and food, Abeeba served and collected the money. Prior to the shop's reopening, Abeeba had tried to convince her husband that they, too, should adopt Abongo's no-credit policy. Sile had quickly frowned upon the idea, claiming that it was inhumane to do such a thing.

The tea seller and his wife debated the matter for three days before they came to a compromise. They agreed to extend credit, but only in special cases and also on condition that the debtor swear by the Koran to pay on time; if a debtor didn't make a payment, he or she would not be given any credit in the future. But, even with the new policy in place, it wasn't long before some of the customers reverted to their old habits and began skipping payments. Then an encounter between Abeeba and one of the defaulters changed everything.

What took place was this: Samadu, the pugnacious sixteen-year-old whose fame had reached every corner of the city, was the tough guy of Zongo Street. He was of medium height, muscular, and a natural-born athlete. For nine months running, no one in the neighborhood had managed to put Samadu's back to the ground in the haphazard wrestling contests held beside the central market's latrine. Samadu's "power" was such that parents paid him to protect their children from other bullies at school. He was also known for having tortured and even killed the livestock of the adults who denounced him.

If they didn't have pets or domestic animals, he harassed their children for several days until he was appeased with cash or goods. Some parents won Samadu's friendship for their children by bribing him with gifts of money, food, or clothing.

Samadu, of course, was deeply in debt to Mallam Sile—he owed him eighty cedis, about four dollars. Early one Tuesday morning, Mallam Sile's wife showed up at Samadu's house to collect the money. Abeeba had tried to collect the debt amicably, but after her third futile attempt she had suggested to Sile that they use force to persuade the boy to pay. Sile had responded by telling his wife, "Stay out of that boy's way—he is dangerous. If he has decided not to pay, let him keep it. He will be the loser in the end."

"But, Mallam, it is an insult what he is doing," Abeeba argued. "I think people to whom we have been generous should only be generous in return. I am getting fed up with their ways, and the sooner the folks here know that even the toad gets sick of filling his belly with the same dirty pond water every day, the better!" Though Sile wasn't sure what his wife meant, he let the matter drop.

When Abeeba arrived at Samadu's house, a number of housewives and young women were busily doing their morning chores in and around the compound—some sweeping and stirring up dust, others fetching water from the tap in the compound's center or lighting up charcoal pots to warm the food left over from the previous night. Abeeba greeted them politely and asked to be shown to the tough guy's door. The women tried to turn Abeeba away, as they feared that Samadu would humiliate her in some way. But Abeeba insisted that she had important business with him, and so the housewives reluctantly directed her to Samadu's room, which, like all the young men's rooms, was situated just outside the main compound.

The usual tactic that the street's teen-age boys used when fighting girls or women was to strip them of the wrapper around their waist, knowing that they would be reluctant to continue fighting half-naked. But Abeeba had heard young boys in the shop discussing Samadu's bullying ways and had come prepared for anything. She wore a sleeveless shirt and a pair of tight-fitting khaki shorts, and, for the first time ever, she had left her veil at home.

"You rogue! If you call yourself a man, come out and pay your debt!" Abeeba shouted, as she pounded on Samadu's door.

"Who do you think you are, ruining my sleep because of some useless eighty cedis?" Samadu screamed from inside.

"The money may be useless, but it is certainly worthier than you, and that's why you haven't been able to pay, you rubbish heap of a man!" Abeeba's voice was coarse and full of menace. The veins on her neck stood out, like those of the *juju* fighters at the annual wrestling contest. Her eyes moved rapidly inside her head, as though she were having a fit of some sort.

One of the onlookers, a famished-looking housewife, pleaded with the tea seller's wife, "Go back to your house, woman. Don't fight him, he will disgrace you in public." Another woman in the background added, "What kind of a woman thinks she can fight a man? Be careful, oh!"

Abeeba didn't pay any attention to the women's admonitions. Just then, a loud bang was heard inside the room. The door swung open, and Samadu stormed out, his face red with anger. "No one gets away with insulting me. No one!" he shouted. There was a line of dried drool on his right cheek, and whitish mucus had gathered in the corners of his eyes. "You ugly elephant-woman. After I am done with you today, you'll learn a lesson or two about why women don't grow beards!"

"Ha, you teach me a lesson? You?" Abeeba said. "I, too, will educate you about the need to have money in your pocket before you flag the candy man!" With this, she lunged at Samadu.

The women placed their palms on their breasts, and their bodies shook with dread. "Where are the men on the street? Come and separate the fight, oh! Men, come out, oh!" they shouted. The children in the compound, though freshly aroused from sleep, hopped about excitedly, as if they were watching a ritual. Half of them called out, *"Piri pirin-pi!,"* while the other half responded, *"Wein son!,"* as they chanted and cheered for Samadu.

Samadu knew immediately that if he engaged Abeeba in a wrestling match she would use her bulky mass to force him to the ground. His strategy, therefore, was to throw punches and kicks from a safe distance, thereby avoiding close contact. But Abeeba was a lot quicker than he imagined, and she managed to dodge the first five punches he threw. He threw a sixth punch, and missed. He stumbled over his own foot when he tried to connect the seventh, and landed inches from Abeeba. With blinding quickness, she seized him by the sleeping wrapper tied around his neck and began to punch him. The exuberant crowd was hushed by this unexpected turn of events.

But Samadu wasn't heralded as the street's tough guy for nothing. He threw a sharp jab at Abeeba's stomach and succeeded in releasing himself from her grip by deftly undoing the knot of his sleeping cloth. He was topless now, clad only in a pair of corduroy knickers. He danced on his feet, swung his arms, and moved his torso from side to side, the way true boxers do. The crowd got excited again and picked up the fight song, *"Piri pirin-pi, Wein son! Piri pirin-pi, Wein son!"* Some among them shouted "Ali! Ali! Ali!" as Samadu danced and pranced, carefully avoiding Abeeba, who watched his movements with the keenness of a hungry lioness.

The women in the crowd went from holding their breasts to slapping their massive thighs. They jumped about nervously, moving their bodies in rhythm to the chants. The boys booed Abeeba, calling her all sorts of names for the beasts of the jungle. "Destroy that elephant!" they shouted.

The harder the crowd cheered for Samadu, the fancier his footwork became. He finally threw a punch that landed on Abeeba's left shoulder, though she seemed completely unfazed and continued to chase him around the small circle created by the spectators. When Samadu next threw his fist, Abeeba anticipated it. She dodged, then grabbed his wrist and twisted his arm with such force that he let out a high-pitched cry: "*Wayyo* Allah!" The crowd gasped as the tough guy attempted to extricate himself from Abeeba's grip. He tightened all the muscles in his body and craned his neck. But her strength was just too much for him.

The crowd booed, "Wooh, ugly rhinoceros." Then, in a sudden, swift motion, Abeeba lifted the tough guy off the ground, raised him above her head (the crowd booed louder), and dumped him back down like a sack of rice. She then jumped on top of him and began to whack him violently.

The women, now frantic, shouted, "Where are the men in this house?" Men, come out, oh! There is a fight!"

A handful of men came running to the scene, followed by many more a few minutes later.

Meanwhile, with each punch Abeeba asked, "Where is our money?"

"I don't have it, and wouldn't pay even if I did!" Samadu responded. The men drew nearer and tried to pull Abeeba off, but her grip on Samadu's waistband was too firm. The men pleaded with Abeeba to let go. "I will not release him until he pays us back our money!" she shouted. "And if he doesn't I'll drag his ass all the way to the Zongo police station."

On hearing this, an elderly man who lived in Samadu's compound ran inside the house; he returned a few minutes later with eighty cedis, which he placed in the palm of Abeeba's free hand. With one hand gripping Samadu's waistband, she used the fingers of the other to flip and count the money. Once she was sure the amount was right, she released the boy, giving him a mean, hard look as she left. The crowd watched silently, mouths agape, as though they had just witnessed something from a cinema reel.

Mallam Sile was still engaged in his morning *zikhr*, or meditation, when Abeeba returned to the shack. He, of course, had no inkling of what had taken place. Later, when Abeeba told him that Samadu had paid the money he owed, the tea seller, though surprised, didn't think to ask how this had happened. In his naïveté, he concluded that Samadu had finally been entered by the love and fear of God. Abeeba's news therefore confirmed Mallam Sile's long-standing belief that every man was capable of goodness, just as he was capable of evil.

The tea seller's belief was further solidified when he ran into Samadu a fortnight later. The tough guy greeted him politely, something he had never done before. When Mallam Sile related this to his wife, she restrained herself from telling him the truth. Abeeba knew that Sile would be quite displeased with her methods. Just a week ago, he had spoken to her about the pointlessness of using fire to put out fire, of how it "worsens rather than extinguishes the original flame." Abeeba prayed that no one else would tell her husband about her duel with Samadu, although the entire city seemed to know about it by now. Tough guys from other neighborhoods came to the tea shop just to steal a glance at the woman who had conquered the tough guy of Zongo Street.

Then one night during the fasting month of Ramadan, some two months after the fight, a voice in Mallam Sile's head asked, "Why is everyone calling my wife 'the man checker'? How come people I give credit to suddenly pay me on time? Why am I being treated with such respect, even by the worst and most stubborn rascals on the street?" Sile was lying in bed with his wife when these questions came to him. But, in his usual fashion, he didn't try to answer them. Instead, he drew in a deep breath and began to pray. He smiled and thanked Allahu-Raheemu, the Merciful One, for curing the street folks of the prejudice they had nursed against him for so long. Mallam Sile also thanked Allah for giving his neighbors the will and the courage to finally accept him just as he was created. He flashed a grin in the darkness and moved closer to his slumbering wife. He buried his small body in her massive, protective frame and soon fell into a deep, dreamless sleep.

CRITICAL EYE

▶ For Discussion

a. What commentary is the author making about relying on faith and taking a situation into one's own hands?

b. If Mallam had come to know the truth about why everyone's treatment toward him changed so drastically, could he still consider himself a *man*?

c. Indeed, men hold the power throughout many lands worldwide, but why is it that Mallam, although a man by birthright, is treated with so little respect?

▶ Re-approaching the Reading

Considering that, generally, women are not celebrated for aggressive or overly "manish" behavior, make the argument that Mallam's wife has overstepped her boundary as a woman.

▶ Writing Assignment

Is it important for a man to assert himself physically in order to be taken seriously? If so, why? Why are the rules for manhood so specific? What is at stake for them should they fall short?

Religion

THE BOOK OF MATTHEW

THE SERMON ON THE MOUNT

5

And seeing the multitudes, he went up into a mountain: and when he was set, his disciples came unto him:

2 And he opened his mouth, and taught them, saying,

3 Blessed *are* the poor in spirit: for theirs is the kingdom of heaven.

4 Blessed *are* they that mourn: for they shall be comforted.

5 Blessed *are* the meek: for they shall inherit the earth.

6 Blessed *are* they which do hunger and thirst after righteousness: for they shall be filled.

7 Blessed *are* the merciful: for they shall obtain mercy.

8 Blessed *are* the pure in heart: for they shall see God.

9 Blessed *are* the peacemakers: for they shall be called the children of God.

10 Blessed *are* they which are persecuted for righteousness' sake: for theirs is the kingdom of heaven.

11 Blessed are ye, when *men* shall revile you, and persecute *you*, and shall say all manner of evil against you falsely, for my sake.

12 Rejoice, and be exceedingly glad: for great is your reward in heaven: for so persecuted they the prophets which were before you.

13 Ye are the salt of the earth: but if the salt have lost his savor, wherewith shall it be salted? It is thenceforth good for nothing, but to be cast out, and to be trodden under foot of men.

14 Ye are the light of the world. A city that is set on a hill cannot be hid.

15 Neither do men light a candle, and put it under a bushel, but on a candlestick; and it giveth light unto all that are in the house.

16 Let your light so shine before men, that they may see your good works, and glorify your Father which is in heaven.

17 Think not that I am come to destroy the law, or the prophets: I am not come to destroy, but to fulfil.

18 For verily I say unto you, Till heaven and earth pass, one jot or one tittle shall in no wise pass from the law, till all be fulfilled.

19 Whosoever therefore shall break one of these least commandments, and shall teach men so, he shall be called the least in the kingdom of heaven: but whosoever shall do and teach *them*, the same shall be called great in the kingdom of heaven.

20 For I say unto you, That except your righteousness shall exceed *the righteousness* of the scribes and Pharisees, ye shall in no case enter into the kingdom of heaven.

21 Ye have heard that it was said by them of old time, Thou shalt not kill; and whosoever shall kill shall be in danger of the judgment:

22 But I say unto you, That whosoever is angry with his brother without a cause shall be in danger of the judgment: and whosoever shall say to his brother, Raca, shall be in danger of the council: but whosoever shall say, Thou fool, shall be in danger of hell fire.

23 Therefore if thou bring thy gift to the altar, and there rememberest that thy brother hath aught against thee;

24 Leave there thy gift before the altar, and go thy way; first be reconciled to thy brother, and then come and offer thy gift.

25 Agree with thine adversary quickly, while thou art in the way with him; lest at any time the adversary deliver thee to the judge, and the judge deliver thee to the officer, and thou be cast into prison.

26 Verily I say unto thee, Thou shalt by no means come out thence, till thou hast paid the uttermost farthing.

27 Ye have heard that it was said by them of old time, Thou shall not commit adultery:

28 But I say unto you, That whosoever looketh on a woman to lust after her hath committed adultery with her already in his heart.

29 And if thy right eye offend thee, pluck it out, and cast *it* from thee: for it is profitable for thee that one of thy members should perish, and not *that* thy whole body should be cast into hell.

30 And if thy right hand offend thee, cut it off, and cast *it* from thee: for it is profitable for thee that one of thy members should perish, and not *that* thy whole body should be cast into hell.

31 It hath been said, Whosoever shall put away his wife, let him give her a writing of divorcement:

32 But I say unto you, That whosoever shall put away his wife, saving for the cause of fornication, causeth her to commit adultery: and whosoever shall marry her that is divorced committeth adultery.

33 Again, ye have heard that it hath been said by them of old time, Thou shall not forswear thyself, but shalt perform unto the Lord thine oaths:

34 But I say unto you, Swear not at all; neither by heaven; for it is God's throne:

35 Nor by the earth; for it is his footstool: neither by Jerusalem; for it is the city of the great King.

36 Neither shalt thou swear by thy head, because thou canst not make one hair white or black.

37 But let your communication be, Yea, yea; Nay, nay: for whatsoever is more than these cometh of evil.

38 Ye have heard that it hath been said, An eye for an eye, and a tooth for a tooth:

39 But I say unto you, That ye resist not evil: but whosoever shall smite thee on thy right cheek, turn to him the other also.

40 And if any man will sue thee at the law, and take away thy coat, let him have *thy* cloak also.

41 And whosoever shall compel thee to go a mile, go with him twain.

42 Give to him that asketh thee, and from him that would borrow of thee turn not thou away.

43 Ye have heard that it hath been said, Thou shalt love thy neighbor, and hate thine enemy.

44 But I say unto you, Love your enemies, bless them that curse you, do good to them that hate you, and pray for them which despitefully use you, and persecute you;

45 That ye may be the children of your Father which is in heaven: for he maketh his sun to rise on the evil and on the good, and sendeth rain on the just and on the unjust.

46 For if ye love them which love you, what reward have ye? do not even the publicans do the same?

Religion

47 And if ye salute your brethren only, what do ye more *than others?* do not even the publicans so?

48 Be ye therefore perfect, even as your Father which is in heaven is perfect.

6

Take heed that ye do not do your alms before men, to be seen of them: otherwise ye have no reward of your Father which is in heaven.

2 Therefore when thou doest *thine* alms, do not sound a trumpet before thee, as the hypocrites do in the synagogues and in the streets, that they may have glory of men. Verily I say unto you, They have their reward.

3 But when thou doest alms, let not thy left hand know what thy right hand doeth:

4 That thine alms may be in secret: and thy Father which seeth in secret himself shall reward thee openly.

5 And when thou prayest, thou shalt not be as the hypocrites *are:* for they love to pray standing in the synagogues and in the corners of the streets, that they may be seen of men. Verily I say unto you, They have their reward.

6 But thou, when thou prayest, enter into thy closet, and when thou hast shut thy door, pray to thy Father which is in secret, and thy Father which seeth in secret shall reward thee openly.

7 But when ye pray, use not vain repetitions, as the heathen *do:* for they think that they shall be heard for their much speaking.

8 Be not ye therefore like unto them: for your Father knoweth what things ye have need of, before ye ask him.

9 After this manner therefore pray ye: Our father which art in heaven, Hallowed be thy name.

10 Thy kingdom come. Thy will be done in earth, as it *is* in heaven.

11 Give us this day our daily bread.

12 And forgive us our debts, as we forgive our debtors.

13 And lead us not into temptation, but deliver us from evil: For thine is the kingdom, and the power, and the glory, for ever. Amen.

14 For if ye forgive men their trespasses, your heavenly Father will also forgive you:

15 But if ye forgive not men their trespasses, neither will your Father forgive your trespasses.

16 Moreover when ye fast, be not, as the hypocrites, of a sad countenance: for they disfigure their faces, that they may appear unto men to fast. Verily I say unto you, They have their reward.

17 But thou, when thou fastest, anoint thine head, and wash thy face;

18 That thou appear not unto men to fast, but unto thy Father which is in secret: and thy Father which seeth in secret shall reward thee openly.

19 Lay not up for yourselves treasures upon earth, where moth and rust doth corrupt, and where thieves break through and steal:

20 But lay up for yourselves treasures in heaven, where neither moth nor rust doth corrupt, and where thieves do not break through nor steal:

21 For where your treasure is, there will your heart be also.

22 The light of the body is the eye: if therefore thine eye be single, thy whole body shall be full of light.

23 But if thine eye be evil, thy whole body shall be full of darkness. If therefore the light that is in thee be darkness, how great is that darkness!

24 No man can serve two masters: for either he will hate the one, and love the other; or else he will hold to the one, and despise the other. Ye cannot serve God and mammon.

25 Therefore I say unto you, Take no thought for your life, what ye shall eat, or what ye shall drink; nor yet for your body, what ye shall put on. Is not the life more than meat, and the body than raiment?

26 Behold the fowls of the air: for they sow not, neither do they reap, nor gather into barns; yet your heavenly Father feedeth them. Are ye not much better than they?

27 Which of you by taking thought can add one cubit unto his stature?

28 And why take ye thought for raiment? Consider the lilies of the field, how they grow; they toil not, neither do they spin:

29 And yet I say unto you, That even Solomon in all his glory was not arrayed like one of these.

30 Wherefore, if God so clothe the grass of the field, which today is, and tomorrow is cast into the oven, *shall he* not much more *clothe* you, O ye of little faith?

31 Therefore take no thought, saying, What shall we eat? or, What shall we drink? or, Wherewithal shall we be clothed?

32 (For after all these things do the Gentiles seek:) for your heavenly Father knoweth that ye have need of all these things.

33 But seek ye first the kingdom of God, and his righteousness; and all these things shall be added unto you.

34 Take therefore no thought for the morrow: for the morrow shall take thought for the things of itself. Sufficient unto the day *is* the evil thereof.

7

Judge not, that ye be not judged.

2 For with what judgment ye judge, ye shall be judged: and with what measure ye mete, it shall be measured to you again.

3 And why beholdest thou the mote that is in thy brother's eye, but considerest not the beam that is in thine own eye?

4 Or how wilt thou say to thy brother, Let me pull out the mote out of thine eye; and, behold, a beam *is* in thine own eye?

5 Thou hypocrite, first cast out the beam out of thine own eye; and then shalt thou see clearly to cast out the mote out of thy brother's eye.

6 Give not that which is holy unto the dogs, neither cast ye your pearls before swine, lest they trample them under their feet, and turn again and rend you.

7 Ask, and it shall be given you; seek, and ye shall find; knock, and it shall be opened unto you:

8 For every one that asketh receiveth; and he that seeketh findeth; and to him that knocketh it shall be opened.

9 Or what man is there of you, whom if his son ask bread, will he give him a stone?

10 Or if he ask a fish, will he give him a serpent?

11 If ye then, being evil, know how to give good gifts unto your children, how much more shall your Father which is in heaven give good things to them that ask him?

12 Therefore all things whatsoever ye would that men should do to you, do ye even so to them: for this is the law and the prophets.

13 Enter ye in at the strait gate: for wide *is* the gate, and broad *is* the way, that leadeth to destruction, and many there be which go in thereat:

14 Because strait *is* the gate, and narrow *is* the way, which leadeth unto life, and few there be that find it.

15 Beware of false prophets, which come to you in sheep's clothing, but inwardly they are ravening wolves.

16 Ye shall know them by their fruits. Do men gather grapes of thorns, or figs of thistles?

17 Even so every good tree bringeth forth good fruit; but a corrupt tree bringeth forth evil fruit.

18 A good tree cannot bring forth evil fruit, neither *can* a corrupt tree bring forth good fruit.

19 Every tree that bringeth not forth good fruit is hewn down, and cast into the fire.

20 Wherefore by their fruits ye shall know them.

21 Not every one that saith unto me, Lord, Lord, shall enter into the kingdom of heaven; but he that doeth the will of my Father which is in heaven.

22 Many will say to me in that day, Lord, Lord, have we not prophesied in thy name? and in thy name have cast out devils? and in thy name done many wonderful works?

23 And then will I profess unto them, I never knew you: depart from me, ye that work iniquity.

24 Therefore whosoever heareth these sayings of mine, and doeth them, I will liken him unto a wise man, which built his house upon a rock:

25 And the rain descended, and the floods came, and the winds blew, and beat upon that house; and it fell not: for it was founded upon a rock.

26 And every one that heareth these sayings of mine, and doeth them not, shall be likened unto a foolish man, which built his house upon the sand:

27 And the rain descended, and the floods came, and the winds blew, and beat upon that house; and it fell: and great was the fall of it.

28 And it came to pass, when Jesus had ended these sayings, the people were astonished at his doctrine:

29 For he taught them as *one* having authority, and not as the scribes.

Critical Eye

▶ For Discussion

a. One goal of this speech is to promise a sense of judgment and justice. To whom are the judgment and justice promised, and why were these images so important to convey?

b. Why is it so very important for human beings to believe that there is another world that is better than this one?

c. This passage is specific in many ways, favoring the weak over the powerful and the poor over the rich. Why, then, are we so obsessed with power and wealth?

▶ Re-approaching the Reading

Read this text alongside the selection from the Koran. What are the similarities?

▶ Writing Assignment

What would be the value of people using their diverging faiths to bring them together as opposed to keeping them separate?

THE PROPHET MOHAMMED
From
THE KORAN

The Believer

In the Name of God, the Compassionate, the Merciful

Hāmōn. This Book is revealed by God, the Mighty One, the All-knowing, who forgives sin and accepts repentance.

His punishment is stern, and His bounty infinite. There is no god but Him. All shall return to Him.

None but the unbelievers dispute the revelations of God. Do not be deceived by their prosperous dealings in the land. Long before them the people of Noah denied Our revelations, and so did the factions after them. Every nation strove to slay their apostle, seeking with false arguments to refute the truth; but I smote them, and how stern was My punishment! Thus shall the word of your Lord be fulfilled concerning the unbelievers: they are the heirs of the Fire.

Those who bear the Throne and those who stand around it give glory to their Lord and believe in Him. They implore forgiveness for the faithful, saying: "Lord, you embrace all things with Your mercy and Your knowledge. Forgive those that repent and follow Your path. Shield them from the scourge of Hell. Admit them, Lord, to the gardens of Eden which You have promised them, together with all the righteous among their fathers, their spouses, and their descendants. You are the Almighty, the Wise One. Deliver them from all evil. He whom You will deliver from evil on that day will surely earn Your mercy. That is the supreme triumph."

But to the unbelievers a voice will cry: "God's abhorrence of you is greater than your hatred of yourselves. You were called to the Faith, but you denied it."

They shall say: "Lord, twice have You made us die, and twice have You given us life. We now confess our sins. Is there no way out?"

They shall be answered: "This is because when God was invoked alone, you disbelieved; but when you were bidden to serve other gods besides Him you believed in them. Today judgement rests with God, the Most High, the Supreme One."

It is He who reveals His signs to you, and sends down sustenance from the sky for you. Yet none takes heed except the repentant. Pray, then, to God and worship none but Him, however much the unbelievers may dislike it.

Exalted and throned on high, He lets the Spirit descend at His behest on those of His servants whom He chooses, that He may warn them of the day when they shall meet Him; the day when they shall rise up from their graves with nothing hidden from God. And who shall reign supreme on that day? God, the One, the Almighty.

"The Believer" from *The Koran* translated by N. J. Dawood (Penguin Classics 1956, Fifth revised edition 1990). Copyright © N. J. Daewood, 1956, 1959, 1966, 1968, 1974, 1990, 1993, 1997, 1999, 2003. Reproduced by permission of Penguin Books Ltd.

On that day every soul shall be paid back according to what it did. On that day none shall be wronged. Swift is God's reckoning.

Forewarn them of the approaching day, when men's hearts will leap up to their throats and choke them; when the wrongdoers will have neither friend nor intercessor to be heard. He knows the furtive look and the secret thought. God will judge with fairness, but the idols to which they pray besides Him can judge nothing. God alone hears all and observes all.

Have they never journeyed through the land and seen what was the end of those who have gone before them, nations far greater in prowess and in splendour? God scourged them for their sins, and from God they had none to protect them. That was because their apostles had come to them with clear revelations and they denied them. So God smote them. Mighty is God, and stern His retribution.

We sent forth Moses with Our signs and with clear authority to Pharaoh, Haman, and Korah. But they said: "A sorcerer, a teller of lies."

And when he brought them the Truth from Ourself, they said: "Put to death the sons of those who share his faith, and spare only their daughters." Futile were the schemes of the unbelievers.

Pharaoh said: "Let me slay Moses, and then let him invoke his god! I fear that he will change your religion and spread disorder in the land."

Moses said: "I take refuge in my Lord and in your Lord from every tyrant who denies the Day of Reckoning."

But one of Pharaoh's kinsmen, who in secret was a true believer, said: "Would you slay a man merely because he says: 'My Lord is God'? He has brought you evident signs from your Lord. If he is lying, may his lie be on his head; but if he is speaking the truth, a part at least of what he threatens will smite you. God does not guide the lying transgressor. Today you are the masters, my people, illustrious throughout the earth. But who will save us from the might of God when it bears down upon us?"

Pharaoh said: "I have told you what I think. I will surely guide you to the right path."

He who was a true believer said: "I warn you, my people, against the fate which overtook the factions: the people of Noah, 'Ad, and Thamūd, and those that came after them. God does not seek to wrong His servants.

"I warn you, my people, against the day when men will cry out to one another, when you will turn and flee, with none to defend you against God. He whom God confounds shall have none to guide him. Long before this, Joseph came to you with veritable signs, but you never ceased to doubt them; and when he died you said: 'After him God will never send another apostle.' Thus God confounds the doubting transgressor. Those who dispute God's revelations, with no authority vouchsafed to them, are held in deep abhorrence by God and by the faithful. Thus God seals up the heart of every scornful tyrant."

Pharaoh said to Haman: "Build me a tower that I may reach the highways—the very highways—of the heavens, and look upon the god of Moses. I am convinced that he is lying."

Thus was Pharaoh seduced by his foul deeds, and he was turned away from the right path. Pharaoh's cunning led to nothing but perdition.

He who was a true believer said: "Follow me, my people, that I may guide you to the right path. My people, the life of this world is a fleeting comfort, but the life to come is an everlasting mansion. Those that do evil shall be rewarded with like evil; but those that have faith and do good works, both men and women, shall enter the gardens of Paradise and therein receive blessings without number.

"My people, how is it that I call you to salvation, while you call me to the Fire? You bid me deny God and serve other gods I know nothing of; while I exhort you to serve the Almighty, the Benignant One. Indeed, the gods to whom you call me can be invoked neither in this world nor in the hereafter. To God we shall return. The transgressors are the heirs of the Fire.

"Bear in mind what I have told you. To God I commend myself. God is cognizant of all His servants."

God delivered him from the evils which they planned, and a grievous scourge encompassed Pharaoh's people. They shall be brought before the Fire morning and evening, and on the day the Hour strikes, a voice will cry: "Mete out to the people of Pharaoh the sternest punishment!"

And when they argue in the Fire, the humble will say to those who deemed themselves mighty: "We have been your followers: will you now ward off from us some of these flames?" But those who deemed themselves mighty will reply: "Here are all of us now. God has judged His servants."

And those in the Fire will say to the keepers of Hell: "Implore your Lord to relieve our torment for one day!"

"But did your apostles not come to you with undoubted signs?" they will ask.

"Yes," they will answer. And their keepers will say: "Then offer your prayers." But vain shall be the prayers of the unbelievers.

We shall help Our apostles and the true believers both in this world and on the day when the witnesses rise to testify. On that day no excuse will avail the guilty. The Curse shall be their lot, and the scourge of the hereafter.

We gave Moses Our guidance and the Israelites the Book to inherit: a guide and an admonition to men of understanding. Therefore have patience; God's promise is surely true. Implore forgiveness for your sins, and celebrate the praise of your Lord evening and morning.

As for those who dispute the revelations of God, with no authority vouchsafed to them, they nurture in their hearts ambitions they shall never attain. Therefore seek refuge in God; it is He that hears all and observes all.

Surely, the creation of the heavens and the earth is greater than the creation of man; yet most men have no knowledge.

The blind and the seeing are not equal, nor are the wicked the equal of those that have faith and do good works. Yet do you seldom give thought.

The Hour of Doom is sure to come: of this there is no doubt; and yet most men do not believe.

Your Lord has said: "Call on me and I will answer you. Those that disdain My service shall enter Hell with all humility."

It was God who made for you the night to rest in and the day to give you light. God is bountiful to men, yet most men do not give thanks.

Such is God your Lord, the Creator of all things. There is no god but Him. How then can you turn away from Him? Yet even thus the men who deny God's revelations turn away from Him.

It is God who has made the earth a dwelling-place for you, and the sky a ceiling. He has moulded your bodies into a comely shape and provided you with good things.

Such is God, your Lord. Blessed be God, Lord of the Universe.

He is the Living One; there is no god but Him. Pray to Him, then, and worship none besides Him. Praise be to God, Lord of the Universe!

Say: "I am forbidden to serve your idols, now that clear proofs have been given me from my Lord. I am commanded to surrender myself to the Lord of the Universe."

It was He who created you from dust, then from a little germ, and then from a clot of blood. He brings you infants into the world; you reach manhood, then decline into old age (though some of you die young), so that you may complete your appointed term and grow in wisdom.

It is He who ordains life and death. If He decrees a thing, He need only say: "Be," and it is.

Do you not see how those who dispute the revelations of God turn away from the right path? Those who have denied the Book and the message We sent through Our apostles shall realize the truth hereafter: when, with chains and shackles round their necks, they shall be dragged through scalding water and burnt in the fire of Hell.

They will be asked: "Where are the gods whom you have served besides God?"

"They have forsaken us," they will reply. "Indeed, they were nothing, those gods to whom we prayed." Thus God confounds the unbelievers.

And they will be told: "That is because on earth you took delight in falsehoods, and led a wanton life. Enter the gates of Hell and stay therein for ever. Evil is the home of the arrogant."

Therefore have patience: God's promise is surely true. Whether We let you glimpse in some measure the scourge We threaten them with, or call you back to Us before We smite them, to Us they shall return.

We sent forth other apostles before your time; of some We have already told you, of others We have not yet told you. None of those apostles could bring a sign except by God's leave. And when God's will was done, justice prevailed and there and then the disbelievers lost.

It is God who has provided you with beasts, that you may ride on some and eat the flesh of others. You put them to many uses; they take you where you wish to go, carrying you by land as ships carry you by sea.

He reveals to you His signs. Which of God's signs do you deny?

Have they never journeyed through the land and seen what was the end of those who have gone before them? More numerous were they in the land, and far greater in prowess and in splendour; yet all their labours proved of no avail to them.

When their apostles brought them veritable signs they proudly boasted of their own knowledge; but soon the scourge at which they scoffed encompassed them. And when they beheld Our might they said: "We now believe in God alone. We deny the idols which We served besides Him."

But their new faith was of no use to them, when they beheld Our might: such being the way of God with His creatures; and there and then the unbelievers lost.

CRITICAL EYE

▶ For Discussion

a. Are there any similarities between Islam and Christianity? If so, why do we struggle to reconcile the two? For that matter, why do we struggle reconciling all faiths?

b. How important is faith to an individual's development?

▶ Re-approaching the Reading

For nations where Islam is the dominant religion, there is no separation between the ruling/political body or the faith that governs the land. How does that compare with a country such as the United States, where we have a separation between church and state?

▶ Writing Assignment

Why, in your opinion, does there appear to be such conflict between Islam and other faiths?

THOMAS PAINE

AGE OF REASON

Part I

Luxembourg, 8th Pluviose, Second Year of the French Republic, one and indivisible. January 27, O. S. 1794.

To My Fellow-Citizens of the United States of America:

I put the following work under your protection. It contains my opinions upon Religion. You will do me the justice to remember, that I have always strenuously supported the Right of every Man to his own opinion, however different that opinion might be to mine. He who denies to another this right, makes a slave of himself to his present opinion, because he precludes himself the right of changing it.

The most formidable weapon against errors of every kind is Reason. I have never used any other, and I trust I never shall.

Your affectionate friend and fellow-citizen,

Thomas Paine

It has been my intention, for several years past, to publish my thoughts upon religion. I am well aware of the difficulties that attend the subject, and from that consideration, had reserved it to a more advanced period of life. I intended it to be the last offering I should make to my fellow-citizens of all nations, and that at a time when the purity of the motive that induced me to it, could not admit of a question, even by those who might disapprove the work.

The circumstance that has now taken place in France, of the total abolition of the whole national order of priesthood, and of everything appertaining to compulsive systems of religion, and compulsive articles of faith, has not only precipitated my intention, but rendered a work of this kind exceedingly necessary, lest in the general wreck of superstition, of false systems of government, and false theology, we lose sight of morality, of humanity, and of the theology that is true.

As several of my colleagues, and others of my fellow-citizens of France have given me the example of making their voluntary and individual profession of faith, I also will make mine; and I do this with all that sincerity and frankness with which the mind of man communicates with itself.

I believe in one God, and no more; and I hope for happiness beyond this life.

I believe in the equality of man; and I believe that religious duties consist in doing justice, loving mercy, and endeavoring to make our fellow-creatures happy.

But, lest it should be supposed that I believe many other things in addition to these, I shall, in the progress of this work, declare the things I do not believe, and my reasons for not believing them.

I do not believe in the creed professed by the Jewish church, by the Roman church, by the Greek church, by the Turkish church, by the Protestant church, nor by any church that I know of. My own mind is my own church.

All national institutions of churches, whether Jewish, Christian or Turkish, appear to me no other than human inventions set up to terrify and enslave mankind, and monopolize power and profit.

I do not mean by this declaration to condemn those who believe otherwise; they have the same right to their belief as I have to mine. But it is necessary to the happiness of man, that he be mentally faithful to himself. Infidelity does not consist in believing, or in disbelieving; it consists in professing to believe what he does not believe.

It is impossible to calculate the moral mischief, if I may so express it, that mental lying has produced in society. When a man has so far corrupted and prostituted the chastity of his mind, as to subscribe his professional belief to things he does not believe, he has prepared himself for the commission of every other crime. He takes up the trade of a priest for the sake of gain, and in order to qualify himself for that trade, he begins with a perjury. Can we conceive any thing more destructive to morality than this?

Soon after I had published the pamphlet Common Sense, in America, I saw the exceeding probability that a revolution in the system of government would be followed by a revolution in the system of religion. The adulterous connection of church and state, wherever it had taken place, whether Jewish, Christian, or Turkish, had so effectually prohibited by pains and penalties, every discussion upon established creeds, and upon first principles of religion, that until the system of government should be changed, those subjects could not be brought fairly and openly before the world; but that whenever this should be done, a revolution in the system of religion would follow. Human inventions and priestcraft would be detected; and man would return to the pure, unmixed and unadulterated belief of one God, and no more.

Every national church or religion has established itself by pretending some special mission from God, communicated to certain individuals. The Jews have their Moses; the Christians their Jesus Christ, their apostles and saints; and the Turks their Mahomet, as if the way to God was not open to every man alike.

Each of those churches shows certain books, which they call revelation, or the word of God. The Jews say that their word of God was given by God to Moses, face to face; the Christians say, that their word of God came by divine inspiration; and the Turks say, that their word of God (the Koran) was brought by an angel from Heaven. Each of those churches accuses the other of unbelief; and for my own part, I disbelieve them all.

As it is necessary to affix right ideas to words, I will, before I proceed further into the subject, offer some observations on the word revelation. Revelation, when applied to religion, means something communicated immediately from God to man.

No one will deny or dispute the power of the Almighty to make such a communication, if he pleases. But admitting, for the sake of a case, that something has been revealed to a certain person, and not revealed to any other person, it is revelation to that person only. When he tells it to a second person, a second to a third, a third to a fourth, and so on, it ceases to be a revelation to all those persons. It is revelation to the first person only, and hearsay to every other, and consequently they are not obliged to believe it.

It is a contradiction in terms and ideas, to call anything a revelation that comes to us at second-hand, either verbally or in writing. Revelation is necessarily limited to the first communication—after this, it is only an account of something which that person says was a revelation made to him; and though he may find himself obliged to believe it, it cannot be incumbent on me to believe it in the same manner; for it was not a revelation made to me, and I have only his word for it that it was made to him.

When Moses told the children of Israel that he received the two tables of the commandments from the hand of God, they were not obliged to believe him, because they had no other authority for it than his telling them so; and I have no other authority for it than some historian telling me so. The commandments carrying no internal evidence of divinity with them; they contain some good moral precepts, such as any man qualified to be a lawgiver, or a legislator, could produce himself, without having recourse to supernatural intervention.*

> *It is, however, necessary to accept the declamation which says that God visits the sins of the fathers upon the children it is contrary to every principle of moral justice.

When I am told that the Koran was written in Heaven, and brought to Mahomet by an angel, the account comes too near the same kind of hearsay evidence and second-hand authority as the former. I did not see the angel myself, and, therefore, I have a right not to believe it.

When also I am told that a woman, called the Virgin Mary, said, or gave out, that she was with child without any cohabitation with a man, and that her betrothed husband, Joseph, said that an angel told him so, I have a right to believe them or not; such a circumstance required a much stronger evidence than their bare word for it; but we have not even this—for neither Joseph nor Mary wrote any such matter themselves—it is only reported by others that they said so—it is hearsay upon hearsay, and I do not chose to rest my belief upon such evidence.

It is, however, not difficult to account for the credit that was given to the story of Jesus Christ being the son of God. He was born when the heathen mythology had still some fashion and repute in the world, and that mythology had prepared the people for the belief of such a story. Almost all the extraordinary men that lived under the heathen mythology were reputed to be the sons of some of their gods. It was not a new thing, at that time, to believe a man to have been celestially begotten; the intercourse of gods with women was then a matter of familiar opinion. Their Jupiter, according to their accounts, had cohabited with hundreds: the story, therefore, had nothing in it either new, wonderful, or obscene; it was conformable to the opinions that then prevailed among the people called Gentiles, or Mythologists, and it was those people only that believed it. The Jews who had kept strictly to the belief of one God, and no more, and who had always rejected the heathen mythology, never credited the story.

It is curious to observe how the theory of what is called the Christian Church sprung out of the tail of the heathen mythology. A direct incorporation took place in the first instance, by making the reputed founder to be celestially begotten. The trinity of gods that then followed was no other than a reduction of the former plurality, which was about twenty or thirty thousand; the statue of Mary succeeded the statue of Diana of Ephesus; the deification of heroes changed into the canonization of saints; the Mythologists had gods for everything; the Christian Mythologists had saints for everything; the church became as crowded with the one, as the Pantheon had been with the other, and Rome was the place of both. The Christian theory is little else than the idolatry of the ancient Mythologists, accommodated to the purposes of power and revenue; and it yet remains to reason and philosophy to abolish the amphibious fraud.

Nothing that is here said can apply, even with the most distant disrespect, to the real character of Jesus Christ. He was a virtuous and an amiable man. The morality that he preached and practiced was of the most benevolent kind; and though similar systems of morality had been preached by Confucius, and by some of the Greek philosophers, many years before; by the Quakers since; and by many good men in all ages, it has not been exceeded by any.

Jesus Christ wrote no account of himself, of his birth, parentage, or anything else; not a line of what is called the New Testament is of his writing. The history of him is altogether the work of other people; and as to the account given of his resurrection and ascension, it was the necessary counterpart to the story of his birth. His historians having brought him into the world in a supernatural manner, were obliged to take him out again in the same manner, or the first part of the story must have fallen to the ground.

The wretched contrivance with which this latter part is told exceeds every thing that went before it. The first part, that of the miraculous conception, was not a thing that admitted of publicity; and therefore the tellers of this part of the story had this advantage, that though they might not be credited, they could not be detected. They could not be expected to prove it, because it was not one of those things that admitted of proof, and it was impossible that the person of whom it was told could prove it himself.

But the resurrection of a dead person from the grave, and his ascension through the air, is a thing very different as to the evidence it admits of, to the invisible conception of a child in the womb. The resurrection and ascension, supposing them to have taken place, admitted of public and ocular demonstration, like that of the ascension of a balloon, or the sun at noon-day, to all Jerusalem at least. A thing which everybody is required to believe, requires that the proof and evidence of it should be equal to all, and universal; and as the public visibility of this last related act was the only evidence that could give sanction to the former part, the whole of it falls to the ground, because that evidence never was given. Instead of this, a small number of persons, not more than eight or nine, are introduced as proxies for the whole world, to say they saw it, and all the rest of the world are called upon to believe it. But it appears that Thomas did not believe the resurrection, and, as they say, would not believe without having ocular and manual demonstration himself. So neither will I, and the reason is equally as good for me, and for every other person, as for Thomas.

It is in vain to attempt to palliate or disguise this matter. The story, so far as relates to the supernatural part, has every mark of fraud and imposition stamped upon the face of it. Who were the authors of it is as impossible for us now to know, as it is for us to be assured that the books in which the account is related were written by the persons whose names they bear; the best surviving evidence we now have respecting this affair is the Jews. They are regularly descended from the people who lived in the times this resurrection and ascension is said to have happened, and they say, it is not true. It has long appeared to me a strange inconsistency to cite the Jews as a proof of the truth of the story. It is just the same as if a man were to say, I will prove the truth of what I have told you, by producing the people who say it is false.

That such a person as Jesus Christ existed, and that he was crucified, which was the mode of execution at that day, are historical relations strictly within the limits of probability. He preached most excellent morality, and the equality of man; but he preached also against the corruptions and avarice of the Jewish priests, and this brought upon him the hatred and vengeance of the whole order of priesthood. The accusation which those priests brought against him was that of sedition and conspiracy against the Roman government, to which the Jews were then subject and tributary; and it is not improbable that the Roman government might have some secret apprehensions of the effects of his doctrine, as well as the Jewish priests; neither is it improbable that Jesus Christ had in contemplation the delivery of the Jewish nation from the bondage of the Romans. Between the two, however, this virtuous reformer and revolutionist lost his life. It is upon this plain narrative of facts, together with another case I am going to mention, that the Christian Mythologists, calling themselves the Christian Church, have erected their fable, which, for absurdity and extravagance, is not exceeded by anything that is to be found in the mythology of the ancients.

The ancient Mythologists tell us that the race of Giants made war against Jupiter, and that one of them threw a hundred rocks against him at one throw; that Jupiter defeated him with thunder, and confined him afterwards under Mount Etna, and that every time the Giant turns himself Mount Etna belches fire.

It is here easy to see that the circumstance of the mountain, that of its being a volcano, suggested the idea of the fable; and that the fable is made to fit and wind itself up with that circumstance.

The Christian mythologists tell us that their Satan made war against the Almighty, who defeated him, and confined him afterward, not under a mountain, but in a pit. It is here easy to see that the first fable suggested the idea of the second; for the fable of Jupiter and the Giants was told many hundred years before that of Satan. Thus far the ancient and the Christian Mythologists differ very little from each other. But the latter have contrived to carry the matter much farther. They have contrived to connect the fabulous part of the story of Jesus Christ with the fable originating from Mount Etna; and in order to make all the parts of the story tie together, they have taken to their aid the traditions of the Jews; for the Christian mythology is made up partly from the ancient mythology and partly from the Jewish traditions.

The Christian Mythologists, after having confined Satan in a pit, were obliged to let him out again to bring on the sequel of the fable. He is then introduced into the Garden of Eden in the shape of a snake or a serpent, and in that shape he enters into familiar conversation with Eve, who is no way surprised to hear a snake talk; and the issue of this tete-a-tete is that he persuades her to eat an apple, and the eating of that apple damns all mankind.

After giving Satan this triumph over the whole creation, one would have supposed that the Church Mythologists would have been kind enough to send him back again to the pit; or, if they had not done this, that they would have put a mountain upon him (for they say that their faith can remove a mountain), or have put him under a mountain, as the former mythologists had done, to prevent his getting again among the women and doing more mischief. But instead of this they leave him at large, without even obliging him to give his parole—the secret of which is, that they could not do without him; and after being at the trouble of making him, they bribed him to stay. They promised him ALL the Jews, ALL the Turks by anticipation, nine-tenths of the world beside, and Mahomet into the bargain. After this, who can doubt the bountifulness of the Christian Mythology?

Having thus made an insurrection and a battle in Heaven, in which none of the combatants could be either killed or wounded—put Satan into the pit—let him out again—giving him a triumph over the whole creation—damned all mankind by the eating of an apple, these Christian Mythologists bring the two ends of their fable together. They represent this virtuous and amiable man, Jesus Christ, to be at once both God and Man, and also the Son of God, celestially begotten, on purpose to be sacrificed, because they say that Eve in her longing had eaten an apple.

Putting aside everything that might excite laughter by its absurdity, or detestation by its profaneness, and confining ourselves merely to an examination of the parts, it is impossible to conceive a story more derogatory to the Almighty, more inconsistent with his wisdom, more contradictory to his power, than this story is. In order to make for it a foundation to rise upon, the inventors were under the necessity of giving to the being whom they call Satan, a power equally as great, if not greater, than they attribute to the Almighty. They have not only given him the power of liberating himself from the pit, after what they call his fall, but they have made that power increase afterward to infinity. Before this fall they represent him only as an angel of limited existence, as they represent the rest. After his fall, he becomes, by their account, omnipresent. He exists everywhere, and at the same time. He occupies the whole immensity of space.

Not content with this deification of Satan, they represent him as defeating, by stratagem, in the shape of an animal of the creation, all the power and wisdom of the Almighty. They represent him as having compelled the Almighty to the direct necessity either of surrendering the whole of the creation to the government and sovereignty of this Satan, or of capitulating for its redemption by coming down upon earth, and exhibiting himself upon a cross in the shape of a man.

Had the inventors of this story told it the contrary way, that is, had they represented the Almighty as compelling Satan to exhibit himself on a cross, in the shape of a snake, as a punishment for his new transgression, the story would have been less absurd—less contradictory. But instead of this, they make the transgressor triumph, and the Almighty fall.

That many good men have believed this strange fable, and lived very good lives under that belief (for credulity is not a crime), is what I have no doubt of. In the first place, they were educated to believe it, and they would have believed anything else in the same manner. There are also many who have been so enthusiastically enraptured by what they conceived to be the infinite love of God to man, in making a sacrifice of himself, that the vehemence of the idea has forbidden and deterred them from examining into the absurdity and profaneness of the story. The more unnatural anything is, the more is it capable of becoming the object of dismal admiration.

But if objects for gratitude and admiration are our desire, do they not present themselves every hour to our eyes? Do we not see a fair creation prepared to receive us the instant we are born—a world furnished to our hands, that cost us nothing? Is it we that light up the sun, that pour down the rain, and fill the earth with abundance? Whether we sleep or wake, the vast machinery of the universe still goes on. Are these things, and the blessings they indicate in future, nothing to us? Can our gross feelings be excited by no other subjects than tragedy and suicide? Or is the gloomy pride of man become so intolerable, that nothing can flatter it but a sacrifice of the Creator?

I know that this bold investigation will alarm many, but it would be paying too great a compliment to their credulity to forbear it on that account; the times and the subject demand it to be done. The suspicion that the theory of what is called the Christian Church is fabulous is becoming very extensive in all countries; and it will be a consolation to men staggering under that suspicion, and doubting what to believe and what to disbelieve, to see the subject freely investigated. I therefore pass on to an examination of the books called the Old and the New Testament.

These books, beginning with Genesis and ending with Revelation (which, by the by, is a book of riddles that requires a revelation to explain it) are, we are told, the word of God. It is, therefore, proper for us to know who told us so, that we may know what credit to give to the report. The answer to this question is, that nobody can tell, except that we tell one another so. The case, however, historically appears to be as follows:

When the church mythologists established their system, they collected all the writings they could find, and managed them as they pleased. It is a matter altogether of uncertainty to us whether such of the writings as now appear under the name of the Old and New Testament are in the same state in which those collectors say they found them, or whether they added, altered, abridged, or dressed them up.

Be this as it may, they decided by vote which of the books out of the collection they had made should be the WORD OF GOD, and which should not. They rejected several; they voted others to be doubtful, such as the books called the Apocrypha; and those books which had a majority of votes, were voted to be the word of God. Had they voted otherwise, all the people, since calling themselves Christians, had believed otherwise—for the belief of the one comes from the vote of the other. Who the people were that did all this, we know nothing of; they called themselves by the general name of the Church and this is all we know of the matter.

As we have no other external evidence or authority for believing these books to be the word of God than what I have mentioned, which is no evidence or authority at all, I come, in the next place, to examine the internal evidence contained in the books themselves. In the former part of this Essay, I have spoken of revelation; I now proceed further with that subject, for the purpose of applying it to the books in question.

Revelation is a communication of something which the person to whom that thing is revealed did not know before. For if I have done a thing, or seen it done, it needs no revelation to tell me I have done it, or seen it, nor to enable me to tell it, or to write it.

Revelation, therefore, cannot be applied to anything done upon earth, of which man is himself the actor or the witness; and consequently all the historical and anecdotal parts of the Bible, which is almost the whole of it, is not within the meaning and compass of the word revelation, and, therefore, is not the word of God.

When Samson ran off with the gate-posts of Gaza, if he ever did so (and whether he did or not is nothing to us), or when he visited his Delilah, or caught his foxes, or did any thing else, what has revelation to do with these things? If they were facts, he could tell them himself or his secretary, if he kept one, could write them, if they were worth either telling or writing; and if they were fictions, revelation could not make them true; and whether true or not, we are neither the better nor the wiser for knowing them. When we contemplate the immensity of that Being who directs and governs the incomprehensible WHOLE, of which the utmost ken of human sight can discover but a part, we ought to feel shame at calling such paltry stories the word of God.

As to the account of the Creation, with which the Book of Genesis opens, it has all the appearance of being a tradition which the Israelites had among them before they came into Egypt; and after their departure from that country they put it at the head of their history, without telling (as it is most probable) that they did not know how they came by it. The manner in which the account opens, shows it to be traditionary. It begins abruptly; it is nobody that speaks; it is nobody that hears; it is addressed to nobody; it has neither first, second, nor third person; it has every criterion of being a tradition; it has no voucher. Moses does not take it upon himself by introducing it with the formality that he uses on other occasions, such as that of saying, "The Lord spake unto Moses, saying."

Why it has been called the Mosaic account of the Creation, I am at a loss to conceive. Moses, I believe, was too good a judge of such subjects to put his name to that account. He had been educated among the Egyptians, who were a people as well skilled in science, and particularly in astronomy, as any people of their day; and the silence and caution that Moses observes, in not authenticating the account, is a good negative evidence that he neither told it nor believed it. The case is, that every nation of people has been world-makers, and the Israelites had as much right to set up the trade of world-making as any of the rest; and as Moses was not an Israelite, he might not chose to contradict the tradition. The account, however, is harmless; and this is more than can be said for many other parts of the Bible.

Whenever we read the obscene stories, the voluptuous debaucheries, the cruel and torturous executions, the unrelenting vindictiveness, with which more than half the Bible is filled, it would be more consistent that we called it the word of a demon, than the word of God. It is a history of wickedness, that has served to corrupt and brutalize mankind; and, for my own part, I sincerely detest it, as I detest everything that is cruel.

We scarcely meet with anything, a few phrases excepted, but what deserves either our abhorrence or our contempt, till we come to the miscellaneous parts of the Bible. In the anonymous publications, the Psalms, and the Book of Job, more particularly in the latter, we find a great deal of elevated sentiment reverentially expressed of the power and benignity of the Almighty; but they stand on no higher rank than many other compositions on similar subjects, as well before that time as since.

The Proverbs which are said to be Solomon's, though most probably a collection (because they discover a knowledge of life which his situation excluded him from knowing), are an instructive table of ethics. They are inferior in keenness to the proverbs of the Spaniards, and not more wise and economical than those of the American Franklin.

All the remaining parts of the Bible, generally known by the name of the Prophets, are the works of the Jewish poets and itinerant preachers, who mixed poetry,* anecdote, and devotion together—and those works still retain the air and style of poetry, though in translation.

> *As there are many readers who do not see that a composition is poetry unless it be in rhyme, it is for their information that I add this note. Poetry consists principally in two things—imagery and composition. The composition of poetry differs from that of prose in the manner of mixing long and short syllables together. Take a long syllable out of a line of poetry, and put a short one in the room of it, or put a long syllable where a short one should be, and that line will lose its poetical harmony. It will have an effect upon the line like that of misplacing a note in a song. The imagery in these books, called the Prophets, appertains altogether to poetry. It is fictitious, and often extravagant, and not admissible in any other kind of writing than poetry. To show that these writings are composed in poetical numbers, I will take ten syllables, as they stand in the book, and make a line of the same number of syllables, (heroic measure) that shall rhyme with the last word. It will then be seen that the composition of those books is poetical measure. The instance I shall first produce is from Isaiah:
> "Hear, O ye heavens, and give ear, O earth"
> Tis God himself that calls attention forth.

Another instance I shall quote is from the mournful Jeremiah, to which I shall add two other lines, for the purpose of carrying out the figure, and showing the intention of the poet:

> "O! that mine head were waters and mine eyes"
> Were fountains flowing like the liquid skies;
> Then would I give the mighty flood release
> And weep a deluge for the human race.

There is not, throughout the whole book called the Bible, any word that describes to us what we call a poet, nor any word that describes what we call poetry. The case is, that the word prophet, to which latter times have affixed a new idea, was the Bible word for poet, and the word 'prophesying' meant the art of making poetry. It also meant the art of playing poetry to a tune upon any instrument of music.

We read of prophesying with pipes, tabrets, and horns—of prophesying with harps, with psalteries, with cymbals, and with every other instrument of music then in fashion. Were we now to speak of prophesying with a fiddle, or with a pipe and tabor, the expression would have no meaning or would appear ridiculous, and to some people contemptuous, because we have changed the meaning of the word.

We are told of Saul being among the prophets, and also that he prophesied; but we are not told what they prophesied, nor what he prophesied. The case is, there was nothing to tell; for these prophets were a company of musicians and poets, and Saul joined in the concert, and this was called prophesying.

The account given of this affair in the book called Samuel is, that Saul met a company of prophets; a whole company of them! coming down with a psaltery, a tabret, a pipe and a harp, and that they prophesied, and that he prophesied with them. But it appears afterwards, that Saul prophesied badly; that is, he performed his part badly; for it is said that an "evil spirit from God"* came upon Saul, and he prophesied.

> *As those men who call themselves divines and commentators, are very fond of puzzling one another, I leave them to contest the meaning of the first part of the phrase, that of an evil spirit from God. I keep to my text—I keep to the meaning of the word prophesy.

Now, were there no other passage in the book called the Bible than this, to demonstrate to us that we have lost the original meaning of the word prophesy, and substituted another meaning in its place, this alone would be sufficient; for it is impossible to use and apply the word prophesy, in the place it is here used and applied, if we give to it the sense which latter times have affixed to it. The manner in which it is here used strips it of all religious meaning, and shows that a man might then be a prophet, or he might prophesy, as he may now be a poet or a musician, without any regard to the morality or the immorality of his character. The word was originally a term of science, promiscuously applied to poetry and to music, and not restricted to any subject upon which poetry and music might be exercised.

Deborah and Barak are called prophets, not because they predicted anything, but because they composed the poem or song that bears their name, in celebration of an act already done. David is ranked among the prophets, for he was a musician, and was also reputed to be (though perhaps very erroneously) the author of the Psalms. But Abraham, Isaac, and Jacob are not called prophets; it does not appear from any accounts we have that they could either sing, play music, or make poetry.

We are told of the greater and the lesser prophets. They might as well tell us of the greater and the lesser God; for there cannot be degrees in prophesying consistently with its modern sense. But there are degrees in poetry, and therefore the phrase is reconcilable to the case, when we understand by it the greater and the lesser poets.

It is altogether unnecessary, after this, to offer any observations upon what those men, styled propliets, have written. The axe goes at once to the root, by showing that the original meaning of the word has been mistaken and consequently all the inferences that have been drawn from those books, the devotional respect that has been paid to them, and the labored commentaries that have been written upon them, under that mistaken meaning, are not worth disputing about. In many things, however, the writings of the Jewish poets deserve a better fate than that of being bound up, as they now are with the trash that accompanies them, under the abused name of the word of God.

If we permit ourselves to conceive right ideas of things, we must necessarily affix the idea, not only of unchangeableness, but of the utter impossibility of any change taking place, by any means or accident whatever, in that which we would honor with the name of the word of God; and therefore the word of God cannot exist in any written or human language.

The continually progressive change to which the meaning of words is subject, the want of a universal language which renders translation necessary, the errors to which translations are again subject, the mistakes of copyists and printers, together with the possibility of willful alteration, are of themselves evidences that the human language, whether in speech or in print, cannot be the vehicle of the word of God. The word of God exists in something else.

Did the book called the Bible excel in purity of ideas and expression all the books now extant in the world, I would not take it for my rule of faith, as being the word of God, because the possibility would nevertheless exist of my being imposed upon. But when I see throughout the greatest part of this book scarcely anything but a history of the grossest vices and a collection of the most paltry and contemptible tales, I cannot dishonor my Creator by calling it by his name.

Thus much for the Bible; I now go on to the book called the New Testament. The new Testament! that is, the new will, as if there could be two wills of the Creator.

Had it been the object or the intention of Jesus Christ to establish a new religion, he would undoubtedly have written the system himself, or procured it to be written in his life-time. But there is no publication extant authenticated with his name. All the books called the New Testament were written after his death. He was a Jew by birth and by profession; and he was the son of God in like manner that every other person is—for the Creator is the Father of All.

The first four books, called Matthew, Mark, Luke, and John, do not give a history of the life of Jesus Christ, but only detached anecdotes of him. It appears from these books that the whole time of his being a preacher was not more than eighteen months; and it was only during this short time that these men became acquainted with him. They make mention of him at the age of twelve years, sitting, they say, among the Jewish doctors, asking and answering questions. As this was several years before their acquaintance with him began, it is most probable they had this anecdote from his parents. From this time there is no account of him for about sixteen years. Where he lived, or how he employed himself during this interval, is not known. Most probably he was working at his father's trade, which was that of a carpenter. It does not appear that he had any school education, and the probability is, that he could not write, for his parents were extremely poor, as appears from their not being able to pay for a bed when he was born.

It is somewhat curious that the three persons whose names are the most universally recorded, were of very obscure parentage. Moses was a foundling; Jesus Christ was born in a stable; and Mahomet was a mule driver. The first and the last of these men were founders of different systems of religion; but Jesus Christ founded no new system. He called men to the practice of moral virtues, and the belief of one God. The great trait in his character is philanthropy.

The manner in which he was apprehended shows that he was not much known at that time; and it shows also, that the meetings he then held with his followers were in secret; and that he had given over or suspended preaching publicly. Judas could no otherwise betray him than by giving information where he was, and pointing him out to the officers that went to arrest him; and the reason for employing and paying Judas to do this could arise only from the causes already mentioned, that of his not being much known and living concealed.

The idea of his concealment, not only agrees very ill with his reputed divinity, but associates with it something of pusillanimity; and his being betrayed, or in other words, his being apprehended, on the information of one of his followers, shows that he did not intend to be apprehended, and consequently that he did not intend to be crucified.

The Christian Mythologists tell us, that Christ died for the sins of the world, and that he came on purpose to die. Would it not then have been the same if he had died of a fever or of the small-pox, of old age, or of anything else?

The declaratory sentence which, they say, was passed upon Adam, in case he eat of the apple, was not, that thou shalt surely be crucified, but thou shalt surely die—the sentence of death, and not the manner of dying. Crucifixion, therefore, or any other particular manner of dying, made no part of the sentence that Adam was to suffer, and consequently, even upon their own tactics, it could make no part of the sentence that Christ was to suffer in the room of Adam. A fever would have done as well as a cross, if there was any occasion for either.

This sentence of death, which they tell us was thus passed upon Adam must either have meant dying naturally, that is, ceasing to live, or have meant what these Mythologists call damnation; and, consequently, the act of dying on the part of Jesus Christ, must, according to their system, apply as a prevention to one or other of these two things happening to Adam and to us.

That it does not prevent our dying is evident, because we all die; and if their accounts of longevity be true, men die faster since the crucifixion than before: and with respect to the second explanation (including with it the natural death of Jesus Christ as a substitute for the eternal death or damnation of all mankind), it is impertinently representing the Creator as coming off, or revoking the sentence, by a pun or a quibble upon the word death. That manufacturer of quibbles, St. Paul, if he wrote the books that bear his name, has helped this quibble on by making another quibble upon the word Adam. He makes there to be two Adams; the one who sins in fact, and suffers by proxy; the other who sins by proxy, and suffers in fact. A religion thus interlarded with quibble, subterfuge, and pun has a tendency to instruct its professors in the practice of these arts. They acquire the habit without being aware of the cause.

If Jesus Christ was the being which those Mythologists tell us he was, and that he came into this world to suffer, which is a word they sometimes use instead of to die, the only real suffering he could have endured would have been to live. His existence here was a state of exilement or transportation from Heaven, and the way back to his original country was to die. In finè, everything in this strange system is the reverse of what it pretends to be. It is the reverse of truth, and I become so tired of examining into its inconsistencies and absurdities, that I hasten to the conclusion of it, in order to proceed to something better.

How much or what parts of the books called the New Testament, were written by the persons whose names they bear, is what we can know nothing of; neither are we certain in what language they were originally written. The matters they now contain may be classed under two heads—anecdote and epistolary correspondence.

The four books already mentioned, Matthew, Mark, Luke, and John, are altogether anecdotal. They relate events after they had taken place. They tell what Jesus Christ did and said, and what others did and said to him; and in several instances they relate the same event differently. Revelation is necessarily out of the question with respect to those books; not only because of the disagreement of the writers, but because revelation cannot be applied to the relating of facts by the person who saw them done, nor to the relating or recording of any discourse or conversation by those who heard it. The book called the Acts of the Apostles (an anonymous work) belongs also to the anecdotal part.

All the other parts of the New Testament, except the book of enigmas, called the Revelations, are a collection of letters under the name of epistles; and the forgery of letters has been such a common practice in the world, that the probability is at least equal, whether they are genuine or forged. One thing, however, is much less equivocal, which is, that out of the matters contained in those books, together with the assistance of some old stories, the Church has set up a system of religion very contradictory to the character of the person whose name it bears. It has set up a religion of pomp and of revenue, in pretended imitation of a person whose life was humility and poverty.

The invention of a purgatory, and of the releasing of souls therefrom by prayers bought of the church with money; the selling of pardons, dispensations, and indulgences, are revenue laws, without bearing that name or carrying that appearance. But the case nevertheless is, that those things derive their origin from the paroxysm of the crucifixion and the theory deduced therefrom, which was that one person could stand in the place of another, and could perform meritorious services for him. The probability, therefore, is, that the whole theory or doctrine of what is called the redemption (which is said to have been accomplished by the act of one person in the room of another) was originally fabricated on purpose to bring forward and build all those secondary and pecuniary redemptions upon; and that the passages in the books, upon which the idea or theory of redemption is built, have been manufactured and fabricated for that purpose. Why are we to give this Church Credit when she tells us that those books are genuine in every part, any more than we give her credit for everything else she has told us, or for the miracles she says she had performed? That she could fabricate writings is certain, because she could write; and the composition of the writings in question, is of that kind that anybody might do it; and that she did fabricate them is not more inconsistent with probability than that she could tell us, as she has done, that she could and did work miracles.

Since, then no external evidence can, at this long distance of time, be produced to prove whether the Church fabricated the doctrines called redemption or not (for such evidence, whether for or against, would be subject to the same suspicion of being fabricated), the case can only be referred to the internal evidence which the thing carries of itself; and this affords a very strong presumption of its being a fabrication. For the internal evidence is that the theory or doctrine of redemption has for its basis an idea of pecuniary Justice, and not that of moral Justice.

If I owe a person money, and cannot pay him, and he threatens to put me in prison, another person can take the debt upon himself, and pay it for me; but if I have committed a crime, every circumstance of the case is changed; moral Justice cannot take the innocent for the guilty, even if the innocent would offer itself.

To suppose Justice to do this, is to destroy the principle of its existence, which is the thing itself; it is then no longer Justice, it is indiscriminate revenge.

This single reflection will show, that the doctrine of redemption is founded on a mere pecuniary idea corresponding to that of a debt which another person might pay; and as this pecuniary idea corresponds again with the system of second redemption, obtained through the means of money given to the Church for pardons, the probability is that the same persons fabricated both the one and the other of those theories; and that, in truth there is no such thing as redemption—that it is fabulous, and that man stands in the same relative condition with his Maker he ever did stand since man existed, and that it is his greatest consolation to think so.

Let him believe this, and he will live more consistently and morally than by any other system; it is by his being taught to contemplate himself as an outlaw, as an outcast, as a beggar, as a mumper, as one thrown, as it were, on a dunghill at an immense distance from his Creator, and who must make his approaches by creeping and cringing to intermediate beings, that he conceives either a contemptuous disregard for everything under the name of religion, or becomes indifferent, or turns what he calls devout. In the latter case, he consumes his life in grief, or the affectation of it; his prayers are reproaches; his humility is ingratitude; he calls himself a worm, and the fertile earth a dunghill; and all the blessings of life by the thankless name of vanities; he despises the choicest gift of God to man, the GIFT OF REASON; and having endeavored to force upon himself the belief of a system against which reason revolts, he ungratefully calls it human reason, as if man could give reason to himself.

Yet, with all this strange appearance of humility and this contempt for human reason, he ventures into the boldest presumptions; he finds fault with everything; his selfishness is never satisfied; his ingratitude is never at an end. He takes on himself to direct the Almighty what to do, even in the government of the universe; he prays dictatorially; when it is sunshine, he prays for rain, and when it is rain, he prays for sunshine; he follows the same idea in everything that he prays for; for what is the amount of all his prayers, but an attempt to make the Almighty change his mind, and act otherwise than he does? It is as if he were to say: Thou knowest not so well as I.

But some, perhaps will say: Are we to have no word of God—no revelation? I answer, Yes; there is a word of God; there is a revelation.

THE WORD OF GOD IS THE CREATION WE BEHOLD and it is in this word, which no human invention can counterfeit or alter, that God speaketh universally to man.

Human language is local and changeable, and is therefore incapable of being used as the means of unchangeable and universal information. The idea that God sent Jesus Christ to publish, as they say, the glad tidings to all nations, from one end of the earth unto the other, is consistent only with the ignorance of those who knew nothing of the extent of the world, and who believed, as those world-saviours believed, and continued to believe for several centuries (and that in contradiction to the discoveries of philosophers and the experience of navigators), that the earth was flat like a trencher, and that a man might walk to the end of it.

But how was Jesus Christ to make anything known to all nations? He could speak but one language; which was Hebrew and there are in the world several hundred languages. Scarcely any two nations speak the same language, or understand each other; and as to translations, every man who knows anything of languages knows that it is impossible to translate from one language into another, not only without losing a great part of the original, but frequently of mistaking the sense; and besides all this, the art of printing was wholly unknown at the time Christ lived.

It is always necessary that the means that are to accomplish any end be equal to the accomplishment of that end, or the end cannot be accomplished. It is in this that the difference between finite and infinite power and wisdom discovers itself. Man frequently fails in accomplishing his ends, from a natural inability of the power to the purpose, and frequently from the want of wisdom to apply power properly. But it is impossible for infinite power and wisdom to fail as man faileth. The means it useth are always equal to the end; but human language, more especially as there is not a universal language, is incapable of being used as a universal means of unchangeable and uniform information, and therefore it is not the means that God useth in manifesting himself universally to man.

It is only in the CREATION that all our ideas and conceptions of a word of God can unite. The Creation speaketh a universal language, independently of human speech or human language, multiplied and various as they may be. It is an ever-existing original, which every man can read. It cannot be forged; it cannot be counterfeited; it cannot be lost; it cannot be altered; it cannot be suppressed. It does not depend upon the will of man whether it shall be published or not; it publishes itself from one end of the earth to the other. It preaches to all nations and to all worlds; and this word of God reveals to man all that is necessary for man to know of God.

Do we want to contemplate his power? We see it in the immensity of the Creation. Do we want to contemplate his wisdom? We see it in the unchangeable order by which the incomprehensible whole is governed! Do we want to contemplate his munificence? We see it in the abundance with which he fills the earth. Do we want to contemplate his mercy? We see it in his not withholding that abundance even from the unthankful. In finè, do we want to know what God is? Search not the book called the Scripture, which any human hand might make, but the Scripture called the Creation.

The only idea man can affix to the name of God is that of a first cause, the cause of all things. And incomprehensible and difficult as it is for a man to conceive what a first cause is, he arrives at the belief of it from the tenfold greater difficulty of disbelieving it. It is difficult beyond description to conceive that space can have no end; but it is more difficult to conceive an end. It is difficult beyond the power of man to conceive an eternal duration of what we call time; but it is more impossible to conceive a time when there shall be no time.

In like manner of reasoning, everything we behold carries in itself the internal evidence that it did not make itself. Every man is an evidence to himself that he did not make himself; neither could his father make himself, nor his grandfather, nor any of his race; neither could any tree, plant, or animal make itself; and it is the conviction arising from this evidence that carries us on, as it were, by necessity to the belief of a first cause eternally existing, of a nature totally different to any material existence we know of, and by the power of which all things exist; and this first cause man calls God.

It is only by the exercise of reason that man can discover God. Take away that reason, and he would be incapable of understanding anything; and in this case it would be just as consistent to read even the book called the Bible to a horse as to a man. How then is it that those people pretend to reject reason?

Almost the only parts in the book called the Bible that convey to us any idea of God, are some chapters in Job, and the 19th Psalm; I recollect no other. Those parts are true deistical compositions, for they treat of the

Deity through his works. They take the book of Creation as the word of God, they refer to no other book, and all the inferences they make are drawn from that volume.

I insert in this place the 19th Psalm, as paraphrased into English verse by Addison. I recollect not the prose, and where I write this I have not the opportunity of seeing it.

> "The spacious firmament on high,
> With all the blue ethereal sky,
> And spangled heavens, a shining frame,
> Their great original proclaim.
> The unwearied sun, from day to day,
> Does his Creator's power display;
> And publishes to every land
> The work of an Almighty hand.
>
> "Soon as the evening shades prevail,
> The moon takes up the wondrous tale,
> And nightly to the list'ning earth
> Repeats the story of her birth;
> Whilst all the stars that round her burn,
> And all the planets, in their turn,
> Confirm the tidings as they roll,
> And spread the truth from pole to pole.
>
> "What though in solemn silence all
> Move round this dark terrestrial ball?
> What though no real voice, or sound,
> Amidst their radiant orbs be found
> In reason's ear they all rejoice
> And utter forth a glorious voice,
> Forever singing, as they shine,
> THE HAND THAT MADE US IS DIVINE."

What more does man want to know, than that the hand or power that made these things is divine, is omnipotent? Let him believe this with the force it is impossible to repel, if he permits his reason to act, and his rule of moral life will follow of course.

The allusions in Job have, all of them, the same tendency with this Psalm; that of deducing or proving a truth that would be otherwise unknown, from truths already known.

I recollect not enough of the passages in Job to insert them correctly; but there is one that occurs to me that is applicable to the subject I am speaking upon. "Canst thou by searching find out God? Canst thou find out the Almighty to perfection?"

I know not how the printers have pointed this passage, for I keep no Bible; but it contains two distinct questions that admit of distinct answers.

First,—Canst thou by searching find out God? Yes; because, in the first place, I know I did not make myself, and yet I have existence; and by searching into the nature of other things, I find that no other thing could make itself; and yet millions of other things exist; therefore it is, that I know, by positive conclusion resulting from this search, that there is a power superior to all those things, and that power is God.

Secondly,—Canst thou find out the Almighty to perfection? No; not only because the power and wisdom He has manifested in the structure of the Creation that I behold is to me incomprehensible, but because even this manifestation, great as it is, is probably but a small display of that immensity of power and wisdom by which millions of other worlds, to me invisible by their distance, were created and continue to exist.

It is evident that both of these questions were put to the reason of the person to whom they are supposed to have been addressed; and it is only by admitting the first question to be answered affirmatively, that the second could follow. It would have been unnecessary and even absurd, to have put a second question, more difficult than the first, if the first question had been answered negatively. The two questions have different objects; the first refers to the existence of God, the second to his attributes; reason can discover the one, but it falls infinitely short in discovering the whole of the other.

I recollect not a single passage in all the writings ascribed to the men called apostles, that conveys any idea of what God is. Those writings are chiefly controversial; and the subjects they dwell upon, that of a man dying in agony on a cross, is better suited to the gloomy genius of a monk in a cell, by whom it is not impossible they were written, than to any man breathing the open air of the Creation. The only passage that occurs to me, that has any reference to the works of God, by which only his power and wisdom can be known, is related to have been spoken by Jesus Christ, as a remedy against distrustful care. "Behold the lilies of the field, they toil not, neither do they spin." This, however, is far inferior to the allusions in Job and in the 19th Psalm; but it is similar in idea, and the modesty of the imagery is correspondent to the modesty of the man.

As to the Christian system of faith, it appears to me as a species of Atheism—a sort of religious denial of God. It professes to believe in a man rather than in God. It is a compound made up chiefly of Manism with but little Deism, and is as near to Atheism as twilight is to darkness. It introduces between man and his Maker an opaque body, which it calls a Redeemer, as the moon introduces her opaque self between the earth and the sun, and it produces by this means a religious, or an irreligious, eclipse of light. It has put the whole orbit of reason into shade.

The effect of this obscurity has been that of turning everything upside down, and representing it in reverse, and among the revolutions it has thus magically produced, it has made a revolution in theology.

That which is now called natural philosophy, embracing the whole circle of science, of which astronomy occupies the chief place, is the study of the works of God, and of the power and wisdom of God in his works, and is the true theology.

As to the theology that is now studied in its place, it is the study of human opinions and of human fancies concerning God. It is not the study of God himself in the works that he has made, but in the works or writings that man has made; and it is not among the least of the mischiefs that the Christian system has done to the world, that it has abandoned the original and beautiful system of theology, like a beautiful innocent, to distress and reproach, to make room for the hag of superstition.

The Book of Job and the 19th Psalm, which even the Church admits to be more ancient than the chronological order in which they stand in the book called the Bible, are theological orations conformable to the original system of theology. The internal evidence of those orations proves to a demonstration that the study and contemplation of the works of creation, and of the power and wisdom of God, revealed and manifested in those works, made a great part of the religious devotion of the times in which they were written; and it was this devotional study and contemplation that led to the discovery of the principles upon which what are now called sciences are established; and it is to the discovery of these principles that almost all the arts that contribute to the convenience of human life owe their existence. Every principal art has some science for its parent, though the person who mechanically performs the work does not always, and but very seldom, perceive the connection.

It is a fraud of the Christian system to call the sciences human inventions; it is only the application of them that is human. Every science has for its basis a system of principles as fixed and unalterable as those by which the universe is regulated and governed. Man cannot make principles, he can only discover them.

For example: Every person who looks at an almanac sees an account when an eclipse will take place, and he sees also that it never fails to take place according to the account there given. This shows that man is acquainted with the laws by which the heavenly bodies move. But it would be something worse than ignorance, were any Church on earth to say that those laws are a human invention. It would also be ignorance, or something worse, to say that the scientific principles by the aid of which man is enabled to calculate and foreknow when an eclipse will take place, are a human invention. Man cannot invent any thing that is eternal and immutable; and the scientific principles he employs for this purpose must be, and are of necessity, as eternal and immutable as the laws by which the heavenly bodies move, or they could not be used as they are to ascertain the time when, and the manner how, an eclipse will take place.

The scientific principles that man employs to obtain the foreknowledge of an eclipse, or of anything else relating to the motion of the heavenly bodies, are contained chiefly in that part of science that is called trigonometry, or the properties of a triangle, which, when applied to the study of the heavenly bodies, is called astronomy; when applied to direct the course of a ship on the ocean, it is called navigation; when applied to the construction of figures drawn by a rule and compass, it is called geometry; when applied to the construction of plans of edifices, it is called architecture; when applied to the measurement of any portion of the surface of the earth, it is called land-surveying. In finè, it is the soul of science; it is an eternal truth; it contains the mathematical demonstration of which man speaks, and the extent of its uses are unknown.

It may be said that man can make or draw a triangle, and therefore a triangle is a human invention.

But the triangle, when drawn, is no other than the image of the principle; it is a delineation to the eye, and from thence to the mind, of a principle that would otherwise be imperceptible. The triangle does not make the principle, any more than a candle taken into a room that was dark makes the chairs and tables that before were invisible. All the properties of a triangle exist independently of the figure, and existed before any triangle was drawn or thought of by man. Man had no more to do in the formation of those properties or principles, than he had to do in making the laws by which the heavenly bodies move; and therefore the one must have the same Divine origin as the other.

In the same manner, as it may be said, that man can make a triangle, so also, may it be said, he can make the mechanical instrument called a lever; but the principle by which the lever acts is a thing distinct from the instrument, and would exist if the instrument did not; it attaches itself to the instrument after it is made; the instrument, therefore, cannot act otherwise than it does act; neither can all the efforts of human invention make it act otherwise; that which, in all such cases, man calls the effect is no other than the principle itself rendered perceptible to the senses.

Since, then, man cannot make principles, from whence did he gain a knowledge of them, so as to be able to apply them, not only to things on earth, but to ascertain the motion of bodies so immensely distant from him as all the heavenly bodies are? From whence, I ask, could he gain that knowledge, but from the study of the true theology?

It is the structure of the universe that has taught this knowledge to man. That structure is an ever-existing exhibition of every principle upon which every part of mathematical science is founded. The offspring of this science is mechanics; for mechanics is no other than the principles of science applied practically. The man who proportions the several parts of a mill, uses the same scientific principles as if he had the power of constructing a universe; but as he cannot give to matter that invisible agency by which all the component parts of the immense machine of the universe have influence upon each other, and act in motional unison together, without any apparent contact, and to which man has given the name of attraction, gravitation, and repulsion, he supplies the place of that agency by the humble imitation of teeth and cogs. All the parts of man's microcosm must visibly touch; but could he gain a knowledge of that agency, so as to be able to apply it in practice, we might then say that another canonical book of the Word of God had been discovered.

If man could alter the properties of the lever, so also could he alter the properties of the triangle: for a lever (taking that sort of lever which is called a steelyard, for the sake of explanation) forms, when in motion, a triangle. The line it descends from (one point of that line being in the fulcrum), the line it descends to, and the chord of the arc which the end of the lever describes in the air, are the three sides of a triangle. The other arm of the lever describes also a triangle; and the corresponding sides of those two triangles, calculated scientifically, or measured geometrically, and also the sines, tangents, and secants generated from the angles, and geometrically measured, have the same proportions to each other, as the different weights have that will balance each other on the lever, leaving the weight of the lever out of the case.

It may also be said, that man can make a wheel and axis; that he can put wheels of different magnitudes together, and produce a mill. Still the case comes back to the same point, which is, that he did not make the principle that gives the wheels those powers. This principle is as unalterable as in the former case or rather it is the same principle under a different appearance to the eye.

The power that two wheels of different magnitudes have upon each other, is in the same proportion as if the semi-diameter of the two wheels were joined together and made into that kind of lever I have described, suspended at the part where the semi-diameters join; for the two wheels, scientifically considered, are no other than the two circles generated by the motion of the compound lever.

It is from the study of the true theology that all our knowledge of science is derived, and it is from that knowledge that all the arts have originated.

The Almighty Lecturer, by displaying the principles of science in the structure of the universe, has invited man to study and to imitation. It is as if He had said to the inhabitants of this globe that we call ours, "I have made an earth for man to dwell upon, and I have rendered the starry heavens visible, to teach him science and the arts. He can now provide for his own comfort, AND LEARN FROM MY MUNIFICENCE TO ALL, TO BE KIND TO EACH OTHER."

Of what use is it, unless it be to teach man something, that his eye is endowed with the power of beholding to an incomprehensible distance, an immensity of worlds revolving in the ocean of space? Or of what use is it that this immensity of worlds is visible to man? What has man to do with the Pleiades, with Orion, with Sirius, with the star he calls the North Star, with the moving orbs he has named Saturn, Jupiter, Mars, Venus, and Mercury, if no uses are to follow from their being visible? A less power of vision would have been sufficient for man, if the immensity he now possesses were given only to waste itself, as it were, on an immense desert of space glittering with shows.

It is only by contemplating what he calls the starry heavens, as the book and school of science, that he discovers any use in their being visible to him, or any advantage resulting from his immensity of vision. But when be contemplates the subject in this light, he sees an additional motive for saying, that nothing was made in vain; for in vain would be this power of vision if it taught man nothing.

As the Christian system of faith has made a revolution in theology, so also bas it made a revolution in the state of learning. That which is now called learning, was not learning originally. Learning does not consist, as the schools now make it consist, in the knowledge of languages, but in the knowledge of things to which language gives names.

The Greeks were a learned people, but learning with them did not consist in speaking Greek, any more than in a Roman's speaking Latin, or a Frenchman's speaking French, or an Englishman's speaking English. From what we know of the Greeks, it does not appear that they knew or studied any language but their own, and this was one cause of their becoming so learned: it afforded them more time to apply themselves to better studies. The schools of the Greeks were schools of science and philosophy, and not of languages; and it is in the knowledge of the things that science and philosophy teach, that learning consists.

Almost all the scientific learning that now exists came to us from the Greeks, or the people who spoke the Greek language. It, therefore, became necessary for the people of other nations who spoke a different language that some among them should learn the Greek language, in order that the learning the Greeks had, might be made known in those nations, by translating the Greek books of science and philosophy into the mother tongue of each nation.

The study, therefore, of the Greek language (and in the same manner for the Latin) was no other than the drudgery business of a linguist; and the language thus obtained, was no other than the means, or as it were the tools, employed to obtain the learning the Greeks had. It made no part of the learning itself, and was so distinct from it, as to make it exceedingly probable that the persons who had studied Greek sufficiently to translate those works, such, for instance as Euclid's Elements, did not understand any of the learning the works contained.

As there is now nothing new to be learned from the dead languages, all the useful books being already translated, the languages are become useless, and the time expended in teaching and in learning them is wasted. So far as the study of languages may contribute to the progress and communication of knowledge, (for it has nothing to do with the creation of knowledge), it is only in the living languages that new knowledge is to be found; and certain it is that, in general, a youth will learn more of a living language in one year, than of a dead language in seven, and it is but seldom that the teacher knows much of it himself. The difficulty of learning the dead languages does not arise from any superior abstruseness in the languages themselves, but in their being dead, and the pronunciation entirely lost. It would be the same thing with any other language when it becomes dead. The best Greek linguist that now exists does not understand Greek so well as a Grecian plowman did, or a Grecian milkmaid; and the same for the Latin, compared with a plowman or a milkmaid of the Romans; it would therefore be advantageous to the state of learning to abolish the study of the dead languages, and to make learning consist, as it originally did, in scientific knowledge.

The apology that is sometimes made for continuing to teach the dead languages is, that they are taught at a time when a child is not capable of exerting any other mental faculty than that of memory; but that is altogether erroneous. The human mind has a natural disposition to scientific knowledge, and to the things connected with it. The first and favourite amusement of a child, even before it begins to play, is that of imitating the works of man. It builds houses with cards or sticks; it navigates the little ocean of a bowl of water with a paper boat, or dams the stream of a gutter and contrives something which it calls a mill; and it interests itself in the fate of its works with a care that resembles affection. It afterwards goes to school, where its genius is killed by the barren study of a dead language, and the philosopher is lost in the linguist.

But the apology that is now made for continuing to teach the dead languages, could not be the cause, at first, of cutting down learning to the narrow and humble sphere of linguistry; the cause, therefore, must be sought for elsewhere. In all researches of this kind, the best evidence that can be produced, is the internal evidence the thing carries with itself, and the evidence of circumstances that unites with it; both of which, in this case, are not difficult to be discovered.

Putting then aside, as a matter of distinct consideration, the outrage offered to the moral justice of God by supposing him to make the innocent suffer for the guilty, and also the loose morality and low contrivance of supposing him to change himself into the shape of a man, in order to make an excuse to himself for not executing his supposed sentence upon Adam—putting, I say, those things aside as a matter of distinct consideration, it is certain that what is called the Christian system of faith, including in it the whimsical account of the creation—the strange story of Eve—the snake, and the apple—the amphibious idea of a man-god—the corporeal idea of the death of a god—the mythological idea of a family of gods, and the Christian system of arithmetic, that three are one, and one is three, are all irreconcilable, not only to the divine gift of reason that God, has given to man, but to the knowledge that man gains of the power and wisdom of God by the aid of the sciences and by studying the structure of the universe that God has made.

The setters-up, therefore, and the advocates of the Christian system of faith could not but foresee that the continually progressive knowledge that man would gain, by the aid of science, of the power and wisdom of God, manifested in the structure of the universe and in all the works of Creation, would militate against, and call into question, the truth of their system of faith; and therefore it became necessary to their purpose to cut learning down to a size less dangerous to their project, and this they effected by restricting the idea of learning to the dead study of dead languages.

They not only rejected the study of science out of the Christian schools, but they persecuted it, and it is only within about the last two centuries that the study has been revived. So late as 1610, Galileo, a Florentine, discovered and introduced the use of telescopes, and by applying them to observe the motions and appearances of the heavenly bodies, afforded additional means for ascertaining the true structure of the universe. Instead of being esteemed for these discoveries, he was sentenced to renounce them, or the opinions resulting from them, as a damnable heresy. And, prior to that time, Virgilius was condemned to be burned for asserting the antipodes, or in other words that the earth was a globe, and habitable in every part where there was land; yet the truth of this is now too well known even to be told.

If the belief of errors not morally bad did no mischief, it would make no part of the moral duty of man to oppose and remove them. There was no moral ill in believing the earth was flat like a trencher, any more than there was moral virtue in believing it was round like a globe; neither was there any moral ill in believing that the Creator made no other world than this, any more than there was moral virtue in believing that he made millions, and that the infinity of space is filled with worlds. But when a system of religion is made to grow out of a supposed system of creation that is not true, and to unite itself therewith in a manner almost inseparable therefrom, the case assumes an entirely different ground. It is then that errors not morally bad become fraught with the same mischiefs as if they were. It is then that the truth, though otherwise indifferent itself, becomes an essential by becoming the criterion that either confirms by corresponding evidence, or denies by contradictory evidence, the reality of the religion itself. In this view of the case it is the moral duty of man to obtain every possible evidence that the structure of the heavens, or any other part of creation affords, with respect to systems of religion. But this, the supporters or partisans of the Christian system, as if dreading the result, incessantly opposed, and not only rejected the sciences, but persecuted the professors. Had Newton or Descartes lived three or four hundred years ago, and pursued their studies as they did, it is most probable they would not have lived to finish them; and had Franklin drawn lightning from the clouds at the same time, it would have been at the hazard of expiring for it in flames.

Later times have laid all the blame upon the Goths and Vandals; but, however unwilling the partisans of the Christian system may be to believe or to acknowledge it, it is nevertheless true, that the age of ignorance commenced with the Christian system. There was more knowledge in the world before that period than for many centuries afterwards; and as to religious knowledge, the Christian system, as already said was only another species of mythology, and the mythology to which it succeeded was a corruption of an ancient system of theism.*

> *It is impossible for us now to know at what time the heathen mythology began; but it is certain, from the internal evidence that it carries, that it did not begin in the same state or condition in which it ended. All the gods of that mythology, except Saturn, were of modern invention. The supposed reign of Saturn was prior to that which is called the heathen mythology, and was so far a species of theism, that it admitted the belief of only one God. Saturn is supposed to have abdicated the government in favor of his three sons and one daughter, Jupiter, Pluto, Neptune, and Juno; after this, thousands of other Gods and demigods were imaginarily created, and the calendar of gods increased as fast as the calendar of saints and the calendar of courts have increased since. All the corruptions that have taken place, in theology and in religion, have been produced by admitting of what man calls revealed religion. The Mythologists pretended to more revealed religion than the Christians do. They had their oracles and their priests, who were supposed to receive and deliver the word of God verbally, on almost all occasions. Since, then, all corruptions, down from Moloch to modern predestinarianism, and the human sacrifices of the heathens to the Christian sacrifice of the Creator, have been produced by admitting of what is called revealed religion, the most effectual means to prevent all such evils and impositions is not to admit of any other revelation than that which is manifested in the book of creation, and to contemplate the creation as the only true and real word of God that ever did or ever will exist; and everything else called the word of God, is fable and imposition.

It is owing to this long interregnum of science, and to no other cause, that we have now to look back through a vast chasm of many hundred years to the respectable characters we call the ancients. Had the progression of knowledge gone on proportionably with the stock that before existed, that chasm would have been filled up with characters rising superior in knowledge to each other; and those ancients we now so much admire would have appeared respectably in the background of the scene. But the Christian system laid all waste; and if we take our stand about the beginning of the sixteenth century, we look back through that long chasm, to the times of the ancients, as over a vast sandy desert, in which not a shrub appears to intercept the vision to the fertile hills beyond.

It is an inconsistency scarcely possible to be credited, that any thing should exist, under the name of a religion, that held it to be irreligious to study and contemplate the structure of the universe that God has made. But the fact is too well established to be denied. The event that served more than any other to break the first link in this long chain of despotic ignorance is that known by the name of the Reformation by Luther. From that time, though it does not appear to have made any part of the intention of Luther, or of those who are called reformers, the sciences began to revive, and liberality, their natural associate, began to appear. This was the only public good the Reformation did; for with respect to religious good, it might as well not have taken place. The mythology still continued the same, and a multiplicity of National Popes grew out of the downfall of the Pope of Christendom.

Having thus shown from the internal evidence of things the cause that produced a change in the state of learning, and the motive for substituting the study of the dead languages in the place of the sciences, I proceed, in addition to the several observations already made in the former part of this work, to compare, or rather to confront, the evidence that the structure of the universe affords with the Christian system of religion; but, as I cannot begin this part better than by referring to the ideas that occurred to me at an early part of life, and which I doubt not have occurred in some degree to almost every other person at one time or other, I shall state what those ideas were, and add thereto such other matter as shall arise out of the subject, giving to the whole, by way of preface, a short introduction.

My father being of the Quaker profession, it was my good fortune to have an exceedingly good moral education, and a tolerable stock of useful learning. Though I went to the grammar school,* I did not learn Latin, not only because I had no inclination to learn languages, but because of the objection the Quakers have against the books in which the language is taught. But this did not prevent me from being acquainted with the subjects of all the Latin books used in the school.

> *The same school, Thetford In Norfolk that the present Counsellor Mingay went to and under the same master.

The natural bent of my mind was to science. I had some turn, and I believe some talent for poetry; but this I rather repressed than encouraged, as leading too much into the field of imagination. As soon as I was able I purchased a pair of globes, and attended the philosophical lectures of Martin and Ferguson, and became afterwards acquainted with Dr. Bevis, of the society called the Royal Society, then living in the Temple, and an excellent astronomer.

I had no disposition for what was called politics. It presented to my mind no other idea than is contained in the word Jockeyship. When therefore I turned my thoughts toward matters of government, I had to form a system for myself that accorded with the moral and philosophic principles in which I had been educated. I saw, or at least I thought I saw, a vast scene opening itself to the world in the affairs of America, and it appeared to me that unless the Americans changed the plan they were then pursuing with respect to the government of England, and declared themselves independent, they would not only involve themselves in a multiplicity of new difficulties, but shut out the prospect that was then offering itself to mankind through their means. It was from these motives that I published the work known by the name of Common Sense, which is the first work I ever did publish; and so far as I can judge of myself,

I believe I should never have been known in the world as an author, on any subject whatever, had it not been for the affairs of America. I wrote Common Sense the latter end of the year 1775, and published it the first of January, 1776. Independence was declared the fourth of July following.

Any person who has made observations on the state and progress of the human mind, by observing his own, can not but have observed that there are two distinct classes of what are called thoughts—those that we produce in ourselves by reflection and the act of thinking, and those that bolt into the mind of their own accord. I have always made it a rule to treat those voluntary visitors with civility, taking care to examine, as well as I was able, if they were worth entertaining, and it is from them I have acquired almost all the knowledge that I have. As to the learning that any person gains from school education, it serves only, like a small capital, to put him in the way of beginning learning for himself afterward. Every person of learning is finally his own teacher, the reason of which is that principles, being of a distinct quality to circumstances, cannot be impressed upon the memory; their place of mental residence is the understanding and they are never so lasting as when they begin by conception. Thus much for the introductory part.

From the time I was capable of conceiving an idea and acting upon it by reflection, I either doubted the truth of the Christian system or thought it to be a strange affair; I scarcely knew which it was, but I well remember, when about seven or eight years of age, hearing a sermon read by a relation of mine, who was a great devotee of the Church, upon the subject of what is called redemption by the death of the Son of God. After the sermon was ended, I went into the garden, and as I was going down the garden steps (for I perfectly recollect the spot) I revolted at the recollection of what I had heard, and thought to myself that it was making God Almighty act like a passionate man, that killed his son when he could not revenge himself any other way, and as I was sure a man would be hanged that did such a thing, I could not see for what purpose they preached such sermons. This was not one of those kind of thoughts that had anything in it of childish levity; it was to me a serious reflection, arising from the idea I had that God was too good to do such an action, and also too almighty to be under any necessity of doing it. I believe in the same manner to this moment; and I moreover believe, that any system of religion that has anything in it that shocks the mind of a child, cannot be a true system.

It seems as if parents of the Christian profession were ashamed to tell their children anything about the principles of their religion. They sometimes instruct them in morals, and talk to them of the goodness of what they call Providence, for the Christian mythology has five deities—there is God the Father, God the Son, God the Holy Ghost, the God Providence, and the Goddess Nature. But the Christian story of God the Father putting his son to death, or employing people to do it (for that is the plain language of the story) cannot be told by a parent to a child; and to tell him that it was done to make mankind happier and better is making the story still worse—as if mankind could be improved by the example of murder; and to tell him that all this is a mystery is only making an excuse for the incredibility of it.

How different is this to the pure and simple profession of Deism! The true Deist has but one Deity, and his religion consists in contemplating the power, wisdom, and benignity of the Deity in his works, and in endeavouring to imitate him in everything moral, scientifical, and mechanical.

The religion that approaches the nearest of all others to true Deism, in the moral and benign part thereof, is that professed by the Quakers; but they have contracted themselves too much, by leaving the works of God out of their system. Though I reverence their philanthropy, I cannot help smiling at the conceit, that if the taste of a Quaker could have been consulted at the creation, what a silent and drab-colored creation it would have been! Not a flower would have blossomed its gayeties, nor a bird been permitted to sing. Quitting these reflections, I proceed to other matters. After I had made myself master of the use of the globes, and of the orrery,* and conceived an idea of the infinity of space, and of the eternal divisibility of matter, and obtained at least a general knowledge of what was called natural philosophy, I began to compare, or, as I have before said, to confront, the internal evidence those things afford with the Christian system of faith.

> *As this book may fall into the bands of persons who do not know what an orrery is, it is for their information I add this note, as the name gives no idea of the uses of the thing. The orrery has its name from the person who invented it. It is a machinery of clock-work, representing the universe in miniature, and in which the revolution of the earth round itself and round the sun, the revolution of the moon round the earth, the revolution of the planets round the sun, their relative distances from the sun, as the centre of the whole system, their relative distances from each other, and their different magnitudes, are represented as they really exist in what we call the heavens.

Though it is not a direct article of the Christian system that this world that we inhabit is the whole of the habitable creation, yet it is so worked up therewith, from what is called the Mosaic account of the Creation, the story of Eve and the apple, and the counterpart of that story, the death of the Son of God, that to believe otherwise, that is, to believe that God created a plurality of worlds, at least as numerous as what we call stars, renders the Christian system of faith at once little and ridiculous, and scatters it in the mind like feathers in the air. The two beliefs cannot be held together in the same mind, and he who thinks that be believes both, has thought but little of either.

Though the belief of a plurality of worlds was familiar to the ancients, it is only within the last three centuries that the extent and dimensions of this globe that we inhabit have been ascertained. Several vessels, following the tract of the ocean, have sailed entirely round the world, as a man may march in a circle, and come round by the contrary side of the circle to the spot he set out from. The circular dimensions of our world, in the widest part, as a man would measure the widest round of an apple, or a ball, is only twenty-five thousand and twenty English miles, reckoning sixty-nine miles and a half to an equatorial degree, and may be sailed round in the space of about three years.*

> *Allowing a ship to sail, on an average, three miles in an hour, she would sail entirely round the world in less than one year, if she could sail in a direct circle; but she is obliged to follow the course of the ocean.

A world of this extent may, at first thought, appear to us to be great; but if we compare it with the immensity of space in which it is suspended, like a bubble or a balloon in the air, it is infinitely less in proportion than the smallest grain of sand is to the size of the world, or the finest particle of dew to the whole ocean, and is therefore but small; and, as will be hereafter shown, is only one of a system of worlds of which the universal creation is composed.

It is not difficult to gain some faint idea of the immensity of space in which this and all the other worlds are suspended, if we follow a progression of ideas. When we think of the size or dimensions of a room, our ideas limit themselves to the walls, and there they stop; but when our eye or our imagination darts into space, that is, when it looks upward into what we call the open air, we cannot conceive any walls or boundaries it can have, and if for the sake of resting our ideas, we suppose a boundary, the question immediately renews itself, and asks, what is beyond that boundary? and in the same manner, what is beyond the next boundary? and so on till the fatigued imagination returns and says, There is no end. Certainly, then, the Creator was not pent for room when he made this world no larger than it is, and we have to seek the reason in something else.

If we take a survey of our own world, or rather of this, of which the Creator has given us the use as our portion in the immense system of creation, we find every part of it—the earth, the waters, and the air that surround it—filled and, as it were crowded with life, down from the largest animals that we know of to the smallest insects the naked eye can behold, and from thence to others still smaller, and totally invisible without the assistance of the microscope. Every tree, every plant, every leaf, serves not only as a habitation but as a world to some numerous race, till animal existence becomes so exceedingly refined that the effluvia of a blade of grass would be food for thousands.

Since, then, no part of our earth is left unoccupied, why is it to be supposed that the immensity of space is a naked void, lying in eternal waste? There is room for millions of worlds as large or larger than ours, and each of them millions of miles apart from each other.

Having now arrived at this point, if we carry our ideas only one thought further, we shall see, perhaps, the true reason, at least a very good reason for our happiness, why the Creator, instead of making one immense world extending over an immense quantity of space, has preferred dividing that quantity of matter into several distinct and separate worlds, which we call planets, of which our earth is one. But before I explain my ideas upon this subject, it is necessary (not for the sake of those that already know, but for those who do not) to show what the system of the universe is.

That part of the universe that is called the solar system (meaning the system of worlds to which our earth belongs, and of which Sol, or in English language, the Sun, is the centre) consists, besides the Sun, of six distinct orbs, or planets, or worlds, besides the secondary called the satellites or moons, of which our earth has one that attends her in her annual revolution round the Sun, in like manner as the other satellites or moons attend the planets or worlds to which they severally belong, as may be seen by the assistance of the telescope.

The Sun is the centre round which those six worlds or planets revolve at different distances therefrom, and in circles concentric to each other. Each world keeps constantly in nearly the same track round the Sun, and continues, at the same time, turning round itself in nearly an upright position, as a top turns round itself when it is spinning on the ground, and leans a little sideways.

It is this leaning of the earth (23.5 degrees) that occasions summer and winter, and the different length of days and nights. If the earth turned round itself in a position perpendicular to the plane or level of the circle it moves in a round the Sun, as a top turns round when it stands erect on the ground, the days and nights would be always of the same length, twelve hours day and twelve hours night, and the season would be uniformly the same throughout the year.

Every time that a planet (our earth for example) turns round itself, it makes what we call day and night; and every time it goes entirely round the Sun it makes what we call a year; consequently our world turns three hundred and sixty-five times round itself, in going once round the Sun.*

*Those who supposed that the sun went round the earth every 24 hours made the same mistake in idea that a cook would do in fact, that should make the fire go round the meat, instead of the meat turning round itself toward the fire.

The names that the ancients gave to those six worlds, and which are still called by the same names, are Mercury, Venus, this world that we call ours, Mars, Jupiter, and Saturn. They appear larger to the eye than the stars, being many million miles nearer to our earth than any of the stars are. The planet Venus is that which is called the evening star, and sometimes the morning star, as she happens to set after or rise before the Sun, which in either case is never more than three hours.

The Sun as before said, being the centre, the planet or world nearest the Sun is Mercury; his distance from the Sun is thirty-four million miles, and he moves round in a circle always at that distance from the Sun, as a top may be supposed to spin round in the track in which a horse goes in a mill. The second world is Venus; she is fifty-seven million miles distant from the Sun, and consequently moves round in a circle much greater than that of Mercury. The third world is this that we inhabit, and which is eighty-eight million miles distant from the Sun, and consequently moves round in a circle greater than that of Venus. The fourth world is Mars; he is distant from the Sun one hundred and thirty-four million miles, and consequently moves round in a circle greater than that of our earth. The fifth is Jupiter; he is distant from the Sun five hundred and fifty-seven million miles, and consequently moves round in a circle greater than that of Mars. The sixth world is Saturn; he is distant from the Sun seven hundred and sixty-three million miles, and consequently moves round in a circle that surrounds the circles, or orbits, of all the other worlds or planets.

The space, therefore, in the air, or in the immensity of space, that our solar system takes up for the several worlds to perform their revolutions in round the Sun, is of the extent in a straight line of the whole diameter of the orbit or circle, in which Saturn moves round the Sun, which being double his distance from the Sun, is fifteen hundred and twenty-six million miles, and its circular extent is nearly five thousand million, and its globular contents is almost three thousand five hundred million times three thousand five hundred million square miles.*

*If it should be asked, how can man know these things? I have one plain answer to give, which is, that man knows how to calculate an eclipse, and also how to calculate to a minute of time when the planet Venus, in making her revolutions round the sun, will come in a straight line between our earth and the sun, and will appear to us about the size of a large pea passing across the face of the sun. This happens but twice in about a hundred years, at the distance of about eight years from each other, and has happened twice in our time, both of which were foreknown by calculation. It can also be known when they will happen again for a thousand years to come, or to any other portion of time. As therefore, man could not be able to do these things if he did not understand the solar system, and the manner in which the revolutions of the several planets or worlds are performed, the fact of calculating an eclipse, or a transit of Venus, is a proof in point that the knowledge exists; and as to a few thousand, or even a few million miles, more or less, it makes scarcely any sensible difference in such immense distances.

But this, immense as it is, is only one system of worlds. Beyond this, at a vast distance into space, far beyond all power of calculation, are the stars called the fixed stars. They are called fixed, because they have no revolutionary motion, as the six worlds or planets have that I have been describing. Those fixed stars continue always at the same distance from each other, and always in the same place, as the Sun does in the centre of our system. The probability, therefore, is, that each of those fixed stars is also a Sun, round which another system of worlds or planets, though too remote for us to discover, performs its revolutions, as our system of worlds does round our central Sun.

By this easy progression of ideas, the immensity of space will appear to us to be filled with systems of worlds, and that no part of space lies at waste, any more than any part of our globe of earth and water is left unoccupied.

Having thus endeavoured to convey, in a familiar and easy manner, some idea of the structure of the universe, I return to explain what I before alluded to, namely, the great benefits arising to man in consequence of the Creator having made a plurality of worlds, such as our system is, consisting of a central Sun and six worlds, besides satellites, in preference to that of creating one world only of a vast extent.

It is an idea I have never lost sight of, that all our knowledge of science is derived from the revolutions (exhibited to our eye and from thence to our understanding) which those several planets or worlds of which our system is composed make in their circuit round the Sun.

Had, then, the quantity of matter which these six worlds contain been blended into one solitary globe, the consequence to us would have been, that either no revolutionary motion would have existed, or not a sufficiency of it to give us the ideas and the knowledge of science we now have; and it is from the sciences that all the mechanical arts that contribute so much to our earthly felicity and comfort are derived.

As, therefore, the Creator made nothing in vain, so also must it be believed that he organized the structure of the universe in the most advantageous manner for the benefit of man; and as we see, and from experience feel, the benefits we derive from the structure of the universe formed as it is, which benefits we should not have had the opportunity of enjoying, if the structure, so far as relates to our system, had been a solitary globe—we can discover at least one reason why a plurality of worlds has been made, and that reason calls forth the devotional gratitude of man, as well as his admiration.

But it is not to us, the inhabitants of this globe, only, that the benefits arising from a plurality of worlds are limited. The inhabitants of each of the worlds of which our system is composed enjoy the same opportunities of knowledge as we do. They behold the revolutionary motions of our earth, as we behold theirs. All the planets revolve in sight of each other, and, therefore, the same universal school of science presents itself to all.

Neither does the knowledge stop here. The system of worlds next to us exhibits, in its revolutions, the same principles and school of science to the inhabitants of their system, as our system does to us, and in like manner throughout the immensity of space.

Our ideas, not only of the almightiness of the Creator, but of his wisdom and his beneficence, become enlarged in proportion as we contemplate the extent and the structure of the universe. The solitary idea of a solitary world, rolling or at rest in the immense ocean of space, gives place to the cheerful idea of a society of worlds, so happily contrived as to administer, even by their motion, instruction to man. We see our own earth filled with abundance, but we forget to consider how much of that abundance is owing to the scientific knowledge the vast machinery of the universe has unfolded.

But, in the midst of those reflections, what are we to think of the Christian system of faith, that forms itself upon the idea of only one world, and that of no greater extent, as is before shown, than twenty-five thousand miles.

An extent which a man walking at the rate of three miles an hour, for twelve hours in the day, could he keep on in a circular direction, would walk entirely round in less than two years. Alas! what is this to the mighty ocean of space, and the almighty power of the Creator?

From whence, then, could arise the solitary and strange conceit that the Almighty, who had millions of worlds equally dependent on his protection, should quit the care of all the rest, and come to die in our world, because, they say, one man and one woman had eaten an apple? And, on the other hand, are we to suppose that every world in the boundless creation had an Eve, an apple, a serpent, and a redeemer? In this case, the person who is irreverently called the Son of God, and sometimes God himself, would have nothing else to do than to travel from world to world, in an endless succession of deaths, with scarcely a momentary interval of life.

It has been by rejecting the evidence that the word or works of God in the creation affords to our senses, and the action of our reason upon that evidence, that so many wild and whimsical systems of faith and of religion, have been fabricated and set up. There may be many systems of religion that, so far from being morally bad, are in many respects morally good; but there can be but ONE that is true; and that one necessarily must, as it ever will, be in all things consistent with the ever-existing word of God that we behold in his works. But such is the strange construction of the Christian system of faith that every evidence the Heavens affords to man either directly contradicts it or renders it absurd.

It is possible to believe, and I always feel pleasure in encouraging myself to believe it, that there have been men in the world who persuade themselves that what is called a pious fraud might, at least under particular circumstances, be productive of some good. But the fraud being once established, could not afterwards be explained, for it is with a pious fraud as with a bad action, it begets a calamitous necessity of going on.

The persons who first preached the Christian system of faith, and in some measure combined with it the morality preached by Jesus Christ, might persuade themselves that it was better than the heathen mythology that then prevailed. From the first preachers the fraud went on to the second, and to the third, till the idea of its being a pious fraud became lost in the belief of its being true; and that belief became again encouraged by the interest of those who made a livelihood by preaching it.

But though such a belief might by such means be rendered almost general among the laity, it is next to impossible to account for the continual persecution carried on by the Church, for several hundred years, against the sciences and against the professors of science, if the Church had not some record or tradition that it was originally no other than a pious fraud, or did not foresee that it could not be maintained against the evidence that the structure of the universe afforded.

Having thus shown the irreconcileable inconsistencies between the real word of God existing in the universe, and that which is called the Word of God, as shown to us in a printed book that any man might make, I proceed to speak of the three principal means that have been employed in all ages, and perhaps in all countries, to impose upon mankind.

Those three means are Mystery, Miracle, and Prophecy, The first two are incompatible with true religion, and the third ought always to be suspected.

With respect to mystery, everything we behold is, in one sense, a mystery to us. Our own existence is a mystery; the whole vegetable world is a mystery. We cannot account how it is that an acorn, when put into the ground, is made to develop itself and become an oak. We know not how it is that the seed we sow unfolds and multiplies itself, and returns to us such an abundant interest for so small a capital.

The fact, however, as distinct from the operating cause, is not a mystery, because we see it, and we know also the means we are to use, which is no other than putting the seed in the ground. We know, therefore, as much as is necessary for us to know; and that part of the operation that we do not know, and which, if we did, we could not perform, the Creator takes upon himself and performs it for us. We are, therefore, better off than if we had been let into the secret, and left to do it for ourselves.

But though every created thing is, in this sense, a mystery, the word mystery cannot be applied to moral truth, any more than obscurity can be applied to light. The God in whom we believe is a God of moral truth, and not a God of mystery or obscurity. Mystery is the antagonist of truth. It is a fog of human invention, that obscures truth, and represents it in distortion. Truth never envelops itself in mystery, and the mystery in which it is at any time enveloped is the work of its antagonist, and never of itself.

Religion, therefore, being the belief of a God, and the practice of moral truth, cannot have connection with mystery. The belief of a God, so far from having any thing of mystery in it, is of all beliefs the most easy, because it arises to us, as is before observed, out of necessity. And the practice of moral truth, or, in other words, a practical imitation of the moral goodness of God, is no other than our acting toward each other as he acts benignly toward all. We cannot serve God in the manner we serve those who cannot do without such service; and, therefore, the only idea we can have of serving God, is that of contributing to the happiness of the living creation that God has made. This cannot be done by retiring ourselves from the society of the world and spending a recluse life in selfish devotion.

The very nature and design of religion, if I may so express it, prove even to demonstration that it must be free from every thing of mystery, and unencumbered with everything that is mysterious. Religion, considered as a duty, is incumbent upon every living soul alike, and, therefore, must be on a level to the understanding and comprehension of all. Man does not learn religion as he learns the secrets and mysteries of a trade. He learns the theory of religion by reflection. It arises out of the action of his own mind upon the things which he sees, or upon what he may happen to hear or to read, and the practice joins itself thereto.

When men, whether from policy or pious fraud, set up systems of religion incompatible with the word or works of God in the creation, and not only above, but repugnant to human comprehension, they were under the necessity of inventing or adopting a word that should serve as a bar to all questions, inquiries and speculations. The word mystery answered this purpose, and thus it has happened that religion, which is in itself without mystery, has been corrupted into a fog of mysteries.

As mystery answered all general purposes, miracle followed as an occasional auxiliary. The former served to bewilder the mind, the latter to puzzle the senses. The one was the lingo, the other the legerdemain.

But before going further into this subject, it will be proper to inquire what is to be understood by a miracle.

In the same sense that everything may be said to be a mystery, so also may it be said that everything is a miracle, and that no one thing is a greater miracle than another. The elephant, though larger, is not a greater miracle than a mite, nor a mountain a greater miracle than an atom. To an almighty power, it is no more difficult to make the one than the other, and no more difficult to make a millions of worlds than to make one. Everything, therefore, is a miracle, in one sense, whilst in the other sense, there is no such thing as a miracle. It is a miracle when compared to our power and to our comprehension; if not a miracle compared to the power that performs it; but as nothing in this description conveys the idea that is affixed to the word miracle, it is necessary to carry the inquiry further.

Mankind have conceived to themselves certain laws, by which what they call nature is supposed to act; and that a miracle is something contrary to the operation and effect of those laws; but unless we know the whole extent of those laws, and of what are commonly called the powers of nature, we are not able to judge whether any thing that may appear to us wonderful or miraculous be within, or be beyond, or be contrary to, her natural power of acting.

The ascension of a man several miles high into the air would have everything in it that constitutes the idea of a miracle, if it were not known that a species of air can be generated, several times lighter than the common atmospheric air, and yet possess elasticity enough to prevent the balloon in which that light air is enclosed from being compressed into as many times less bulk, by the common air that surrounds it. In like manner, extracting flashes or sparks of fire from the human body, as visible as from a steel struck with a flint, and causing iron or steel to move without any visible agent, would also give the idea of a miracle, if we were not acquainted with electricity and magnetism. So also would many other experiments in natural philosophy, to those who are not acquainted with the subject. The restoring persons to life who are to appearance dead as is practised upon drowned persons, would also be a miracle, if it were not known that animation is capable of being suspended without being extinct.

Besides these, there are performances be slight-of-hand, and by persons acting in concert, that have a miraculous appearance, which when known are thought nothing of. And besides these, there are mechanical and optical deceptions. There is now an exhibition in Paris of ghosts or spectres, which, though it is not imposed upon the spectators as a fact, has an astonishing appearance. As, therefore, we know not the extent to which either nature or art can go, there is no criterion to determine what a miracle is, and mankind, in giving credit to appearances, under the idea of their being miracles, are subject to be continually imposed upon.

Since, then, appearances are so capable of deceiving, and things not real have a strong resemblance to things that are, nothing can be more inconsistent than to suppose that the Almighty would make use of means such as are called miracles, that would subject the person who performed them to the suspicion of being an impostor, and the person who related them to be suspected of lying, and the doctrine intended to be supported thereby to be suspected as a fabulous invention.

Of all the modes of evidence that ever were invented to obtain belief to any system or opinion to which the name of religion has been given, that of miracle, however successful the imposition may have been, is the most inconsistent. For, in the first place, whenever recourse is had to show, for the purpose of procuring that belief, (for a miracle, under any idea of the word, is a show), it implies a lameness or weakness in the doctrine that is preached. And, in the second place, it is degrading the Almighty into the character of a showman, playing tricks to amuse and make the people stare and wonder. It is also the most equivocal sort of evidence that can be set up; for the belief is not to depend upon the thing called a miracle, but upon the credit of the reporter who says that he saw it; and, therefore, the thing, were it true, would have no better chance of being believed than if it were a lie.

Suppose I were to say, that when I sat down to write this book, a hand presented itself in the air, took up the pen, and wrote every word that is herein written; would anybody believe me? Certainly they would not. Would they believe me a whit the more if the thing had been a fact? Certainly they would not. Since, then, a real miracle, were it to happen, would be subject to the same fate as the falsehood, the inconsistency becomes the greater of supposing the Almighty would make use of means that would not answer the purpose for which they were intended, even if they were real.

If we are to suppose a miracle to be something so entirely out of the course of what is called nature, that she must go out of that course to accomplish it, and we see an account given of such a miracle by the person who said he saw it, it raises a question in the mind very easily decided, which is, is it more probable that nature should go out of her course, or that a man should tell a lie? We have never seen, in our time, nature go out of her course; but we have good reason to believe that millions of lies have been told in the same time; it is therefore, at least millions to one, that the reporter of a miracle tells a lie.

The story of the whale swallowing Jonah, though a whale is large enough to do it, borders greatly on the marvellous; but it would have approached nearer to the idea of a miracle, if Jonah had swallowed the whale. In this, which may serve for all cases of miracles, the matter would decide itself, as before stated, namely, is it more probable that a man should have swallowed a whale or told a lie?

But suppose that Jonah had really swallowed the whale, and gone with it in his belly to Nineveh, and to convince the people that it was true, had cast it up in their sight, of the full length and size of a whale, would they not have believed him to have been the devil, instead of a prophet? Or if the whale had carried Jonah to Nineveh, and cast him up in the same public manner, would they not have believed the whale to have been the devil, and Jonah one of his imps?

The most extraordinary of all the things called miracles, related in the New Testament, is that of the devil flying away with Jesus Christ, and carrying him to the top of a high mountain, and to the top of the highest pinnacle of the temple, and showing him and promising to him all the kingdoms of the World. How happened it that he did not discover America, or is it only with kingdoms that his sooty highness has any interest?

I have too much respect for the moral character of Christ to believe that he told this whale of a miracle himself; neither is it easy to account for what purpose it could have been fabricated, unless it were to impose upon the connoisseurs of Queen Anne's farthings and collectors of relics and antiquities; or to render the belief of miracles ridiculous, by outdoing miracles, as Don Quixote outdid chivalry; or to embarrass the belief of miracles, by making it doubtful by what power, whether of God or of the devil, anything called a miracle was performed. It requires, however, a great deal of faith in the devil to believe this miracle.

In every point of view in which those things called miracles can be placed and considered, the reality of them is improbable and their existence unnecessary. They would not, as before observed, answer any useful purpose, even if they were true; for it is more difficult to obtain belief to a miracle, than to a principle evidently moral without any miracle. Moral principle speaks universally for itself. Miracle could be but a thing of the moment, and seen but by a few; after this it requires a transfer of faith from God to man to believe a miracle upon man's report. Instead, therefore, of admitting the recitals of miracles as evidence of any system of religion being true, they ought to be considered as symptoms of its being fabulous. It is necessary to the full and upright character of truth that it rejects the crutch, and it is consistent with the character of fable to seek the aid that truth rejects. Thus much for mystery and miracle.

As mystery and miracle took charge of the past and the present, prophecy took charge of the future and rounded the tenses of faith. It was not sufficient to know what had been done, but what would be done. The supposed prophet was the supposed historian of times to come; and if he happened, in shooting with a long bow of a thousand years, to strike within a thousand miles of a mark, the ingenuity of posterity could make it point-blank; and if he happened to be directly wrong, it was only to suppose, as in the case of Jonah and Nineveh, that God had repented himself and changed his mind. What a fool do fabulous systems make of man!

It has been shown, in a former part of this work, that the original meaning of the words prophet and prophesying has been changed, and that a prophet, in the sense of the word as now used, is a creature of modern invention; and it is owing to this change in the meaning of the words, that the flights and metaphors of the Jewish poets, and phrases and expressions now rendered obscure by our not being acquainted with the local circumstances to which they applied at the time they were used, have been erected into prophecies, and made to bend to explanations at the will and whimsical conceits of sectaries, expounders, and commentators. Everything unintelligible was prophetical, and everything insignificant was typical. A blunder would have served for a prophecy, and a dish-clout for a type.

If by a prophet we are to suppose a man to whom the Almighty communicated some event that would take place in the future, either there were such men or there were not. If there were, it is consistent to believe that the event so communicated would be told in terms that could be understood, and not related in such a loose and obscure manner as to be out of the comprehension of those that heard it, and so equivocal as to fit almost any circumstance that might happen afterward. It is conceiving very irreverently of the Almighty, to suppose he would deal in this jesting manner with mankind, yet all the things called prophecies in the book called the Bible come under this description.

But it is with prophecy as it is with miracle; it could not answer the purpose even if it were real. Those to whom a prophecy should be told, could not tell whether the man prophesied or lied, or whether it had been revealed to him, or whether he conceited it; and if the thing that he prophesied, or intended to prophesy, should happen, or something like it, among the multitude of things that are daily happening, nobody could again know whether he foreknew it, or guessed at it, or whether it was accidental. A prophet, therefore, is a character useless and unnecessary; and the safe side of the case is to guard against being imposed upon by not giving credit to such relations.

Upon the whole, mystery, miracle, and prophecy are appendages that belong to fabulous and not to true religion. They are the means by which so many Lo, heres! and Lo, theres! have been spread about the world, and religion been made into a trade. The success of one impostor gave encouragement to another, and the quieting salvo of doing some good by keeping up a pious fraud protected them from remorse.

Having now extended the subject to a greater length than I first intended, I shall bring it to a close by abstracting a summary from the whole.

First—That the idea or belief of a word of God existing in print, or in writing, or in speech, is inconsistent in itself for the reasons already assigned. These reasons, among many others, are the want of a universal language; the mutability of language; the errors to which translations are subject; the possibility of totally suppressing such a word; the probability of altering it, or of fabricating the whole, and imposing it upon the world.

Secondly—That the Creation we behold is the real and ever-existing word of God, in which we cannot be deceived. It proclaimeth his power, it demonstrates his wisdom, it manifests his goodness and beneficence.

Thirdly—That the moral duty of man consists in imitating the moral goodness and beneficence of God manifested in the creation toward all his creatures. That seeing, as we daily do, the goodness of God to all men, it is an example calling upon all men to practise the same toward each other; and, consequently, that everything of persecution and revenge between man and man, and everything of cruelty to animals, is a violation of moral duty.

I trouble not myself about the manner of future existence. I content myself with believing, even to positive conviction, that the Power that gave me existence is able to continue it, in any form and manner he pleases, either with or without this body; and it appears more probable to me that I shall continue to exist hereafter, than that I should have had existence, as I now have, before that existence began.

It is certain that, in one point, all nations of the earth and all religions agree—all believe in a God; the things in which they disagree, are the redundancies annexed to that belief; and therefore, if ever an universal religion should prevail, it will not be believing anything new, but in getting rid of redundancies, and believing as man believed at first. Adam, if ever there was such a man, was created a Deist; but in the meantime, let every man follow, as he has a right to do, the religion and worship he prefers.

CRITICAL EYE

▶ For Discussion

a. Paine claims "my own mind is my own church." What exactly does he mean? Is this assertion important?

b. Many viewed Paine's work as following early eighteenth century British Deism. What does this approach outline? Do you think it is an appropriate way to approach religion, or is it, as many claimed, blasphemy?

▶ Re-approaching the Reading

Many claim that religion is the foundation of any civilized society; as such, how does Paine's approach to religion speak to his juxtaposition of "common sense" and spirituality?

▶ Writing Assignment

Researching Paine's life, how does the treatment he received—social expulsion, prison, not allowing his body to be buried on American soil—speak to religious indignation? Are Americans overly-religious and, as a result, intolerant, or have we truly evolved into a country where a person can worship however they choose without fear of repercussion?

CHAPTER 6

Gender, Sex, and Sexuality

Being Powerful is like being a lady. If you have to tell people you are, you aren't.
Margaret Thatcher

Whether women are better than men I cannot say—but I can say they are certainly no worse.
Golda Meir

Why can't they have gay people in the army? Personally, I think they are just afraid of a thousand guys with M16s going, "Who'd you call a faggot?"
John Stewart

We live in a world of only two genders. As the 21st century progresses, societies continue to explore and define what a male and female's roles should be. Within the confines of our respective cultures, we embrace, expect, and exclude members based on these expectations of whom and, just as importantly, what its members should represent. Understanding how people should behave and look, as well as who we should become as citizens of nations, or, for that matter, who we can be intimate with, are mandates—either codified in law or unsaid but understood—that allow us to not only embrace our partners and neighbors, but punish them as well. Understanding how powerful sex is, how personally and socially defining it is—within the confines of our homes, schools, and religions—remains one of the most influential issues our world continues to grapple with.

Perhaps what is most perplexing about the issue of gender is that, in many ways, we are still holding fast to stereotypes that stagnate our identities. Should we still, in the 21st century, be arguing that men were born to do one thing and women another? Are we at a point where one's sexuality or sexual orientation can be viewed separately and distinctly from what makes them male or female? Moreover, should we consider that our sexual stereotyping is placing lives in danger?

The works presented here should help navigate the global ramifications of gender, sex, and sexuality in an attempt to help readers determine whether the old adage holds any truth. In short, "have we really come a long way, baby?"

LOUIE CREW

Thriving as an Outsider, Even as an Outcast, in Smalltown America

From 1973 to 1979, my spouse and I lived in Fort Valley, a town of 12,000 people, the seat of Peach County, sixty miles northeast of Plains, right in the geographic center of Georgia. I taught English at a local black college and my spouse was variously a nurse, hairdresser, choreographer for the college majorettes, caterer, and fashion designer.

The two of us have often been asked how we survived as a gay, racially integrated couple living openly in that small town. We are still perhaps too close to the Georgia experience and very much caught up in our similar struggles in central Wisconsin to offer a definite explanation, but our tentative conjectures should interest anyone who values the role of the dissident in our democracy.

Survive we did. We even throve before our departure. Professionally, my colleagues and the Regents of the University System of Georgia awarded me tenure, and the Chamber of Commerce awarded my spouse a career medal in cosmetology. Socially, we had friends from the full range of the economic classes in the community. We had attended six farewell parties in our honor before we called a halt to further fetes, especially several planned at too great a sacrifice by some of the poorest folks in the town. Furthermore, I had been away only four months when the college brought me back to address an assembly of Georgia judges, majors, police chiefs, and wardens. We are still called two to three times a week by scores of people seeking my spouse's advice on fashion, cooking, or the like.

It was not always so. In 1974 my spouse and I were denied housing which we had "secured" earlier before the realtor saw my spouse's color. HUD documented that the realtor thought that "the black man looked like a criminal." Once the town was up in arms when a bishop accused the two of us of causing a tornado which had hit the town early in 1975, an accusation which appeared on the front page of the newspaper. "This is the voice of God. The town of Fort Valley is harboring Sodomists. Would one expect God to keep silent when homosexuals are tolerated? We remember what He did to Sodom and Gomorrah" (*The Macon Herald*, March 20, 1975; 1). A year later my Episcopal vestry asked me to leave the parish, and my own bishop summoned me for discipline for releasing to the national press correspondence related to the vestry's back-room maneuvers. Prompted in part by such officials, the local citizens for years routinely heckled us in public, sometimes threw rocks at our apartment, trained their children to spit on us from their bicycles if we dared to jog, and badgered us with hate calls on an average of six to eight times a week.

"Thriving as an Outsider, even as an Outcast, in Smalltown America," by Louie Crew. Used by permission of the author.

One such episode offers a partial clue to the cause of our survival. It was late summer, 1975 or 1976. I was on my motorcycle to post mail at the street-side box just before the one daily pickup at 6:00 P.M. About fifty yards away, fully audible to about seventy pedestrians milling about the court house and other public buildings, a group of police officers, all men, began shouting at me from the steps of their headquarters: "Louise! Faggot! Queer!"

Anyone who has ever tried to ease a motorcycle from a still position without revving the engine knows that the feat is impossible: try as I did to avoid the suggestion, I sounded as if I were riding off in a huff. About half-way up the street, I thought to myself, "I'd rather rot in jail than feel the way I do now." I turned around, drove back—the policemen still shouting and laughing—and parked in the lot of the station. When I walked to the steps, only the lone black policeman remained.

"Did you speak to me?" I asked him.

"No, sir," he replied emphatically.

Inside I badgered the desk sergeant to tell her chief to call me as soon as she could locate him, and I indicated that I would press charges if necessary to prevent a recurrence. I explained that the police misconduct was an open invitation to more violent hoodlums to act out the officers' fantasies with impunity in the dark. Later, I persuaded a black city commissioner and a white one, the latter our grocer and the former our mortician, to threaten the culprits with suspension if ever such misconduct occurred again.

Over a year later, late one Friday after his payday, a black friend of my spouse knocked at our door to offer a share of his Scotch to celebrate his raise—or so he said. Thus primed, he asked me, "You don't recognize me, do you?"

"No," I admitted.

"I'm the lone black policeman that day you were heckled. I came by really because I thought you two might want to know what happened inside when Louie stormed up to the sergeant."

"Yes," we said.

"Well, all the guys were crouching behind the partition to keep you from seeing that they were listening. Their eyes bulged when you threatened to bring in the K.B.I. and such. Then when you left, one spoke for all when he said, 'But sissies aren't supposed to do things like that!'"

Ironically, I believe that a major reason for our thriving on our own terms of candor about our relationship has been our commitment to resist the intimidation heaped upon us. For too long lesbians and gay males have unwillingly encouraged abuses against ourselves by serving advance notice to any bullies, be they the barnyard-playground variety, or the Bible-wielding pulpiteers, that we would whimper or run into hiding when confronted with even the threat of exposure. It is easy to confuse sensible nonviolence with cowardly nonresistance.

In my view, violent resistance would be counter-productive, especially for lesbians and gays who are outnumbered 10 to 1 by heterosexuals, according to Kinsey's statistics. Yet our personal experience suggests that special kinds of creative nonviolent resistance are a major source of hope if lesbians and gay males are going to reverse the physical and mental intimidation which is our daily portion in this culture.

Resistance to oppression can be random and spontaneous, as in part was my decision to return to confront the police hecklers, or organized and sustained, as more typically has been the resistance by which my spouse and I have survived. I believe that only organized and sustained resistance offers much hope for long-range change in any community. The random act is too soon forgotten or too easily romanticized.

Once we had committed ourselves to one another, my spouse and I never gave much thought for ourselves to the traditional device most gays have used for survival, the notorious "closet" in which one hides one's identity from all but a select group of friends. In the first place, a black man and a white man integrating a Georgia small town simply cannot be inconspicuous. More importantly, the joint checking account and other equitable economies fundamental to the quality of our marriage are public, not private acts. Our denial of the obvious would have secured closet space only for our suffocation; we would have lied, "We are ashamed and live in secret."

All of our resistance stems from our sense of our own worth, our conviction that we and our kind do not deserve the suffering which heterosexuals continue to encourage or condone for sexual outcasts. Dr. Martin Luther King used to say, "Those who go to the back of the bus, deserve the back of the bus."

Our survival on our own terms has depended very much on our knowing and respecting many of the rules of the system which we resist. We are not simply dissenters, but conscientious ones.

For example, we are both very hard workers. As a controversial person, I know that my professionalism comes under far more scrutiny than that of others. I learned early in my career that I could secure space for my differences by handling routine matters carefully. If one stays on good terms with secretaries, meets all deadlines, and willingly does one's fair share of the busy work of institutions, one is usually already well on the way towards earning collegial space, if not collegial support. In Georgia, I routinely volunteered to be secretary for most committees on which I served, thereby having enormous influence in the final form of the groups' deliberations without monopolizing the forum as most other molders of policy do. My spouse's many talents and sensibilities made him an invaluable advisor and confidante to scores of people in the community. Of course, living as we did in a hairdresser's salon, we knew a great deal more about the rest of the public than that public knew about us.

My spouse and I are fortunate in the fact that we like the enormous amount of work which we do. We are not mere opportunists working hard only as a gimmick to exploit the public for lesbian and gay issues. Both of us worked intensely at our professional assignments long before we were acknowledged dissidents with new excessive pressures to excel. We feel that now we must, however unfairly, be twice as effective as our competitors just to remain employed at all.

Our survival has also depended very much on our thorough knowledge of the system, often knowledge more thorough than that of those who would use the system against us. For example, when my bishop summoned me for discipline, I was able to show him that his own canons give him no authority to discipline a lay person except by excommunication. In fact, so hierarchical have the canons of his diocese become, that the only laity who exist worthy of their mention are the few lay persons on vestries.

Especially helpful has been our knowledge of communication procedures. For example, when an area minister attacked lesbians and gays on a TV talk show, I requested actual time; so well received was my response that for two more years I was a regular panelist on the talk show, thereby reaching most residents of the entire middle Georgia area as a known gay person, yet one speaking not just to sexual issues, but to a full range of religious and social topics.

When I was occasionally denied access to media, as in the parish or diocese or as on campus when gossip flared, I knew the value of candid explanations thoughtfully prepared, xeroxed, and circulated to enough folks to assure that the gossips would have access to the truthful version. For example, the vestry, which acted in secret, was caught by surprise when I sent copies of their hateful letter to most other parishioners, together with a copy of a psalm which I wrote protesting their turning the House of Prayer into a Court House. I also was able to explain that I continued to attend, not in defiance of their withdrawn invitation, but in obedience to the much higher invitation issued to us all by the real head of the Church. In January, 1979, in the first open meeting of the parish since the vestry's letter of unwelcome three years earlier, the entire parish voted to censure the vestry for that action and to extend to me the full welcome which the vestry had tried to deny. Only three voted against censure, all three of them a minority of the vestry being censured.

My spouse and I have been very conscious of the risks of our convictions. We have viewed our credentials—my doctorate and his professional licenses—not as badges of comfortable respectability, but as assets to be invested in social change. Dr. King did not sit crying in the Albany jail, "Why don't these folk respect me? How did his happen? What am I doing here?" When my spouse and I have been denied jobs for which we were the most qualified applicants, we have not naively asked how such things could be, nor have we dwelled overly long on self-pity, for we have known in advance the prices we might have to pay, even if to lose our lives. Our realism about danger and risk has helped us to preserve our sanity when everyone about us has seemed insane. I remember the joy which my spouse shared with me over the fact that he had just been fired for his efforts to organize other black nurses to protest their being treated as orderlies by the white managers of a local hospital.

Never, however, have we affirmed the injustices. Initially, we simply cannot be surprised by any evil and are thus less likely to be intimidated by it. Hence, we find ourselves heirs to a special hybrid of courage, a form of courage too often ignored by the heterosexual majority, but widely manifest among sexual outcasts, not the courage of bravado on battlegrounds or sportsfields, but the delicate courage of the lone person who patiently waits out the stupidity of the herd, the cagey courage that has operated many an underground railway station.

Our survival in smalltown America has been helped least, I suspect, by our annoying insistence that potential friends receive us not only in our own right, but also as members of the larger lesbian/gay and black communities of which we are a part. Too many whites and heterosexuals are prepared to single us out as "good queers" or "good niggers," offering us thereby the "rewards" of their friendship only at too great a cost to our integrity. My priest did not whip up the vestry against me the first year we lived openly together. He was perfectly happy to have one of his "clever queers" to dress his wife's hair and the other to help him write his annual report. We became scandalous only when the two of us began to organize the national group of lesbian and gay-male Episcopalians, known as INTEGRITY; then we were no longer just quaint. We threatened his image of himself as the arbiter of community morality, especially as he faced scores of queries from brother priests elsewhere.

Many lesbians and gay males are tamed by dependencies upon carefully selected heterosexual friends with whom they have shared their secret, often never realizing that in themselves alone, they could provide far more affirmation and discover far more strength than is being cultivated by the terms of these "friendships." Lesbians and gay males have always been taught to survive on the heterosexuals' terms, rarely on one's own terms, and almost never on the terms of a community shared with other lesbians and gay males.

Heterosexuals are often thus the losers. The heterosexual acquaintances close to us early on when we were less visible who dropped us later as our notoriety spread were in most cases folks of demonstrably much less character strength than those heterosexuals who remained our friends even as we asserted our difference with thoughtful independence.

My spouse and I have never been exclusive nor aspired to move to any ghetto. In December, 1978, on the night the Macon rabbi and I had successfully organized the area's Jews and gays to protest a concert by Anita Bryant, I returned home to watch the videotape of the march on the late news in the company of eight house guests invited by my spouse for a surprise party, not one of them gay (for some strange reason nine out of ten folks are not), not one of them obligated to be at the earlier march, and not one of them uneasy, as most of our acquaintances would have been a few years earlier before we had undertaken this reeducation together.

Folks who work for social change need to be very careful to allow room for it to happen, not to allow realistic appraisals of risks to prevent their cultivation of the very change which they germinate.

Our survival has been helped in no small way by our candor and clarity in response to rumor and gossip, which are among our biggest enemies. On my campus in Georgia, I voluntarily spoke about sexual issues to an average of 50 classes per year outside my discipline. Initially, those encounters sharpened my wits for tougher national forums, but long after I no longer needed these occasions personally for rehearsal, I continued to accept the invitations, thereby reaching a vast majority of the citizens of the small town where we continued to live. I used to enjoy the humor of sharing with such groups facts which would make my day-to-day life more pleasant. For example, I routinely noted that when a male student is shocked at my simple public "Hello," he would look both ways to see who might have seen him being friendly with the gay professor. By doing this he is telling me and all other knowledgeable folks far more new information about his own body chemistry than he is finding out about mine. More informed male students would reply, "Hello" when greeted. With this method I disarmed the hatefulness of one of their more debilitating weapons of ostracism.

All personal references in public discussions inevitably invade one's privacy, but I have usually found the invasion a small price to pay for the opportunity to educate the public to the fact that the issues which most concern sexual outcasts are not genital, as the casters-out have so lewdly imagined, but issues of justice and simple fairness.

Resistance is ultimately an art which no one masters to perfection. Early in my struggles, I said to a gay colleague living openly in rural Nebraska, "We must stamp on every snake." Wisely he counseled, "Only if you want to get foot poisoning." I often wish I had more of the wisdom mentioned in *Ecclesiastes*, the ability to judge accurately, "The time to speak and the time to refrain from speaking." Much of the time I think it wise to pass public hecklers without acknowledging their taunts, especially when they are cowardly hiding in a crowd. When I have faced bullies head-on, I have tried to do so patiently, disarming them by my own control of the situation. Of course, I am not guaranteed that their violence can thus be aborted every time.

Two major sources of our survival are essentially very private—one, the intense care and love my spouse and I share, and the other, our strong faith in God as Unbounding Love. To these we prefer to make our secular witness, more by what we do than by what we say.

I am not a masochist. I would never choose the hard lot of the sexual outcast in small-town

America. Had I the choice to change myself but not the world, I would return as a white male heterosexual city-slicker millionaire, not because whites, males, heterosexuals, city-slickers, and millionaires are better, but because they have it easier.

Yet everyone faces a different choice: accept the world the way you find it, or change it. For year after year I dissented, right in my own neighborhood.

America preserves an ideal of freedom, although it denies freedom in scores of instances. My eighth-grade civics teacher in Alabama did not mention the price I would have to pay for the freedom of speech she taught me to value. I know now that the docile and ignorant dislike you fiercely when you speak truth they prefer not to hear. But I had a good civics class, one that showed me how to change our government. I rejoice.

Sometimes I think it's society's critics must appreciate the society far more than others, for the critics typically take very seriously the society's idle promises and forgotten dreams. When I occasionally see them, I certainly don't find many of my heterosexual eighth-grade classmates probing much farther than the issues of our common Form 1040 headaches and the issues as delivered by the evening news. Their lives seem often far duller than ours and the main adventures in pioneering they experience come vicariously, through television, the movies, and for a few, through books. In defining me as a criminal, my society may well have hidden a major blessing in its curse by forcing me out of lethargy into an on-going, rigorous questioning of the entire process. Not only do I teach *The Adventures of Huckleberry Finn,* my spouse and I have in an important sense had the chance to be Huck and Jim fleeing a different form of slavery and injustice in a very real present.

Critical Eye

▶ For Discussion

a. Despite Crew's civil right to live as he pleases, did the town have the right to express their views about his lifestyle?

b. Can you ask someone to adjust his or her faith in order to accommodate someone else's lifestyle?

c. Can/should a faith that strictly forbids someone's lifestyle still embrace the individual?

▶ Re-approaching the Reading

Imagine that Crew is telling the story from the viewpoint of a Muslim. Would the account be worse or the same?

▶ Writing Assignment

Crew asserts that those who discriminate are often bullies who need to be confronted. Is this notion true or false? Furthermore, what are the dangers of challenging bullies in this day and age?

JAMES BALDWIN

From the Novel
GIOVANNI'S ROOM

The person who appeared, and whom I did not know very well, was a girl named Sue, blonde and rather puffy, with the quality, in spite of the fact that she was not pretty, of the girls who are selected each year to be Miss Rheingold. She wore her curly blond hair cut very short, she had small breasts and a big behind, and in order, no doubt, to indicate to the world how little she cared for appearance or sensuality, she almost always wore tight blue jeans. I think she came from Philadelphia and her family was very rich. Sometimes, when she was drunk, she reviled them, and, sometimes, drunk in another way, she extolled their virtues of thrift and fidelity. I was both dismayed and relieved to see her. The moment she appeared I began, mentally, to take off all her clothes.

'Sit down,' I said. 'Have a drink.'

'I'm glad to *see* you,' she cried, sitting down, and looking about for the waiter. 'You'd rather dropped out of sight. How've you been?'— abandoning her search for the waiter and leaning forward to me with a friendly grin.

'I've been fine,' I told her. 'And you?'

'Oh, *me!* Nothing ever happens to me.' And she turned down the corners of her rather predatory and also vulnerable mouth to indicate that she was both joking and not joking. 'I'm built like a brick stone wall.' We both laughed. She peered at me. 'They tell me you're living way out at the end of Paris, near the zoo.'

'I found a maid's room out there. Very cheap.'

'Are you living alone?'

I did not know whether she knew about Giovanni or not. I felt a hint of sweat on my forehead. 'Sort of,' I said.

'Sort of? What the hell does *that* mean? Do you have a monkey with you, or something?'

I grinned, 'No. But this French kid I know, he lives with his mistress, but they fight a lot and it's really *his* room so sometimes, when his mistress throws him out, he bunks with me for a couple of days.'

'Ah!' she sighed. '*Chagrin d'amour!*'

'He's having a good time,' I said. 'He loves it.' I looked at her. 'Aren't you?'

'Stone walls,' she said, 'are impenetrable.'

The waiter arrived. 'Doesn't it,' I dared, 'depend on the weapon?'

'What are you buying me to drink?' she asked.

'What do you want?' We were both grinning. The waiter stood above us, manifesting a kind of surly *joie de vivre*.

'I believe I'll have'—she batted the eyelashes of her tight blue eyes—'*un ricard*. With a hell of a lot of ice.'

From *Giovanni's Room* by James Baldwin, copyright © 1956 by James Baldwin. Used by permission of Doubleday, a division of Random House, Inc.

'*Deux ricards,*' I said to the waiter '*avec beaucoup de la glace.*'

'*Oui, monsieur.*' I was sure he despised us both. I thought of Giovanni and of how many times in an evening the phrase, *Oui, monsieur* fell from his lips. With this fleeting thought there came another, equally fleeting: a new sense of Giovanni, his private life and pain, and all that moved like a flood in him when we lay together at night.

'To continue,' I said.

'To continue?' She made her eyes very wide and blank. 'Where were we?' She was trying to be coquettish and she was trying to be hard-headed. I felt that I was doing something very cruel.

But I could not stop. 'We were talking about stone walls and how they could be entered.'

'I never knew,' she simpered, 'that you had any interest in stone walls.'

'There's a lot about me you don't know.' The waiter returned with our drinks. 'Don't you think discoveries are fun?'

She stared discontentedly at her drink. 'Frankly,' she said, turning toward me again, with those eyes, 'no.'

'Oh, you're much too young for that,' I said. '*Everything* should be a discovery.'

She was silent for a moment. She sipped her drink. 'I've made,' she said, finally, 'all the discoveries that I can stand.' But I watched the way her thighs moved against the cloth of her jeans.

'But you can't just go on being a brick stone wall forever.'

'I don't see why not,' she said. 'Nor do I see *how* not.'

'Baby,' I said, 'I'm making you a proposition.'

She picked up her glass again and sipped it, staring straight outward at the boulevard. 'And what's the proposition?'

'Invite me for a drink. *Chez toi.*'

'I don't believe,' she said, turning to me, 'that I've got anything in the house.'

'We can pick up something on the way,' I said.

She stared at me for a long time. I forced myself not to drop my eyes. 'I'm sure that I shouldn't,' she said at last.

'Why not?'

She made a small, helpless movement in the wicker chair. 'I don't know. I don't know what you want.'

I laughed. 'If you invite me home for a drink,' I said, 'I'll show you.'

'I think you're being impossible,' she said, and for the first time there was something genuine in her eyes and voice.

'Well,' I said, 'I think *you* are.' I looked at her with a smile which was, I hoped, both boyish and insistent. 'I don't know what I've said that's so impossible. I've put all my cards on the table. But you're still holding yours. I don't know why you should think a man's being impossible when he declares himself attracted to you.'

'Oh, please,' she said, and finished her drink, 'I'm sure it's just the summer sun.'

'The summer sun,' I said, 'has nothing to do with it.' And when she still made no answer, 'All you've got to do,' I said desperately, 'is decide whether we'll have another drink here or at your place.'

She snapped her fingers abruptly but did not succeed in appearing jaunty. 'Come along,' she said. 'I'm certain to regret it. But you really will have to buy something to drink. There *isn't* anything in the house. And that way,' she added, after a moment, 'I'll be sure to get something out of the deal.'

It was I, then, who felt a dreadful holding back. To avoid looking at her, I made a great show of getting the waiter. And he came, as surly as ever, and I paid him, and we rose and started walking towards the rue de Sèvres, where Sue had a small apartment.

Her apartment was dark and full of furniture. 'None of it is mine,' she said. 'It all belongs to the French lady of a certain age from whom I rented it, who is now in Monte Carlo for her nerves.' She was very nervous, too, and I saw that this nervousness could be, for a little while, a great help to me. I had bought a small bottle of cognac and I put it down on her marble-topped table and took her in my arms. For some reason I was terribly aware that it was after seven in the evening, that soon the sun would have disappeared from the river, that all the Paris night was about to begin, and that Giovanni was now at work.

She was very big and she was disquietingly fluid—fluid without, however, being able to flow. I felt a hardness and a constriction in her, a grave distrust, created already by too many men like me ever to be conquered now. What we were about to do would not be pretty.

And, as though she felt this, she moved away from me. 'Let's have a drink' she said. 'Unless, of course, you're in a hurry. I'll try not to keep you any longer than absolutely necessary.'

She smiled and I smiled, too. We were as close in that instant as we would ever get—like two thieves. 'Let's have several drinks.' I said.

'But not *too* many,' she said, and simpered again suggestively, like a broken-down movie queen facing the cruel cameras again after a long eclipse.

She took the cognac and disappeared into her corner of a kitchen. 'Make yourself comfortable,' she shouted out to me. 'Take off your shoes. Take off your socks. Look at my books—I often wonder what I'd do if there weren't any books in the world.'

I took off my shoes and lay back on her sofa. I tried not to think. But I was thinking that what I did with Giovanni could not possibly be more immoral than what I was about to do with Sue.

She came back with two great brandy snifters. She came close to me on the sofa and we touched glasses. We drank a little, she watching me all the while, and then I touched her breasts. Her lips parted and she put her glass down with extraordinary clumsiness and lay against me. It was a gesture of great despair and I knew that she was giving herself, not to me, but to that lover who would never come.

And I—I thought of many things, lying coupled with Sue in that dark place. I wondered if she had done anything to prevent herself from becoming pregnant; and the thought of a child belonging to Sue and me, of my being trapped that way—in the very act, so to speak, of trying to escape—almost precipitated a laughing jag. I wondered if her blue jeans had been thrown on top of the cigarette she had been smoking. I wondered if anyone else had a key to her apartment, if we could be heard through the inadequate walls, how much in a few moments, we would hate each other. I also approached Sue as though she were a job of work, a job which it was necessary to do in an unforgettable manner. Somewhere, at the very bottom of myself, I realized that I was doing something awful to her and it became a matter of my honor not to let this fact become too obvious. I tried to convey, through this grisly act of love, the intelligence, at least, that it was not her, not *her* flesh, that I despised—it would not be her I could not face when we became vertical again. Again, somewhere at the bottom of me, I realized that my fears had been excessive and groundless and, in effect, a lie: it became clearer every instant that what I had been afraid of had nothing to do with my body. Sue was not Hella and she did not lessen my terror of what would happen when Hella came: she increased it, she made it more real than it had been before. At the same time, I realized that my performance with Sue was succeeding even too well, and I tried not to despise her for feeling so little what her laborer felt. I travelled through a network of Sue's cries, of Sue's tom-tom fists on my back, and judged by means of her thighs, by means of her legs, how soon I could be free. Then I thought, *The end is coming soon*, her sobs became even higher and harsher, I was terribly aware of the small of my back and the cold sweat there, I thought, *Well, let her have it for Christ sake, get it over with;* then it was ending and I hated her and me, then it was over, and the dark, tiny room rushed back. And I wanted only to get out of there.

She lay still for a long time. I felt the night outside and it was calling me. I leaned up at last and found a cigarette.

'Perhaps,' she said, 'we should finish our drinks.'

She sat up and switched on the lamp which stood beside her bed. I had been dreading this moment. But she saw nothing in my eyes—she stared at me as though I had made a long journey on a white charger all the way to her prison house. She lifted her glass.

'*À la votre*,' I said.

'*À la votre?*' She giggled. '*À la tienne, chéri!*' She leaned over and kissed me on the mouth. Then, for a moment, she felt something; she leaned back and stared at me, her eyes not quite tightening yet; and she said, lightly, 'Do you suppose we could do this again sometime?'

'I don't see why not,' I told her, trying to laugh. 'We carry our own equipment.'

She was silent. Then: 'Could we have supper together—tonight?'

'I'm sorry,' I said. 'I'm really sorry, Sue, but I've got a date.'

'Oh. Tomorrow, maybe?'

'Look, Sue. I hate to make dates. I'll just surprise you.'

She finished her drink. 'I doubt that,' she said.

She got up and walked away from me. 'I'll just put on some clothes and come down with you.'

She disappeared and I heard the water running. I sat there, still naked, but with my socks on, and poured myself another brandy. Now I was afraid to go out into that night which had seemed to be calling me only a few moments before.

When she came back she was wearing a dress and some real shoes, and she had sort of fluffed up her hair. I had to admit she looked better that way, really more like a girl, like a school-girl. I rose and started putting on my clothes. 'You look nice,' I said.

There was a great many things she wanted to say, but she forced herself to say nothing. I could scarcely bear to watch the struggle occurring in her face, it made me so ashamed. 'Maybe you'll be lonely again,' she said, finally. 'I guess I won't mind if you come looking for me.' She wore the strangest smile I had ever seen. It was pained and vindictive and humiliated, but she inexpertly smeared across this grimace a bright, girlish gaiety—as rigid as the skeleton beneath her flabby body. If fate ever allowed Sue to reach me, she would kill me with just that smile.

'Keep a candle,' I said, 'in the window'—and she opened her door and we passed out into the streets.

CRITICAL EYE

▶ For Discussion

a. In what way is the character dealing with his own self-hatred as he tries to reach out for human contact?

b. Is this text condemning casual sex or revealing a kind of enlightenment that comes as a result of it?

▶ Re-approaching the Reading

While we are not made aware of it in this section, the text reveals that the main character is a homosexual. How does that impact your reading of this section?

▶ Writing Assignment

In what ways are we all leading two lives? Is it almost necessary to do so in order to protect ourselves from the scrutiny and abuse of others?

DAVID MURA

HOW AMERICA UNSEXES THE ASIAN MALE

The Japanese-American actor Marc Hayashi once said to me: "Every culture needs its eunuchs. And we're it. Asian-American men are the eunuchs of America." I felt an instant shock of recognition.

To my chagrin, I came close to being one such eunuch on screen in the Coen brothers' movie "Fargo."

The call for the role seemed perfect: a Japanese-American man, in his late 30's, a bit portly, who speaks with a Minnesota accent.

I am a sansei, a third-generation Japanese-American. I've lived in Minnesota for 20 years. Though not portly, I'm not thin. A writer and a performance artist, I had done one small film for PBS.

After I passed the first two readings, my wife and I talked about what other parts might follow and even joked about moving to Hollywood. But in the end, the Coens found another Asian-American actor.

But when I saw the much-acclaimed "Fargo," I said to myself, "Thank God I didn't get the part." The character I would have played is Mike Yanagita, a Japanese-American who speaks with a thick Minnesota accent and awkwardly attempts a pass at an old high school friend, Marge Gunderson, a rural police chief who is visibly pregnant.

He then tells of marrying a mutual acquaintance from high school and of her recent death from cancer. A few scenes later, Marge learns that his marriage was fiction: the acquaintance is not only alive, but has also complained to the police that Mike has been harassing her.

The Japanese-American character has no relevance to Margie's investigation. He is there mainly for humor. The humor is based on his derangement and his obvious illusions that Marge or their acquaintance would ever find him attractive.

I recognized this character as only the latest in a long line of Asian and Asian-American male nerds. Often, as in "Fargo," such a character will pant after white women, ridiculous in his desires. In the movies, as in the culture as a whole, Asian-American men seem to have no sexual clout. Or sexual presence.

Americans rarely talk about race and sex together. It's still taboo. Yet, I often wonder what people make of me and my wife, who is three-quarters WASP and one-quarter Hungarian Jew. Recently we went shopping with my sister Linda and our children. Several people, all white, mistook Linda for the wife, the mother. Was that because many whites find it difficult to picture an Asian-American man with a white woman?

"How America Unsexes the Asian Male" by David Mura. Reprinted by permission of the author.

In fiction, when East meets West, it is almost always a Western man meeting an Asian woman. There is constant reinforcement for the image of the East as feminine and the stereotype of Asian women as exotic, submissive and sensual. From "Madame Butterfly" to "The Karate Kid, Part II" and "Miss Saigon," the white man who falls in love with an Asian woman has been used to proffer the view that racial barriers cannot block the heart's affections.

But such pairings simply place white men at the screen's center and reinforce a hierarchy of power and sexual attractiveness. They play on the stereotype of the East as feminine. And where does that leave Asian men?

A salient feature of the play "M. Butterfly" is that it affirms this feminine view of Asian men. In it, a French diplomat conducts a lengthy love affair with someone he believes is a woman but is actually a Chinese transvestite. The affair proves that Asian manhood is indeed difficult to find, at least for white Westerners. And when the "mistress" strips to a highly buffed and masculine body, it is not just the diplomat who gasps, but the audience as well.

And the stereotypes continue. In the sitcom "All-American Girl," Margaret Cho played a hip Korean-American who dated white boys in defiance of her mother's wishes. The brother was a studious, obsequious geek who dated no one.

Asian and Asian-American men are simply not seen as attractive or sexual beings by the mainstream culture. What could be attractive about the horny, thick-glassed, nerdy Asian guy, ridiculous in his desires for white women?

How little things change. As a boy I watched Mickey Rooney as the Japanese buffoon neighbor in "Breakfast at Tiffany's" and knew I never wanted to be associated with this snarling, bucktoothed creature who shouted at Audrey Hepburn, "Miss Gorrightry, Miss Gorrightry," and panted when she offered to let him photograph her; I identified with John Wayne against the Japs; in "Have Gun Will Travel," I was a cowboy like Paladin, not the Chinese messenger who ran into the hotel lobby shouting, "Terragram for Mr. Paradin."

To me as a child, Asian features, Asian accents—these were all undesirable. They weren't part of my image of a real all-American boy.

For a while this seemed to work. My parents, interned during World War II, wanted to distance themselves from their ethnic roots. We lived in an all-white suburb, where I generally felt like one of the crowd. Then came adolescence, and my first boy-girl party. As usual, I was the only Asian-American and person of color in the room. But when we began to play spin the bottle, I felt a new sense of difference from the others. And then the bottle I'd spun pointed to a girl I had a crush on, and she refused to kiss me.

Did that have to do with race? I had no language to express how race factored into the way the others perceived me, nor did they. But if the culture had told me Asian men were nerds or goofy houseboys, the white kids at the party must have received the same message.

In college, in the early 1970's, my reaction to the sexual place assigned to me took the form of compulsive sexuality: rampant promiscuity with white women and an obsession with pornography. There was definitely a racial component to it: my desires focused specifically on white women. I thought if I was with a white woman, then I would be as "good" as a white guy.

It took me years to figure out what was going on. It helped to read Frantz Fanon, the great Caribbean author and psychiatrist. In "Black Skin, White Masks," he writes of how the black man who constantly sleeps with white women has the illusion that his feelings of inferiority will somehow be erased by this act.

Gradually, I began to ask questions about how I learned what was sexually attractive and what images the culture gave me of myself.

How, for instance, does race factor in attraction? A popular way around such questions is to say that love sees no color.

I don't believe that. We are taught to see and process race early on. Race may not be the sole determinant in interracial relationships, but it is a factor. When I look at my wife, for example, I'm aware my desires for her cannot be separated from the ways the culture has inculcated me with standards of white beauty.

And when I told Alexs Pate, an African-American novelist, about Marc Hayashi's comment about the eunuchization of Asian-American men, he replied, "And black men are the sexual demons."

One is undersexed, the other, oversexed. Everyone knows who possesses a normal, healthy sense of sexuality.

Recently, after a panel discussion on "identity art," an elderly white man came up and complimented me on a performance I'd appeared in with my friend Alexs. Then he asked, "Weren't you in 'Fargo,' too?"

"No," I replied. "That wasn't me."

CRITICAL EYE

▶ For Discussion

a. The author posits that being stereotyped sexually is just as offensive and prejudiced as any form of racism. Why might this be true?

b. Would you argue that the images of what can be construed as "attractive," "beautiful," or "normal" are received from television and film and that these images in turn affect how we view those who are outside of these constructs?

c. What other myths have we constructed about Asian people, and how have these images come about?

▶ Re-approaching the Reading

Mura's assertion is that America, as a whole, has a fixed viewpoint of all Asian men as eunichs and all Asian women as exotic. Has he presented enough information to substantiate his claims? If he has, explore. If he hasn't, explain.

▶ Writing Assignment

Think of other ethnic groups in this country who have undergone some form of racial/ethnic stereotyping. Is what any of these groups has endured any different than what Mura writes about?

JUNOT DIAZ

FIESTA 1980

Mami's youngest sister—my tía Yrma—finally made it to the United States that year. She and tío Miguel got themselves an apartment in the Bronx, off the Grand Concourse and everybody decided that we should have a party. Actually, my pops decided, but everybody—meaning Mami, tía Yrma, tío Miguel and their neighbors—thought it a dope idea. On the afternoon of the party Papi came back from work around six. Right on time. We were all dressed by then, which was a smart move on our part. If Papi had walked in and caught us lounging around in our underwear, he would have kicked our asses something serious.

He didn't say nothing to nobody, not even my moms. He just pushed past her, held up his hand when she tried to talk to him and headed right into the shower. Rafa gave me the look and I gave it back to him; we both knew Papi had been with that Puerto Rican woman he was seeing and wanted to wash off the evidence quick.

Mami looked really nice that day. The United States had finally put some meat on her; she was no longer the same flaca who had arrived here three years before. She had cut her hair short and was wearing tons of cheap-ass jewelry which on her didn't look too lousy. She smelled like herself, like the wind through a tree. She always waited until the last possible minute to put on her perfume because she said it was a waste to spray it on early and then have to spray it on again once you got to the party.

We—meaning me, my brother, my little sister and Mami—waited for Papi to finish his shower. Mami seemed anxious, in her usual dispassionate way. Her hands adjusted the buckle of her belt over and over again. That morning, when she had gotten us up for school, Mami told us that she wanted to have a good time at the party. I want to dance, she said, but now, with the sun sliding out of the sky like spit off a wall, she seemed ready just to get this over with.

Rafa didn't much want to go to no party either, and me, I never wanted to go anywhere with my family. There was a baseball game in the parking lot outside and we could hear our friends, yelling, Hey, and, Cabrón, to one another. We heard the pop of a ball as it sailed over the cars, the clatter of an aluminum bat dropping to the concrete. Not that me or Rafa loved baseball; we just liked playing with the local kids, thrashing them at anything they were doing. By the sounds of the shouting, we both knew the game was close, either of us could have made a difference. Rafa frowned and when I frowned back, he put up his fist. Don't you mirror me, he said.

Don't you mirror me, I said.

He punched me—I would have hit him back but Papi marched into the living room with his

---

"Fiesta 1980," from *Drown* by Junot Diaz, copyright © 1996 by Junot Diaz. Used by permission of Riverhead Books, an imprint of Penguin Group (USA) Inc.

towel around his waist, looking a lot smaller than he did when he was dressed. He had a few strands of hair around his nipples and a surly closed-mouth expression, like maybe he'd scalded his tongue or something.

Have they eaten? he asked Mami.

She nodded. I made you something.

You didn't let him eat, did you?

Ay, Dios mío, she said, letting her arms fall to her side.

Ay, Dios mío is right, Papi said.

I was never supposed to eat before our car trips, but earlier, when she had put out our dinner of rice, beans and sweet platanos, guess who had been the first one to clean his plate? You couldn't blame Mami really, she had been busy—cooking, getting ready, dressing my sister Madai. I should have reminded her not to feed me but I wasn't that sort of son.

Papi turned to me. Coño, muchacho, why did you eat?

Rafa had already started inching away from me. I'd once told him I considered him a low-down chickenshit for moving out of the way every time Papi was going to smack me.

Collateral damage, Rafa had said. Ever heard of it?

No.

Look it up.

Chickenshit or not, I didn't dare glance at him. Papi was old-fashioned; he expected your undivided attention when you were getting your ass whupped. You couldn't look him in the eye either—that wasn't allowed. Better to stare at his belly button, which was perfectly round and immaculate. Papi pulled me to my feet by my ear.

If you throw up—

I won't, I cried, tears in my eyes, more out of reflex than pain.

Ya, Ramón, ya. It's not his fault, Mami said.

They've known about this party forever. How did they think we were going to get there? Fly?

He finally let go of my ear and I sat back down. Madai was too scared to open her eyes. Being around Papi all her life had turned her into a major-league wuss. Anytime Papi raised his voice her lip would start trembling, like some specialized tuning fork. Rafa pretended that he had knuckles to crack and when I shoved him, he gave me a *Don't start* look. But even that little bit of recognition made me feel better.

I was the one who was always in trouble with my dad. It was like my God-given duty to piss him off, to do everything the way he hated. Our fights didn't bother me too much. I still wanted him to love me, something that never seemed strange or contradictory until years later, when he was out of our lives.

By the time my ear stopped stinging Papi was dressed and Mami was crossing each one of us, solemnly, like we were heading off to war. We said, in turn, Bendición, Mami, and she poked us in our five cardinal spots while saying, Que Dios te bendiga.

This was how all our trips began, the words that followed me every time I left the house.

None of us spoke until we were inside Papi's Volkswagen van. Brand-new, lime-green and bought to impress. Oh, we were impressed, but me, every time I was in that VW and Papi went above twenty miles an hour, I vomited. I'd never had trouble with cars before—that van was like my curse. Mami suspected it was the upholstery. In her mind, American things—appliances, mouthwash, funny-looking upholstery—all seemed to have an intrinsic badness about them. Papi was careful about taking me anywhere in the VW, but when he had to, I rode up front in Mami's usual seat so I could throw up out a window.

¿Cómo te sientas? Mami asked over my shoulder when Papi pulled onto the turnpike. She had her hand on the base of my neck. One thing about Mami, her palms never sweated.

I'm OK, I said, keeping my eyes straight ahead. I definitely didn't want to trade glances with Papi. He had this one look, furious and sharp, that always left me feeling bruised.

Toma. Mami handed me four mentas. She had thrown three out her window at the beginning of our trip, an offering to Eshú; the rest were for me.

I took one and sucked it slowly, my tongue knocking it up against my teeth. We passed Newark Airport without any incident. If Madai had been awake she would have cried because the planes flew so close to the cars.

How's he feeling? Papi asked.

Fine, I said. I glanced back at Rafa and he pretended like he didn't see me. That was the way he was, at school and at home. When I was in trouble, he didn't know me. Madai was solidly asleep, but even with her face all wrinkled up and drooling she looked cute, her hair all separated into twists.

I turned around and concentrated on the candy. Papi even started to joke that we might not have to scrub the van out tonight. He was beginning to loosen up, not checking his watch too much. Maybe he was thinking about that Puerto Rican woman or maybe he was just happy that we were all together. I could never tell. At the toll, he was feeling positive enough to actually get out of the van and search around under the basket for dropped coins. It was something he had once done to amuse Madai, but now it was habit. Cars behind us honked their horns and I slid down in my seat. Rafa didn't care; he grinned back at the other cars and waved. His actual job was to make sure no cops were coming. Mami shook Madai awake and as soon as she saw Papi stooping for a couple of quarters she let out this screech of delight that almost took off the top of my head.

That was the end of the good times. Just outside the Washington Bridge, I started feeling woozy. The smell of the upholstery got all up inside my head and I found myself with a mouthful of saliva. Mami's hand tensed on my shoulder and when I caught Papi's eye, he was like, No way. Don't do it.

The first time I got sick in the van Papi was taking me to the library, Rafa was with us and he couldn't believe I threw up. I was famous for my steel-lined stomach. A third-world childhood could give you that. Papi was worried enough that just as quick as Rafa could drop off the books we were on our way home. Mami fixed me one of her honey-and-onion concoctions and that made my stomach feel better. A week later we tried the library again and on this go-around I couldn't get the window open in time. When Papi got me home, he went and cleaned out the van himself, an expression of askho on his face. This was a big deal, since Papi almost never cleaned anything himself. He came back inside and found me sitting on the couch feeling like hell.

It's the car, he said to Mami. It's making him sick.

This time the damage was pretty minimal, nothing Papi couldn't wash off the door with a blast of the hose. He was pissed, though; he jammed his finger into my cheek, a nice solid thrust. That was the way he was with his punishments: imaginative. Earlier that year I'd written an essay in school called "My Father the Torturer," but the teacher made me write a new one. She thought I was kidding.

We drove the rest of the way to the Bronx in silence. We only stopped once, so I could brush my teeth. Mami had brought along my toothbrush and a tube of toothpaste and while every car known to man sped by us she stood outside with me so I wouldn't feel alone.

Tío Miguel was about seven feet tall and had his hair combed up and out, into a demi-fro. He gave me and Rafa big spleen-crushing hugs and then kissed Mami and finally ended up with Madai on his shoulder. The last time I'd seen Tío was at the airport, his first day in the United States. I remembered how he hadn't seemed all that troubled to be in another country.

He looked down at me. Carajo, Yunior, you look horrible!

He threw up, my brother explained.

I pushed Rafa. Thanks a lot, ass-face.

Hey, he said. Tío asked.

Tío clapped a bricklayer's hand on my shoulder. Everybody gets sick sometimes, he said. You should have seen me on the plane over here. Dios mio! He rolled his Asian-looking eyes for emphasis. I thought we were all going to die.

Everybody could tell he was lying. I smiled like he was making me feel better.

Do you want me to get you a drink? Tío asked. We got beer and rum.

Miguel, Mami said. He's young.

Young? Back in Santo Domingo, he'd be getting laid by now.

Mami thinned her lips, which took some doing.

Well, it's true, Tío said.

So, Mami, I said. When do I get to go visit the D.R.?

That's enough, Yunior.

Its the only pussy you'll ever get, Rafa said to me in English.

Not counting your girlfriend, of course.

Rafa smiled. He had to give me that one.

Papi came in from parking the van. He and Miguel gave each other the sort of handshakes that would have turned my fingers into Wonder bread.

Coño, compa'i, ¿cómo va todo? they said to each other.

Tía came out then, with an apron on and maybe the longest Lee Press-On Nails I've ever seen in my life. There was this one guru motherfucker in the *Guinness Book of World Records* who had longer nails, but I tell you, it was close. She gave everybody kisses, told me and Rafa how guapo we were—Rafa, of course, believed her—told Madai how bella she was, but when she got to Papi, she froze a little, like maybe she'd seen a wasp on the tip of his nose, but then kissed him all the same.

Mami told us to join the other kids in the living room. Tío said, Wait a minute, I want to show you the apartment. I was glad Tía said, Hold on, because from what I'd seen so far, the place had been furnished in Contemporary Dominican Tacky. The less I saw, the better. I mean, I liked plastic sofa covers but damn, Tío and Tía had taken it to another level. They had a disco ball hanging in the living room and the type of stucco ceilings that looked like stalactite heaven. The sofas all had golden tassels dangling from their edges. Tía came out of the kitchen with some people I didn't know and by the time she got done introducing everybody, only Papi and Mami were given the guided tour of the four-room third-floor apartment. Me and Rafa joined the kids in the living room. They'd already started eating. We were hungry, one of the girls explained, a pastelito in hand. The boy was about three years younger than me but the girl who'd spoken, Leti, was my age. She and another girl were on the sofa together and they were cute as hell.

Leti introduced them: the boy was her brother Wilquins and the other girl was her neighbor Mari. Leti had some serious tetas and I could tell that my brother was going to gun for her. His taste in girls was predictable. He sat down right between Leti and Mari and by the way they were smiling at him I knew he'd do fine. Neither of the girls gave me more than a cursory one-two, which didn't bother me. Sure, I liked girls but I was always too terrified to speak to them unless we were arguing or I was calling them stupidos, which was one of my favorite words that year. I turned to Wilquins and asked him what there was to do around here. Mari, who had the lowest voice I'd ever heard, said, He can't speak.

What does that mean?

He's mute.

I looked at Wilquins incredulously. He smiled and nodded, as if he'd won a prize or something.

Does he understand? I asked.

Of course he understands, Rafa said. He's not dumb.

I could tell Rafa had said that just to score points with the girls. Both of them nodded. Low-voice Mari said, He's the best student in his grade.

I thought, Not bad for a mute. I sat next to Wilquins. After about two seconds of TV Wilquins whipped out a bag of dominos and motioned to me. Did I want to play? Sure. Me and him played Rafa and Leti and we whupped their collective asses twice, which put Rafa in a real bad mood. He looked at me like maybe he wanted to take a swing, just one to make him feel better. Leti kept whispering into Rafa's ear, telling him it was OK.

In the kitchen I could hear my parents slipping into their usual modes. Papi's voice was loud and argumentative; you didn't have to be anywhere near him to catch his drift. And Mami, you had to put cups to your ears to hear hers. I went into the kitchen a few times—once so the tíos could show off how much bullshit I'd been able to cram in my head the last few years; another time for a bucket-sized cup of soda. Mami and Tía were frying tostones and the last of the pastelitos. She appeared happier now and the way her hands worked on our dinner you would think she had a life somewhere else making rare and precious things. She nudged Tía every now and then, shit they must have been doing all their lives. As soon as Mami saw me though, she gave me the eye. Don't stay long, that eye said. Don't piss your old man off.

Papi was too busy arguing about Elvis to notice me. Then somebody mentioned María Montez and Papi barked, María Montez? Let me tell *you* about María Montez, compa'i.

Maybe I was used to him. His voice—louder than most adults'—didn't bother me none, though the other kids shifted uneasily in their seats. Wilquins was about to raise the volume on the TV, but Rafa said, I wouldn't do that. Muteboy had balls, though. He did it anyway and then sat down. Wilquins's pop came into the living room a second later, a bottle of Presidente in hand. That dude must have had Spider-senses or something. Did you raise that? he asked Wilquins and Wilquins nodded.

Is this your house? his pops asked. He looked ready to beat Wilquins silly but he lowered the volume instead.

See, Rafa said. You nearly got your *ass kicked*.

I met the Puerto Rican woman right after Papi had gotten the van. He was taking me on short trips, trying to cure me of my vomiting. It wasn't really working but I looked forward to our trips, even though at the end of each one I'd be sick. These were the only times me and Papi did anything together. When we were alone he treated me much better, like maybe I was his son or something.

Before each drive Mami would cross me.

Bendición, Mami, I'd say.

She'd kiss my forehead. Que Dios te bendiga. And then she would give me a handful of mentas because she wanted me to be OK. Mami didn't think these excursions would cure anything, but the one time she had brought it up to Papi he had told her to shut up, what did she know about anything anyway?

Me and Papi didn't talk much. We just drove around our neighborhood. Occasionally he'd ask, How is it?

And I'd nod, no matter how I felt.

One day I was sick outside of Perth Amboy. Instead of taking me home he went the other way on Industrial Avenue, stopping a few minutes later in front of a light blue house I didn't recognize. It reminded me of the Easter eggs we colored at school, the ones we threw out the bus windows at other cars.

The Puerto Rican woman was there and she helped me clean up. She had dry papery hands and when she rubbed the towel on my chest, she did it hard, like I was a bumper she was waxing. She was very thin and had a cloud of brown hair rising above her narrow face and the sharpest blackest eyes you've ever seen.

He's cute, she said to Papi.

Not when he's throwing up, Papi said.

What's your name? she asked me. Are you Rafa?

I shook my head.

Then it's Yunior, right?

I nodded.

You're the smart one, she said, suddenly happy with herself. Maybe you want to see my books?

They weren't hers. I recognized them as ones my father must have left in her house. Papi was a voracious reader, couldn't even go cheating without a paperback in his pocket.

Why don't you go watch TV? Papi suggested. He was looking at her like she was the last piece of chicken on earth.

We got plenty of channels, she said. Use the remote if you want.

The two of them went upstairs and I was too scared of what was happening to poke around. I just sat there, ashamed, expecting something big and fiery to crash down on our heads. I watched a whole hour of the news before Papi came downstairs and said, Let's go.

About two hours later the women laid out the food and like always nobody but the kids thanked them. It must be some Dominican tradition or something. There was everything I liked—chicharrones, fried chicken, tostones, sancocho, rice, fried cheese, yuca, avocado, potato salad, a meteor-sized hunk of pernil, even a tossed salad which I could do without—but when I joined the other kids around the serving table, Papi said, Oh no you don't, and took the paper plate out of my hand. His fingers weren't gentle.

What's wrong now? Tía asked, handing me another plate.

He ain't eating, Papi said. Mami pretended to help Rafa with the pernil.

Why can't he eat?

Because I said so.

The adults who didn't know us made like they hadn't heard a thing and Tío just smiled sheepishly and told everybody to go ahead and eat. All the kids—about ten of them now—trooped back into the living room with their plates a-heaping and all the adults ducked into the kitchen and the dining room, where the radio was playing loud-ass bachatas. I was the only one without a plate. Papi stopped me before I could get away from him. He kept his voice nice and low so nobody else could hear him.

If you eat anything, I'm going to beat you. ¿Entiendes?

I nodded.

And if your brother gives you any food, I'll beat him too. Right here in front of everybody. ¿Entiendes?

I nodded again. I wanted to kill him and he must have sensed it because he gave my head a little shove.

All the kids watched me come in and sit down in front of the TV.

What's wrong with your dad? Leti asked.

He's a dick, I said.

Rafa shook his head. Don't say that shit in front of people.

Easy for you to be nice when you're eating, I said.

Hey, if I was a pukey little baby, I wouldn't get no food either.

I almost said something back but I concentrated on the TV. I wasn't going to start it. No fucking way. So I watched Bruce Lee beat Chuck Norris into the floor of the Colosseum and tried to pretend that there was no food anywhere in the house. It was Tía who finally saved me. She came into the living room and said, Since you ain't eating, Yunior, you can at least help me get some ice.

I didn't want to, but she mistook my reluctance for something else.

I already asked your father.

She held my hand while we walked; Tía didn't have any kids but I could tell she wanted them. She was the sort of relative who always remembered your birthday but who you only went to visit because you had to. We didn't get past the first-floor landing before she opened her pocketbook and handed me the first of three pastelitos she had smuggled out of the apartment.

Go ahead, she said. And as soon as you get inside make sure you brush your teeth.

Thanks a lot, Tía, I said.

Those pastelitos didn't stand a chance.

She sat next to me on the stairs and smoked her cigarette. All the way down on the first floor and we could still hear the music and the adults and the television. Tía looked a ton like Mami; the two of them were both short and light-skinned. Tía smiled a lot and that was what set them apart the most.

How is it at home, Yunior?

What do you mean?

How's it going in the apartment? Are you kids OK?

I knew an interrogation when I heard one, no matter how sugar-coated it was. I didn't say anything. Don't get me wrong, I loved my tía, but something told me to keep my mouth shut. Maybe it was family loyalty, maybe I just wanted to protect Mami or I was afraid that Papi would find out—it could have been anything really.

Is your mom all right?

I shrugged.

Have there been lots of fights?

None, I said. Too many shrugs would have been just as bad as an answer. Papi's at work too much.

Work, Tía said, like it was somebody's name she didn't like.

Me and Rafa, we didn't talk much about the Puerto Rican woman. When we ate dinner at her house, the few times Papi had taken us over there, we still acted like nothing was out of the ordinary. Pass the ketchup, man. No sweat, bro. The affair was like a hole in our living room floor, one we'd gotten so used to circumnavigating that we sometimes forgot it was there.

By midnight all the adults were crazy dancing. I was sitting outside Tía's bedroom—where Madai was sleeping—trying not to attract attention. Rafa had me guarding the door; he and Leti were in there too, with some of the other kids, getting busy no doubt. Wilquins had gone across the hall to bed so I had me and the roaches to mess around with.

Whenever I peered into the main room I saw about twenty moms and dads dancing and drinking beers. Every now and then somebody yelled, Quisqueya! And then everybody else would yell and stomp their feet. From what I could see my parents seemed to be enjoying themselves.

Mami and Tía spent a lot of time side by side, whispering, and I kept expecting something to come of this, a brawl maybe. I'd never once been out with my family when it hadn't turned to shit. We weren't even theatrical or straight crazy like other families. We fought like sixth-graders, without any real dignity. I guess the whole night I'd been waiting for a blowup, something between Papi and Mami. This was how I always figured Papi would be exposed, out in public, where everybody would know.

You're a cheater!

But everything was calmer than usual. And Mami didn't look like she was about to say anything to Papi. The two of them danced every now and then but they never lasted more than a song before Mami joined Tía again in whatever conversation they were having.

I tried to imagine Mami before Papi. Maybe I was tired, or just sad, thinking about the way my family was. Maybe I already knew how it would all end up in a few years, Mami without Papi, and that was why I did it. Picturing her alone wasn't easy. It seemed like Papi had always been with her, even when we were waiting in Santo Domingo for him to send for us.

The only photograph our family had of Mami as a young woman, before she married Papi, was the one that somebody took of her at an election party that I found one day while rummaging for money to go to the arcade. Mami had it tucked into her immigration papers. In the photo, she's surrounded by laughing cousins I will never meet, who are all shiny from dancing, whose clothes are rumpled and loose. You can tell it's night and hot and that the mosquitos have been biting. She sits straight and even in a crowd she stands out, smiling quietly like maybe she's the one everybody's celebrating. You can't see her hands but I imagined they're knotting a straw or a bit of thread. This was the woman my father met a year later on the Malecón, the woman Mami thought she'd always be.

Mami must have caught me studying her because she stopped what she was doing and gave me a smile, maybe her first one of the night. Suddenly I wanted to go over and hug her, for no other reason than I loved her, but there were about eleven fat jiggling bodies between us. So I sat down on the tiled floor and waited.

I must have fallen asleep because the next thing I knew Rafa was kicking me and saying, Let's go. He looked like he'd been hitting those girls off; he was all smiles. I got to my feet in time to kiss Tía and Tío good-bye. Mami was holding the serving dish she had brought with her.

Where's Papi? I asked,

He's downstairs, bringing the van around. Mami leaned down to kiss me.

You were good today, she said.

And then Papi burst in and told us to get the hell downstairs before some pendejo cop gave him a ticket. More kisses, more handshakes and then we were gone.

I don't remember being out of sorts after I met the Puerto Rican woman, but I must have been because Mami only asked me questions when she thought something was wrong in my life. It took her about ten passes but finally she cornered me one afternoon when we were alone in the apartment. Our upstairs neighbors were beating the crap out of their kids, and me and her had been listening to it all afternoon. She put her hand on mine and said, Is everything OK, Yunior? Have you been fighting with your brother?

Me and Rafa had already talked. We'd been in the basement, where our parents couldn't hear us. He told me that yeah, he knew about her.

Papi's taken me there twice now, he said.

Why didn't you tell me? I asked.

What the hell was I going to say? *Hey, Yunior, guess what happened yesterday? I met Papi's sucia!*

I didn't say anything to Mami either. She watched me, very very closely. Later I would think, maybe if I had told her, she would have confronted him, would have done something, but who can know these things? I said I'd been having trouble in school and like that everything was back to normal between us. She put her hand on my shoulder and squeezed and that was that.

We were on the turnpike, just past Exit 11, when I started feeling it again. I sat up from leaning against Rafa. His fingers smelled and he'd gone to sleep almost as soon as he got into the van. Madai was out too but at least she wasn't snoring.

In the darkness, I saw that Papi had a hand on Mami's knee and that the two of them were quiet and still. They weren't slumped back or anything; they were both wide awake, bolted into their seats. I couldn't see either of their faces and no matter how hard I tried I could not imagine their expressions. Neither of them moved. Every now and then the van was filled with the bright rush of somebody else's headlights. Finally I said, Mami, and they both looked back, already knowing what was happening.

CRITICAL EYE

▶ **For Discussion**

a. Why, in your opinion, does the father seem comfortable flaunting his secret in front of his sons?

b. Can the way the father treats his son be construed as child abuse or discipline?

▶ **Re-approaching the Reading**

Examine Cheever's "The Reunion" alongside Diaz's story. Are the two sons suffering from similar burdens?

▶ **Writing Assignment**

Should a child still love and respect a parent, even after discovering something shameful about the adult who is supposed to stand as a shining example of how to live?

JULIAN WILLIAMS

The New Breed

A few days ago I found myself engaged in an awkward conversation with a group of people I continuously encounter at a neighborhood bar on what seems like every Thursday. We meet with no planned invitation, and there are no official announcements about the next meeting. Now that I think about it, we—in true New York fashion—never meet for dinner or visit each other's apartments before or after drinks. And no, we do not communicate via email or texts. We are simply a group of casual drunks who, for well over a year, seem to find themselves in familiar proximity of each other on the same day of every week.

On this night, we were spaced out comfortably, having beaten the after-work-rush, discussing the ever puzzling yet seemingly simplistic phenomenon known as parenting.

One of our more vocal members is a woman named Nicole. She is a former Wall Street analyst who consciously, going on ten years, opted to become a fulltime housewife. She is a woman who's stinging and frequently derisive views have exposed her as a resentful babysitter with too much education and no one around during the day to really notice. In retrospect, she is a relatively young, married White woman who drinks far too much. She likes red wine in abundance, and it tends to make her face flush as she rocks from side to side twirling a lock of her shoulder length hair that, less than a month ago, was neck length hair.

Looking at her, Nicole has a decent figure—which, given that she can stay home and exercise all day, she should—but she is not nearly as cute as she thinks. During our abbreviated time together she tends to speak very loudly and exudes a smug and patronizing demeanor, which everyone whispers about when she leaves to go outside for one of her many smoking breaks. While unintentional on her part, Nicole is often abrupt and haughty in her demeanor—and, well, when she talks to you she can be a little condescending when she is attempting to appear insightful. "My husband always says . . ." or "Our place upstate . . ." or "When I was in charge of the Hershman account—you know Hershman, don't you? Hello, the billionaire developer. Anyway . . ."

Not unlike her deluded perception regarding her looks, her discernment on matters of life and living are rudimentary and overly opinionated. And, the more she drinks, the louder she gets. Sober, she is a close talker. Drunk, she practically spits in your mouth.

Truthfully, I am not uncomfortable around Nicole—and I am definitely not denying her acumen with numbers—but I believe she needs to learn that over-talking other people while engaging in social conversation is rude.

It was Nicole who introduced the topic of parenting, just as she had guided us towards a discussion on the true nature of Islam the week before. I'm sure I am not the only one who wonders if she picks a focus ahead of time and prepares herself so that she can appear more insightful than the rest of us. "Well, actually, from the oasis cities of Makkah and Madinah in the Arabian desert—centuries before the Turks embraced it—Islam spread with electrifying speed within a half century of the Prophet's death. If I'm not mistaken, and I'm sure I'm not, this was during the 6th century," she explained off-handedly after Simone had simply asked if anyone knew where the best place to get Middle Eastern food was.

On tonight's topic she claimed that when it comes to raising kids, "parents are the first line of defense." "It's the job of a mother and father to make sure that their kids grow up to be productive members of society," she asserted.

In a somewhat disinterested tone, I asked her, "Well, what sacrifice does that entail for the parent?"

Tilting her head, she eyed me as if I had asked if her own kids—two supposedly "adorable" tots, one male, the other not, of five and seven years—were well-adjusted and, if not, they would like to come and live with me. Her response was—in her special, condescending way—quick and brief.

She said, "Everything."

The others, who were now eager to become involved in the discussion, nodded and agreed, even though out of the seven people present, only one other was a parent. I pressed the issue.

"Well, what exactly is everything?"

The room was now a-buzz. This is just the type of discussion people of a certain age in these types of settings—those past twenty-five with a drink nearby—hope to find on a Thursday after work which, in New York, actually begins the weekend. This gathering, like so many others in bars across the city, provides an outlet where those who often feel unappreciated at work or home can now assert themselves in a conversation where they can be witty and droll without fear of know-it-all spouses or bosses.

As Elif, our heavily accented Romanian chain smoker, arrived, they caught her up on the discussion. While she ordered a drink and expressed how thankful she was that she hadn't missed much, I caught a glimpse of something that I had, until that moment, never really noticed—something that I'm now sure is a constant during our talks.

Elif, like the rest of them, was sitting directly in front of me. Facing me head on. From my vantage point, I now sat alone.

This was fine, I guess, especially since no one ever really seems too eager to take-up my argument. Yet, as I reflect on our past conversations, I now see that, at some point, I usually become odd member out. By asking my simple questions, I somehow position myself as the Thursday night nitwit—the antagonist who never seems to quite agree with the rest. As I scanned the reactions of the group—the eyes rolled upward, brows creased, lips twisted —I knew, as I have always known, that these people don't think I'm as bright as they are.

Feeling a little played, I asked again, "Well, what the hell does everything mean?"

John, a male flight attendant who insists on always wearing several silver arm bangles of various sizes that are far too feminine for my taste but, otherwise, a seemingly good guy, responded through a chuckle, "Well, everything means everything."

In my mind's eye, it was here that I should have recognized we had arrived at my stop. I should have pressed the buzzer, exited, happy to dismount the conversation. Instead . . .

"I'm still not sure what 'everything' entails," I said. "Do you mean that parents should have no lives other than their children; that from the moment the child plops outta the mother and gulps its first thankful breath, the parents should resign to quit their jobs, turn over their gym memberships, and send out 'gone til child can fend for self' notices?" I asked.

"Is this the 'everything' you mean?" I inquired, face frowning, distaste written all over my brow.

At the time I wasn't really sure why I was becoming worked up about this issue, but I began to feel as if I was presenting the air of one who had been insulted. Yet, when I think back, their faces showed no sign of worry—not regarding my questioning or their understanding of the matter. See, this group is a mixture of seemingly intelligent—at the very least, educated—and somewhat successful drinkers who consider themselves well-versed in many different areas of, both, fact and trivia. In other words, these are people who know what they know. And in our year of sharing stories and opinions, they have come to know that I am joker, a kidder, a sarcastic satirist who couldn't possibly think half the stuff I express. Quite simply, our time together has made them believe they have insight into my person.

What I often find interesting are the types of relationships we have with people. This gathered group of Thursday night warriors knows me, but don't really know me. They are merely acquaintances that, over time, assume they have figured me out. They are like the people we work with but never associate with outside of work. They call you friend and, probably in their limited minds, actually believe that is what you are. But the reality is different. These are individuals who you would never share real secrets with or talk about anything of importance late into the night. You would never invite them to hang out where you're actually from, nor would you allow them to see what you look like away from the office.

My Thursday group has heard me speak of fatherhood, children, the state of the union and have giggled or waved a dismissive hand at me—as if I were too intellectually inept to comprehend their more insightful views on the ways of family, politics, or religion—time and again. Yet, as this night's conversation matured and I became more and more agitated, I could see in the faces of a few that they were beginning to wonder if some of my biting commentary on these subjects had not merely been banter for laughs and shock value.

"C'mon. Y'all talk a good game, but I mean—c'mon. Really now, it takes more to raise little monsters than just some empty concept—a bit of 'everything,'" I said drolly.

One of our motley crew is a very short, extremely small-breasted woman with an unusually wide nose and an overbite that borders on buck-toothedness. For the life of me, I can never remember her name. When this happens to me, and it happens often, I tend to reference people, at least to myself, based upon some physical trait.

She is lil' Bucky.

Lil' Bucky's eyes started at my feet and eventually rested on my forehead. Once she'd scanned me completely, she snickered, "You weren't kidding when you said you don't like kids."

I didn't really see how that comment was a fitting response. Not that it's not true. Sure, I've said it a million times. But her saying it was awkward. It just wasn't timed right.

When trying to make a point, timing is crucial, no?

As I was preparing my witty retort, the delicious looking Dominican bartender, whose breasts couldn't possibly sit up or out like that without the help of a better than average bra or a surgeon's skillful hand, came, took drink orders, and chimed in as if this was a discussion open to the public, saying, "I know what you all means. I do's everything wit' my kids. If you don't, you yusedem to the streets. I mean, hell, you got ta' watch em' all de time—watchem' like haw-kes. If you don't, errested or molested, I always say."

High fives were exchanged. Laughs turned to bellows. Both men and women agreed. After thinking about what she had said, I rose and looked behind the bar, then angled my head towards the back of the bar, and then towards the front. After surveying the premises, I looked the bartender in her big blue eyes which, I'd guess, had to be colored contacts, and asked, "If that's true, where are your kids now?"

One day I'll stop, I swear.

Looking at me as if I'd asked, "Does that thong ride up your back only when you bend over or are you just high-hipped?" she went to pour our drinks. Dana, the motherless mother hen of the groups asked me, "Why do you have to be so crass?"

Truthfully, I didn't actually think I was being crass, and, since I didn't want to be an asshole, I considered her question.

Rude? Maybe. Insensitive? I could argue for or against. Silly? I could see.

But crass? C'mon.

I responded, "If I had said, 'If that's true, seems like yo sexy lil ass should be with your kids instead of shaking those stuffed melons and pouring drinks for dollar bills!' now that, that would have been crass."

After wet napkins were thrown and boos were lauded my way, Jan and Amir, the married couple of our outing, piped up: "I mean, you can't be with them twenty-four-seven. You gotta have a life," Amir claimed.

Jan added, "Yeah, hell, what are grandparents for?" Taking his cue as only a couple that spends too much time together can, Amir—a one cosmopolitan drunk if ever there was one—slurred, "When we have our kids, they'll be with us as much as possible. Dana will take the first two years off and stay home but, after that, we've got to go on living."

Slapping Amir's groping hand off her shoulder with a shocked and somewhat flushed look on her face, one that indicated a late night conversation about the sexist views from "the man I married," Dana said, with a pitch of annoyance, "Uh, yeah. The point is you have to get a support system until you eventually drop them off at school. You gotta have help. You'd go crazy if you didn't get away from them sometimes."

Hoisting her drink in the air, Nicole screamed "Ain't that the truth, girl."

Turning to face Nicole, I drooped my shoulders, presented a confused and defeated posture, and said, "But I thought you said that the sacrifice entailed 'everything.'"

Staring me straight in the face, Nicole—who I noticed for the first time is a wee bit cross-eyed—said to me, and I quote, "Well, I didn't mean EV...ER...Y...THING. What I meant was, well, everything."

To her comment they all nodded in some form of agreement. To Nicole's assessment I, too, acted as if I understood—as if her simple words had shined a holy light upon my sinning eyes. But what I understood and what they thought I understood was vastly different. My nodding was more of an inner conversation, a self-confirming clarity on their final concord, which was just what I had assumed when I pressed the issue. Their opinions on the matter were just what I thought they would be.

Before leaving my Thursday night bunch with my knickers in a bunch, having switched to bottled beer from my staple of Kettle One on the rocks because I was afraid I might get a special and unwanted mystery taste courtesy of the bartender—who, consequently, I left a big tip—I summed up what these people, either parents or hoping-to-be-parents-as-soon-as-it-fits, had told me. Apparently, what must happen before and after having kids is a knowledge they all seemed of one mind about: A). You must sacrifice EV...ER...Y...THING, but not everything; B). Kids need constant love and affection, but parents need to breathe sometimes, too; C). There needs to be a good babysitting connection, and grandparents work best; D). School is the eventual daycare center that they can't wait to drop their children off at, leaving the kids attended to during the day and giving the grandparents a much needed break; E). There is no I in team, and, when kids arrive, there is no longer a "me" either until. . . .

Walking down Lexington Ave, I was overwhelmed by the contradictions, the hypocrisy of it all. The opinions, the supposed deep thinking of this drunken bunch were, for me, another sobering nod for birth control.

Honestly, Lil Bucky was right. In my routine, throughout the course of any given day, I am liable to say aloud that I do not like children. One of my favorite quips is, "The only thing I hate worse than kids are teenagers." Men often think I say this to shock people, but that it couldn't possibly be a truism. Women think my sentiment is actually a twisted code for, "I really want kids, but I'm too insecure and embarrassed to express my real nature." But those who know me, the real me, understand that my slant on the subject comes from years of thoughtful observation. More than anything, as a student of human behavior, I have come to realize that what keeps psychiatrists and psychologists in overpriced offices on Fifth Ave. and lavish summer homes in the Hamptons is what my compadres had all just confirmed: today's generation of parents don't know shit.

Four days later, I was on the train headed to Queens.

Twice a week—because I must prostitute my only marketable skill to make ends meet—I am forced to ride the E train, which connects on the East Side at 51st Street, to teach an Art history course entitled Greece, Mythology, and the Artistry of an Empire. As a supposed academic, riding these trains to teach these types of classes seems to be my fate. This course is not even in my field, but, as the saying goes, "Beggars can't be choosers—so they just keep begging."

In order to get to the college, I have to ride a train I hate more than most with people I despise wholeheartedly. While walking through the tunnel from the no. 6 train to the E—on my consistently monotonous quest to make the donuts—I actually feel my body undergo a physical change: my ass tightens, my teeth become locked, and my out-on-the-street scowl grows more fearsome looking.

This transformation is because I know that they are there, waiting, hyperly looking forward to the presence of those they can intimidate, disrespect, or shock. As I trod towards the down escalator, dragging my feet like an insolent child approaching the dentist's office, I see many of them. I recognize them instantly. They are my greatest nemeses next to the state lottery people who refuse to acknowledge me as the rightful winner of all those millions I deserve. They are horribly loathsome creatures, and I would love to have a mass killing of them all—an organized shoving onto the tracks, a strangling, one by one, as the rest wait patiently in line. The way they smell. The way they move. The aggressive nature of these postpubescent misfits makes my journey to Queens one that is as uncomfortable as it is unfortunate.

It's 2:30 PM. The bell has rung. The beasts have been released from their cages.

After waiting on the crowded platform, the E pulls into the station. I have positioned myself so that I am on the last car or, when put into perspective, the first car to exit at Jamaica Center, the final stop. When the doors open, a few enter with me.

The car is crowded, always crowded, and we are all forced to stand. The surrounding hellions who have entered the car with me make noise and entertain themselves. This assembly atmosphere resembles a flock of cackling ducks whose soul purpose is to disrupt those either reading or trying to catch a quick nap. At any moment you expect someone to yell, "Shut the fuck up!"—to assert their right to peace and quiet during their journey. But alas, these flapping mongrels are allowed to continue.

Their presence is, in reality, not that bad. Not overwhelming. They are the tamed beasts, the ones who are wearing uniforms. They do not represent the threat to come. No, these are the private school irritants with high-pitched voices, blue and checkered print bottoms, knee socks and black shoes. They are a part of the world I despise, but they are more grating than anything.

"I mean, man, like, I hate Jennifer," the blond with the pink barrettes and severely red lipstick declares.

"I know," her Asian confidant responds, "I know. Shesu-ha-bitch."

Lord, they have corrupted the Asians, the last hope for their kind.

These types of conversations make you want to catch their eye and mouth a threatening "Quiet, child," followed with a look that says, "Hey, don't make me have to come over there and straighten you out."

Luckily, a paternal browbeating is unnecessary. This bunch is basically innocuous to the rest of us because, while their actions contain maddening manners, there is no real malice. But then we approach the Roosevelt Ave. station, and the sense that they are coming, the terrible ones, builds. Head down, reading my book, I hear them enter before I see them. They rush the door before it fully opens, brushing aggressively passed anyone exiting the train. To a novice, they immediately reflect their "Fuck you, we rule!" attitude. But to an experienced rider, a veteran of this war, it is more than that.

These are students of dark skin, Black teenagers—with a sprinkling of Puerto Rican, Haitian, and Dominican here and there—whose message is, "We'll gather as a group and stomp anyone who doesn't like what we are saying, what we stand for. Just look us in the eye if you dare!"

Growling, they walk slumped and crooked, bouncing up and down the length of the car. One of them is in possession of a radio that is as big as an adult torso—a monstrosity covered in lights and dials that must run on no less than fifty dollars worth of batteries. He is blaring a song by some ignorant misogynist, an individual whose main lyrics seem to be about "riding" and "dropping it" and "sweat" and—"balls?" The louder the music plays, the more incited they become. And the more excited they get, the more powerful and righteous their behavior becomes—as if challenging anyone who looks their way to dare and criticize their taste in music.

New York is funny. It is the only place I know where people without skateboards or sandy beaches and boardwalks still carry boom boxes in this age of iPods.

As music fills the car, the savage ones rant and rave, hoop and holler, pacing between cars as if high on some drug that's main jolts are surges of stupidity and profanity. As the frantic pounding continues throughout the car, people still act as if they are reading. But as I know—a pretender myself—this is no longer really possible.

I try not to stare, make no eye contact. I look away and keep my head low. I do this not because I am afraid, but, more so, because I am—maybe I am afraid. As I skim the car between moments of feigning as if I'm reading the lines on my now lifeless book's pages, I notice the most horrific and outrageous conversation—the one which spews hatred and overflows with recognizable anger and vileness that is appalling, yet no longer surprising—is coming from a group near the door across from me. This loud and profanely despicable monologue is led as a vulgar donation to the rest of us by the most vicious of the creatures. Clearly, the tone emanating is different than the rest. Yelling at a deafening pitch, we cannot not hear this discourse. We are all—those of us who were dumb enough to have not run for, if not our lives, our tender sensibilities—witnesses to the unrehearsed production of what has emerged in the past years as the most untamed, shrewdest, and dangerous of the bunch. Speaking is the predator to be watched most closely, truly the most despicable of their kind—a new breed of animal.

She is around 5'3. Her hair is pulled back in micro braids and she is wearing too much makeup. Her skin is riddled with poc-marks, as if she were in the habit of bursting pimples as soon as they arrive and flicking off the morning scabs, leaving a pink mark blending in with her other darker ones. She is of a dark complexion, with a huge behind and heavy breasts. She is wearing what appears to be pink calf-length high top sneakerish type shoes—with pump heels? I try not to look anymore, but it's like a car accident—and everybody has to look at a wreck. As I continue to slyly take the measure of my captor, I note that she has black with white tipped painted fingernails that, if I'm not mistaken, seem to have a picture of her own face superimposed on the thumbs. Noticing all this as I covertly examine her person, I am ever leery to any sudden moves she might make. As she continues to roar, I note that her teeth are not so much yellow as sepia in coloring, and her breath, though I cannot smell it, is most assuredly foul. She is neither large in stature nor bearing any apparent weapons, but, like the pack leading hyena, she is dangerous—undeniably dangerous.

As I look over, I note that her bag is on the floor, leaning heavily against the leg of a nervous looking Indian woman coming from or going to work. My only hope is that this is not the woman's first trip with these filthy mammals, for it is a scarring adventure for the faint of heart.

"I woulda' cut dat bitch. I will fuck that hoe and her fat ass sista up. Let them hoes come round tomorrow. Shit, you know I don't care. Fuck, fuck, fuck," she roared.

And then came the threat.

As if her stomach was rumbling and she was desperate to relieve herself, the loathsome creature said, "Oooooooooo, I'mahaveta smack me a muthafucka before I see dem hoes. Shit, I gotta get this out."

Slowly shifting my head from side to side, I'm sure I wasn't the only person wondering whom exactly she might choose to express herself upon.

Slowly, as I turned back toward her, it seemed, at least for a moment, that she was staring at me with an annoyed yet wondering look.

The rest of the pack exhorted her on, and she gathered explosive energy from their combinations of sweat and indignant support.

But surely, I thought, there is a sense of animus that some of them must keep hidden from her. For though she seems to lead this group of hooligans or, at the very least, she is the voice that represents the twisted pragmatism of her peers, they cannot like or respect her. I refuse to believe that's possible. Deep down, they have to despise her.

I need to believe this.

And, if true, there has to be something else that links those obviously less vocal to her. My brain says that sex is involved, but I quickly dismiss it. I find her presence so offensive that I can't imagine how anyone would want her in an intimate way. Besides, her aggression is so unattractive and nakedly obvious that I can only imagine that sex is…I shake my head and almost laugh at myself. Rubbing my hand over my face, I look up and catch her tapping the tall guy with the boom box and pointing in my direction.

Fear is an interesting factor to come to grips with. Some people are afraid of bugs. For some, it's animals. Some, it's heights. Some people are, I've heard, afraid of success. But most people are afraid of confrontation. It is not an unwise course of awareness, this fear, because there are many angry, crazed folks out there, hoping that you're not insightful enough to know that you should look away. It is, however, not fear of imminent physical danger that makes this bunch so bad. What is worse than being afraid of anyone, let alone a group of anyones, is when you catch yourself behaving timidly and unsure around people who are so much younger, so much dumber, and, often, who look similar—though horribly evolved—to pictures in the photo albums located in your own parents' home. This awakening is, undeniably, humiliating.

As the young carnivore scanned the car sniffing and snorting, possibly sending warning signals or mating calls to her kind, you could actually see in her face how she reveled in the environment she was creating. The creatures that resembled her but who were from another world—those who had boarded the train earlier—clearly found the monster and her minions amusing. As I looked to the other end of the train where they were, I noted how they giggled, snickered, and nodded their approval at the scene the more barbarous members of their species performed. Having observed both groups extensively, I knew, at that very moment, that these privileged teens had so much and nothing at all in common with these terrorists of a darker hue. In a sense, the private school kids were like White kids who dress Black and imitate Black trends in clothes and speech. While thinking it is cool to rail and offend the majority, they have a buried knowledge in their subconscious, a sense of knowing that betrays their jovial mood, their defiant body language. Inevitably, this insight will appear like a wise specter in the coming years and whisper, "This act was cute at one point, but it is time to step away from this silliness, straighten up, and assume your rightful role as productive and respectful citizen." Once they actually reach this realization, they can cut their hair, remove their gaudy earrings, cover their tattoos, pull up their pants, put on a suit or a knee-length skirt, and then presto-changeo—like it never happened.

I don't know which group I hate worse.

As the music blared about bitches and cars, and how bitches like cars, and about how much crissy and bling and bitches could be ridden inside cars, the walls shrank inward and those who were not part of this spectacle were smushed together against the windows looking as if they were contemplating breaking the glass and leaping onto the safety of the tracks. Refusing to move and bracing any of the encroaching hostage takers with my evil stare, I—standing erect, back to door, chest poked forward—stood amid a few of the braver souls. While not reading the book I was desperately trying to read, I noticed that the young female...thing—I really don't know what to call her at this point, her behavior so repulsive, her presence so offensive—had adjusted her position so that she would be the first-line, the welcoming party standing in front of the opening doors to meet and greet any new passengers.

Many straphangers opted to run and enter another car. Some eventually gathered their belongings and walked through the connecting doors. And then there were those who squeezed passed the menacing gauntlet, either aggressively pushing forward and showing little dread or giving off the scent of coward and thus having to put up with the subjective whims of this gang of hoodlums led by a girl gone wild and ugly.

It was a tense thirty-minute ride, one that often made me consider changing cars. But being a man of full height and body weight—a least as full of size as my thin 5'10, 155 pounds will ever reach—I stood my ground and waited for it to get worse.

Somehow, I never expected what was to come. With eyes lowered, I saw the whole disgusting act. It was the moment when she proved herself—this leader, this monster—to me, us all, what she thought of life.

"I can't wait to get to da crib and light up. Gots some straight up flame that needs smoking. Skunk, babyyyyy. Y'all trying to . . . damn, I need something to drink cus my mouth is dry as hell," she said.

Coughing, "Dog, my . . ." was the sentence she didn't complete.

The words seemed to catch in her throat. The hope that maybe she had swallowed her tongue and was going to strangle on her own vomit became a dream too pleasing to share. Instead she hocked loudly and, as she extended her chin forward, looking down towards the tiled floor, her discolored incisors extending as she pursed her lips—parting them some—she spit, or is it spat, on the car's floor.

Well I'll be damned.

I didn't look around. I didn't let my eyes wander. I remained frozen because I didn't want to appear as grossed out as I actually was. So, instead, eyes locked, I just stared at the thick yellow and brown and—is that blood, too?

I felt my face flush and my shoulders hunch upward as my stomach turned over. Shaking my head slightly, I brushed it off and quickly regained my composure. I didn't move a muscle. Instead, I gawked at the result, waiting for the alien's acid laced saliva to burn a hole through the floor of the car down onto the tracks. When that didn't happen, I slowly looked up and turned towards the door that separates the train cars.

And I waited.

I waited for the police to come and drag her away because, I'm almost positive, spitting on the train is a crime. I waited for someone to reach out and smack her face, to let her know that this was not the act of a human being on a train—at least not an act performed in the company of other human beings. But mostly, I waited for her to at least seem abashed in some way—to, with head held low, wipe her mouth and offer an apology to those of us who were witnesses to this atrocious behavior.

Luckily the train ride was almost over—because if she was forced to ride any further, since she obviously had no sense of what is done where and when, her next attention getting trick might have been a dropping of trough accompanied by a solid bowel movement.

Laughing at herself, she leaned into the car doors. As another bass thumping song came on, she, obviously a fan, turned one of the dials on the boom box. Suddenly the music cranked up even louder. She had her eyes closed, one hand held over her head while her hips swayed to the hip hop song that consumed the car from end to end.

Mouth open, I slowly raised my head and shamefully locked eyes with a White woman sitting across from me. Her look was one that pleaded with me to act, to speak, to pull out a weapon and slay the beast before it could breed. "Kill her! Lynch the griffin while it is unaware. Slay the Chimera, now!" her eyes begged. But I simply lowered my eyes, embarrassed that this girl would reduce me to this sense of cultural shame, that her behavior would bring the pity and rage of those around us who somehow automatically grouped me as—if no longer one of them—one who had been one of them.

As the train pulled into Jamaica Center, the people disembarked, most leaving through a different door, or circling a wide ark around the yellowish phlegm that was gelling precariously on the floor. Taking my time as to avoid any further interaction with the savage brutes, I hung back, allowing the car to empty out. When I exited, I saw them all hoopin' and hollarin', led by this new breed of teenager—who was now minus the unacknowledged support from her uniformed conspirators who had exited at an earlier stop, retreating to homes and, possibly, meals prepared by hand.

Thinking of this contrast as I approached the line for the platform escalator, I found that I was more than my usually perturbed self. This was definitely a different sensation, not like the daily irritation I usually feel due to the offending presence of those who keep riding the train talking, eating, laughing—breathing. What I felt this time was a strange sense of sadness, and this led to me reflecting on the conversation I'd had with my fellow Thursday night drunkards. Thinking about our conversation on parenting, I began to earnestly reflect on that word—the one that now hung in my mind like an impenetrable mushroom cloud—which all of my cronies kept repeating, as if the term had a power all its own: "everything."

Had this young girl—for surely, before mutating into the thing she had become, she had to have been an innocent, one who wanted nothing more than to be read bedtime stories and who blushed at those who said, "Well aren't you pretty"—been given "everything"? As I thought about that, my curiosity peaked. I really began to consider if the person who for that last half-hour had been the very bane of my existence, had received the "everything" that Nicole and the others had so snootily carried on about?

Was she loved and cared for? Fed at all hours? Spoiled endlessly with toys and affection? Had she been helped with her homework? Had she been given airplane spins on the flats of a parent's feet?

As I shuffled passed the resident platform ranting Jesus Freak, the man holding his worn Bible, screaming at people about how the Lord was coming, and how disgusted he was going to be with us heathens, I wondered about the creature—the girl— that had already exited the station.

Had anyone told her that, no matter what, everything was going to be okay? Was there someone in her life who looked her in the eye and promised that, no matter what, they would be there for her? Had she been given direction? Taught discretion? Punished when insolent and hugged just for being? Was there a party who represented her interests during parent/teacher conferences—someone who was actually stressed about how she was performing in school? Surely there was a person, once upon a time, who cared if she was learning?

Certainly someone taught her to bathe, that brushing prevents gingivitis, and that proper hygiene is important—the whole cleanliness/Godliness spiel.

Someone must have shown her how to insert a tampon. Or told her about the best types of pads to buy. Or explained, at the very least, to never wear white on those uncomfortable days—or, for that matter, after Labor Day. Of course there was a hand that showed her how to cook, how to clean, and how by simply lighting a match in the bathroom the air becomes more breathable and the rest of the house is spared one's most personal intestinal smell.

As I strolled off the escalator into the main hub, I wondered more. Inane questions now flooded my brain.

Wasn't there a trust fund set up to bring her comfort in her latter years? Wouldn't she grow up and strive to find her own voice, even though her family would want her to join the legacy that was their empire? Wouldn't she fight to find a love all her own, instead of the young man from the prestigious family her parents had been hoping she would wed—possibly heir to an import/export fortune?

Or was this all just a cruel fantasy, one that a person like her could never truly fancy?

At the very least, surely there had to be figure at home that pressed her about test scores and reminded her that college was a necessity.

But if all of this were true, didn't someone tell her how to carry herself, how to behave?

For the love of God, didn't someone tell her not to spit on the train?

"Everything."

In less than an hour, this hopelessly angry and ill-mannered misanthrope had confirmed why I was so pessimistic and defensive about the naïve responses of those who tossed around the word as if it was the solution to a life of balance and success.

"Everything?" What the hell is it? Who can actually provide it? Is it even possible? While a great notion, a wonderful fantasy, it seems to be impossible. Or, am I simply so bitter about the world that I can no longer even see how something like "everything" can exist?

Now my curiosity began to bubble my buried resentment. I mean, could they—those who dismissed me as the jaded guy who one day would probably be alone and crotchety—actually offer "everything?"

No, surely the reality remains the same. Of course they can't. They had just as well admitted it that night.

"You have to guide them and be firm about stuff. I read this book about silence as discipline. I think it's the approach I'll take,"Elif declared.

"I'm not sure how I'll tell my kid not to do drugs—as much dope as I smoked when I was a teenager? Shit. Just tell em' not to do it and hope for the best," was Joel's solution.

But it was Nicole who summed it up best, who had really poked her finger in my eye that night: "Just buy them the best stuff and get them the best help. If I decide to go back to work, I want be sure they have the best of everything. Please, I'm just trying to get them to leave the house more, get off those damn computers in their rooms, and get outta my face!" she laughed.

Computers? Rooms? Plural? Wow.

Did the terror of the E-line have a computer in her home? I now pondered. Did she even have a room of her own, a space where she could be private with her own thoughts? Hell, for that matter, I wondered if both her parents were in her life. I wondered if she even knew who her father was.

I walked through the station. There was a line to exit, so I waited. I could smell peanuts and see smoke spewing at the top of the escalator from the pretzel cart upstairs. A white haired woman on a child-sized kick scooter rolled passed me. She looked ridiculous.

Suddenly, I heard hip hop music coming from somewhere. This brought me right back to thoughts of the girl I was clearly becoming too focused on.

Does she have a sense of privilege about anything?

Maybe that's why she behaved the way she did. Maybe harassing a trainload of people was her way of saying, "Hey, nobody ever gave me shit. I ain't got nuthin' and ain't gonna be nuthin'."

I wondered if she ever thought about what it would be like to have someone even discussing her and the silliness of "everything" in the same breath. I bet she would have liked to see somebody at least fail at the effort. Maybe subjecting the rest of us to her diatribe of anger and disdain was as close to feeling apart of the world as she could reach.

As I looked at two male transit policemen who were talking way too familiarly with a couple of tight jean wearing teenagers, I'm pretty sure I know why I became so sensitive last week. It was because I know, having come from a world not completely dissimilar than the misguided monsters, that there is no such thing as "everything." And, for some, there is nothing that even comes close. For the poor, the under-educated, the ones that can never escape the stigmas and stereotypes of their culture—overcome them, maybe, but never escape them—isn't "everything" as ridiculous an illusion to low-income people of color as those White co-workers who return every Monday declaring they have just had a "great weekend"?

Was I upset because the people who were talking last Thursday were like those privileged private school kids? Was I upset because I know that they all had or might have a chance, an actual real live chance, to provide their kids with so much stuff, so many advantages, that it might actually resemble "everything"? Maybe I'd gotten a little heated the previous Thursday because I knew—know— that the "everything" my typically heterogeneous Manhattan group, people who are only urban because they live in a major metropolis, not because they have lived the veiled and coded "urban" life, was more of a possibility than I'd ever known—than this angry future woman would ever be privy. See, my Thursday night crew could never understand that the real reason I have opted never to have children directly correlates with my own failure to conceive of the reality of our topic, all while grasping the utter importance of it.

Or, maybe I got mad because I think that the opposite of everything, no matter how much you give, is sometimes nothing at all.

As I lumbered towards the school, my head throbbed and I felt despondent beyond words. Just as I was beginning to really feel sorry for the girl who society had robbed of a childhood, of opportunities, of love, I heard someone call me. Well, I assume that I was the addressee only because, "Say, bitch!" was shouted so loudly in my direction that it snapped me out of my haze.

As I looked around, I saw her, along with about ten of her devilish minions, step out from under the viaduct near the college. If I didn't know any better—well, rather, if I didn't think it possible—I would have to assume they had been patiently waiting for me. As I smelled the remnants of marijuana smoke filtering the air, I was shocked more than frightened. But more than anything, I was quickly reminded why I hate this group more than any other social irritant in New York—a place overrun with homeless beggars, cons, freaks, and deviants.

Looking her in the face, I could see the challenge in her dilated pupils. "You was looking all crazy at me and shit like you had beef on da train. We gots a problem, mutherfucka?" As she said these things to me, her flippant behavior and exaggerated movements brought "oooos" and "aahhhhhs" from her peers.

Not being a peer, I found myself less than amused. At first, I could not figure out my next move. While not a physically imposing man—besides being one who hasn't had a fistfight since the eighth grade—I was extremely nervous about tussling with a group of teenagers who, obviously, were bold enough to accost me in broad daylight.

Now, at the same time, I am also a grown man, and I'm pretty sure I'd find it more than difficult to live with myself if I allowed a teenager—a girl, no less—to strip away my manhood.

As she hopped around, dancing and flailing herself about for her friends' amusement, I decided to act like an adult and walk through the gauntlet they had made. I would not be intimidated. Plainly, whatever was going to happen was going to happen.

I mean, lets be real. What was she going to do, hit me?

As I took two steps toward the future leaders of our country, our great youthful brain trust,

I felt her move quickly, possessed, I must assume, by the drug she had recently smoked coupled with her generally nasty attitude. In a blink, she had swung upward, trying to snatch off my, as she put it, "lil hoe ass hat."

Before I realized what I was doing, I had pivoted on one foot and pushed her off with my left hand. Falling back as if she couldn't believe I had laid hands on her, as if I was the one bothering her person, her face changed to one of pure and irrational fury, contorting and transforming the same way a housecat hunches its back and bares its pointy little teeth, hissing angrily as if to remind its owner that it is the descendent of a long line of warrior felines. As she lunged forward, the crowd backed away—almost as if they were going to let the two of us go head-to-head without any interference. Like we were two men arguing outside a bar near a deserted truck stop.

She tugged at her ears furiously, yanking at her earrings and cursing incessantly: "This muthafucka dun pushed me! Me! Hell to da fucknaw! I'makill this skinny bitch nigga!"

Her fists were balled tightly and her mouth was wide open. Charging wildly, she came straight ahead.

Well, nobody ever said this new breed was bright. My punch landed flush, right under her left eye. Her skin split instantly. Because she had charged forward, she was already off balance. So, instead of falling backwards, the punch plus her own momentum sent her spiraling downward. When she hit the ground, her face actually scraped the concrete, removing a nice patch of skin from her forehead.

Shit.

Just as a few of her friends were trying to decide if they would take up the battle, I heard the wailing of a siren barreling towards us. As the crowd widened, two police officers, one White, the other of Spanish speaking descent—I couldn't tell if she was Puerto Rican or Columbian or, possibly, a very fair skinned Mexican—came charging over to find me standing over a bleeding teenage girl. As they helped her to her feet, her curses grew more contemptible and the officers actually had to restrain her as she wildly kicked and clawed her way at me, screaming through a foaming mouth about how she was going kill me.

While one officer radioed for an ambulance, the other started asking me a barrage of questions: "What happened? Why did you hit her? Who else was involved? Did they attack you?"

As the questions came flying at me and I attempted to answer, my mind and my mouth could not gather pace with one another. I was in the mist of telling the cop that she, the girl, and her friends were waiting for me and that I was just defending myself when I began to sweat uncontrollably. And the more and more I said, the more my nerves frayed.

And then I lost it.

I rambled off about how she had held the train hostage. When his partner walked back over, I told them how I was an adult and how she was a dirty train spitter. I tried to tell them how nobody cared about her and how she was just lashing out and that this wasn't her fault.

I mean, my fault.

I tried to tell them how she was unloved and poor and under-educated and how no one cared and how she shared a room with several siblings and how no one had ever spun her with their feet and how she shouldn't wear white after Labor Day and . . .

Whoa. Listening to myself, I could now see that what I had done was nothing more than stereotype this young savage's life to suit my own needs and somehow make her actions justifiable. My words were actually nothing more than imaginative, self-deluding drivel. So much so, my goings-on even made the girl shut up, tilt her head and scrunch her face with one of those, "What the hell are you talking about?" looks. At that moment, I must have appeared as out of control as she did.

Was I really so desperate to justify my reactions last Thursday that I made up a life story for this hateful little ogre? Maybe whatever Nicole and the rest saw when I spoke wasn't so crazy after all.

Shit.

I tried to explain more to the police, but I was nervous and angry, so the last forty minutes came out in a flood of emotion. As the ambulance pulled onto the sidewalk to take the girl away, the police, shaking their heads, handcuffed me and placed me in the back of the patrol car. Inside there was an open bag of tacos and a half-eaten enchilada covered with extra beans and cheese sitting on the dashboard. The smell was strong and it made saliva swell in my throat. For some reason this made me even more nervous. As they stood outside talking to the ambulance driver and another squad car that had pulled up, I was tempted to ask if they would be so kind as to go and tell the office secretary to post a sign for my class, but I figured that silence was what the moment demanded. As people circled the car and tried to peek inside, I found myself sliding down in the seat. This was extremely uncomfortable because of the cuffs restraining me behind my back.

When they entered and started the car, they talked amongst themselves. The driver grabbed a taco and took a bite. I could see him take a hard swallow and then, as if he didn't like it, tossed the tortilla back in the bag. He looked at me in the mirror with pinched eyes, and I wondered if he blamed me for his food being cold.

I honestly don't know if I have ever felt more out of sorts in my life.

As we drove off—away from the school, the college where I teach, as a professor, with an office and everything—I had to assume I was going to jail. I had to guess that I, too, had been stereotyped, and that these officers looked at me, at us, as a product of Black bestiality run-a-muck on the streets of NYC, once again.

Or, maybe I'd been arrested because I'd just cold-cocked a sixteen-year old female.

Tomato, Tomatoe.

Much to my surprise, however, after traveling no further than around the corner, the cops pulled into what appeared to be a car impound lot right off Jamaica Ave. near Guy Brewer Blvd.

Shit.

As I was becoming more and more afraid, I could sense that soon, not yet, but soon, I might actually shed a tear. Deep in the back of my brain, I was sure that another stereotype was getting ready to play out. And that this one was really going to be painful.

Suddenly the car braked and I was thrown forward. Opening the door, the male officer grabbed me under my armpit and stood me up. As I braced myself, I was hoping that, at the very least, I would not piss myself. As I squeezed my eyes tightly and waited for the cop to hurt me in some way, one of the officers spun me around.

That's when the female removed my cuffs. Although a little surprised, this was nothing in the realm of the unexpected—not when you consider what happened next. Before I could open my mouth, the taller of the two officers opened his arms and, before I could react, squeezed me into a bear hug. Then his partner, a small pug of a woman, reached in and hugged me, too.

I can only imagine what a sight we must have been. After the embrace was broken, they applauded me for, how did she put it, "letting that group of filthy animals know dat dey do not own de world." After hearing her speak, I wondered if she might be Panamanian.

Her partner, who was shaking me like a proud father, said, "Hell yeah! We're forced to patrol this area during after school hours. Three til six. Five fuckn' days a week. And then we watch them act like rabid animals—every damn day around this time! We break em up, make em disperse, but they just flip us the bird and talk about their rights—like we ain't the fukn' cops! Bet they go out and buy a can of respect for next time!" he bellowed.

Laughing themselves teary-eyed, they then proceeded to shake my hand.

I was too stunned. As they drove away, I could see them high-fiving each other, appreciating the moment as if it were designed just for them. Before they turned the corner, she, riding in the passenger seat, actually leaned her entire torso out of the window and continuously bowed at me as if I had just been crowned and knighted prince of the NYPD.

For real.

I swear.

I couldn't make this stuff up.

Picking my mouth up off the ground, I didn't know if I was happy or disgusted. I mean, really?

I'd just assaulted a young girl. I had hit a developing mind on the streets of Queens, New York. I had just violated someone and, simply because they didn't like her and her friends, the coppers let me go.

Really?

I mean, where was the justice? Where was the humanity? Where was Al Sharpton?

Sometimes I crack myself up.

As I walked back to the college, I felt exhausted. After all that, after running the gambit of emotions—anticipation, apprehension, disgust, pity, wrath, and, ultimately, fear—all I knew for sure was that I needed a drink. Looking over my shoulder, in case there were any other young brutish girls that needed a good beat down, I knew that while I understand how a monster like that is made—madcap stereotyping, if I do say—it doesn't matter. Bad manners, intimidating and overbearing behavior would no longer be tolerated in my world. I would forever more defend my space, and the space of the weaker.

As I walked ahead, I got more and more worked up. Bobbing my head up and down, I said to myself, "That's right. From now on, I'll defend those who have been forced to act meek and ashamed in the presence of such overbearingly hostile conduct. Maybe I'll become like a superhero against rude and intolerable behavior—smacking young girls everywhere I go. I could be . . . the SMACKAHOE AVENGER!"

A couple walking by turned and looked at me.

Okay, maybe not.

I entered the front of the building and, as quickly as I could before being spotted, made a b-line downstairs and right out of the lower-level's back door. Once outside, I called the secretary and, in my best hoarse voice, tried to sound sick. Even though I was sure she could hear the distinct sound of bullshit in my voice, she said she would post a notice, but not before explaining in a huff about how I should have given more notice than thirty minutes before class started. I apologized.

When I hung up I mumbled, "Bitch," to myself. Oddly, this made me feel a little better, too.

With today's class canceled, I made my way back to the very train I had just exited. I was hoping that my ride back into the city would be a little less eventful. When I walked passed a group of high school girls making noise, their butt cracks showing, full sized panties visible now that the reign of the thong had lost its youthful allure, I slowed my pace. When they looked at me, I stared back. They looked away, yet I heard them laughing as I walked by. But I didn't care because I hadn't felt the need to look away.

Maybe I would go and get a drink. Riding the escalator down to the platform level, I wondered if any of the gang ever shows up at the bar on Mondays. Smiling for the first time in days, I wondered what we would talk about next.

CRITICAL EYE

▶ For Discussion

a. How valid is the "cultural shame" the narrator says he experiences while on the train? In short, is it ever possible to feel ashamed of the race or culture one descends from? Moreover, at what point do we cease being responsible for the sins committed by people who "look" like us?

b. While in the bar, the author learns that children must have "everything" in order to become functional adults. But, can we argue that today's children have way too much of everything at their disposal and, as a result, have become spoiled beyond measure?

c. Is parenting a skill, or is it merely a game of trial and error in which most parents simply hope for the best?

▶ Re-approaching the Reading

How is this story a manifesto against having children? And is not having a child necessarily a bad thing?

▶ Writing Assignment

In the text, the author makes a clear distinction between the "good kids" and the "bad kids." The "good kids" he asserts, take on the appearance, vernacular, and sometimes the culture of other groups but will one day shrug off these characteristics and become functional members of society. The so-called "good kids," he suggests, are perhaps worse than the "bad kids." How valid is this assumption?

From the Novel Indian Killer
HIGHER EDUCATION

As a result of brutal and ritualistic killings perpetrated against White males, the city of Seattle is gripped by fear and suspicion; as such, the historical wounds between Whites and Indians have opened. The Indian Killer has made it impossible for neighbors and family members to trust one another. And in this case, the murders, and a discussion about Indian Identity, have locked a White professor and his Indian student in a heated theoretical battle about what it means to be Indian.

Marie sat in an uncomfortable chair in the office of Dr. Faulkner, the department chair. Faulkner and Dr. Clarence Mather sat opposite her, while Bernice Zamora, the department secretary, was busy taking Rotes. A replay of Reggie's meeting, except this time Marie was the hostile Indian.

"Well, since it is your class, Dr. Mather," said Faulkner, "and since you did file the complaint against Ms. Polatkin, we'd like you to start."

Mather sat up straight, adjusted his bolo tie, and cleared his throat.

"Well, first of all, I'd like to point out that I have the highest respect for Ms. Polatkin. She is an extremely intelligent girl. And certainly ambitious. But I think her ambitions outweigh her intellect. She is very much like a relative of hers, Reggie Polatkin, who we have some experience with."

"I don't know Reggie Polatkin," said Marie. "I mean, he's my cousin, but I've only met him once or twice. I don't know anything about him."

"As you know," continued Mather, "I am teaching the evening course of the Introduction to Native American Literature class this semester. As a tenured full professor, I certainly don't have to be teaching an evening class, and as an anthropology professor, I certainly don't have to be teaching a literature class. But I felt there was a need the University simply wasn't meeting. I took it upon myself. to fill that need. Ms. Polatkin obviously had a need for such a class, and enrolled in my section."

"Excuse me," said Marie.

"Yes," said Faulkner.

"Why isn't an Indian teaching the class?"

"Why would you ask that?" asked Faulkner.

"Well, when I take a chemistry course, I certainly hope the teacher is a chemist. Women teach women's lit at this university, don't they? And I hope that African-Americans teach African-American lit."

"Do you understand why I have problems with her?" Mather said. "She is incapable of reasoned discussion. I simply will not have her questioning my authority in my class. She must be forced to drop it."

"Ms. Polatkin," said Faulkner. "Dr. Mather is an expert in Native American studies. He has published many books and countless articles. He has worked with dozens of Indian tribes. He has been teaching for twenty years."

Excerpt from *Indian Killer*, copyright © 1996 by Sherman Alexie. Used by permission of Grove/Atlantic, Inc.

"I have been involved with Native Americans longer than you've been alive," Mather said to Marie.

"Listen," said Marie. "As long as I've been alive, I've been an Indian."

"I hardly think this is appropriate," said Mather with a dismissive wave of his hand. "Why should I have to prove myself to a student, and an undergraduate at that?"

"You really think you know about Indians, don't you? You're such an arrogant jerk."

"Ms. Polatkin, I fail to see where this is getting us," said Faulkner. "I mean, in light of the tension this Indian Killer situation is causing, I think we should reschedule this meeting for a more appropriate time."

"I've been adopted into a Lakota Sioux family," protested Mather.

"That just proves some Indians have no taste."

"Ms. Polatkin, please!" said Faulkner.

"You really think you know about Indians, don't you?" Marie asked Mather. "You think you know about the Indian Killer, huh? Well, do you know about the Ghost Dance?"

"Of course."

"Yeah, and you know that Wovoka said if all Indians Ghost Danced, then all the Europeans would disappear, right?"

"Yes, it was a beautiful, and ultimately desperate, act."

"Yeah, you don't believe in the Ghost Dance, do you? Oh, you like its symbolism. You admire its metaphorical beauty, enit? You just love Indians so much. You love Indians so much you think you're excluded from our hatred. Don't you see? If the Ghost Dance had worked, you wouldn't be here. You'd be dust."

"Dr. Faulkner," Mather said. "Please put an end to this ridiculus digression."

But Faulkner, fascinated by Marie now, was silent.

"So maybe this Indian Killer is a product of the Ghost Dance. Maybe ten Indians are Ghost Dancing. Maybe a hundred. It's just a theory. How many Indians would have to dance to create the Indian Killer? A thousand? Ten thousand? Maybe this is how the Ghost Dance works."

"Ms. Polatkin, the Ghost Dance was not about violence or murder. It was about peace and beauty."

"Peace and beauty? You think Indians are worried about peace and beauty? You really think that? You're so full of shit. If Wovoka came back to life, he'd be so pissed off. If the real Pocahontas camel back, you think she'd be happy about being a cartoon? If Crazy Horse, or Geronimo, or Sitting Bull came back, they'd see what you white people have done to Indians, and they would start a war. They'd see the homeless Indians staggering around downtown. They'd see the fetal-alcohol-syndrome babies. They'd see the sorry-ass reservations. They'd learn about Indian suicide and infant-mortality rates. They'd listen to some dumb-shit Disney song and feel like hurting somebody. They'd read books by assholes like Wilson, and they would start killing themselves some white people, and then kill some asshole Indians, too.

"Dr. Mather, if the Ghost Dance worked, there would be no exceptions. All you white people would disappear. All of you. If those dead Indians came back to life, they wouldn't crawl into a sweathouse with you. They wouldn't smoke the pipe with you. They wouldn't go to the movies and munch popcorn with you. They'd kill you. They'd gut you and eat your heart."

CRITICAL EYE

▶ For Discussion

a. Is Marie Polatkin's anger justified?

b. Is the ethnic dynamic of the meeting and its discussion racist?

c. Although her points may be valid, does Marie's anger and vitriol make it almost impossible to take her side?

▶ Re-approaching the Reading

Examine the texts from Dr. Mather's perspective. Although Marie has a unique cultural perspective as an Indian woman, isn't he the "true" authority in his classroom?

▶ Writing Assignment

Marie declares that a White man has no business teaching an Indian Studies course? Is she right? Should teachers/professors be members of the cultural community that they are teaching about?

From the Novel
PUSH

I was left back when I was twelve because I had a baby for my fahver. That was in 1983. I was out of school for a year. This gonna be my second baby. My daughter got Down Sinder. She's retarded. I had got left back in the second grade too, when I was seven, 'cause I couldn't read (and I still peed on myself). I should be in the eleventh grade, getting ready to go into the twelf' grade so I can gone 'n graduate. But I'm not. I'm in the ninfe grade.

I got suspended from school 'cause I'm pregnant which I don't think is fair. I ain' did nothin'!

My name is Claireece Precious Jones. I don't know why I'm telling you that. Guess 'cause I don't know how far I'm gonna go with this story; or whether it's even a story or why I'm talkin'; whether I'm gonna start from the beginning or right from here or two weeks from now. Two weeks from now? Sure you can do anything when you talking or writing, it's not like living when you can only do what you doing. Some people tell a story 'n it don't make no sense or be true. But I'm gonna try to make sense and tell the truth, else what's the fucking use? Ain' enough lies and shit out there already?

So, OK, it's Thursday, September twenty-four 1987 and I'm walking down the hall. I look good, smell good—fresh, clean. It's hot but I do not take off my leather jacket even though it's hot, it might get stolen or lost. Indian summer, Mr Wicher say. I don't know why he call it that. What he mean is, it's *hot*, 90 degrees, like summer days. And there is no, none, I mean *none*, air conditioning in this mutherfucking building. The building I'm talking about is, of course, I.S. 146 on 134th Street between Lenox Avenue and Adam Clayton Powell Jr Blvd. I am walking down the hall from homeroom to first period maff. Why they put some shit like maff first period I do not know. Maybe to gone 'n git it over with. I actually don't mind maff as much as I had thought I would. I jus' fall in Mr Wicher's class sit down. We don't have assigned seats in Mr Wicher's class, we can sit anywhere we want. I sit in the same seat everyday, in the back, last row, next to the door. Even though I know that back door be locked. I don't say nuffin' to him. He don't say nuffin' to me, *now*. First day he say, "Class turn the book pages to page 122 please." I don't move. He say, "Miss Jones, I said turn the book pages to page 122." I say, "Motherfucker I ain't deaf." The whole class laugh. He turn red. He slam his han' down on the book and say, "Try to have some discipline." He a skinny little white man about five feets four inches. A peckerwood as my mother would say. I look at him 'n say, "I can slam too. You wanna slam?" 'N I pick up my book 'n slam it down on the desk hard. The class laugh some more. He say, "Miss Jones I would appreciate

From *Push* by Sapphire, copyright © 1996 by Sapphire/Romana Lofton. Used by permission of Alfred A. Knopf, a division of Random House, Inc.

it if you would leave the room right NOW" I say, "I ain' going nowhere mutherfucker till the bell ring. I came here to learn maff and you gon' teach me." He look like a bitch just got a train pult on her. He don't know what to do. He try to recoup, be cool, say, "Well, if you want to learn, calm down—" "I'm calm," I tell him. He say, "If you want to learn, shut up and open your book." His face is red, he is shaking. I back off. I have won. I guess.

I didn't want to hurt him or embarrass him like that you know. But I couldn't let him, anybody, know, page 122 look like page 152, 22, 3, 6, 5—all the pages look alike to me. 'N I really do want to learn. Everyday I tell myself something gonna happen, some shit like on TV I'm gonna break through or somebody gonna break through to me—I'm gonna learn, catch up, be normal, change my seat to the front of the class. But again, it has not been that day.

But thas the first day I'm telling you about. Today is not the first day and like I said I was on my way to maff class when Mrs Lichenstein snatch me out the hall to her office. I'm really mad 'cause actually I like maff even though I don't do nuffin', don't open my book even. I jus' sit there for fifty minutes. I don't cause trouble. In fac' some of the other natives get restless I break on 'em. I say, "Shut up mutherfuckers I'm tryin' to learn something." First they laugh like trying to pull me into fuckin' with Mr 'Wicher and disrupting the class. Then I get up 'n say, "Shut up mutherfuckers I'm tryin' to learn something." The coons clowning look confuse, Mr Wicher look confuse. But I'm big, five feet nine-ten, I weigh over two hundred pounds. Kids is scared of me. "Coon fool," I tell one kid done jumped up. "Sit down, stop ackin' silly." Mr Wicher look at me confuse but grateful. I'm like the polices for Mr Wicher. I keep law and order. I like him, I pretend he is my husband and we live together in Weschesser, wherever that is.

I can see by his eyes Mr Wicher like me too. I wish I could tell him about all the pages being the same but I can't. I'm getting pretty good grades. I usually do. I just wanna gone get the fuck out of I.S. 146 and go to high school and get my diploma.

Anyway I'm in Mrs Lichenstein's office. She's looking at me, I'm looking at her. I don't say nuffin'. Finally she say, "So Claireece, I see we're expecting a little visitor." But it's not like a question, she's telling me. I still don't say nuffin'. She staring at me, from behind her big wooden desk, she got her white bitch hands folded together on top her desk.

"Claireece."

Everybody call me Precious. I got three names—Claireece Precious Jones. Only mutherfuckers I hate call me Claireece.

"How old are you Claireece?"

White cunt box got my file on her desk. I see it. I ain't that late to lunch. Bitch know how old I am.

"Sixteen is ahh rather ahh"—she clear her throat—"*old* to still be in junior high school."

I still don't say nuffin'. She know so much let her ass do the talking.

"Come now, you are pregnant, aren't you Claireece?"

She asking now, a few seconds ago the hoe just knew what I was.

"Claireece?"

She tryin' to talk all gentle now and shit.

"Claireece, I'm talking to you."

I still don't say nuffin'. This hoe is keeping me from maff class. I like maff class. Mr Wicher like me in there, need me to keep those rowdy niggers in line. He nice, wear a dope suit every day. He do not come to school looking like some of these other nasty ass teachers.

"I don't want to miss no more of maff class," I tell stupid ass Mrs Lichenstein.

Gender, Sex, and Sexuality

She look at me like I said I wanna suck a dog's dick or some shit. What's with this cunt bucket? (That's what my muver call women she don't like, cunt buckets. I kinda get it and I kinda don't get it, but I like the way it sounds so I say it too.)

I get up to go, Mrs Lichenstein ax me to please sit down, she not through with me yet. But I'm through with her, thas what she don't get.

"This is your second baby?" she says. I wonder what else it say in that file with my name on it. I hate her.

"I think we should have a parent-teacher conference Claireece—me, you, and your mom."

"For what?" I say. "I ain' done nuffin'. I doose my work. I ain' in no trouble. My grades is good."

Mrs Lichenstein look at me like I got three arms or a bad odor out my pussy or something.

What my muver gon' do I want to say. What is she gonna do? But I don't say that. I jus' say, "My muver is busy."

"Well maybe I could arrange to come to your house—" The look on my face musta hit her, which is what I was gonna do if she said one more word. Come to my house! Nosy ass white bitch! I don't think so! We don't be coming to your house in Weschesser or wherever the fuck you freaks live. Well I be damned, I done heard everything, white bitch wanna visit.

"Well then Claireece, I'm afraid I'm going to have to suspend you—"

"For what!"

"You're pregnant and—"

"You can't suspend me for being pregnant, I got rights!"

"Your attitude Claireece is one of total uncooperation—"

I reached over the desk. I was gonna yank her fat ass out that chair. She fell backwards trying to get away from me 'n started screaming, "SECURITY SECURITY!"

I was out the door and on the street and I could still hear her stupid ass screaming, "SECURITY SECURITY!"

"Precious!" That's my mother calling me.

I don't say nothin'. She been staring at my stomach. I know what's coming. I keep washing dishes. We had fried chicken, mashed potatoes, gravy, green beans, and Wonder bread for dinner. I don't know how many months pregnant I am. I don't wanna stand here 'n hear Mama call me slut. Holler 'n shout on me all day like she did the last time. Slut! Nasty ass tramp! What you been doin'! Who! Who! WHOoooo like owl in Walt Disney movie I seen one time. Whooo? Ya wanna know who—

"Claireece Precious Jones I'm talkin' to you!"

I still don't answer her. I was standing at this sink the last time I was pregnant when them pains hit, wump! Ahh wump! I never felt no shit like that before. Sweat was breaking out on my forehead, pain like fire was eating me up. I jus' standing there 'n pain hit me, then pain go sit down, then pain git up 'n hit me harder! 'N she standing there screaming at me, "Slut! Goddam slut! You fuckin' cow! I don't believe this, right under my nose. You been high tailing it round here." Pain hit me again, then *she* hit me. I'm on the floor groaning, "Mommy please, Mommy please, please Mommy! Mommy! Mommy! MOMMY!" Then she KICK me side of my face! "Whore! Whore!" she screamin'. Then Miz West live down the hall pounding on the door, hollering "Mary! Mary! What you doin'! You gonna kill that chile! She need help not no beating, is you crazy!"

Mama say, "She shoulda tole me she was pregnant!" "Jezus Mary, you didn't know.

I knew, the whole building knew. Are you crazy—"

"Don't tell me nothin' about my own chile—"

"Nine-one-one! Nine-one-one! Nine-one-one!" Miz West screamin' now. She call Mama a fool.

Pain walking on me now. jus' stomping on me. I can't see hear, I jus' screamin', "Mommy! Mommy!"

Some mens, these ambulance mens, I don't see 'em or hear 'em come in. But I look up from the pain and he dere. This Spanish guy in EMS uniform. He push me back on a cushion. I'm like in a ball from the pain. He say, "RELAX!" The pain stabbing me wif a knife and this spic talking 'bout relax.

He touch my forehead put his other hand on the side of my belly. "What's your name?" he say. "Huh?" I say. "Your name?" "Precious," I say. He say, "Precious, it's almost here. I want you to push, you hear me momi, when that shit hit you again, go with it and push, Preshecita. *Push.*"

And I did.

And always after that I look for someone with his face and eyes in Spanish people. He coffee-cream color, good hair. I remember that. God. I think he was god.

CRITICAL EYE

▶ For Discussion

a. What prevents people from helping Claireece Precious Jones?

b. Based on this excerpt, how likely is it that Precious will be able to overcome her circumstances?

▶ Re-approaching the Reading

If Precious was male—same ethnicity, same socio-economic background—how different would her life have been?

▶ Writing Assignment

The author's sequel, *The Kid*, looks at Precious' son and the effects having her as a mother has had on his life. In your opinion, how does that book speak to the continued legacy of poor and unsupported teen mothers and the generations of children they're having.

CHAPTER 7

Fork in the Road

One day Alice came to a fork in the road and saw a Cheshire cat in a tree. Which road do I take? she asked. Where do you want to go? was his response. I don't know, Alice answered. Then, said the cat, it doesn't matter.
Lewis Carroll

The Fish Trap exists because of the fish. Once you've gotten the fish, you can forget the trap. The rabbit snare exists because of the rabbit. Once you've gotten the rabbit, you can forget the snare. Words exist because of meaning. Once you've got the meaning, you can forget the words. Where can I find a man who has forgotten words so I can talk to him?
Chuang Tzu

Who am I? What should I do with my life? How did I get to this point? These are the questions that fill our lives—those often unanswered life evaluations that beg to be addressed. And, as we go through life wondering, hoping for more, we find ourselves pondering the prolific utterance that Jack Nicholson's movie made famous, "Is this as good as it gets?"

The average preteen has already discovered that life is tough, and that it, all too frequently, is unfair. If you ask teenagers about love, marriage, or adulthood in general, they will explain to you that one day they plan to get married, get a good job, have children, buy a home, and become productive members of their communities. If you talk with them further, these same young, maturing people will explain how they anticipate being unhappy with their chosen careers, that marriage and children are "hard work," and that some level of misery is to be expected.

Apparently, living our lives is a paved road filled with potholes, sometimes even landmines that appear primed to explode. As a result, we find ourselves going through life desperately trying to figure out how to make sense of our socioeconomic status, our complex home environments, love, death, education, work, and, yes, even where and how to vacation—all the while looking for that path that will shine a light into our shaded eyes. So many of us hope for a better way of being. So many of us want to break a cycle and rise up, evolve, and display that we are better than before—stronger, smarter, capable of leaping where we once stumbled. So many of us look at the way the world divides the "have" and the "have nots," leaving us moored to a fixed post. Summed up, so many of us want things to change. Yet, at some point, many of us trip over the "fork"—the opening pathway that signals that a new day, be it cognizant recognition or physical transformation, is offering a new opportunity; the one that, when recognized, will change everything.

Clearly, one point remains a constant: No matter how you slice it, the proverbial "fork in the road" and the choices one makes upon it end up being character definers. As you read these selected works, you will note the following: Some people do not like what they find out about themselves; others welcome the challenge, and may find that those around them—whom they consider "constant"—fail them at every turn.

SIR ARTHUR CONAN DOYLE

From the Novel
A STUDY IN SCARLET

Chapter I. Mr. Sherlock Holmes.

IN the year 1878 I took my degree of Doctor of Medicine of the University of London, and proceeded to Netley to go through the course prescribed for surgeons in the army. Having completed my studies there, I was duly attached to the Fifth Northumberland Fusiliers as Assistant Surgeon. The regiment was stationed in India at the time, and before I could join it, the second Afghan war had broken out. On landing at Bombay, I learned that my corps had advanced through the passes, and was already deep in the enemy's country. I followed, however, with many other officers who were in the same situation as myself, and succeeded in reaching Candahar in safety, where I found my regiment, and at once entered upon my new duties.

The campaign brought honours and promotion to many, but for me it had nothing but misfortune and disaster. I was removed from my brigade and attached to the Berkshires, with whom I served at the fatal battle of Maiwand. There I was struck on the shoulder by a Jezail bullet, which shattered the bone and grazed the subclavian artery. I should have fallen into the hands of the murderous Ghazis had it not been for the devotion and courage shown by Murray, my orderly, who threw me across a pack-horse, and succeeded in bringing me safely to the British lines.

Worn with pain, and weak from the prolonged hardships which I had undergone, I was removed, with a great train of wounded sufferers, to the base hospital at Peshawar. Here I rallied, and had already improved so far as to be able to walk about the wards, and even to bask a little upon the verandah, when I was struck down by enteric fever, that curse of our Indian possessions. For months my life was despaired of, and when at last I came to myself and became convalescent, I was so weak and emaciated that a medical board determined that not a day should be lost in sending me back to England. I was dispatched, accordingly, in the troopship "Orontes," and landed a month later on Portsmouth jetty, with my health irretrievably ruined, but with permission from a paternal government to spend the next nine months in attempting to improve it.

I had neither kith nor kin in England, and was therefore as free as air—or as free as an income of eleven shillings and sixpence a day will permit a man to be. Under such circumstances, I naturally gravitated to London, that great cesspool into which all the loungers and idlers of the Empire are irresistibly drained. There I stayed for some time at a private hotel in the Strand, leading a comfortless, meaningless existence, and spending such money as I had, considerably more freely than I ought. So alarming did the state of my finances become, that I soon realized that I must either leave the metropolis and rusticate somewhere in the country, or that I must make a complete alteration in my style of living. Choosing the latter alternative, I began by making up my mind to leave the hotel, and to take up my quarters in some less pretentious and less expensive domicile.

On the very day that I had come to this conclusion, I was standing at the Criterion Bar, when some one tapped me on the shoulder, and turning round I recognized young Stamford, who had been a dresser under me at Barts. The sight of a friendly face in the great wilderness of London is a pleasant thing indeed to a lonely man. In old days Stamford had never been a particular crony of mine, but now I hailed him with enthusiasm, and he, in his turn, appeared to be delighted to see me. In the exuberance of my joy, I asked him to lunch with me at the Holborn, and we started off together in a hansom.

"Whatever have you been doing with yourself, Watson?" he asked in undisguised wonder, as we rattled through the crowded London streets. "You are as thin as a lath and as brown as a nut."

I gave him a short sketch of my adventures, and had hardly concluded it by the time that we reached our destination.

"Poor devil!" he said, commiseratingly, after he had listened to my misfortunes. "What are you up to now?"

"Looking for lodgings." I answered. "Trying to solve the problem as to whether it is possible to get comfortable rooms at a reasonable price."

"That's a strange thing," remarked my companion; "you are the second man to-day that has used that expression to me."

"And who was the first?" I asked.

"A fellow who is working at the chemical laboratory up at the hospital. He was bemoaning himself this morning because he could not get someone to go halves with him in some nice rooms which he had found, and which were too much for his purse."

"By Jove!" I cried, "if he really wants someone to share the rooms and the expense, I am the very man for him. I should prefer having a partner to being alone."

Young Stamford looked rather strangely at me over his wine-glass. "You don't know Sherlock Holmes yet," he said; "perhaps you would not care for him as a constant companion."

"Why, what is there against him?"

"Oh, I didn't say there was anything against him. He is a little queer in his ideas—an enthusiast in some branches of science. As far as I know he is a decent fellow enough."

"A medical student, I suppose?" said I.

"No—I have no idea what he intends to go in for. I believe he is well up in anatomy, and he is a first-class chemist; but, as far as I know, he has never taken out any systematic medical classes. His studies are very desultory and eccentric, but he has amassed a lot of out-of-the way knowledge which would astonish his professors."

"Did you never ask him what he was going in for?" I asked.

"No; he is not a man that it is easy to draw out, though he can be communicative enough when the fancy seizes him."

"I should like to meet him," I said. "If I am to lodge with anyone, I should prefer a man of studious and quiet habits. I am not strong enough yet to stand much noise or excitement. I had enough of both in Afghanistan to last me for the remainder of my natural existence. How could I meet this friend of yours?"

"He is sure to be at the laboratory," returned my companion. "He either avoids the place for

Fork in the Road

weeks, or else he works there from morning to night. If you like, we shall drive round together after luncheon."

"Certainly," I answered, and the conversation drifted away into other channels.

As we made our way to the hospital after leaving the Holborn, Stamford gave me a few more particulars about the gentleman whom I proposed to take as a fellow-lodger.

"You mustn't blame me if you don't get on with him," he said; "I know nothing more of him than I have learned from meeting him occasionally in the laboratory. You proposed this arrangement, so you must not hold me responsible."

"If we don't get on it will be easy to part company," I answered. "It seems to me, Stamford," I added, looking hard at my companion, "that you have some reason for washing your hands of the matter. Is this fellow's temper so formidable, or what is it? Don't be mealy-mouthed about it."

"It is not easy to express the inexpressible," he answered with a laugh. "Holmes is a little too scientific for my tastes—it approaches to cold-bloodedness. I could imagine his giving a friend a little pinch of the latest vegetable alkaloid, not out of malevolence, you understand, but simply out of a spirit of inquiry in order to have an accurate idea of the effects. To do him justice, I think that he would take it himself with the same readiness. He appears to have a passion for definite and exact knowledge."

"Very right too."

"Yes, but it may be pushed to excess. When it comes to beating the subjects in the dissecting-rooms with a stick, it is certainly taking rather a bizarre shape."

"Beating the subjects!"

"Yes, to verify how far bruises may be produced after death. I saw him at it with my own eyes."

"And yet you say he is not a medical student?"

"No. Heaven knows what the objects of his studies are. But here we are, and you must form your own impressions about him." As he spoke, we turned down a narrow lane and passed through a small side-door, which opened into a wing of the great hospital. It was familiar ground to me, and I needed no guiding as we ascended the bleak stone staircase and made our way down the long corridor with its vista of whitewashed wall and dun-coloured doors. Near the further end a low arched passage branched away from it and led to the chemical laboratory.

This was a lofty chamber, lined and littered with countless bottles. Broad, low tables were scattered about, which bristled with retorts, test-tubes, and little Bunsen lamps, with their blue flickering flames. There was only one student in the room, who was bending over a distant table absorbed in his work. At the sound of our steps he glanced round and sprang to his feet with a cry of pleasure. "I've found it! I've found it," he shouted to my companion, running towards us with a test-tube in his hand. "I have found a re-agent which is precipitated by hoemoglobin, 4 and by nothing else." Had he discovered a gold mine, greater delight could not have shone upon his features.

"Dr. Watson, Mr. Sherlock Holmes," said Stamford, introducing us.

"How are you?" he said cordially, gripping my hand with a strength for which I should hardly have given him credit. "You have been in Afghanistan, I perceive."

"How on earth did you know that?" I asked in astonishment.

"Never mind," said he, chuckling to himself. "The question now is about hoemoglobin. No doubt you see the significance of this discovery of mine?"

"It is interesting, chemically, no doubt," I answered, "but practically——"

"Why, man, it is the most practical medico-legal discovery for years. Don't you see that it gives us an infallible test for blood stains. Come over here now!" He seized me by the coat-sleeve in his eagerness, and drew me over to the table at which he had been working. "Let us have some fresh blood," he said, digging a long bodkin into his finger, and drawing off the resulting drop of blood in a chemical pipette. "Now, I add this small quantity of blood to a litre of water. You perceive that the resulting mixture has the appearance of pure water. The proportion of blood cannot be more than one in a million. I have no doubt, however, that we shall be able to obtain the characteristic reaction." As he spoke, he threw into the vessel a few white crystals, and then added some drops of a transparent fluid. In an instant the contents assumed a dull mahogany colour, and a brownish dust was precipitated to the bottom of the glass jar.

"Ha! ha!" he cried, clapping his hands, and looking as delighted as a child with a new toy. "What do you think of that?"

"It seems to be a very delicate test," I remarked.

"Beautiful! beautiful! The old Guiacum test was very clumsy and uncertain. So is the microscopic examination for blood corpuscles. The latter is valueless if the stains are a few hours old. Now, this appears to act as well whether the blood is old or new. Had this test been invented, there are hundreds of men now walking the earth who would long ago have paid the penalty of their crimes."

"Indeed!" I murmured.

"Criminal cases are continually hinging upon that one point. A man is suspected of a crime months perhaps after it has been committed. His linen or clothes are examined, and brownish stains discovered upon them. Are they blood stains, or mud stains, or rust stains, or fruit stains, or what are they? That is a question which has puzzled many an expert, and why? Because there was no reliable test. Now we have the Sherlock Holmes' test, and there will no longer be any difficulty."

His eyes fairly glittered as he spoke, and he put his hand over his heart and bowed as if to some applauding crowd conjured up by his imagination.

"You are to be congratulated," I remarked, considerably surprised at his enthusiasm.

"There was the case of Von Bischoff at Frankfort last year. He would certainly have been hung had this test been in existence. Then there was Mason of Bradford, and the notorious Muller, and Lefevre of Montpellier, and Samson of new Orleans. I could name a score of cases in which it would have been decisive."

"You seem to be a walking calendar of crime," said Stamford with a laugh. "You might start a paper on those lines. Call it the 'Police News of the Past.'"

"Very interesting reading it might be made, too," remarked Sherlock Holmes, sticking a small piece of plaster over the prick on his finger. "I have to be careful," he continued, turning to me with a smile, "for I dabble with poisons a good deal." He held out his hand as he spoke, and I noticed that it was all mottled over with similar pieces of plaster, and discoloured with strong acids.

"We came here on business," said Stamford, sitting down on a high three-legged stool, and pushing another one in my direction with his foot. "My friend here wants to take diggings, and as you were complaining that you could get no one to go halves with you, I thought that I had better bring you together."

Sherlock Holmes seemed delighted at the idea of sharing his rooms with me. "I have my eye on a suite in Baker Street," he said, "which would suit us down to the ground. You don't mind the smell of strong tobacco, I hope?"

"I always smoke 'ship's' myself," I answered.

"That's good enough. I generally have chemicals about, and occasionally do experiments. Would that annoy you?"

"By no means."

"Let me see—what are my other shortcomings. I get in the dumps at times, and don't open my mouth for days on end. You must not think I am sulky when I do that. Just let me alone, and I'll soon be right. What have you to confess now? It's just as well for two fellows to know the worst of one another before they begin to live together."

I laughed at this cross-examination. "I keep a bull pup," I said, "and I object to rows because my nerves are shaken, and I get up at all sorts of ungodly hours, and I am extremely lazy. I have another set of vices when I'm well, but those are the principal ones at present."

"Do you include violin-playing in your category of rows?" he asked, anxiously.

"It depends on the player," I answered. "A well-played violin is a treat for the gods—a badly-played one——"

"Oh, that's all right," he cried, with a merry laugh. "I think we may consider the thing as settled—that is, if the rooms are agreeable to you."

"When shall we see them?"

"Call for me here at noon to-morrow, and we'll go together and settle everything," he answered.

"All right—noon exactly," said I, shaking his hand.

We left him working among his chemicals, and we walked together towards my hotel.

"By the way," I asked suddenly, stopping and turning upon Stamford, "how the deuce did he know that I had come from Afghanistan?"

My companion smiled an enigmatical smile. "That's just his little peculiarity," he said. "A good many people have wanted to know how he finds things out."

"Oh! a mystery is it?" I cried, rubbing my hands. "This is very piquant. I am much obliged to you for bringing us together. 'The proper study of mankind is man,' you know."

"You must study him, then," Stamford said, as he bade me good-bye. "You'll find him a knotty problem, though. I'll wager he learns more about you than you about him. Good-bye."

"Good-bye," I answered, and strolled on to my hotel, considerably interested in my new acquaintance.

Chapter II. The Science of Deduction.

WE met next day as he had arranged, and inspected the rooms at No. 221B, 5 Baker Street, of which he had spoken at our meeting. They consisted of a couple of comfortable bed-rooms and a single large airy sitting-room, cheerfully furnished, and illuminated by two broad windows. So desirable in every way were the apartments, and so moderate did the terms seem when divided between us, that the bargain was concluded upon the spot, and we at once entered into possession. That very evening I moved my things round from the hotel, and on the following morning Sherlock Holmes followed me with several boxes and portmanteaus. For a day or two we were busily employed in unpacking and laying out our property to the best advantage. That done, we gradually began to settle down and to accommodate ourselves to our new surroundings.

Holmes was certainly not a difficult man to live with. He was quiet in his ways, and his habits were regular. It was rare for him to be up after ten at night, and he had invariably breakfasted and gone out before I rose in the morning. Sometimes he spent his day at the chemical laboratory, sometimes in the dissecting-rooms, and occasionally in long walks, which appeared to take him into the lowest portions of the City. Nothing could exceed his energy when the working fit was upon him; but now and again a reaction would seize him, and for days on end he would lie upon the sofa in the sitting-room, hardly uttering a word or moving a muscle from morning to night. On these occasions I have noticed such a dreamy, vacant expression in his eyes, that I might have suspected him of being addicted to the use of some narcotic, had not the temperance and cleanliness of his whole life forbidden such a notion.

As the weeks went by, my interest in him and my curiosity as to his aims in life, gradually deepened and increased. His very person and appearance were such as to strike the attention of the most casual observer. In height he was rather over six feet, and so excessively lean that he seemed to be considerably taller. His eyes were sharp and piercing, save during those intervals of torpor to which I have alluded; and his thin, hawk-like nose gave his whole expression an air of alertness and decision. His chin, too, had the prominence and squareness which mark the man of determination. His hands were invariably blotted with ink and stained with chemicals, yet he was possessed of extraordinary delicacy of touch, as I frequently had occasion to observe when I watched him manipulating his fragile philosophical instruments.

The reader may set me down as a hopeless busybody, when I confess how much this man stimulated my curiosity, and how often I endeavoured to break through the reticence which he showed on all that concerned himself. Before pronouncing judgment, however, be it remembered, how objectless was my life, and how little there was to engage my attention. My health forbade me from venturing out unless the weather was exceptionally genial, and I had no friends who would call upon me and break the monotony of my daily existence. Under these circumstances, I eagerly hailed the little mystery which hung around my companion, and spent much of my time in endeavouring to unravel it.

He was not studying medicine. He had himself, in reply to a question, confirmed Stamford's opinion upon that point. Neither did he appear to have pursued any course of reading which might fit him for a degree in science or any other recognized portal which would give him an entrance into the learned world. Yet his zeal for certain studies was remarkable, and within eccentric limits his knowledge was so extraordinarily ample and minute that his observations have fairly astounded me. Surely no man would work so hard or attain such precise information unless he had some definite end in view. Desultory readers are seldom remarkable for the exactness of their learning. No man burdens his mind with small matters unless he has some very good reason for doing so.

His ignorance was as remarkable as his knowledge. Of contemporary literature, philosophy and politics he appeared to know next to nothing. Upon my quoting Thomas Carlyle, he inquired in the naivest way who he might be and what he had done. My surprise reached a climax, however, when I found incidentally that he was ignorant of the Copernican Theory and of the composition of the Solar System. That any civilized human being in this nineteenth century should not be aware that the earth travelled round the sun appeared to be to me such an extraordinary fact that I could hardly realize it.

"You appear to be astonished," he said, smiling at my expression of surprise. "Now that I do know it I shall do my best to forget it."

"To forget it!"

"You see," he explained, "I consider that a man's brain originally is like a little empty attic, and you have to stock it with such furniture as you choose. A fool takes in all the lumber of every sort that he comes across, so that the knowledge which might be useful to him gets crowded out, or at best is jumbled up with a lot of other things so that he has a difficulty in laying his hands upon it. Now the skilful workman is very careful indeed as to what he takes into his brain-attic. He will have nothing but the tools which may help him in doing his work, but of these he has a large assortment, and all in the most perfect order. It is a mistake to think that that little room has elastic walls and can distend to any extent. Depend upon it there comes a time when for every addition of knowledge you forget something that you knew before. It is of the highest importance, therefore, not to have useless facts elbowing out the useful ones."

"But the Solar System!" I protested.

"What the deuce is it to me?" he interrupted impatiently; "you say that we go round the sun. If we went round the moon it would not make a pennyworth of difference to me or to my work."

I was on the point of asking him what that work might be, but something in his manner showed me that the question would be an unwelcome one. I pondered over our short conversation, however, and endeavoured to draw my deductions from it. He said that he would acquire no knowledge which did not bear upon his object. Therefore all the knowledge which he possessed was such as would be useful to him. I enumerated in my own mind all the various points upon which he had shown me that he was exceptionally well-informed. I even took a pencil and jotted them down. I could not help smiling at the document when I had completed it. It ran in this way—

SHERLOCK HOLMES—his limits.

1. Knowledge of Literature.—Nil.
2. Philosophy.—Nil.
3. Astronomy.—Nil.
4. Politics.—Feeble.
5. Botany.—Variable. Well up in belladonna, opium, and poisons generally. Knows nothing of practical gardening.
6. Geology.—Practical, but limited. Tells at a glance different soils from each other. After walks has shown me splashes upon his trousers, and told me by their colour and consistence in what part of London he had received them.
7. Chemistry.—Profound.
8. Anatomy.—Accurate, but unsystematic.
9. Sensational Literature.—Immense. He appears to know every detail of every horror perpetrated in the century.
10. Plays the violin well.
11. Is an expert singlestick player, boxer, and swordsman.
12. Has a good practical knowledge of British law.

When I had got so far in my list I threw it into the fire in despair. "If I can only find what the fellow is driving at by reconciling all these accomplishments, and discovering a calling which needs them all," I said to myself, "I may as well give up the attempt at once."

I see that I have alluded above to his powers upon the violin. These were very remarkable, but as eccentric as all his other accomplishments. That he could play pieces, and difficult pieces, I knew well, because at my request he has played me some of Mendelssohn's Lieder, and other favourites. When left to himself, however, he would seldom produce any music or attempt any recognized air. Leaning back in his arm-chair of an evening, he would close his eyes and scrape carelessly at the fiddle which was thrown across his knee. Sometimes the chords were sonorous and melancholy. Occasionally they were fantastic and cheerful. Clearly they reflected the thoughts which possessed him, but whether the music aided those thoughts, or whether the playing was simply the result of a whim or fancy was more than I could determine. I might have rebelled against these exasperating solos had it not been that he usually terminated them by playing in quick succession a whole series of my favourite airs as a slight compensation for the trial upon my patience.

During the first week or so we had no callers, and I had begun to think that my companion was as friendless a man as I was myself. Presently, however, I found that he had many acquaintances, and those in the most different classes of society. There was one little sallow rat-faced, dark-eyed fellow who was introduced to me as Mr. Lestrade, and who came three or four times in a single week. One morning a young girl called, fashionably dressed, and stayed for half an hour or more. The same afternoon brought a grey-headed, seedy visitor, looking like a Jew pedlar, who appeared to me to be much excited, and who was closely followed by a slip-shod elderly woman. On another occasion an old white-haired gentleman had an interview with my companion; and on another a railway porter in his velveteen uniform. When any of these nondescript individuals put in an appearance, Sherlock Holmes used to beg for the use of the sitting-room, and I would retire to my bed-room. He always apologized to me for putting me to this inconvenience. "I have to use this room as a place of business," he said, "and these people are my clients." Again I had an opportunity of asking him a point blank question, and again my delicacy prevented me from forcing another man to confide in me. I imagined at the time that he had some strong reason for not alluding to it, but he soon dispelled the idea by coming round to the subject of his own accord.

It was upon the 4th of March, as I have good reason to remember, that I rose somewhat earlier than usual, and found that Sherlock Holmes had not yet finished his breakfast. The landlady had become so accustomed to my late habits that my place had not been laid nor my coffee prepared. With the unreasonable petulance of mankind I rang the bell and gave a curt intimation that I was ready. Then I picked up a magazine from the table and attempted to while away the time with it, while my companion munched silently at his toast. One of the articles had a pencil mark at the heading, and I naturally began to run my eye through it.

Its somewhat ambitious title was "The Book of Life," and it attempted to show how much an observant man might learn by an accurate and systematic examination of all that came in his way. It struck me as being a remarkable mixture of shrewdness and of absurdity. The reasoning was close and intense, but the deductions appeared to me to be far-fetched and exaggerated. The writer claimed by a momentary expression, a twitch of a muscle or a glance of an eye, to fathom a man's inmost thoughts. Deceit, according to him, was an impossibility in the case of one trained to observation and analysis. His conclusions were as infallible as so many propositions of Euclid. So startling would his results appear to the uninitiated that until they learned the processes by which he had arrived at them they might well consider him as a necromancer.

"From a drop of water," said the writer, "a logician could infer the possibility of an Atlantic or a Niagara without having seen or heard of one or the other. So all life is a great chain, the nature of which is known whenever we are shown a single link of it. Like all other arts, the Science of Deduction and Analysis is one which can only be acquired by long and patient study nor is life long enough to allow any mortal to attain the highest possible perfection in it. Before turning to those moral and mental aspects of the matter which present the greatest difficulties, let the enquirer begin by mastering more elementary problems. Let him, on meeting a fellow-mortal, learn at a glance to distinguish the history of the man, and the trade or profession to which he belongs. Puerile as such an exercise may seem, it sharpens the faculties of observation, and teaches one where to look and what to look for. By a man's finger nails, by his coat-sleeve, by his boot, by his trouser knees, by the callosities of his forefinger and thumb, by his expression, by his shirt cuffs—by each of these things a man's calling is plainly revealed. That all united should fail to enlighten the competent enquirer in any case is almost inconceivable."

"What ineffable twaddle!" I cried, slapping the magazine down on the table, "I never read such rubbish in my life."

"What is it?" asked Sherlock Holmes.

"Why, this article," I said, pointing at it with my egg spoon as I sat down to my breakfast. "I see that you have read it since you have marked it. I don't deny that it is smartly written. It irritates me though. It is evidently the theory of some arm-chair lounger who evolves all these neat little paradoxes in the seclusion of his own study. It is not practical. I should like to see him clapped down in a third class carriage on the Underground, and asked to give the trades of all his fellow-travellers. I would lay a thousand to one against him."

"You would lose your money," Sherlock Holmes remarked calmly. "As for the article I wrote it myself."

"You!"

"Yes, I have a turn both for observation and for deduction. The theories which I have expressed there, and which appear to you to be so chimerical are really extremely practical—so practical that I depend upon them for my bread and cheese."

"And how?" I asked involuntarily.

"Well, I have a trade of my own. I suppose I am the only one in the world. I'm a consulting detective, if you can understand what that is. Here in London we have lots of Government detectives and lots of private ones. When these fellows are at fault they come to me, and I manage to put them on the right scent. They lay all the evidence before me, and I am generally able, by the help of my knowledge of the history of crime, to set them straight. There is a strong family resemblance about misdeeds, and if you have all the details of a thousand at your finger ends, it is odd if you can't unravel the thousand and first. Lestrade is a well-known detective. He got himself into a fog recently over a forgery case, and that was what brought him here."

"And these other people?"

"They are mostly sent on by private inquiry agencies. They are all people who are in trouble about something, and want a little enlightening. I listen to their story, they listen to my comments, and then I pocket my fee."

"But do you mean to say," I said, "that without leaving your room you can unravel some knot which other men can make nothing of, although they have seen every detail for themselves?"

"Quite so. I have a kind of intuition that way. Now and again a case turns up which is a little more complex. Then I have to bustle about and see things with my own eyes. You see I have a lot of special knowledge which I apply to the problem, and which facilitates matters wonderfully. Those rules of deduction laid down in that article which aroused your scorn, are invaluable to me in practical work. Observation with me is second nature. You appeared to be surprised when I told you, on our first meeting, that you had come from Afghanistan."

"You were told, no doubt."

"Nothing of the sort. I knew you came from Afghanistan. From long habit the train of thoughts ran so swiftly through my mind, that I arrived at the conclusion without being conscious of intermediate steps. There were such steps, however. The train of reasoning ran, 'Here is a gentleman of a medical type, but with the air of a military man. Clearly an army doctor, then. He has just come from the tropics, for his face is dark, and that is not the natural tint of his skin, for his wrists are fair. He has undergone hardship and sickness, as his haggard face says clearly. His left arm has been injured. He holds it in a stiff and unnatural manner. Where in the tropics could an English army doctor have seen much hardship and got his arm wounded? Clearly in Afghanistan.' The whole train of thought did not occupy a second. I then remarked that you came from Afghanistan, and you were astonished."

"It is simple enough as you explain it," I said, smiling. "You remind me of Edgar Allen Poe's Dupin. I had no idea that such individuals did exist outside of stories."

Sherlock Holmes rose and lit his pipe. "No doubt you think that you are complimenting me in comparing me to Dupin," he observed. "Now, in my opinion, Dupin was a very inferior fellow. That trick of his of breaking in on his friends' thoughts with an apropos remark after a quarter of an hour's silence is really very showy and superficial. He had some analytical genius, no doubt; but he was by no means such a phenomenon as Poe appeared to imagine."

"Have you read Gaboriau's works?" I asked. "Does Lecoq come up to your idea of a detective?"

Sherlock Holmes sniffed sardonically. "Lecoq was a miserable bungler," he said, in an angry voice; "he had only one thing to recommend him, and that was his energy. That book made me positively ill. The question was how to identify an unknown prisoner. I could have done it in twenty-four hours. Lecoq took six months or so. It might be made a text-book for detectives to teach them what to avoid."

I felt rather indignant at having two characters whom I had admired treated in this cavalier style. I walked over to the window, and stood looking out into the busy street. "This fellow may be very clever," I said to myself, "but he is certainly very conceited."

"There are no crimes and no criminals in these days," he said, querulously. "What is the use of having brains in our profession. I know well that I have it in me to make my name famous. No man lives or has ever lived who has brought the same amount of study and of natural talent to the detection of crime which I have done. And what is the result? There is no crime to detect, or, at most, some bungling villany with a motive so transparent that even a Scotland Yard official can see through it."

I was still annoyed at his bumptious style of conversation. I thought it best to change the topic.

"I wonder what that fellow is looking for?" I asked, pointing to a stalwart, plainly-dressed individual who was walking slowly down the other side of the street, looking anxiously at the numbers. He had a large blue envelope in his hand, and was evidently the bearer of a message.

"You mean the retired sergeant of Marines," said Sherlock Holmes.

"Brag and bounce!" thought I to myself. "He knows that I cannot verify his guess."

The thought had hardly passed through my mind when the man whom we were watching caught sight of the number on our door, and ran rapidly across the roadway. We heard a loud knock, a deep voice below, and heavy steps ascending the stair.

"For Mr. Sherlock Holmes," he said, stepping into the room and handing my friend the letter.

Here was an opportunity of taking the conceit out of him. He little thought of this when he made that random shot. "May I ask, my lad," I said, in the blandest voice, "what your trade may be?"

"Commissionaire, sir," he said, gruffly. "Uniform away for repairs."

"And you were?" I asked, with a slightly malicious glance at my companion.

"A sergeant, sir, Royal Marine Light Infantry, sir. No answer? Right, sir."

He clicked his heels together, raised his hand in a salute, and was gone.

Chapter III. The Lauriston Garden Mystery

I CONFESS that I was considerably startled by this fresh proof of the practical nature of my companion's theories. My respect for his powers of analysis increased wondrously. There still remained some lurking suspicion in my mind, however, that the whole thing was a pre-arranged episode, intended to dazzle me, though what earthly object he could have in taking me in was past my comprehension. When I looked at him he had finished reading the note, and his eyes had assumed the vacant, lack-lustre expression which showed mental abstraction.

"How in the world did you deduce that?" I asked.

"Deduce what?" said he, petulantly.

"Why, that he was a retired sergeant of Marines."

"I have no time for trifles," he answered, brusquely; then with a smile, "Excuse my rudeness. You broke the thread of my thoughts; but perhaps it is as well. So you actually were not able to see that that man was a sergeant of Marines?"

"No, indeed."

"It was easier to know it than to explain why I knew it. If you were asked to prove that two and two made four, you might find some difficulty, and yet you are quite sure of the fact. Even across the street I could see a great blue anchor tattooed on the back of the fellow's hand. That smacked of the sea. He had a military carriage, however, and regulation side whiskers. There we have the marine. He was a man with some amount of self-importance and a certain air of command. You must have observed the way in which he held his head and swung his cane. A steady, respectable, middle-aged man, too, on the face of him—all facts which led me to believe that he had been a sergeant."

"Wonderful!" I ejaculated.

"Commonplace," said Holmes, though I thought from his expression that he was pleased at my evident surprise and admiration. "I said just now that there were no criminals. It appears that I am wrong—look at this!" He threw me over the note which the commissionaire had brought.

"Why," I cried, as I cast my eye over it, "this is terrible!"

"It does seem to be a little out of the common," he remarked, calmly. "Would you mind reading it to me aloud?"

This is the letter which I read to him——

"MY DEAR MR. SHERLOCK HOLMES,—

"There has been a bad business during the night at 3, Lauriston Gardens, off the Brixton Road. Our man on the beat saw a light there about two in the morning, and as the house was an empty one, suspected that something was amiss. He found the door open, and in the front room, which is bare of furniture, discovered the body of a gentleman, well dressed, and having cards in his pocket bearing the name of 'Enoch J. Drebber, Cleveland, Ohio, U.S.A.' There had been no robbery, nor is there any evidence as to how the man met his death. There are marks of blood in the room, but there is no wound upon his person. We are at a loss as to how he came into the empty house; indeed, the whole affair is a puzzler. If you can come round to the house any time before twelve, you will find me there. I have left everything in status quo until I hear from you. If you are unable to come I shall give you fuller details, and would esteem it a great kindness if you would favour me with your opinion. Yours faithfully,

"TOBIAS GREGSON."

"Gregson is the smartest of the Scotland Yarders," my friend remarked; "he and Lestrade are the pick of a bad lot. They are both quick and energetic, but conventional—shockingly so. They have their knives into one another, too. They are as jealous as a pair of professional beauties. There will be some fun over this case if they are both put upon the scent."

I was amazed at the calm way in which he rippled on. "Surely there is not a moment to be lost," I cried, "shall I go and order you a cab?"

"I'm not sure about whether I shall go. I am the most incurably lazy devil that ever stood in shoe leather—that is, when the fit is on me, for I can be spry enough at times."

"Why, it is just such a chance as you have been longing for."

"My dear fellow, what does it matter to me. Supposing I unravel the whole matter, you may be sure that Gregson, Lestrade, and Co. will pocket all the credit. That comes of being an unofficial personage."

"But he begs you to help him."

"Yes. He knows that I am his superior, and acknowledges it to me; but he would cut his tongue out before he would own it to any third person. However, we may as well go and have a look. I shall work it out on my own hook. I may have a laugh at them if I have nothing else. Come on!"

He hustled on his overcoat, and bustled about in a way that showed that an energetic fit had superseded the apathetic one.

"Get your hat," he said.

"You wish me to come?"

"Yes, if you have nothing better to do." A minute later we were both in a hansom, driving furiously for the Brixton Road.

It was a foggy, cloudy morning, and a dun-coloured veil hung over the house-tops, looking like the reflection of the mud-coloured streets beneath. My companion was in the best of spirits, and prattled away about Cremona fiddles, and the difference between a Stradivarius and an Amati. As for myself, I was silent, for the dull weather and the melancholy business upon which we were engaged, depressed my spirits.

"You don't seem to give much thought to the matter in hand," I said at last, interrupting Holmes' musical disquisition.

"No data yet," he answered. "It is a capital mistake to theorize before you have all the evidence. It biases the judgment."

"You will have your data soon," I remarked, pointing with my finger; "this is the Brixton Road, and that is the house, if I am not very much mistaken."

"So it is. Stop, driver, stop!" We were still a hundred yards or so from it, but he insisted upon our alighting, and we finished our journey upon foot.

Number 3, Lauriston Gardens wore an ill-omened and minatory look. It was one of four which stood back some little way from the street, two being occupied and two empty. The latter looked out with three tiers of vacant melancholy windows, which were blank and dreary, save that here and there a "To Let" card had developed like a cataract upon the bleared panes. A small garden sprinkled over with a scattered eruption of sickly plants separated each of these houses from the street, and was traversed by a narrow pathway, yellowish in colour, and consisting apparently of a mixture of clay and of gravel. The whole place was very sloppy from the rain which had fallen through the night. The garden was bounded by a three-foot brick wall with a fringe of wood rails upon the top, and against this wall was leaning a stalwart police constable, surrounded by a small knot of loafers, who craned their necks and strained their eyes in the vain hope of catching some glimpse of the proceedings within.

I had imagined that Sherlock Holmes would at once have hurried into the house and plunged into a study of the mystery. Nothing appeared to be further from his intention. With an air of nonchalance which, under the circumstances, seemed to me to border upon affectation, he lounged up and down the pavement, and gazed vacantly at the ground, the sky, the opposite houses and the line of railings. Having finished his scrutiny, he proceeded slowly down the path, or rather down the fringe of grass which flanked the path, keeping his eyes riveted upon the ground. Twice he stopped, and once I saw him smile, and heard him utter an exclamation of satisfaction. There were many marks of footsteps upon the wet clayey soil, but since the police had been coming and going over it, I was unable to see how my companion could hope to learn anything from it. Still I had had such extraordinary evidence of the quickness of his perceptive faculties, that I had no doubt that he could see a great deal which was hidden from me.

At the door of the house we were met by a tall, white-faced, flaxen-haired man, with a notebook in his hand, who rushed forward and wrung my companion's hand with effusion. "It is indeed kind of you to come," he said, "I have had everything left untouched."

"Except that!" my friend answered, pointing at the pathway. "If a herd of buffaloes had passed along there could not be a greater mess. No doubt, however, you had drawn your own conclusions, Gregson, before you permitted this."

"I have had so much to do inside the house," the detective said evasively. "My colleague, Mr. Lestrade, is here. I had relied upon him to look after this."

Holmes glanced at me and raised his eyebrows sardonically. "With two such men as yourself and Lestrade upon the ground, there will not be much for a third party to find out," he said.

Gregson rubbed his hands in a self-satisfied way. "I think we have done all that can be done," he answered; "it's a queer case though, and I knew your taste for such things."

"You did not come here in a cab?" asked Sherlock Holmes.

"No, sir."

"Nor Lestrade?"

"No, sir."

"Then let us go and look at the room." With which inconsequent remark he strode on into the house, followed by Gregson, whose features expressed his astonishment.

A short passage, bare planked and dusty, led to the kitchen and offices. Two doors opened out of it to the left and to the right. One of these had obviously been closed for many weeks. The other belonged to the dining-room, which was the apartment in which the mysterious affair had occurred. Holmes walked in, and I followed him with that subdued feeling at my heart which the presence of death inspires.

It was a large square room, looking all the larger from the absence of all furniture. A vulgar flaring paper adorned the walls, but it was blotched in places with mildew, and here and there great strips had become detached and hung down, exposing the yellow plaster beneath. Opposite the door was a showy fireplace, surmounted by a mantelpiece of imitation white marble. On one corner of this was stuck the stump of a red wax candle. The solitary window was so dirty that the light was hazy and uncertain, giving a dull grey tinge to everything, which was intensified by the thick layer of dust which coated the whole apartment.

All these details I observed afterwards. At present my attention was centred upon the single grim motionless figure which lay stretched upon the boards, with vacant sightless eyes staring up at the discoloured ceiling. It was that of a man about forty-three or forty-four years of age, middle-sized, broad shouldered, with crisp curling black hair, and a short stubbly beard. He was dressed in a heavy broadcloth frock coat and waistcoat, with light-coloured trousers, and immaculate collar and cuffs. A top hat, well brushed and trim, was placed upon the floor beside him. His hands were clenched and his arms thrown abroad, while his lower limbs were interlocked as though his death struggle had been a grievous one. On his rigid face there stood an expression of horror, and as it seemed to me, of hatred, such as I have never seen upon human features. This malignant and terrible contortion, combined with the low forehead, blunt nose, and prognathous jaw gave the dead man a singularly simious and ape-like appearance, which was increased by his writhing, unnatural posture. I have seen death in many forms, but never has it appeared to me in a more fearsome aspect than in that dark grimy apartment, which looked out upon one of the main arteries of suburban London.

Lestrade, lean and ferret-like as ever, was standing by the doorway, and greeted my companion and myself.

"This case will make a stir, sir," he remarked. "It beats anything I have seen, and I am no chicken."

"There is no clue?" said Gregson.

"None at all," chimed in Lestrade.

Sherlock Holmes approached the body, and, kneeling down, examined it intently. "You are sure that there is no wound?" he asked, pointing to numerous gouts and splashes of blood which lay all round.

"Positive!" cried both detectives.

"Then, of course, this blood belongs to a second individual—presumably the murderer, if murder has been committed. It reminds me of the circumstances attendant on the death of Van Jansen, in Utrecht, in the year '34. Do you remember the case, Gregson?"

"No, sir."

"Read it up—you really should. There is nothing new under the sun. It has all been done before."

As he spoke, his nimble fingers were flying here, there, and everywhere, feeling, pressing, unbuttoning, examining, while his eyes wore the same far-away expression which I have already remarked upon. So swiftly was the examination made, that one would hardly have guessed the minuteness with which it was conducted. Finally, he sniffed the dead man's lips, and then glanced at the soles of his patent leather boots.

"He has not been moved at all?" he asked.

"No more than was necessary for the purposes of our examination."

"You can take him to the mortuary now," he said. "There is nothing more to be learned."

Gregson had a stretcher and four men at hand. At his call they entered the room, and the stranger was lifted and carried out. As they raised him, a ring tinkled down and rolled across the floor. Lestrade grabbed it up and stared at it with mystified eyes.

"There's been a woman here," he cried. "It's a woman's wedding-ring."

He held it out, as he spoke, upon the palm of his hand. We all gathered round him and gazed at it. There could be no doubt that that circlet of plain gold had once adorned the finger of a bride.

"This complicates matters," said Gregson. "Heaven knows, they were complicated enough before."

"You're sure it doesn't simplify them?" observed Holmes. "There's nothing to be learned by staring at it. What did you find in his pockets?"

"We have it all here," said Gregson, pointing to a litter of objects upon one of the bottom steps of the stairs. "A gold watch, No. 97163, by Barraud, of London. Gold Albert chain, very heavy and solid. Gold ring, with masonic device. Gold pin—bull-dog's head, with rubies as eyes. Russian leather card-case, with cards of Enoch J. Drebber of Cleveland, corresponding with the E. J. D. upon the linen. No purse, but loose money to the extent of seven pounds thirteen. Pocket edition of Boccaccio's 'Decameron,' with name of Joseph Stangerson upon the fly-leaf. Two letters—one addressed to E. J. Drebber and one to Joseph Stangerson."

"At what address?"

"American Exchange, Strand—to be left till called for. They are both from the Guion Steamship Company, and refer to the sailing of their boats from Liverpool. It is clear that this unfortunate man was about to return to New York."

"Have you made any inquiries as to this man, Stangerson?"

"I did it at once, sir," said Gregson. "I have had advertisements sent to all the newspapers, and one of my men has gone to the American Exchange, but he has not returned yet."

"Have you sent to Cleveland?"

"We telegraphed this morning."

"How did you word your inquiries?"

"We simply detailed the circumstances, and said that we should be glad of any information which could help us."

"You did not ask for particulars on any point which appeared to you to be crucial?"

"I asked about Stangerson."

"Nothing else? Is there no circumstance on which this whole case appears to hinge? Will you not telegraph again?"

"I have said all I have to say," said Gregson, in an offended voice.

Sherlock Holmes chuckled to himself, and appeared to be about to make some remark, when Lestrade, who had been in the front room while we were holding this conversation in the hall, reappeared upon the scene, rubbing his hands in a pompous and self-satisfied manner.

"Mr. Gregson," he said, "I have just made a discovery of the highest importance, and one which would have been overlooked had I not made a careful examination of the walls."

The little man's eyes sparkled as he spoke, and he was evidently in a state of suppressed exultation at having scored a point against his colleague.

"Come here," he said, bustling back into the room, the atmosphere of which felt clearer since the removal of its ghastly inmate. "Now, stand there!"

He struck a match on his boot and held it up against the wall.

"Look at that!" he said, triumphantly.

I have remarked that the paper had fallen away in parts. In this particular corner of the room a large piece had peeled off, leaving a yellow square of coarse plastering. Across this bare space there was scrawled in blood-red letters a single word—

RACHE.

"What do you think of that?" cried the detective, with the air of a showman exhibiting his show. "This was overlooked because it was in the darkest corner of the room, and no one thought of looking there. The murderer has written it with his or her own blood. See this smear where it has trickled down the wall! That disposes of the idea of suicide anyhow. Why was that corner chosen to write it on? I will tell you. See that candle on the mantelpiece. It was lit at the time, and if it was lit this corner would be the brightest instead of the darkest portion of the wall."

"And what does it mean now that you have found it?" asked Gregson in a depreciatory voice.

"Mean? Why, it means that the writer was going to put the female name Rachel, but was disturbed before he or she had time to finish. You mark my words, when this case comes to be cleared up you will find that a woman named Rachel has something to do with it. It's all very well for you to laugh, Mr. Sherlock Holmes. You may be very smart and clever, but the old hound is the best, when all is said and done."

"I really beg your pardon!" said my companion, who had ruffled the little man's temper by bursting into an explosion of laughter. "You certainly have the credit of being the first of us to find this out, and, as you say, it bears every mark of having been written by the other participant in last night's mystery. I have not had time to examine this room yet, but with your permission I shall do so now."

As he spoke, he whipped a tape measure and a large round magnifying glass from his pocket. With these two implements he trotted noiselessly about the room, sometimes stopping, occasionally kneeling, and once lying flat upon his face. So engrossed was he with his occupation that he appeared to have forgotten our presence, for he chattered away to himself under his breath the whole time, keeping up a running fire of exclamations, groans, whistles, and little cries suggestive of encouragement and of hope. As I watched him I was irresistibly reminded of a pure-blooded well-trained foxhound as it dashes backwards and forwards through the covert, whining in its eagerness, until it comes across the lost scent. For twenty minutes or more he continued his researches, measuring with the most exact care the distance between marks which were entirely invisible to me, and occasionally applying his tape to the walls in an equally incomprehensible manner. In one place he gathered up very carefully a little pile of grey dust from the floor, and packed it away in an envelope. Finally, he examined with his glass the word upon the wall, going over every letter of it with the most minute exactness. This done, he appeared to be satisfied, for he replaced his tape and his glass in his pocket.

"They say that genius is an infinite capacity for taking pains," he remarked with a smile. "It's a very bad definition, but it does apply to detective work."

Gregson and Lestrade had watched the manoeuvres of their amateur companion with considerable curiosity and some contempt. They evidently failed to appreciate the fact, which I had begun to realize, that Sherlock Holmes' smallest actions were all directed towards some definite and practical end.

"What do you think of it, sir?" they both asked.

"It would be robbing you of the credit of the case if I was to presume to help you," remarked my friend. "You are doing so well now that it would be a pity for anyone to interfere." There was a world of sarcasm in his voice as he spoke. "If you will let me know how your investigations go," he continued, "I shall be happy to give you any help I can. In the meantime I should like to speak to the constable who found the body. Can you give me his name and address?"

Lestrade glanced at his note-book. "John Rance," he said. "He is off duty now. You will find him at 46, Audley Court, Kennington Park Gate."

Holmes took a note of the address.

"Come along, Doctor," he said; "we shall go and look him up. I'll tell you one thing which may help you in the case," he continued, turning to the two detectives. "There has been murder done, and the murderer was a man. He was more than six feet high, was in the prime of life, had small feet for his height, wore coarse, square-toed boots and smoked a Trichinopoly cigar. He came here with his victim in a four-wheeled cab, which was drawn by a horse with three old shoes and one new one on his off fore leg. In all probability the murderer had a florid face, and the finger-nails of his right hand were remarkably long. These are only a few indications, but they may assist you."

Lestrade and Gregson glanced at each other with an incredulous smile.

"If this man was murdered, how was it done?" asked the former.

"Poison," said Sherlock Holmes curtly, and strode off. "One other thing, Lestrade," he added, turning round at the door: "'Rache,' is the German for 'revenge;' so don't lose your time looking for Miss Rachel."

With which Parthian shot he walked away, leaving the two rivals open-mouthed behind him.

Chapter IV. What John Rance Had To Tell.

IT was one o'clock when we left No. 3, Lauriston Gardens. Sherlock Holmes led me to the nearest telegraph office, whence he dispatched a long telegram. He then hailed a cab, and ordered the driver to take us to the address given us by Lestrade.

"There is nothing like first hand evidence," he remarked; "as a matter of fact, my mind is entirely made up upon the case, but still we may as well learn all that is to be learned."

"You amaze me, Holmes," said I. "Surely you are not as sure as you pretend to be of all those particulars which you gave."

"There's no room for a mistake," he answered. "The very first thing which I observed on arriving there was that a cab had made two ruts with its wheels close to the curb. Now, up to last night, we have had no rain for a week, so that those wheels which left such a deep impression must have been there during the night. There were the marks of the horse's hoofs, too, the outline of one of which was far more clearly cut than that of the other three, showing that that was a new shoe. Since the cab was there after the rain began, and was not there at any time during the morning—I have Gregson's word for that—it follows that it must have been there during the night, and, therefore, that it brought those two individuals to the house."

"That seems simple enough," said I; "but how about the other man's height?"

"Why, the height of a man, in nine cases out of ten, can be told from the length of his stride. It is a simple calculation enough, though there is no use my boring you with figures. I had this fellow's stride both on the clay outside and on the dust within. Then I had a way of checking my calculation. When a man writes on a wall, his instinct leads him to write about the level of his own eyes. Now that writing was just over six feet from the ground. It was child's play."

"And his age?" I asked.

"Well, if a man can stride four and a-half feet without the smallest effort, he can't be quite in the sere and yellow. That was the breadth of a puddle on the garden walk which he had evidently walked across. Patent-leather boots had gone round, and Square-toes had hopped over. There is no mystery about it at all. I am simply applying to ordinary life a few of those precepts of observation and deduction which I advocated in that article. Is there anything else that puzzles you?"

"The finger nails and the Trichinopoly," I suggested.

"The writing on the wall was done with a man's forefinger dipped in blood. My glass allowed me to observe that the plaster was slightly scratched in doing it, which would not have been the case if the man's nail had been trimmed. I gathered up some scattered ash from the floor. It was dark in colour and flakey—such an ash as is only made by a Trichinopoly. I have made a special study of cigar ashes—in fact, I have written a monograph upon the subject. I flatter myself that I can distinguish at a glance the ash of any known brand, either of cigar or of tobacco. It is just in such details that the skilled detective differs from the Gregson and Lestrade type."

"And the florid face?" I asked.

"Ah, that was a more daring shot, though I have no doubt that I was right. You must not ask me that at the present state of the affair."

I passed my hand over my brow. "My head is in a whirl," I remarked; "the more one thinks of it the more mysterious it grows. How came these two men—if there were two men—into an empty house? What has become of the cabman who drove them? How could one man compel another to take poison? Where did the blood come from? What was the object of the murderer, since robbery had no part in it? How came the woman's ring there? Above all, why should the second man write up the German word RACHE before decamping? I confess that I cannot see any possible way of reconciling all these facts."

My companion smiled approvingly.

"You sum up the difficulties of the situation succinctly and well," he said. "There is much that is still obscure, though I have quite made up my mind on the main facts. As to poor Lestrade's discovery it was simply a blind intended to put the police upon a wrong track, by suggesting Socialism and secret societies. It was not done by a German. The A, if you noticed, was printed somewhat after the German fashion. Now, a real German invariably prints in the Latin character, so that we may safely say that this was not written by one, but by a clumsy imitator who overdid his part. It was simply a ruse to divert inquiry into a wrong channel. I'm not going to tell you much more of the case, Doctor. You know a conjuror gets no credit when once he has explained his trick, and if I show you too much of my method of working, you will come to the conclusion that I am a very ordinary individual after all."

"I shall never do that," I answered; "you have brought detection as near an exact science as it ever will be brought in this world."

My companion flushed up with pleasure at my words, and the earnest way in which I uttered them. I had already observed that he was as sensitive to flattery on the score of his art as any girl could be of her beauty.

"I'll tell you one other thing," he said. "Patent leathers and Square-toes came in the same cab, and they walked down the pathway together as friendly as possible—arm-in-arm, in all probability. When they got inside they walked up and down the room—or rather, Patent-leathers stood still while Square-toes walked up and down. I could read all that in the dust; and I could read that as he walked he grew more and more excited. That is shown by the increased length of his strides. He was talking all the while, and working himself up, no doubt, into a fury. Then the tragedy occurred. I've told you all I know myself now, for the rest is mere surmise and conjecture. We have a good working basis, however, on which to start. We must hurry up, for I want to go to Halle's concert to hear Norman Neruda this afternoon."

This conversation had occurred while our cab had been threading its way through a long succession of dingy streets and dreary by-ways. In the dingiest and dreariest of them our driver suddenly came to a stand. "That's Audley Court in there," he said, pointing to a narrow slit in the line of dead-coloured brick. "You'll find me here when you come back."

Audley Court was not an attractive locality. The narrow passage led us into a quadrangle paved with flags and lined by sordid dwellings. We picked our way among groups of dirty children, and through lines of discoloured linen, until we came to Number 46, the door of which was decorated with a small slip of brass on which the name Rance was engraved. On enquiry we found that the constable was in bed, and we were shown into a little front parlour to await his coming.

He appeared presently, looking a little irritable at being disturbed in his slumbers. "I made my report at the office," he said.

Holmes took a half-sovereign from his pocket and played with it pensively. "We thought that we should like to hear it all from your own lips," he said.

"I shall be most happy to tell you anything I can," the constable answered with his eyes upon the little golden disk.

"Just let us hear it all in your own way as it occurred."

Rance sat down on the horsehair sofa, and knitted his brows as though determined not to omit anything in his narrative.

"I'll tell it ye from the beginning," he said. "My time is from ten at night to six in the morning. At eleven there was a fight at the 'White Hart'; but bar that all was quiet enough on the beat. At one o'clock it began to rain, and I met Harry Murcher—him who has the Holland Grove beat—and we stood together at the corner of Henrietta Street a-talkin'. Presently—maybe about two or a little after—I thought I would take a look round and see that all was right down the Brixton Road. It was precious dirty and lonely. Not a soul did I meet all the way down, though a cab or two went past me. I was a strollin' down, thinkin' between ourselves how uncommon handy a four of gin hot would be, when suddenly the glint of a light caught my eye in the window of that same house. Now, I knew that them two houses in Lauriston Gardens was empty on account of him that owns them who won't have the drains seed to, though the very last tenant what lived in one of them died o' typhoid fever. I was knocked all in a heap therefore at seeing a light in the window, and I suspected as something was wrong. When I got to the door——"

"You stopped, and then walked back to the garden gate," my companion interrupted. "What did you do that for?"

Rance gave a violent jump, and stared at Sherlock Holmes with the utmost amazement upon his features.

"Why, that's true, sir," he said; "though how you come to know it, Heaven only knows. Ye see, when I got up to the door it was so still and so lonesome, that I thought I'd be none the worse for some one with me. I ain't afeared of anything on this side o' the grave; but I thought that maybe it was him that died o' the typhoid inspecting the drains what killed him. The thought gave me a kind o' turn, and I walked back to the gate to see if I could see Murcher's lantern, but there wasn't no sign of him nor of anyone else."

"There was no one in the street?"

"Not a livin' soul, sir, nor as much as a dog. Then I pulled myself together and went back and pushed the door open. All was quiet inside, so I went into the room where the light was a-burnin'. There was a candle flickerin' on the mantelpiece—a red wax one—and by its light I saw——"

"Yes, I know all that you saw. You walked round the room several times, and you knelt down by the body, and then you walked through and tried the kitchen door, and then——"

John Rance sprang to his feet with a frightened face and suspicion in his eyes. "Where was you hid to see all that?" he cried. "It seems to me that you knows a deal more than you should."

Holmes laughed and threw his card across the table to the constable. "Don't get arresting me for the murder," he said. "I am one of the hounds and not the wolf; Mr. Gregson or Mr. Lestrade will answer for that. Go on, though. What did you do next?"

Rance resumed his seat, without however losing his mystified expression. "I went back to the gate and sounded my whistle. That brought Murcher and two more to the spot."

"Was the street empty then?"

"Well, it was, as far as anybody that could be of any good goes."

"What do you mean?"

The constable's features broadened into a grin. "I've seen many a drunk chap in my time," he said, "but never anyone so cryin' drunk as that cove. He was at the gate when I came out, a-leanin' up agin the railings, and a-singin' at the pitch o' his lungs about Columbine's New-fangled Banner, or some such stuff. He couldn't stand, far less help."

"What sort of a man was he?" asked Sherlock Holmes.

John Rance appeared to be somewhat irritated at this digression. "He was an uncommon drunk sort o' man," he said. "He'd ha' found hisself in the station if we hadn't been so took up."

"His face—his dress—didn't you notice them?" Holmes broke in impatiently.

"I should think I did notice them, seeing that I had to prop him up—me and Murcher between us. He was a long chap, with a red face, the lower part muffled round——"

"That will do," cried Holmes. "What became of him?"

"We'd enough to do without lookin' after him," the policeman said, in an aggrieved voice. "I'll wager he found his way home all right."

"How was he dressed?"

"A brown overcoat."

"Had he a whip in his hand?"

"A whip—no."

"He must have left it behind," muttered my companion. "You didn't happen to see or hear a cab after that?"

"No."

"There's a half-sovereign for you," my companion said, standing up and taking his hat. "I am afraid, Rance, that you will never rise in the force. That head of yours should be for use as well as ornament. You might have gained your sergeant's stripes last night. The man whom you held in your hands is the man who holds the clue of this mystery, and whom we are seeking. There is no use of arguing about it now; I tell you that it is so. Come along, Doctor."

We started off for the cab together, leaving our informant incredulous, but obviously uncomfortable.

"The blundering fool," Holmes said, bitterly, as we drove back to our lodgings. "Just to think of his having such an incomparable bit of good luck, and not taking advantage of it."

"I am rather in the dark still. It is true that the description of this man tallies with your idea of the second party in this mystery. But why should he come back to the house after leaving it? That is not the way of criminals."

"The ring, man, the ring: that was what he came back for. If we have no other way of catching him, we can always bait our line with the ring. I shall have him, Doctor—I'll lay you two to one that I have him. I must thank you for it all. I might not have gone but for you, and so have missed the finest study I ever came across: a study in scarlet, eh? Why shouldn't we use a little art jargon. There's the scarlet thread of murder running through the colourless skein of life, and our duty is to unravel it, and isolate it, and expose every inch of it. And now for lunch, and then for Norman Neruda. Her attack and her bowing are splendid. What's that little thing of Chopin's she plays so magnificently: Tra-la-la-lira-lira-lay."

Leaning back in the cab, this amateur bloodhound carolled away like a lark while I meditated upon the many-sidedness of the human mind.

Chapter V. Our Advertisement Brings a Visitor.

OUR morning's exertions had been too much for my weak health, and I was tired out in the afternoon. After Holmes' departure for the concert, I lay down upon the sofa and endeavoured to get a couple of hours' sleep. It was a useless attempt. My mind had been too much excited by all that had occurred, and the strangest fancies and surmises crowded into it. Every time that I closed my eyes I saw before me the distorted baboon-like countenance of the murdered man. So sinister was the impression which that face had produced upon me that I found it difficult to feel anything but gratitude for him who had removed its owner from the world. If ever human features bespoke vice of the most malignant type, they were certainly those of Enoch J. Drebber, of Cleveland. Still I recognized that justice must be done, and that the depravity of the victim was no condonment in the eyes of the law.

The more I thought of it the more extraordinary did my companion's hypothesis, that the man had been poisoned, appear. I remembered how he had sniffed his lips, and had no doubt that he had detected something which had given rise to the idea. Then, again, if not poison, what had caused the man's death, since there was neither wound nor marks of strangulation? But, on the other hand, whose blood was that which lay so thickly upon the floor? There were no signs of a struggle, nor had the victim any weapon with which he might have wounded an antagonist. As long as all these questions were unsolved, I felt that sleep would be no easy matter, either for Holmes or myself. His quiet self-confident manner convinced me that he had already formed a theory which explained all the facts, though what it was I could not for an instant conjecture.

He was very late in returning—so late, that I knew that the concert could not have detained him all the time. Dinner was on the table before he appeared.

"It was magnificent," he said, as he took his seat. "Do you remember what Darwin says about music? He claims that the power of producing and appreciating it existed among the human race long before the power of speech was arrived at. Perhaps that is why we are so subtly influenced by it. There are vague memories in our souls of those misty centuries when the world was in its childhood."

"That's rather a broad idea," I remarked.

"One's ideas must be as broad as Nature if they are to interpret Nature," he answered. "What's the matter? You're not looking quite yourself. This Brixton Road affair has upset you."

"To tell the truth, it has," I said. "I ought to be more case-hardened after my Afghan experiences. I saw my own comrades hacked to pieces at Maiwand without losing my nerve."

"I can understand. There is a mystery about this which stimulates the imagination; where there is no imagination there is no horror. Have you seen the evening paper?"

"No."

"It gives a fairly good account of the affair. It does not mention the fact that when the man was raised up, a woman's wedding ring fell upon the floor. It is just as well it does not."

"Why?"

"Look at this advertisement," he answered. "I had one sent to every paper this morning immediately after the affair."

He threw the paper across to me and I glanced at the place indicated. It was the first announcement in the "Found" column. "In Brixton Road, this morning," it ran, "a plain gold wedding ring, found in the roadway between the 'White Hart' Tavern and Holland Grove. Apply Dr. Watson, 221B, Baker Street, between eight and nine this evening."

"Excuse my using your name," he said. "If I used my own some of these dunderheads would recognize it, and want to meddle in the affair."

"That is all right," I answered. "But supposing anyone applies, I have no ring."

"Oh yes, you have," said he, handing me one. "This will do very well. It is almost a facsimile."

"And who do you expect will answer this advertisement."

"Why, the man in the brown coat—our florid friend with the square toes. If he does not come himself he will send an accomplice."

"Would he not consider it as too dangerous?"

"Not at all. If my view of the case is correct, and I have every reason to believe that it is, this man would rather risk anything than lose the ring. According to my notion he dropped it while stooping over Drebber's body, and did not miss it at the time. After leaving the house he discovered his loss and hurried back, but found the police already in possession, owing to his own folly in leaving the candle burning. He had to pretend to be drunk in order to allay the suspicions which might have been aroused by his appearance at the gate. Now put yourself in that man's place. On thinking the matter over, it must have occurred to him that it was possible that he had lost the ring in the road after leaving the house. What would he do, then? He would eagerly look out for the evening papers in the hope of seeing it among the articles found. His eye, of course, would light upon this. He would be overjoyed. Why should he fear a trap? There would be no reason in his eyes why the finding of the ring should be connected with the murder. He would come. He will come. You shall see him within an hour?"

"And then?" I asked.

"Oh, you can leave me to deal with him then. Have you any arms?"

"I have my old service revolver and a few cartridges."

"You had better clean it and load it. He will be a desperate man, and though I shall take him unawares, it is as well to be ready for anything."

I went to my bedroom and followed his advice. When I returned with the pistol the table had been cleared, and Holmes was engaged in his favourite occupation of scraping upon his violin.

"The plot thickens," he said, as I entered; "I have just had an answer to my American telegram. My view of the case is the correct one."

"And that is?" I asked eagerly.

"My fiddle would be the better for new strings," he remarked. "Put your pistol in your pocket.

Fork in the Road

When the fellow comes speak to him in an ordinary way. Leave the rest to me. Don't frighten him by looking at him too hard."

"It is eight o'clock now," I said, glancing at my watch.

"Yes. He will probably be here in a few minutes. Open the door slightly. That will do. Now put the key on the inside. Thank you! This is a queer old book I picked up at a stall yesterday—'De Jure inter Gentes'—published in Latin at Liege in the Lowlands, in 1642. Charles' head was still firm on his shoulders when this little brown-backed volume was struck off."

"Who is the printer?"

"Philippe de Croy, whoever he may have been. On the fly-leaf, in very faded ink, is written 'Ex libris Guliolmi Whyte.' I wonder who William Whyte was. Some pragmatical seventeenth century lawyer, I suppose. His writing has a legal twist about it. Here comes our man, I think."

As he spoke there was a sharp ring at the bell. Sherlock Holmes rose softly and moved his chair in the direction of the door. We heard the servant pass along the hall, and the sharp click of the latch as she opened it.

"Does Dr. Watson live here?" asked a clear but rather harsh voice. We could not hear the servant's reply, but the door closed, and some one began to ascend the stairs. The footfall was an uncertain and shuffling one. A look of surprise passed over the face of my companion as he listened to it. It came slowly along the passage, and there was a feeble tap at the door.

"Come in," I cried.

At my summons, instead of the man of violence whom we expected, a very old and wrinkled woman hobbled into the apartment. She appeared to be dazzled by the sudden blaze of light, and after dropping a curtsey, she stood blinking at us with her bleared eyes and fumbling in her pocket with nervous, shaky fingers. I glanced at my companion, and his face had assumed such a disconsolate expression that it was all I could do to keep my countenance.

The old crone drew out an evening paper, and pointed at our advertisement. "It's this as has brought me, good gentlemen," she said, dropping another curtsey; "a gold wedding ring in the Brixton Road. It belongs to my girl Sally, as was married only this time twelvemonth, which her husband is steward aboard a Union boat, and what he'd say if he come 'ome and found her without her ring is more than I can think, he being short enough at the best o' times, but more especially when he has the drink. If it please you, she went to the circus last night along with——"

"Is that her ring?" I asked.

"The Lord be thanked!" cried the old woman; "Sally will be a glad woman this night. That's the ring."

"And what may your address be?" I inquired, taking up a pencil.

"13, Duncan Street, Houndsditch. A weary way from here."

"The Brixton Road does not lie between any circus and Houndsditch," said Sherlock Holmes sharply.

The old woman faced round and looked keenly at him from her little red-rimmed eyes. "The gentleman asked me for my address," she said. "Sally lives in lodgings at 3, Mayfield Place, Peckham."

"And your name is——?"

"My name is Sawyer—her's is Dennis, which Tom Dennis married her—and a smart, clean lad, too, as long as he's at sea, and no steward in the company more thought of; but when on shore, what with the women and what with liquor shops——"

"Here is your ring, Mrs. Sawyer," I interrupted, in obedience to a sign from my companion; "it clearly belongs to your daughter, and I am glad to be able to restore it to the rightful owner."

With many mumbled blessings and protestations of gratitude the old crone packed it away in her pocket, and shuffled off down the stairs. Sherlock Holmes sprang to his feet the moment that she was gone and rushed into his room. He returned in a few seconds enveloped in an ulster and a cravat. "I'll follow her," he said, hurriedly; "she must be an accomplice, and will lead me to him. Wait up for me." The hall door had hardly slammed behind our visitor before Holmes had descended the stair. Looking through the window I could see her walking feebly along the other side, while her pursuer dogged her some little distance behind. "Either his whole theory is incorrect," I thought to myself, "or else he will be led now to the heart of the mystery." There was no need for him to ask me to wait up for him, for I felt that sleep was impossible until I heard the result of his adventure.

It was close upon nine when he set out. I had no idea how long he might be, but I sat stolidly puffing at my pipe and skipping over the pages of Henri Murger's "Vie de Bohème." Ten o'clock passed, and I heard the footsteps of the maid as they pattered off to bed. Eleven, and the more stately tread of the landlady passed my door, bound for the same destination. It was close upon twelve before I heard the sharp sound of his latch-key. The instant he entered I saw by his face that he had not been successful. Amusement and chagrin seemed to be struggling for the mastery, until the former suddenly carried the day, and he burst into a hearty laugh.

"I wouldn't have the Scotland Yarders know it for the world," he cried, dropping into his chair; "I have chaffed them so much that they would never have let me hear the end of it. I can afford to laugh, because I know that I will be even with them in the long run."

"What is it then?" I asked.

"Oh, I don't mind telling a story against myself. That creature had gone a little way when she began to limp and show every sign of being foot-sore. Presently she came to a halt, and hailed a four-wheeler which was passing. I managed to be close to her so as to hear the address, but I need not have been so anxious, for she sang it out loud enough to be heard at the other side of the street, 'Drive to 13, Duncan Street, Houndsditch,' she cried. This begins to look genuine, I thought, and having seen her safely inside, I perched myself behind. That's an art which every detective should be an expert at. Well, away we rattled, and never drew rein until we reached the street in question. I hopped off before we came to the door, and strolled down the street in an easy, lounging way. I saw the cab pull up. The driver jumped down, and I saw him open the door and stand expectantly. Nothing came out though. When I reached him he was groping about frantically in the empty cab, and giving vent to the finest assorted collection of oaths that ever I listened to. There was no sign or trace of his passenger, and I fear it will be some time before he gets his fare. On inquiring at Number 13 we found that the house belonged to a respectable paperhanger, named Keswick, and that no one of the name either of Sawyer or Dennis had ever been heard of there."

"You don't mean to say," I cried, in amazement, "that that tottering, feeble old woman was able to get out of the cab while it was in motion, without either you or the driver seeing her?"

"Old woman be damned!" said Sherlock Holmes, sharply. "We were the old women to be so taken in. It must have been a young man, and an active one, too, besides being an incomparable actor. The get-up was inimitable.

He saw that he was followed, no doubt, and used this means of giving me the slip. It shows that the man we are after is not as lonely as I imagined he was, but has friends who are ready to risk something for him. Now, Doctor, you are looking done-up. Take my advice and turn in."

I was certainly feeling very weary, so I obeyed his injunction. I left Holmes seated in front of the smouldering fire, and long into the watches of the night I heard the low, melancholy wailings of his violin, and knew that he was still pondering over the strange problem which he had set himself to unravel.

CRITICAL EYE

▶ For Discussion

a. Why is Dr. Watson thrilled to dedicate himself to Holmes and a lifelong pursuit of endless danger?

b. Why does Watson find it so difficult to acclimate after the war?

▶ Re-approaching the Reading

Sherlock Holmes was such an appealing character that, over time, people began to believe that he was a real man. What is it about Holmes and his adventures that have made him larger than the page?

▶ Writing Assignment

Detective fiction as a genre deals with the search for truth. What is it about the genius, an individual who can perceive what the average person cannot, that forces them to intercede in the face of deception?

FRANCES A. ALTHAUS

FEMALE CIRCUMCISION: RITE OF PASSAGE OR VIOLATION OF RIGHTS?

Female circumcision, the partial or total cutting away of the external female genitalia, has been practiced for centuries in parts of Africa, generally as one element of a rite of passage preparing young girls for womanhood and marriage. Often performed without anesthetic under septic conditions by lay practitioners with little or no knowledge of human anatomy or medicine, female circumcision can cause death or permanent health problems as well as severe pain. Despite these grave risks, its practitioners look on it as an integral part of their cultural and ethnic identity, and some perceive it as a religious obligation.

Opponents of female genital cutting, however, emphasize that the practice is detrimental to women's health and well-being. Some consider female circumcision a ritualized form of child abuse and violence against women, a violation of human rights.

The debate over female circumcision is relatively recent. The practice was rarely spoken of in Africa and little known in the West until the second half of this century. In the 1950s and 1960s, however, African activists and medical practitioners brought the health consequences of female circumcision to the attention of international organizations such as the United Nations and the World Health Organization (WHO). Still, it was not until 1979 that any formal policy statement was made: A seminar organized by WHO in Khartoum to address traditional practices affecting the health of women and children issued recommendations that governments work to eliminate the practice.

During the following decade, the widespread silence surrounding female circumcision was broken. After African women's organizations met in Dakar, Senegal, in 1984 to discuss female circumcision and other detrimental cultural practices, the Inter African Committee Against Harmful Traditional Practices (IAC) was formed. With national committees in more than 20 countries, the IAC has been important in bringing the harmful effects of female circumcision to the attention of African governments. In addition, other African women's networks and organizations that had focused primarily on such issues as reproductive health, women's rights and legal justice became involved in working against the practice. Such groups as Mandalaeo Ya Wanawake in Kenya, NOW in Nigeria and New Woman in Egypt now include the elimination of female circumcision among their goals.

In part because these groups brought fresh perspectives to the issue, the emphasis in discussions of female circumcision

Althaus FA, Female Circumcision: Rite of passage or violation of rights? *International Family Planning Perspectives,* 1997, 23 (3): 130–133.

shifted to encompass women's human and reproductive rights as well as their health. International consensus statements and treaties such as the Convention to Eliminate All Forms of Discrimination Against Women, the Convention on the Rights of the Child and the African Charter on the Rights and Welfare of the Child began to include language applicable to female circumcision. These documents, however, did not directly mention the practice, focusing instead on broad categories such as detrimental practices, violence and rights violations.

With shifts in emphasis came new language: Although activists and clinicians continued to refer to female circumcision when working directly with women in the community, policy statements and other documents began to use the term "female genital mutilation." That term was used in the first international document to specifically address the practice, the Programme of Action adopted by the International Conference on Population and Development in Cairo in 1994. The Program refers to female genital mutilation as a "basic rights violation" and urges governments to "prohibit and urgently stop the practice . . . wherever it exists."

In the Platform of the Fourth World Conference on Women, held in Beijing in 1995, female genital mutilation was cited as both a threat to women's reproductive health and a violation of their human rights. In addition to making general recommendations, the Platform specifically called on governments to "enact and enforce legislation against the perpetrators of practices and acts of violence against women, such as female genital mutilation. . . ." Notably, the drive to include language specifically condemning female genital mutilation in the Platform was led by Africans.

Against this background of activity and changing emphasis, the plight of Fauziya Kassindja, a 17-year-old woman from Togo, focused public attention in the United States on female circumcision. More important, her case was instrumental in redefining the practice as gender-based violence that could be grounds for the granting of political asylum. Kassindja, who fled her homeland in October 1994 to avoid an arranged marriage and the genital cutting that would be part of the marriage rites, was placed in a detention center after arriving in the United States under a false passport and asking for asylum. She was released a year and a half later and granted asylum after intensive media coverage of her situation.

Prevalence

Female circumcision is currently practiced in at least 28 countries stretching across the center of Africa north of the equator; it is not found in southern Africa or in the Arabic-speaking nations of North Africa, with the exception of Egypt. Female circumcision occurs among Muslims, Christians, animists and one Jewish sect, although no religion requires it.

The availability of reliable figures on the prevalence of female circumcision has increased greatly in recent years: National data have now been collected in the Demographic and Health Survey (DHS) program for six countries—the Central African Republic. Côte d'Ivoire, Egypt, Eritrea, Mali and Sudan. In these countries, from 43% to 97% of reproductive-age women have been circumcised. Within countries, prevalence may vary across ethnic groups; in Mali, for example, where the overall proportion of women who have undergone circumcision is 94%, only 17% of women of Tamachek ethnicity have been circumcised.

Estimates for other countries are generally based on local surveys or anecdotal information. The estimated proportion of women who have undergone circumcision in these countries ranges from 5% in Uganda and the Congo (formerly Zaire) to 98% in Djibouti and Somalia. Both because of wide variations in prevalence across social and demographic subgroups and because of data limitations, these figures should be interpreted with caution.

Types of Circumcision

Although circumcision may be performed during infancy, during adolescence or even during a woman's first pregnancy, the procedure is usually carried out on girls between ages four and 12. In the countries for which DHS data are available, the median age at excision ranges from less than two months in Eritrea to about six years in Mali and almost 10 years in Egypt. The operation is generally performed by a traditional birth attendant or an *exciseuse*, an elder village woman.

There are three basic types of genital excision, although practices vary widely. In the first type, clitoridectomy, part or all of the clitoris is amputated, while in the second (often referred to as excision), both the clitoris and the labia minora are removed. Infibulation, the third type, is the most severe: After excision of the clitoris and the labia minora, the labia majora are cut or scraped away to create raw surfaces, which are held in contact until they heal, either by stitching the edges of the wound or by tying the legs together. As the wounds heal, scar tissue joins the labia and covers the urethra and most of the vaginal orifice, leaving an opening that may be as small as a matchstick for the passage of urine and menstrual blood.

The overall proportion of women who have undergone each type of circumcision is not known, although clitoridectomy appears to be by far the most common procedure. It is estimated that about 15% of all circumcised women have been infibulated, although an estimated 80–90% of all circumcisions in Djibouti, Somalia and the Sudan are of this type.

Consequences of Excision

In the conditions under which female circumcision is generally performed in Africa, even the less extensive types of genital cutting can lead to potentially fatal complications, such as hemorrhage, infection and shock. The inability to pass urine because of pain, swelling and inflammation following the operation may lead to urinary tract infection. A woman may suffer from abscesses and pain from damaged nerve endings long after the initial wound has healed.

Infibulation is particularly likely to cause long-term health problems. Because the urethral opening is covered, repeated urinary tract infections are common, and stones may form in the urethra and bladder because of obstruction and infection. If the opening is very small, menstrual flow may be blocked, leading to reproductive tract infections and lowered fertility or sterility. One early study estimated that 20–25% of cases of sterility in northern Sudan can be linked to infibulation.

Without deinfibulation before childbirth, obstructed labor may occur, causing life-threatening complications for both mother and infant. Because birthrates are high in many countries where infibulation is practiced, a woman's infibulation scar may be cut and resewn many times during her reproductive years.

In addition, the amputation of the clitoris and other sensitive tissue reduces a woman's ability to experience sexual pleasure. For infibulated women, the consummation of marriage is likely to be painful because of the small vaginal opening and the lack of elasticity in the scar tissue that forms it. Tearing and bleeding may occur, or the infibulation scar may have to be cut open to allow penetration.

Infibulation may make intercourse unsatisfying for men as well as women: In a study of 300 polygynous Sudanese men, each of whom had one wife who had been infibulated and one or more who had not, 266 expressed a definite sexual preference for the uninfibulated wife; in addition, 60 said they had married a second, uninfibulated wife because of the penetration difficulties they experienced with their first wife, whose scarred vaginal opening became progressively more inelastic after each birth. Under such conditions, marital dissolution may occur, especially if a woman's fertility is affected. In Sudan, for example, one study found that infibulated women are almost twice as likely as other women to have lower fertility and more than twice as likely to be divorced. Thus, a practice that is justified as making girls marriageable and safeguarding their fertility may actually increase the risk of marital dissolution and subfertility.

Given the medical complications and related consequences of female circumcision, why does the practice continue? First, it is unclear how frequently such problems occur, for few data exist and those that are available come from small studies or are based on self-reports. Second, in societies in which few women remain uncircumcised, problems arising from female circumcision are likely to be seen as a normal part of a woman's life and may not even be associated with circumcision. The most important reasons, however, probably lie in the social and economic conditions of women's lives.

Social Context

Female circumcision is an integral part of the societies that practice it, where patriarchal authority and control of female sexuality and fertility are givens. In communities where a person's place in society is determined by lineage traced through fathers, female circumcision reduces the uncertainty surrounding paternity by discouraging or preventing women's sexual activity outside of marriage. Although the societies that practice circumcision vary in many ways, most girls receive little education and are valued primarily for their future role as sources of labor and producers of children. In some communities, the prospective husband's family pays a brideprice to the family of the bride, giving his family the right to her labor and her children; she herself has no right to or control over either.

A girl's virginity may be considered essential to her family's ability to arrange her marriage and receive a brideprice, as well as to family honor. In Somalia, for example, a prospective husband's family may have the right to inspect the bride's body prior to marriage, and mothers regularly check their infibulated daughters to ensure that they are still "closed." In this context, parents see both infibulation and early marriage as means of ensuring that their daughter remains "pure" and thus worthy of the brideprice.

In many cultures, considerable social pressure is brought to bear on families who resist conforming to the tradition of female circumcision. In Man, a town in the interior of Côte d'Ivoire, a Yacouba girl who has not been circumcised is not considered marriageable. Among the Samburu of Kenya, who consider uncircumcised girls unclean, promiscuous and immature, girls are generally circumcised at age 14 or 15, usually just before they are married. A girl with a younger brother may undergo circumcision if she remains unmarried by her late teens, since custom dictates that a boy with an uncircumcised older sister may not be initiated into the warrior class.

Girls' desires to conform to peer norms may make them eager to undergo circumcision, since those who remain uncut may be teased and looked down on by their age mates. In addition, the ritual cutting is often embedded in ceremonies in which the girls are feted and showered with presents and their families are honored. A girl's wishes, in any case, are often irrelevant; it is her family—often the father or elder female relatives—who decide whether she will undergo circumcision. According to one Yacouba father, "[My daughter] has no choice. I decide. Her viewpoint is not important."

Indeed, girls have very little choice. Given their age and their lack of education and resources, they are dependent on their parents, and later on their husband, for the basic necessities of life. Those who resist may be cut by force. If they remain uncircumcised and their families are therefore unable to arrange a marriage, they may be cast out without any means of subsistence.

Because of their lack of choice and the powerful influence of tradition, many girls accept circumcision as a necessary, and even natural part of life, and adopt the rationales given for its existence. Of the five countries for which DHS data are available on women's opinions toward excision, the Central African Republic is the only one in which the majority favor discontinuation. A variety of justifications are given by DHS respondents who favor continuation of the practice, including preservation of virginity before marriage, fidelity after marriage, enhancement of the husband's sexual pleasure, enhancement of fertility, prevention of infant and child mortality, cleanliness and religious requirements, but tradition is by far the most commonly mentioned reason.

As these data show, women themselves are involved in perpetuating the practice of female genital cutting. Data on the attitudes of men have been collected only in Eritrea and Sudan. DHS data for Eritrea show that men are slightly more likely than women to favor discontinuation, and that men who believe the practice should be stopped are about twice as likely as their female counterparts to cite medical complications and lack of sexual satisfaction as reasons. In Sudan, a 1981 study found that men are somewhat more likely than women to believe female genital cutting should continue, but are less than half as likely as women to prefer infibulation.

Working for Change

Efforts to eliminate female circumcision have often been unsuccessful because opponents of the practice ignored its social and economic context. In some cases, external intervention has strengthened the resolve of communities to continue their genital cutting rituals as a way of resisting what they perceive as cultural imperialism.

During the era of colonial rule in Africa, some governments attempted to ban female circumcision and met with resistance. In Sudan, when a law banning infibulation was about to be proclaimed in 1946, many parents rushed to midwives to have their daughters infibulated in case it should become impossible later on. When some midwives were arrested for performing circumcision, anticolonial protests broke out. The British colonial government, fearing a massive nationalist revolt such as those that had occurred in Egypt and Kenya, eventually let the law go unenforced.

More recently, calls to action by Western feminists and human rights activists have provoked similar negative reactions. African women have perceived many of these efforts as condescending and derogatory toward their culture. In the words of one infibulated Somali woman. "If Somali women change, it will be a change done by us, among us. When they order us to stop, tell us what we must do, it is offensive to the black person or the Muslim person who believes in circumcision. To advise is good, but not to order."

In many Western publications dealing with female circumcision, one anthropologist observes, "African women are . . . depicted as aberrant, while intact Western women have their sexuality affirmed as the norm." Yet, as Nahid Toubia points out, Western women also subject themselves to medically unnecessary, hazardous procedures, such as cosmetic surgery and the insertion of breast implants, to increase their sexual desirability.

The strong reactions against depictions of cultures practicing female circumcision as savage, violent and abusive of women and children have led to new ways of approaching the issue. Some international organizations working against the practice are supporting local activist groups with funding, training and technical expertise rather than choosing direct involvement. Numerous projects have been mounted to eliminate female circumcision, although none have included rigorous evaluations to determine their success. The following approaches are typical:

- *Community education.* A nationwide study conducted in 1985–1986 by the National Association of Nigerian Nurses and Midwives found that female circumcision was practiced in all states and that in five of the then 11 states at least 90% of the women had been cut. In response to this information, the organization designed an eradication campaign with support from Population Action International and the Program for Appropriate Technology in Health. The project trained health workers to teach individuals about the harmful effects of female circumcision and to work through religious organizations, women's organizations and social clubs to mobilize communities against the practice.

- *Alternative rituals.* The organization Maendeleo Ya Wanawake carried out a pilot project in the Meru district of Kenya in 1996 to develop an alternative initiation ritual. Some 25 mother-daughter pairs participated in a six-day training session that included information on the consequences of female circumcision and how to defend the decision not to be cut. The session culminated in a coming-of-age celebration planned by the community, excluding circumcision but including gifts and special T-shirts for the initiates, skits, and "books of wisdom" prepared by the parents of each girl.

- *Drama.* In Burkina Faso, the director of a local theater group developed a play, based on the experience of his niece, on the consequences of female circumcision; the play is aimed particularly at men. A grant from the Research Action and Information Network for Bodily Integrity of Women (RAINBO) enabled him to videotape the play and show it throughout the region.

Prospects for the Future

The available data provide little evidence that the practice of female circumcision will decline substantially in the near future. The Central African Republic, where prevalence is moderate, is the only country in which steady decline seems to be occurring. Young women in Côte d'Ivoire, Egypt, Eritrea and Mali appear to be no less likely than older women to have undergone circumcision. In Sudan, the sole country for which longitudinal comparisons can be made, prevalence appears to have declined slightly, from 96% to 89%, between the 1978–1979 Sudan Fertility Survey and the 1989–1990 Sudan DHS. Nevertheless, the DHS data do not indicate any differences between younger and older women.

Despite the overall lack of change in the percentages of girls who undergo circumcision, changes in attitudes and practices seem to be occurring in some countries. In Eritrea, for example, women and men younger than 25 are much more likely than those in their 40s to believe that the tradition should be discontinued. In Sudan, where the great majority of women have traditionally been infibulated, there appears to be a small shift toward clitoridectomy.

Given the lack of enforcement of most laws against female circumcision, it is unclear whether a purely legal approach is effective in itself. While legislation may be enforceable in countries where only a small minority adhere to the practice, that is unlikely to be the case when the majority follow the tradition. As Toubia points out, "Clear policy declarations by government and professional bodies are essential to send a strong message of disapproval, but if the majority of the society is still convinced that female genital mutilation serves the common good, legal sanctions that incriminate practitioners and families may be counterproductive." In such countries, she suggests, public information campaigns and counseling of families about the effects of the practice on children may be more useful.

Substantial change is likely to occur only with improvements in the status of women in society. According to Rogaia Abusharaf. "To get married and have children, which on the surface fulfills gender expectations and the reproductive potential of females, is, in reality, a survival strategy in a society plagued with poverty, disease, and illiteracy. . . . The socio economic dependency of women on men affects their response to female circumcision."

This view is born out by the DHS data: In most countries, women with higher levels of education and those who have income of their own are less likely than other women to have been circumcised and are also less likely to have had their daughters circumcised. As Toubia comments, "this one violation of women's rights cannot [be abolished] without placing it firmly within the context of efforts to address the social and economic injustice women face the world over. If women are to be considered as equal and responsible members of society, no aspect of their physical, psychological or sexual integrity can be compromised."

CRITICAL EYE

▶ **For Discussion**

a. If every cultural practice can be questioned and changed, what is the purpose of tradition?

b. How can female circumcision be justified/viewed as a rite of passage?

c. The statistics tell us that women and children are the most abused and poorest people on the planet. Given this certainty, if we, as a global society, rise to eliminate one evil that women face, won't another merely take its place?

▶ **Re-approaching the Reading**

In what ways can those African nations that still practice female circumcision see outside interference and concern as a disregard for a culture westerners fail to understand?

▶ **Writing Assignment**

Overt sexism, racism, and discrimination against the disabled are practices that America has engaged in. In your opinion, what other American practices need to be questioned in order to create reform and change?

JOHN CHEEVER

REUNION

The last time I saw my father was in Grand Central Station. I was going from my grandmother's in the Adirondacks to a cottage on the Cape that my mother had rented, and I wrote my father that I would be in New York between trains for an hour and a half, and asked if we could have lunch together. His secretary wrote to say that he would meet me at the information booth at noon, and at twelve o'clock sharp I saw him coming through the crowd. He was a stranger to me—my mother divorced him three years ago and I hadn't been with him since—but as soon as I saw him I felt that he was my father, my flesh and blood, my future and my doom. I knew that when I was grown I would be something like him; I would have to plan my campaigns within his limitations. He was a big, good-looking man, and I was terribly happy to see him again. He struck me on the back and shook my hand. "Hi, Charlie," he said. "Hi, boy. I'd like to take you up to my club, but it's in the Sixties, and if you have to catch an early train I guess we'd better get something to eat around here." He put his arm around me, and I smelled my father the way my mother sniffs a rose. It was a rich compound of whiskey, after-shave lotion, shoe polish, woolens, and the rankness of a mature male. I hoped that someone would see us together. I wished that we could be photographed. I wanted some record of our having been together.

We went out of the station and up a side street to a restaurant. It was still early, and the place was empty. The bartender was quarreling with a delivery boy, and there was one very old waiter in a red coat down by the kitchen door. We sat down, and my father hailed the waiter in a loud voice. "*Kellner!*" he shouted. "*Garçon! Cameriere! You!*" His boisterousness in the empty restaurant seemed out of place. "Could we have a little service here!" he shouted. "Chop-chop." Then he clapped his hands. This caught the waiter's attention, and he shuffled over to our table.

"Were you clapping your hands at me?" he asked.

"Calm down, calm down, *sommelier*," my father said. "If it isn't too much to ask of you—if it wouldn't be too much above and beyond the call of duty, we would like a couple of Beefeater Gibsons."

"I don't like to be clapped at," the waiter said.

"I should have brought my whistle," my father said. "I have a whistle that is audible only to the ears of old waiters. Now, take out your little pad and your little pencil and see if you can get this straight: two Beefeater Gibsons. Repeat after me: two Beefeater Gibsons."

"I think you'd better go somewhere else," the waiter said quietly.

From *The Stories of John Cheever* by John Cheever, copyright © 1978 by John Cheever. Used by permission of Alfred A. Knopf, a division of Random House, Inc.

"That," said my father, "is one of the most brilliant suggestions I have ever heard. Come on, Charlie, let's get the hell out of here!"

I followed my father out of that restaurant into another. He was not so boisterous this time. Our drinks came, and he cross-questioned me about the baseball season. He then struck the edge of his empty glass with his knife and began shouting again. "*Garçon! Kellner! Cameriere! You!* Could we trouble you to bring us two more of the same."

"How old is the boy?" the waiter asked.

"That," my father said, "is none of your God-damned business."

"I'm sorry, sir," the waiter said, "but I won't serve the boy another drink."

"Well, I have some news for you," my father said. "I have some very interesting news for you. This doesn't happen to be the only restaurant in New York. They've opened another on the corner. Come on, Charlie."

He paid the bill, and I followed him out of that restaurant into another. Here the waiters wore pink jackets like hunting coats, and there was a lot of horse tack on the walls. We sat down, and my father began to shout again. "Master of the hounds! Tallyhoo and all that sort of thing. We'd like a little something in the way of a stirrup cup. Namely, two Bibson Geefeaters."

"Two Bibson Geefeaters?" the waiter asked, smiling.

"You know damned well what I want," my father said angrily. "I want two Beefeater Gibsons, and make it snappy. Things have changed in jolly old England. So my friend the duke tells me. Let's see what England can produce in the way of a cocktail."

"This isn't England," the waiter said.

"Don't argue with me," my father said. "Just do as you're told."

"I just thought you might like to know where you are," the waiter said.

"If there is one thing I cannot tolerate," my father said, "it is an impudent domestic. Come on, Charlie."

The fourth place we went to was Italian. "*Buon giorno,*" my father said. "*Per favore, possiamo avere due cocktail americani, forti, forti. Molto gin, poco vermut.*"

"I don't understand Italian," the waiter said.

"Oh, come off it," my father said. "You understand Italian, and you know damned well you do. *Vogliamo due cocktail americani. Subito.*"

The waiter left us and spoke with the captain, who came over to our table and said, "I'm sorry, sir, but this table is reserved."

"All right," my father said. "Get us another table."

"All the tables are reserved," the captain said.

"I get it," my father said. "You don't desire our patronage. Is that it? Well, the hell with you. *Vada all' inferno.* Let's go, Charlie."

"I have to get my train," I said.

"I'm sorry, sonny," my father said. "I'm terribly sorry." He put his arm around me and pressed me against him. "I'll walk you back to the station. If there had only been time to go up to my club."

"That's all right, Daddy," I said.

"I'll get you a paper," he said. "I'll get you a paper to read on the train."

Then he went up to a newsstand and said, "Kind sir, will you be good enough to favor me with one of your God-damned, no-good, ten-cent afternoon papers?" The clerk turned away from him and stared at a magazine cover. "Is it asking too much, kind sir," my father said, "is it asking too much for you to sell me one of your disgusting specimens of yellow journalism?"

"I have to go, Daddy," I said. "It's late."

"Now, just wait a second, sonny," he said. "Just wait a second. I want to get a rise out of this chap."

"Goodbye, Daddy," I said, and I went down the stairs and got my train, and that was the last time I saw my father.

CRITICAL EYE

▶ **For Discussion**

a. How is this a text about failed expectations for the father and the son?

b. Why does the father feel that power/strength comes from humiliation?

▶ **Re-approaching the Reading**

Examine Cheever's story alongside of "Fiesta 1980" by Junot Diaz. In what way(s) are the two stories similar? What do the two sons want or need from their respective fathers?

▶ **Writing Assignment**

We often hear about fathers feeling disappointed in their sons, but what is at stake when a son is disappointed in his father?

JONATHAN KOZOL

THE HUMAN COST OF AN ILLITERATE SOCIETY

> *Precautions, Read Before Using. Poison; Contains sodium hydroxide (caustic soda-lye). Corrosive: Causes severe eye and skin damage, may cause blindness. Harmful or fatal if swallowed. If swallowed, give large quantities of milk or water. Do not induce vomiting. Important: Keep water out of can at all times to prevent contents from violently erupting. . . .*
> —Warning on a can of Drano

Questions of literacy, in Socrates' belief, must at length be judged as matters of morality. Socrates could not have had in mind the moral compromise peculiar to a nation like our own. Some of our Founding Fathers did, however, have this question in their minds. One of the wisest of those Founding Fathers (one who may not have been most compassionate but surely was more prescient than some of his peers) recognized the special dangers that illiteracy would pose to basic equity in the political construction that he helped to shape.

"A people who mean to be their own governors," James Madison wrote, "must arm themselves with the power knowledge gives. A popular government without popular information or the means of acquiring it, is but a prologue to a farce or a tragedy, or perhaps both."

Tragedy looms larger than farce in the United States today. Illiterate citizens seldom vote. Those who do are forced to cast a vote of questionable worth. They cannot make informed decisions based on serious print information. Sometimes they can be alerted to their interests by aggressive voter education. More frequently, they vote for a face, a smile, or a style, not for a mind or character or body of beliefs.

The number of illiterate adults exceeds by 16 million the entire vote cast for the winner in the 1980 presidential contest. If even one third of all illiterates could vote, and read enough and do sufficient math to vote in their self-interest, Ronald Reagan would not likely have been chosen president. There is, of course, no way to know for sure. We do know this; Democracy is a mendacious term when used by those who are prepared to countenance the forced exclusion of one third of our electorate. So long as 60 million people are denied significant participation, the government is neither of nor for, nor by, the people. It is a government, at best, of those two thirds whose wealth, skin color, or parental privilege allows them opportunity to profit from the provocation and instruction of the written word.

"The Human Cost of an Illiterate Society", from *Illiterate America* by Jonathan Kozol, copyright © 1985 by Jonathan Kozol. Used by permission of Doubleday, a division of Random House, Inc.

The undermining of democracy in the United States is one "expense" that sensitive Americans can easily deplore because it represents a contradiction that endangers citizens of all political positions. The human price is not so obvious at first.

Since I first immersed myself within this work I have often had the following dream: I find that I am in a railroad station or a large department store within a city that is utterly unknown to me and where I cannot understand the printed words. None of the signs or symbols is familiar. Everything looks strange: like mirror writing of some kind. Gradually I understand that I am in the Soviet Union. All the letters on the walls around me are Cyrillic. I look for my pocket dictionary but I find that it has been mislaid. Where have I left it? Then I recall that I forgot to bring it with me when I packed my bags in Boston. I struggle to remember the name of my hotel. I try to ask somebody for directions. One person stops and looks at me in a peculiar way. I lose the nerve to ask. At last I reach into my wallet for an ID card. The card is missing. Have I lost it? Then I remember that my card was confiscated for some reason, many years before. Around this point, I wake up in a panic.

This panic is not so different from the misery that millions of adult illiterates experience each day within the course of their routine existence in the U.S.A.

Illiterates cannot read the menu in a restaurant.

They cannot read the cost of items on the menu in the *window* of the restaurant before they enter.

Illiterates cannot read the letters that their children bring home from their teachers. They cannot study school department circulars that tell them of the courses that their children must be taking if they hope to pass the SAT exams. They cannot help with homework. They cannot write a letter to the teacher. They are afraid to visit in the classroom. They do not want to humiliate their child or themselves.

Illiterates cannot read instructions on a bottle of prescription medicine. They cannot find out when a medicine is past the year of safe consumption; nor can they read of allergenic risks, warnings to diabetics, or the potential sedative effect of certain kinds of nonprescription pills. They cannot observe preventive health care admonitions. They cannot read about "the seven warning signs of cancer" or the indications of blood-sugar fluctuations or the risks of eating certain foods that aggravate the likelihood of cardiac arrest.

Illiterates live, in more than literal ways, an uninsured existence. They cannot understand the written details on a health insurance form. They cannot read the waivers that they sign preceding surgical procedures. Several women I have known in Boston have entered a slum hospital with the intention of obtaining a tubal ligation and have emerged a few days later after having been subjected to a hysterectomy. Unaware of their rights, incognizant of jargon, intimidated by the unfamiliar air of fear and atmosphere of ether that so many of us find oppressive in the confines even of the most attractive and expensive medical facilities, they have signed their names to documents they could not read and which nobody, in the hectic situation that prevails so often in those overcrowded hospitals that serve the urban poor, had even bothered to explain.

Childbirth might seem to be the last inalienable right of any female citizen within a civilized society. Illiterate mothers, as we shall see, already have been cheated of the power to protect their progeny against the likelihood of demolition in deficient public schools and, as a result, against the verbal servitude within which they themselves exist. Surgical denial of the right to bear that child in the first place represents an ultimate denial, an unspeakable metaphor, a final darkness that denies even the twilight gleamings of our own humanity. What greater violation of our biological, our biblical, our spiritual humanity could possibly exist than that which takes place nightly, perhaps hourly these days, within such overburdened and benighted institutions as the Boston City Hospital? Illiteracy has many costs; few are so irreversible as this.

Even the roof above one's head, the gas or other fuel for heating that protects the residents of northern city slums against the threat of illness in the winter months become uncertain guarantees. Illiterates cannot read the lease that they must sign to live in an apartment which, too often, they cannot afford. They cannot manage check accounts and therefore seldom pay for anything by mail. Hours and entire days of difficult travel (and the cost of bus or other public transit) must be added to the real cost of whatever they consume. Loss of interest on the check accounts they do not have, and could not manage if they did, must be regarded as another of the excess costs paid by the citizen who is excluded from the common instruments of commerce in a numerate society.

"I couldn't understand the bills," a woman in Washington, D.C., reports, "and then I couldn't write the checks to pay them. We signed things we didn't know what they were."

Illiterates cannot read the notices that they receive from welfare offices or from the IRS. They must depend on word-of-mouth instruction from the welfare worker—or from other persons whom they have good reason to mistrust. They do not know what rights they have, what deadlines and requirements they face, what options they might choose to exercise. They are half-citizens. Their rights exist in print but not in fact.

Illiterates cannot look up numbers in a telephone directory. Even if they can find the names of friends, few possess the sorting skills to make use of the yellow pages; categories are bewildering and trade names are beyond decoding capabilities for million of nonreaders. Even the emergency numbers listed on the first page of the phone book—"Ambulance," "Police," and "Fire"—are too frequently beyond the recognition of nonreaders.

Many illiterates cannot read the admonition on a pack of cigarettes. Neither the Surgeon General's warning nor its reproduction on the package can alert them to the risks. Although most people learn by word of mouth that smoking is related to a number of grave physical disorders, they do not get the chance to read the detailed stories which can document this danger with the vividness that turns concern into determination to resist. They can see the handsome cowboy or the slim Virginia lady lighting up a filter cigarette; they cannot heed the words that tell them that this product is (not "may be") dangerous to their health. Sixty million men and women are condemned to be the unalerted, high-risk candidates for cancer.

Illiterates do not buy "no-name" products in the supermarkets. They must depend on photographs or the familiar logos that are printed on the packages of brand-name groceries. The poorest people, therefore, are denied the benefits of the least costly products.

Illiterates depend almost entirely upon label recognition. Many labels, however, are not easy to distinguish. Dozens of different kinds of Campbell's soup appear identical to the nonreader. The purchaser who cannot read and does not dare to ask for help, out of the fear of being stigmatized (a fear which is unfortunately realistic), frequently comes home with something which she never wanted and her family never tasted.

Illiterates cannot read instructions on a pack of frozen food. Packages sometimes provide an illustration to explain the cooking preparations; but illustrations are of little help to someone who must "boil water, drop the food—*within* its plastic wrapper—in the boiling water, wait for it to simmer, instantly remove."

Even when labels are seemingly clear, they may be easily mistaken. A woman in Detroit brought home a gallon of Crisco for her children's dinner. She thought that she had bought the chicken that was pictured on the label. She had enough Crisco now to last a year—but no more money to go back and buy the food for dinner.

Recipes provided on the packages of certain staples sometimes tempt a semiliterate person to prepare a meal her children have not tasted. The longing to vary the uniform and often starchy content of low-budget meals provided to the family that relies on food stamps commonly leads to ruinous results. Scarce funds have been wasted and the food must be thrown out. The same applies to distribution of food-surplus produce in emergency conditions. Government inducements to poor people to "explore the ways" by which to make a tasty meal from tasteless noodles, surplus cheese, and powdered milk are useless to nonreaders. Intended as benevolent advice, such recommendations mock reality and foster deeper feelings of resentment and of inability to cope. (Those, on the other hand, who cautiously refrain from "innovative" recipes in preparation of their children's meals must suffer the opprobrium of "laziness," "lack of imagination. . . .")

Illiterates cannot travel freely. When they attempt to do so, they encounter risks that few of us can dream of. They cannot read traffic signs and, while they often learn to recognize and to decipher symbols, they cannot manage street names which they haven't seen before. The same is true for bus and subway stops. While ingenuity can sometimes help a man or woman to discern directions from familiar landmarks, buildings, cemeteries, churches, and the like, most illiterates are virtually immobilized. They seldom wander past the streets and neighborhoods they know. Geographical paralysis becomes a bitter metaphor for their entire existence. They are immobilized in almost every sense we can imagine. They can't move up. They can't move out. They cannot see beyond. Illiterates may take an oral test for drivers' permits in most sections of America. It is a questionable concession. Where will they go? How will they get there? How will they get home? Could it be that some of us might like it better if they stayed where they belong?

Travel is only one of many instances of circumscribed existence. Choice, in almost all its facets, is diminished in the life of an illiterate adult. Even the printed TV schedule, which provides most people with the luxury of preselection, does not belong within the arsenal of options in illiterate existence. One consequence is that the viewer watches only what appears at moments when he happens to have time to turn the switch. Another consequence, a lot more common, is that the TV set remains in operation night and day. Whatever the program offered at the hour when he walks into the room will be the nutriment that he accepts and swallows. Thus, to passivity, is added frequency—indeed, almost uninterrupted continuity. Freedom to select is no more possible here than in the choice of home or surgery or food.

"You don't choose," said one illiterate woman. "You take your wishes from somebody else." Whether in perusal of a menu, selection of highways, purchase of groceries, or determination of affordable enjoyment, illiterate Americans must trust somebody else; a friend, a relative, a stranger on the street, a grocery clerk, a TV copywriter.

"All of our mail we get, it's hard for her to read. Settin' down and writing a letter, she can't do it. Like if we get a bill . . . we take it over to my sister-in-law. . . . My sister-in-law reads it."

Billing agencies harass poor people for the payment of the bills for purchases that might have taken place six months before. Utility companies offer an agreement for a staggered payment schedule on a bill past due. "You have to trust them," one man said. Precisely for this reason, you end up by trusting no one and suspecting everyone of possible deceit. A submerged sense of distrust becomes the corollary to a constant need to trust. "They are cheating me . . . I have been tricked . . . I do not know . . ."

Not knowing: This is a familiar theme. Not knowing the right word for the right thing at the right time is one form of subjugation. Not knowing the world that lies concealed behind those words is a more terrifying feeling. The longitude and latitude of one's existence are beyond all easy apprehension. Even the hard, cold stars within the firmament above one's head begin to mock the possibilities for self-location. Where am I? Where did I come from? Where will I go?

"I've lost a lot of jobs," one man explains. "Today, even if you're a janitor, there's still reading and writing. . . . They leave a note saying, 'Go to room so-and-so . . .' You can't do it. You can't read it. You don't know."

"The hardest thing about it is that I've been places where I didn't know where I was. You don't know where you are. . . . You're lost."

"Like I said: I have two kids. What do I do if one of my kids starts choking? I go running to the phone . . . I can't look up the hospital phone number. That's if we're at home. Out on the street, I can't read the sign. I get to a pay phone. Okay, tell us where you are. We'll send an ambulance.' I look at the street sign. Right there, I can't tell you what it says. I'd have to spell it out, letter for letter. By that time, one of my kids would be dead. . . . These are the kinds of fears you go with, every single day . . ."

"Reading directions, I suffer with. I work with chemicals. . . . That's scary to begin with . . ."

"You sit down. They throw the menu in front of you. Where do you go from there? Nine times out of ten you say, 'Go ahead. Pick out something for the both of us.' I've eaten some weird things, let me tell you!"

Menus. Chemicals. A child choking while his mother searches for a word she does not know to find assistance that will come too late. Another mother speaks about the inability to help her kids to read; "I can't read to them. Of course that's leaving them out of something they should have. Oh, it matters. You *believe* it matters! I ordered all these books. The kids belong to a book club. Donny wanted me to read a book to him. I told Donny: 'I can't read.' He said: 'Mommy, you sit down. I'll read it to you.' I tried it one day, reading from the pictures. Donny looked at me. He said, 'Mommy, that's not right.' He's only five. He knew I couldn't read . . .'"

A landlord tells a woman that her lease allows him to evict her if her baby cries and causes inconvenience to her neighbors. The consequence of challenging his words conveys a danger which appears, unlikely as it seems, even more alarming than the danger of eviction. Once she admits that she can't read, in the desire to maneuver for the time in which to call a friend, she will have defined herself in terms of an explicit impotence that she cannot endure. Capitulation in this case is preferable to self-humiliation. Resisting the definition of oneself in terms of what one cannot do, what others take for granted, represents a need so great that other imperatives (even one so urgent as the need to keep one's home in winter's cold) evaporate and fall away in face of fear. Even the loss of home and shelter, in this case, is not so terrifying as the loss of self.

"I come out of school. I was sixteen. They had their meetings. The directors meet. They said that I was wasting their school paper. I was wasting pencils . . ."

Another illiterate, looking back, believes she was not worthy of her teacher's time. She believes that it was wrong of her to take up space within her school. She believes that it was right to leave in order that somebody more deserving could receive her place.

Children choke. Their mother chokes another way: on more than chicken bones.

People eat what others order, know what others tell them, struggle not to see themselves as they believe the world perceives them. A man in California speaks about his own loss of identity, of self-location, definition:

"I stood at the bottom of the ramp. My car had broke down on the freeway. There was a phone. I asked for the police. They was nice. They said to tell them where I was. I looked up at the signs. There was one that I had seen before. I read it to them: ONE WAY STREET. They thought it was a joke. I told them I couldn't read. There was other signs above the ramp. They told me to try. I looked around for somebody to help. All the cars was going by real fast. I couldn't make them understand that I was lost. The cop was nice. He told me: 'Try once more.' I did my best. I couldn't read. I only knew the sign above my head. The cop was trying to be nice. He knew that I was trapped. 'I can't send out a car to you if you can't tell me where you are.' I felt afraid. I nearly cried. I'm forty-eight years old. I only said: 'I'm on a one-way street, . . .'"

The legal problems and the courtroom complications that confront illiterate adults have been discussed above. The anguish that may underlie such matters was brought home to me this year while I was working on this book. I have spoken, in the introduction, of a sudden phone call from one of my former students, now in prison for a criminal offense. Stephen is not a boy today. He is twenty-eight years old. He called to ask me to assist him in his trial, which comes up next fall. He will be on trial for murder. He has just knifed and killed a man who first enticed him to his home, then cheated him, and then insulted him—as "an illiterate subhuman."

Stephen now faces twenty years to life. Stephen's mother was illiterate. His grandparents were illiterate as well. What parental curse did not destroy was killed off finally by the schools. Silent violence is repaid with interest. It will cost us $25,000 yearly to maintain this broken soul in prison. But what is the price that has been paid by Stephen's victim? What is the price that will be paid by Stephen?

Perhaps we might slow down a moment here and look at the realities described above. This is the nation that we live in. This is a society that most of us did not create but which our President and other leaders have been willing to sustain by virtue of malign neglect. Do we possess the character and courage to address a problem which so many nations, poorer than our own, have found it natural to correct?

The answers to these questions represent a reasonable test of our belief in the democracy to which we have been asked in public school to swear allegiance.

Critical Eye

▶ For Discussion

a. Are we deeply concerned with the illiteracy of others, or do we believe it to be "their" problem?

b. The author paints a rather apocalyptic view for those who are outside of the literacy construct. Is it really that devastating?

c. In order to combat this issue, what must we do? In essence, who bears the most responsibility?

d. Since this essay was written, America has slipped even further academically as a world leader. Why is this happening? Is there any real hope for recovery?

▶ Re-approaching the Reading

The author suggests that those most in danger of falling into the illiteracy hole are those who do not speak English. Do we make it difficult for the immigrant to succeed? In short, are we patient and helpful with their "assimilation"?

▶ Writing Assignment

Do policies like President George Bush's *No Child Left Behind Act* and President Barack Obama's *Waiver Plan* help the situation of illiteracy in this country?

MONIQUE FERRELL

Go Brooklyn!

This story begins with a whimper and ends with a bang—literally and figuratively on both accounts. I had come into Manhattan with a camera crew to visit the law offices of Mason, Furman, & Shaw. It was an all-purpose, high-end firm that handled everything from divorces to murder cases.

Traditionally, the law firm had always been an "all-boys" club, but it had just added two new partners: Corrin Thomas and Madelyn Schwartz. Corrin was Black and bi-sexual. She had jet-black dreadlocks that hung to the middle of her back and was also tall with a runway model's body and looks to match. Madelyn, another tall beauty, had a head full of "I should be doing hair care commercials" blonde hair. She had piercing green eyes that I'm sure contributed to her many wins. Not because she used them to mesmerize but, instead, to intimidate and confuse juries and witnesses. While undeniably attractive, this woman seemed to be so much more, at least initially, than a "dumb blonde." The firm had hit the jackpot when they lured them from the competition. By adding these two ladies, they were firmly embracing political correctness and kissing every left-wing liberal in the mouth. The senior partners had covered almost every base. Women. Homosexuality. Race. I wondered if the men in charge had longed for one of them to develop a degenerative limp so they could corner the disability niche. A winning firm with those kinds of demographics would be unstoppable. Maybe the partners would pay someone to bust one of their kneecaps.

In the courtroom, Corrin and Madelyn were quite dangerous and were often referred to as the Tiger Lady and the Shark Woman respectively. I liked what I'd heard about them, their professionalism, and their antics in the courtroom. Surprise witnesses. The ability to break the opposition's witnesses. The ability to find just the right evidence at just the right time. They were both legal wunderkinds. So great were each at their jobs that when they once battled each other, the judge had to declare a mistrial because the jury was hung. Articulate. Savvy. Smart. Beautiful. Sexy. Isn't that what we want in our lawyers? What keeps us glued to our television sets watching ill-written one hour law dramas? Corrin and Madlyn had it all, and they were the only undefeated women lawyers in the city. Mason, Furman, & Shaw wanted them, and they got them. Believe me, they paid dearly to get them. It cost a very high six figures a piece just to sign them.

I thought a story on these two would fit in nicely on my current affairs news program, *The Issue At Hand*. Corrine and Madelyn were serving as co-counsel on a murder case. A well-known football player had been accused of murdering his ex-fiancé. The collective brain matter of the country was dulled by the feeling that we had all been here before. At the time, my show was the highest rated program on the highest rated news channel on cable television. So, I wasn't doing too badly myself. Some critics were heralding me as the "new" Oprah Winfrey, and, at only thirty-four years old, it was a moniker I was willing to take on.

I was a poor kid from the projects whose mother and father struggled to send me to the best schools and to ballet class twice a week to, as they called it, "keep me out of trouble, off my back, and from having some deadbeat nigga's baby." My parents are a hoot, but they meant well. They had seen too many of the young girls in our neighborhood succumb to the kinds of clichés that are the norm in "the hood."

And because of their commitment to me, I did them proud. With a Bachelor's and a Master's degree in Communications, I worked my way up from gopher and coffee getter to the host of my own number one show. I guess that's what peaked my interest in Corrin and Madelyn. Initially, they appeared to be women after my own heart—go-getters. And, halleluiah, the gender had come far, but we still had a long way to go as women. I wanted to be a part of that and help other women along the way if I could, no matter where they hailed from on the planet. So I thought it was my duty as a fellow go-getting woman to promote Corrine and Madelyn.

The news van pulled up in front of the office building on Friday at 1:00 P.M. sharp with time to spare for our 2:00 P.M. interview. This would give my camera people enough time to set up and me a chance to review my notes. As we headed toward the building, I noticed a young Hispanic woman de-boarding a city bus—briefcase and shopping bag in hand. She raced to the building's gold and brass doors looking harried and talking to herself. Once inside the building, we found her waiting at the elevator. When the elevator doors closed behind us, she pressed her floor and, noticing the cameras, asked, "Has something happened somewhere in the building?"

"No," I said, "I'm here to interview Corrin Thomas and Madelyn Schwartz."

"My goodness," she said with recognition in her eyes. "You're Desiree Mandel. You're here for Corrin and Madelyn? I'm their assistant, Bethany. They didn't tell me you were coming."

While I could tell that she was a bit astonished to see someone from television in her office space, I was sure I also detected the fact that she was a bit pissed off because no one had told her I was coming.

"Listen, why don't you get yourself settled in? It looks like you're coming back from lunch. Take a few minutes, and then let them know we're here."

She looked relieved. Hurt and relieved. The doors opened on the fiftieth floor, and Bethany led us to a lavish waiting area. She placed her briefcase behind her desk and took a shopping bag from Ellington's with her and walked into a huge meeting room where two women, clearly the women of the hour, could be seen and heard discussing what had to be a case.

"Corrin. Madelyn. Desiree Mandel is here to interview you. Oh, and Madelyn, here is your blouse."

Okay. Strike one.

Did these heffas send their assistant out to pick up a personal item?

I've been told by people over the years that I have a sixth sense. Sometimes, I can tell when a story is a dud or when a source is being less than truthful. In my personal life, I can tell by the first date if the guy is a dud or is being less than truthful—which was probably why I hadn't had a date in six months. My parents could never keep the Christmas gifts hidden, so they took to buying them on Christmas Eve. I could also read someone's character instantly. My nose twitched. Really, it did. The twitch was imperceptible to those who didn't know me well, but it was there nonetheless—a slight movement at the end of my button nose.

Both women bounced out of the office well-dressed and full of smiles. I despised them instantly. I'd been in the news game for a very long time. I can spot a good story and a bad one. This was a bad one. I hated to think it, but I was sure that these were two of the biggest bitches on planet Earth. And I had the strangest feeling that they each tortured Bethany in special ways every day. How do you not tell your assistant—who is usually the right hand in any office—that a camera crew is coming? How do you send that same assistant out to buy your damn blouse during her lunch break? They looked shocked to see her back so soon. And then it suddenly dawned on me; they hadn't *wanted* her here to greet me.

With much pomp and circumstance, they thanked me for coming. Then they told me how happy they were to meet me and asked Bethany to show us into the conference room where we could set up.

By the time the interview was over, I hated these women with everything within me. They weren't *real* women. They were two sets of breasts with sharp teeth and long claws. They fawned over each other in the interview—each heaping phony praise on the other. Puffing up their respective chests with answers that, if you listened closely, seemed to say, "Enough about me, what do think about me?"

Madelyn actually said, "It's really important for us to be here. Just think of all of the opportunities we're able to give other women. Like our assistant, Bethany. She's a minority. What chances are there for her in the legal field that doesn't involve finger-printing and a mug shot? I mean, I kid, but that's how some people see things. They don't see that she's a capable, bright woman. They may just see her Dominican face and hear her accent." Once finished, she flipped her hair over her shoulders and giggled like a five-year-old cheerleader in knee socks. Traditional dingbat move.

"Yes, this is so true," chimed in Corrin with an above-it-all and dismissive edge in her voice, all the while talking with her hands. "We still have some very serious Civil Rights issues at hand in this country. I think working here enables Bethany to see the possibilities of her life and reminds her to stay focused. We're trying to coax her into going to law school."

Wellfuckme. Yes, that's what they actually said about that very intelligent woman that my crew and I encountered on the elevator, who spoke perfect English, had no visible accent, and was not Dominican. I ought to know because I'm half Black and half Dominican, and I know my own people.

The tip of my nose was on fire.

After my time with them, I went on to interview the male partners of the firm. It was a welcome relief. They stuck to the situation at hand, being rather frank about the importance of having Corrin and Madelyn in the firm as partners. They were even honest about the fact that some of their clients were concerned about having two relatively young women in the firm. Because, as they said, women get married. Have babies. Change their priorities. In other words, men get married, have babies, never change their priorities and, most of all, they don't have periods. Horace Mason, son of founding father Davis Mason, damn near floated out of his seat every time he mentioned Madelyn's name. No question about what was going on there. Same old game. I guess casting couches were in law offices, too. A token Negro and a Dingbat. As smart as they were in the courtroom, they were nothing more than clichés. And mean-spirited at that.

After wrapping up the interview, I said my goodbyes and made my way to the bathroom. I wanted to fill a sink with cold water and dunk my head in. Once there, I looked into the mirror and shook my head at my reflection. I was already thinking of ways to edit this piece so that these very important women didn't come off looking like the assholes they were. Yeah, they probably deserved to be outed, but men have been protecting each other for generations—wasn't it our turn? I ran my fingers through my shoulder length twists and exhaled. Then I heard it.

Whimpering. Someone was crying.

"Excuse me, is someone in here?" I asked.

The far end stall door opened and out walked Bethany.

"I'm sorry Ms. Mandel. I'm so embarrassed. And I know it's unprofessional to cry at work, but I'm just a little overwhelmed today. I have a lot on my mind."

"I bet you do, meja," I said with a smirk.

I checked every stall in the bathroom and then handed her a paper towel.

"Toma. And stop apologizing. I know what's going on here. I'm not a reporter for nothing."

"Where are you from?" she asked.

"From here. My father is Black and my mother is from the D.R. What about you? *They* seem to think you're Dominican."

"They think I'm Dominican?" she laughed loudly. "Of course they do. I'm Puerto Rican, first generation New Yorican. And my Spanish is horrible."

"Why are you in here crying?" As if I didn't already know.

"I just feel trapped. I feel like I'm never going to be the one in the office with the big cases. I just don't feel like anyone sees me. Hell, I don't even see me any more. When I leave here, I have to go to law school at night. I work like an unappreciated dog here all day. I work like a dog at school. Home is a mess. I'm just so tired, and I'm very embarrassed to be breaking down and telling you this."

"And I bet they don't make it any easier huh?"

She didn't answer. Still protective of the lady barracudas even though they had each shown her no loyalty or respect at all. That's what happens when you're powerless; you tend to protect those who hold your future in their hands.

"Listen, Bethany, whatever you discuss with me stays within the walls of this bathroom. I know integrity is not something that many reporters have any more, but I do. Hear what I am saying. There are 365 days in the year, which means that it is statistically impossible for you to be wrong every single one of them. Sometimes it is not you; it *is* them. Get away from these people before they kill everything that is good and strong in you."

With that, I reached into my bag and pulled out my business card.

"Call me on Monday. We have a legal department over at the station. I'm sure we can use you. Sometimes, it's who you know. Tu sabe? Knowing people seems to work around here, just ask Madelyn."

Her eyes opened wide as saucers. How had I known? Was I going to reveal it on the show? She just stood there amazed that her life had just turned on a dime. It's like that sometimes.

My own life was about to make a sudden change, and I didn't even know it.

"You're right," I said, turning to leave. "It's bad to be around people who don't see you, but you're wrong about one thing—I see you. I see you very clearly."

Once downstairs, we loaded the van and discussed bar options. We all desperately needed to get drunk to wash ourselves clean of the Tiger Lady and the Shark Woman. I turned to look at the corner where I'd seen Bethany exit her bus and hoped against hope that she'd never have to take a bus to run someone else's errands again.

Suddenly, for the second time that day, something on a city bus caught my attention.

The poster on the side of the just-arriving bus was an advertisement for an upcoming movie for a rap artist called Big Ru. The film was called *Bullet Proof*. I'd heard of the artist before. I'd even heard some of his lyrics and, as usual, I was not impressed. Moreover, I was insulted as a Black woman and as a Black person. Hell, I was insulted as a human being who walked the earth. To say I hated rap music was an understatement. These artists, if you can call them that, embarrassed me—giving me a cultural shame that I couldn't even begin to define.

But this so-called artist was special. Everyone knew him as Big Ru.

But if my eyes were not deceiving me, the man on the bus was Darnel Quincy, and, if I had my way, he was going to be in big trouble on live, national television.

The tip of my nose was on fire.

I boarded the van, cylinders clicking, already working on what I knew would be my next story and what I hoped would change the face of Hip Hop music—maybe even bring it to its knees.

Two weeks later, the story about Corrin and Madelyn aired making them look like the brilliant minds they *thought* they were. They each sent me flowers, long-winded individual *thank you* notes, and invitations to dinner with the other partners. They even seemed to forgive the fact that I'd stolen Bethany. So, I had made some powerful friends.

I was already wrapped up in my next story. I had my assistants Matt and Gloria digging up every piece of information on Big Ru, or as I knew him to be called, Darnel Quincy, that they could find. His record company, *Body Blow Records*, created a bio on Ru, a pseudonym for their constructed bad boy Alvin Jenkins, which rivaled any fairytale on the market. They had to create a life for Ru because no actual birth certificate existed. How the media had neglected to research this man thoroughly was beyond me. But how shocked could I really be? This is the madness that we had descended into as a once honorable profession. We no longer pushed stories that celebrated profound world-changing ideas or brilliant discoveries. Instead, we focused on barely researched stories that reflected our chaotic and loud drift towards mediocrity.

According to *Body Blow*, Big Ru was from the mean streets of Bed-Stuy Brooklyn. His father was doing life in prison for armed bank robbery and for killing two guards and a civilian when Ru was five. His mother was killed while turning tricks in an alley in the Bronx's Hunts Point area when he was nine. Apparently, his mother became a prostitute to support herself and Ru in his father's absence. Once an orphan, Ru's grandparents took him in, where they raised him to the best of their ability in the Paul Gleeson Housing Projects on Laurleton Street—notoriously one of the worst neighborhoods and housing developments in Brooklyn. To support himself and to protect his aging grandparents, who worked at a paper factory by the Brooklyn docks, Ru began establishing himself as a major contender in the drug game. He was merciless to those who stole from him and was determined to rule all of Brooklyn's drug trade. And then came that fateful night during his seventeenth year.

According to legend, and I do mean legend, it was a deal gone bad. Ru was supposedly set up by his nemesis, a guy named Black from a rivaling neighborhood. It was to be a swap of money and drugs, but, instead, Ru and his crew were met by handguns and semi-automatics in an abandoned building. Most of his "boys" were killed—including his nemesis—and Ru, always strapped, pulled out his gat and busted a cap in those mother.... I'm being facetious, but isn't that always how the cliché goes?

So he fights his way out, takes a bullet in the leg and one in the hand. He turns a corner, trying to get home and hears someone behind him. Now, here is where the street fiction comes into play—the ghetto scuttlebutt that Matt and Gloria helped me dig up. Scared and injured after the shootout, Ru turns and fires without looking and hits a boy. A ten-year-old named Darius Mead. It is then that Ru throws the gun in the sewer and, despite the fact that he hears police cars coming around the corner, he stays with the little boy, who cannot or will not say who shot him. Ru tells the cops they were both shot by the same assailant. The police, with no gun in sight, could not pin the crime on him. But, they find the drugs, and he does a nickel in a New York State prison. The child survives the gun wound and never tells the truth. Supposedly, another reason why no one could tie him to the events of that fated evening was that Ru was a background boss. A mastermind, if you will. He let his minions do his work, and, therefore, people never knew just who the top dog really was.

Clark Kent. Superman.

Back to the *Body Blow Records* biographical account. While in jail, apparently Ru has a dream. In it, his grandfather comes to him and tells him to, and I am quoting here, "Get out of his own way." He also tells him "There are all kinds of ways to make people rue the day they met you. Not all of it has to do with bloodshed."

The next eventful day behind bars, he receives word that his grandfather died the previous night from heart failure, and Ru decides to leave his life of crime behind. He also takes his grandfather's words to heart and becomes Big Ru, as in rue the day. And, poof, just like that, a Hip Hop legend was born. And who can refute the story? Everyone from the neighborhood, so-called enemies and friends alike, are dead. And the low level drug dealers who remained all wanted to attest to the fact that they both *knew* and *rolled* with Big Ru.

Welcomed by today's angry, confused, disenfranchised youth—Black, White, and everything in between—Ru became the poet of his generation. He was welcomed because everyone believed that he came up from the streets, made it, and proved his manhood.

As I read the bio *Body Blow* sent along with the notes Matt and Gloria put together, I almost peed my pants.

"Oh, what a hunk of bullshit!" I said to the papers in my hand.

"What, Des?" Matt asked with a jump. He often sat in my office while I read the research he'd help me gather. If there was something wrong or missing, he wanted to be there to explain it or to fix it.

Poor Matt. He wanted more than anything to be a reporter and was convinced that somehow he was failing me at every turn. The kid had a great mind. He was a Dean's List sophomore at one of the leading universities in the city and was interning with me. He had an eye for news, and he could write.

I didn't answer him. I just kept reading.

"Lies. Lies. Lies. Damn, how had I missed this? How long has Big Ru been putting out records?" I looked at Gloria.

"Five years now. His last two albums have all but skyrocketed him off the planet. This guy is Hip Hop, Desiree. And, this movie he's in, *Bullet Proof*, is about to change everything. This man is about to become *the* wealthiest rap artist ever. And he's barely thirty."

Gloria Liu was a senior researcher for the *Issue At Hand* and was next in line to become the producer of my show. The media business was about as cutthroat as everything else, but Gloria didn't take any shit and she knew her field and how to work with reporters. At 110 pounds soaking wet, and the ripe statuesque height of 4'10, this was no easy task. But she was good at her job. She was also good at training Matt. He worshiped her and thought she was brilliant.

"Okay, people," I said, snapping out of my trance. "Here's our next story."

"You want to do a story on Big Ru?"

"Yes, Matt, I do. And let me tell you why . . ."

I don't think I'd ever been so smug, but this was a big one. And, with that, I reached into my desk and pulled out my own file on Big Ru complete with interviews I'd been conducting for about two weeks. I had been calling all of my old high school friends and teachers. I even took a walk down to a precinct in good old Brooklyn and asked them about an old case involving a fourteen-year-old-boy named Darnel Quincy. And, while I was there, I asked about a notorious dealer from Bed-Stuy and his antics and found that the reason no cop or FBI or DEA agent ever came knocking at Big Ru's mansion was because they didn't know who or what the hell he was talking about. A journalist is nothing without good sources. And, once again, mine at the Public Records office located two sets of birth certificates and social security numbers that could be traced back to Darnel Quincy.

I was able to obtain college transcripts and old college identification cards. And then I pulled out my high school year book and, with a shit eating grin, I opened it to a picture of a fourteen-year-old boy dressed in his catholic school uniform. He was smiling and was surrounded by his chess teammates. The trophy, off to the side and awaiting a winner, was extravagant and taller than either of the players who, locked in a heated chess battle, were framed forever in the photo. Above him, the high school newspaper headline read, "King Me." It was the 1994 New York City High School Chess Championship, and Darnel Quincy was about to make a chess move that has yet to be bested in the subsequent years. It was probably the last day he was ever really happy.

Matt and Gloria looked at the picture.

"Who is the cute kid?" Gloria asked.

I reached into the folder and pulled out a color copy of Darnel Quincy's college I.D. "They look kinda the same. They related?" Matt asked.

And then I picked up an enlarged color photo for the cover art of Big Ru's latest album.

"He's had his nose done. That's because it was broken when he was fourteen. He's dyed his hair. He was a redhead like his mother. He's also had something done to his eyes. Reconstructive surgery. I'm sure he's had to have quite a bit of it done over the years due to his injuries. But, this my friends . . ."

". . . is fucken' Big Ru," Gloria gasped. "The chess geek is fucken' Big Ru!" As it often did whenever she got excited, I could hear a smidgen of her Chinese accent come out.

"This is a big deal. The 'slap dem bitches,' 'I'm from the hood,' 'I did time in jail,' big-time gangsta went to Catholic School? He's Catholic? And a dirty nerdy chess player, too?"

"Yep."

"But," said Matt "the Catholic Church reveres the Virgin Mary. He talks about women like, well, like they're animals. I've never seen a woman with her clothes on in his videos. At best, this is interesting. It's trippy. All rap artists lie about their reps. Not to ruin the moment for you, boss, but what's the big deal? Sure, it'll hurt him, maybe even ruin his career. Get us some extra ratings. But it won't get us an Emmy or snagged by a bigger network or change the face of Hip Hop all that much."

"Oh, but wait. There is indeed more." And then I let it all fly . . .

When I was done, they both sat in silence with their mouths open. They could not believe that I knew this man when he was a boy—before something, a moment in time, changed his

Fork in the Road

life. That's all we are, when you come to think of it, a series of moments that can maim or strengthen us. He chose his path, and now I was about to change mine.

"Are we really going to do this, Desiree?" Matt said. The Hip Hop community is going to crucify you. You'll get everything journalists dream of, but some people are going to call you a sell-out—and this may just destroy the Hip Hop industry. Or make some artists do even worse shit to prove just how *hard* they are."

"A sell-out to what, Matt? A music that hates women—women that look like me? A music that turned Black men into animals and makes it so that you—my young brown friend—can't even walk down the street without someone thinking you're a criminal? Do you think the world out there sees you, Matt? Or do you think they see a 'ghetto nigga' from one of these videos? No, it's time. Right is right. Wrong is wrong. Somebody has got to stand up. And as far as toppling *the industry*, the industry, if you can call it that, needs to be cleaned up! It, like The Black Television Network, is a disgrace to the Black people it pretends to serve and has created little more than a pimp/whore relationship between them and all of us. And, for the record, fuck an Emmy. I'm sick of that being the moment of glory for so-called journalists. I smelled a story and went after it! I did the research. I looked at a simple poster on the side of a city bus and found the story of the year because I have an eidetic memory and great journalistic savvy—that's the job. Whatever happened to getting the story? Whatever happened to finding the truth? Speaking to the cultural consciousness of our nation? We're so god-damned scared of the truth that we lie every time the camera comes on, or we love pushing someone else's lie. No sir, not me."

"I'll make the call." Having said that, Gloria picked up the phone and called the big wigs at *Body Blow Records* to ask Big Ru's people for an interview. Given the release of his new movie and its soundtrack and the status of my show, how could they say no?

When we were done, it was after 6:00 P.M. on a Friday. I asked Matt and Gloria if they wanted to get drinks and dinner. We went to *Solstice* across the street. I'd been drinking a lot lately. I knew something was coming. It was literally one of those days when you could feel your future shifting. It was like those damn stairs at Hogwarts in those *Harry Potter* books. They moved without telling you, taking you off somewhere into a new distance. And that's how I felt, like the ground was shifting beneath me. But I wasn't quite sure where I was going or how I was going to feel once I got there.

The next ten days were a haze of activity. We checked and re-checked with the legal department to make sure our asses were covered and to make sure that all of our facts were solid. After all, you can't bring down a label, slit the throat of an entire genre of music, and destroy an artist without expecting some serious repercussions.

I asked that Bethany be assigned to check each and every legal aspect of the pending show. She was happy to and was flourishing in the legal wing of my network. Because she was extra grateful to me, she went above and beyond to make sure my ass was covered. If this went as I knew it would, Matt and Gloria would be promoted, and I would start getting offers from other networks. And, of course, more money, too.

It all came together. Big Ru's company wanted him on my show. It was the imagery of it all that made their mouths water. What a coup it was going to be: the new major player in Hip Hop, fresh from prison and the ghetto, with a bevy of number one hits and a soon-to-be released movie face-to-face with the new Belle of cable news—a *sister*, at that. Even better, a half and half sister. Hip Hop spoke to both the Black and Latino youth of our country, didn't it? We shall overcome. Black is beautiful. Latino is Lovely. You can get some, too, White folks. And so can every other racial group in the middle. Up with the people. Malcolm, Martin and Mandela would have been so proud.

One of the great advantages of doing what I was going to do is that my show airs live. There would be no second takes. No editing. His first response would be his only one, and everyone who was watching would see every stutter and stammer. They'd see the tick around his eyes and mouth as I revealed every lie he'd ever told.

The night before the show, I lay in bed unable to sleep. While I date occasionally, and have had my share of serious relationships, the most recent, which lasted for three years, had ended because his job moved to France and I wouldn't go with him. I'm not one of those women that feel that she has to give it all up for love. There is nothing cute or romantic about sacrificing everything you worked for just so you can have a man in your bed. Logically, it didn't make sense. And, I knew, that just as I'd loved him, I would love someone else.

Let's face it, not only am I a feminist, but I'm also a womanist, and I am not impressed by men. Neither do I feel them to be a necessary component of a woman's life, any more than I believe that we are necessary to men. I believe that relationships complement us. They do not complete us. And, if we allow ourselves to be defined by who we have in our beds, we miss the larger picture of who we are and what we have to offer.

But I must admit, that night, I gave in to every feminine stereotype there was, because I wanted a man in my bed. I wanted to be held.

Instead, I was alone. Wide awake. Wondering.

I was doing the right thing, wasn't I? This wasn't a gimmick, was it? I wasn't doing to Darnell what Corrin and Madelyn had done to Bethany, was I? Wouldn't everybody see that I was trying to right an egregious wrong that people had learned to live with? There wasn't an ounce of cruelty in my intentions, but, rather, I just wanted the madness and the validation of that madness to stop. The end result would be good for Black people—it had to be. There are two million people in prison in this country, and over a million of them are Black. And, big frigging surprise, the majority of their crimes are drug related. And *this* fool was standing before the entire world glorifying all of this. What was worse was that he was speaking to and about a world he could never lay claim to—feeding an already helpless generation more crooked fodder for their needy veins. Rap music wasn't the cause of all of the evil that befell Black folk, but it damn sure wasn't helping. Perhaps pulling the plug on a destructive industry would free the captives so that they could get down to the work of saving their own lives. Right?

I rose the next morning after only three hours sleep. I told myself that I was just nervous because of the weight of what I was about to do. Perhaps, I thought to myself, I'd been experiencing a little racial guilt. Wasn't I selling out a Black man, a brother, for the infamous, omnipresent Man? What right did I have?

But, the other side of me, the woman in me, growing more furious by the minute, was tired of men using women as the ass rag of their world. I was tired of being inundated with catcalls on the street, the possibility of being sexually assaulted just *because*. I was tired of being paid less, of being challenged at every turn because men still didn't think we had the intestinal fortitude to defend ourselves. And, finally, music—which should have been a bastion of fair play— had been turned into a haven of misogyny and sexism. We were making these men rich beyond all imagination and allowing them to lie and beef up their reputations by way of keeping us on our backs.

Well, I wasn't a turtle. I wasn't going to lie defenseless and tuck my head inside while hoping no one would see me and run me over on the road. I'd thrown the gauntlet down—and it was going to stay there.

Big Ru arrived promptly at 7:00 P.M. He came with his manager, a White man named Skip Peterson of all things, and his album producer, Kevin Davis. He was also White. Creepy factoids: Most of the labels that produce Hip Hop are owned by White men, and most Hip Hop music is bought by White men. So, the influence and capital of the music are held by those who don't live the set of circumstances discussed in the music. They do not hail from the race and culture they profit from. Additionally, those at the forefront who perform the music are often soon parted from their money, do not seem to comprehend or care about the cultural damage they inflict on the national conscience, and are unaware of the sick cyclical nature of it all.

The three men waited in the green room after we made our introductions. Big Ru showed no signs of recognizing me. But, why would he? Darnel had spent most of his life avoiding the eyes of others—especially after that fateful day.

He was about six feet tall and had clearly been working out quite a bit. He still had those hazel eyes that almost turned green when the light hit them at a certain angle. He wore a T-shirt advertising his new movie and a pair of jeans low on his waist. He also wore a white baseball cap that read simply in bright bold, black letters: MINE. I should have paid attention to that.

The first twenty-five minutes of the program went off without a hitch. Correspondents from the field gave their reports and segued into their pre-recorded interviews. Then the real fun began. We came back from commercial, and I introduced the world to Big Ru and a little boy named Darnel Quincy.

"Good evening and welcome back to *The Issue At Hand*. Tonight, I am pleased to have the leading Hip Hop artist of all time, Big Ru. Now, should I call you Big Ru or Ru?"

"Ru is fine." He smiled revealing two rows of perfectly white, even teeth. I'd heard that ladies loved his smile and his dimples. It's easy to have a smile like that when your teeth are not your own, I thought.

"Okay, so I'll start with the obvious. One of the major and most compelling things about you, which seems to make you speak to both genders and transcend color lines, is that people seem to appreciate your rise from poverty."

"Yeah, I mean people, my fans, see me as the real deal. Maybe they look at me and think if he did it, maybe I can, too."

"But, what's so compelling about your story? It's certainly no different or any more painful than most people's. Why you?"

His face twitched.

"I think people are into me because I spit the truth. And, I turned it all around. I showed them that the world didn't break me. I broke the world."

"And, just how did you do that?"

He leaned forward in his chair and smiled. Using his hands to help articulate his reply.

"Are you kidding? I sell mad records. There are artists who have been around longer than me and I've outsold them. I'm rich. *Real* rich. I took my people wit' me up from the ghetto. And now I'm going to be a movie star. I have changed the face of Hip Hop—again. And, I did it better."

"True, but some would argue that you've done all of that on the backs of *your* people, women, and by lying."

"I hear that all of the time. Why? Because I say nigga? Ooh, can I say that on television?"

"You just did. But, you're all about keeping it real. So let's dispense with the P.C. use of the N- word. Yes, you say nigger."

"Nigga."

"Oh stop. You know the words are the same. Let's not insult each other's intelligence. I've listened to your album, and you actually say nigger or 'nigga,' over the course of 14 songs, 213 times. Don't you think that's overkill? I say this because, as you've pointed out, you are a major contender in music..."

"*THE* contender."

"Okay, *THE* contender. Doesn't that mean you are very influential? That you are allowing and perpetuating racism, demeaning your own people, and encouraging others who are not Black to use the word? What, if anything, is your social responsibility? Or, is it just about selling albums?"

SILENCE

"So," he said, leaning forward. "This is going to be one of those interviews?"

"Meaning?"

"Meaning, you're one of those women."

"Meaning?"

"Your one of dem Feminazis. You take the music too literally and get all upset when no one is talking about *you* specifically."

"Oh, Mr. Ru—please. Don't tell me you're going to be one of those artists?"

"Meaning?" He said with a smile. Thinking I was the mouse in his cat's game.

"Meaning you are filled with double-talk and become condescending when you've painted yourself into a corner."

He smiled. All teeth now. He looked over at his manager. Not for support but, as if to say, "do you believe this bitch?"

"You see Ru, *I* am from Bed-Stuy. *I* am a child of the projects. I've got as much nerve as you think you have—and maybe a bit more. So, when you say I'm a Feminazi, I take great umbrage, because whatever you say about *any* women, you say about me. Unfortunately, we live in a society that does not always make the distinction between who *you* call a bitch and a ho and me. We have outrageous statistics when it comes to violence against women. So when you talk about smacking bitches and keeping them in their place, you have to be talking about me and informing men about how to respond to me."

"It's just a form of expression. It means to keep your situation straight and in order. In essence, you run things—nobody else."

"And you keep your house in order by smacking a woman and busting a cap?"

"Again, you're being too literal."

"But aren't you? This is the life you're 'up from.' The majority of Blacks and Hispanics who listen to you are living through what you say you've come 'up from.' Aren't you validating their experiences of violence, or of being violated? And, since the majority of your records—hell, most rap records—are bought by White middleclass men, aren't you perpetuating a stereotype of Black men?"

"I've done all that? Are *you* serious?"

"*Are you?* Your last album went diamond. If you never sell another album again, you'll never have to worry about money. Your image and those you portray in videos are cast around the globe. People in Africa and the Ukraine know who you are. You are a man of influence. I have never once heard you rap, 'pick up a book and go to college.' And you know why you don't? Because there is more money in being you."

"Because no one wants to hear that bull," he snapped and then, just as quickly, collected himself. "The world is a real place and things happen to people. People want to hear how you struggle up through that sh...stuff to make a better life."

"And, the way to do that is kill, sell dope, and smack women?"

"Sometimes. Sometimes there are no other options. It isn't pretty, but you have to tell the truth."

"The truth? That's an insult!"

"When did the truth ever become an insult?"

"The truth isn't an insult. *Pretending* to tell the truth is. Truth is relative, and the merit of what it reveals is all in the telling and the teller. No one has the right to kidnap a generation's future based upon a lie. As I've said, I'm from where you *say* you are from. I've seen what you *say* you've lived through, and it was never my truth. I wouldn't let it be. But, since you are all about truth and, believe me, the truth is very important to me, why don't you tell your fans *your* real truth? Don't you think that would help them?"

I have always believed that in a moment of crisis, backed into a corner, forced to trip over the lies you've told, you become who you really are. In Ru's case, who he *really was*, was a well-educated, articulate young man. And, everyone who was watching or listening could hear his roughneck, ebonic speech leave his verbiage.

Gloria and Matt were pacing back and forth behind the cameras. This was the moment. Ru's manager and producer knew that something was up.

"What do you mean? You are acting as if I am still a part of *that* life. Can't I be judged for who I am now? And how on earth have I become a kidnapper of a generation? Now I'm evil incarnate?"

"You are absolutely correct; I am doing my absolute best to judge everything about you. And, I'd be careful about all of the fancy talk, Darnel. Your true level of education is beginning to show."

"I'm sorry, who?"

First, he nervously shifted from side to side in his chair. And then he leaned forward. I didn't take my eyes off of him. I didn't move. I've heard that some animals turn and run when confronted by a predator. Some bury their heads in the dirt adopting the "if I can't see them, they can't see me" strategy. Others choose the stand-off, locking themselves in an eye-to-eye confrontation. For them it becomes a matter of waiting to see who makes the first move and then responding accordingly. This mode of defense was about drawing first blood and living to tell the story.

I continued.

"Darnel. Darnel Quincy. That is your real name, is it not? You are Darnel Quincy?"

Darnel's manager, Skip, took a seat in one of the studio folding chairs while his producer nudged him, miming, "What's wrong?"

But Ru was no fool. The first rule of a lie is to keep it going until the other player reveals their his or her hand. Maybe, I *didn't* know everything. So what, I knew his *real* legal name. I couldn't know everything. That his parents had changed his name after the incident or that the other name was constructed by the record company. He wasn't the same. His face was different. He was older. He'd successfully assumed another personality with a fraudulent name, Social Security number, birthday, and bio twice in one lifetime. I couldn't know everything unless I was there. But, the trouble for Big Ru, alias James Clark before college and Alvin Jenkins pre Big Ru, was that I had been there. I was a witness, and he didn't recognize me.

He played his hand.

"Suddenly we've gone from an interview to an interrogation?"

"Answer the question, or let's move on. Are you Darnel Quincy? Are you this young boy?"

And behind us, on the big full-screen monitor there sat pictures of Darnel at his chess match,

Darnel as James Clark on his college I.D. card, and at his college graduation from Billford University—one of the top colleges in this country.

"You see, my question is, why is this little boy, this man, nothing to rap about? Why is Ru more of a celebration than this boy and his story? Ru is an invention. It's the same tired, redundant, irresponsible M.O. But, this boy, he has a survival story."

Darnel leaned back in his chair. He seemed neither defeated nor afraid. Actually, he seemed relieved.

"You sure you wanna go here, Miss Reporter Lady? I mean you're from the mean streets, but are you ready for me?"

It was at this point that I should have realized that Ru had left Darnel behind. He had nothing else available to him except the man he'd constructed out of the ashes of his life.

I continued.

"Is it true that you are really Darnel Quincy? That your parents were, are, quite wealthy? At one time they were both lawyers for the *top* law firm in this state. If I am correct, and I am pretty sure that I am, you grew up in the Heights section of Brooklyn where your family owned a brownstone worth well over a million dollars. Your street bio says that you were born and raised in 'the hood' and that your father is in jail and your mother, a prostitute, is deceased. But, in truth, your father is a White man named Evan Quincy. And your mother is very much alive, isn't she? My investigation also unearthed that you haven't spoken to your family since you've taken on this persona. I can see how they would want to distance themselves from you and you from them. Apparently, your father didn't much get you when you were a child, and I'm sure he's rather disgusted by you now. How could he, *they*, claim you now? How could they explain you to their colleagues and wealthy friends? They barely survived the scandal of your childhood."

I turned once again to the screen, pointing to the pictures of the young Darnel. The youthful face was both different and the same from the man who sat before me. The adult face, changed in so many ways by the skillful hand of a cosmetic surgeon, could not completely erase what the finger of God had both molded and etched while Darnel grew in his mother's womb. We are who we are. Anyone looking at the photos of the teenage boy and the so-called artist who sat before me had to see the truth.

I continued.

"Is it true that *this* boy went to a Catholic high school in Brooklyn, and that he was sweet, kind, a chess champion? Many called you a borderline genius. And, because he wasn't cool, wasn't entirely comfortable with the Black kids or the White kids but, was instead, just your run-of-the-mill American nerd, he was often bullied and beaten up? Wasn't he a science and math geek? A loner who felt more comfortable with his teachers than his peers because those who were too ignorant to understand or comprehend his beauty or intellect mistreated him?

Is it true that these same bullies dragged this beautiful boy into a bathroom, and, as mobs often do, things got way out of hand and he was beaten unmercifully? Causing him to receive reconstructive surgery, especially around his nose and mouth?"

Still nothing.

"Isn't it true, Darnel, that your school underestimated just how brutal and sadistic this particular group of bullies was? That because the victimized students were so terrified of retaliation, those young tyrants literally ruled your high school unbeknownst to the administration and faculty? And isn't it true, Darnel, that to further humiliate that beautiful little boy that they sodomized him? That they made him perform oral sex on all five of them before they left him in a pool of his own blood to be found by another student? Is it true that the school was sued, lost all funding, and was subsequently closed because no one could believe that the caretakers of our students could be that oblivious? Didn't you and your parents go into hiding for a time because of the scandal and, also, to give you time to heal? Isn't it true that you've changed your name at least twice? Once before you entered college and once again before you became Ru? Do you even know who you are anymore?"

He didn't move.

"Maybe I'm wrong. Maybe Ru is real. Maybe he is Darnel's rage. I understand how rap music became appealing to you. It was the opposite of everything you used to be—everything that you believed led to your abuse and subsequent victimization. It was strong where you were weak. Irreverent where you had always been a follower of rules. Vengeance in the face of your weakness. I was there, Darnel. I went to your school. My family scrimped and saved to send me there, but I was there. Three years ahead of you. I want you to tell me, Darnel, what does truth mean to you now?"

"Well, Miss Reporter Lady, it means this," he said, pulling out a gun.

Gloria screamed and sent someone for security.

"Ru, man, don't do this!" his agent yelled.

Ru turned to the camera man and hissed, "If you shut off one camera, or leave this room, this bitch is dead."

"Leave it on," I said. "I am not scared. I'm not scared of Darnel at all."

And I wasn't. Neither was Darnel. The truth was that both of us, in our own way, were truly exhausted. Darnel was tired of carrying around three extra identities. It couldn't have been easy running away from a self that beheld the worst of everything imaginable. And then covering that same self up with another identity constructed to pretend it all away. And finally, in a last ditch effort to kill the darkness of his own soul, making a bigger and badder self that was, hopefully, mightier than every bully in the world.

Me? Maybe I was just sick and tired of being sick and tired. Maybe I'd lost all of my convictions. Maybe I didn't believe in "the truth" anymore. Perhaps all of that grandstanding in my office about the truth and change was subterfuge and bullshit. Here I was unearthing Darnel's secrets while I let the world believe a lie about Corrin and Madelyn. And it wasn't the first time I'd done it either—sculpted an impression for my viewers. I guess I just had this vision of the world, about how it *should* be, and about how it *should* feel about itself. I wanted to make that vision a reality because it seemed best. The truth is, I was beginning to lose my faith in people. We weren't making good choices anymore. We wanted "things" over the humanity of our own souls. We were being led by and emulating silly celebutants. Our children, barely able to read, comprehend science, or compute mathematical equations were the most uninspired entitled brats who believed that their parents owed them nothing less than everything. Every single economist, scientist, and poll taker had attested to the fact that as a nation we were getting dumber and fatter and, even worse, greedier.

And how do you lead a nation like that? How do you reason with them five days a week for ninety minutes? Well, sometimes you have to lie to them. Sometimes, you have to tell them the truth, but sometimes, more often than not, you have to shock the hell out of them to get them to listen or take a good hard look at themselves. In that moment with Darnel, I understood why all of our nation's presidents go almost completely gray after only a short time in office. Someone pulls them into a quiet space outside of the Oval Office and tells them what they're up against—and then they realize what they'll have to do in order to really do the job—and it scares the fuck out of them.

And that's what I'd been doing. What I was doing with Darnel. Someone had to see what we were doing to ourselves. How what we say and listen to matters. How our own ignorance and unwillingness to see had pushed this man to the brink because his supposed manhood had been challenged and we were never going to allow him to forget it. And because we weren't going to forget, he would never heal. I wanted everyone to see that all of this began with bullying. While Darnel's bullies were a bunch of rich, tyrannical sociopaths who did a few years in juvenile detention and then had their records sealed, we were all facing our own tyrants each and every day. Some of them were the drivers of our politics. Others were our bosses, spouses—hell even the unknown passersby on the street. But the bullies alone didn't hold all of the cards. It's the ill-fated maneuvers that we make in order to deal with them, or our ignoring them altogether that causes the most harm. I guess that's the point I was trying to make. Together, Darnel and I were about to find out which one of us had chosen the best option.

Darnel had not moved from his seat.

"*This* bitch is bold, huh?" he said to no one in particular. "Oh, I'm sorry," he continued, "I forgot how much you hate *that* word."

He was laughing now. That sound you emit from your throat when that fine thread between sanity and going over the deep end is all but frayed. He rose to his feet, placing the barrel of the gun to my forehead, and then, just as quickly, he stepped back and looked at me.

"Don't worry about me, Darnel. I'm a big girl. As an *actual* child of the streets, I've seen a gun before. I've seen what they can do, and I've seen them in the hands of angrier and more violent men than you."

I was pretty cocky for someone whose life was in imminent danger, no? Darnel attempted to remedy the insolence. He slapped me with his free hand. Matt yelled out for him not to hurt me. Gloria, dumbstruck, covered both sides of her face with her hands.

Ru's people did their best to calm him down. I heard my producer asking how in the hell he'd gotten a gun into the building. Everyone was afraid. But, no one left me. No one hit the deck. Everyone stayed. I'd like to believe that I'd earned the loyalty—that they cared for me as opposed to being afraid that he'd shoot each and every one of them in the back if they tried to flee to safety.

"I have to say, one day I knew this would all come out. My mother always said 'everything always comes out in the wash.' What, nothing else to say, Reporter Lady?"

I could taste the blood in my mouth. I'd bitten my lip and could feel my cheek begin to swell. I rose to face him.

"So, what do you want Darnel? What do you wish to accomplish here, and with a gun at that? They are never going to let you get out of this building. It's over. All of it."

"It's all over because you are a nosey bitch!" he screamed.

He lurched forward as if to strike me again. I stepped back and took a defensive posture.

"Darnel, if you hit me again, I'm going to make you shoot me."

There was that insolence again. When in the corner, become who you really are. And I was a fighter. If this was it, I was going to leave the world kicking and screaming.

"Oh, and she's a tough bitch, too. You think you got me all figured out? You gonna make some money offa me, Reporter Lady? Get yourself some big old ratings—maybe be a bigger star than me?"

"Oh, please, you think this is about ratings?"

I was screaming now and was losing all sense of the danger I was in.

"You think I give a shit about some damn ratings? I did this because I am sick of you! I'm sick of people like you! You keep touching the world in all of these dark and dangerous ways, and you don't give a damn about the mayhem you leave behind. I get it, something bad happened to you, and it should never have happened. But, you could have found a way to deal with it. The way millions of women are told to and made to every god-damned day! But no, you had to create a whole other way of living in the world. You could have been a real man and told your story in a million different ways, but, instead, you've got millions of people bobbing their heads to a bunch of nonsense. You could have really made a difference—said something important . . ."

"What the fuck have I got to say, lady? Who the fuck would have listened to me then, and who gone listen to me now? You took my shit. You stripped me of my manhood. Again! Men act! I'm not a man. Do you know what happened to me in that bathroom? Bitch, you're standing here feeding me and them nothing but bullshit."

He turned to face the main camera.

"Put that shit on me, man," he said to one of the cameramen. "This society only respects a man when he's attached to money and power. Ain't that right, America? And please, let's not pretend we don't expect men to lead with a mighty hand. We don't respect a man unless he's willing to smack someone in the mouth. We don't want to know anything about little boys getting raped in bathrooms or men getting attacked in jails, right? 'Cuz then he's some kind of fag, right? Do you know my father could barely look at me after it happened? He was always disappointed in me, thought I was small and weak because I liked to read. Because I was smart. He saw all of that as a weakness. I didn't like sports. I didn't like fighting. So what, that made me fucking unlovable? Do you know he actually asked my mother why I hadn't fought back? Five against one, and he wanted to know why I hadn't fought. And you gone stand here and judge me, too? I had a right to do whatever I needed to forget. So what now, Reporter Lady? What am I supposed to do now? You gone get me therapy?"

He pointed at Skip and Davis.

"They took a chance on me. To them, I was just some suburban kid who could flow. And they invested in that. They saw something special in me," he said pounding his chest. "They made me into something. I didn't have to remember nothing about my childhood; all I had to do was make my music. So what if they made some shit up to get me some street cred? You can't sell my kind of music without none. I wasn't hurting anyone."

"Yes, you did. You hurt yourself. Look at you. You're standing here with a gun. You have three different personalities, and, in the end, you're still that little boy that no one bothered to protect. What do you need a gun for, Darnel? You aren't Ru. You don't have any enemies. You haven't been to jail. *Your* life isn't real. Everybody has got their *something* Darnel. We all get bad news, have the blues, and have a set of bad memories. You aren't better than anyone else, and you damned sure aren't entitled to any more happiness than anyone on the planet."

I turned to the screen and pointed to the newspaper clipping of him at the chess match.

"Look, Darnel, I was there when you won that trophy. Look at the screen, Darnel. I'm in the picture. I'm standing right behind you. When I think about that little boy, I don't remember the tragedy, I remember that moment. I remember his intellect. I remember a young Black kid who was bound for big things."

He stopped and looked. Suddenly, a brief smile covered his face. Just then the police entered with their guns drawn. Great, just what the situation needed, more guns. Darnel had a loaded gun on me. There were now no less than five guns trained on Darnel. I could hear more people with guns outside of the studio doors. Somewhere on the other side of the camera one of the viewers was probably cleaning a gun or using one to scratch his ass.

"Don't come up in here. So help me God! I will kill her. Stay back. I'm not done talking yet!"

"I'm okay." I said. I raised my hands as if to say "let's all just relax." I was trying to diffuse what I was certain was about to happen. "Please stop. Do not kill him. Please, I'm alright. He's not going to hurt me, and you don't need to hurt him. Right, Darnel? We're okay up here, right?"

"Put the gun down, son," one of the officers said. "No one has to get hurt here."

"Shut up, man." Darnel said. The gun was still fixed on me. "I got some shit to say. You leave that camera on."

The officers began clearing the studio. Isaac, the cameraman who always filmed my best side, agreed to stay. "I won't leave you," he mouthed. They had to drag Gloria and Matt out.

"Son, you don't want to hurt anyone. And you don't want to hurt anyone in front of all of your fans, do you?"

"Nigga, fuck you. I ain't your son."

And then he turned to the camera, speaking to a man he hadn't seen in years. He ain't my daddy, is he Pop?" he said meanly.

Turning back to the officer that had just addressed him, he said, "Man, don't try to con me. Half of my fans will cheer. The other half will move on to the next rapper. Ain't that right, Miss Reporter Lady? It's just a game. It's just a game. It was just a game all of those years ago, too. It started because someone grabbed my book bag. As usual, that's all they ever did. But this time. I got mad and hit back. You see, people only understand violence. But they had to teach me a lesson. There is a pecking order, and no one is supposed to step out of their place. I wasn't supposed to get strong."

"Darnel," I said "this isn't strength now. Ru is a lie. He lies to people. He exists because you couldn't live with what happened—something that was beyond your control. But you survived, you went to college. You . . ."

"But, I couldn't get the shit out of my mind. Don't you see? I couldn't get the shit out of my mind." He started slapping himself in the forehead with his free hand. "Darnel never grew up. He's still fourteen, laid out on a bathroom floor. He still has his mouth wired shut. His nose is still hanging off of his face. Do you know that those fuckers did juvey? Fuckenjuvey? And then they got out. And then their records were sealed. They went on and lived. They're men. Darnel isn't a man, but Ru is. Hip Hop is full of men—even if they have to pretend. No one fucks with them because of the threat of what they might do. You see, you think you know, but you don't know. And you don't know shit about being a Black man."

"Darnel. This is not being a Black man. You have been manipulating people into believing that you are a jailbird, a murderer, and a drug dealer—hoping that no one will notice that you're terrified. You were born into money, were well-educated, never hungry a day in your life, and you're a multimillionaire many times over. Your responsibility was to survive, live on, and help someone else. You sold your soul because you were too weak to live with the fact that you survived."

He shook his head and then looked me in the eyes.

"But, you didn't have the right to tell it!"

The gun began to shake in his hand. He began looking around. First at me, then at the monitor displaying the pictures, and then, finally, at the cops. He seemed stuck between worlds. He didn't know who he was anymore.

Fork in the Road

"That's enough, Darnell. Let's stop now. If you were going to shoot me, you would have done it already. I'll walk out of here with you. I won't leave your side, whatever happens. You were not born to be this, Darnel. You are not a killer. You are a chess player."

I had decided that we were both right.

And that we were both wrong.

He nodded at me. I was bridging the gap between us. The police kept screaming at me to sit down. I placed my hand on the gun.

I was reaching him.

"Put it down, Darnel. Tell the truth, and teach these people who call themselves your fans what it really means to be a man. Please. If you don't, who will?"

He didn't let go, but I sensed his resolve beginning to fade. Things would have been okay except one of the officers came too close to the stage. Darnel turned, and his eyes went wide. He didn't mean to, but he squeezed the trigger. It was an involuntary reflex. Even the camera saw that. And that's important because I want them to know that he—Darnel Quincy—did not shoot me on purpose. But I did get shot. And it was bad. And, then Darnel turned the gun on himself. And, the police officers—in their zest to stop him—shot him in the head.

We lay there in a heap, almost on top of each other, until the police closed in and separated our bleeding bodies. There was so much chaos. And so much blood. Walkie-talkies were buzzing all around me. I remember the EMS workers showing up. I remember saying, "don't let him die."

I remember an officer saying, "What did she believe would happen bringing someone like him in here?" I remember reaching out to touch Darnel as we lay side by side on our stretchers. He smiled at me through his oxygen mask. He looked so peaceful. We were being wheeled to the elevators. Matt and Gloria were at my side telling me to hold on. Darnel reached back for me.

We had said so much about truth and about who has the right to speak it. I guess I don't know what the truth is. But I know what beauty is. It's a Black man at peace. Hell, maybe it's any man at peace—unburdened of all of the trappings we heap upon them. My God, who will our little boys become if we do not let them cry?

As they wheeled him out, I remember seeing Darnel smile at me before closing his eyes for what I knew would be the very last time.

And, as for me, all the rest was silence.

CRITICAL EYE

▶ **For Discussion**

a. Our main character says that she is deeply concerned with how Black and Hispanic men and women are portrayed in the Hip Hop industry, but what gives her the right to speak for these groups?

b. By the end of the story, our main character admits that she lies to her viewers in order to push her own agenda. Is she right to do so? Must we lie to the citizens of the world in order to make them better people?

c. Whether or not you agree with the main character's deeds, can you argue that her behavior is justified?

▶ **Re-approaching the Reading**

Examine this story alongside of Crouch's article "Taking Back The Music." What points are the two texts making about the dangerous and far-reaching implications of Hip Hop music?

▶ **Writing Assignment**

Consider the story from Darnel's perspective. Is he right? Why must he keep what happened to him as a child hidden? Why couldn't he "sell" his triumph over his childhood adversity? What are the consequences for him as a man after Desiree reveals his past?

CHAPTER 8

Manmade and Natural Disasters

In today's turbulent world, we live in constant fear. This unease is a result of our inability to control the environment under our very feet—one that, as time passes, continues to spiral out of control. For centuries, we have been afraid of those we deem different. Because of this, humanity has created a world of crime and violence—a world that is literally at war with itself. If there is a higher being, a creator—a God—then human beings are arguably our maker's most destructive mistake. We will slaughter each other for land and profit, for personal offenses and text-based judgments, for ethnic and cultural dissimilarities, as well as sexual hostility and perversion. We attack each other. We hate and destroy. We are not above the complete decimation of species we deem weaker or less important than ourselves. We are cruel more than not, and our indifference towards destruction is the basis for the extinction of creatures we hunt for sport.

In the last decade, nature, which humans constantly tamper with, has finally become fed up. In recent years, the world community has suffered tremendously as water and wind rage across the globe. Hurricanes, Tsunami's, tornadoes, and flooding have devastated property and killed hundreds, thousands, in the blink of an eye. Cities and countries are still in disrepair—the result of natural disasters coupled with human neglect. People are displaced. The wetlands have been polluted. The polar ice caps are melting. All of this natural annihilation is happening while politicians argue over aide and, even more ridiculously, government and corporation culpability. Fascinatingly, many people in power even dismiss the notion that Global Warming exists.

This chapter will look at the devastation, both manmade and natural, that has slashed a path of destruction across the globe—damage that, if it continues at this rate, may possibly result in humanity's annihilation.

THE BOOK OF GENESIS
THE GREAT FLOOD

Sons of God, Daughters of Men

1 And it came to pass, when men began to multiply on the face of the earth, and daughters were born unto them,

2 That the sons of God saw the daughters of men that they were fair; and they took them wives of all which they chose.

3 And the LORD said, My spirit shall not always strive with man, for that he also is flesh: yet his days shall be an hundred and twenty years.

4 There were giants in the earth in those days; and also after that, when the sons of God came in unto the daughters of men, and they bare children to them, the same became mighty men which were of old, men of renown.

5 And GOD saw that the wickedness of man was great in the earth, and that every imagination of the thoughts of his heart was only evil continually.

6 And it repented the LORD that he had made man on the earth, and it grieved him at his heart.

7 And the LORD said, I will destroy man whom I have created from the face of the earth; both man, and beast, and the creeping thing, and the fowls of the air; for it repenteth me that I have made them.

Noah, Shem, Ham, and Japheth

8 But Noah found grace in the eyes of the LORD.

9 These are the generations of Noah: Noah was a just man and perfect in his generations, and Noah walked with God.

10 And Noah begat three sons, Shem, Ham, and Japheth.

11 The earth also was corrupt before God, and the earth was filled with violence.

12 And God looked upon the earth, and, behold, it was corrupt; for all flesh had corrupted his way upon the earth.

13 And God said unto Noah, The end of all flesh is come before me; for the earth is filled with violence through them; and, behold, I will destroy them with the earth.

Cubit, Pitch, and Gopher Wood

14 Make thee an ark of gopher wood; rooms shalt thou make in the ark, and shalt pitch it within and without with pitch.

15 And this is the fashion which thou shalt make it of The length of the ark shall be three hundred cubits, the breadth of it fifty cubits, and the height of it thirty cubits.

16 A window shalt thou make to the ark, and in a cubit shalt thou finish it above; and the door of the ark shalt thou set in the side thereof; with lower, second, and third stories shalt thou make it.

17 And, behold, I, even I, do bring a flood of waters upon the earth, to destroy all flesh, wherein is the breath of life, from under heaven; and every thing that is in the earth shall die.

18 But with thee will I establish covenant; and thou shalt come into the ark, thou, and thy sons, and wife, and thy sons' wives with thee.

19 And of every living thing of all flesh, two of every sort shalt thou bring into the ark, to keep them alive with thee; they shall be male and female.

20 Of fowls after their kind, and of cattle after their kind, of every creeping thing of the earth after his kind, two of every sort shall come unto thee to keep them alive.

21 And take thou unto thee of all food that is eaten, and thou shalt gather it to thee; and it shall be for food for thee, and for them.

22 Thus did Noah; according to all that God commanded him, so did he.

The Deluge

1 And the LORD said unto Noah, Come thou and all thy house into the ark; for thee have I seen righteous before me in this generation.

2 Of every clean beast thou shalt take to thee by sevens, the male and his female: and of beasts that are not clean by two, the male and his female.

3 Of fowls also of the air by sevens, the male and the female; to keep seed alive upon the face of all the earth.

4 For yet seven days, and I will cause it to rain upon the earth forty days and forty nights; and every living substance that I have made will I destroy from off the face of the earth.

5 And Noah did according unto all that the LORD commanded him.

6 And Noah was six hundred years old when the flood of waters was upon the earth.

7 And Noah went in, and his sons, and his wife, and his sons' wives with him, into the ark, because of the waters of the flood.

8 Of clean beasts, and of beasts that are not clean, and of fowls, and of every thing that creepeth upon the earth,

9 There went in two and two unto Noah into the ark, the male and the female, as God had commanded Noah.

10 And it came to pass after seven days, that the waters of the flood were upon the earth.

11 In the six hundredth year of Noah's life, in the second month, the seventeenth day of the month, the same day were all the fountains of the great deep broken up, and the windows of heaven were opened.

12 And the rain was upon the earth forty days and forty nights.

13 In the selfsame day entered Noah, and Shem, and Ham, and Japheth, the sons of Noah, and Noah's wife, and the three wives of his sons with them, into the ark;

14 They, and every beast after his kind, and all the cattle after their kind, and every creeping thing that creepeth upon the earth after his kind, and every fowl after his kind, every bird of every sort.

15 And they went in unto Noah into the ark, two and two of all flesh, wherein is the breath of life.

16 And they that went in, went in male and female of all flesh, as God had commanded him: and the LORD shut him in.

17 And the flood was forty days upon the earth; and the waters increased, and bare up the ark, and it was lift up above the earth.

18 And the waters prevailed, and were increased greatly upon the earth; and the ark went upon the face of the waters.

19 And the waters prevailed exceedingly upon the earth; and all the high hills, that were under the whole heaven, were covered.

20 Fifteen cubits upward did the waters prevail; and the mountains were covered.

21 And all flesh died that moved upon the earth, both of fowl, and of cattle, and of beast, and of every creeping thing that creepeth upon the earth, and every man:

22 All in whose nostrils was the breath of life, of all that was in the dry land, died.

23 And every living substance was destroyed which was upon the face of the ground, both man, and cattle, and the creeping things, and the fowl of the heaven; and they were destroyed from the earth: and Noah only remained alive, and they that were with him in the ark,

24 And the waters prevailed upon the earth an hundred and fifty days.

Waters Assuaged

1 And God remembered Noah, and every living thing, and all the cattle that was with him in the ark: and God made a wind to pass over the earth, and the waters asswaged;

2 The fountains also of the deep and the windows of heaven were stopped, and the rain from heaven was restrained;

3 And the waters returned from off the earth continually: and after the end of the hundred and fifty days the waters were abated.

An Ark in Mountains of Ararat

4 And the ark rested in the seventh month, on the seventeenth day of the month, upon the mountains of Ararat.

5 And the waters decreased continually until the tenth month: in the tenth month, on the first day of the month, were the tops of the mountains seen.

6 And it came to pass at the end of forty days, that Noah opened the window of the ark which he had made:

7 And he sent forth a raven, which went forth to and fro, until the waters were dried up from off the earth.

8 Also he sent forth a dove from him, to see if the waters were abated from off the face of the ground;

9 But the dove found no rest for the sole of her foot, and she returned unto him into the ark, for the waters were on the face of the whole earth: then he put forth his hand, and took her, and pulled, her in unto him into the ark.

10 And he stayed yet other seven days; and again he sent forth the dove out of the ark;

11 And the dove came in to him in the evening, and, lo, in her mouth was an olive leaf pluckt off: so Noah knew that the waters were abated from off the earth.

12 And he stayed yet other seven days; and. sent forth the dove; which returned not again unto him any more.

13 And it came to pass in the six hundreth and first year, in the first month, the first day of the month, the waters were dried up from off the earth: and Noah removed the covering of the ark, and looked, and, behold, the face of the ground was dry.

The Replenishing of the Earth

14 And in the second month, on the seven and twentieth day of the month, was the earth dried.

15 And God spake unto Noah, saying,

16 Go forth of the ark, thou, and thy wife, and thy sons, and thy sons' wives with thee.

17 Bring forth with thee every living thing that is with thee, of all flesh, both of fowl, and of cattle, and of every creeping thing that creepeth upon the earth; that they may breed abundantly in the earth; and be fruitful, and multiply upon the earth.

18 And Noah went forth, and his sons, and his wife, and his sons' wives with him:

19 Every beast, every creeping thing, and every fowl, and whatsoever creepeth upon the earth, after their kinds, went forth out of the ark.

20 And Noah builded an altar unto the LORD; and took of every clean beast, and of every clean fowl, and offered burnt offerings on the altar.

21 And the LORD smelled a sweet savour; and the LORD said in his heart, I will not again curse the ground any more for man's sake; for the imagination of man's heart is evil from his youth; neither will I again smite any more every thing living, as I have done.

22 While the earth remaineth, seedtime and harvest, and cold and heat, and summer and winter, and day and night shall not cease.

Death of Noah

1 And God blessed Noah and his sons, and said unto them, Be fruitful, and multiply, and replenish the earth.

2 And the fear of you and the dread of you shall be upon every beast of the earth, and every fowl of the air, upon all that moveth upon the earth, and upon all the fishes of the sea; into your hand are they delivered.

3 Every moving thing that liveth shall be meat for you; even as the green herb have I given you all things.

4 But flesh with the life thereof, which is the blood thereof, shall ye not eat.

5 And surely your blood of your lives will I require; at the hand of every beast will I require it, and at the hand of man; at the hand of every man's brother will I require the life of man.

6 Who so sheddeth man's blood, by man shall his blood be shed: for in the image of God made he man.

7 And you, be ye fruitful, and multiply; bring forth abundantly in the earth, and multiply therein.

8 And God spake unto Noah, and to his sons with him, saying,

9 And I, behold, I establish my covenant with you, and with your seed after you;

10 And with every living creature that is with you, of the fowl, of The cattle, and of every beast of the earth with you; from all that go out of the ark, to every beast of the earth.

11 And I will establish my covenant with you; neither shall all flesh be cut off any more by the waters of a flood; neither shall there any more be a flood to destroy the earth.

12 And God said, This is the token of the covenant which I make between me and you and every living creature that is with you, for perpetual generations:

13 I do set my bow in the cloud, and it shall be for a token of a covenant between me and the earth.

14 And it shall come to pass, when I bring a cloud over the earth, that the bow shall be seen in the cloud:

15 And I will remember my covenant, which is between me and you and every living creature of all flesh; and the waters shall no more become a flood to destroy all flesh.

16 And the bow shall be in the cloud; and I will look upon it, that I may remember the everlasting covenant between God and every living creature of all flesh that is upon the earth.

17 And God said unto Noah, This is the token of the covenant, which I have established between Me and all flesh that is upon the earth.

18 And the sons of Noah, that went forth of the ark, were Shem, and Ham, and Japheth: and Ham is the Noah: and of them was the whole earth overspread.

CRITICAL EYE

▶ For Discussion

a. Consider the stories of Mallim Sile and Noah. How do these men use their respective faiths to get them through trying times?

b. In this excerpt, God seems to echo the exact same sentiment expressed by many of the writers in this anthology; namely, that mankind is wicked. If God has little to no faith in humanity, how can we?

c. At the end of the text, God assures Noah that he will never again destroy the planet Earth and its inhabitants. If so, why then are so many people predicting and waiting for the end of the world?

▶ Re-approaching the Reading

Examine this excerpt from the book of *Genesis* alongside of Twain's "The Lowest Animal," "Aesop's Fable," "A Lion and Other Animals Go Hunting," and the excerpt for Sherman Alexie's *Indian Killer*. Although written at different points in our global history, each seems to argue against humanity's ability to treat each other with respect and kindness. How is this true? Be specific.

▶ Writing Assignment

If all of mankind is wicked, why is that God relies upon one man to help save humankind?

CESAR ILLIANO AND TERRY WADE

Chilean Miners Rescued After 69 Days Underground

(Reuters)—Chile's trapped miners were shuttled up a narrow escape shaft to freedom and joyous reunions on Wednesday in a meticulously planned rescue operation that ended their two-month ordeal deep underground.

One by one, the miners climbed into a specially designed steel capsule barely wider than a man's shoulders and took a 15-minute journey through 2,050 feet of rock to the surface.

With 29 of the 33 miners freed in a rescue operation that advanced rapidly without hitches, officials expected to have the remaining men out by the end of the day instead of in 48 hours as originally estimated.

Scenes of jubilation erupted each time a miner arrived to a hero's welcome above the San Jose gold and copper mine in Chile's northern Atacama desert.

One of the latest miners to reach the surface was Franklin Lobos, a former professional soccer player. He received autographed jerseys from teams around the world during his two months underground. He was passed a soccer ball as soon as he left the rescue capsule and juggled it briefly with his feet.

"This was the toughest match of my life," he said.

Church bells rang out in Chile when the first miner was extricated and Chileans were glued to their televisions through the night, proud of their nation's ability to save the men.

"It's dangerous to say but things are going extraordinarily well," Chilean Health Minister Jaime Manalich said.

Large video screens were set up in public places across Chile to let people watch and cheer as each miner was hauled to the surface and freed.

The miners were whisked away for medical checkups and found to be in "more than satisfactory" health, except for one who has pneumonia and is being treated with antibiotics, the minister said.

That man is thought to be the oldest, 63-year-old Mario Gomez, who suffers from the lung disease silicosis. He was brought to the surface breathing from an oxygen mask.

Gomez, who has worked as miner for 50 years, was helped out of the escape capsule, and immediately dropped to his knees to pray. "I never lost faith that they would find us," he said.

Esteban Rojas also knelt and prayed on arrival. The 44-year-old had promised to wed his wife formally in church if he got out alive, to seal their civil marriage.

From *Reuters*, October 13, 2010. © 2010 Reuters. All rights reserved. Used by permission and protected by the Copyright Laws of the United States. The printing, copying, redistribution, or retransmission of the material without express written permission is prohibited.

Once Believed Dead

Euphoric rescuers, relatives and friends broke into cheers—and tears—as the miners emerged to breathe fresh air for the first time since the mine caved in on Aug 5.

"This is a miracle from God," said Alberto Avalos, the uncle of Florencio Avalos, a father of two who was the first to emerge shortly after midnight.

The miners have spent a record 69 days in the hot, humid bowels of the collapsed mine and, for the first 17 days, they were all believed to be dead.

Their story of survival captured global attention. Some 1,500 journalists were at the mine to report on the rescue operation, which was broadcast live around the world, including dramatic live images of the miners hugging rescuers who traveled down the shaft to their refuge deep in the mine.

Rescuers had found the men miraculously alive with a bore hole the width of a grapefruit. It served as a lifeline to pass hydration gels, water and food, as well as bibles, letters from their families and soccer videos to keep their spirits up.

Engineers deployed the escape capsule, dubbed "Phoenix" after the mythical bird that rose from the ashes, after boring the shaft down to the miners and reinforcing it with metal casing to prevent rocks from falling and blocking it.

Each man's journey to safety was taking about 15 minutes. The capsule traveled at about 3 feet (1 meter) per second, or a casual walking pace, and could speed to 10 feet a second if the miner being carried gets into trouble.

The miners could communicate with rescue teams using an intercom in the capsule. After emerging, they were taken to a nearby hospital for two days observation.

Each of the miners wore dark glasses to protect their eyes after spending so long in the dimly lit tunnel.

World Inspiration

The flawless rescue was a big success for Chilean President Sebastian Pinera, who waited at the mouth of the shaft through the night and morning to greet and hug the men as they emerged from the red, white and blue capsule—the Chilean colors.

Pinera, a billionaire entrepreneur who took office in March, ordered an overhaul of Chile's mine safety regulations after the accident. His popularity ratings have surged and his government has won praise for its handling of the crisis.

Among millions of people who watched television coverage of the rescue of the first miner was U.S. President Barack Obama, who hailed the operation as an inspiration to the world.

"This rescue is a tribute not only to the determination of the rescue workers and the Chilean government but also the unity and resolve of the Chilean people who have inspired the world," Obama said in Washington.

Thirty-two of the miners are Chilean but one is from neighboring Bolivia and the rescue has helped improve ties between the two countries, locked in a dispute for more than a century over Bolivia's demands for access to the Pacific.

Bolivia's president, Evo Morales, was at the mine to welcome Bolivian miner Carlos Mamani as he was lifted to safety and he thanked Pinera and his government for rescuing him.

"I and the Bolivian people will never forget this great effort," Morales said at a news conference with Pinera.

Chile will continue to shut old, decrepit mines after the miners' saga, but the clampdown is unlikely to hit output in the world's top copper producer, industry insiders say.

The mining industry has played a central and often tragic role in Latin American history, starting with the hunger for gold and silver that drove the Spanish conquest and led to the enslavement of indigenous peoples.

For centuries, conditions in Latin American mines were miserable but they have improved dramatically in recent decades and the industry over the past 10 years has helped fuel a boom in some of the region's economies, including Chile.

CRITICAL EYE

▶ **For Discussion**

a. Why is it that a national tragedy has the power to bring a nation together? Why isn't this kind of altruistic behavior commonplace year round?

b. As you see it, did the leaders of Chile and Bolivia politicize this tragedy?

c. Why did this event gain worldwide attention?

▶ **Re-approaching the Reading**

While the rescue garnered most of the attention, this article does not spend an equal amount of time discussing the everyday plight of miners in countries like Chile. Would you argue that the journalists should have used this article as a platform to discuss Miner's Rights in order to prevent future disasters?

▶ **Writing Assignment**

The article takes time to include President Obama's perspective on the tragedy and the eventual rescue. Why is this? What is accomplished by including his remarks? What are the political implications?

SCOTT GOLD

Little to Reclaim in the Lower 9th

The sun was still burning off the fog Thursday morning when 88-year-old Nelson Meyers climbed five stairs onto a concrete porch he had built four decades ago. The railing was there. The house was gone.

The 25-foot wall of water that burst through the levee forming the western boundary of New Orleans' Lower 9th Ward after Hurricane Katrina lifted the home off its foundation. The house landed in the neighbor's yard, on top of a car, caked in mud, its lacy curtains shredded into filthy ribbons.

"A man's home is his castle," Meyers said. "And this is what we've got."

Currently living with 28 other relatives in Florida, Meyers and three family members drove to New Orleans to take up Mayor C. Ray Nagin on his offer to sift through the wreckage, to salvage what they could.

The Lower 9th had been closed since the flooding, and residents had grown agitated over not being able to get to their property. Nagin relented, cautioning that the neighborhood—probably the pocket of the city hit the hardest—was not stable enough for people to move back. But, he said: "Everybody can get their stuff."

So for two hours, Meyers and his family rumbled through the Lower 9th in a small convoy, stopping at four family homes that dated back five generations. They all had their wish lists: the lovely picture of Meyers and his wife enjoying a picnic, taken in the '40s. The family Bible. Birth certificates.

They came away with nothing.

Like hundreds of other families, they did not—could not—salvage a single item.

Little more than three months ago, few outside of New Orleans had heard of the 9th Ward. Today, the neighborhood remains a singular testament to the wrath of Katrina's flood, a mind-boggling heap of splintered houses, upside-down cars, refrigerators stuck on rooftops and, across Jourdan Avenue, a massive barge that floated through the levee breach and settled atop a school bus.

The mayor's "look and leave" program could do little to stem the pain—or to extinguish the anger among many residents, who feel that they were forgotten even as politicians' promises were echoing off the deserted streets.

"We heard so many words," said Linda Garth Llopis, 60, as she stood outside her partially collapsed home on Deslonde Street. "Our president said he was going to help. Everybody said they were going to help. We are citizens of the United States. And we've just been thrown away."

It is popular in New Orleans these days to remind people that they should feel blessed to

From *Los Angeles Times*, December 2, 2005. Reprinted with permission of Los Angeles Times.

have survived, that material possessions can be replaced. But such reassurances sounded empty Thursday to those who had lost everything.

Llopis is living in a hotel, with no job and no hope for rebuilding. At her feet was a small pile of belongings that her husband was able to retrieve from their home—a handful of costume jewelry, a batch of his heart medicine, most likely ruined.

"We had a nice life," she said. "We had marble countertops. I had a mink hat for church."

She and many of her neighbors say they are fighting the conventional wisdom that the 9th isn't worth saving, that it was dirty and crime-ridden anyway, that the storm's silver lining was that it washed away the city's blight.

Like most poor neighborhoods, the 9th had its troubles. But it was a community, said Barbara Ponder, 50, who had never lived anywhere but the 1900 block of Deslonde. Just about everybody owned their home; there were very few renters. There was a preschool down the street from Ponder's house. Several nearby houses had been remodeled in recent years.

Ponder lived a few hundred feet from the levee lining the Inner Harbor Navigational Canal. Her daughter used to play there, often skidding down its sloped, grassy bank on flattened cardboard boxes.

On Thursday, Ponder stood on a flattened lot. There was no sign of her house. The few remnants of life where her home once stood—some dishes, a bashed-in stove, a flyswatter—were not hers. They had floated in from elsewhere.

She had made her final mortgage payment in July.

"We had our crimes and everything—car thefts and things—but this was my home," she said. "Now it's gone. My whole life, everything I owned, everything I have ever accomplished, has vanished."

Much of the destruction in New Orleans, particularly in the Central Business District, was brought by a slow, seeping flood. That was not true in the Lower 9th, much of which was crushed instantly by a wave of water when an 800-foot-wide section of the levee collapsed early in the storm. Close to the canal, entire blocks are gone. Even a mile or so east, houses have been reduced to rubble, as if a giant stomped through town.

Here, the notion of rebuilding seems faint at best. Almost all of the houses above Claiborne Avenue—an 11-by 25-square-block area—will be demolished. Most were below sea level, and it is far from certain that the neighborhood will ever be rebuilt.

Nelson Meyers and his relatives knew it was going to be bad. But, he said, they were not prepared for what they found Thursday.

They began at a single-story home on Caffin Avenue, where his daughter, 58-year-old Patricia Meyers Washington, lived. Five generations of the family had lived in that house. Washington's grandmother had lived there for years, until she died recently at 105. The garden she had tended to was still there—tomato plants and turnip greens.

"It was beautiful," Washington said. "There were flowers everywhere."

With nothing to recover, the relatives hopped in their cars. Their next stop was a relative's four-bedroom home in the 1800 block of Lizardi Street, five blocks southwest, or "Upriver," as they say around here. Washington leapt out of the car.

"It's gone," she said.

It was a vacant lot. A blue jacket and a pair of pink tennis shoes belonging to Washington's granddaughter were the only reminders that the family had ever lived there—until Dewitt Lucas, another relative, spotted the home about 200 feet away.

"There it is!" he said, pointing and standing on the bumper of a car. "That looks like the front door over there."

The house had collapsed on itself. They couldn't get inside, and didn't need to bother anyway.

They hung a right on North Derbigny Street, past the skeletal remains of a couple of businesses—"Po Boys and Hot Plates," one sign read—and a house where rescuers had spray-painted "**POSSIBLE BODY**" on an outside wall. They headed to another home owned by Washington, where more relatives had lived. She had decorated and maintained the house, and it contained a slew of her possessions, including antique tables and a painting she had bought in the French Quarter.

They pulled up. Someone's shed had been carried into the yard. Lucas squeezed inside the blown-out front door as Washington stood on the porch and peered in behind him. Thick, dried mud coated the floors and walls. She pointed to items that she thought she might be able to save as Lucas climbed over the jumbled furniture, including a picture of her grandson, Cornell.

Lucas handed her the small gold frame. Inside, the picture was curdled and faded.

"This was a picture of my baby," Washington said with a smile. "It was taken on Easter, when he was 2. There was an Easter Bunny down there." She pointed to a large white blob in the corner of the photo.

"What about those picture books, the albums?" she asked, pointing to a bookcase that was still standing. Lucas climbed across the room.

"No, Pat," he said. "I'm sorry."

Their last stop held their greatest hope. It was on the 1600 block of Gordon Street, farther east of the levee breach.

Like the first house they stopped at, which had floated off its foundation, Meyers built this one himself, in 1952, and he had raised five children there. Meyers had added storm braces to the walls—2-by-4s crisscrossed inside the walls—and they had done their job. The house was still standing, though the walls were beginning to separate from the floor.

The mud, however, had gotten inside. The dining room table was upside down, though there were still bills dating back to August on top of the television. Meyers dispatched Lucas into a back bedroom to retrieve two boxes containing the family's papers, birth certificates, deeds and the like. But the floor of the attic had collapsed, burying the room in debris, so he couldn't get there.

Everyone went outside except for Washington, who was desperate to come away with some token of what had been their lives. She lingered for a few minutes, pawing at framed photos, scraping away slime and mold to see if any could be saved. No luck. In the corner, she spotted the thick family Bible. It had been around for as long as anyone could remember. Important dates—birthdays, weddings—had been written on the inside cover.

"Daddy! I found your Bible," she shouted.

CRITICAL EYE

▶ For Discussion

a. Given the slow government response, why should the people interviewed in the article believe anything their government says? How does one move forward when everything is lost and the government sworn to protect its citizens abandons them?

b. How do Class and racial matters play into the role of rebuilding? Why has New Orleans still not been rebuilt?

▶ Re-approaching the Reading

Consider the fact that most of the residents in the lower 9th owned their homes, a reality that is indicative of the American dream. How, after losing everything—alongside being displaced and seemingly forgotten by their government—should these citizens view their place in society? Juxtapose your response with Alan Parker's *Mississippi Burning* and Spike Lee's documentary about the hurricane and its aftermath, *When the Levees Broke*.

▶ Writing Assignment

Historically speaking, Blacks have been treated, following slavery, as second class citizens. In an age of change, how do the events of Katrina speak to the growing alarm for Black people in America? Keeping in mind that the promise of "40 acres and a mule" has never been fulfilled, what options—socially, politically, economically—do those who feel like "other" in society really have?

SIMON ROMERO

Quake Accentuated Chasm That Has Defined Haiti

PORT-AU-PRINCE, Haiti—The lights of the casino above this wrecked city beckoned as gamblers in freshly pressed clothes streamed to the roulette table and slot machines. In a restaurant nearby, diners quaffed Veuve Clicquot Ponsardin Champagne and ate New Zealand lamb chops at prices rivaling those in Manhattan.

A few yards away, hundreds of families displaced by the earthquake languished under tents and tarps, bathing themselves from buckets and relieving themselves in the street as barefoot children frolicked on pavement strewn with garbage.

This is the Pétionville district of Port-au-Prince, a hillside bastion of Haiti's well-heeled where a mangled sense of normalcy has taken hold after the earthquake in January. Business is bustling at the lavish boutiques, restaurants and nightclubs that have reopened in the breezy hills above the capital, while thousands of homeless and hungry people camp in the streets around them, sometimes literally on their doorstep.

"The rich people sometimes need to step over us to get inside," said Judith Pierre, 28, a maid who has lived for weeks in a tent with her two daughters in front of Magdoos, a chic Lebanese restaurant where diners relax in a garden and smoke flavored tobacco from hookahs. Chauffeurs for some of the customers inside lined up sport utility vehicles next to Ms. Pierre's tent on the sidewalk near the entrance.

Haiti has long had glaring inequality, with tiny pockets of wealth persisting amid extreme poverty, and Pétionville itself was economically mixed before the earthquake, with poor families living near the gated mansions and villas of the rich.

But the disaster has focused new attention on this gap, making for surreal contrasts along the streets above Port-au-Prince's central districts. People in tent camps reeking of sewage are living in areas where prosperous Haitians, foreign aid workers and diplomats come to spend their money and unwind. Often, just a gate and a private guard armed with a 12-gauge shotgun separate the newly homeless from establishments like Les Galeries Rivoli, a boutique where wealthy Haitians and foreigners shop for Raymond Weil watches and Izod shirts.

"There's nothing logical about what's going on right now," said Tatiana Wah, a Haitian planning expert at Columbia University who is living in Pétionville and working as an adviser to Haiti's government. Ms. Wah said the revelry at some nightclubs near her home, which are frequented by rich Haitians and foreigners, was now as loud—or louder—than before the earthquake.

From *New York Times,* March 27, 2010. © 2010 New York Times. All rights reserved. Used by permission and protected by the Copyright Laws of the United States. The printing, copying, redistribution, or retransmission of the material without express written permission is prohibited.

The nongovernmental organizations "are flooding the local economy with their spending," she said, "but it's not clear if much of it is trickling down."

Aleksandr Dobrianskiy, the Ukrainian owner of the Bagheera casino here in the hills, smiled as customers flowed in one recent Saturday evening, drinking Cuba Libres and plunking tokens into slot machines.

He said business had never been better, attributing the uptick at his casino to the money coming into Haiti for relief projects. That spending is percolating through select areas of the economy, as some educated Haitians get jobs working with relief agencies and foreigners bring in cash from abroad, using it on housing, security, transportation and entertainment.

"Haiti's like a submarine that just hit the bottom of the sea," said Mr. Dobrianskiy, 39, who moved here a year ago and carries a semiautomatic Glock handgun for protection. "It's got nowhere to go but up."

Sometimes the worlds of haves and have-nots collide. Violent crime and kidnappings have been relatively low since the earthquake. But when two European relief workers from Doctors Without Borders were abducted outside the exclusive Plantation restaurant this month and held for five days, the episode served as a reminder of how Haiti's poverty could give rise to resentment and crime.

The breadth of Haiti's economic misery seemed incomprehensible to many before the quake, with almost 80 percent of the population living on less than $2 a day. A small elite in gated mansions here in Pétionville and other hillside districts wields vast economic power.

But with parts of Port-au-Prince now in ruins, tens of thousands of people displaced by the quake are camping directly in the bulwarks once associated with power and wealth, like Place St.-Pierre (across from the elegant Kinam Hotel) and the grounds of Prime Minister Jean-Max Bellerive's office.

The city's biggest tent camp, with more than 40,000 displaced people, sprawls over the hills of the Pétionville Club, a country club with a golf course that before the quake had its own Facebook page for former members. ("Had the best Citronade; I bet I drank thousands of them, no exaggeration," one reminiscence said.)

Pétionville's boutiques and restaurants stand in stark contrast to the parallel economic reality in the camp now at the Pétionville Club. Throughout its maze of tents, merchants sell dried fish and yams for a fraction of what the French cuisine costs in exclusive restaurants nearby like Quartier Latin or La Souvenance.

Manicurists in the camp do nails. A stylist in a hovel applies hair extensions. The camp even has its own Paradis Ciné, set up in a tent with space for as many as 30 people. It charges admission of about $1.50 for screenings of "2012," the end-of-times disaster movie known here as "Apocalypse."

"The people in the camp need their diversion, too," said Cined Milien, 22, the operator of Paradis Ciné.

Still, a ticket to see "Apocalypse" is a luxury out of the grasp of most people who lost their homes in the earthquake. Some of the well-off in Pétionville who have reopened their businesses have done so cautiously, aware of the misfortune that persists on their doorstep.

"It's kind of hard for people to dance and have fun," said Anastasia Chassagne, 27, the Florida-educated owner of a trendy bar in Pétionville. "I put music, but really low, so like the people walking outside the street don't hear, like, 'Hey, these people are having fun.'"

Not everyone in Pétionville has such qualms. Mr. Dobrianskiy, the casino entrepreneur, said he was pleased that Haiti's currency, the gourde, had recently strengthened against the dollar to a value higher than before the quake, in part because of the influx of money from abroad.

And on the floor above Mr. Dobrianskiy's casino, a nightclub called Barak, with blaring music and Miami-priced cocktails, caters to a different elite here: United Nations employees and foreigners working for aid groups. They mingle with dozens of suggestively clad Haitian women and a few moneyed Haitian men taking in the scene.

As hundreds of displaced families gathered under tents a few yards away, the music of Barak continued into the night. A bartender could not keep up with orders for Presidente beers.

"Those who are gone are gone and buried, and we can't do anything about that," said Michel Sejoure, 21, a Haitian enjoying a drink at Barak. Asked about the displaced-persons camp down the street, he said, "I would want to help but I don't have enough, and the government should be the ones that are actually helping these people out."

"But," he said over the booming music, "they're not."

CRITICAL EYE

▶ For Discussion

a. The Island nation of Haiti was already struggling with issues of extreme poverty and political corruption prior to the earthquake. As you see it, who is most to blame for the country's slow recovery?

b. In many ways, the article highlights how the people of Haiti are attempting to return to some kind of normalcy in the face of decimation and loss. Why is this crucial? Would you argue that doing so prevents Haiti's citizens from slipping into the abyss of anarchy, violence, and chaos?

c. Once again, in the face of such a national catastrophe, the world opened its heart and its wallets to aid those who were in need. As such, why has so little changed in Haiti?

▶ Re-approaching the Reading

We have now had a massive earthquake in Haiti, a devastating hurricane in New Orleans, and crippling tsunami in Japan. As you see it, have our world leaders learned anything about how to respond to natural disasters?

▶ Writing Assignment

Shockingly, the attention and scrutiny of the media highlighted how the factors of race and poverty are often linked in America. Has anything changed for the disenfranchised of New Orleans? Or, has the media simply moved on to its next big and sensationalized story?

STEVEN ERLANGER

Amid Tears, Flickering Candles and Flowers, a Shaken Norway Mourns

OSLO—Sunday was a day of remembrance and self-examination for Norway, a small country shaken by the massacre of at least 93 of its people, many of them children, by one of its own.

The royal family and average citizens alike, some traveling long distances, came to a memorial service for the dead in the Oslo Cathedral. Long lines of people of all ages and colors waited patiently and quietly, some of them crying, to lay flowers or light candles at the spreading blanket of bouquets in front of the cathedral. Someone propped up a radio on a post so those waiting could listen to the service inside.

At the same time, the Norwegian police and security services faced numerous questions about their slow response to the reports of shooting on the island of Utoya, where the country's governing Labor Party was holding its annual political summer camp, considered Norway's nursery school for future leaders. The police took an hour to arrive on the island after the first reports, and officials said that it was hard to find boats and that their helicopters were only capable of surveillance, not of shooting down the killer.

Anders Behring Breivik, 32, the only suspect arrested, admits to the shootings on Utoya and the fatal bombing of government offices in Oslo, his lawyer, Geir Lippestad, told Norwegian news media, but rejects "criminal responsibility." Mr. Lippestad said that Mr. Breivik insists that he acted alone, and alone wrote his mammoth manifesto — rambling from a hostile historical look at Islam to recipes (and price lists) for bomb manufacture to his family's pressure on him to date.

"He has said that he believed the actions were atrocious, but that in his head they were necessary," the lawyer said. "He wanted a change in society and, from his perspective, he needed to force through a revolution. He wished to attack society and the structure of society."

He also clearly wants to leave a legacy and thinks he will create some kind of mass following, said Tore Bjorgo, one of Norway's most respected scholars of right-wing extremism. "He had this strange idea that he will provoke a mass following, despite the violence, which is why I put it in a Christian frame," said Mr. Bjorgo, a professor at the Norwegian Police University College.

Mr. Breivik, who has cooperated with the police, has asked for an open hearing in the City Court of Oslo on Monday morning, when the police will seek to detain him for another

From *New York Times*, July 24, 2011. © 2011 Reuters. All rights reserved. Used by permission and protected by the Copyright Laws of the United States. The printing, copying, redistribution, or retransmission of the material without express written permission is prohibited.

four weeks on suspicion of terrorism—longer if necessary for the investigation—before the prosecution brings formal charges.

Some speculated that Mr. Breivik is seeking another public platform for his anti-immigrant, anti-Muslim ideas, which center around the conservation of cultural and Christian values in the face of what he sees as a continuing effort by Islam to conquer Europe since the Ottomans were stopped at the gates of Vienna in 1683. His manifesto, called "2083—A European Declaration of Independence," seemed intended to reflect the 400th anniversary of the siege.

Mr. Breivik was said by analysts to have been an occasional commenter on a blog, Gates of Vienna, which is topped by these words: "At the siege of Vienna in 1683 Islam seemed poised to overrun Christian Europe. We are in a new phase of a very old war."

According to the police, when he surrendered, Mr. Breivik was carrying an automatic rifle and a pistol and he still retained "a considerable amount of ammunition." Doctors have said that he was apparently using dumdum bullets, expanding rounds designed to inflict the deadliest wounds possible in unarmored victims.

With no death penalty and the longest prison term possible in Norway set at 21 years, some Norwegians wondered how best to punish Mr. Breivik.

Hedda Felin, a political scientist and human resources manager, said that giving Mr. Breivik an open platform "was more of a reward than a punishment." He said in his manifesto that he considered killing Norway's top journalists at their yearly meeting, she said, for not listening to him and his arguments.

"He wants an open trial to be listened to, so journalists will now write about his ideas," Ms. Felin said. "A real punishment would be not to write about him at all."

There were church services all over Norway on Sunday. At the Oslo Cathedral, King Harald V and Queen Sonja of Norway were both in tears, and they were hardly alone. Prime Minister Jens Stoltenberg, who knew many of the dead, said, "We are crying with you, we feel for you." The brief period since the killings "feels like an eternity—hours and days and nights filled with shock and angst and weeping," he said.

"Each and every one of those who has left us is a tragedy," Mr. Stoltenberg added. "Together, it is a national tragedy."

Outside, among the mourners, Tured Mong, a pensioner, said she drove 40 miles with her husband to bring flowers from her garden and a candle she wanted to light. "I only want to lay them down here," Ms. Mong said. "I am sorry for all the parents waiting to find some news who don't know about their children." She added: "I wanted to bring the flowers and light a candle. It's very hard to just sit and watch the TV. I feel like I'm doing something."

Another mourner, Evy Andersen, from Oslo, brought a sunflower from her garden. "I have a niece who has been to this camp twice, and she has many friends who are missing," she said. "She is wondering about them. I did this for her and for myself."

Ms. Andersen said there would be useful introspection for a country that thinks of itself as favored and far from the world's worst problems. "We've been in such a favorable position, we've forgotten a bit about the others among us," she said. "We're a bit spoiled."

Borge Wilhemsen, a Labor Party activist, said he drove for five hours to be at the memorial service, along with his 6-year-old daughter. "You can't take them away from everything," he said, referring to his daughter. "They have to learn that life is sometimes hard. I have not told her everything. I told her that there were two big accidents."

Mr. Wilhemsen said he knew a number of those killed at the island camp. Some of them were as young as 12, he said.

There were also many mourners who were immigrants or children of mixed race. Le Lemeo, a refugee from Vietnam 21 years ago, said: "Norway helped the Vietnamese people to come here. They were very welcoming." Mr. Le said he was a well-known sushi chef here. "I have a job and a family, and I wanted to come," he said. "It is very sad for all the young people."

Marina Heier, 15, is the product of a Norwegian mother and a South African father; she was born here and is a native Norwegian speaker as well as fluent in English. She, too, brought flowers from her garden. "It's important that everyone in Norway stands together," Marina said. "This is a reminder of the danger of hatred."

CRITICAL EYE

▶ For Discussion

a. We often believe that issues of race and bigotry are specific to our own immediate part of the world. How does the Norwegian tragedy disprove that claim?

b. More often than not, this level of violence changes a people irrevocably. Given their law enforcement agency's slow response to the crime scene, what do you believe the people of Norway need to do differently? Will making these kinds of changes—in order to prepare for a more violent world—make this nation more like us?

▶ Re-approaching the Reading

There is no death penalty in Norway, and the most that any one individual can spend in jail is 21 years. Is something wrong with this policy? Do they need to institute a death penalty policy immediately in order to bring Mr. Breivik to justice?

▶ Writing Assignment

When individuals like Breivik commit these kinds of crimes, we often wonder just how sane the individual actually is. Is insanity ever a plausible excuse in the face of such depraved inhumanity? In order to deter them from committing these kinds of crimes, what should we do to punish them when these murderous individuals act out?

FREDERICK DOUGLASS

What to the Slave Is the 4th of July?

From Independence Day Speech at Rochester, 1852

Fellow citizens, pardon me, allow me to ask, why am I called upon to speak here today? What have I, or those I represent, to do with your national independence? Are the great principles of political freedom and of natural justice, embodied in that Declaration of Independence, extended to us? and am I, therefore, called upon to bring our humble offering to the national altar, and to confess the benefits and express devout gratitude for the blessings resulting from your independence to us?

Would to God, both for your sakes and ours, that an affirmative answer could be truthfully returned to these questions! Then would my task be light, and my burden easy and delightful. For who is there so cold that a nation's sympathy could not warm him? Who so obdurate and dead to the claims of gratitude that would not thankfully acknowledge such priceless benefits? Who so stolid and selfish that would not give his voice to swell the hallelujahs of a nation's jubilee, when the chains of servitude had been torn from his limbs? I am not that man. In a case like that the dumb might eloquently speak and the "lame man leap as an hart."

But such is not the state of the case. I say it with a sad sense of the disparity between us. I am not included within the pale of this glorious anniversary! Your high independence only reveals the immeasurable distance between us. The blessings in which you, this day, rejoice are not enjoyed in common. The rich inheritance of justice, liberty, prosperity, and independence bequeathed by your fathers is shared by you, not by me. The sunlight that brought light and healing to you has brought stripes and death to me. This Fourth of July is yours, not mine. You may rejoice, I must mourn. To drag a man in fetters into the grand illuminated temple of liberty, and call upon him to join you in joyous anthems, were inhuman mockery and sacrilegious irony. Do you mean, citizens, to mock me by asking me to speak today? If so, there is a parallel to your conduct. And let me warn that it is dangerous to copy the example of a nation whose crimes, towering up to heaven, were thrown down by the breath of the Almighty, burying that nation in irrevocable ruin! I can today take up the plaintive lament of a peeled and woe-smitten people.

"By the rivers of Babylon, there we sat down. Yea! We wept when we remembered Zion. We hanged our harps upon the willows in the midst thereof. For there, they that carried us away captive, required of us a song; and they who wasted us required of us mirth, saying, Sing us one of the songs of Zion. How can we sing the Lord's song in a strange land? If I forget thee, O Jerusalem, let my right hand forget her cunning. If do not remember thee, let my tongue cleave to the roof of my mouth."

Fellow citizens, above your national, tumultuous joy, I hear the mournful wail of millions! Whose chains, heavy and grievous yesterday, are, today, rendered more intolerable by the jubilee shouts that reach them. If I do forget, if I do not faithfully remember those bleeding children of sorry this day, "may my right hand cleave to the roof of my mouth"! To forget them, to pass lightly over their wrongs, and to chime in with the popular theme would be treason most scandalous and shocking, and would make me a reproach before God and the world. My subject, then, fellow citizens, is American slavery. I shall see this day and its popular characteristics from the slave's point of view. Standing there identified with the American bondman, making his wrongs mine. I do not hesitate to declare with all my soul that the character and conduct of this nation never looked blacker to me than on this Fourth of July! Whether we turn to the declarations of the past or to the professions of the present, the conduct of the nation seems equally hideous and revolting. America is false to the past, false to the present, and solemnly binds herself to be false to the future. Standing with God and the crushed and bleeding slave on this occasion, I will, in the name of humanity which is outraged, in the name of liberty which is fettered, in the name of the Constitution and the Bible which are disregarded and trampled upon, dare to call in question and to denounce, with all the emphasis I can command, everything that serves to perpetuate slavery- the great sin and shame of America! "I will not equivocate, I will not excuse"; I will use the severest language I can command; and yet not one word shall escape me that any man, whose judgment is not blinded by prejudice, shall not confess to be right and just....

For the present, it is enough to affirm the equal manhood of the Negro race. Is it not as astonishing that, while we are plowing, planting, and reaping, using all kinds of mechanical tools, erecting houses, constructing bridges, building ships, working in metals of brass, iron, copper, and secretaries, having among us lawyers doctors, ministers, poets, authors, editors, orators, and teachers; and that, while we are engaged in all manner of enterprises common to other men, digging gold in California, capturing the whale in the Pacific, feeding sheep and cattle on the hillside, living, moving, acting, thinking, planning, living in families as husbands, wives, and children, and above all, confessing and worshiping the Christian's God, and looking hopefully for life and immortality beyond the grave, we are called upon to prove that we are men!...

What, am I to argue that it is wrong to make men brutes, to rob them of their liberty, to work them without wages, to keep them ignorant of their relations to their fellow men, to beat them with sticks, to flay their flesh with the lash, to load their limbs with irons, to hunt them with dogs, to sell them at auction, to sunder their families, to knock out their teeth, to burn their flesh, to starve them into obedience and submission to their masters? Must I argue that a system thus marked with blood, and stained with pollution, is wrong? No! I will not. I have better employment for my time and strength than such arguments would imply....

What, to the American slave, is your Fourth of July? I answer: a day that reveals to him, more than all other days in the year, the gross injustice and cruelty to which he is the constant victim. To him, your celebration is a sham; your boasted liberty, an unholy license; your national greatness, swelling vanity; your sounds of rejoicing are empty and heartless; your denunciation of tyrants, brass-fronted impudence; your shouts of liberty and equality, hollow mockery; your prayers and hymns, your sermons and thanksgivings, with all your religious parade and solemnity, are, to Him, mere bombast, fraud, deception, impiety, and hypocrisy-a thin veil to cover up crimes which would disgrace a nation of savages. There is not a nation of savages. There is not a nation on the earth guilty of practices more shocking and bloody than are the people of the United States at this very hour.

Go where you may, search where you will, roam through all the monarchies and despotisms- of the Old World, travel through South America, search out every abuse, and when you have found the last, lay your facts by the side of the everyday practices of this nation, and you will say with me that, for revolting barbarity and shameless hypocrisy, America reigns without a rival.

CRITICAL EYE

▶ For Discussion

a. Can Douglass' speech be interpreted as a patriotic speech? Consider this point, keeping in mind that seeking to become involved with the betterment of one's country can be construed as the ultimate example of love for one's country.

b. Would you argue that Blacks are still disenfranchised from obtaining their portion of the American Dream?

c. Why do different cultural groups seem to have diverging and, at times, negative view points about inclusion and patriotism?

▶ Re-approaching the Reading

Examine the argument set forth by Douglass alongside of Barack Obama's "A More Perfect Union" (download) speech. How are these two documents similar? In essence, in what way(s) are these men examining the same highly charged race matters between Blacks and Whites? Does the Obama speech signal the strides that have been made along the lines of racial harmony, or is he arguing that not nearly enough has changed for either side?

▶ Writing Assignment

Examine the myriad of so-called "racial minority groups" within America; determine whether or not they can all make the charge that somehow "true" inclusion has evaded them.

JEEVAN VASAGAR

The Nightwalkers

Every evening, in war-torn northern Uganda, 40,000 children leave home and trek to the safety of special night shelters.

Mary Aciro has spent the day gathering sheaves of grass to feed the cattle, weeding the vegetable patch and helping her mother cook dinner over a charcoal fire: the life of any African girl in any African village. But as daylight begins to fade, Mary slips away from the family's tiny mud hut and strides down a sandy track into the nearest town. The adults in the town of Lacor in northern Uganda are going home for dinner on buses which spray plumes of dust over Mary's face and clothes as she walks. Mary, along with hundreds of other children, is going the other way. The children are dressed in rags and flip-flops; some carry sacks or rolled-up blankets on their shoulders. They scramble over grassy banks and hurry down the sun-scorched roadside on the way to the night shelters, which are guarded by government troops.

In any other country, a 14-year-old girl leaving her home and an anxious mother for the night would spell rebellion. Here, it's simply about survival. "We fear the rebels, we fear thugs and robbers who come at night to disturb us," says Mary as she walks with a swinging stride.

On a troubled continent, the war in this region stands out. It is Africa's longest-running civil war, and perhaps the only conflict in history where children are both the main victims and the principal aggressors. Mary and the other children walk to safety every night because they fear, with very good reason, abduction by the Lord's Resistance Army, a Christian fundamentalist rebel group which uses children as soldiers, porters and sexual slaves. The LRA carries out its raids at night, storming into villages from the surrounding bush, killing adults and forcing children to bludgeon their parents before marching them away to camps deep in the bush.

Mary's 15-year-old brother Geoffrey was abducted by the rebels; he was held for three months. "They made him carry heavy loads, beat him at times, he went without food," their mother Agnes says. Geoffrey only escaped when a government helicopter gunship strafed the rebels holding him. Mary's neighbour, a girl named Florence, was abducted too. She spent three years with the rebels: she was forced into sexual slavery and became pregnant.

Desperate to keep the child-snatchers from their doors, parents in northern Uganda began sending their children into nearby towns at night in 2002. Back then, children used to sleep on the pavements, curling up together for warmth. They came in vast numbers: 40,000 children across northern Uganda started walking into towns to sleep. Aid agencies set up shelters to give them somewhere safe to go, and it's one of these that Mary is heading for.

Copyright Guardian News & Media Ltd 2006.

As she approaches Lacor town, she walks past bars lit by a single, bare lightbulb, where a few drinkers sit outside on white plastic chairs sipping fizzy drinks or local beers, past tiny shops whose wooden shelves are crammed with cooking oil, salt, soap powder and mobile phone top-up cards. As the shadows spread, the shopkeepers are bolting their thief-proof metal doors and stepping out on to the chipped concrete pavements.

Mary lives near the town and follows the main road, but some of the other children walk for hours to reach safety, following winding unlit paths between mango trees and thickets of scrub. When she reaches the shelter, it is already full of children, some of them barely toddlers, others in their late teens. The shelter is made up of stark concrete buildings, bare as a barn inside, as well as rows of giant white canvas tents propped up by wooden stakes. The children give them names such as Pope Paul II and Moon Star Hall.

Lillian Apiyo, 14, is already inside. "I come here for protection," she says, sitting on a concrete step. "I always get new friends from here. There is nowhere to stay at home." The children filter through the gates looking subdued, but a party atmosphere soon develops. A dozen or so children begin dancing, gyrating their hips and nodding their heads. At other shelters there is frenetic singing of hymns or motivational songs, accompanied by the beating of cowhide drums. In one camp, adult volunteers chant: "Who are you? Who are you?" as the children arrive, and they shriek back: "I'm a winner - a winner!"

At Mary's shelter, groups of boys are washing themselves beneath communal taps, their wet bodies glistening in the semi-darkness provided by the moon and a sprinkling of lightbulbs.

The children are not given anything to eat. The shelters are busy enough as it is, and if food were provided they would be overwhelmed. Adult wardens patrol with torches, breaking up the occasional fight over a blanket and checking on children who look scared or upset.

Often, children feel more looked after here than they do at home. "When I am here, I feel I am somebody," says Gabriel Oloya, who studies his schoolbooks in the dim light. "When I am at home I'm always upset. I feel lonely and so many thoughts come into my mind. Here I tend to forget such things." Gabriel is head of his family, responsible for the four younger brothers who walk with him to the shelter. "My parents are dead, killed by the rebels," he says.

Childhood is short in rural Africa - boys in their teens will herd cattle and girls of 10 must fetch water - but it is rare for children to be thrown so completely on their own resources as they are in this war-damaged society.

Gabriel receives food handouts from the UN. Together with his even smaller brothers, the skinny 15-year-old hauls bricks for a little money. "What worries me most is the absence of my parents," he says. "I have to be responsible for taking care of my brothers."

The children who come to the shelters crave affection. Many of them are cuckoos at home - orphans whose parents were murdered by the rebels and have been taken in by their extended family. Freed from the responsibility of caring for younger siblings, or working in vegetable gardens, they can be young again in the shelters. The girls comb and braid each other's hair while the boys spin bottle-tops or engage in play-fights.

Collins Ocen, a tiny 13-year-old who looks scarecrow-like in an oversized coat, ragged shorts and flip-flops, comes partly for the fun. "I like playing, sharing stories with others and bathing," he says.

Elsewhere, teenage hormones are going wild. A crowd of watching children gathers around the gaggle of dancers. In the villages, dances such as these were courtship rituals; a chance for teenage boys and girls to sneak glances at each other in a setting approved by their elders. In the shelter, the wardens keep boys and girls apart, but outside its metal gates young couples are cuddling in the semi-darkness.

This sort of thing does worry Mary's mother. "We can't follow our children up to the shelter," Agnes says. "Sometimes a girl says she has gone there, but she has gone to a boyfriend, and she becomes pregnant and drops out of school." But then there are more serious things to worry about than teenage boys in the night shelters; in this land of lost innocence the troops who are meant to guard the children have been known to press girls into prostitution, or shoot boys merely for leaving the huts at night.

Mary's shelter fills up quickly. There are soon more than 1,000 children here, more boys than girls, and the adults are busy making sure everyone has a place to sleep. The boys and girls sleep in separate dormitories, spreading mats or blankets they have brought from home across the bare floors. By 10pm they have settled down for the night and the lights go out. Some are already half-asleep; many are exhausted from the walk in. A few of the small ones are agitated; they seem to be having nightmares, and cuddle up against older brothers or sisters for comfort.

The Acholi and Lango tribes of northern Uganda were once peasant farmers, living in small, scattered villages amid their herds of long-horned cattle and fields of maize. But 19 years of war have warped everything: virtually the entire population of the north, some 1.5 million people, has been displaced into crowded, dusty encampments on the outskirts of the main towns. Families live pressed together in tiny mud huts with thatched roofs. There is little space to farm or keep their cattle. Despair has bred alcoholism and domestic violence; the horror of war is part and parcel of life. It is so common, in fact, to have lost both parents that children here talk about it in calm, steady voices.

As the older generation dies out, so does the hope of anyone here returning to a normal life. This is a culture with few written records, which relies on memories rather than maps to place the boundaries of farmland and the distance to the nearest stream. When their parents are gone, the children's link with their original villages will be broken for ever.

"Half of the population of people in the camps are under 15," says Father Carlos Rodriguez Soto, a Roman Catholic priest who has spent 18 years in Uganda. "[They] are losing memory of the original demarcation of their land. For me, the worst thing that may happen here is a situation where officially there is no war, but everybody remains in the camps."

The sun has not quite risen when the adult wardens rouse the children. There is laughter and the sound of scuffling from inside the tents as they get dressed and hurry outside, turning on the washing taps in the raw pre-dawn light.

The new day begins with a communal prayer, led by the adults. Some children raise their right hands in the air, a gesture common among the evangelical churches sweeping up souls in the most desperate corners of Africa. Some crouch down and cover their faces, a symbol, the adult wardens explain, of being "humble before God". Surveying this crowd of skinny children in second-hand rags, it is hard to imagine any group of people on earth more humble.

After the prayer, the children who have blankets roll them on to their shoulders, the older ones gather up younger brothers and sisters and they begin to slip out of the gates and stream on to the road. By 9am the sun will burn and sweat will drip from every forehead, but now it is gentle. It is a good time to walk home.

CRITICAL EYE

▶ For Discussion

a. Research and statistics tell us that women and children are the poorest and most abused people on the planet. The plight of the Ugandan children is known worldwide. If we know that the world's children are often prey for the villains of our global community, why don't we do more to protect them?

b. How can the world community best help the nation of Uganda?

▶ Re-approaching the Reading

Consider this article alongside of the one about the Haiti. As they both relate to the citizens and how they move forward in the face of grave danger and tragedy, in what way(s) are they similar?

▶ Writing Assignment

Recently, there has been a call for the world's leaders to arrest Uganda's Joseph Kony, the leader of the Lord's Resistance Army (LRA), for war crimes. Why aren't the world's leaders quickly moving to bring this man to justice—especially when the lives of children are at stake?

IAN URBINA

Mobs Are Born as Word Grows by Text Message

PHILADELPHIA—It started innocently enough seven years ago as an act of performance art where people linked through social-networking Web sites and text messaging suddenly gathered on the streets for impromptu pillow fights in New York, group disco routines in London, and even a huge snowball fight in Washington.

But these so-called flash mobs have taken a more aggressive and raucous turn here as hundreds of teenagers have been converging downtown for a ritual that is part bullying, part running of the bulls: sprinting down the block, the teenagers sometimes pause to brawl with one another, assault pedestrians or vandalize property.

On Wednesday, the police here said that they had had enough. They announced plans to step up enforcement of a curfew already on the books, and to tighten it if there is another incident.

They added that they planned to hold parents legally responsible for their children's actions. They are also considering making free transit passes for students invalid after 4 P.M., instead of 7 P.M., to limit teenagers' ability to ride downtown.

"This is bad decision making by a small group of young people who are doing silly but dangerous stuff," Mayor Michael A. Nutter said in an interview Wednesday. "We intend to do something about it immediately."

Flash mobs are not unique to Philadelphia, but they have been more frequent here than elsewhere. Others that resulted in arrests and injuries have been reported over the past year in Boston, South Orange, N.J., and Brooklyn.

Philadelphia officials added that they had also begun getting help from the Federal Bureau of Investigation to monitor social-media networks. And television and radio stations are helping to recruit hip-hop artists to make public service announcements imploring teenagers to end the practice.

In the past year, at least four of the flash mobs have broken out in the city, including one on Saturday in which roving teenagers broke into fights, several onlookers were injured and at least three people were arrested.

"It was like a tsunami of kids," said Seth Kaufman, 20, a pizza deliveryman at Olympia II Pizza & Restaurant on South Street. He lifted his shirt to show gashes along his back and arm. He also had bruises on his forehead he said were from kicks and punches he suffered while trying to keep a rowdy crowd from entering the shop, where a fight was already under way.

"By the time you could hear them yelling, they were flooding the streets and the stores and the sidewalks," Mr. Kaufman said.

From *New York Times*, March 24, 2010. © 2010 New York Times. All rights reserved. Used by permission and protected by the Copyright Laws of the United States. The printing, copying, redistribution, or retransmission of the material without express written permission is prohibited.

The ad hoc gangs have scared many pedestrians off the streets.

City residents are also starting to complain about the number of unsupervised children, and child advocates are asking if there are enough activities to keep young people busy after school.

"We definitely need more jobs for kids, we need more summer jobs for kids, we need more after-school programming, and we need more parent support," said Shelly Yanoff, executive director of Public Citizens for Children and Youth, a children's advocacy group in Philadelphia.

Ms. Yanoff added that libraries and after-school programs had been reduced and a program for youth offenders had been cut sharply. On Friday, officials said, two preteenagers assaulted a woman as part of a violent game called "Catch and Wreck," in which children pick out people who appear homeless and then beat them and take any money they have.

The police, who say these assaults are unrelated to flash mobs, arrested an 11-year-old boy and a 12-year-old girl in the attack. The police said they also planned to charge the boy in an attack on a 73-year-old man who was beaten and robbed in the same area on March 13.

The flash mobs have raised questions about race and class.

Most of the teenagers who have taken part in them are black and from poor neighborhoods. Most of the areas hit have been predominantly white business districts.

In the flash mob on Saturday, groups of teenagers were chanting "black boys" and "burn the city," bystanders said.

In a Feb. 16 melee, 150 teenagers spilled out of the Gallery shopping mall east of City Hall during rush hour and rampaged through Macy's, knocking down customers and damaging displays.

The police arrested 15 of the teenagers and, according to one report, some had not been allowed to call their parents six hours after they were detained.

Clay Yeager, a juvenile justice consultant and former director of the Office of Juvenile Justice and Delinquency Prevention in Pennsylvania, said he believed the flash mobs were partly a result of a decline in state money for youth violence prevention programs.

Financing for the programs has dropped 93 percent to $1.2 million in this year's budget compared with $16 million in 2002. City financing for such programs has dropped to $1.9 million in the past three years compared with $4.1 million from 1999 through 2002, a 53 percent drop.

Mayor Nutter, who is black, rejected the notion that race or the city cut in services was a factor.

"I don't think people should be finding excuses for inappropriate behavior," Mr. Nutter said. "There is no racial component to stupid behavior, and parents should not be looking to the government to provide entertainment for their children."

Violent crime in Philadelphia has dropped 12 percent and homicides have fallen 23 percent since 2008.

Bill Wasik, a senior editor at Harper's who is credited with introducing the notion of a flash mob in 2003, said he was surprised by the new focus of some of the gatherings.

Mr. Wasik said the mobs started as a kind of playful social experiment meant to encourage spontaneity and big gatherings to temporarily take over commercial and public areas simply to show that they could.

"It's terrible that these Philly mobs have turned violent," he said.

CRITICAL EYE

▶ For Discussion

a. Initially, media pundits began to make these violent eruptions about race and class. Is Mayor Nutter correct about these events being more about bad parenting?

b. What commentary is this article making about young people and their use of social media, if any?

▶ Re-approaching the Reading

Examine this text alongside of Williams' "The New Breed" and determine whether or not the behavior of the teens is indicative of what we have come to expect of all modern day American teenagers. In essence, is this kind of bad social behavior the new norm?

▶ Writing Assignment

In order to protect his city, Mayor Nutter determined that parents of offending teens should be held financially responsible for any damage done by their teen(s). Is this a logical response? Are parents responsible for what their children do when they are not with them?

Index

A

abuse, sexual, 389–92
Adventures of Huckleberry Finn (Twain), 82–86
Aesop, 92–93
Age of Reason (Paine), 306–39
Alexie, Sherman, 386–88
Ali, Mohammed Naseehu, 286–94
Althaus, Frances A., 423–30
"Amid Tears, Flickering Candles and Flowers, a Shaken Norway Mourns" (Erlanger), 481–84
Asian males, emasculation and, 306–39
assimilation, religion and, 278–85
Awakening, The (Chopin), 204–12

B

"bad girl" social construct, 53–58
Baldwin, James, 350–54
"Believer, The" (The Koran), 301–5
Bidpai, 45–46
biracial children, 109–13
biracial couples, 295–300
birth control, 47–52
Book of Genesis, 463–68
Book of Matthew, 295–300
"Brave We Are" (Naqvi), 109–13

C

"Camel and His Friends, The" (Bidpai), 45–46
Cheever, John, 431–34
childrearing, 369–85
"Chilean Miners Rescued after 69 Days Underground" (Illiano, Wade), 469–72
choices, making. see "Fork in the Road"
Chopin, Kate, 204–12
class and the culture of power, 199–267
    "An Evening Visit" (Chestnut), 259–67
    The Awakening (Chopin), 204–12
    Decolonising the Mind (Thoing'o), 213–18
    Fantomina: Or, Love In a Maze (Haywood), 227–44
    Frankenstein (Shelley), 219–26
    Interpreter of Maladies (Lahiri), 245–58
    "The Lowest Animal" (Twain), 199–203

colonialism, 97–101
concentration camps, 87–91
country unification, 191–95
Crew, Louie, 343–49
Crouch, Stanley, 3–5
culture of power. see class and the culture of power

D

death and violence, 59–93
   Adventures of Huckleberry Finn (Twain), 82–86
   "A Lion and Other Animals Go Hunting" (Aesop), 92–93
   "Home Soil" (Zabytko), 76–81
   "Mother Savage" (de Maupassant), 70–75
   Paradise (Morrison), 64–69
   The Shawl (Ozick), 87–91
   "What LaShanda Armstrong Teaches Us About Teen Pregnancy Ten Years Out" (Lowen), 61–63
Decolonising the Mind (Thoing'o), 213–18
de Maupassant, Guy, 70–75
Diaz, Junot, 359–68
disasters. see manmade and natural disasters
Douglass, Frederick, 485–87
Doyle, Sir Arthur Conan, 397–422

E

Emerson, Ralph Waldo, 9–24
Erlanger, Steven, 481–84
ethnic identity, class and, 245–58
ethnic shame, 369–85
"Evening Visit, An" (Chestnut), 259–67
expectations, for fathers, 431–34

F

Fantomina: Or, Love In a Maze (Haywood), 227–44
"Father, A" (Mukherjee), 278–85
"Female Circumcision: Rite of Passage or Violation of Rights?" (Althaus), 423–30
Ferrell, Monique, 442–60
"Fiesta 1980" (Diaz), 359–68
"Fork in the Road," 395–460
   "Female Circumcision: Rite of Passage or Violation of Rights?" (Althaus), 423–30
   "Go Brooklyn!" (Ferrell), 442–60
   "Reunion" (Cheever), 431–34
   A Study in Scarlett (Doyle), 397–422
   "The Human Cost of an Illiterate Society" (Kozol), 435–41
Frankenstein (Shelley), 219–26

G

gender, sex, and sexuality, 341–93
   "Fiesta 1980" (Diaz), 359–68
   Giovanni's Room (Baldwin), 350–54
   "Higher Education" from the novel *Indian Killer*, 386–88
   "How America Unsexes the Asian Male" (Mura), 355–58
   Push (Sapphire), 389–92
   "The New Breed" (Williams), 369–85
   "Thriving as an Outsider, even as an Outcast, in Smalltown America" (Crew), 343–49
genital cutting, 423–30
"Ghost Dance Songs" (author unknown), 271–72
Giovanni's Room (Baldwin), 350–54
"Go Brooklyn!" (Ferrell), 442–60
Gold, Scott, 473–76
"Great Flood, The" (Book of Genesis), 463–68

H

Haiti, earthquake in, 477–80
Haywood, Eliza, 227–44
"Higher Education" (Alexie), 386–88
hip hop music, 442–60
Hispanics, racial affiliation and, 102–4
"Home Soil" (Zabytko), 76–81
Homosexuality, 295–300, 350–54
Hosseini, Khaled, 25–44
"House Divided Speech" (Lincoln), 191–95
"How America Unsexes the Asian Male" (Mura), 355–58
"Human Cost of an Illiterate Society, The" (Kozol), 435–41
Hurricane Katrina, 473–76

I

Illiano, Cesar, 469–72
illiteracy, 435–41
Indigenous religious songs, 271–72
infidelity, 359–68
Interpreter of Maladies (Lahiri), 245–58
"It's Hard Enough Being Me" (Raya), 102–4

J

Jesus, 295–300

K

Kingston, Maxine Hong, 105–8
Kite Runner, The (Hosseini), 25–44
Koran, The, 301–5
Kozol, Jonathan, 435–41

L

Lahiri, Jhumpa, 245–58
Larsen, Nella, 6–8
Lincoln, Abraham, 191–95
"Lion and Other Animals Go Hunting, A" (Aesop), 92–93
"Little to Reclaim in the Lower 9th" (Gold), 473–76
Lowen, Linda, 61–63
"Lowest Animal, The" (Twain), 199–203

M

"Making of a Slut, The" (Wolf), 53–58
"Mallam Sile" (Ali), 286–94
manmade and natural disasters, 461–94
    "Amid Tears, Flickering Candles and Flowers, a Shaken Norway Mourns" (Erlanger), 481–84
    "Chilean Miners Rescued after 69 Days Underground" (Illiano, Wade), 469–72
    "Little to Reclaim in the Lower 9th" (Gold), 473–76
    "Mobs Are Born as Word Grows by Text Message" (Urbina), 492
    "Quake Accentuated Chasm That Has Defined Haiti" (Romero), 477–80
    "The Great Flood" (Book of Genesis), 463–68
    "The Nightwalkers" (Vasagar), 488–91

"What to the Slave Is the 4th of July?" (Douglass), 485–87
marriage, 204–12
mass murder, 70–75, 481–84
"Misery of Silence, The" (Kingston), 105–8
mob mentality, 82–86
"Mobs Are Born as Word Grows by Text Message" (Urbina), 492
Mohammed (prophet), 301–5
Morrison, Toni, 64–69
motherhood, 204–12
"Mother Savage" (de Maupassant), 70–75
Mukherjee, Bharati, 278–85
Mura, David, 355–58
murder, 61–63, 70–75, 481–84

N

Naqvi, Tahiri, 109–13
Native Americans, 271–72, 369–85
natural disasters. see manmade and natural disasters
"New Breed, The" (Williams), 369–85
"Nightwalkers, The" (Vasagar), 488–91
Noah, story of, 463–68
Norway, mass murder in, 481–84

O

oppression, religion and, 273–77
Ozick, Cynthia, 87–91

P

Paine, Thomas, 306–39
Paradise (Morrison), 64–69
Passing (Larsen), 6–8
power. *see* class and the culture of power
prejudice, 219–26, 286–94. *see also* class and the culture of power; gender, sex, and sexuality; racial matters; religion
Push (Sapphire), 389–92

R

race, 259–67. see also class and the culture of power
Race in North America (Smedley), 273–77
racial matters, 95–198
    "Brave We Are" (Naqvi), 109–13

"House Divided Speech" (Lincoln), 191–95
"It's Hard Enough Being Me" (Raya), 102–4
Othello, the Moor of Venice (Shakespeare), 114–90
"The Misery of Silence" (Kingston), 105–8
"Young Men, Got Out and Fight Them" (Wooden Leg), 97–101

racism, 6–8. see also racial matters
rap music, 3–5
Raya, Anna Lisa, 102–4
religion, 269–339
- "A Father" (Mukherjee), 278–85
- *Age of Reason* (Paine), 306–39
- "Ghost Dance Songs" (author unknown), 271–72
- "Mallam Sile" (Ali), 286–94
- *Race in North America* (Smedley), 273–77
- "The Believer" (The Koran), 301–5
- "The Sermon on the Mount" (Book of Matthew), 295–300

"Reunion" (Cheever), 431–34
Romero, Simon, 477–80

S

Sanger, Margaret, 47–52
Sapphire, 389–92
second-language learners, 105–8, 213–18
"Self-Reliance" (Emerson), 9–24
self-sacrifice, 45–46
"Sermon on the Mount, the" (Jesus, from Book of Matthew), 295–300
sex and sexuality. see gender, sex, and sexuality
sexism, 204–12, 227–44
Shakespeare, William, 114–90
Shawl, The (Ozick), 87–91
Shelley, Mary, 219–26
slavery
- Uganda, 488–91
- United States, 485–87

Smedley, Audrey, 273–77
social media, violence and, 492
social responsibility, 1–58
- *The Kite Runner* (Hosseini), 25–44
- *Passing* (Larsen), 6–8
- "Self-Reliance" (Emerson), 9–24
- "Taking Back the Music" (Crouch), 3–5
- "The Camel and His Friends" (Bidpai), 45–46

"The Making of a Slut" (Wolf), 53–58
"The Turbid Ebb and Flow of Misery" (Sanger), 47–52
speciesism, 199–203
Study in Scarlet, A (Doyle), 397–422
suicide, 61–63

T

"Taking Back the Music" (Crouch), 3–5
teen pregnancy, 61–63
Thoing'o, Ngugi Wa, 213–18
"Thriving as an Outsider, even as an Outcast, in Smalltown America" (Crew), 343–49
"Turbid Ebb and Flow of Misery, The" (Sanger), 47–52
Twain, Mark
- *Adventures of Huckleberry Finn*, 82–86
- "The Lowest Animal," 199–203

U

Uganda, child slaves in, 488–91
Urbina, Ian, 492–494

V

Vasagar, Jeevan, 488–91
violence. see death and violence

W

Wade, Terry, 469–72
war, 70–75, 76–81, 97–101
"What LaShandra Armstrong Teaches Us About Teen Pregnancy Ten Years Out" (Lowen), 61–63
"What to the Slave Is the 4th of July?" (Douglass), 485–87
Williams, Julian, 369–85
Wolf, Naomi, 53–58
women, violence against, 64–69
Wooden Leg, 97–101

Y

"Young Men, Got Out and Fight Them" (Wooden Leg), 97–101

Z

Zabytko, Irene, 76–81